MONTGOMERY COLLEGE LIBRARY
ROCKVILLE CAMPUS

ENGLISH LETTERS AND
LETTER-WRITERS

Autotype.

HENRIETTA HOBART, COUNTESS OF SUFFOLK.

FROM THE ORIGINAL BY JARVIS IN THE COLLECTION AT STRAWBERRY HILL.

From a Print in the British Museum.

ENGLISH LETTERS AND LETTER-WRITERS

OF THE

EIGHTEENTH CENTURY.

WITH EXPLANATORY NOTES.

BY

HOWARD WILLIAMS

ILLUSTRATED WITH PORTRAITS AND FACSIMILES.

FIRST SERIES.

SWIFT AND POPE.

Essay Index Reprint Series

BOOKS FOR LIBRARIES PRESS
PLAINVIEW, NEW YORK

First Published 1886
Reprinted 1973

Library of Congress Cataloging in Publication Data

Williams, Howard, 1837-1931, ed.
  English letters and letter-writers of the eighteenth century.

  (Essay index reprint series)
  No more published.
  Reprint of the 1886 ed.
  CONTENTS: Life and writings of Swift.--Letters of Swift.--Life and writings of Pope.--Letters of Pope.
  1. Swift, Jonathan, 1667-1745. 2. Pope, Alexander 1688-1744. I. Swift, Jonathan, 1667-1745. II. Pope, Alexander, 1688-1744. III. Title.
PR3726.A49 1973   821'.5 [B]   73-1483
ISBN 0-518-10068-5

PRINTED IN THE UNITED STATES OF AMERICA

PREFACE.

FOR the most part, the Literature of Letter-Writing, properly so-called, falls within quite modern times. From Antiquity have come down to us several Collections of "Letters"; but, with two or three notable exceptions, such only in name, they are chiefly moral or political essays, descriptive pieces, and rhetorical declamations. In Greek Literature, one of the earliest of them bears the magic name of Plato. Modern criticism, generally, holds them to be forgeries; and their intrinsic merit or interest is not so high as to make their genuineness or spuriousness matter of very great concern. Equally spurious, but more entertaining, are the *Letters* of the Scythian or Tartar prince, Anacharsis, the enterprising traveller of the Sixth Century, B.C.[1] Next, in order of time, come the so-called *Letters* of Alkiphron (of the Second or Third Century of the Christian era), the most entertaining and valuable of the species. As pictures of Athenian life and manners, of the New Comedy period, high interest attaches to them; and for elegance of style, and picturesqueness of description, they have a deserved repute. Not much later, probably, were composed the *Love-Letters* of Aristænetus. In their day, they seem to have had some vogue. Not more, however, than the *Epistles* of Alkiphron do they

---

[1] Others, of more or less fame, are those of Phalaris, the Greek prince of Agrigentum, so celebrated by the Bentley-Boyle controversy; of Theano, the wife of Pythagoras; and of Philostratus, the author of the *Life of Apollonius of Tyana*. Only the last are genuine.

possess any claim to the modern title, or to be regarded as other than artificial productions intended for the public eye. For the most part, they are imitations and adaptations from Plato, Menander, Lucian, and other distinguished and popular writers. Of Greek Collections, which have more right to the title, most celebrated, perhaps, are the *Epistles* of the famous rhetorician Libanius—the friend and correspondent of the Emperor Julian, Athanasius, and Chrysostom—and those of Julian himself.

Latin Literature, which owes so much to its Greek parent, can boast, in (genuine) epistolary productions, greater fame as well as greater fertility. It includes the *Letters* of Cicero; of Seneca (which, however, are, in fact, admirable moral treatises evidently intended for publication); of the Younger Pliny, the correspondent of the Emperor Trajan; of the eminent rhetorician, Fronto, the preceptor and correspondent of the Emperor Marcus Aurelius; of the erudite Symmachus, the apologist of the fallen but still surviving religion of Jupiter; and, finally, of Sidonius, the last poet of the disrupted Roman Empire. Of these, the *Letters* of Cicero and of Pliny alone bear much resemblance to the modern type; and they may be reckoned among the most interesting lesser remains—among the most entertaining *parerga*—of the Roman Literature. The *Letters* of the great Orator, and the more studied, but, at the same time, more varied and entertaining ones of the friend of Trajan, remained the standard and model, more admired than imitated, of the Epistolary style.

Barren as they were in all the higher species of prose

Literature, the long ages preceding the Renaissance produced, also, little of interest or of importance in this class—until the Eleventh Century, nothing at all. To that Age belong a few, perhaps half-a-dozen, Collections of some value. Excepting the (Latin) *Letters* of Heloisa and Abélard, which have been generally, but rather too hastily, received as genuine, none of them acquired or deserved any popularity or special fame. The *Letters* of Petrarca, to whom we owe the discovery of Cicero's *Epistles to his Familiar Friends*, and the *Letters* of the famous scholar Poggio Bracciolini, who has earned even greater gratitude from the reading world by his recovery of several of the lost *Comedies* of Plautus, among others, represent the Epistolary Art during the Fourteenth and Fifteenth Centuries; while the *Epistles* of the illustrious Erasmus remain the best representatives of it in the next Age. In the vernacular languages, nothing of the kind, hitherto, had been produced at all.

The first Collection of English Letters is that of the Paston Family, written during the latter half of the Fifteenth Century. At first suspected, their genuineness is now fairly established. But, valuable as they are to the Antiquarian, neither their archaic style nor their rather dry matter attracts the unarchæological reader. Still less entertaining or edifying, and of merely historic or biographic value, such as it may be, must be adjudged the vast majority of the published Letters of eminent personages of the next Century—princes, statesmen, scholars, or savans. Few things, in fact, make duller or drearier reading than these ponderous productions of formalism and pedantry. Modelling their style according to the minute regulations laid down by the legislators of the Art, these epistolographers would almost as soon have thought of asserting the right of free-thinking as of free letter-writing; of discrediting the miracles of Herodotus or of Livy as of departing from the received canons of Epistolary forms. Among other Codes, in the " Art of Letter-Writing " (*De Epistolis Conscribendis*) of the philosophic, as well as erudite, Erasmus these laws have been displayed in detail. The witty author of the *Praise of Folly*, it may reasonably be presumed, would weary his readers considerably less than the rest of the Epistolary authorities: yet his rules and regulations leave little license to the individual imagination and fancy. As for the legislators most in esteem, they divide the whole Art into five principal departments:—the *Didactic*, the *Deliberative*, the *Demonstrative*, the *Judicial*, and the *Familiar*. These they sub-divide into twenty-one varieties:—the *Congratulatory*, the *Laudatory*, the *Consolatory*, the *Denunciatory*, the *Comminatory*, the *Petitionary*, the *Mandatory*, the *Officious*, the *Jocose*, &c. Spontaneity and freedom, of the very essence of the species of writing, to them would have seemed but as outward and visible signs of barbarism and *Philistinism*.

Until the middle of the Seventeenth Century, pedantic forms continued to characterise the epistolary productions of eminent personages, whether in society or in letters. To produce and maintain this sort of conventionalism in this country, two causes concurred: on the one hand, the *English* pedantry of the Court of Elizabeth and of the first Stuart (of which the famous

Euphues of Lilly, that long served as the text-book of polite language, was at once cause and effect); and, on the other, the *Latin* pedantry of the schools. But, principally, the universal maintenance of Latin, as the medium of intercourse among scholars, checked and fettered the use of the vernacular idioms. The one remarkable exception to the prevailing conventional formalism are the *Letters* of Howell (1616-1660). So modern an air have they, as compared with those of his contemporaries, that, but for evidence to the contrary, his earlier ones might be suspected to be forgeries by a later hand. In the second half of the Century, as reverence for authority decreased, and the national languages came into greater cultivation and repute, Letter-Writing began to throw off the fetters imposed upon it; and it assumed an ease and freedom scarcely known before. If English Letter-Writing of that period, in peculiar graces of style—owed still more to the genius of the language than to that of the individual—does not boast a Mde. de Sévigné, or even a Balzac, yet the letters of Lady Rachel Russell, or of Locke, in point of style may claim some merit; while, in the expression of thought or feeling, they far excel the trifling and vapid matter of Balzac and his School. With the Eighteenth Century and with Swift, from whom the Art (if, in his hands, it can be called an *Art*) in England received a new ease and vigour, may be said to begin the English classical letter-writers.

Few words are necessary to explain the plan and scope of the present volume, which will be followed by others, completing the series. 1.—No Letters have been included, which have not seemed to possess for the ordinary reader some especial interest, whether biographic, social, literary, or historic. 2.—A biographical sketch of each Letter-Writer, as comprehensive and, at the same time, as concise as possible, forming a summary of the most interesting or important facts of his life, with illustrative extracts from his principal public writings, has been prefixed. Without such introduction, for the greater number of readers the interest, and even the intelligibility, of his epistolary remains is considerably lessened. 3.—Explanatory and illustrative Notes (including extracts from the letters of correspondents), wherever they have seemed to be necessary or useful for elucidating the text, have been freely supplied. 4.—A full and complete Index appears at the end of each volume.

If the best letters of the Masters of the Art form one of the most entertaining kinds of lighter literature, that commonplace productions of the species offer one of the dullest and least edifying sorts of reading is equally true. The Collections of many of the most celebrated contributors to this popular kind of writing illustrate the truth with sufficient force; and in no department of literature, perhaps, can the principle of selection be more conveniently or advantageously applied. In the cases of some of the more voluminous—of Pope, of Chesterfield, in particular, —the applicability of the principle is especially apparent, a fact which, probably, will be recognised by most persons who have been at the pains of exploring the entire mass of their published letters.

Care has been taken in ascertaining, as far as possible, the genuine text of the *Letters* of Pope. The ordinary Collections, published before the minute researches of his more recent critics and editors, have become, to a considerable extent, of little value, in respect of their chronology and addresses, as well as in relative significance. But, in fact, of a large proportion of the whole body of them the interest for any but the biographer is slight.

It is intended to include in the Series only the most eminent Letter-Writers, with two or three of the most distinguished names in English Literature, whose Letters possess especial interest, derived as well from the matter as from the fame of the writer. The Series, when completed, will exhibit, it is believed, a varied and lively picture of the Eighteenth Century life, manners, literature, politics, and society generally—as they appeared to some of its most distinguished representatives in English Letters or Society—such as rarely has been displayed in the same limit of space.

It remains to add that the publication of the present volume has been unavoidably delayed, the plan of the work having been formed, and the larger part of the matter having been arranged, four years ago.

December, 1885.

CONTENTS.

I.—THE LIFE AND WRITINGS OF SWIFT.

An extraordinary interest in the life and productions of Swift constantly displayed—Perplexities for his biographer—Variety of opinion as to the purposes of his two masterpieces—Recent critical examination of his character and Writings—His family and birth—At the Kilkenny School—At the Dublin University—Pedantry and Scholasticism prevalent at the Universities—Mythical accounts of Swift's life at Trinity College, derived from Lord Orrery and Dr. Barrett, exploded by a recently discovered document—Swift leaves Ireland, and goes to visit his mother at Leicester—Finds an asylum with Sir William Temple—His first love-affair at Leicester—His position with Temple—The residents at Moor Park—Mrs. Johnson and her two daughters—Esther Johnson—Mrs. Dingley—Swift returns to Ireland—His first attacks of giddiness and deafness, and their fancied origin—A Letter of Temple to the Secretary for Ireland recommending him—Again at Leicester—Re-enters Temple's service—His better position at Moor Park—Macaulay's misrepresentation of his and Esther Johnson's position there—Swift takes the degree of Master of Arts at Oxford—His multifarious reading—Publishes *Pindaric Odes*—Attends King William III. at Moor Park—Sent by Temple to the Court on a political mission—Addresses an *Ode* to Congreve—Leaves Moor Park in anger, visits Leicester, and then returns to Ireland—Takes Orders, and obtains the Prebend of Kilroot—Makes the acquaintance of Miss Waring—His first letter to her—His letter to her with an offer of marriage—Re-enters Temple's service—Esther Johnson at the age of fifteen—Swift's description of her—Strong affection between Swift and her—His letter to Mrs. Johnson—Writes the *Tale of a Tub* and *Battle of the Books*—Temple's death—Swift returns to Ireland as Secretary to the Lord-Lieutenant, Lord Berkeley—The ladies of the Castle—Takes the degree of D.D. at the Dublin University—Breaks with Miss Waring—His insulting letter to her—Obtains a Prebend and two small Livings in Ireland—Returns to England with Lord Berkeley—Publishes his first political Tract, *A Discourse of the Dissensions*, &c.—Becomes known to the leading Whig Ministers—His political and ecclesiastical principles—Induces Esther Johnson to reside in Ireland—His account of the matter—Publishes the *Tale of a Tub* and the *Battle of the Books*—Some account of those Satires—Beginning of Swift's friendship with Addison and Steele—Begins a correspondence with Dr. King, Archbishop of Dublin—Satirical verses on Vanbrugh—*Baucis and Philemon*—Returns to Ireland—Occupations and friends at Laracor and in Dublin—Again in England—Publishes a *Letter upon the Sacramental Test*—His *Argument Against the Abolition of Christianity*—Assails Anthony Collins in a pamphlet, *Collins's Discourse of Free Thinking*, &c.—His attitude in theological controversy—The *Argument* quoted—Swift's theological sincerity in question—*Predictions of Isaac Bickerstaff*—John Partridge and *Merlinus Liberatus*—The *Predictions* burned by the *Holy Office* at Lisbon—Addison, Steele, and other wits, join with Swift in the ridicule of Partridge and the astrological prophets—Swift publishes his *Project for the Advancement of Religion and Reformation of Manners*—Exposes the general corruption of Society in the Government, the Army, and the Magistracy—Proposes means for checking the enormous evils of Drunkenness—Denounces the prevalence of Fraud among Traders and Shopkeepers—England pre-eminent in Europe for all kinds of Fraud—Swift thinks of emigrating to America, his design of going to Vienna on a diplomatic mission being at an end—A letter to Col. Hunter quoted—His life in London—Visits to the Vanhomrighs—A letter to Ambrose Philips quoted—Frequent reference in his note-books to attacks of giddiness, &c.—Returns to Ireland—Writes to Lord Halifax, asking for preferment—Halifax's reply—Probable reasons for Swift's non-advancement—Writes for the *Tatler*—The Sacheverell agitation raises the hopes of the Anglo-Irish Clergy—Swift appointed on a Commission to negociate for remission of "First-Fruits," &c.—His journal-letters to Esther Johnson—Entertains for her, at this time, a real affection—Arrives in London, and goes over to the Tories—Motives for this secession—The Tories in power—Swift receives unceasing flattery from, and obtains extraordinary influence with, their leaders—Writes for the *Examiner*—Holds up the late Government (the Duke of Marlborough, in particular) to contempt and detestation—On intimate terms with the Tory Ministers—His character of them—Describes St. John (Lord Bolingbroke) and Lord Peterborough—Moves from St. James's to Chelsea—Renews acquaintance with the Vanhomrighs—Acts as preceptor to Hester Vanhomrigh—His relations with her—Only twice mentions her in letters to her rival—Various topics of the journal-letters to Esther Johnson—Sits for his portrait to Jervas—Other portraits of him—His powerful frame and physique, and vigorous exercise, consist with painful and fatal maladies—A member of the *October* Club—Frequently changes his lodgings—A letter from Archbishop King—Swift's grief at the death of Lady Ashburnham—Appointed to the Deanery of St. Patrick's—The *Aliquid Amari*—Embarrassments from his doubtful relations with the two rival ladies—With Steele at Laracor—His letter to Vanessa—Gladly returns to England—His counsels needed by the dissentient Tories—The *Scriblerus* Club and its members—Origin of *Martin Scriblerus*—Queen Anne's death puts an end to the Tory Government, and disperses Swift's friends—Returns to his Deanery—Perplexities of his position in regard to Stella and Vanessa—Vanessa, left unprotected, goes to Ireland—Her appeals of despairing affection to Swift—Extreme caution and secrecy observed and enjoined by him in their correspondence—His visits to her at Cellbridge—Reproaches of Esther Johnson and entreaties for marriage—Swift, as alleged, at length consents to a private marriage-ceremony—Testimony for and against it—Hester Vanhomrigh's death—Alleged visit of Swift and a suitor to her—Her indignant rejection of the latter—She retires to Cellbridge, and indulges in solitude her fatal passion—Her letters—Swift publishes his poem, *Cadenus and Vanessa*—Extracts from the poem—Character of the relationship of Swift and Hester Vanhomrigh disputed and uncertain—Conflicting theories—Her Will—A view of the state of Ireland at this time—Swift takes up the cause of the Anglo-Irish—His *Proposal for the Universal Use of Irish Manufactures*—The *Drapier Letters*—Extracts from those pamphlets—Swift compels the withdrawal of the obnoxious coinage—The *Drapier Letters* followed by a succession of political pamphlets and broadsheets from his hand—Mixed motives of his war against the Whig Government—Visits England as the guest of Pope and of Lord Bolingbroke—Welcomed at the rival Court at Leicester House, and in high favour with the Princess of Wales and Mrs. Howard—Contributes, with Pope and Arbuthnot, to the *Miscellanies*—Returns to Ireland—Again visits London—Publishes his *Travels of Lemuel Gulliver*—His reputation and popularity raised to the highest point—Extraordinary and almost unexampled success of the Satire—Pirated editions—Its simultaneous publication in a periodical called *Parker's Penny Post*—Undergoes many revisions—First taken in hand in 1720—References to it while still in manuscript—The French translation of the Abbé Desfontaines—His letter to Swift—Swift's reply—Desfontaines produces a continuation of the *Travels*, under the title of *Le Nouveau Gulliver*—Scott's notice of it—Dr. Arbuthnot's witty Gulliverian pamphlets—The Satire well received at Leicester House—Gay's letter to Swift reporting the universal popularity of the book—The author, in a Preface, ironically complains of the publisher's alterations and excisions—Cause of the enduring fame and popularity of the Satire—Swift increases the *vraisemblance* by inserting a portrait of the hero and maps—His revisions—His own account of his purpose in the Satire—A curiously-interesting letter from him to the publisher upon suggested illustrations of the *Travels* —Again visits London, for the last time, as the guest of Pope and of Lord Oxford—Supplies the *Beggar's Opera* with two of its songs—His hopes of higher preferment, at the death of George I., disappointed— Leaves England in disgust—His recently-printed *Journal* at Holyhead—Extracts from it—Dangerous illness of Stella—Despairing letter from Swift to Sheridan respecting her—Shrinks from her death-bed— Doubtful stories of his conduct during her last days—Remarkable silence of himself and his friends, in their correspondence, regarding her—Strange contradictions on all sides—Esther Johnson's Will— Swift's *Birthday Poems* quoted—He is present neither at her last moments nor at her interment—Notice of her death in his *Character of Mrs. Johnson*—His settled melancholy and gloom after her death— A rapid succession of political pamphlets, satires, and tracts—Indignant alike at the misgovernment of the rulers and the apathetic indifference of the people of Ireland—Exposes the disastrous folly of the general neglect of Agriculture—More's *Utopia* quoted—Swift's *Modest Proposal* "one of the most terrific Satires ever written"—Extracts from it—Swift's later verse-satires—Correspondence with his friends in England—With Gay and Lord Bolingbroke—A letter from Bolingbroke quoted—Letters from Lady Betty Germaine—Swift's chief Irish friends, Drs. Sheridan and Delany—A notice of Sheridan—The *Art of Punning* quoted—Other Irish friends—Literary ladies of Swift's acquaintance in Dublin—Bindon's portrait of him at Howth Castle— His relations to the poor in his jurisdiction—His contemptuousness of manner not confined to his official inferiors—His *Polite Conversation* and *Directions for Servants* noticed—His poems—*The Grand Question Debated* and the *Day of Judgment* quoted—Sir Walter Scott alleges the only possible excuse for the extreme grossness of some of the Swift poems—Some of them said to be stolen copies, not intended for publication—Their extraordinary correctness of versification, wit, and naturalness—His *Verses on the Death of Dr. Swift* quoted—His mental disease begins to appear in the year 1736—Not gradual, as usually supposed, but the immediate consequence of paralysis—Dr. Wilde's theory of its origin—Swift's last words in writing—Buried in St. Patrick's Cathedral, in the same grave with Stella—Disinterment of the remains—Curiosity excited in fashionable society by their exhibition—Strange contrasts in the character of Swift—His ecclesiastical orthodoxy—His *Sermons* quoted—His place as a letter-writer—His

Correspondence—The letters to and from Esther Johnson (the journal-letters excepted), unhappily for the gratification of the public curiosity, destroyed—His journal-letters—Correspondence with Hester Vanhomrigh only partially preserved—His most elaborate biographer, Mr. Forster, had access to a mass of unpublished letters in various hands, but did not live to complete his work—Few additions made to the published letters since the edition of Scott—Two or three of interest appear in Mr. Craik's biography—The most interesting addition, in the bibliography of Swift, the large paper copy of the first edition of *Gulliver's Travels*, now in the South Kensington Museum—The handwriting of Swift . . . . 1-68.

II.—Letters of Swift.

To the Rev. J. Kendall. Swift defends his conduct at Leicester—His literary activity—Not in love—His ideas on marriage . . 71-74

To William Swift. Expresses satisfaction at the civilities accorded to him at the University of Oxford—When the King (William III.) gives him a prebend, he intends to take Orders—Dissatisfied with Sir William Temple—Concerned that he is so distant from his friends 72-75

To Deane Swift. On superstition in Portugal—Leaves Moor Park—Temple's resentment—Intends to enter the Church—Asks his cousin to procure him a Chaplaincy at Lisbon 75-76

To the Rev. Dr. Tisdall. Strong party feeling in the metropolis on the Bill Against Occasional Conformity—The ladies divided into High Church and Low Church—Swift interviews Lords Somers and Peterborough, the Bishop of Salisbury, and others upon the Bill—Proposes speedy return to Ireland—Sends legal advice to Miss Johnson—Imparts to Tisdall a new way of being witty . . . 77-79

To the Rev. Dr. Tisdall. Declares Miss Johnson and Mrs. Dingley to be the first considered in his correspondence—Scolds him for shewing his letter to the Archbishop of Dublin—Quotes Montaigne's device—Snubs him for his presumption with the ladies, and illustrates his meaning by an anecdote—Remarks on Esther Johnson's punning—On theological pamphlet-writing—Dissuades him from publishing—On

Dissenters and Independents—Whigs and Tories—Sends his service
to the Primate and other friends 79-82
To ARCHBISHOP KING. Informs him of Court-intrigues and Party-
politics in London—The confusion of Parties—Narrates the intrigues
of Harley 82-85
To COLONEL HUNTER (prisoner of war in Paris). Puts the blame of
his delay in writing on Addison—*Persiflage*—News of town friends,
Addison and others—Fires on the frozen Thames—Atterbury's displeasure at the prorogation of Convocation, of which he was to have
been Prolocutor—Swift's occupations—Addison and he sometimes
"steal to a pint of bad wine"—Party-feeling—The Italian Opera—Lords
Somers and Halifax—Lord Dorset and Prior—Steele sends his "service"
—Swift denies authorship of the *Letters on Enthusiasm* . . 85-88
To DEAN STERNE. Excuses himself for failing to attend at the Chapter
—The ladies of St. Mary's—About to preach to an audience of fifteen
persons—Summarises his parishioners' occupations . . 88-89
To JOSEPH ADDISON. News from Dublin—Addison's great popularity
in Ireland—Swift, the Bishop of Clogher, and Paget dine at the
Castle—Remarks on a volume of the *Tatler*—Hints to Addison his
wishes for preferment—The place of Historiographer, or Dr. South's
prebend and sinecure, eligible—On Mrs. Manley's *Memoirs of Europe*
—The Lord Lieutenant recalled—Swift desires the memory of Lord
Halifax to be refreshed 89-91
To DEAN STERNE. Reports Cabinet changes—Criticises his friends,
the Whig Ministers—Patrick's report—Lord Godolphin, the Premier,
the worst dissembler of his Party—Flying rumours—Pamphlets and
squibs in increasing abundance—The Whigs begin to skirmish faintly—
Deserters daily coming in—All the virtues fly over to the Office-
holders—Swift intends to begin the business of the Irish Church, and
desires the Archbishop's instructions—Regrets for Ireland—Weary of
the caresses of great men out of place 92-93
To ESTHER JOHNSON. His numerous invitations and engagements
upon his arrival in town—Sends a long letter to the *Tatler* on corruptions of the English language—Cursory remarks on their mutual
acquaintance—Exhorts her to take care of her eyes—Denounces Patrick, his servant, for drunkenness—Threatens to dismiss him—Dines
with Addison and Jervas at Addison's country-place—Engaged on
his lampoon, *Sid Hamet*—Writes a *Tatler*—Gossip—Lodges in Bury
Street—His powers on the Irish Commission . . . 93-98
To ESTHER JOHNSON. Interview with Harley—Dines with the Vanhomrighs, and visits the Ladies Butler—Inquires as to the reception
of his *City Shower* in Ireland—Spends an evening with Addison and
Wortley Montagu—His high position among the Tories—The *Rod of
Sid Hamet* and *Ballad on the Westminster Election*—Acknowledges

receipt of her fourth letter—Condoles with her on her suffering from headaches, &c.—Dines with Harley and Lord Peterborough—Transacts business of "First-Fruits," &c., with Harley—Desires to know the feeling in Ireland about it—His good offices on Steele's behalf—Visits Addison, whom he finds suspicious and reticent—Reflects on Steele's ingratitude—Sees the Duke of Ormond and Lord Berkeley—Behaves coldly to Addison—Dines with Addison, and Steele, and Addison's sister—Visits Congreve, and reports his blindness and gout—His love for china cooled—Exhorts Stella not to injure her eyes by writing—Dines with his cousin Leach—Advises Stella on money-matters—Lady Giffard's debt to her—Dines with Rowe and Prior—Meets Congreve, Temple, and others at a tavern—A drinking bout, himself prudently abstemious—Dines with Garth and Addison at a hedge-tavern—Calls on Harley, the Ladies Butler, and others—Dreads the return of the Whigs to power as ruinous to the Church and Clergy—At the Vanhomrighs'—Writes to Mrs. Long—A later letter from him mourning her death—Dines with Addison and others, who get "half-fuddled."—*Persiflage* 98–107

To ESTHER JOHNSON. Dines with Mr. Secretary St. John—Harley becomes Earl of Oxford, Earl of Mortimer, and Lord Harley of Wigmore Castle, and expects the Lord Treasurer's Staff—A wet walk home to Chelsea—Visits his neighbour Dr. Atterbury—His lodging at Chelsea—Returns to town by water—His troubles with Patrick—Visits Lord Oxford, and declines the offer of a private chaplaincy—Patrick again—Swift counter-orders a suit of livery for him at the tailor's, and knows not what to do with him—Lady Ashburnham forgets her invitation, and he dines at the Vanhomrighs'—Walks in the Park with Lord Harley till a late hour—Lord Oxford becomes Prime Minister—Swift notes his breaking with Addison, Steele, Somers, Halifax, and the Whigs—Receives a long letter from the Archbishop respecting a squabble in choosing a Lord Mayor for Dublin—Remarks his frequent visits to the Vanhomrighs—Baulked of an intended swim at Chelsea—Excessive heat—Goes to the Premier's—Meets Lady Betty Butler and Lady Ashburnham at the Vanhomrighs'—Insupportable heat—Visits the Duke of Ormond and St. John—Expected changes in the Government—Lord Oxford now at the top of power and popularity—A swimming adventure—Dines with Lady B. Germaine and Lady Berkeley, who play off tricks upon him—A crowd of visits—In a passion from the heat—Swimming difficulties—St. John's critical position in the Cabinet—On snuff and tobacco . . . 107–114

To ESTHER JOHNSON. Accompanies the Premier to Windsor—Occupies Mr. Secretary St. John's apartments—Borrows one of St. John's shirts to go to Court in—Dines with Mr. Masham—Patrick takes a holiday, and leaves him without clothes—Patrick again—His opinion of Windsor—His agent Walls and his wife—Desires Stella to give him particulars of her visit to Wexford—Meets Addison and Steele again at Tonson's—Jacob Tonson pays court to him—On easy terms with Addison and Steele, to the latter of whom he had written a "biting letter"—With St. John to Windsor, with whom he lodges—Complains of Patrick again—Never was in a greater passion—Indignant at an offer from the Ministry—At Court—A dunce preaches before the Queen, which often happens—Great company at the Sunday dinners at Windsor—Reports Patrick drunk three times in five days—Resolves to dismiss him, and to use him without pity—The Duchess of Shrewsbury gives Swift the name of Presto—On a visit to St. John in Berkshire—*Badinage* with the Premier and the Secretary at a *levée* of the former at Windsor—Attends the Queen's Drawing Room in her bedchamber—Dines at the "Green Cloth"—Dr. Arbuthnot acts as his *chaperon*—They meet Miss Forester, Maid of Honour, and the Queen 114-121

To ESTHER JOHNSON. Noisy company at the Green Cloth Table after the Races—Letter from the Archbishop of Dublin on the matter of the "First-Fruits," &c.—Indignant at the ingratitude of Convocation—Anxious about Mrs. Masham's health—Her death would be a terrible thing—Complains again of the ingratitude of the Clergy in Convocation—Dines with the Premier and Mrs. Masham—The Premier's unbusinesslike habits—Laments his expenditure in fees to butlers and footmen—The Queen has the gout—She orders an expenditure of twenty thousand pounds on the completion of Blenheim . 121-124

To ESTHER JOHNSON. Dines with the Mashams and Miss Hill—Boxes Patrick's ears—With a riding-party in the Park—Arbuthnot and his excruciating malady 124-125

To ARCHBISHOP KING. Expected settlement of the Treaty of Utrecht—Certain "unlucky circumstances," not to be trusted to a letter, have retarded the Peace—Five millions to be borrowed by the Government—Swift objects to the proposed tax upon paper and imported books—Political and Diplomatic news—The Irish *Houghers* and the English *Mohawks*—Duke of Marlborough not to be impeached—Less talk of the Pretender—Harley, the Premier's son, sent on a mission to Hanover—The Whigs threaten to have the Premier's head—Discontent of the Tories with their Chief—Swift prays for the Queen's health—A "projector" and the longitude—Writes a letter (of thirty pages) to the Premier proposing an Academy for the improvement of the English language—A Commission appointed by Lord Oxford and himself for the purpose 125-128

To ESTHER JOHNSON. Pledges himself to write oftener for the future—Impatient at the neglect of his interests by his political friends—Returns of his old maladies—Anti-ministerial newspapers suppressed by taxation—Engaged on a contemporary History—Despairs of the Tory Government—Dissensions and critical condition of the Tories—Loses his money among the ladies—His friends and himself alarmed by the Queen's illness—Death of L l Godolphin, and the sudden discovery of his virtues—Lady Orkney and himself grow great friends—Duke of Marlborough ill with *diabetes*—Rising hopes of the Ministry—Complains of Stella's delay in writing—A new Viceroy for Ireland—Swift's sister leaves Lady Giffard—He inquires about Dublin gossip—The Duchess of Hamilton works him a pocket for a snuff-box—Lady Masham makes the Queen send him preserved ginger—Finds fault with Parvisol, his agent—Lady Masham goes to Kensington to lie in—Her accident—An anxious time for himself and his Tory friends **128-133**

To HESTER VANHOMRIGH. Gossip—Loses his money at Ombre with the Duke and Duchess of Shrewsbury—Conjectures how Vanessa passes her time—Despatches from Lord Bolingbroke from Utrecht—Vanessa with her mother and sister intends to visit Windsor—Expense of journey and living—Advice to Vanessa and her sister—*Badinage* **134-135**

To ESTHER JOHNSON. Fears for the safety of Charles XII., King of Sweden, among the Turks—Prevails on Bolingbroke to invite Addison to dine with him on Good Friday—Addison preparing to bring out his *Cato*—Swift dines, with Addison, at Bolingbroke's—Steele brings out a new daily paper, the *Guardian*—The Peace signed—With Addison and others at Lord Bolingbroke's—Addison and his host—Mutual contentment—Passion week—Swift reads Sacheverell's "long dull sermon"—Sacheverell's first *Sermon* since his suspension—At a rehearsal of *Cato*—Mrs. Oldfield as Cato's daughter—Other news **135-137**

To ESTHER JOHNSON. Dines with the Premier and his Saturday company—The Duchess of Marlborough and the Queen's portrait—Goes to Court with Mr. Berkeley, for whom he intends to do all he can with the Government—Court and diplomatic news—Threatens the Tory Chiefs to return to Ireland—Dines at the Duke of Ormond's, who promises him the Deanery—Expects to be in Dublin before the end of April, 1713—Lady Masham's lamentations at his near departure—Dines with Arbuthnot and Berkeley—Lady Masham promises to speak to the Queen for him—Dines with Lady Masham, who intercedes with the Queen—The Queen promises to decide the matter with the Premier—Swift professes indifference, and prepares to set out for Ireland—Irritated at delays he shuns his Tory patrons—Dines at an ale-house with Berkeley and Parnell—The Queen at length orders the warrants—Her angry resolve—Further delay, and Swift's misgivings—At length announces his departure for Dublin . . . **138-141**

To JOSEPH ADDISON. Complains to him of Steele's attacks in the *Guardian*—Denies writing in the *Examiner*—Accuses Steele of ingratitude 141-142

To RICHARD STEELE. On the eve of starting for Ireland—Complains of being called "an Infidel"—Declares he seldom sees the *Examiner*, and his innocence of any assaults upon Steele in that paper—Calls the Tory Ministers to witness to his good offices on behalf of his old Whig friends—Professes himself still a Whig in politics—Has often defended the Duke of Marlborough—Reminds Steele of the eulogy given him in the Letter on the English Language—Reply of Steele, and another letter from Swift (*note*.) 142-144

To MRS. VANHOMRIGH. *Badinage*—His journey to Chester—Reminiscences of Dunstable—Visits a cousin, an old *belle*, at Chester—Desires to know what visitors Vanessa receives—His head somewhat the better for the journey, but fatigued 145-146

To HESTER VANHOMRIGH. His brief stay in Dublin—The visits paid him are all to the *Dean*—Hates the thoughts of Dublin, and prefers the discomforts of Laracor—Intends to pass the greater part of his stay in Ireland in that village—Will not visit England again unless sent for ;—Horribly melancholy during his installation as Dean—Describes Laracor—Vanessa a good politician—His *History of the Peace*—Occupations on his farm—Davila—The coming Assizes at Trim—Trim acquaintance 147-148

To DR. ARBUTHNOT. His usual way of treating his best friends—In no happy state—Familiar allusions to his Tory friends—*Martin Scriblerus* Arbuthnot's proper work, at least, as regards the sciences—Disqualifications of Pope, Gay, and Parnell for it—His own capabilities regarding it—Uncertain in his literary plans—As for his *History*; he will not again let it out of his hands, and will revise it, if he lives—Arbuthnot's hints on Medicine admirable—Court-life—Has written to Oxford a "very odd and serious" letter—Intends to visit him in Herefordshire—Ironical references to the Proclamation against the Pretender—Wishes the Kingdom, as well as the Succession, taken account of—Country politics doubly insupportable—The crops and dairy at Chawdry 149-151

To HESTER VANHOMRIGH. *Badinage*—Goes, not to Bath but, into Herefordshire to Lord Oxford's—Bolingbroke's prospects of the Premiership—Doubts his zeal for his (Swift's) preferment—Disappointed as to the post of Historiographer, which is gone to a "worthless rogue"—Refuses to rejoin the Party in power—Lord Oxford begs a visit from him—Oxford's faults as Minister, but his kindness to Swift "excessive"—A moving letter from him—Personal matters—Congratulates Vanessa on her legal knowledge—An illegible letter 151-152

To HESTER VANHOMRIGH. Sets out for Ireland to take the oaths—Blames her for visiting Wantage—Enjoins the greatest secrecy in correspondence—Warns her that in Ireland he shall very seldom see her—Ireland not a place for secrets—May meet her in London—The late political events (death of Queen, &c.) depress him . . 153

To LORD BOLINGBROKE. Holds him to be greater in retirement than at the head of affairs—Suspects the Post Office—Chagrin at the past blunders of the Tory Ministry—Bolingbroke has left no Elisha in the House of Commons—Compares the late Queen to the Giant Longaron of Rabelais—Bolingbroke the only possible saviour of his country—Agricultural prospects—Imagines his friend smoking with his "humdrum" squire—Invites him to the Deanery, promises food and lodging—Two good sixpenny pamphlets spoiled—How he shall be cured of loving England—Ruinous state of his Laracor parsonage—Lives solitarily in Dublin—Parsons not bad company when under subjection—Suffers only such parsons to come near him—Reflects upon the indolence and indifference of his Tory friends. . 154-156

To HESTER VANHOMRIGH. Excuses his avoidance of her—Fears for her health—Compares her Irish and English experiences—Letter from her to Swift (*note*) 156-157

To ALEXANDER POPE. Reasons for infrequent letters to England—Compares Pope's political prospects with his own—His great affection for Oxford, Bolingbroke, and Ormond—Anxiety for their safety—The eclipse of August 1—Borrows Pope's *Homer*—Blames him for bad rhymes, and for his triplets—The Notes and Preface perfectly good—Remarks on Pope's boldness in mentioning Bolingbroke—Notices the *Key to the Lock*—His dislike for the Irish Parliament—Not in a fit state for *Scriblerus*—Describes his household at the Deanery—His relations with the Archbishop, and with his Choir 158-160

To ALEXANDER POPE. Interrogates Ford as to Pope's political principles—Dedications to men in power, or none, the measure of the independence of writers—Power confers Virtue as five of the Popish Sacraments do *Grace*—On poets and wine-drinkers—Ireland not Paradise—On Pope's enemies, the publishers, and others—Has long had a design on Curll's ears—Exhorts Pope not to take service with the Turks—A hint for Quaker *Pastorals*—Newgate, footmen, &c., also afford material for a *Pastoral*—His mental depression 160-163

To HESTER VANHOMRIGH. *Badinage*—Sends some verses of his *Cadenus and Vanessa*—Alludes to Mary Vanhomrigh's ill health—An epigram on Dorinda—Vanessa's age for loving parsons not yet arrived—His illegible and, in some parts, unintelligible letter 164-165

To ARCHBISHOP KING. Refuses to believe Bolingbroke has turned "informer"—Bolingbroke's disqualification for that office, even if he wished for it—Confident of the innocence of his Tory friends of

Jacobitism—Clears himself of such suspicions—Surprised that the Archbishop could so many years have corresponded with him, believing him all the time to be a Jacobite—Had there been a plot he must have had some suspicion of it—Opportunities of the Tory Ministry—Himself always opposed to the Pretender's claims, and why 165-167

To JOSEPH ADDISON. Congratulates him on his appointment as Secretary of State—His appointment agreeable to many thousands of persons as a guarantee of the maintenance of Church and State—Obliged by Addison's good intentions towards him irrespective of Party—Professes high esteem and affection for him—Feels no vanity in being known to a Secretary of State—Concerned to see him stand single—To rise by merit a prodigious singularity—Great utility of such appointments 167-168

To HESTER VANHOMRIGH (in French). On a visit to some friends for the restoration of his health—Protests devotion to her wishes and commands—Anxious for her health—Promises her verses—Compliments her sister who likes tales and Latin—Compliments herself on her perfection in French—Some new perfection of hers always appearing—Ashamed of his own French—Her superlative merits—Blames her for hiding them from the world—Her great superiority, in all respects, even to the best of her sex—Impossible for him not to esteem her above the rest of the human species. 168—169

To HESTER VANHOMRIGH. Extraordinarily bad weather prevents walking or riding—Compliments her on her business and legal capacities—Advises her to drive away melancholy with diverting books as he himself does—His riding—Why she must not shake him by the hand—Doubts that any Christian family will receive him—Results of a "northern journey"—Not so nice in his conversation and company as she is—*Cadenus* the only conversable creature in Ireland—Politeness and cleanliness equally rare—Imagines himself and her together again—Her amusements—Her best company—Has been reading a vast amount of trash—Reminiscences of their London meetings—Extracts from an earlier letter from him and from Vanessa (*notes*) 170-173

To ROBERT COPE. Strange revolutions—Political reverses of his friends—A Bishop born to be his tormentor—The Whig Ministry wish him to give a benefice to one of their "hang-dogs"—His dilemma in regard to his Cathedral Chapter—The Brazen Image—General belief in Jacobite plots—Ireland drained of money—A narrow escape from hanging decides him against writing treason—Lions and bears and uncircumcised Philistines—Lord Orrery's Jacobitism—Swift's elm-plantations—Irish informers—Informing will be the best trade in London—Hates the Tories now, but also pities them as fools—Ironical eulogy of the royal clemency—Dublin gossip . . . 173-175

To JOHN GAY. Regrets for his English friends—Hatred of his Dublin life—Reasons for not visiting England—Inquires as to Gay's manner of living—Recommends to him temperance and exercise—His giddiness—Desires news of his old acquaintance—Pope's independence—Why poets are so bad courtiers—Inquires as to Gay's *Pastorals*—On Government patronage—Advises Gay to seek employment in Ireland, and assures him a welcome—Exhorts him either to be more moderate in his expenses, or to turn parson and get a bishopric 176-178

To LORD CARTERET. Apologises for not appearing at the Castle—Thanks him and Lady Carteret for their great civilities—Prefers a request for Dr. Sheridan, and vouches for his scholarship and virtues—Sheridan's greatest fault a wife and four children—The former, however, thought necessary for a schoolmaster—Sheridan, without some preferment, will starve 179-180

To DR. SHERIDAN. Stella and himself agree in exhorting Sheridan to a great appearance of temperance abroad, and observance of "all grave forms"—Cautions him not to pledge toasts in company of the Bishop of Cork—Mr. Addison's maxim in office—Swift lectures Sheridan on extravagance—Admonishes him not to lie in bed reading Homer—To stick to his school—Desires him to send the school-exercises for his correction—Exhorts him to preach at his own church, and be very devout—To keep regular hours, and hold evening-prayers . . 180-181

To DR. SHERIDAN. Lectures him on his inadvertences—Safer to blaspheme than to be of a party out of power—Quotes Don Quixote's authority—Scolds Sheridan for his rash sermon—The way of the world—Reminds him of his domestic disadvantages and inaptitude to bear ill-fortune—Lays down rules for his guidance and mode of life—Not to dream of printing his unlucky sermon—Lord Oxford's *bon mot*—An exhortation to make friends of the "Mammon of Unrighteousness" 182-184

To ALEXANDER POPE. His ecclesiastical occupations, and bursarial jurisdiction at St. Patrick's—Employed in finishing and revising his *Gulliver's Travels*—His design in writing the work—Pope and translations—Swift professes and defines his misanthropy—Definition of the human animal—Notices the *Odyssey*—Why less valued by him—Pope's grotto and garden—Allegory of a Court lady—Arbuthnot's illness—Arbuthnot has but one fault, illustrated from Bede—On Gay—Ambrose Philips writes *flams* on Miss Carteret—A Dublin blacksmith follows his example—Reasons for not subscribing his name to his letters—Accident to Bolingbroke 184-187

To WORRALL. Desires a draft on his bankers—His grief at the news of Stella's dangerous illness—His long intimacy with her—Has for two months seen through Mrs. Dingley's *disguises*—If Stella dies in his absence, intends to postpone his return to Ireland—Wishes she would make a Will—Her intended legacies—Could not endure to be at her death-bed—Fears her death at the Deanery, and consequent scandal—Enjoins on Worrall to write every week, and to observe the utmost secrecy—Shrinks from the thought of Stella's dying—Buys her a repeating gold watch—Holds too great and intimate friendship to be foolish—Renewed injunctions to secrecy—Other matters—Good news of Stella would be more welcome than the offer of Canterbury—Extract from his letter to Dr. Stopford reporting his reception by the Whigs in London, and interviews with the Princess of Wales and Walpole (*note*) 187-190

To DR. SHERIDAN. News of the dangerous illness of Stella long expected by him with the greatest agony of mind—Wished her to try Montpelier, Bath, or Tunbridge, or, at least, to come to London—The greatest event that could ever happen to him—His long intimacy with Stella—Her superlative merit—Could not endure to see her—Already forbodes her death—Interrupted by a visitor—Weary of the world—Stella's affection for Sheridan, in great measure, the cause of Swift's regard for him . . . 190-191

To THE HON. MRS. HOWARD. Sends her a piece of Irish plaid—The Parliament-men must not know, lest they cut off the weaver's fingers—Offers to make the same present to the Princess—His pledge if she will wear it—No courtier—Mrs. Howard's headaches—Extracts from letter of Mrs. Howard (*note*) 191-193

To THE HON. MRS. HOWARD. Obliquity of Mrs. Howard's handwriting—Affects ignorance of the meaning of her allusions to *Gulliver's Travels*—Refuses money-payment for her plaids, being a proselyte of the Houyhnhnms—Only mercenary Yahoos fond of *shining pebbles*—Is not a prostitute flatterer like Gulliver—Duty on the plaids already paid—Parables from *Gulliver*—Interprets certain prodigies—Letter from Lord Peterborough on the *Travels* (*note*) . . . 194-196

To ALEXANDER POPE. Affects ignorance of authorship of *Gulliver's Travels*—Criticises it—An episcopal criticism—*Tedium* of his life in Ireland—Gay's dilatoriness—Assists the Archbishop in degrading a parson for "coupling beggars"—A hint to Gulliver's friends . 197-198

To THE HON. MRS. HOWARD. Thanks her for her championship of *Gulliver*—Begs the continuance of her favour in making his peace with the Maids of Honour—Pretends ignorance of his offence—His insignificance at the Brobdingnagian Court, and the consequent contempt of its ladies for him—Submits his cause to Mrs. Howard, and lays the crown of Lilliput at her feet—Wishes all courtiers would imitate his honesty on a memorable occasion . . . 198-199.

To MARTHA BLOUNT. *Badinage* on their proposed correspondence—London extravagance and country management—Gossip about his

London friends—Of Pope and herself—Advises her to get out of Pope's jurisdiction—Twits her for taking up with an antiquated dean and a sickly poet—Inadvertently inserts a paragraph to Gay, and apologises—She is to threaten to turn heretic if Pope scolds—Wishes they would live with him, and promises them "hospitality"—The Catholic Dean of St. Patrick's should be her confessor . . 199–201

To Dr. Sheridan. Complains that his letters are often stopped and opened—Stella's dangerous cold—The Tories design to assail the Government—Walpole's agents in the Press—Greatly displeased with the Whig Minister and his party—Advised not to visit France—Walpole and the Viceroy's Irish bishops—Uncertainty of war-rumours—Heavy taxes in prospect—Walpole's indifference—Interview with the Princess of Wales—She retains her old civility, and himself his freedom—She taxes him with the authorship of *Gulliver*, but, no less than the Prince, is well pleased with every part of it—Affects to disown the book—Keeps bad company—Enjoins on Sheridan great care of Stella—Desires copies of his *Drapiers* . 202–203

To Dr. Sheridan. Vindicates his character as a correspondent—Pope reading Sheridan's *Persius* under difficulties—His own advice about it—Has informed Stella of the King's death—Intends to elude the Archbishop—Declines political intrigues—His old maladies—Proposes the Prince of Wales as Chancellor of the Dublin University—Desires Sheridan to copy his verses to Stella for his *Miscellany*—Alarmed for her health—Purchases for Irish friends—Braves the Archbishop's mandates—A visit to Paris prevented—Scolds Sheridan for sending the *Drapiers* bound—Desires it to be publicly known in Ireland that he never goes to Court—Why he wants the Poem to Stella—A challenge to Sheridan 203–206

To Worrall. Expects every day news of the death of Stella—Has cautioned his housekeeper, from fear of scandal—Too unwell to travel—Mrs. Dingley to be supplied with necessary money—Doubts his ability to return to Ireland before his license expires, which, therefore, is to be renewed for another year—Possible visit to France—Injunctions as to receiving his rent 206–207

To Benjamin Motte. Increased deafness—Suggestions for the illustration of *Gulliver's Travels*—The Voyage to Lilliput better fitted for illustration than the Brobdingnagian part—Instances possible woodcuts for the latter—Criticises some he has seen—Wotton the painter's criticism—Illustrations for the Flying Island—The Country of Horses might furnish many examples—The publisher is to consult Gay, Wotton, and others—His share in the *Miscellany*—His poetry worth printing to be found there—Rejection of some pieces by Pope's advice—Pope intends a pleasant Discourse on Poetry in the *Miscellany* 207–209

CONTENTS.

To ALEXANDER POPE. Describes the Achesons—Lady Acheson his pupil—His "libels" on her—Sees nobody in Dublin—False rumours of a new Viceroy—His grief for Congreve's death, but, under the circumstances, the event a "happy release"—Character of Dr. Helsham, his *bon-vivantism*, "hospitality," and easy indifferentism—Envies but does not love his character—Gay's contempt for advice 210-212

To ALEXANDER POPE. Eight months in the country with the Achesons —Returns of giddiness and deafness, which prevent him from visiting his Chapter and "punishing enormities"—None the less he has to pay for the Visitation Dinner—Peculiarity of his disorders—Contempt for a decision of the House of Lords—Ill health prevents his wintering in England—Inducements to Pope to cross the Channel—Shrinks from going to France because of his difficulty in conversing in the language —Gay's rude health—Asthma worse than deafness—Hopes Gay will not print his new Opera before it is acted—His "libels" on Lady Acheson not intended for the public eye—Allusions to some of his fugitive pieces—His part in the *Intelligencer*—His genius depressed by the circumstances of his life—Keeps humble company for want of means—Not at home to people of title—His Sunday evening entertainments—Begs Pope to come to him—Sends services to his friends in England—Angry with Mrs. Howard and the Queen for neglecting him—Mrs. Pope's illness—His letter really a reply to Ford's, whose handwriting he mistakes for Pope's 212-216

To LORD BOLINGBROKE. Acknowledges "travelling letters"—Deprecates his friend's affectations as to old age, &c.—Himself much older—Bolingbroke, not Oxford, his hero—Bolingbroke taught him to love the latter, and defended him—Suggests a Vindicatory History to the ex-Secretary—Daily reflects on death—Compares his own and his friend's birth and advantages—His love and esteem for him greater now, in his disgrace, than ever before in his exaltation—His contempt for money—Repudiates Bolingbroke's pretence at a stoical philosophy —Invites him to the Deanery—Laughs at his friend's faulty arithmetic—Can live on fifty pounds a year (wine excluded)—His only ambition—Only one or two in an age can expect immortality—Mingled pleasure and pain in writing to his friend—In default of philosophy desires stupefaction—Extracts from letters of Bolingbroke (*note*) 216-219

To JOHN GAY. Complains of rarity of Gay's letters—Letters to Gay or Pope meant for both—Impossibility of sending a letter to Gay in Scotland—Scotland in what respects worse than Ireland—Definition of Ireland—All exportation of Irish manufactures prohibited—Has heard of the "Wife of Bath," in Shakspeare, he thinks—Dissuades Gay from reviving his Opera of that name—Plenty of other subjects to choose among follies and vices—Poets, or creators, why so called—Pope, and Gay's debts—An unreasonable edition of De Thou —Why angry with Lord Burlington—Vindicates the honesty, present and prospective, of his Chapter—Gay turned out of his lodgings at Whitehall—Walpole's magnanimity—A cargo of violent colds— Regrets he does not know the Duchess of Queensberry—Her own fault—Her dignity and spirit—Excuses himself to her for his *solecism* in eating—Hopes she will be Gay's guardian, and take care of his purse—Remembrances to his friends in England . . . 219-223

To ALEXANDER POPE. An account of three citizens' wives, his friends—Mrs. Grierson, Mrs. Barber, and Mrs. Sykins—No such triumfeminate in London—Mrs. Sykins's ambition to "interview" Pope as the only remaining *Estrich* in England—Appoints Lewis his agent in dealing with his publisher Motte—Eulogy of Pope's mother —*A Libel on Dr. Delany and Lord Carteret*—Imputes his epistolary shortcomings to the climate, and to the prostitute slavery of the Irish Parliament 223-225

To LADY SUFFOLK (Mrs. Howard). His letter a history—Calls her to witness he has not played the courtier—His modest requests—The medal promised by the Queen never received—Nothing less than a portrait by Jervas will now satisfy him—Desires that she may be told this, although he is now under her displeasure—His only complaint against Lady Suffolk herself—Her virtues and accomplishments— Angry with the Queen for sacrificing Gay to Walpole—Gay's services merited for him better treatment—The Queen's promises about Ireland unfulfilled—That country now on the brink of ruin—Has never asked more than a trifle for himself—Congratulates Lady Suffolk on her release from court-servitude, and the uncertain position of a favourite —She will no longer be worried by sinecure-seekers, &c.—Has always credited her with sincerity, but heartily pledged her only for beauty, wit, and an unblemished character—Criticises Court morality —Desires his remarks be reported to the Queen—But for good manners, could have predicted Lady Suffolk's reverse of fortune— At least three ladies of his acquaintance equally unfortunate—Court ladies as "scaffoldings"—Inspiration of his letter—Esteems Lady Suffolk before all her sex, with a single exception—Has reason to complain of the Queen, but "venerates her great qualities" . 225-229

To ALEXANDER POPE. His lowness of spirits—Solitude and company equally displease him—All his papers left, in his Will, at Pope's disposal—Various literary schemes unaccomplished—More averse from writing every day—"Accidental" pieces never intended for publication —Starts the *Intelligencer* with Sheridan—Reasons for its short life— Identifies his own pieces—Enumerates some of his other productions —Disowns the *Scheme for Paying public Debts by a Tax on Vices*—

The actual author borrows the idea from *Gulliver*—The most promising young man they have, and his grand ambition to see Pope—Swift's poetic fountain dried up—*Polite Conversation*—*Directions to Servants*—Concerned for Lady Bolingbroke's health—Dawley without her—Why old men are said to be in second childhood—Condoles with Pope on his mother's illness . . 229-232

To LORD ORRERY. Excise on Tobacco Bill—Further taxes imminent—A pamphlet out in defence of the tax—Has sent Pope's epitaph on Gay to be copied, of which some lines ought to be corrected—Pope's *Imitation* of Horace, and his Essay on the *Use of Riches*, considered by his friends his *chefs d'œuvre*—Has chid Gay for writing a sequel to the *Beggar's Opera* and *Achilles*—Prophesies little good of the second part of the *Fables*—The first thoughts of a poet usually the most natural—Burnet's parody on Pope's *Imitation* . 233-234

To ALEXANDER POPE. Condoles with him on the loss of his mother—Hoped to see him in Ireland, but hears he is afraid of being killed there with eating and drinking—Limited number of unofficial persons able to give dinners—Employments in Church and State almost entirely in English hands—Dr. Delany the chief Apicius—Dublin in what superior to London—Promises Pope the attentions of his friends and of some "orderly females"—Himself unable to visit England—Not rich enough to live comfortably in that country—Greater civility shewn him in Ireland than in England—Chooses to be a free man among slaves rather than to be a slave among free men—His popularity and power in Dublin—Occasional feuds with the Archbishop—His vigour in youth 234-236

To MRS. PENDARVES. His disorders—Salutary effects of her letters—Her goodness in writing to him, and constancy in the general desertion—Extract from letter from her (*note*)—He cannot now "make shifts," and rough it as formerly—Strong expressions of regret at her absence—Wishes she were forced to take refuge in Dublin—A pernicious heresy prevalent as to women—Women themselves almost as heretical as the men—Reason for giving up his purpose of writing against this heresy—Herself would be the best contradiction to the prejudice—She may be silly for half an hour a week, if she will come—Lord Carteret in danger of being spoiled by riches—Lord Bathurst's friendship—Even Bolingbroke and Pope begin to fail him—Her immaculateness most vexes him—Explains meaning of the French *Boutade*—Has experienced it from many ladies—Commands her to come over for one year—Disappointed in the Duke of Chandos—No reply from the Duke to his exceptionally civil letter—Desires to know the reason from Lord Lansdowne—Professes great esteem for Mrs. Pendarves—Promises to be in residence, if she will come over 237-241

CONTENTS. xxix.

To MRS. PENDARVES. Reasons for not going to Bath—Seldom visited and seldomer visits—Dines alone like a king—His few acquaintance—Dublin not the same since her departure—Paradise, what and where—How often brought back by wives—Critical faculty and learning not necessarily synonymous, usually the contrary—Scolds her for taking him to be a pedant—Ladies improve in reading and writing—Hopes that gaming, dressing, and other accomplishments may soon restore their old ignorance—How a great lady among his correspondents scrawled and spelled—Knows several ladies of very high quality with the same defect—Mrs. Barber's circumstances and virtues—Delany and his friends—Could never weary of Mrs. Pendarves's company 241-243

To THOMAS BEACH. Like all poets, his correspondent no favourite of fortune—Approves of his poem, *Eugenio*, but points out its faults—Condemns the *triplet*, and blames Dryden for using it and the *Alexandrine*—Himself banished them by a *triplet* in his *City Shower*—Prevailed on Pope, Gay, and others to reject them—Pope uses them in his *Homer* only, and in one or two of his latest poems—Denounces certain abbreviations in Poetry—An author can best correct his own productions—Dissuades Beach from publishing in Dublin, and recommends Motte or Lintot—His own Works printed in Dublin against his wish—The London publishers' chagrin—His letter to Pulteney (*note*) 244-246

To LADY BETTY GERMAINE. Apologises for failing memory—The House of Lords and Curll—Wonders how Curll got hold of the Pope letters—Has not yet seen them—Burned all the letters received from Ministers he could find—Has preserved hers, because entertaining—Some letters from others kept out of friendship, in spite of bad sense and spelling—Hates to forget dead friends—All letters of Somers burned—All those of Halifax but one—Good sense of her own letters—Has never printed any of his own or correspondents' letters—Puzzled by a passage in her letter, and begs explanation—Affects anger with her niece, Lady Vere Beauclerc—Threatens to send all the letters of the latter to Curll, unless she apologise—Complains of the Duke of Dorset (Lord-Lieut.) for not replying to his letters—Imagines reasons for his incivility—His own letters to him few and disinterested—Little approves of the Government in either country—Takes credit for not using his influence in Ireland to be troublesome—Has ceased entirely to interfere in Irish politics, from despair—The loyal Irish Whigs, and Government emoluments—Letters of Lady B. Germaine to Swift (*notes*) 246-250

To LORD ORRERY. Bad health the cause of his retirement—Settling his affairs like a dying man—His whole fortune bequeathed in trust for the building and maintaining a Lunatic Asylum—Saves the

expense of a Chaplain and almost of a Physician—A real King—
"Trifler" Sheridan his greatest loss—The fright of the Bishop's
Chaplain—Sees little company, except on Sunday evenings—Drs.
Helsham and Delany—Squire Hughes's poetry—Out of patience with
the present set of *Whifflers*—Desires Orrery, as he traverses his
estates, to compute the increasing poverty and misery of the poor
Irish tenants—Still greater misery in the neighbourhood of the
Capital—His wish for the City of Cork—Unusual quiet of the Capital
—A compliment equal to any in the *Polite Conversation* . 250-252

To DR. SHERIDAN. A rhyming letter—A prophetic calendar in verse
—St. Patrick's bells celebrating the election of a Master of the
Corporation of Butchers 252-253

To DR. SHERIDAN. Joint letter of *persiflage* of Swift and Mrs.
Whiteway—Poem on the *Legion Club* announced—Consists of 240
lines, and is sold at threepence—He signs a petition to the Government—Makes a long speech at the Tholsel 254-255

To DR. SHERIDAN. Challenges him to a friendly duel—Sheridan's
arithmetic—Sheridan as a schoolmaster—Advises and scolds him on
various domestic concerns—Mrs. Whiteway and Sheridan—Obstacles
to Swift's leaving home and travelling—His affairs terribly embroiled
—His scheme of living at Cavan, or going to Bath, during the Session
of the Irish Parliament—Detests the follies and corruptions of the
Legislature—Exhorts Sheridan to business habits—A military plague
—Mrs. Acheson's relapse—Dr. Grattan's ailment—Philosopher
Webster 255-257

To JOHN TEMPLE. Mrs. Dingley and her troubles—Lely's portrait of
Lady Giffard—Pleads for Mrs. Dingley—Her merits—Ignorant of the
present Temple family—Approves the keeping up the family-place at
Moor Park, and hears it is much improved—The elm on which he
carved a Latin hemistich—His rough correspondence with Lord
Palmerston—Forgets the cause of it—Lord Castledurrow . 257-259

To ALEXANDER POPE. Pope not only his best but his only friend
left—Indifferentism of ordinary friends—Social selfishness—Annoyed
by conventional compliments—The poor more constant than the rich
—His popularity with his "lower friends"—Without the love, or
even civility, of the people in place or power—Boasts of exchanging
no visits with lords, spiritual or temporal—His own cathedral his only
patronage—Thanks Pope for his version of the Horatian *Singula de
nobis anni prædantur euntes*, &c.—Most pleased with his celebration
in the *Dunciad*—Miscarriage of letters—The greatest rogue in England—Virtue not proof against place and power—The new
Pharoah 259-260

To WILLIAM PULTENEY. Pulteney's letter from Bath not received—
Suspects meddlers at the post office—Agrees with him respecting

physicians—Arbuthnot the only physician from whom he has ever got benefit—His medical dietetic prescription—Does not profess himself *philanthropus*, and why—Another Duke as Viceroy—Pulteney's motto and modesty—The Duke of Dorset as Viceroy—Has ceased all communication with him—Useless applications to the Duke—Lord Bolingbroke's father likely to outlive his son—The most worthless man in England—Reasons for not visiting England—Spreads the story of Mrs. Mapp—Will Carteret oppose arbitrary power?—The deceitfulness of riches—Letter from Pulteney (*note*) . . 260-263

To LORD OXFORD. Narrates the origin of his *History of the Four Last Years*—His unsuccessful mediation between Bolingbroke and Oxford's father at Lord Masham's—Goes to Oxford and then into Berkshire till the Queen's death—The Tories and the *History*—Determined to publish it now in London—Has had the best means and opportunities of learning the facts—In the highest confidence of the Tory chiefs—His *History* based on official documents and information from the Government—Characterises Lord Oxford (the Premier)—Offers to print in an appendix any letters or suitable material—His disinterested attachment to the first Lord Oxford—Prides himself on his English origin—Congratulates his correspondent on his marriage—Repeats his own qualifications as historian—One great design of his *History*—No hope of seeing England again—His domestic way of life—Laments his lot in an oppressed and miserable country—Ireland not made miserable by Nature—Good wishes for the present Lord Oxford and his family—Will watch his career with interest, but expects his own life, of which he is heartily weary, will soon end—Hears that England is as fully corrupt as enslaved Ireland—Letters from Lord Oxford (*note*) 263-266

To ERASMUS LEWIS. Why he has not written to him for so many years—Repeats the origin and reason of his *History*, and adds further particulars—Unnecessary anxiety of (the present) Lord Oxford as to his father's appearance in the book—The author more likely to be charged with partiality to the late Minister—Lord Oxford could know nothing more of importance—Lewis himself the only important witness—Difficulty of transmitting his MS.—The present possessor tenacious of it, but consents to let it be read to either Oxford or Lewis—Himself could satisfy them both, if he could get to London—Bolingbroke now in France, writing the *History of his Own Times*—Bolingbroke's hatred of Oxford—Swift's grief at the deaths of Arbuthnot, Gay, and other friends—Pities Lord Masham, and dislikes the education of his son—Inquires as to other friends—Increasing deafness and giddiness—Thinks deafness worse than blindness—Writing no longer amuses him—Always dines at home with his housekeeper—Sometimes receives one or two friends and a female cousin—Letter of Lewis (*note*) 267-269

To ALDERMAN BARBER. Reports a letter from Pope, and a few lines from Bolingbroke—The sale of Dawley—Desires to know Bolingbroke's state of affairs—Reflects upon his extravagance—Inquires after Lady Bolingbroke—Anxious to see Bolingbroke's *History*—Approves Pope's last poem, MDCCXXXVIII.—His obscure way of life hinders recognition of its allusions—His great affection for the Oxfords—Lord Oxford's extravagance unendurable: the dupe of a land-jobber—Sends his "services" to the Oxfords and to Lord Bathurst—His walking powers—But for his deafness would ride through Ireland and through half England—His aversion for the term "Great Britain" 270-271

III.—THE LIFE AND WRITINGS OF POPE.

His place among the letter-writers—His letters laboured and artificial—The Poet of Art and Epigram—After Shakspeare, the most often quoted of English Poets—His parentage—Claims descent from an Earl of Downe—His parents both Papist—Brought up in that Church, and his earliest friends members of it—Inherited feebleness and deformity of body—Alleged sweetness of his disposition in childhood—His first teaching and schools—Indebted mainly to his own early efforts—His father retires to Binfield with a considerable fortune—Pope's studies there—Precocious powers of versification common to all the great poets—Reads Homer and Ovid in Ogilby and Sandys—Dryden his chief model—Uncertainty as to dates of his earliest productions—His account of them to Spence—Origin of the *Pastorals*—Eulogies of his friends and the critics—His early patrons—First appearance of the *Pastorals* in Tonson's *Miscellany*—Letter to Walsh on borrowing in literature—To Henry Cromwell in praise of Philips—Sends an ironical paper to the *Guardian*—Publishes in Tonson's *Miscellany* imitations of Chaucer and specimen-versions of the *Iliad*—Publishes his *Essay on Criticism*—Its principles—Allusions to superstition—Attacks Dennis—Publishes *Windsor Forest* and *Messiah*, and, in Lintot's *Miscellany*, verse translations and imitations of Ovid and Statius, and *Rape of the Lock*—*Ode on St. Cecilia's Day*, Prologue to *Cato*—Contributes Essay to the *Guardian* on the cruelties of Butchering and "Sport"—Becomes known to the chief literary and political persons of the day—His friendship and correspondence with Swift—Replies to Swift's proposition to him to join the Established Church—Writes to Steele—Papers in the *Guardian*—Satirises Dennis—An alleged letter to Addison—His satire of him—Intimacy with Arbuthnot, Gay, Parnell, Prior, Harley, and Bolingbroke—Associates himself with the Tory Party—His Papist friends—Letters to Caryll on sectarian intolerance and on political partisanship—Reference to *Cato*—Friendship with the Blounts—Pays court to both sisters—His affectation of gallantry to women—Denies truth of reports in regard to Martha Blount—Writes to Caryll on the same subject—Addresses a poetical epistle to Teresa Blount—Another to

c

her under the name of Zephalinda—An ecstatic letter to Martha Blount—Correspondence with Wycherley—With Henry Cromwell—Publishes revised edition of the *Rape of the Lock*—Its models—Enthusiastic praises of it—His representation of Miss Fermor as Belinda—Her marriage—Her portrait—Pope puts forth a *Key to the Lock*—Contributes to Steele's *Miscellanies* more translations and imitations from the *Odyssey* and Chaucer—His *Iliad*—Letters from him during the progress of the work—Difficulties in the translation and with engravers—His assistants—Works consulted by him—His *Odyssey*—Pecuniary profits—Congratulations of friends—An indignant letter on Addison's preference and partiality for Tickell—Ceases to be on friendly terms with Addison—Makes the acquaintance of Jervas—His early sketches and remaining specimens of his paintings—*A Farewell to London*—Migrates from Binfield to Chiswick—Visits the Princess's Court at Richmond, and his aristocratic friends—His *Elegy to the Memory of an Unfortunate Lady*, and *Eloisa to Abelard*—Sources of the latter poem—Makes the acquaintance of Lady M. W. Montagu—Of the Maids of Honour—Joins them in their parties of diversion, which he describes in a letter to Teresa Blount—Periodical visits to Bath—Describes to Teresa Blount the manner of taking the bath *à la mode*—Visits Oxford—Humorous letter on his adventures with his publisher on the road—Carries on incessant war with authors and publishers—Origin of his quarrel with Curll—His ridicule of him—Quarrels with Cibber—Moves from Chiswick to Twickenham—Improvements in the villa and grounds—Letters to Edward Blount describing his *Grotto*—Ridicules the fashionable gardening—Not insensible to the charms of landscape, as evidenced in letters to the Blounts, Digby, and others—Celebrates Miss Judith Cowper under the name of Erinna—Corresponds with her—Sends her a copy of verses—His edition of Shakspeare—Origin of his feud with Theobald and enmity to critics and commentators—Publishes his translation of the *Odyssey*—Makes the acquaintance of Spence—Entertains Swift at Twickenham—Associated with Swift, Gay, and Arbuthnot in the *Miscellanies*—His chief contributions to them—Relates the history of his *Treatise on the Bathos*, and the enmities incurred by it—The original of the *Dunciad*—Witty parodies on *Gulliver's Travels*—Narrow escape from drowning—Relations with Voltaire—Origin of the *Dunciad*—First ascertained edition—Announces to Swift its intended publication—Ingenious methods for obtaining notoriety for it—His account of its reception by its victims—Various persons figuring in the *Dunciad*—Adds a Fourth Book—Theobald dethroned in favour of Cibber—The satire directed against personal rather than public wrongs—Continues the war in the *Grub Street Journal*—Publishes his *Epistles*, 1731-35—Satirises Lady M

W. Montagu, the Duchess of Marlborough, Lady Suffolk, and others—The *Epistles* rather Satires than Moral Essays—Visits Lord Peterborough at Bevis Mount—His friendship and connexion with Lord Bolingbroke—Character of the Pope-Bolingbroke correspondence—Obligations to his friend in the *Essay on Man*—His alterations of certain passages in the *Essay*—Acknowledges Warburton's championship—First meets him at Twickenham—Procures for him a rich wife and, indirectly, a Bishopric—Character of the Pope-Warburton correspondence—Alarmed by the attack of De Crousaz on the heterodoxy of the Poem—Inspires an apologetic letter to Louis Racine—Also writes apologetically to Caryll—Merits of the *Essay*—Human arrogance ridiculed—World-wide Humanitarianism—Numerous alterations and revisions—Not always improvements—*The Universal Prayer*—Dedicates Prologue to his *Epistles* to Arbuthnot—Letter to Caryll on an *Imitation* of Horace—*Parerga,* Epigrams, &c.—Epitaphs on his friends and himself—Replies to Lord Hervey's *Epistle*—Letter to Swift noticing his *Letter to a Noble Lord*—Satirises Hervey in *Grub Street Journal* and in *Epistle to Arbuthnot*—Visits to his friends—Letters from Bristol and Clifton—Savage at Bristol—Frequent visits to Lord Bathurst at Cirencester, and to Lord Peterborough at Southampton—With Lord Chesterfield visits the old Duchess of Marlborough—With Martha Blount a guest of the Allens at Bath—His letter to her upon a quarrel with their hosts—Last visits to Bolingbroke at Battersea—Last letters—Last letter to Martha Blount—Retains his energy to the end—Conforms to the rites of his Church—Buried at Twickenham—His Will and legacies—Alleged breach of trust in regard to Bolingbroke's Writings—Furious controversy between the latter and Warburton—Pope's numerous biographers and editors—Various estimates of his place among the Poets—Principal critics on either side—His two most eminent eulogists, Voltaire and Byron—Their opinions quoted—His Editors—Warburton's Edition—Ruffhead's *Life of Pope*—Johnson's *Life*—Wakefield's unfinished Edition—Warton's Edition—Bowles's Edition—Campbell defends Pope from the criticisms of the latter—The long and heated controversy upon Pope—Byron the most distinguished combatant—Roscoe's Edition—Croker's intended Edition—Elwin's Edition—The most adverse critics of Pope unite in enthusiastic eulogy of the *Rape of the Lock* and the *Eloisa to Abelard*—C. W. Dilke's investigations—Edition of Carruthers—Faults in the *Essay on Criticism* and *Essay on Man* pointed out, in detail, by his latest Editor—Adverse critics err in not considering enough the Age, education, and circumstances of Pope—The poet of Society and of Epigram *par excellence*—His many defective rhymes and harsh inversions—His ethics superior to his metaphysics—His large contribution to English proverbial phrases—His character and place as a letter-writer—No other correspondence the cause of so much perplexity and controversy to biographers and editors—First discoveries of Pope's epistolary insincerity—Sketch of the history of his epistolary frauds—The Wycherley correspondence—His first acknowledged corrected Edition of his correspondence—A second revised Edition—Publishes his reasons for bringing it out—The Atterbury correspondence—Swift correspondence—The Caryll Letters—Motives of his epistolary insincerity and frauds—His good qualities—A certain humaneness in his philosophical system—Thackeray's opinion of him—Chesterfield's testimony—Correspondence with Bolingbroke, Warburton, and Atterbury criticised—Alleged letters to Addison—Correspondence with Lady Mary Wortley Montagu—Absurd affectations of gallantry—Letters to the Blount sisters and to Judith Cowper—Letters to Digby and Fortescue—A large proportion of his letters and correspondence have interest for the biographer rather than for the general reader—With few exceptions, his correspondents' letters not distinguished by any special merit—His physical defects satirised by himself in the *Guardian*—His portraits—Handwriting 276-348

IV.—LETTERS OF POPE.

To WILLIAM WALSH. On his *Pastorals* and on *Pastoral* poetry—The *Aminta* and *Pastor Fido*—Innocence of the pastoral character imaginary—On the liberty of borrowing in literature—Praises his friend's *Eclogues* 351-353

To THE REV. RALPH BRIDGES. Thanks him for his criticism of his Homer translations—Led into deviations from the Greek by Chapman and Hobbes—Remarks on their translations—Adopts his friendly critic's suggestions, even in opposition to Dryden—Values one live poet above twenty critics or commentators—The latter, however, necessary to him—Distinguishing excellences of Homer—Homer and Virgil compared—Homer's beauty of language—Apologises for his pedantry 353-355

To HENRY CROMWELL. Delays to write in order to send him the *Miscellanies* and his Statius—Authors and publishers—A poetic flux upon him—Modern bards in Spring—Their productions compared to flowers cut for the market—Covent Garden and the poetical Magazines similarly supplied—The publishing enterprise of Hills, of Blackfriars—A modern "Sappho"—Submits his verses to Cromwell's criticism, and promises deference to his judgment for the future—Desires him to mark the criticised passages—Pledges himself to avoid *Hiatus* as far as possible—Malherbe convinces him of its non-necessity—Dryden does not follow his own rule—Sends his services to Wycherley . 356-358

To HENRY CROMWELL. Describes his adventure in a coach—A sick lady—His shortsightedness—The lady proves to be an interesting companion—Never till now had any ambition to be a "doctor"—Prescribes a dose of forbidden fruit, and effects an immediate cure in spite of the "doctors"—The story of the devil and Eve, with a difference 359-360

To RICHARD STEELE. Passes Christmas with certain honest country gentlemen, who never read the *Spectator*—Has, therefore, not earlier acknowledged Steele's eulogy of his *Essay*—Thanks him for his candour no less than for his good opinion—A common method of pretenders to taste or learning—Engages to adopt Steele's corrections—Conscious of the faults of the poem—Some encouragement needed by a young writer—Steele's lavish praises dictated by partiality—Expresses esteem for and gratitude to him—Steele's reply . 360-361

To THE HON. JAMES CRAGGS. Mrs. Weston—The unfortunate most need sympathy and consideration, yet most neglected by the world—Cannot excuse the conduct of some of his family or friends in regard to Mrs. Weston—Sympathy of mind a greater bond than blood-relationship—Craggs's compassion for Mrs. Weston more appreciated by Pope than all his former kindnesses—Letter from Craggs (*note*) . 362-363

To RICHARD STEELE. Gratified by Steele's praises of the *Temple of Fame*—Will be still more obliged by his friend's severity—No errors too trivial for correction—Many of them in his poem—Steele's panegyric neither merited nor expected—His *Temple of Fame* long in manuscript—Shrinks from publishing anything unworthy of his readers' acceptance—Replies to Steele's request for his co-operation in the new *Guardian*—Sends compliments to Addison—Letter from Steele (*note*) 363-364

To JOHN CARYLL. Congratulates himself on their increased friendship—Follows Caryll's advice, and takes lessons in painting from Jervas—Idle as a poet—The enthusiastic reception of Addison's *Cato* by Whigs and Tories alike—The Prologue-writer clapped into a Whig against his will—Bolingbroke and Booth—The Whigs "on their mettle"—Dr. Garth's *bon mot*—*Cato* just published—Cried about the streets and sold in the parks—An instance of the infection of popularity 364-366

To JOHN CARYLL. Deprecates the fame of his papers in the *Guardian*
—Too few to be worth the credit or discredit they bring him—
His association with Steele taken very ill by the Tories and Jacobites
—Expects calumnies from it—Himself scorns political partisanship—
Nullius addictus jurare in verba Magistri—If he has renounced
reason in theology, will not renounce it in anything else—Mr. Englefield's want of civility—Expects such annoyances in the course of his
life—Usually employs his mornings in painting at Jervas's in Cleveland
Court, and his evenings in society without distinction of sect or
party—Encloses his imitation of the Epigram of Hadrian *Ad Animam*,
with two others 366-369

To JOHN GAY. Becoming an ardent pupil of Jervas—Discontented with his
attempts at portraiture of Swift, the Ladies Bridgwater, Duchess of
Montagu, and others—Attempts at a Crucifixion and a Madonna—A
rival of St. Luke himself—Not obnoxious to the penalty of the "Second
Commandment"—Gay's *Fan*, and Pope's advice—Use of the fan in
China 369-370

To JOHN GAY. Complains of perpetual sickness—Immortality of the
soul his constant speculation—Seneca—Dr. Parnell promises contributions to Tonson's *Miscellany*—Dr. Swift approves of his design of a
periodical to be called *The Works of the Unlearned*—The *Fan*—
Deeply engaged in poetry—Expects his friend Fortescue   - 371-372

To DEAN SWIFT. Swift lays him under two special obligations, by
correspondence and by his munificent proselytising bribe—No clergyman ever so generous with his purse in the cause of any religion—
His bribe almost as large as that accepted by Judas of Iscara—A
better speculation would be to propose a change of religion, than
to propose a translation of Homer, by subscription—Proposes his conditions—A poet and good Christian irreconcilable—The Whigs as
much wish to make him the one as Swift the other—On what terms
he will become a convert—Recognises the disinterestedness and zeal
of the Government on behalf of truth—Confers upon the Dean full
authority to transact the business in his name—The conditions
detailed—Reserves one article (Masses for the Dead), out of regard
for his friends' salvation—Those for whom he happens to be most
concerned are heretics, schismatics, poets, and painters—Expense of
delivering them from Purgatory all the greater—Particularly in the
cases of Dryden, Walsh, and L'Estrange—Why the Tories ought not
to grudge the purgatorial tax for the last—Sum total of the expense
of the ransoms—A further consideration of the cases of certain friends,
such as Jervas and Gay—An extra expense—The most costly of all
the residents in Purgatory will be the Dean himself, who, by his
own confession, has composed more libels than sermons—Reason for
hoping his safety after all—Pope thinks his soul undeserving to be

saved, if he did not try to save that of one to whom he is so much
obliged—Montaigne's apophthegm—According to it, Swift is his
debtor rather than creditor—Completion of the *Rape of the
Lock* 372-375
To JOHN CARYLL. Congratulates him upon the birth of an heir—
Obligations to him as a solicitor for subscription for the Homer—
Requests a list of the subscriptions by the opening of Parliament—
The list to be then printed—Confident of warm support—Flatters
himself he has skilfully managed the Dedication of the *Rape of the
Lock*—Written with great deliberation—Miss Fermor approves—
Has taken the best advice in the kingdom respecting it—His intended
Preface superseded by the Dedication—Fools, however, will talk—
Rentes viagères—Intends to revenge himself on the "Great
Monarch" in his Homer—Proposes to be in London all the
winter 375-377
To JOHN CARYLL. Too much devoted to Homer to visit Ladyholt—
The long siege of Troy not a pleasing prospect—The Greek not so
formidable as he had feared—Commentators and critics a troublesome
sort of auxiliaries—A method of dispensing with their services—
Caryll soliciting subscriptions—Unfriendly critics charge him with
ignorance of Greek—Refuted by his specimen translations already
before the public—Charges of Popery and of Toryism—At a loss
to account for the former accusation—Accused, on the other
side, of Whiggism—A reasonable inference—Partisanship and
Sectarianism dominant—Finds it a misfortune to have been bred a
Papist—Between two fires—His indifference and impartiality—Independence of mind worth more than all the virtues of Bigotry 377-380
To JOHN GAY. Invites him to Binfield where Parnell is a guest—Mr.
Harcourt's bad report of Gay's health—Dr. Parnell's liturgical error
—Parnell and himself in exemplary harmony, warned by the Greeks
before Troy—The effects of Homeric studies upon his looks—Young
himself of not more tragic aspect—Cannot consent to the publication
of a certain burlesque—Sends his remembrances to the Dean, Arbuthnot, and others 380-381
To ARABELLA FERMOR. The *Rape of the Lock* designed only to amuse
a few young ladies, who can laugh at their sex's follies and their own
—Reason of the hasty publication of the first incomplete edition—
Explains the meaning of *machinery* in poetry—The ancient poets
and many modern young ladies compared—The Rosicrucians—*Le
Comte de Gabalis*—Sylphs, Gnomes, Nymphs, and Salamanders—The
poem wholly fictitious—Belinda and Miss Fermor have nothing in
common but beauty—Miss Fermor's immaculateness . . 381-383
To ARABELLA FERMOR.—One man of merit worth a thousand common-
place adorers—The happy fortune of her accepted lover—Felicitates

her—More her well-wisher than a pretender to celebrate her beauty—She has more happiness to come than that of being a fine lady—To be addressed now in the language of truth—Felicitations again 383-384

To Dr. Parnell. Entreats him to return to Binfield—Entirely depends upon him in the matter of Homer—Homer's commentators overwhelm him—Curses them all, and even blasphemes Homer himself—Begs Parnell to come quickly and prevent further impiety—Parnell's miracles—If Parnell cannot come to him, he must go to Parnell—His time never more precious—Compares himself as unacademic with his academic and Greek-learned friend—The one a mere wit, the other a reverend parson—His learned friend, in fine, is Dr. *Parnell* 384-386

To Dr. Arbuthnot. Hot weather and headaches—Has read Arbuthnot's verses on the Dust-Plague—*Scriblerus* must be postponed to the winter—No disadvantage, since the world will be affording fresh materials—Reports a recent visit to the Dean at Letcombe—The Dean in the character of an Epicurean deity—Swift's methods of passing his time—Experiments and mystic signs on the votes and bills of the House of Commons—Concludes with an epigram in the Scriblerian manner 386-389

To Charles Jervas. Reports a visit to Oxford—All very honest fellows there—Their great consternation at the news of the Queen's death—No panegyrics yet ready for the new King at the University—Admires Jervas's Whig principles of resistance—Quotes Addison's verses on Liberty—Thanks Jervas for his good offices with Addison—Reflects on Philips' conduct towards him—Expects nothing more than mere civility from Addison—Would scorn to receive a favour from any man having so low an opinion of him as to consider him as a mere partisan—Leaves his reputation to Time to vindicate—Addison sure of his respect at all times, and of his real friendship when he chooses to claim it—The nature of his connexion and correspondence with Swift—Obligations forced him to show gratitude—Anathematises *Party*—Wishes there may be an end of it . . 389-391

To Edward Blount—However occupied, incapable of forgetting him—His Homeric task increased by his addition of Notes, and the necessity of a visit to the Oxford Libraries—Lord Harcourt—Dr. Clarke seduces him from his proper occupation—The Geographers and their Maps, and the Libraries—His engraver's shortcomings—Writes to him in a highly imperious style—Inconveniences of being a Papist—A dangerously-powerful subject—Barcelona the rival of Troy—Why *Machinery* in a *Barceloniad* would be juster—Professes astonishment at the co-existence of so much heroism and so much superstition in the same breasts—A trip of curiosity to London at the Queen's death—His political and philosophical indifferentism—Cosmopolitanism proof against the agitations of Party—Hopes that Toryism and Whiggism may be things of the past—Regrets that Roman Catholics have not been imbued with the spirit of tolerance—*Quicquid delirant reges, plectuntur Achivi*—The madness of the many the gain of the few 391-394

To WILLIAM FORTESCUE. His lawyer-friend does not deserve the diabolic motto, *circuit quærens quem devoret*—The travelling experience of a barrister—His own inferiority as a rambler—Fortescue's report of a legal *case* entertains some ladies of their acquaintance—Reports of the same kind continued would be more diverting than half the novels read by ladies—They would have a happy union of truth and scandal—Bath itself yields to circuit experience—An eminent judge's precedent unheeded 394-395

To TERESA BLOUNT. Declares an impartial and divided affection for herself and her sister—In love with them from infancy—Queens-regent by turn—His practice is to write to the Sovereign for the time being—Dr. Radcliffe's prescription, and her sister's obstinacy—When virtues and vices exchange places—Her sister as Undine—At Bath ambitious ladies must leave their proper element—Martha Blount and Queen Christina of Sweden compared—The best mermaid in Christendom excelled—Teresa in the character of Undine—Exhorts her to conquer by water as well as by land—Buckram and German Ruffs—The tyranny of fashion becomes easy by habit—A delightful story, and an ineffectual *recipe* 395-397

To DR. ARBUTHNOT. A joint letter from Parnell and himself—*Scriblerus* much neglected by Parnell at present—Hopes the late political changes will not deprive the world of the further lucubrations of Martin—Pledges himself to advance the work as much as he can—The campaign before Troy almost ended—Rejoices at his approaching freedom—Gay, though he has lost his diplomatic secretaryship, will still act as secretary to Martin Scriblerus—No greater glory—Recollections of the meetings of the *Scriblerus* Club at St. James's Palace—Reply of Arbuthnot (*note*) 397-398

To JOHN GAY. Welcomes him on his return from Hanover—Offers him a retreat at Binfield—Whether Whig or Tory, equally welcome—Real friends do not need the assurance of frequent letter-writing—The late surprising political *bouleversement* sufficiently accounts for the epistolary shortcomings of Gay's friends—Even himself affected by the late excitement—His own reasons for not writing to his friend—Invites him to assist in celebrating the end of the Homeric labours at Binfield—*Badinage* upon Gay's *Pastorals*—The Blouzelindas of the Hague and the Rosalindas of Britain—Hanover Philips and his

Rosalind—Parnell and himself at the Bath and inseparable—Offers to pay Gay's expenses if he will join them—Advises him to make his fortune by some Court-ode or other 399-401

To MARTHA BLOUNT. Writes from the Bath—Neglects a large company of ladies for that purpose—Commands a prospect of a bevy of them from the window—The finest promenade in the world—His dissipations at Bath—Why no lampoon out on the Bath ladies—His late travelling companion the prettiest of them—Mrs. Gage does him double honour—Endeavours to be agreeable by imitating the beaux, in particular Gascoigne and Nash—A deluded Adonis—Nash and Gascoigne his chief male acquaintance—Is so much of a rake as to be ashamed to be seen with Dr. Parnell—Better company expected—A disgraced Earl's health drunk by certain ladies—Libels and intrigues under disguise of " drinking the waters "—The public man who deserves a monument—A week's dissipation—Intends to visit Longleat and Lord Lansdowne—The two sisters never so much in his thoughts as now—Differently regarded by him at Binfield, London, and Bath—Her narrow escape from death has revealed all her value to him—Expresses admiration for both sisters—Their superiority to the rest of their sex 401-403

To JOHN CARYLL. Caryll in a fit of the gout—Harcourt also a gouty subject—Gay and himself suffering from an attack of criticism—Some intervals of ease and laughter—Critics and tarantulas produce the same effects—Burnet's *Homerides*—The same critic attacks *What-d'ye-Call-It*—The Pope and his *Homer* not yet burned by the hangman, and Gay's Farce not yet silenced by the Lord Chamberlain—Productions destined to survive those of the critic's father, the Bishop of Salisbury—The Bishop's fate according to Sacheverell and the Church of Rome—Town news—Invited to see the lions at the Tower—The invitation comes from a lord who shortly expects to have a lodging there—Gay's Farce—To be acted at Lincoln's-Inn-Fields in spite of Steele 403-405

To DR. PARNELL. Numerous complaints from Parnell's correspondents—Variety of conjectures at the reasons for his silence— The only valid excuse his occupation on the *Life of Zoilus*—Witty allusion to Parnell's translation of the *Batrachomyomachia*—Acknowledges receipt of Parnell's poem through Addison—A packet of various new literature 405-407

To JOHN CARYLL. Just arrived, much fatigued, at Bath with Parnell—Represents himself as a stranger and foreigner there—Nothing remarkable in the shape of visitors or lampoons—His own genius not at all turned to that sort of satire—His laborious Translation would extinguish any such kind of emotion—Quotes the case of Dryden—On the whole, as innocent and as little dreaded as Wycherley, who is now at

Bath—Wycherley's encomium of Caryll justified—Doubts the advantage either to his Homer or to his health from his Bath dissipations—Hopes to visit Ladyholt—Writes in the midst of a number of noisy friends at a tavern 407-409

To MARTHA BLOUNT. At Stanton Harcourt—Describes a journey and visit to Oxford—Sentimental reflections—A black gown and a salary would transform him into a University don—Conforms to the University way of living—His vanity excited by the respectful reception given to him—Asks himself what College or Library he had founded—Doubts the expediency of returning to the world again, and of forsaking the Library for a lady's feet—A piece of Euphuism—Stanton Harcourt harbours an angel—The angel a relative of his Lordship, who offers her to him as wife—Declines politely—In love with both sisters at Mapledurham 409-411

To DEAN SWIFT. Jervas, the bearer of the letter, can best express all his affection and esteem—Compares Swift, in Ireland, to a patron-spirit in another world—The susceptibilities of a Protestant divine need not be offended at such a comparison—Suffers many things, as an author militant, with Swift—Has no hopes of the Cardinalate, though he suffers for his religion in almost every weekly paper—Alludes to his version of the first *Psalm*—Proposes to take service under the Marquis de Langallerie in Turkey—Hopes, if he turn Mohammedan, there will be no breach between them—A man must live—The Church of Rome appears to be now in a declining condition, as well from many modern symptoms as from ancient prophecies—The Church of England in as bad a state—Churches sink like European banks, and for the same reason—Truth a sort of contraband commodity 411-412

To LADY MARY WORTLEY MONTAGU. The fourth letter he has written to her abroad—His constant thought of her obliges him to write again —Euphuisms and affectations of gallantry—His addresses to her like a poor papist's prayers to his patron-saint—Celestial and terrestrial *Beaux*—The rest of the world engrossed with the affairs of the Turks, himself only with hers—Anxious for her safety—The Court of Vienna and the Camps of Hungary two very different things—No Pacha so hateful to him as Count Volkra—Ambassadors' wives not exempt from human accidents—Perils among Turks and Tartars—Wishes Mr. Walpole and she could be diverted from Constantinople—Prepared to give up the Circassian slave, if she will abandon her journey—More after the manner of *Euphues*—Capable of following his mistress even to those parts of India where the ugliest men are said to be in the greatest favour with women—But needs greater encouragement than he can hope for—Draws an example from the *Orlando Furioso*—Ready to set out for Italy, if she is to pass through that ladies' climate—

Compares Lady Mary and himself to the fair Princess and the Dwarf of the tale—Concludes with more Euphuism 413-416

To LADY MARY WORTLEY MONTAGU. Finds himself growing more and more *romantic*—Truth alone, not flattery, can overtake her at so great a distance—A generous piece of Popery—The very extravagance of it must be owned a sort of piety—Regards her now as a beatified being, and addresses his prayers to her—More Euphuism— Miss Macfarland's immolation of her lover—Lucretia and Portia— Angry at the petty criticism of her travelling costume, &c., by her most intimate friends—Cares only for her own charms—Loveliness unadorned—Not in the least interested by her notices of relics and shrines—Would much rather go on a pilgrimage to see one such face as hers than to see two St. John the Baptist's heads—Wishes she might have the Golden Image of Nebuchadnezzar on one condition—The Court of Vienna and its ladies—Expects to hear of Lady Mary's gradual relinquishment of the *Thirty-nine Articles*, as she approaches the regions of Infidelity—Desires to know the effect upon her of a Sunday Opera at High Mass—And whether she still retains reverence for Sternhold and Hopkins—Assumes that her chaplain will be discharged before he is left without any *cure*—Imagines her adopting the customs of the Faithful—Why the Dervish country must be a peculiarly happy one for young and gay women—Pictures her enthusiastic reception by the Pacha at Belgrade on her pronuncing *Allah* and *Mohammed*—Her husband, as representative of his Britannic Majesty, can not conveniently conform—Anticipated visions of Mohammed's Paradise at Pera —Has written, as he has often in her company talked, himself into a good humour 416-419

To CHARLES JERVAS. A ramble to Oxford the cause of his late silence —Jervas in repute even in that Tory stronghold—Dr. Clarke acts as Pope's chaperon—Original designs of Inigo Jones—Sees at Oxford some of Jervas's first pieces—Inquires after Parnell and his *Frogs*— " The world forgetting," &c., Horace's but not his own motto, Parnell and Swift surviving—Congratulates Jervas upon the admiration won by him in his native country, Ireland—Fame not often acquired by prophets or poets—Jervas has the advantage of them— Recommends to him the story of St. Patrick and the vermin—Longs to see him an historical painter—The public and Antiquity now claim his talents—Pope in possession of Jervas's house—Why secure in that rickety building—Consoles himself with the Irishman's comfort 420-422

To THE HON. ROBERT DIGBY. Sickness—Intends to resort to his friend's physicians, as grave as any of the Faculty—Ridicule has little effect upon opinion—Asses as doctors, and doctors as asses—Glad of his friend's health—The world without Digby, and others of his kind, not worth living in—Most men of wit or honesty very lean—How his friend may find comfort for his leanness—Warton induces Pope to take up *Gorboduc*—Much credit to himself from the undertaking—Dryden and Oldham's failure in it—Blames them for their contempt of that drama—About to be absorbed in the histories of Briseis, Agamemnon, and Achilles—The noble ambition of a late Recorder of the City of London—Heartily wishes the deaths of all Homer's heroes—A pious ejaculation and request . . . 422-424

TO LADY MARY WORTLEY MONTAGU. Her image and their former intimacy daily in his thoughts—Uncertainty and unsatisfactoriness of their correspondence—His letters convey but a faint shadow of his actual feeling—Waiting for postal conveyance—Indebted to Congreve for the discovery of one—Inquiries at Mr. Methuen's office—Providing against postal accidents—Defective vision obliges him to cease all correspondence but with herself—A letter from her little less than a miracle for him—A dream worth more than most of the dull realities of life—Effect of ill-health and ill-fortune upon him—Desires her compassion for a poet who has lost all but a few romantic ideas—Hero and Leander—A Jew beheaded as a spy—Jacob Tonson—Lady Mary in a position to enlighten him on many passages in Homer—She is in the midst of Homeric memories, and in view of the scenes of his epics—Sends her the third volume of his *Iliad* and his other Works—Calls her attention to a passage in his *Eloisa*—London news—Heidegger's masquerades at the Haymarket—Lady Mohun's adventures and marriage—Lady Rich and Miss Griffith will have anticipated him—Political parties—The quarrel between the King and the Prince of Wales—Coalition of parties only at the masquerade—The Princess a dissenter from the fashionable diversion—She has but a very small following in so unmodish a heresy—Lady Mary's last letter dated Peterwaradin—Its never-to-be-forgotten generosity—A very melancholy letter sent by himself just before—Has received only four of her letters, as against several from him—Begs her to write as often as possible—Any sort of news from her pleasing 424-427

TO DR. PARNELL. No apologies or ceremony needed between friends for epistolary shortcomings—Approbation of Parnell's *Batrachomyomachia* universal—Himself suggested the Work—Other pieces of his friend religiously guarded—Parnell in the character of a patron-saint—Homer's salvation depends upon him—Begs for suggestions in regard to some books of the *Iliad*—Very backward in this year's task, through a variety of causes to be imparted only to an intimate friend—These causes prevent his joining his friend in Ireland—Violence and intensity of Party-feeling—The Muses all run mad—Unseasonable moment for publishing—His obligations to the Dean of St. Patrick's—

Desires the expression of his esteem and affection to him—Gay goes to France with Pulteney—Himself remains at Chiswick occupied with business and poetry 427-429

To TERESA AND MARTHA BLOUNT. A dull companion and a dull correspondent—Undertakes to give some account of his pilgrimage after the manner of Purchas or Bunyan—Travels to Hampton Court by water—Meets the Prince of Wales, with all his ladies, coming from hunting—Taken under the protection of Miss Bellenden and Miss Lepell, who give him a dinner—Converses with Mrs. Howard—The life of a Maid of Honour—Her diversions qualify her to be an excellent fox-hunter's wife—Court life—Walks three hours by moonlight with Miss Lepell—Meets only the King and his Vice-Chamberlain *sub divo*—An invitation to Madame Kilmansegg's—An excellent discourse of Quackery—Further adventures in Windsor Forest—Dr. Radcliffe gone the way of all his patients—His miserably unwieldy estate—Garth's *bon mot*—Dr. Shadwell's wit, and the lady's repartee 429-431

To THE DUCHESS OF HAMILTON. Mrs. Whitworth and her epitaph—A portrait of the Duchess—His mystification and obscurity of allusion calculated to delight a statesman or a divine—Lord Selkirk—Descends from the oracular style and explains himself—Unspeakably pleased with the portrait—The Duchess how compared to an elephant—Lady Orkney's distinguished feature—Dr. Logg, the new chaplain to the Blounts—A model confessor—After the Order of Melchizedec—A possible result of the expected abolition of the Christian religion—Has no hope of the Duchess's conversion—The best reason with some people for going to church—Wishes her to call upon the Blounts—Begs for a letter and her early appearance in town . . 432-434

To BISHOP ATTERBURY. Obliged to him for condolences on his father's death, and for his invitation to join the Established Church—Acknowledges the Bishop's interest at once in his spiritual and his temporal advantage, and frankly replies—His father not his only bond to the Old Church—His mother still survives—With Euryalus, he could not withstand a parent's tears—A merely "carnal tie," he acknowledges, from the point of view of a divine—More certain, however, of the obligation to consult his aged mother's happiness than of any merely speculative matter—As ignorant, too, as Euryalus of the result of such an adventure, in spite of the most positive divinity—Uncertainty of the spiritual advantages to him in exchanging one Church for another—All the controversies between the two Churches already read by him in his youth—In consequence, a Papist and a Protestant by turns—Converting and outwitting—The Bishop would gain little glory by his conversion—His theological or ecclesiastical indifferentism—Acknowledges the *temporal* advantages to be all on the Bishop's side—But he has little talent for active life, still less health or inclination—Contemplative life his choice and habit—Ordinary ambition appears to him stooping rather than climbing—Delivers his profession of faith, political and religious—How not a Papist—A Catholic in the true sense of the word—Professes a proper sense of the excellence of the British Constitution—His ideal Catholicism in religion and politics a *sermo ad clerum* 434-437

To THE HON. ROBERT DIGBY. A usual preface—Wit now-a-days all thrown away—Writing as little regarded as Preaching—All that writers can hope for, is to be read with decency and patience once a week in the country—Fine writing and *Sermons* almost equally contemned—The Stage alone excites enthusiasm—Effusive loyalty there—All other virtues at a discount—Triumphant vices—Lady Scudamore—Cibber's *Nonjuror* not yet seen by her—How she has raised his hopes for the welfare of Satire—His friend's happiness excites his envy 437-438

To THE HON. ROBERT DIGBY. Ill health again—Lady Scudamore's note to him a sort of beatific vision—Promises a better life in the Elysian fields of Cirencester—Adopts the style of the pulpit—Ejaculations and benedictions—Milton on the life of the Celestials—Huntingfinery—Osborne's representation of King James I.—Digby's superiority to all the various abounding money-grabbers and *hoc genus omne*—Invites him to turn from this mercenary scene to philosophy, gardening, and marriage—Betakes himself to water-gruel and Palladio—Letter from Digby (*note*) 439-440

To BISHOP ATTERBURY. A present of sulphur and two volumes of Gay—Sends a copy of the *Arabian Nights' Entertainment*—Solomon and the Bishop compared—The Oracle and Prophet of Bromley—The catastrophe of the South Sea Company—All feared but none prepared for the *finale*—Retribution—The *auri sacra fames* their common ruin —Recommends Hesiod's maxim—*Job* and the *Psalmist* quoted—The ruin of the guiltless and industrious part of the community only to be lamented—The South Sea unlike the Old Deluge—Congratulates himself that he is not of the unrighteous remnant—Arbuthnot's observation—A letter from Dr. Atterbury (*note*) 441-443

To JOHN CARYLL.—On Caryll the younger—Misses seeing Lady Mary Wortley Montagu—Twickenham under water—His situation very much like that of Noah's Ark—Isolated from all society—Reflections on the crimes and calamities of the South Sea Company—Protests his own innocence and satisfaction—Begs his friend to pay him his debt—More in need of money than ever before—Arbuthnot on the South Sea Company 443-444

To LORD OXFORD. Takes advantage of the permission to write—A grateful and faithful servant—Requests permission to dedicate Parnell's *Remains* to him—Bearing testimony to truth a pleasure and an excusable vanity—Sends the volume itself—Declares it to be the only *Dedication* he has ever written—Resolved never to bow the knee to a less man than Oxford, and expects to see no greater man—Prepared to comply with his decision 444-446

To BISHOP ATTERBURY. Extremely sensible of the favours of Atterbury's kind letters—Certain of his goodwill—Invites him to Twickenham—In the character of Diabolus and of Nebuchadnezzar—Aspires to be innocent rather than great—Quarles and the Devil at Bowls—The Bishop's favourite diversion—The charms of Twickenham—Atterbury and the Fathers of the Desert—Quotes *Paradise Regained*, and Milton's allusion to a frugal diet—Promises Atterbury the use of a coach, and privacy 447-449

To THE HON. ROBERT DIGBY. Epistolary apologies and compliments on both sides—Proposes to visit his friend at Sherbourne—Hopes to be Miss Digby's guide through Cirencester Wood—Looks upon himself as the magician of that enchanted forest—The prospective glories of the place—Proposed junction of the Thames and Severn—The finest wood in England—The different attractions of London—Women of quality turned camp-followers—Hyde Park—The Park the resort of all the town—The ladies of Scythia and the ladies of London—The latter in the character of Spartan matrons—*Est ferrum quod amant*—Black broth, however, not in vogue—Mars in the ascendant—His Twickenham life of a different kind—Wholly engaged with the Homeric heroes—The Bishop of Rochester, his guest, gives him leave to write this letter 449-451

To HUGH BETHEL. Conventional compliments—Humanity and sympathy preferable to the common-place virtues of Society—His *Odyssey*—Bethel's travels compared with those of Ulysses—Recommends Wollaston's *Religion of Nature*—Promises to send it with the *Odyssey*—Its popularity with women—Their enthusiasm for truth as inconstant as it is for health—Their ephemeral enthusiasm for Dr. Cheyne's books 451-454

To JUDITH COWPER. Angry at her literary modesty—His regard for her originates with himself alone—Challenges psychical relationship with her—Claims kinship in Apollo—But aspires still more to personal than to poetical friendship—What natures make the best friends—Intellect and morality—Deprecates compliments—Could make her a great many, but spares her modesty—Herself still more estimable than her writings—Slips into the complimentary style—Sends her verses on her portrait—The brightest wit, without the affections of the heart, destined to be eclipsed . . . 453-454

To JUDITH COWPER. On conventional compliments again—An illustration from Sancho Panza's experience—Parnassus enriched—Mrs. Howard and sincerity—Mrs. Howard's discretion—Miss Cowper's imitation of Shakspeare—His impartial appraisement of it—Its true but melancholy view of human life—She is too young to indulge that way of thinking—Town life suitable for her age—The proper period for country retirement—The *pis-aller* of public men—Lines on his grotto—La Bruyère's *Charactères*—Progress of his *Shakspeare*—Method of editing—Not to be finished within the year—Acknowledges Miss Cowper's compliments upon it—His gradual sinking—Longs for her return to town 454-456

To JUDITH COWPER. Mrs. Howard's news of her—Her retirement from authorship fortunate for himself and other writers—Her commemoration of Twitenham—Mrs. Howard's residence at Richmond—The former a paltry hermitage—She has spoiled its owner for being a *solitaire*—Leaves him without hope—He adores her stolen picture—Why he does not make verses to it 457-458

To JUDITH COWPER. Ashamed of his epistolary shortcomings—Poetical compliments—Forming a wish for a lady's happiness—Sends her and Mrs Howard copies of verses, "To a Lady on her Birthday"—Invites her to improve them 458-459

To LORD BOLINGBROKE. His severe sickness—The improvement of the English Language, and the glory of its Poetry, must depend on other hands—Pleads guilty to being a convicted translator—His Homer a sort of *parergon*—Easier to him than Pliny to De Sacy—More anxious to consult his happiness than his fame—Quiet happiness—Contentment—An author's self satisfaction ought to be in inverse proportion to public applause—Why an author is the unhappiest man—Ambition and its sacrifices—To be one of the immortals in literature, it is necessary to leave all and cleave only to the Muses—Literary martyrdom—The service of the Muses incompatible with "good fellowship"—The present Age not worth the sacrifice—Indebted to his country and to posterity in the same degree—Why he owns no debt to the former—On the possibility of fixing a language—Languages more enduring than Governments—How Greek and Latin were spread—Vitality of the Greek and English languages compared—Dissents from Bolingbroke's estimate of the influence of English classic writers—Government by party injurious to literature—English more corrupted by party-writers than by any other cause, and why—Only just recovered enough to read the *Henriade* attentively—His double obligations to the author and to the giver of the poem—Why he cannot pretend to judge authoritatively of its *poetic* merits—Can estimate only the design, conduct, and sentiments of the poem—On the introduction of allegorical personages in modern poetry—Wishes the *Henriade* had more of the *fictitious* and of description and speeches—The book on the love-story of Gabrielle the most poetical part—Thinks some personages and parts not made enough of—The actions and sentiments of the characters excellent and the *forte* of the poem—Its superiority to the *Pharsalia*—Lofty and philosophical views—Voltaire not less a poet for being a writer of sense and judgment—Grounds of his especial esteem for the author—Holds him to be worthy of Bolingbroke's friendship and intimacy—Expects responses from the Oracle of La Source—Paraphrases verses of an Ode of Horace . . . 459-465

To WILLIAM FORTESCUE. Delighted at his long-delayed letter and news of his family—Good wishes for their welfare—Ignorant of his friend's locality—His mother's illness—His own health—Gay at the Bath with Arbuthnot—Mrs. Howard and Marble Hill—Prince William wants Miss Fortescue as a play-fellow—Expects Fortescue at Twit'nam—His Devonshire man-servant—*Auri sacra fames*—Intended visit to Lord Oxford and Cobham—Consequent hurry—The *Odyssey* advanced to the Eighth Book—His Gardens improve more than his Writings—His devotion to Mrs. Howard—*Adieus* 465

To WILLIAM FORTESCUE. The Ninth *beatitude*—Illustrated by Gay—Walpole and his reputation—Wishes the Premier were Gay's friend—Replies to Fortescue's inquiry as to Walpole's visit to Twickenham with Peterborough—Walpole's oath—A Statesman's promise—Has never returned the Premier's visit—Reasons for his indifference—An accident 466-467

To EDWARD BLOUNT. Silence not forgetfulness—Wishes for the presence of his friend's daughters at Twickenham—The Gardens and Grotto at length finished—Description of them—The inscription for the Grotto—The place owes little to art . . . 467-469

To DEAN SWIFT. An encomium on Stopford the bearer of his letter—The *Miscellany* completed and printed—Prodigiously pleased with his association with Swift, and their descending to posterity together—Not in the usual flattering and formal style of learned authors, but in an easy and diverting manner—The third volume contains only verses distinguished by some peculiar merit—Solomon's *dictum* on books—Applies still more to *Miscellanies*—On the "Twelve Thousand"—His verses suggested by *Gulliver*—Political zeal—Does not read newspapers or pamphlets—Sends Swift a whole parcel of them for his diversion—At Glubdubbdrib—In rather better health—Injuries to his hands—Lady Bolingbroke's long letter—Her bad, and her husband's good, health—Peterborough writes twice to Swift—Lost or intercepted letters?—Ten thousand things to say—Begs Swift to come over in the Spring—No sooner found than lost—Ireland the receptacle of all he values 469-471

To LORD BATHURST. Quotes Plato and a Spanish bishop *de irâ*—Acts upon their precept—Takes Lord Bathurst to task for neglecting engagements—Nebuchadnezzar and John Coryate—His visit to Cirencester—Caustic criticism on Bathurst's "improvements"—Proves his placability by offering architectural advice—The Church Steeple difficulty—How his friend may at once satisfy Taste and conciliate the Dissenters and Quakers—How he may pay court to the Walpole Administration—Urges him to do something *éclatant* in the House of Lords—Mrs. Erasmus Lewis a good match for his Lordship—Offers to take lodgings for Lady Bathurst at Bath—His testimony to the sobriety and steadiness of herself and the young ladies—Lewis and he fix a day for their visit to Cirencester—Forgives and forgets 471-474

To JOHN KNIGHT. Bad weather—Fashionable diversions—The Coronation of George II.—Coronations and Harlequinades—Madame Tussaud anticipated—A Puppet-Show and Waxwork Exhibition of the nobility—No Punch or Showman necessary—No news of more importance in the metropolis—Craggs' statue in Westminster Abbey—The statue up and the statuary down—The inscription for the Urn not yet done—Unaccountable delay 474-476

To LORD PETERBOROUGH. Beauties vegetable, animal, and rational—Some very *rational* ones at Bevis Mount—Felicitates Peterborough on his leisure and gardening—Alludes to Bolingbroke's disgrace—Agriculture most akin to Philosophy—Titular prefixes—The Great Turk and Peterborough compared—The two Paradises—Nothing stirring—Court-journals and royal feasts, &c —Plenty of the *Chroniques Scandaleuses* for posterity—Does not court Sir Robert Walpole —Great men's impartial obliviousness 476-478

To JOHN KNIGHT. On a visit to Stowe—"A demi-paradise"—More beautiful than ever—Mrs. Knight toasted—Lord Cobham sends his services with an invitation to her—Diminution of happiness—Regrets his boon companions—Mr. Mallet and his gain—Miss Patty Blount and her dietary—Regrets her absence—Her sister on town-life—His rambles do not improve his health—Takes no medicine but mental —His next visit to Bevis Mount—Lady Peterborough, as a Catholic friend, will take care of his soul—An incomparable Jesuit . 478-479

To JONATHAN RICHARDSON. His mother's health—Requests his friend to paint her portrait—Kneller's painter's prayer—Anti-Sabbatarianism—Richardson's many kind offices to human oxen and asses 480-481

To JOHN CARYLL. Building a portico—Caryll as Nestor—"The time of the singing of Birds"—In Spring he yields to them, and is silent—His last piece of song received with a flood of flattery—A slight thing, the work of two days—The *Epistle* to Bathurst a two years' work—The priests "gravelled" by an expression in his last thing—Their discernment at fault—Writing for fools—*Qui legit intelligat,* an unreasonable demand—A new poem, the *Essay on Man,* all the rage of the town—Affects ignorance of its authorship—Criticises it—Attempts to patch up its orthodoxy—Requests Caryll's careful opinion—A faction to set up the anonymous author against himself—Morality Pope's only concern—The generality of readers like a seasoning of satire 481-483

To JONATHAN RICHARDSON. Announces his mother's death—An innocent life and an easy decease—Requests his friend to come to Twit'nam and sketch her face—Urges him to come at once 483-484

To HUGH BETHEL. His mother's death left him no heart for writing—Twickenham deserted—Wandering about all the Summer—In Essex, and at Dawley—Going to Cirencester and Southampton—Regrets leaving Martha Blount—She is not happily situated—His other acquaintances—Mr. Cleland—His friend in his Yorkshire home—His only care is to finish his *Essay on Man*—Commemorates Bethel in it—A condition—Bethel's modesty, and his own greatest pleasure—A poet as the eulogiser of virtue—A *laudator temporis acti* 484-485

To AARON HILL. His old enemy Dennis in distress—Forgivingly disposed towards him—Acknowledges with thanks Hill's present to his Grotto, his agreeable letter, and his excellent translation of Voltaire's *Zaïre*—Absorbed in the perusal of Thomson's new poem—Miss Uranie—A letter from Hill on the tragedy of *Zaïre* (note) . 485-486

To JONATHAN RICHARDSON. In town on business with Dr. Mead—Looks forward to winter evenings with his friend—A more flattering comparison for old men than Homer's Grasshoppers—His sleepiness and sleeplessness—Despairs of his health—Twickenham and Bath, as sanitary resorts, compared—Only the outskirts of Bath, at Mr. Allen's, endurable for a few weeks—Has little liking for the place—Friendship alone has drawn h m there—Battersea his home of late . 487

To MRS. KNIGHT. Writes from Bevis Mount—All that letters are ever good for—Mrs. Elliott—His information at Stowe of the abominable roads, after his recent experience of road-travelling, frightens him from an intended journey to the Knights—A clerical alarmist—His bad state of health—Finds rest, where least to be expected, under Lord Peterborough—The natural charms of Bevis Mount—A very good Catholic lady in the house—Their prayers together for Mrs. Knight's salvation—The Duchess of Montagu a near neighbour—Bewley finely situated on the sea—Visit planned there with his host—Miss Patty Blount on a visit to a papist lady in Surrey—Other news—Desires Mrs. Elliott's prayers. 488-489

To RALPH ALLEN. On two pictures of the old Masters—A hint as to the ornamentation of Prior House—Not only taste but virtue in question in ornamentation—Didactic Art—The walls of a rich man's house might easily be made more didactic than his conversation—" Sermons

in stones "—Zeal of the ecclesiastical Reformers ill-directed—Epitaphs
and pictures in churches compared—Lying trophies—The subscription
for his *Letters*—An intended visit to Lady Peterborough—The publication of his *Letters* by subscription not an agreeable task . 489-490
To AARON HILL. Wandering in earthly paradises—Hill's less pleasing
experiences—Receiving and answering letters—Republicanism in
literature—Welcomes free criticism of his own writings—Acknowledges the honour done him by Hill in submitting his manuscript
Essay to him—Insists on impartial treatment of himself in it—Deprecates any suspicion of *pique* against Theobald—Never supposed the
Play, censured in the *Treatise of the Bathos*, to be Theobald's, but of
the Shakspearian Age—Arbuthnot responsible for many of the criticisms in the *Treatise*—Regrets that Hill seems to know him better as
a poet than as a man—His censure or contempt inspired by public not
personal feeling—Not his political, but his personal, character an
object of concern to him—Protests the sincerity of his declarations
—Hill too partial a critic of his Poetry—Prefers the affection to the
admiration of a good man 490-492
To DEAN SWIFT. Miscarriage of letters—Swift asks questions already
answered—In particular, in regard to Lord Bolingbroke—Both Bolingbroke and himself have written to him—Dawley sold—Bolingbroke
now living in the finest part of France—His manner of life there—
Lady Bolingbroke's division of her time—Her daughter an abbess of
a royal convent—Bolingbroke's epicurean indifferentism—His Introduction to his *History*—The *History* itself—The author's fear respecting Swift's *History*—Swift and his Twickenham friends—His
presence would afford perfect contentment—Mr. Jervas and his
value of his friends—Mr. Lewis—Miss Arbuthnot—Miss Patty
Blount—Comprehensive classification of the rest of the feminine world
—On other friends—The Prince of Wales and Pope—The Prince's
presents to him—Indifferent to the assaults of Ministerial writers—
Relations with the courtiers—The Duchess of Marlborough—Young
and old people's friends—Sinking fast into prose—Anything he may
write now ought to be valuable in matter rather than in manner—His
health and amusements—Lives between London and Twickenham—
Lord Bathurst—Mr. Pulteney—Summer rambles to Stowe or Bath—
Reminiscences of Swift and Gay—Why he cannot cross the Channel—
His first and last experience of the sea in Peterborough's yacht—
Assures Swift none the less of his entire affection and esteem—
Finishes his letter at Lord Orrery's—The Provost of St. Mary Hall,
Oxford, his fellow guest—Mr. Swift 492-496
To MARTHA BLOUNT. Dates from Stowe—Miss Blount going into the
country—Her Court friends—A hamper for Mrs. Dryden at Lord Cob-
ham's in Hanover Square—His next address Sir Thomas Lyttelton's at

CONTENTS.

Hagley—Mr. Lyttleton expects Mr. Grenville—Stowe at its best—Not the less wishes to rejoin her—Dreads the journey to Worcester and the frightful roads—The Duke of Argyll's report of the roads—The Duke at the happiest period of his life—The gardens at Stowe beyond description—Spends almost every hour in them—Laments the absence of his friend—Lady Cobham and Mrs. Speed expect him as eagerly as they do their dresses—A Castle of Indolence and Liberty Hall—She is constantly, as always, in his thoughts—Pineapples from Twickenham—Postal inconvenience—Starting for the Elysian Fields to dream of her 497-499

To MARTHA BLOUNT. At Bristol. His manner of life there—A visit to the Bath from Prior Park—Lady Cox and Mrs. Slingsby Bethel—At a loss to describe the scenery from Bath to Bristol—Nothing but a picture can do justice to it—Some account of the road and of Bristol itself—The road to Clifton described—The village of Clifton—Remembrances to Lady Gerard—Wishes Martha Blount would visit Bristol and Clifton in the next summer—She would be charmed by what would frighten most ladies—Mr. Allen expected—Remembrances to Lord Lyttelton and other friends 499-501

To MARTHA BLOUNT. Another letter from Bristol—A graphic description of the village of Clifton—Picturesque scenery—Crossing the Severn into Wales—Mr. Allen and Mr. Hook's enterprising excursion—The city of Bristol described—Seldom writes to anyone—Going to Bath—Dr. Cheyne and Mead—Drinking the waters—Inconveniences of a winter residence at Clifton Wells—Assurances of affection—Requests a letter every Thursday 501-503

To THE REV. WILLIAM WARBURTON. Assurances of friendship and esteem—The use of letter-writing—Wishes for an opportunity of doing Warburton some real services—Fortune's niggardliness to the deserving—Wishes his champion had a benefice nearer the Thames—A nobleman's good intentions, and an incumbent's inconsiderate longevity—Thanks Warburton for his hints—Almost tempted by them to become an author anew or, rather, a new author—Professes dissatisfaction with his past productions—Warburton's expected honorary degree, and the delay on the part of the University of Oxford to confer it—Dr. King believes it is only delayed—Pope refuses to receive a similar honour, if his friend is rejected—Will be *doctored* with him or not at all—Neither princes nor priests can confer honour on the undeserving 504-505

To THE REV. WILLIAM WARBURTON. Lord Chesterfield, the good-intentioned nobleman—His incontrovertible judgment—A pleasure and not a shame, in such a case, to be indebted—Regrets that he himself has only good wishes to offer—His consolation—Apologises for his panegyric—His *Dunciad*—If completed, will be published entire in the general edition of his Poems—Congratulates himself on the prospect of going down to posterity with Warburton—The poor moderns—*Vitæ summa brevis*—The Commentator's crutch—They will take their degrees together in Fame, if not at the University 505-506

To the Rev. William Warburton. Friendship needs no epistolary assurance—His own and Mr. Lyttelton's satisfaction at Warburton's retirement from the contest with Dr. Middleton—A divine who loves peace more than victory—Lyttelton's admiration—Recommends a publisher—Invites Warburton to the Allens' at Prior Park—Inducements to the visit—His host presses the invitation—Allen's merits—The best season for Bath—An episcopal friend of Warburton expected—The various accommodations at Prior Park—Pope lays down the *route* for Warburton—A journey of three days on horseback from Newark—Engages to convey him back to London—Allen's house near to Bath—His brother, the postmaster . 506-508

To the Rev. William Warburton. No news worth writing, either public or personal—His increasing asthma confines him entirely to the fireside—Sees scarcely any one but the Bolingbrokes—His time chiefly spent at Battersea—Desires Warburton as a ghostly comforter—*Paullo minus ab angelis*—His maladies engage almost all his attention—Preparing a general edition of his Poems with Warburton's Notes—Specifies certain of his productions—Bowyer wrongly counsels delay—An expected attack from the Laureate—Warburton also threatened—Cibber's Pamphlet as good as a dose of hartshorn to him—Affects concern at the offence taken by the Clergy of the Establishment at one or two of his verses—The verses in question harder upon his own Church than on theirs—Concerned more for Warburton's safety, in the clerical onslaught, than for his own—His debt to him—The Allens' health 508-510

To Ralph Allen. Reconciliation—The Government proclamation against the Pretender—Forced by it to remove further from the metropolis—Consequently unable to receive the Allens at Twickenham—Invites them to his present residence—A method of evading the law—To come to town would be imprudent and "contumacious"—Offers his friend a warm reception—His possible flight to Battersea with Warburton—Engages to introduce Warburton to Lord Bolingbroke.

THE LIFE AND WRITINGS OF SWIFT.

In the History of English Literature scarcely any celebrated writer can be named, in whose life and productions more interest has been displayed than in those of the most famous of English satirists; Pope, perhaps, excepted, there is none with whose career so many contradictions, and perplexities for the biographer, are connected. Of the most conspicuous events in his life—his political conversion, and his relations with the two women with whom his memory remains inextricably entwined—the estimates of readers and critics have been, and, from the nature of the case, will continue to be, of the most differing kind. Of his two most celebrated productions, the *Tale of a Tub* and *Gulliver's Travels*, opinions as to the intention and scope have been equally various, and they still excite controversy. Within recent years, especially, critical attention has been drawn to his life and the character of his writings by further examination of new materials and documents, and of his extensive correspondence.

Settled first in Yorkshire, the family of Swift in the sixteenth century branched into two principal divisions—one fixed itself in Kent, the other in Herefordshire. One of the name, Barnum Swift, became notorious by his eccentric humour, and from Charles I. obtained the title of Viscount Carlingford. It is his grandfather, however, whom his distinguished descendant, in his autobiographical anecdotes, has chosen particularly to commemorate—Thomas Swift, the militant incumbent of Goodrich, in Herefordshire, who, by his aggressive attitude, brought down upon himself the vengeance of the Republicans. Thomas Swift left four daughters and two sons. The eldest brother, Godwin, having married into the Ormond family, obtained from them the post of Attorney-General in the "palatinate" of Tipperary. Jonathan Swift, the father of the most renowned of the name, was the seventh or eighth son. With Godwin, and others of the family, upon his father's death, he migrated to Ireland, at the age of fourteen. He married a lady of an old but poor Leicestershire family, Abigail Erick or Herrick; depending upon such chance occupation in the Law Courts as his eldest brother could procure for him. At length he gained the post of Steward of the King's Inns in Dublin. Six months before the birth of Jonathan Swift (who had been preceded by a sister), 1667, his father died, and left his widow dependent, in great measure, upon the good feeling of his more prosperous relatives, and his children to the guardianship of his uncles; of whom, on the maternal side, Dryden was one. The birth of Jonathan Swift the younger took place in a house in Hoey's Court, near to the Castle Grounds, at that time a fashionable part of the city.

He was only a year old when his nurse, not wishing to part from him, secretly carried him away—he himself assures us—to her relatives at Whitehaven, and there he lived three years. By his uncle Godwin, who seems to have conferred his charity grudgingly, and whom he describes as "an ill-pleader but, perhaps, a little too dexterous in the subtle parts of the Law," he was placed, at the age of six years, at the Grammar School of Kilkenny, a few miles distant from the family residence of Swiftsheath. Kilkenny school, as remarked by Mr. Leslie Stephen, can boast of having had as its *alumni*, the greatest satirist, the most brilliant writer of comedies (Congreve, a fellow-pupil of Swift), and the subtlest metaphysician in the English language (Berkeley, who entered the School a few years later). At fourteen Swift proceeded as a pensioner to the Dublin University, (1682). A pedantic and profitless Scholasticism, which he afterwards covered with ridicule in his *Tale of a Tub*, still prevailed, more or less, at the Universities and schools. Neglecting, as far as possible, the established *curriculum*, "for some parts of which," he says, "he had no great relish by nature," the boyish undergraduate[1] seems to have given such time as he gave at all to books to the more pleasing studies of Poetry and History, so that when the time came for taking his degree of Bachelor of Arts, although he had lived, as he declares, "with great regularity, and due observance of the Statutes, he was stopped of his degree for *dulness and insufficiency*, and, at last,

[1] The customary age at which boys were sent to the Universities, up to about the middle of the last century, varied from fifteen to seventeen. Gibbon was entered at Magdalen College, Oxford, in his fifteenth year. Perhaps the most memorable instance of a juvenile undergraduate is that of the great Legal Reformer, Bentham, who *matriculated* at Queen's College, Oxford, at the age of thirteen, and passed his first examination in Arts, in his sixteenth year.

hardly admitted, in a manner little to his credit, which is called in that College *speciali gratiâ*, on the 15th February, 1685, with four more on the same footing; and this discreditable mark, as I am told, stands upon record in their College Registry."

Lord Orrery, the friend of Swift in his later years, but a hostile biographer, originated the legend of Swift's idleness and ignominy at the University.[1] A year later (1756), Deane Swift (a cousin), in his *Essay*, repeated it. Sheridan, the son of Swift's friend, a highly eulogistic biographer, who published his life in 1787, gave fresh currency to the report. But the most important (alleged) evidence was that of Dr. Barrett, Vice-Provost of the University. A published letter of Richardson, the novelist, in which he states that Swift had been expelled for having "raked up all the scandal against the heads of that University that a severe enquirer, and a still severer temper, could get together into his harangue" [at a College Exercise], had set the Vice-Provost upon an examination of the College Records. Unable to identify the expelled *terrae filius* (as it is called) with Swift, he, nevertheless, elaborately drew the unjustifiable deduction that he must, at all events, have been an accomplice of the offender, because of resemblances in the offensive speech to certain passages in the *Tale of a Tub* and *Gulliver's Travels*, a presumptive sort of proof which Nichols (1808) and Scott (1814) rashly adopted. During the whole period of Jonathan Swift's *status pupillaris* at Trinity College his cousin and senior, Thomas Swift, also resided there as an *alumnus*, a fruitful source of confusion; the

---

[1] Orrery's *Remarks on the Life and Writings of Swift*, the first to appear of the many biographies of Swift, was published in 1751. Mrs. Delany, writing to a friend in November of that year, says: "The remarks of Lord Orrery on Dr. Swift are published, and they have made me very angry. They are much commended, said to be very entertaining, but I am so angry at the unfriendly, ungenerous manner of Swift's being treated, by one who calls himself his friend, that it quite prejudices me against the book, and casts a cloud over all its merit. Every failing is expressed, every fault is magnified, every virtue almost either tarnished or concealed. . . . Yet calls himself his friend ! Such a *friend*, that Brutus-like gives the deepest and the surest wound. I am so angry I can't keep within bounds . . . and I fear there are too many truths in the book! but they do not become my Lord Orrery to publish them, who was *admitted at all times*, and saw him in his *most unguarded moments*." She returns to the attack more than once. See *Life and Correspondence of Mrs. Delany*.

Of Deane Swift's book (*Essay on the Life, Writings, and Character of Dr. Jonathan Swift*) she gives an equally unfavourable report. "We are now engaged," she writes (February, 1755), "in that very extraordinary book, Mr. Deane Swift's account of his cousin the Dean of St. Patrick's life and writings, wherein he mauls my Lord Orrery, and then falls on the author of the *Observations on Lord Orrery* [by Delany] without mercy or decency. But he is so mad and abusive, that his satire loses its sting, and where he is not abusive he is exceedingly dull. It is a book rather to despise and laugh at than to resent."

more so, that they have not been distinguished by their individual names. An important document, overlooked but known to exist by his earlier editors, recently discovered by his most elaborate biographer has, at length, settled the vexed question and relieved the perplexity of future editors.[1] Consciousness of entire dependence upon assistance, grudgingly given to him by his richer relatives, seems even thus early to have embittered his mind; although for other members of his family he retained affection.

In his twenty-first year—the memorable year 1688—"driven by stress of circumstances" (in his own expression), Swift left Ireland for England, and, after twelve months passed with his mother, who now lived at Leicester, and whom he had scarcely seen during fifteen years, he found an asylum in the house of Sir William Temple, with whom his mother, as a relative of Lady Temple, claimed connexion. At Leicester we hear of his first love-affair. Writing, long afterwards, to a friend, he thus represents it: "When I went a lad to my mother, after the Revolution, she brought me to the knowledge of a family where there was a daughter, with whom I was acquainted. My prudent mother was afraid I should be in love with her; but, when I went to London, she married an innkeeper in Loughborough, in that county, by whom she had several children."[2] The young lady, by name Betty Jones, was a cousin of Swift. She seems to have been not the only Leicester siren who charmed him. Before the end of 1689, "a raw and inexperienced youth," as he characterises himself, he arrived at Moor Park; and his first period of residence, with some intervals of absence, lasted

---

[1] A *facsimile*, in part, of the registry of the results of the Examination at Trinity College, which indirectly determined the place of Swift, has been printed by Mr. Forster, in his *Life of Swift*. The subjects are :—Physics, Greek and Latin, and *Thema* (Latin Essay). The two Swifts occupy the 12th and 13th places in a list of 119 candidates. To Jonathan Swift's name is attached, as the result of his examination :—" Ph[ilosophy], *male*; G. & L., *bene*; Th[eology], *negligenter*." From an analysis of the Roll, Mr. Forster declares the fact that, on the whole, Swift takes almost the highest place of the 119 examined ; only one in all three subjects receiving the award of *bene*. The *degree* was obtained in the last resort, as Mr. Craik, his most recent biographer, has pointed out, not by examination, but by a scholastic disputation ; it being also an essential preliminary that a candidate should have completed a certain number of *Terms*, and also passed the usual *terminal* examinations. Hence, in Swift's case, the need of the *speciali gratiâ*.

According to Barrett's minute investigation, the punishments awarded to the younger Swift befel him for non-attendance in chapel, and for missing night-rolls, or " town haunting," (that is, the being out of the College after nine o'clock), for which the several fines are affixed. That he did not proceed to the degree of M.A., has been proved by a letter of Temple, published thirty years ago, to have been owing to the commotions in Dublin consequent upon the Revolution of 1688, which nearly emptied the College.

[2] Letter to Worrall, January, 1729, quoted by Forster.

five years. Under what conditions, or in what position, he first entered the household of Temple, does not clearly appear, but he seems to have made himself generally useful; in particular, as an accountant. Temple lived alternately at his house at Sheen, near Richmond, and at his lately-purchased estate at Moor Park, near Farnham, in Surrey. At the head of the household nominally presided Lady Temple, but actually Temple's widowed sister, Lady Giffard, whose somewhat imperious temper Swift could ill brook, and with whom, eventually, he quarrelled. At some time or other during this first period, his cousin, Thomas Swift, for whom he had no love, became one of the establishment in capacity of Chaplain. But of the residents at Moor Park, by far the most interesting is she whose name and fate biographical history has linked so closely with his—Esther Johnson. Her mother, the widow of a London merchant, had been for some time established as an inmate of Moor Park. Gratitude to her father for certain services, it is said, prompted the hospitality. Scandal, however, had discovered other reasons, but on no sufficient grounds. Mrs. Johnson had two daughters. The elder, Esther, was at this time only eight years of age; and, not until during the period of the second residence, does her history intermingle with Swift's. In an undefined position she lived with her mother and sister, sometimes in the house, sometimes in a cottage on the estate, which has given to the lodge, that has succeeded to it, the name of "Stella's Cottage." Another inmate of the house was Mrs. Rebecca Dingley, a connexion of the Temples, who figures frequently in Swift's correspondence.

At the end of a year Swift went back to Ireland on the plea of ill-health. He had already begun to feel those attacks of giddiness and deafness, which were to be his life-long tormentors, and which became much more severe with advancing years. The sufferer himself had firmly imbibed the belief that they originated in a "surfeit of fruit" in his childhood; but, as Johnson, his critic, observes with much common sense, "the original of diseases is commonly obscure, and almost every boy eats as much fruit as he can get without any inconvenience." The actual or, at least, principal reason of his going away may be pretty safely assigned to a disagreement of some kind with his patron, which did not prevent the latter from recommending his young dependant to the Secretary for Ireland, Sir R. Southwell in a letter of considerable interest:—"This afternoon," writes Temple, "I hear, though by a common hand, that you are going over into Ireland, Secretary of State for that kingdom; upon which I venture to make you the offer of a servant, in case you may have occasion for such an one as this bearer. He was born and bred there (though of a good family in Herefordshire), was near seven years in the College of Dublin, and ready to take his degree of Master of Arts, when he was forced away by the desertion of that College upon the calamities of the country. Since that time he has lived in my house, read to me, writ for me, and kept all accounts as far as my small occasions required. He has Latin and Greek, some French, writes a very good and correct hand, is very honest and diligent, and has good friends, though they have for the present lost their fortunes, in Ireland; and his whole family having been long known to me obliged me thus far to take care of him. If you please to accept him into your service, either as a gentleman to wait on you, or as clerk to write under you, and either to use him so, if you like his services, or, upon any establishment of the College, to recommend him to a Fellowship there, *which he has a just pretence to,* I shall acknowledge it as a great obligation to me as well as to him." [1] Nothing resulted from the recommendation to the Irish Secretary; and in the autumn of the next year, having passed a short time with his mother in Leicester, Swift re-entered the service of Temple, where he now assumed the more certain and satisfactory position of secretary; in his own words, "growing into some confidence, and being trusted with affairs of great importance." [2]

[1] This letter, dated May 29, 1690, first appeared in print in Cunningham's edition of Johnson's *Lives of the Poets* (1854), and is quoted in Forster's *Life of Swift.* The term "servant," as remarked by Forster, is evidently used here, not in the restricted sense of the present day, but in the meaning rather of *employé,* one employed in a subordinate position.

[2] Macaulay's estimate of the position, both of Swift and of Esther or "Hetty" Johnson at Moor Park, Mr. Forster has shown to be not an accurate one. "An eccentric, uncouth, disagreeable young Irishman," writes Macaulay, "who had narrowly escaped plucking at Dublin, attended Sir William as an *amanuensis,* for board and twenty pounds a year, dined at the second table, wrote bad verses in praise of his employer, and made love to a very pretty, dark-eyed, young girl who waited on Lady Giffard. Little did Temple imagine that the coarse exterior of his dependant concealed a genius equally suited to politics or letters, a genius destined to shake great kingdoms, to stir the laughter and the rage of millions, and to leave to Posterity memorials which can perish only with the English language. Little did he think that the flirtation in his servants' hall, which he, perhaps, scarcely deigned to make the subject of a jest, was the beginning of a long unprosperous love, which was to be as widely-famed as the passion of Petrarch or of Abelard." (Article in *Ed. Rev.,* on Sir William Temple, October, 1838). Again (*History of England, vi.*), Macaulay exaggerates the unpleasantness (if such there really were) of the relations between the patron and dependant: "The humble student would not have dared to raise his eyes to a lady of family; but when he had became a clergyman he began, after the fashion of a clergyman of that generation, to make love to a pretty waiting-maid, who was the chief ornament of the servants' hall, and whose name is inseparably associated with his in a sad and mysterious history. . . His spirit had been bowed down, and might seem to have been broken, by calamities and humiliations. The language, which he was in the habit of

Of the superior status and treatment of Swift, in the second period of his residence, his frequent visits to Moor Park after Temple's death, and, in particular, a remark to one of Temple's nephews, while thanking him for an invitation to the house, seem to be some presumptive proof. "I am extremely obliged by your invitation to Moor Park," he replies, "which no time will make me forget or love less."[1] By the good offices of his influential patron, after a residence of a few weeks at Hertford College (then called Hart Hall), he obtained the coveted degree of Master of Arts, which served in a manner to efface the memory of any shortcomings, real or supposed, at Dublin. Swift, in future years, did not forget the good reception accorded to him by the Tory University, any more than he quite forgave the humiliation of his Dublin experiences. At this period he read much and discursively, with some eccentricity of selection. In a letter to a friend, of the same time, he records that already he "had writ, burnt, and writ again, upon all manner of subjects, more, perhaps, than any man in England." His first published attempts, in the taste of the day, *Pindaric Odes*, have not much to distinguish them from the crowd of similar poetic productions, excepting here and there some signs of his developing contempt for pedantry and pretence—the "lumber of the Schools." Some of his best verses, or at least sentiments, in an *Ode to Temple*, may be deemed the following :—

> " You strove to cultivate a barren Court in vain ;
> Your Garden's better worth your nobler pain."

He exposes the shams of Governments, and the too usual conduct of public affairs :—

> "The wily shifts of State, those jugglers' tricks,
> Which we call *deep designs and Politics*."

He had, in fact, already been admitted a little behind the scenes of political life. When the ex-diplomatist found himself laid up with

holding to his patron, as far as we can judge from the specimens which still remain, was that of a lacquey, or rather of a beggar. A sharp word, or a cold look, of the master sufficed to make the servant miserable during several days. But this tameness was merely the tameness with which a tiger caught, caged, and starved, submits to the keeper who brings him food. The humble menial was, at heart, the haughtiest, the most aspiring, the most vindictive, the most despotic of men." This representation has been shewn to be founded on no kind of *positive* evidence. The mother of Esther Johnson occupied, as Scott represented it, rather the position of "friend and companion" than of a "waiting-woman"; nor is there any evidence that Esther Johnson herself acted as a "waiting-maid."

[1] Letter to John Temple, June, 1706; first printed by Forster, 1875.

gout—a not unfrequent event—upon his confidential secretary devolved the office of receiving the King (William III.), on his visits to Moor Park, who, while walking in the grounds, condescended to converse familiarly with the deputy. In the spring of 1693, the important *Triennial Bill*, proposed in the House of Commons, had aroused the jealous opposition of the elect of the Whigs; and Temple, who had been consulted by him, being too ill to attend the Court in person, despatched his secretary to represent his views. Success did not attend Swift's diplomacy; but this first experience of Courts helped to cure him of vanity.

More interesting than any of his former poetical pieces, an Ode addressed to Congreve, in this year, exhibits his impatience of the trifling and petty vices, of which he saw enough around him to stimulate his satirical genius; and two verses, in particular, prophetically reveal his future mission:—

"My hate, whose lash just heaven has long decreed,
Shall, on a day, make sin and folly bleed."

Under a persuasion that Temple did not sufficiently appreciate his services, or regard his interests, Swift, in anger, left him again, in 1694. First visiting his mother, he proceeded to Ireland to take "Orders." Before obtaining them, he had to present a certificate of conduct from his late employer. For this purpose he wrote a humble letter, which became the means of reconciliation. As soon as he had gone through the preliminary ceremony (January, 1695), he acquired, by family influence, the prebend of Kilroot, near Belfast, with an income of a hundred pounds. Among his acquaintances here he had an old University friend, named Waring, of a wealthy Belfast family, with whose sister he fell in love. His first letter to Miss Waring, or *Varina*, as, according to his practice, he poetised her name, is "half-fantastic, half-passionate." Tiring of the monotony of his clerical life, he readily accepted Temple's invitation to return to him, and he set out for England in the spring of 1696. On the eve of departure he addressed a letter to Miss Waring, offering marriage. The strain of this love-letter of his younger days (he had now reached his twenty-eighth year) contrasts remarkably with the calculated style of his letters to Esther Johnson and Hester Vanhomrigh:—

"Listen to what I solemnly protest," he passionately writes, "by all that can be witness to an oath—that if I leave this kingdom before you are mine, I will endure the utmost indignities of fortune rather than ever return again, though the King would send me back his deputy . . . Would to heaven you were but a while sensible of the thoughts into which my present distractions plunge me. They hale me a thousand ways, and I am not able to bear them. It is so, by heaven. The love of Varina is of more tragical consequence than her cruelty. Would to God you had [so] treated and scorned me from the beginning! It was your pity opened the first way to my misfortune; and now your love is finishing my ruin. And is it so then? In one fortnight I must take eternal farewell of Varina, and, I wonder, will she weep at parting a little, to justify her poor pretence of some affection to me. And will my friends still continue reproaching me for the want of gallantry and neglecting a close siege? How comes it that they all wish us married together, they knowing my circumstances and yours extremely well; and, I am sure, love you too well, if it is only for my sake, to wish you anything that might cross your interest or your happiness? . . .

"Would not your conduct make one think you were hugely skilled in all the little politic methods of intrigue? Love, with the gall of too much discretion," he adds, in odd contrast with his own practice afterwards, " is a thousand times worse than none at all. . . . The little disguises, and affected contradictions of yourself, were all (to say the truth), infinitely beneath persons of your pride and mine—paltry maxims that they are, calculated for the rabble of humanity."[1]

Esther Johnson had now attained the interesting age of fifteen, half the number of Swift's years. Remarkable for her charms of manner still more than for beauty, she reigned as one of the *belles* of the London drawing-rooms; for, in spite of her undefined position, with the rest of the Temple family, she mixed in fashionable society. In his *Character of Mrs. Johnson,* as, in the style of the time, he calls Esther Johnson or Swift (as the case may be), drawn up on the day of her death, he has thus described her:—"She was born at Richmond, in Surrey, in the year 1681. Her father was a younger brother of good family in Nottinghamshire; her mother of a lower degree, and, indeed, she had little to boast of her birth.[2] I knew her from six years old, and

---

[1] First printed in Mr. G. Monck Berkeley's *Literary Relics*, 1789.—Note by Scott (*Works of Swift*, xv., 1824). So different is it from Swift's ordinary style, that we are almost tempted to suspect the genuineness of this letter.

[2] The various editions punctuate so as to make it appear that the last words refer to Esther Johnson; but the sense of the passage and probability make the present punctuation preferable.

had some share in her education by directing what books she should read, and perpetually instructing her in the principles of honour and virtue, from which she never swerved in any one action or moment of her life. She was sickly from her childhood until about the age of fifteen, but then grew into perfect health, and was looked upon as one of the most beautiful, graceful, and agreeable young women in London, only a little too fat. Her hair was blacker than a raven, and every feature of her face in perfection. . . . She had a gracefulness somewhat more than human, in every motion, word, and action. Never was so happy a conjunction of civility, freedom, easiness, and sincerity. There seemed to be a combination among all that knew her to treat her with a dignity much beyond her rank; yet people of all sorts were never more easy than in her company. . . She spoke in a most agreeable voice, in the plainest words, never hesitating, except out of modesty, before new faces, where she was somewhat reserved; nor, among her nearest friends, ever spoke much at a time. She was but little versed in the common topics of female chat. Scandal, censure, and detraction, never came out of her mouth. Yet, among a few friends, in private conversation, she made little ceremony in discovering her contempt of a coxcomb, and describing all his folly to the life. But the follies of her own sex she was rather inclined to extenuate or to pity." Orrery, who eulogises her in proportion as he depreciates Hester Vanhomrigh, declares that "virtue was her guide in morality, and sincerity her guide in religion. Her voice, sweet in itself, was rendered more harmonious by what she said. Her manners were polite, easy, and unreserved, wherever she came attracting attention and esteem. She exactly answered the description of Penelope in Homer:—

' A woman, loveliest of the lovely kind—
A body perfect, and complete in mind.' "

Attracted by sympathy, arising out of their dependent position, but still more by opportunities offered, it is not surprising, perhaps, disparity of years notwithstanding, that a feeling of strong affection sprang up between them, which became, however, much more intense, as years went on, on her side than on his. He undertook the superintendence of her reading, as he tell us; and as far, at least, as pupilage was concerned, she became the new Heloise of a new Abélard; although it does not appear, as yet, that the passion of love had been excited. At least, it does not become conspicuous until some years later, when, upon the death of Temple, Swift had to find a new home. Belonging to the beginning of the period of his second residence with Temple, there remains an interesting record of him in the fragments of a letter, written by him in the absence of the family in London. Scott supposes it to be addressed to Esther Johnson herself, but more probably it was addressed to her mother, who was now married to a steward or agent of the estate, a Mr. Mose. He imagines the absent family to have become perfect courtiers, and expects to hear nothing for the next five months but of "we courtiers," and he sends his "love" to the King, and desires to know how he looks. He says that he does not wish them back too soon, for he is living in great state, and the cook comes every day for orders, &c. Some one had reported to him that the great Tsar Peter, who was then in England on his travels, had fallen in love with his correspondent, and he jocosely advises her to provide herself with furs and dress proper for the regions of ice and snow.[1]

During this period Swift composed, or rather completed, two famous books—the *Tale of a Tub* and the *Battle of the Books*—the first-fruits of his satirical genius in prose. The death of Temple in January, 1699, who bequeathed to him the labour of editing his rather voluminous writings delayed their publication, and they did not come out until 1704. Meanwhile he accepted the secretaryship to Lord Berkeley, the new Viceroy of Ireland. Among the ladies of the Castle especially claims notice Lady Betty Berkeley, better known as Lady Betty Germaine, a daughter of the Lord-Lieutenant, with whom he afterwards maintained an intimate correspondence. In 1701 he took his Doctor's degree at Trinity College, and to the same date belongs the termination of his relation with *Varina*. In reply to a letter from her, offering renewal of love, he sent an insulting missive, which redounds little to his credit, making any further advances on her part impossible. One, and only one, excuse, such as it is, can be offered for him—his dread of an imprudent marriage, which might bring with it poverty and humiliation. Of this he had an example in the marriage of his only sister. Her husband, an unsuitable choice to which he had been strongly opposed, died not long afterwards, bankrupt by his extravagance, leaving her in entire dependence upon her brother.[2] During his secretaryship,

[1] Quoted in *Life of Swift* by Forster.
[2] The statement repeated by some of his biographers, that Swift, while giving her a small annuity, sternly refused, after the *mésalliance*, any personal communication with her, although she remained his nearest relative, has been disproved by Forster. After her husband's death, Mrs. Fenton lived with Mrs. Johnson, at Farnham.

Swift obtained, through the interest of Lord Berkeley, a prebend in Dublin Cathedral, and also the incumbency of two small Irish livings, the more famous of which is that of Laracor, near Trim, in East Meath. The parishioners, including every resident, hardly reached to the number of twenty, and the new vicar found ample time for indulging his tastes for gardening, planting, building, fishing, &c. Soon after his return to England with Lord Berkeley, he brought out his first political tract, *A Discourse of the Dissensions between the Nobles and Commons in Athens and Rome* (1701), which at once introduced him to the notice of and to close relationship with the leading Whig statesmen, Somers, Halifax, Godolphin, and with others of less celebrity. The Tories had come into power, and, in the House of Commons, had proceeded to impeach their rivals for their share in the Partition Treaty. The House of Lords, as it happened, now more Whig than the Lower House, resisted the impeachment. Hence the *dissension* and the parallel drawn by Swift. His party principles, as he professed them at this time, embraced, in Church matters, high Anglicanism or rather high Toryism, although not of the extreme " passive obedience" type ; in politics, moderately Whig doctrines. Of the authorship of the *Discourse* Lord Somers and Bishop Burnet were each suspected, and the latter escaped impeachment only by a timely disclaimer. But Swift's Church Toryism was too pronounced to allow him to co-operate cordially with his party, and he never wrote again in their interests.

A far more interesting and important biographical event belongs to this year. At the death of Temple, who had left her a small legacy, and property in Wicklow, Esther Johnson found a double attraction across the Channel, the presence of her lover and the greater easiness of living upon a limited income. Swift saw her at Farnham, and exerted his eloquence to persuade her to the step, which, probably, she took with little reluctance, " very much," as he candidly tells us, " for my own satisfaction, who had few friends or acquaintances in Ireland. I prevailed with her and her dear friend and companion, the other lady [Mrs. Dingley], to draw what money they had into Ireland, a great part of their fortunes being in annuities upon funds. They complied with my advice, and soon after came over; but I happening to continue some time longer in England, they were much discouraged to live in Dublin, where they were wholly strangers. But the adventure looked so like a frolic, the censure held for some time, as if there were a secret history in such a removal ; which, however, soon blew off by her excellent conduct. She came over with her friend in the year 1700, and they both lived together until this day."[1] To avoid scandal the two ladies lived in the town of Trim, from which Laracor lies distant two miles; excepting in the absence of the prebendary, when they occupied his parsonage-house. In the autumn of the same year Swift followed them to Ireland.

Composed seven years earlier, in 1704 appeared the *Tale of a Tub*,[2] together with its lesser companion, the *Battle of the Books*. Although the famous satire (as pointed out by Mr. Craik, the latest biographer of Swift) embraces a much wider scope of ridicule than, perhaps, is commonly recognised—only one-third of the *Tale* being concerned with ecclesiastical history—yet the fact remains that the most prominent and personal part of it sketches, as is well-known, under the allegory of the fortunes of the three brothers, Peter, Martin, and Jack, the histories of the three great Sects of Christendom. Nothwithstanding the fact that the author, while throwing the greatest ridicule upon both Catholics and Calvinists, deals tenderly with the Anglicans (whom Martin represents), the covert but transparent satire upon Christianity itself proved to be, in after years, the one great bar to him to the highest preferment in his Church. With all her high churchism, the orthodox and pious Queen Anne could not forgive, even to the champion of the Church of England, what she conceived to be an insidious attack upon the very foundations upon which its claims were built.

The *Tale of a Tub* has a double dedication to Lord Somers and to Prince Posterity, in which Swift ironically represents the fulsome flatteries of writers, and the vanity of authorship in general in too confidently anticipating the verdict of later ages. Among various writers cited he quotes conspicuously the authority of Lucretius; while to Rabelais he owes a very considerable debt. The book came out anonymously, and for a long time the parentage (the honour of which Lord Somers, among others, received) remained in doubt; a doubt which Dr. Johnson paradoxically revived, in his *Life of Swift*, nearly eighty years after the controversy had ended. The author never explicitly acknowledged his own claims, and the nearest recognition of his authorship occurs in an apparently allusive passage in the *Travels of Gulliver*.

---

[1] *Character of Mrs. Johnson.*

[2] The title is derived from a nautical expression—" to throw a tub to a whale,"—to frighten away the imagined assailant of the ship, and so to save it. As the sailors throw the tub overboard for this purpose, so the author implies that he uses his tub to divert assaults from the Church and State. Sir Thomas More uses the expression, and Ben Jonson wrote a comedy with that title.

But he would not permit any false claimants, and the pretensions of his cousin, the Chaplain, to part-authorship he sharply repressed. Some of the best critics have expressed the highest admiration of the *Tale*. Voltaire, no enthusiastic admirer of Rabelais, pronounced it to be *Rabelais perfectionné*. Hallam thinks it the masterpiece of Swift. Dr. Johnson, who strangely expresses the eulogy as proof that the book did not come from its reputed author, declares that " there is in it such a vigour of mind, such a swarm of thoughts, so much of nature, and art, and life." Contemporary critics displayed equal admiration. Atterbury, the future Bishop, reports to his friend, Bishop Trelawney, that nothing pleased more in London than this book, and shrewdly guesses the source of it, although at Oxford it had been assigned to various names. De Foe speaks of the author as " a walking index of books, who had all the libraries of Europe in his head." His protagonist of the *Battle of the Books*, Wotton, published an elaborate Commentary to show up its mischievousness, with various illustrations; which gave his opponent an opportunity of displaying his characteristic irony, and way of converting the attacks of enemies to his own advantage. "He printed these illustrations as notes contributed to the elucidation of its text by the worthy and ingenious Mr. Wotton, bachelor of divinity; and its most envenomed assailant has thus, in countless editions since, figured as its friendly illustrator."[1]

When, five years afterwards, he was expecting higher preferment in the Church from his Tory friends, he prefixed to his *Tale* an *Apology*, in reply to his orthodox critics, in which he ingeniously seeks to clear himself of the charge of scepticism, and, more successfully, attempts to establish his loyalty to the Church of England. In one of the most famous passages in the Satire he has suggested to Carlyle a hint for the *Sartor Resartus*—the passage where, treating of the fine trimmings tacked on to their coats by the brothers, he descants on the philosophy of clothes in general :—" About this time it happened a Sect arose, whose tenets obtained and spread very far, especially in the *grand monde*, and among every body of good fashion. They worshipped a sort of Idol who, as their doctrine delivered, did daily create men by a kind of manufactory operation. This idol they placed in the highest part of the house, on an altar erected about three feet. . . . . The worshippers of this deity had also a system of their belief, which seemed to turn upon the following fundamentals: They held the Universe

[1] Forster's *Life of Swift*.

to be a large suit of clothes which invests everything; that
the Earth is invested by the Air; the Air is invested by the Stars;
and the Stars are invested by the *Primum Mobile*. . . These *postulata*
being admitted, it will follow, in due course of reasoning, that those
beings, which the world calls improperly *Suits of Clothes,* are, in
reality, the most refined species of animals ; or, to proceed higher, that
they are rational creatures or men. For is it not manifest that they
live, and move, and talk, and perform all other offices of human life ?
Are not beauty, and wit, and mien, and breeding their inseparable pro-
prieties ? In short, we see nothing but them, hear nothing but them.
Is it not they who walk the streets, fill up Parliament, Coffee, and
Play-houses ? It is true, indeed, that these animals, who are vulgarly
called *Suits of Clothes,* or *Dresses,* do, according to certain compositions,
receive different appellations. If one of them be trimmed up with a
gold chain, and a red gown, and a white rod, and a great horse, it is
called a *Lord Mayor* ; if certain ermines and furs be placed in a certain
position, we style them a *Judge*; and so an apt conjunction of lawn and
black satin we entitle a *Bishop*."

In the *Battle of the Books,* in St. James's Library, the main purpose
is a defence of the *Ancients*, or rather of Sir William Temple, their
principal champion, against the *Moderns* with Perrault, Wotton, and
Bentley at their head. But in this Satire, as well as in the *Tale*, the
purpose of ridiculing the absurd pedantry of the schools appears
scarcely less prominent, and, whatever may be thought of the primary
inspiration, the secondary one, at least, must approve itself to the more
critical reason of the present day. Wotton retaliated with a charge of
plagiarism. He asserted that the whole idea, as well as title page, of the
Battle of the Books had been taken from a French work, published in
1688, by De Callières (not Coutray, as Scott calls him). But, in fact,
neither in the title nor in the purpose does the French *brochure* bear
much resemblance to its more celebrated successor; and Swift indignantly
denied any obligation to the Frenchman.[1] From this period dates his

[1] See *Life of Jonathan Swift*, by Henry Craik, 1882. It is interesting to note that the now
famous expression "sweetness and light," made current by Mr. Matthew Arnold, in recent
days, occurs in a passage in the *Battle of the Books*. In the fine episode of the controversy
between the Bee and Spider, Æsop is introduced as deducing the following inferences of
the superiority of the *Ancients* :—" As for us, the Ancients, we are content, with the Bee,
to pretend to nothing of our own beyond our wings and our voice; that is to say, our
flights and our language. For the rest, whatever we have got has been by infinite labour
and research, ranging through every corner of nature. The difference is that, instead of
dirt and poison [like the Spider's], we have rather chosen to fill our hives with honey and
wax—thus furnishing mankind with the two noblest of things, which are *Sweetness and
Light*."

friendship and correspondence with Addison. Lately returned from his travels in Italy, Addison sent him a copy of his *Remarks*, inscribed to "Dr. Jonathan Swift, the most agreeable companion, the truest friend, and the greatest genius of the age!" Until the political conversion of Swift, his intimacy with the Whig essayist continued to be of the closest kind, nor did mutual regard cease upon their political separation. With Steele, too, and others of the Whig *coterie*, he had been brought into close and boon companionship (records of suppers and *symposiums* abound in the *Journal* of 1710-11), which, a few years later, changed into bitter animosity, when the two chief partisan-writers edited their rival Papers. Another conspicuous name in the correspondence of Swift is that of King, the Whig Archbishop of Dublin. At first a little cold, and occasionally even somewhat hostile, their relations became latterly sufficiently friendly, and almost even cordial. Their correspondence ended in 1729, the year of the death of the Archbishop.

Two witty pieces of this date (1705) deserve notice. One a satirical poem on Vanbrugh (the comedy-writer and the architect of Blenheim House, Castle Howard, &c.) who, after manufacturing plays, had taken to manufacturing houses, and had lately built himself a mansion, which the Wits are represented as hunting about in all directions to find; the object of the satire, as exhibited in the original MS. version,[1] being, principally, the easy success of the trifling productions of the Stage as compared with more solid performances. But a wittier piece is the *Baucis and Philemon*, a parody of Ovid's well-known *Metamorphosis*. A special interest belongs to the MS. copy found by Mr. Forster at Narford, as being the original poem before it had been revised and reduced to its printed proportions by Addison.[2] "Two brother hermits, saints by trade," in disguise, one winter's night, put to the proof the Christian hospitality of some poor villagers, and "begged relief which none would grant." At length they come to the cottage of Philemon and Baucis, who at once give them a hearty welcome with food and drink. By way of reward, following the example (with a difference) of their celestial prototypes, the disguised saints convert the humble cottage into a church, the chimney assuming the form of a steeple, the wooden

[1] Formerly in the possession of Mr. Forster.

[2] The printed poem has 178 lines only; the MS. at Narford (the place of Swift's friend, Sir Andrew Fountaine) 230. The variations between the two consist in "the omission of 96 lines, the addition of 44, and the alteration of 22." The alternative title of the Parody reads: *The Ever Lamented Loss of the Two Yew Trees in the parish of Chilthorne, Somerset. Imitated from the Eighth Book of Ovid.* The village, after all, as it appears in the body of the poem, is fixed as "down in Kent."

jack that of a clock; the "groaning" arm-chair becomes the pulpit, and (in the MS.) the crumbling mortar the font: the illustrated ballads hanging on the old walls, the "heraldry of every tribe" (in the printed copy);[1] the pews taking shape out of the ancient bedsteads, "such as our grandfathers use," and still retaining the virtue "of lodging folks disposed to sleep":—

> "The groaning Chair began to crawl,
> Like a huge insect, up the wall;
> There stuck, and to a Pulpit grew,
> But kept its matter and its hue.
> And, mindful of its ancient state,
> Still groans, while tattling gossips prate.
> The Mortar, only changed its name,
> In its old shape, a Font became."

As for the old couple themselves—the "Goodman," at his own request, like his Ovidian prototype, becomes the priest or "parson" of his metamorphosed habitation:—

> "You have raised a Church here in a minute,
> And I would fain continue in it;
> I'm good for little at my days—
> Make me the Parson, if you please."

Straightway, the metamorphosis accomplished:—

> "A trembling, awkward gait he took,
> With a demure dejected look,
> Talked of his Offerings, Tithes, and Dues,
> Could smoke, and drink, and read the news;
> Or sell a goose at the next town,
> Decently hid beneath his gown;
> Contrived to preach old sermons next,
> Changed in the preface and the text;
> At Christenings well could act his part,
> And had the service all by heart;
> Wished women might have children fast,

---

[1] Or better in the MS.:—

> "And now the heraldry describe
> Of a Churchwarden or a Tribe."

The allusion is to the "rude painted inscriptions, so common in old days, of country churches, and to be met occasionally even yet, where Jacob's ensigns may be seen standing for the Tribes of Israel; and here and there an aspiring Churchwarden will have found beside them a place for his own family heraldry."—Forster.

> And thought whose sow had furrowed last ;
> Against Dissenters would repine,
> And stood up firm ' for right divine';
> Carried it to his equals higher,
> But most obsequious to the Squire ;
> Found his head filled with many a system ;
> But Classic authors—he ne'er missed 'em." [1]

In the autumn of 1706 Swift went back to Ireland and there remained till November, 1707, living alternately at Laracor and in Dublin. Among his commonest and discordant occupations were planting and gardening in the country, and dining, and cards, and suppers in the town; some of the members of these clubs, or convivial meetings, being Esther Johnson and Mrs. Dingley ; Sterne, Dean of St. Patrick's ; Archdeacon Walls, his *factotum*, when Swift was in England; the Archdeacon's wife, whom he frequently names in his letters as " Goody Walls, my gossip," and who has acquired fame by her remarkable fecundity, whose house in Dublin Esther Johnson often made her home ; a Dublin Alderman, named Stoyte, afterwards Lord Mayor, and his wife and daughter ; and the Dublin Postmaster, Manley, and his wife: to all of whom he frequently refers in his letters to Esther Johnson (1710-13). Other acquaintance were Raymond, Vicar of Trim, in whose house Esther and her companion occasionally boarded, the Wesleys, Warburton, his curate, the Percevals, &c. At Laracor his official work could not have been severe; his parishioners, with Squire Jones and "other scoundrels" as he calls them familiarly, numbering not twenty. "I am this minute very busy," he writes to Dean Sterne, on the eve of starting for England in 1710, " being to preach to-day before an audience of at least fifteen people, most of them gentle, and all simple." In 1708 he was again in England, mixing in familiar intercourse with political and literary friends, and engaged upon his various political and other essays and pamphlets, which came from the press in rapid succession. His *Letter upon the Sacramental Test* (1708), denouncing relaxation of the repressive laws against Nonconformity, seemed to be a sort of public announcement of his future secession from the Whigs. About the same time he published, as it may briefly be cited, his *Argument against the*

---

[1] "The reason the good man gives for desiring to be made the parson, the gait and the look which he takes thereon, his changes of demeanour to his equals and to the Squire, and the decent uses of his gown on Market-days, are Swift all over. But no trace of them will be found in the [Audison] altered poem."—Forster.

Abolition of Christianity.[1] Equally with Defoe's *Short and Easy Method with Dissenters*, and his own *Proposal for Utilising the Children of the Poor in Ireland*, of a later period, the majority of his readers took it *au grand sérieux*. In this ironical piece, as well as in his pamphlet upon the famous *Discourse of Free-Thinking* of Anthony Collins (1713), which he entitled *Mr. Collins's Discourse of Free-Thinking put into Plain English by way of Abstract for the Use of the Poor*, the conservation of the Christian Creed, obviously enough to the observant reader, becomes a matter of expediency rather than a question of truth; and Swift's cynical remark, that "the bulk of mankind is as well qualified for flying as for thinking," expresses, in brief, his conservative attitude in these controversies. The irony of some parts of the *Argument* is sufficiently marked, as, for instance, in the following passage:—

"I hope no reader imagines me so weak as to stand up in the defence of real Christianity, such as used in *primitive* times (if we may believe the authors of those ages) to have an influence upon men's belief and actions. To offer at the restoring of that would, indeed, be a wild project. It would be to dig up foundations; to destroy, at one blow, all the wit and half the learning of the kingdom; to break the entire frame and constitution of things; to ruin trade; extinguish arts and science, with the professors of them; in short, to turn our courts, exchanges, and shops into deserts. . . Therefore I think this caution was, in itself, altogether unnecessary (which I have inserted only to prevent all possibility of cavilling), since every candid reader will easily understand my discourse to be intended only in defence of *nominal* Christianity; the other having been, for some time, wholly laid aside by general assent as utterly inconsistent with our present schemes of wealth and power. But why we should, therefore, cast off the *name and title* of Christians, although the general opinion and resolution be so violent for it, I confess I cannot (with submission) apprehend, nor is the consequence necessary. . . .

"For the rest, it may, perhaps, admit controversy, whether the banishing of all notions of religion whatsoever would be convenient for the vulgar. Not that I am in the least of opinion with those who hold

---

[1] In its full title: "An Argument to Prove that the Abolishing of Christianity in England may, as all Things now stand, be attended with some Inconveniences, and perhaps not produce those many Good Effects proposed thereby." It has received the praise of Johnson as "very happy and judicious."

religion to have been the invention of politicians, to keep the lower part of the world in awe by the fear of invisible powers, unless mankind was very different to what it is now; for I look upon the mass or body of our people here in England to be as free-thinkers—that is to say, as staunch unbelievers—as any in the highest rank. But I conceive some scattered notions about a superior Power to be of singular use for the common people, as furnishing excellent materials to keep children quiet when they grow peevish, and providing topics of amusement in a tedious winter's night."

What strikes an impartial reader as not so pleasant (in the English meaning of the word), in the controversial writings of Swift, is the imputation of unworthy motives alike to the orthodox and non-orthodox nonconformists. The imputation comes with the less grace from one who allowed to himself sufficiently wide licence in dealing with matters theological.[1] It has too often the disagreeable taste of the zeal of a candidate for ecclesiastical dignities; although, without doubt, his attachment to Anglicanism, as a form of ecclesiastical government, must be admitted to have been entirely sincere. A more worthy essay than his *Letter*, as well as more popular production, is the *Predictions for the Year 1708* by Isaac Bickerstaff, an ironical exposure of the pretences of the Astrologers in general, and of John Partridge, the well-known almanac manufacturer and editor of *Merlinus Liberatus*, in particular. The wit of the *Predictions* consists in this—that, while denouncing the impostures of the diviners and prophets, he gravely sets up a sort of opposition method of divination, by which he fortells a number of political and other events; and, in particular, the death of Partridge himself. Difficult as the fact may be of belief, for those not versed in the history of Diabolism, the *Predictions* received the distinguished honour of being burned in solemn conclave by the Inquisitors of the Faith in Portugal, as a genuine production of diabolatry and the *Black Art*. Swift continued the joke in a succession of narratives of accomplishments, and vindications, recounting in the former, with the

---

[1] A severe critic, the most brilliant satirist of our times, has strongly asserted his belief that Swift's theological orthodoxy was not sincere. "It is my belief," declares Thackeray, "that he suffered frightfully from the consciousness of his own scepticism, and that he had bent his pride so far down as to put his apostasy out to hire. The papers left behind him, called *Thoughts on Religion*, is merely a set of excuses for not professing disbelief [in preternatural Christianity]. He says of his sermons, that he preached pamphlets. They have scarce a Christian characteristic; they might be preached from the steps of a synagogue, or the floor of a mosque, or the box of a coffee house almost. . . . Having put that cassock on, it poisoned him, he was strangled in his bands. He goes through life tearing, like a man possessed with a devil." *Lectures on the English Humourists*.

greatest exactness of time and circumstance, the pretended fact of the decease of the bewildered prophet. All the wits, Addison, Steele, and others, soon joined in this ludicrous combat, and the name of Bickerstaff became famous throughout the reading world of Europe.

To the next year (1709) belongs his *Project for the Advancement of Religion and the Reformation of Manners*.[1] He makes a comprehensive arraignment of the corruptions of the Social State:—

"But all these are trifles in comparison, if we step into other scenes, and consider the fraud and cosenage of trading men and shopkeepers; that insatiable gulf of injustice and oppression, the Law; the open traffic for all Civil and Military employments (I wish it rested there), without the least regard to merit or qualifications; the corrupt management of men in office; the many detestable abuses in choosing those who represent the people, with the management of interest, and factions, among the Representatives; to which I must be bold to add the ignorance of some of the lower clergy; the mean servile temper of others; the pert pragmatical demeanour of several young stagers in divinity, upon their just producing themselves into the world, with many other circumstances needless, or rather, invidious, to mention, which, falling in with the corruptions already related, have, however unjustly, rendered the whole Order contemptible." As for the army: "If gentlemen of that profession were, at least, obliged to some *external* decorum in their conduct; or, even if a profligate life and character were not a means of advancement, and the appearance of piety a most infallible hindrance, it is impossible the corruptions there should be so universal and exorbitant. I have been assured by several great officers, that no troops abroad are so ill-disciplined as the English; which cannot well be otherwise, while the common soldiers have perpetually before their eyes the vicious example of their leaders, and it is hardly possible for those to commit any crime, whereof these are not infinitely more guilty, and with less temptation."

Nor does he give any better account of the administrators of the Laws themselves: "There is one abuse in this town which wonderfully contributes to the promotion of vice—that such men are often put into the Commission of the Peace, whose interest it is that virtue should be utterly banished from among us; who maintain or, at least, enrich them-

[1] Under the pseudonym of a "Person of Quality" he dedicated it to the Countess of Berkeley, upon whom, when Chaplain to her husband, he imposed his clever parody of Boyle's *Meditations*, the *Meditation on a Broomstick*, as a genuine production of that sober savant.

selves by encouraging the grossest immoralities, to whom all the bawds of the Ward pay contribution for shelter and protection from the laws. Thus, these worthy magistrates, instead of lessening enormities, are the occasion of just twice as much debauchery as there would be without them. For these infamous women are *forced upon doubling their work and industry* to answer the double charges of paying the Justice and supporting themselves—like thieves who escape the gallows, and are let out to steal, in order to discharge the gaoler's fees." Peculation and legal robbery prevailed, in almost every branch of the "public service," with impunity. "The many corruptions, at present, in every branch of business are almost inconceivable. I have heard it computed by skilful persons, that of £6,000,000 raised every year, for the service of the public, one-third, at least, is sunk and intercepted through the several classes and subordinations of artful men in office, before the remainder is applied to the proper uses . . . I could name a Commission, where several persons, out of a salary of £500, without other visible revenues, have always lived at the rate of £2000, and laid out £40,000 or £50,000 upon purchases of lands or annuities. A hundred other instances of the same kind might easily be produced."

His remarks upon the incalculable evils proceeding from the unrestricted sale of intoxicating drinks, after the lapse of 170 years, still, in great measure, remain applicable : " In order to reform the vices of this town, which, as we have said, has so mighty an influence on the whole kingdom, it would be very instrumental to have a law made, that all taverns and ale houses, should be obliged to dismiss their company by twelve at night, and shut up their doors ; and, that no woman should be suffered to enter any tavern or ale house, upon any pretence whatsoever. It is easy to conceive what a number of ill consequences such a law would prevent, the mischiefs of quarrels and lewdness, and thefts, and midnight brawls, the diseases of intemperance and venery, and a thousand other evils needless to mention. Nor would it be amiss, if the masters of those public houses were obliged, upon the severest penalties, to give only a *proportioned* quantity of drink to every company ; and, when he found his guests disordered with excess, to refuse them any more." The arts of adulteration, as well as of other fraud, seem to have flourished one hundred and seventy years ago almost as greatly as now : "I believe there is hardly a nation in Christendom, where all kind of fraud is practised in so unmeasurable a degree as with us. The lawyers and the tradesmen have found so many arts to deceive in their several callings, that they have outgrown the common prudence of mankind, which is in no sort able to fence against them. Neither could the legislature in anything more consult the public good than by providing some effectual remedy against this evil, which, in several cases, deserves greater punishment than many crimes that are capital among us. The vintner who, by mixing poison with his wines, destroys more lives than any one disease in the bill of mortality; the lawyer, who persuades you to purchase what he knows is mortgaged for more than the worth, to the ruin of you and your family; the goldsmith or scrivener [banker], who takes all your fortune to dispose of, when he has beforehand resolved to break the following day, do surely deserve the gallows much better than the wretch who is carried thither for stealing a loaf!"

Swift, at this time, balanced between the hope of a foreign secretaryship and a bishopric.[1] He seems to have had some expectation of a bishopric in Virginia, and he writes half seriously, half jocularly, to his friend Hunter, then awaiting his appointment to a governorship somewhere in English America; "vous savez que Monsieur d'Addison, notre bon ami, est fait sécrétaire d'état d'Irlande; and, unless you make haste over and get me my Virginian bishopric, he will persuade me to go with him, for the Vienna project is off, which is a great disappointment to the design I had of displaying my politics at the Emperor's Court." (Feb. 1709.)

While lingering in London he passed his days in a rather desultory manner, finishing his editing of Temple's *Remains,* attending drawing-rooms, joining with his town-friends in dinners and suppers at the clubs, playing picquet at Mrs. Vanhomrigh's, visiting the Berkeleys, discussing politics with his Whig associates, and occasionally going to the opera. For the latter sort of entertainment, and, in fact, for music generally, he had little affection. In a letter to Ambrose Philips he reports that "the town is gone mad after a new opera. Poetry and good sense are dwindling, like Echo, with repetition and voice. Critic Dennis vows to God that operas will be the ruin of the nation, and brings examples from Antiquity to prove it. A good old lady, five miles out of town, asked me the other day what these *uproars* were that her daughter was always going to."[2] His note books contain frequent entries, in these years, of terrible suffering from his peculiar

[1] His friend Addison had lately obtained the post of Secretary for Ireland with £2,000 a year, as well as a sinecure place of £400; while he himself, after all his expectation, had secured only £300 a year from Laracor and his prebend.

[2] From an unprinted letter, quoted in Forster's *Life.*

maladies of sickness and giddiness, and of the remedies which he vainly sought from the physicians.[1]

He returned to Ireland in June, 1709. Before leaving London, he again refreshed the memory of his Whig patron, Halifax, as to the preferment he still expected. His postscript, like the proverbial woman's, contained the gist of the whole letter, in which he half-seriously, half-ironically, and not too ambitiously, writes:—"Pray, my Lord, desire Dr. South [now nearly eighty] to die about the fall of the leaf, for he has a prebend of Westminster (which will make me your neighbour), and a sinecure in the country, both in the Queen's gift, which my friends have often told me would fit me extremely. And forgive me one word, which I know not what extorts from me; that if my Lord President would, in such a juncture, think me worth laying any weight of his credit on, you cannot but think me persuaded that it would be a very easy matter to compass; and I have some sort of pretence, since the late King promised me a prebend of Westminster, when I petitioned him in pursuance of a recommendation I had from Sir William Temple." To which Halifax replies, after a long interval, "I am quite ashamed for myself and friends, to see you left in a place so incapable of tasting you [sic], and to see so much merit, and so great qualities, unrewarded by those who are sensible of them. Mr. Addison and I are entered into a new confederacy never to give over the pursuit, nor to cease reminding those who can serve you, till your worth is placed in that light it ought to shine in. Dr. South holds out still, but he cannot be immortal. The situation of his prebend would make me doubly concerned in serving you; and, upon all occasions that shall offer, I will be your constant solicitor, your sincere admirer, and your unalterable friend."[2]

---

[1] Mr. Forster has printed a curious *fac-simile* of one of these pages of the note books, recording his expenses on this account for four weeks in December, 1708, written in his usual minute hand-writing. Of these brief records of his illnesses the following are samples:—"1708, Nov. 6th to 16th, often giddy. Gd. help me. So to 25th, less. 16th, Brandy for giddiness, 2s. Brandy 3d. Dec. 5th, horrible sick. 12th, much better, thank God and M.D's. prayers. 16th, bad fit at Mrs. Barton's. 24th, Better, but dread a fit. . . . March [1709], headache frequent. April 2, small giddy fitt and swimming in head. M. D., and God help me. August, sick, with giddiness much. 1710. . . . March 14, very ill. July, terrible fitt. Gd. knows what may be the event. Better towards the end." The latest theory as to these maladies will be referred to hereafter. *M.D.* stands for Esther Johnson.

[2] In Forster's *Life*. The letter is endorsed by Swift—"I kept this as a true original of courtiers and court promises." Of the promises of the ministers he elsewhere speaks scornfully, as ending in "only good words and dinners," the latter, according to Swift, being not beyond criticism. One of the perplexities in Swift's career is, how to explain the strange neglect by his party, whether Whig or Tory, to provide for him the usual reward of political service—service, in his case, so important. The opposition of the Queen, on the

Suggested to him by the famous *jeux d'esprit* of "Bickerstaff," Steele had (1709) established his famous periodical, *The Tatler*; and he obtained the assistance of their witty author, who contributed several papers, (Swift's papers in *The Tatler* are twenty in all, the most interesting is No. 290, on abbreviating English), and also permitted the adoption of the popular *nom de plume* by Steele himself. At this moment, the temporary reaction in favour of High Churchism, to which the Sacheverell agitation contributed greatly, inspired hope into the Irish clergy of acquiring, as their English brethren already had done, the "first-fruits" from the Crown; and Swift was joined in a commission with two Irish bishops to prosecute the suit of the Irish Convocation for that purpose.

The letters to Esther Johnson, commonly but improperly styled the *Journal to Stella*,[1] begin at the date of his arrival at Chester, on his way to London. They form, altogether, the most unique and entertaining series of letters in any language; unique by the style and "little language," intended for no eyes but those of his two correspondents, in which the writer uses the familiar expressions of the old days at Moor Park, when the girl to whom he writes was still a mere child.[2] A careful perusal of these private memorials reveals that, whatever may

ground of his freedom of style in dealing with matters theological, alone does not appear to be an adequate cause; nor is the difficulty explained altogether by the fact, that, being a cleric, he could not so easily be supplied with a suitable place, like his lay associates. There were places or offices of dignity or emolument in the patronage of the Government, besides ecclesiastical ones, which might have been found for him. One solution of the problem may be, that the political chiefs wished to keep so exceptionally useful a writer dependent upon them as long as possible.

But it seems that the influence of his personal enemies had no little weight in the matter. According to Sheridan, "the Duchess of Somerset, who entertained implacable hatred against him, determined to move heaven and earth to prevent his promotion. She first prevailed on the Archbishop of York to oppose it, whose remarkable expression to the queen was, *That her majesty should be sure that the man whom she was going to make a bishop was a Christian.*" The Duchess then went to the Queen, we are told, and "throwing herself on her knees, entreated with tears in her eyes, that she would not give the bishopric to Swift, at the same time presenting to her that excessively bitter copy of verses which Swift had written against her, called the *Windsor Prophecy.*"

[1] The title given to it by the biographers and editors. In point of fact, "Stella" does not occur once in all these letters. Swift, probably, derived the poetic name, which he afterwards adopted, from the *Arcadia* of Sydney. It is possible, and characteristic of him, as pointed out by Mr. Forster, that it might have been suggested by the resemblance of *Esther* or *Hester* to the Greek word for Star—*Aster*.

[2] A large part o the curiously spelled words are a mere *onomatopœia*, representing, as nearly as possible, the sounds produced by "making up the mouth," customary with nurses and others in talking to young children. The original spelling, and even whole words, have been altered or omitted by former editors. Mr. Forster has been the first to restore and systematically to attempt to interpret (not always satisfactorily) this "little language."

have been the case at a later time, Swift now entertained for Esther or *M.D.* (as he usually addresses her) a very real affection—terms of affectionate endearment, that would scarcely be used by an indifferent lover, continually occur, and his thoughts constantly revert to her home on the Liffey.

On Sept. 9, 1710, Swift arrived in the capital. With this moment opens a new epoch in his life, and the four next years include the most notable part of his political and public career. From the first day of his appearance upon the scene, his letter-journals exhibit him in a constant stream of dinners, visits, suppers, tavern-symposiums, interviews with his various political associates, especially (at first) with the leading Whigs, Godolphin the ex-Lord Treasurer, Somers, Halifax, &c., and so it went on, without intermission, for the next three months. He came upon the scene in time to witness the fall of his Whig friends, and the triumph of the Tories, with whom, henceforward, he allied himself in the firmest bonds of intimacy. The motives to this political apostasy have too often been discussed, to make it necessary to re-open the question here at length. Nothing leads to the belief that the conversion was either wholly dishonest or wholly disinterested. By constitutional or educational temperament, of conservative bias, he seems to have readily embraced the opportunity offered to him at once of satisfying his ardour for revenge upon his late allies for their neglect of him (with whom perhaps, too, he had acted rather by chance than by conviction), and of publicly adopting the ecclesiastical creed, or rather policy, of the opponents of the Whigs. The new Tory Government came into power in the autumn of 1710. To Somers, Godolphin, Halifax, Cowper, Walpole, and Wharton succeeded Rochester as Lord Treasurer (replaced shortly afterwards by Harley), St. John as Chief Secretary of State, the Duke of Ormond as Viceroy in Ireland, and Granville as Secretary at War. During the four years of their enjoyment of power, the object of unceasing flattery and caresses from the Tory Cabinet, such as never before had fallen to the lot of any literary man, Swift experienced, with something of the power, not a little of the anxiety, of a political partisan writer, to whom everything might be promised, but from whom also everything was expected.

His first overt act of secession appeared in the *Examiner* (of Nov. 2), which he continuedly conducted, unaided, until June, 1711, when the notorious Mrs. Manley, the novelist and play writer, assumed the editorship. Under Swift's management the *Examiner*, if not in solidity of argument, at least in brilliancy, soon asserted its superiority over its political rivals. With unsparing ridicule and contempt he revenged not so much the public as his own wrongs, holding up the late government, in particular the Duke of Marlborough, for the detestation of the country; and he quickly became the ruling spirit, as well as the most trusted supporter of the Harley—St. John Cabinet. He took part in their private councils, and their semi-official Saturday dinners, to which he makes frequent reference in his letters. As one reward of his services he obtained the long-demanded "first-fruits" and "twentieths." Meanwhile his pride, though not his ambition, he satisfied to the fullest extent. In the society of the first Ministers he bore himself not so much as a subordinate as an equal or even superior, and his behaviour towards them was (according to his own representation) occasionally supercilious in the extreme, for he did not permit himself to be deceived by outward show of friendship and familiarity. "They are good, honest, hearty fellows," he describes them to Esther Johnson. "I use them like dogs, because I expect they will use me so. They call me nothing but Jonathan; and I said, I believed they would leave me Jonathan as they found me, and that I never knew a minister do anything for those whom they made companions of their pleasure; and I believe you will find it so, but I care not," he adds with affected indifference.

Among his many new friends he numbered the eccentric Lord Peterborough,[1] whom, without much difficulty, he brought over to the Tory camp, and "Mr. Pope, a papist," as he styles him in one of his letters. Of Bolingbroke, the most prominent political figure of the day, he thus records his earlier impressions (Nov. 3, 1711): "I think Mr. St. John the greatest young man I ever knew—wit, capacity, beauty, quickness of apprehension, good learning, and an excellent taste; the best orator in the House of Commons, admirable conversation, good nature, and good manners, generous, and a despiser of money. His only fault is

[1] In verses addressed to him in 1705 he thus wittily hits off his odd outward person, with an allusion to his extraordinary rapidity of movement:—

> "A skeleton in outward figure
> His meagre corpse, though full of vigour,
> Would halt behind him, were it bigger.
>
> "So wonderful his expedition,
> When you have not the least suspicion,
> He's with you like an apparition."

Swift expresses high regard for the rash but lucky hero of Spain, and they always retained a mutual admiration.

talking to his friends, in a way of complaint, of too great a load of business, which looks a little like affectation, and he endeavours too much to mix the fine gentleman and man of business. What truth and sincerity he may have, I know not. He is now but thirty-two, and has been Secretary above a year." Twelve months before he had written to Esther Johnson of the same distinguished celebrity: "I dined to-day by invitation with the Secretary of State, Mr. St. John. . . . I am thinking what a veneration we used to have for Sir William Temple, because he *might have been* Secretary of State at fifty. And here is a young fellow, hardly thirty, in that employment. His father is a man of pleasure,[1] that walks the Mall, frequents the St. James's Coffee-house and the Chocolate-houses; and the young man is principal Secretary of State. Is there not something very odd in that? He told me," he goes on, "among other things, that Mr. Harley complained he could keep nothing from me—I had the way so much of getting into him. I knew that was a *refinement*, and so I told him; and it was so. Indeed, it is hard to see these great men use me like one was their betters, and the puppies with you in Ireland hardly regarding me."

From St. James's, where he first lodged, he migrated, for the sake of better air and exercise, and to relieve his attacks of giddiness (intensified, doubtless, by his conformity to fashionable living), to Chelsea, where he took up his quarters near Atterbury, who was at this time Dean of Carlisle. In the evening, after his official labours, or some hours passed at one or other of his numerous acquaintances, he walked the distance, through well-known streets and promenades, until he reached the open fields which then conducted to the surburban village. A name now frequently occurs in the *Journal*, destined to occupy a conspicuous place in his biography. Two years before, he had first made the acquaintance of Mrs. Vanhomrigh, the widow of a gentleman of Dutch birth, formerly a Commissioner of the Revenue in Ireland. With her two daughters she lived in Bury Street, St. James's. Hester Vanhomrigh, at this time seventeen years younger than Esther Johnson, seems to have possessed, if not all the personal charms, more than the "accomplishments" of the latter. As with "Stella," so with "Vanessa," as he poetically names her, Swift first gained her affection, and acquired his ascendancy over her mind, by assuming the post of superintendent of her studies. In his letters to Ireland he only once or twice refers to

[1] Sir Henry St. John. In his youth he had been tried and convicted for murder in a duel. He lived to an advanced age.

the principal attractive force which drew him so often to Bury Street—although he frequently mentions the mother—and then only an obscure hint of her existence drops from him. "This was Mrs. Vanhomrigh's daughter's birthday," he notes under date of Feb. 10, 1711, on one of the two occasions on which he divulges the fact of her existence, "and Mr. Ford and I were invited to dinner to keep it, and we spent the evening there drinking punch. That was our way of beginning Lent." How far he had responded to her affection, or pledged himself, we have no certain, direct, evidence. Some of his biographers, as Sheridan and Scott, find proof in his letters to Esther Johnson of his increasing coolness towards that lady, and presumptive evidence of increasing attachment to her rival. His latest biographer, on the other hand, believes the passion to have existed solely on the side of Miss Vanhomrigh.[1] But the indirect evidences, as well as probabilities, hardly bear out this supposition. However it may be, when the moment arrived for his departure for Dublin, proofs of her deep devotion reached him in letters of the most affectionate strain, which became more and more impassioned as time went on.

The letters to Esther Johnson bring us into acquaintance with a number of various people, political, social, and literary. They present, in fact, a highly interesting picture of the times, as they appeared to a keen observer of men and manners, who, himself, took a leading part in them : nor have they less interest as a presentation of himself to us in an easy and most familiar "undress." We are introduced to the more or less conspicuous personages, who make a considerable figure in the history-books of the time, or in the more enduring annals of literature—to Somers, Halifax, St. John, Harley, Marlborough and his almost equally famous Duchess, Addison, Steele, Arbuthnot, Rowe, Congreve, Prior, Garth, Penn, Peterborough, Duke of Ormond, and the ladies Butler, Lord Berkeley and his daughters, Jervas the painter, Wharton, Sacheverell, Mrs. Masham, Lady Falconbridge (a daughter of Oliver Cromwell), Kneller, Atterbury, Carteret, Eugène the Austrian Generalissimo, the Duchess of Hamilton (the young widow of the Duke killed in a duel), and, finally, to the pious Queen Anne, who "hunts in a chaise with one horse, which she drives herself, and drives furiously like Jehu, and is a mighty hunter, like Nimrod." Such are a few of the *epistolarum personæ*. With the writer we enter the taverns (where something less innocent than chocolate was drunk), or chocolate houses, and see

[1] See *Life of Jonathan Swift*, by Henry Craik, 1882.

him seated in familiar talk with Addison, Steele, and the other wits of the day; and observe him prudently (on account of his ill-health) avoiding the excess in drinking, in which the rest of the company indulged themselves. We accompany him to his *tête-à-tête* with the Cabinet ministers (with the Whig at first, but afterwards with the Tory solely), and to the semi-official Saturday dinners at Harley's, and occasionally listen to his scolding at their indifference and remissness in state-affairs; and, afterwards, in the retirement of his modest lodging, see him note down his gratification at his revenge upon his old allies, and his hopes and fears in regard to his new alliance. We are alternately amused or interested in reading about his troubles with his Irish manservant, Patrick, whose drinking habits and incorrigible ways frequently recur; his lamentations over the exactions of great men's great men, in the shape of fees, or over the expenses of coach or chair-hire owing to continuously bad weather; his experiences at book auctions; his annoyances from the dunning of Irish or other friends for his good offices; criticisms of his correspondent's writing and spelling, and allusion to her occupations and friends in Ireland; his contributions to the *Tatler* or to the *Examiner;* the formation of the *October Club,* and its meetings; visits to the Vanhomrighs, as to the cause of which, as they become more frequent, Esther Johnson faintly expresses, it seems, some misgiving.[1] Card parties at drawing rooms, symposiums with his various political or literary associates; his sufferings from his maladies, which were, without doubt, greatly aggravated by "good living;" extemporised proverbs, for which he was famous, given off as though long established and well known; records, constantly occurring, of severe weather, snow, hail, rain, &c., or excessive heats, as notable as any of which complaints nowadays are heard, as if the skies only in these latter times had turned unpropitious. We are variously entertained by descriptions of riding parties at Windsor, of Maids of Honour, and others, whom he accompanies, dressed out in his best; his threatened History of Maids of Honour, which threw them into a

---

[1] Sheridan supposes the beginning of the serious attachment of Swift for Miss Vanhomrigh to be traceable in the latter part of the Journal-Letters to her rival, "in which, from March, 1712, to the end there is a remarkable change in his manner of writing to the two ladies [Miss Johnson and her friend]. We no longer find there any of what he called *the little language,* the playful sallies of an undisguised heart to a bosom friend, no more expressions of tenderness, . . . but, on the contrary, we see nothing but a dry journal continued out of form, made up of trifling incidents, news, or politics, without anything in the matter, or expression, at all interesting to the parties addressed."—*Life of Dr. Jonathan Swift,* by Thomas Sheridan, A.M., 1787.

flutter of excitement; of Sundays at Court, with the official Sacrament-taking, and the succeeding dinners; the fears of himself and his superiors, aroused by the Queen's severe attacks of gout, or other illnesses, with his anathemas against her physicians, whom he has a "mind to turn out for slowly killing her by law—for, in my conscience, they will soon kill her among them;" his occasional appearance at Court, where, "I am so proud, I make all the lords come up to me;" his impressment by St. John to preach before the Queen;[1] his dislike for Lent; the Mohocks or Mohawks and their lawless and licentious acts of savagery, done with impunity in the public streets; his complaints of exactions in the form of "Christmas-boxes;" notice of the new fashion of crinoline;[2] the meetings of the famous *Scriblerus Club;* Sacheverell and his sermons;[3] his rusticating with St. John at that Minister's farm at Bucklersbury; Mrs. Masham and her lying-in troubles at Kensington; descriptions of Prince Eugène, and comments upon the character and conduct of Marlborough, whom he severely attacked in the *Examiner;* references to the *Spectators ;*[4] and, finally, his negociations and vexations in quest of the long-expected preferment, which resulted, to his undisguised disappointment, in the gift of the Irish deanery.

During this period of his residence in London Swift sat for the completion of his portrait, begun by Jervas in 1708 ("who has given it now quite another turn, and now approves it entirely"), and which remains the happiest of all the existing representations of him. Two copies of

[1] Of selected court preachers he remarks on ... occasion: "We had a dunce to preach before the Queen to-day, which often happens."

[2] "Have you got the whalebone petticoats among you yet?" he writes; "I hate them. A woman here may hide a moderate gallant under them."

[3] With this famous ecclesiastic Swift had some correspondence. For procuring for him some reward or other for his services to the Tories Dr. Sacheverell sends from Southwark, Jan. 31, 1712, a letter of thanks, not without the hope of further favours. "I am informed, also," writes Sacheverell, "that I am much indebted to my great countryman, Mr. Secretary St. John, for his generous recommendation of this matter to his lordship. I should be proud of an opportunity of expressing my gratitude to that eminent patriot, for whom no one, that wishes the welfare or honour of his church or country, can have too great a veneration." In a postscript he modestly adds (on behalf of his brother): "I am told there is a place in the Custom House void, called the *Searchers*, which, if proper to ask, I would not presume, but rather leave it to his lordship's disposal."

[4] "The *Spectators*," he reports under date Nov. 2, 1711, "are printing in a larger and smaller volume, so I believe they are going to leave them off; and, indeed, people grow weary of them, though they are often prettily written." And again, on Feb. 8, 1712, referring to attacks upon him: "I will not meddle with the *Spectators*, let him *fair sex* it to the end of the world." The frequent recurrence of the "fair sex" in its pages being a standing joke with Swift. The only part Swift ever had in the *Spectator* was a hint to Steelé for No. 50.

it exist, one in the Bodleian Library in Oxford, the other in the National Portrait Gallery in South Kensington; the latter having been, formerly, in the possession of the late Marquess of Hastings. It is a half-length, in a sitting posture, almost full-face to the spectator. His eyes (different from Pope's account) have a pale blueish-grey colour,[1] his cheeks fresh-coloured, chin double, with a depression in the middle, and bushy eyebrows. He has his right arm upon an open book, his left hand holding a letter or paper. Before him on the table stand copies of Lucian, Horace, Æsop. He is dressed in a blue silk dressing gown and flaxen wig, reaching to his shoulders in long curls, and in clerical bands. The full, round face has an expression of half-amusement, half-satire.[2] In person, as described by Scott, Swift was "tall, strong, and well made, of a dark complexion (but with blue eyes), black and bushy eyebrows, nose somewhat aquiline, and features which remarkably expressed the stern, haughty, and dauntless turn of his mind." According to Pope, "although his face had an expression of dulness, his eyes were very particular; they were as azure as the heavens, and had an unusual expression of acuteness." Johnson describes him as having "a kind of muddy complexion, which, though he washed himself with oriental scrupulosity, did not look clean. He had a countenance sour and severe, which he seldom softened by any appearance of gaiety. He stubbornly resisted any tendency to laughter." According to his biographers, indeed, he was never known to laugh. Besides the portraits of Jervas, there are three by the painter Bindon: one in the Deanery of Dublin; another, full length, in Howth Castle; and a third, which varies in some respects from the other two, and has been said to be a remarkably good likeness, was, in the time of Scott, in the possession of a Dr. Hill.[3] Nothing in the portrait of Jervas reveals the terrible physical and mental suffering

---

[1] It is curious to remark the opposite colours that have been given to the eyes of the same person by different painters. Notably is this the case in the two portraits of Mary Stuart, Queen of Scotland (one by a French, the other by a Scotch artist), the former of which represents her with dark blue, the latter, with hazel eyes; and in the portraits of Pope, in the National Portrait Gallery.

[2] "The characteristic of the face is its keen and nervous force. The features are large and finely formed, with an unusual fulness of curve in lip and chin and nostril. Nowhere in the face is there repose. The eye, even in spite of the heavy eyebrow, is prominent, and its look, as it struck contemporaries, could change at will from the sweetness of azure blue, which it wore to Pope, into something black and threatening that struck the gazer dumb, as Vanessa knew. The lurking corners of the mouth tell of humour, subtle, lively, quick: only there is wanting the calm that gives to humour time to germinate the light that shines from the inner recess, where creation takes body and shape, and that inspires the dramatist or poet." *Life of Swift*, by H. Craik, 1882.

[3] See *Life and Works of Swift*, by Sir Walter Scott, xx., 1824.

to which he is known even then to have been, more or less frequently, subject; and of which, towards the latter part of his life, he became the almost constant prey. A powerful frame and physique, great energy, and vigorous and even violent exercise seemed, on the contrary, to betoken a strong and healthy constitution. But the germs of the fatal malady lay hid, to be developed, as time went on, by the circumstances of his stormy career.

Of the period 1710—13, one of the most interesting literary events in Swift's life is the founding of the *October Club*, as they styled it, by a number of the ultra-Tories, by way of a sort of *caucus*, to keep the ministers up to their mark, and which afterwards came under the direction of the more moderate Tories, Harley, Swift, and others. Either of two qualifications admitted to its membership—party eminence or wit. St. John, Arbuthnot who, as Swift said, "knew his art but not his trade," Gay, Swift, Harley, the Duke of Ormond, Lord Lansdowne, and Masham, formed the association as first established. They met every evening at one of the many eating houses between St. James's and St. Martin's Lane. But dissensions growing up among the political leaders, the *October Club* lost its original character, and re-constituted itself as a Literary Club—which has given its name to the famous Satire of Arbuthnot, the *Memoirs of Martin Scriblerus* (the first name having been prefixed in honour of Swift)—of which Pope, also, became a member. During his three years residence in London Swift changed his lodgings pretty frequently—from Bury Street to Chelsea, from Chelsea to Suffolk Street, and then, to be near the head-quarters of the Premier, to Windsor. His abrupt and odd, but graphic sketches, in the letters, of the manners of Court life, and the various scenes of the fashionable trifling there and elsewhere, form some of the most curious passages. In the midst of all this exciting turmoil, a letter from Archbishop King amuses us by its naïve expression of the wish that he would abandon "his present pursuits, and take to religious writing, and look to his advancement in life." He might, thinks his Grace, write something "both profitable and agreeable, above most things that pass the Press; and, in Dr. Wilkins's *Gifts of Preaching*, he might find a catalogue of useful subjects yet untouched."[1] Late in 1711 he moved to Leicester Fields, and again to Panton Street, in the Haymarket. In January of the following year died quite young his "greatest favourite," as he terms her, Lady Ashburnham, daughter of the Duke of

[1] Quoted in *Life of Swift*, by H. Craik.

Ormond. His grief he bitterly expresses in this wise: "I hate life when I think it exposed to such accidents, and to see so many thousand wretches burdening the earth, while such as her [sic] die, makes me think God did never intend life to be a blessing."

In June, 1713, he set out to take possession of his Deanery of St. Patrick's, which his ministerial friends had, not without much difficulty and delay, extorted for him from the Queen. His letters to Esther Johnson abound in complaints of these delays; but, if he had not secured the highest ecclesiastical preferment or dignities, at least he had enjoyed, what he esteemed hardly less, high influence in the State, and the greatest fame in Literature. The *aliquid amari*, however, constantly arises for him; for now, added to the hostility which his assumption of decanal dignity evoked among the anti-Tory party in Dublin, he began to feel serious embarrassment from his connexion with Miss Vanhomrigh. At Laracor, where he took refuge from his annoyances in Dublin, and where he enjoyed the society of "Stella" (who, with Rebecca Dingley, now lived in the neighbouring town of Trim), he exercises all his epistolary skill in attempts to appease the anxious suspicions of "Vanessa." He tells her he has hidden himself away at the country parsonage from official vexations, choosing "a field-bed and an earthen floor before the great house there [in the capital], which they say is mine," and excuses his silence by the reminder that, "I told you, when I left England, I would endeavour to forget everything there and would write as seldom as I could." Yet, when a summons from his friends in England recalled him, after only a few weeks' possession of his new dignity, he very readily accepted it. Not only had the Tory Government cause to fear the assaults of the Opposition, but, also and still more, the consequences of the dissensions of their own chiefs; and to their late Mentor they looked for help in the dangerous crisis. But, more interesting than the squabbles of politicians and political factions, remains the history of his connexion with the Literary Club. Established soon after his return to London, the *Scriblerus* Society used to meet in St. James's Palace, in the rooms of Dr. Arbuthnot, who filled the post of Court physician: the principal members being Swift, Pope, Arbuthnot, Gay, Parnell, Bolingbroke, and Harley, who lately had been raised to the peerage. To Arbuthnot belongs the fame of the elaboration[1] of Cornelius Scriblerus, his pedantic educational theories.

---

[1] A quite recently published letter of Swift to Arbuthnot (July 3, 1714) implies Pope to have been the original inventor of *Scriblerus*.

and their illustrious exemplification in the person of his more distinguished son, Martin. His *memoirs*, however, remain only as a fragment; and "the memory of that learned Phantom, which is to be immortal" (in Pope's expression) survives chiefly in his more substantial successor. His creator, it is interesting to know, seems to have entertained the idea of completing his history. In a letter to Swift (June 26, 1714) he recalls the memory of the "learned Phantom," and adds: "the ridicule of Medicine is so copious a subject, that I must only here and there touch it," which draws from his *collaborateur* the letter of interesting allusion to *Scriblerus* just noticed.

A sudden and unexpected *bouleversement* put an end to the supremacy of Swift's political friends, and to his own hopes of higher advancement, for the present, at least. By the death of the Queen, in August of 1714, everything was changed. The heads of the Tory and Jacobite faction sought refuge in France, or found themselves lodged in the Tower. Swift retired, not too soon, to the safer refuge of his Deanery. His prospects, sunk from the highest expectations, now appeared gloomy enough. Not only had he lost the society of his principal friends, some of whom, Lords Bolingbroke and Oxford (Harley), the Duke of Ormond, and Bishop Atterbury, had more or less compromised themselves in conspiring against the Protestant succession and the liberties of their countrymen; but he himself fell, though unjustly, under some suspicion of the same criminal intrigues. But what caused him still greater perplexity were his relations with the two rival divinities, or rather devotees, who contended, each unconscious of the other's existence and near neighbourhood, for his affection. Her mother dead, her younger sister in bad health, and her only brother a bankrupt by his extravagance,[1] Hester Vanhomrigh claimed a protection which he could no longer refuse. Her appeals to his affection, and protestation of her deep devotion, beginning from the moment of their separation in June, 1713, when he had set out to be installed as Dean, became more and more passionate and despairing. "If you think I write too often," she addresses him from London, soon after he had left her, on the occasion just referred to, "your only way is to tell me so; or, at least, to write to me again, that I may know you don't quite forget me; for I very much fear that I never employ a thought of yours now, except when you are reading my letters, which makes me ply you with them.

[1] Writing to Swift from Dublin, some time in the year 1714, she speaks of "a wretch of a brother, cunning executors, and importunate creditors of my mother's."

If you are very happy, it is ill-natured of you not to tell me so, except 'tis what *is inconsistent with my own* [happiness]." When, in spite of his protestation that, "it is not a place for freedom, but everything is known in a week, and magnified a hundred times," she had insisted upon following him to Dublin, and found him to have assumed a cold demeanour towards her, she declares: "If you continue to treat me as you do, you will not be made uneasy by me long." When she is told that she is "among fools, and must submit," she protests she would rather "bear the rack than those killing, killing words" of his again:—"Put my passion under the utmost restraint; send me as distant from you as the earth will allow, yet you cannot banish those charming ideas which will stick by me whilst I have the use of memory. Nor is the love I bear you only seated in my soul; for there is not a single atom of my frame that is not blended with it." She entreats him not to suffer her to live "a life that is a languishing death,[1] which is the only life I can lead, if you have lost any of your tenderness for me." In his replies, Swift, it is to be remarked, uses the utmost caution, and a sort of language understood by themselves alone, while he urges the greatest secrecy upon his too ardent correspondent.

Sometimes visiting the capital, she usually resided on a small property of her father's at Marley Abbey, near to the village of Cellbridge, on the Liffey, about ten miles distant, where the spots frequented by the lovers are still pointed out. Here she cherished that passion so fatal to her happiness and her life, and wrote and received those letters, whose ambiguous style has caused so much perplexity to the biographers.[2] While Hester Vanhomrigh thus indulged the vain hope of a "declaration," and languished from unreturned, or, at least, unfulfilled love, in scarcely less torturing doubt lived her unconscious rival. Reproaches and entreaties she long lavished in vain; and not until Esther Johnson seemed almost to be at the point of death did Swift at length consent, as it has been asserted upon strong testimony, and upon still stronger probability, to a private marriage ceremony, under circumstances, and

[1] "A life that is no life,"—in Greek tragic phrase. But Miss Vanhomrigh derives her high-flown language from Mde. Scudori rather than from Euripides.

[2] Lord Orrery, who had never seen her, states of Miss Vanhomrigh:—"Vanessa was exceedingly vain. The character given of her by *Cadenus* is fine painting, but, in general, fictitious. She was fond of dress; impatient to be admired; very romantic in her turn of mind; superior, in her own opinion, to all her sex; full of pertness, gaiety, and pride; not without some agreeable accomplishments; but far from being either beautiful or genteel . . . happy in the thoughts of being Swift's concubine, but still aiming and intending to be his wife."—*Remarks, &c.* "What Lord Orrery says of Vanessa is *barbarous*," comments Mrs. Delany (*Letters*).

upon conditions of the most profound secrecy, two years after his flight from England (1716). The fact of the ceremony has been vehemently disputed; nor is it even now satisfactorily established.¹ The weight of evidence, or rather of probability, however, inclines to the actual performance of the rite, which, it is asserted, took place in the garden of the deanery; the bridegroom's friend, the Bishop of Clogher, officiating. Sheridan, a principal witness for the marriage, explicitly states that, " the whole account of the transaction [the ceremony], was given me by Mrs. Sican, a lady of uncommon understanding, fine taste, and great goodness of heart; on which account she was a great favourite both with the Dean and Mrs. [Miss] Johnson." Dr. Johnson represents the legal tie as Swift's own choice :—" while she was at her own disposal, he did not consider his possession as secure. Resentment, ambition, or caprice might separate them: he was, therefore, resolved to make 'assurance doubly sure,' and to appropriate her by a private marriage, to which he had annexed the expectation of all the pleasures of perfect friendship, without the uneasiness of conjugal restraint. But with this state poor Stella was not satisfied; she never was treated as a wife, and to the world she had the appearance of a mistress."²

¹ Of the extremely conflicting testimonies for and against the marriage ceremony Mr. Craik has drawn up an interesting summary. The marriage is first asserted by Lord Orrery (not the most satisfactory witness), in 1751—six years after Swift's death—in the following words: " Stella was the concealed, but undoubted, wife of Dr. Swift; and, if my informations are correct, she was married to him in the year 1716, by Dr. Ashe, then Bishop of Clogher." Delany, the next witness, seems merely to repeat the assertion of Orrery. Sheridan professes to have had the account from his father, the intimate friend of Swift; but Sheridan is not an altogether unimpeachable authority. Next, in order of time, on the affirmative side, come principally Dr. Johnson, Monck Berkeley, Scott, and Mr. Craik. On the other side are the declarations of Mrs. Dingley, Esther Johnson's executors, Swift's housekeeper, and his physician, Dr. Lyon. As regards the weight of mere *authority*, in spite of the imposing array of influential names in affirmation, it must be conceded that the comparative *lateness*, and still more the character, of the first testimony unfavourably affect its value. Briefly stated, as a writer in a recent number of the *Quarterly Review* (who maintains the unreality of the marriage) has expressed it, the test. mony, on either side, is *traditionary* rather than *documentary*. We have, thus, to fall back, after all, upon indirect evidence, and a balance of probabilities; and it is, at least, very difficult to resist their weight in favour of the performance of the rite. The argument from the use of her maiden name by Esther Johnson in her ordinary signatures, and lastly, in her Will, which has been advanced as conclusive, has been fairly met by the consideration that this was " clearly only part of the *bargain;* and, after it had been finally settled between them, that no publication of the marriage should take place, beyond a very limited circle of friends, it remained for Stella, both out of fidelity to their original bargain, and out of regard for her own dignity, to use that name, and to exercise those free testamentary powers, with which she was quite confident that Swift would never, on the strength of his legal rights, interfere." The destruction, or, at least, the withholding from publication, in their entirety, of her letters to Swift seems to be strong presumptive proof of an important secret not to be divulged.

² *Life of Swift* (in *Lives of the Poets*). See, also, *Life* by T. Sheridan.

Of this (presumed) clandestine marriage Hester Vanhomrigh remained in ignorance four years, and, when the *éclaircissement* came, it is said to have brought her death-blow. She died, at all events, within a few weeks of the (alleged) announcement of the fatal secret (1720). After the marriage, Swift, according to Sheridan's narrative, went to her, with "a gentleman of good fortune [a Mr. Dean Winter] who was her professed admirer, and had made overtures of marriage to her;" and we do not feel much surprise to learn that, "nothing could have been a greater mortification to her love-sick mind than such a visit, as it implied a recommendation of his rival, and an entire renunciation of his own pretensions. She rejected his proposals with disdain, as well as those of every suitor who offered, having centred all her views of happiness in life in the possession of Cadenus." She then retired to Cellbridge, where, "in silence and solitude, she indulged her fatal passion, until it rose almost to a pitch of frenzy."[1] Of her original manuscript letters (said to have been destroyed by Bishop Berkeley, one of her executors) Judge Marshall took copies; from which extracts, from time to time, found their way to the printers and the public.[2] This love-drama, thus tragically closed, had already inspired Swift with the subject for his poem, *Cadenus and Vanessa*,[3] which he composed at Windsor, five years before the death of its heroine; and he now revised and published it. It has something of the appearance of having been designed as a sort of *apologia pro amore suo*. But, if so, the poet has strangely contrived to raise suspicion that the connexion was not altogether so platonic as he elsewhere represents it, and the ambiguousness of meaning of the verses, commemorating their relation of preceptor and pupil, appears to be intentional :—

"She well remembered, to her cost,
That all his lessons were not lost.
Two maxims she could still produce,
And sad experience taught their use :

[1] Sheridan's *Life*, &c. The sensational incidents—of a letter from "Vanessa" to her rival, demanding to know the truth of the report of the marriage, and the sudden irruption of the enraged Swift, and its deadly consequence—related by Sheridan, and often repeated as they have been, appear to rest on no very certain evidence.

[2] The copies, from which Scott's Collection was printed, were transcribed by his friend, Mr. Berwick, of Esher. In whose hands the original copies of Marshall then remained Scott is unable to say. Scott's *Life of Swift*.

[3] *Cadenus* being an anagram of Decanus. *Vanessa* is made up of the first syllable of her surname, and a fanciful form of her Christian name, Hester.

> That Virtue, pleased by being shown,
> Knows nothing which it dares not own;
> Can make us, without fear, disclose
> Our inmost secrets to our foes—
> That common forms were not designed
> Directors to a noble mind."

But the hardest and most disputed lines of all, than which " no more unfortunate ones were ever penned," are found towards the close of the poem :—

> "But what success Vanessa met,
> Is to the world a secret yet.
> Whether the Nymph, to please her Swain,
> Talks in a high romantic strain;
> Or whether he, at last, descends
> To act with less seraphic ends;
> Or, to compound the business better, whether
> They temper love and books together,
> Must never to mankind be told,
> Nor shall the conscious Muse unfold."

It is quite possible, and perhaps quite reasonable, to attach an indifferent meaning to these delphic verses, or to interpret them as the expression of conscious innocence and of contempt for the opinion of the world; but, it must be allowed, they are not happily designed to confirm the theory of pure *platonic* affection. Lord Orrery, while he acquits his (so-called) friend of illicit connexion with Hester Vanhomrigh, at the same time implies, by his remarks, as Sheridan has justly observed, a greater degree of real immorality in the conduct of Swift than would be involved in the more obvious interpretation. Such moral turpitude Sheridan shews to be inconceivable without the supposition of the basest hypocrisy, which he maintains, with much reason, to be entirely foreign to the character of his hero; and he accounts for the extraordinary nature of the relations of Swift, both with Esther Johnson and with Hester Vanhomrigh, by the supposition of a natural coldness of temperament or deficiency: a theory adopted by the writer of the article on *Swift* in the *Ency. Brit.* (Ed. VIII.). Sheridan's statements, that Hester Vanhomrigh, in her last moments, left instructions to her executors to publish *all* her letters (which instructions were prevented from being carried out by the opportune protests of Dr. Sheridan), and also the poem of *Cadenus and Vanessa*, are no less capable of a double interpretation—either as proofs of the confident innocence of her attachment, or of desire for vengeance. That she left her property to strangers (the common report of the revocation of her Will rests on no ascertained fact), may be taken as presumptive evidence of consciousness of injury done to her reputation, and of consequent revenge: but, in every part of this contradictory history, doubts and difficulties occur at every turn.

From the bitterness of grief or remorse Swift sought refuge in solitude for some time, in the south of Ireland. But a contest, in which he strove to forget his own misery, and, in some measure, to atone for the unhappiness he had brought upon his closest connexions, now awaited him: a contest in which he was to acquire more glory than by any of his former writings, dictated by mere partisan feeling or interests. Ireland had been reduced, at this period, to a condition, apparently, even more wretched than any it had previously experienced in its long history of misery and misgovernment. Landlord tyranny and selfishness rampant, unequal laws grinding down the population, the country drained of its proper resources, and, through the grasping avarice of the landowners and their subordinates, left almost without any cultivation, Administrative corruption, consequent extremest destitution and suffering of all kinds for the mass of the people, violence and ruffianism of every sort triumphant—such, in brief, was the state of Ireland, as depicted by credible witnesses of the time, during the greater part, and more especially in the earlier half, of the eighteenth century. One injustice, in particular, which had long weighed down the commercial chances of the country had become more and more apparent—the prohibition by the English Government of the exportation of the Irish woollen manufacture. Swift—inspired, doubtless, with the desire of avenging his private wrongs upon the Whig Government, as well as of avenging the public sufferings—seized upon this particular grievance as the starting-point from which to begin his series of assaults upon the Government and of denounciations of the manifold wrongs of the Irish people, or, rather, of the Anglo-Irish; for to the aboriginal population he does not appear to have much extended his sympathy. His *Proposal for the Universal Use of Irish Manufactures* appeared in 1720. In retaliation of their commercial wrongs, he recommends the people to "utterly renounce and reject every wearable thing" that came from England. He breathes out fierce indignation against their oppressors, and a sort of scorn of the oppressed who tamely submitted to them:—" The *Scripture* tells us that Oppression makes a wise man mad; therefore, consequently speaking, the reason why some men are not mad is, that they are not wise. However, it were to be wished that Oppression would, in time, teach a little wisdom to fools. . . I know not how it comes to pass (and yet, perhaps, I know well enough) that slaves have a natural disposition to be tyrants: and that, when my betters give me a kick, I am apt to revenge it with six upon my footman; although, perhaps, he may be an honest and diligent fellow." He next turns to the governing class of the country, and condemns them as a primary cause of its frightful condition, and declares, "Whoever travels this country, and observes the face of nature, or the faces, and habits [clothing?], and dwellings of the natives will hardly think himself in a land where law, religion, or common humanity is professed."

But they are the *Letters*, which he published under the pseudonym of "M. B. Drapier" [Draper], that have made his name especially famous as the champion of unprotected Irish rights as against English legal injustice. They originated, as is well-known, in the attempt of the Government to force a debased copper currency, known as *Wood's Halfpence* (from the name of the speculator, who had obtained the monopoly by bribing one of the Royal Mistresses), upon the people of Ireland. Addressed to "the Tradesmen, Shopkeepers, Farmers, and Country People, in general, of the Kingdom of Ireland," the first Letter came out in 1724. The writer begins with telling them, that he had ordered the printers to sell it at the lowest rate [twopence]; and reproaches them with their apathy: "It is a great fault with you, that when a person writes with no other intention than to do you good, you will not be at the pains to read his advices. One copy of this paper may serve a dozen of you, which will be less than a farthing apiece. It is your folly, that you have no *common* or *general* interest in your view —not even the wisest among you. Neither do you know, or inquire, or care, who are your friends, or who are your enemies." Having prepared the way, the "Draper," in three succeeding Letters, extends the scope of his denunciations. He addresses the third Letter to the "Nobility and Gentry of Ireland"; and in the fourth and last, the most important of the series, appealing to the "Whole People of Ireland," putting aside mere temporary grievances, he launches out, with more effect, into denunciation of permanent, essential, injustices. "My dear countrymen," he begins, "having already written three Letters upon so disagreeable a subject as Mr. Wood and his Halfpence, I conceived my task was at an end: but I find that cordials must be frequently applied to weak constitutions, political as well as natural. A people, long used to hardships, lose by degrees the very notions of Liberty. They look upon themselves as creatures at mercy, and that all impositions laid on them by a stronger hand are, in the phrase of the Report, legal and obligatory. Hence proceed that poverty and lowness of spirit, to which a kingdom may be subject as well as a particular person—and when Esau came fainting from the field, at the point to die, it is no wonder that he sold his birthright for a mess of potage." . . . "Our neighbours," he sarcastically remarks, "whose understandings are just upon a level with ours (which are, perhaps, none of the brightest), have a strong contempt for most nations; but especially for Ireland. They look upon us as a sort of savage Irish whom our ancestors conquered several hundred years ago." He proceeds so far as to invite the people, if abuses be not swept away, at once to assert their political independence. "All Government, without the consent of the governed," he lays down, "is the very definition of slavery: but, in fact," he significantly adds, "eleven men, well armed, will certainly subdue one single man in his shirt."[1]

Every effort of the Government to discover the audacious offender signally failed. At length they recalled the obnoxious Halfpence; and when the danger had passed, and the secret had been proclaimed, the champion of their rights everywhere received the homage of his grateful clients. Over a long series of years Swift followed up the *Drapier's Letters* with every variety of political pamphlet and broadsheet, by which, apparently, he sought to rouse the miserable people to rebellion. Hatred of his enemies, the Whigs, who happened to be in power, doubtless did much to intensify, if not to excite, his indignation against iniquities which he saw around him; but, also, he had, we may believe, advanced somewhat in political wisdom since the days of his ministerial connexions; although he never got wholly rid of his old Tory prejudices. It has been already noticed that the sympathies of the English pamphle-

---

[1] Compare the still more eloquent and remarkable *Address to the Irish People*, by Shelley, at the age of twenty, which he printed and distributed himself to the poor of Dublin, in 1812. In this marvellously well-considered and well-reasoned *Manifesto*, the youthful Reformer lays down the primary conditions upon which alone an oppressed people can hope for permanent deliverance after ages of bad laws and bad government:—"Do not inquire," he exhorts them, "if a man be a heretic, if he be a Quaker, a Jew, or a heathen, but if he be a virtuous man—if he love Liberty and Truth, if he wish the happiness and peace of the world. If a man be ever so much a *believer*, and love not these things, he is a heartless hypocrite and a knave. . . . It is not a merit to tolerate, but it is a crime to be intolerant. . . . Be free and be happy: *but first be wise and good.*"

teer seem to have been chiefly confined within the *English Pale*, as appears from his own report of his interview with Walpole, the Premier, during his visit to England in 1726, and from various passages in his other letters. In the spring of that year he again mixed with his friends in London, Pope, Arbuthnot, Gay, Bolingbroke, Peterborough, and others. Most of the time he passed with Pope at Twickenham, or with Bolingbroke at Dawley. At Leicester House, where the Prince and Princess of Wales held their Court in open rivalry with St. James's, and bestowed ostentatious honour upon the Tory malcontents, he appeared as a welcome guest. Especially did he find favour with the Princess and with her Maid of Honour, Mrs. Howard, afterwards Countess of Suffolk.

About this time Pope published his *Miscellanies*, to which himself, Arbuthnot, and Swift jointly contributed. In August, 1726, Swift returned to his exile, as he always called it (where great acclamations awaited the author of the *Drapier's Letters*, from the citizens of Dublin); but only for a few months. In the following year he once again escaped from his chagrin and the dulness of the life there to the brilliant frivolousness of the English metropolis, where the recent publication of *The Travels into Several Remote Nations of the World, by Lemuel Gulliver*, had raised his reputation and popularity to the highest point. This masterpiece of Satire appeared, like nearly all Swift's writings, anonymously; but it quickly caused more sensation, in the world of fashion, than any fiction, almost than any book, ever before given to the world. A second edition came out in a few days. Pirated copies abounded in Ireland as well as in England; and the *Travels*, as pointed out by a recent writer,[1] has the singular honour of having been the first classical work of fiction to appear periodically in a newspaper. Almost at the same time with its publication by the authorised bookseller, it came out in the columns of a journal of the day called *Parker's Penny Post*, and thus gained a wider and quicker circulation than otherwise it could have had. With almost all masterpieces of literature, it had undergone many revisions, having been first taken in hand so early as in the year 1720; and references to it while yet in manuscript are traceable in four or five letters before November, 1726. Hester Vanhomrigh is the first to allude to it in a letter somewhere in 1720—1; and Bolingbroke and Pope notice it in 1722 and 1725, respectively. In France, where a translation had been made by the Abbé Desfontaines, at the suggestion of Voltaire, it had a

[1] *Quarterly Review*, July, 1833.

reception almost as eager as in this country. Desfontaines writes to Swift (July, 1727), that already three editions of his translation had been called for, and begs him not to postpone his visit to Paris; for he would find "a people who would esteem you infinitely."[1] Swift replies (in French) to the Abbé, who had taken the liberty of making some omissions and slight alterations, in an ironical strain of gratitude. He begins with saying, "You will permit me to tell you that I have been very much surprised to observe that, while giving me for a fatherland a land in which I chanced to be born (en me donnant pour *patrie* un *pais* dans lequel je suis né), you thought proper to attribute to me a book, which bears the name of its author, who has had the misfortune of displeasing some of our ministers, and which I have never avowed. This complaint which I make of your conduct, in respect to myself personally, does not prevent me from rendering you justice. Translators, for the most part, give excessive praise to works which they translate, and imagine, perhaps, that their reputation depends, in some way, upon that of the author whom they have chosen. But you have felt your strength, which places you above precautions like these. Capable of correcting a bad book, a more difficult undertaking than that of composing a good one, you have not shrunk from giving to the public a translation of a work which you declare to be full of blackguardisms (*polissonneries*), of stupidities, and of puerilities, &c. We agree here that national taste is not always the same; but we are forced to suppose that *good taste* is the same everywhere, where there are people of understanding and wit, of judgment and of knowledge. If, then, the books of Sieur Gulliver are calculated only for the British Islands, that traveller must pass for a very pitiable writer. The same vices and the same follies reign everywhere, in all the civilized countries of Europe; and the author, who writes but for a city, a province, a kingdom, or even a century, so little deserves to be translated, that he does not merit even to be read. . . .

"You may easily imagine that the people of whom I have just spoken to you don't greatly approve of your criticism; and you will, without doubt, be surprised to learn that they regard this ship-surgeon as a grave author who never jokes [*qui ne sort jamais de son sérieux*], who does not borrow any disguise, who does not pique himself upon having

---

[1] Voltaire, who had made Swift's acquaintance in England, writes in May of the same year to him, offering letters of introduction. "I shall certainly," he concludes, "do my best endeavours to serve you, and to let my country know that I have the inestimable honour to be one of your friends."

any wit, and who is content with communicating to the public, in a simple and unsophisticated narrative, his adventures, and the things which he has seen and heard during his voyage." . . .

Desfontaines had mis-stated some fact in the history of the *Drapier Letters*, which induces Swift to protest in conclusion:—"As for the article which regards Lord Carteret, without inquiring from whence you drew your memoirs, I beg to tell you that you have written but half the truth; and that this Drapier, real or imaginary, has saved Ireland, in raising the entire nation against a project, which was to have enriched a certain number of individuals at the expense of the public." He proceeds to add that "severe accidents have prevented me from making the journey to France now. I know I have lost much, and I am very sensible of the loss. The only consolation that remains to me is, in thinking that I shall better endure to remain in the country to which fortune has condemned me." Notwithstanding "all its affectation of superior taste and refinement," remarks Scott, "the French version is very tolerable." The Abbé wrote a continuation of the *Voyages* "in a style, as may easily be conceived, very different from the original." It is entitled *Le Nouveau Gulliver*, and purports to be the travels of John, son of Lemuel.[1] At Leicester House, not least on account of its covert satire upon the King (George I.) and Walpole (in the *Voyage to Lilliput*), it found a warm welcome.

"About ten days ago," writes Gay to Swift, "a book was published here of The Travels of one Gulliver, which hath been the conversation of

---

[1] "Jean Gulliver is merely an uninteresting *voyageur imaginaire*, who travels into one country where the women were the ruling sex; in another, where the life of the inhabitants was ephemeral; into a third where ugliness was the object of desire and admiration. Though sinking far below the originality and spirit of his model, Desfontaines' work displays some fancy and talent."—Scott (*Life and Works of Swift*). In his preface to the translation, the Abbé "modestly craves some mercy for the prodigious fictions which he had undertaken to clothe in the French language: he confesses there were passages at which his pen escaped his hand from actual horror and astonishment at the daring violations of all critical decorums: then he becomes alarmed lest some of Swift's political satire might be applied to the Court of Versailles, and protests, with much circumlocution, that it only concerns the *Toriz* and the *Wigts*, as he is pleased to term them, of the factious kingdom of Britain. Lastly, he assures his readers that not only has he changed many of the incidents to accommodate them to the French taste, but, also, they will not be annoyed, in his translation, with the nautical details—minute particulars so offensive in the original."—Scott. Desfontaines became later, as is well known, a very conspicuous object of Voltaire's severest satire. He edited, for a long period, the *Journal des Sçavans*.

Arbuthnot wrote two witty Gulliverian pamphlets—one "*Gulliver Decyphered*. . . Vindicating the reverend Dean, on whom it is maliciously fathered. With some probable conjectures concerning the real author,"—the other, *Critical Remarks on Captain Gulliver's Travels by Dr. Bentley*. In the latter he asserts the Houyhnhnms to have been known to the Ancients, and adduces, among other, the pretended authority of Chaucer.

the whole town ever since. The whole impression sold in a week: and nothing is more diverting than to hear the different opinions people give of it; though all agree in liking it extremely. It is generally said that you are the author; but, I am told, the bookseller declares that he knows not from what hand it came. From the highest to lowest, it is universally read —from the Cabinet Council to the nursery. . . . Your friend, my Lord Harcourt, commends it very much, though he thinks in some places the matter too for carried. [Sarah] the Duchess Dowager of Marlborough is in raptures at it. She says she can dream of nothing else since she read it. She declares that she hath now found out that her whole life hath been lost in caressing the worst part of mankind, and treating the best as her foes; and that if she knew Gulliver, though he had been the worst enemy she ever had, she would give up her present acquaintance for his friendship.

"You may see by this that you are not much injured by being supposed the author of this piece. If you are, you have disobliged us, and two or three of your best friends, in not giving us the least hint of it while you were with us; and, in particular, Dr. Arbuthnot, who says it is ten thousand pities he had not known it, he could have added such abundance of things upon every subject. Among lady critics, some have found out that Mr. Gulliver had a particular malice to Maids of Honour. Those of them who frequent the Church say his design is impious, and that it is depreciating the works of the Creator. Notwithstanding, I am told, the Princess hath read it with great pleasure. . . It hath passed Lords and Commons, *nemine contradicente*; and the whole town, men, women, and children, are quite full of it."

In the first edition the publisher, upon his own responsibility, had altered or excised several passages. Of this the author complains, ironically, in a preface to the second edition, which served to give to the *Travels* still further an air of reality:—"I do not in the least complain," writes Gulliver to his cousin Sympson, "of my own great want of judgment in being prevailed upon, by the entreaties and false reasonings of you and some others, very much against my own opinion, to suffer my *Travels* to be published. Pray, bring to mind how often I desired you to consider, when you insisted upon the motive of public good, that the Yahoos were species of animals utterly incapable of amendment by precepts and example. And so it has proved: for, instead of seeing a full stop put to all abuses and corruptions, at least in this little island, as I had reason to expect, behold, after above six months warning, I cannot learn that my book has produced one single effect according to mine intentions. I desired you would let me know, by a letter, when party and faction were extinguished, judges learned and upright, pleaders honest and modest, with some tincture of common sense, and Smithfield blazing with pyramids of law books, the young nobility's education entirely changed, the physicians banished," &c. He further demands : "Have not I the most reason to complain, when I see those very Yahoos carried by Houyhnhnms in a vehicle, as if these were *brutes*, and those the *rational* creatures ?'"[1] The cause of its enduring popularity and fame is the extraordinary *naturalness*, and elaborate and inimitable *verisimilitude* of the fiction, and the *universality* of the satire, notwithstanding the frequent allusions to comtemporary history. The least successful part of the *Travels*, obviously, is the *Voyage to Laputa*. The irony, too little discriminating, seems to confound true and false science in one general contempt, although, it may be allowed, the science of the day too often exposed itself to deserved ridicule. In the last part, the extreme severity of the sarcasm tends, perhaps, to weaken its real force. But to represent the human species, so generally unfeeling and tyrannical towards the subject species, for once as subjected to a race of beings superior in power no less than in intelligence and morality, must be admitted to have been a happy as well as original idea.[2]

To add to the air of reality of his volumes, Swift inserted maps of the countries visited by his hero, as well as a portrait of him. The first edition varies from succeeding ones in certain passages—with the exception of a paragraph in the *Voyage to Laputa*, upon the island of Tribnia —all in the *Voyage to the Houyhnhnms ;* and a copy of the first edition, now in the South Kensington Museum, contains the manuscript revisions of the author, who has cancelled the passages which were to be altered for the next edition. One of these alterations concerns the highly interesting interview of Gulliver with his Houyhnhnm master ; where, in place of the words, "I said there was a Society of men among us, bred from their youth in the art of proving by words, multiplied for

[1] How far Swift, like other great writers, lies under obligation to his predecessors—to Lucian, Rabelais, and Bergerac (*Histoire Comique des Etats et des Empires de la Lune, &c.*), in particular, has already been sufficiently pointed out ; but a curiously close imitation, or rather transcription, in the Voyage to Brobdingnag, from a narrative of a storm at sea, found in a little known publication, the *Mariners' Magazine*, 1679, has been lately discovered by the writer of the article in the *Quarterly Review*, July, 1883. In this passage Swift adopts, through several sentences, the very words of the magazine writer.

[2] The *Houyhnhnms*, pronounced *Whinhyms*, as the author carefully informs his readers, signifies, in its etymology, the *perfection of nature*.

the purpose, that White is Black, and Black White," &c., as in the present text, appeared, originally, the following:—"I said that those who made profession of this science [of Law] were exceedingly multiplied, being almost equal to the caterpillars in number, that they were of diverse degrees, distinctions, and denominations. The numerousness of those that dedicated themselves to the Profession was such, that the fair and justifiable advantage, and income, of the Profession was not sufficient for the decent and handsome maintenance of multitudes of those who followed it. Hence it came to pass that it was found needful to supply that by artifice and cunning, which could not be procured by just and honest methods; the better to bring which about, very many men among us were bred up from their youth," &c.

Much has been written, and many theories have been hazarded, to explain the purpose and scope of this great Satire. Whatever may have been the purpose of particular parts, his own words plainly declare the general inspiration of it to have been the gratification of being able (as he imparts to Pope, Sept. 29, 1725) "to vex the world." "Principally," he reiterates, "I hate and detest that animal called *Man*; although I heartily love John, Peter, Thomas. . . . I have got materials towards a treatise, proving the falsity of that definition *animal rationale*, and to show it should be only *rationis capax*. Upon this great foundation of misanthropy (though not in Timon's manner) the whole building of my *Travels* is erected, and I never will have peace till all honest men are of my opinion." In a curiously interesting letter, now first printed, addressed to his publisher Motte, in December, 1727, he gives a number of hints for the illustration of his book. Motte, it seems, had suggested the advisability of thus increasing its popularity; and Swift replies, with some doubt, "You will consider how much it will raise the price of the book. The world glutted itself with that book at first, and now it will go off but soberly; but, I suppose, will not soon be worn out? The part of the *Little* Men will bear cuts much better than that of the *Great*. . . The Country of Horses, I think, would furnish many; Gulliver brought to be compared with the Yahoos; the family at dinner and he waiting; the Grand Council of Horses assembled sitting—one of them standing with a hoof extended, as if he were speaking," &c.

Swift again visited London, and for the last time, in 1727, taking up his quarters with Pope, and with Lord Oxford at Wimpole. One of the most interesting incidents during this visit was his supplying Gay's *Beggar's Opera*, the idea of which he is said to have originated, with two of the songs. In ridicule and a parody of the Italian Opera, which had come into fashion at the beginning of the century, the *Beggar's Opera* now shared with the *Travels* the public favour. The death of George I. for a moment raised the hopes of the Dean of St. Patrick's, hopes that he had derived from the favour of Mrs. Howard; but, unfortunately for him, the influence of the Queen, in this exceptional instance, outweighed that of the Mistress. Disappointed in this last chance, he left England in disgust, never to return. At Holyhead bad weather detained him a week, and the dreariness of his solitude in the inn he relieved by keeping a slight journal, which has been printed, for the first time, by Mr. Craik. Its interest, curious rather than important, lies in its characteristic style, in which the diarist jots down the most trifling thoughts or occurrences as the humour strikes him, apparently with the double purpose of distracting his mind from saddening thoughts and of giving vent to his ennui.[1] Three months only from the date of his arrival in

[1] Life at Holyhead for weather-bound travellers, in the first half of the last century, appears to have been gloomy enough at the best; but accidental circumstances aggravated for Swift the disagreeableness of the situation, e.g.:—"I dare not send my linen to be washed, for fear of being called away at half-an-hour's warning, and then I must leave them behind me, which is a serious point. I live at great expense, without one comfortable bit or sup—I am afraid of joining with passengers, for fear of getting acquainted with Irish. The days are short, and I have five hours at night to spend by myself before I go to bed. I should be glad to converse with farmers or shopkeepers, but none of them speak English. A dog is better company than the Vicar; for I remember him of old. What can I do but write everything that comes into my head? Watt [his servant] is a booby of that species which I dare not suffer to be familiar with me, for he would ramp on my shoulders in half-an-hour. . . I am a little risky [?] from two scurvy disorders, and if I should relapse, there is not a Welsh house-cur that would not have more care taken of him than I, and whose loss would not be more lamented. I confine myself to my narrow chamber in all unwalkable hours. The master of the pacquet-boat, one Jones, hath not treated me with the least civility, although Watt gave him my name. In short, I come from being used like an Emperor to be used worse than a dog at Holyhead. Yet my hat is worn to pieces by answering the civilities of the poor inhabitants as they pass by. The women might be safe enough, who all wear hats, yet, never pull them off, if the dirty streets did not foul their petticoats by courtseying so low. On my conscience, you may know a Welsh dog as well as a Welsh-man or woman by its peevish, passionate way of barking. . . .

If the Vicar could but play at back-gammon, I were an Emperor; but I know him not, I am as insignificant here as parson Brooke is in Dublin. By my conscience, I believe Cæsar would be the same without his army at his back. Whoever would wish to live long should live here, for a day is longer than a week; and, if the weather be foul, as long as a fortnight. Yet here I could live with two or three friends, in a warm house, and good wine,—much better than being a slave in Ireland. But my misery is, that I am in the worst part of Wales, under the very worst circumstances; afraid of a relapse; in utmost solitude; impatient for the condition of our friend [Stella]; not a soul to converse with; hindered from exercise by rain; cooped up in a room not half so large as one of the Deanery closets. My room smokes into the bargain, and the other is too cold and moist to be without a fire." Prefixed to the journal are a number of verses, the most interesting part of the note-book, in which he expresses, in no complimentary terms, his bitter detestation of all parties in his native country who were everlastingly wrangling for place and power, in the midst of the general misery:—

E

Dublin, after long and painful lingering in a condition between life and death, the woman, who had sacrificed her reputation and devoted her whole life to him, at last ended her unhappy days—after how much secret suffering, who can say? How much anguish of soul he himself felt his letters sufficiently reveal. Eighteen months before the closing scene came, while still in England, news had reached him of her even then almost dying state, and he writes to Dr. Sheridan, who had sent him the melancholy report:—"I have yours just now of the 19th [July, 1726], and the account you give me is nothing but what I have some time expected with the utmost agonies, and there is one aggravation of constraint—that, where I am, I am forced to put on an easy countenance. It was, at this time, the best office your friendship could do—not to deceive me. . . I look upon this to be the greatest event that can ever happen to me; but all my preparations will not suffice to make me bear it like a philosopher, nor altogether like a Christian. . . Nay, if I were now near her, I would not see her. I could not behave myself tolerably, and should redouble her sorrow. Judge in what a temper of mind I write this. The very time I am writing, I conclude the fairest soul in the world has left its body."[1]

Such expressions of deep agony of mind serve to account for, what otherwise would be inexplicable, his shrinking from her presence during her last moments; for the story of his violent behaviour at the bed of the dying Stella is all but incredible, and happily rests upon no sure evidence. Yet, strange contradictions, difficult to reconcile, meet us on this occasion, equally as in the case of the death of Hester

> "This land of slaves,
> Where all are fools and all are knaves.
> * * * * *
> Where Whig and Tory fiercely fight
> Who's in the wrong, who in the right."

Printed from MS., formerly belonging to Mr. Forster, now in the South Kensington Museum. *Life of Jon. Swift*, by H. Craik, 1882.

[1] When we consider how much her life was bound up with his, it is strange, as Mr. Craik has pointed out, that scarcely any reference to her is found in Swift's correspondence with his friends. The only one of them that mentions her name is Lord Bolingbroke, two or three times, and then only in jest, *e.g.*, in Sept., 1724, he invites his friend, in Horatian fashion, to mourn her absence over his wine cups :—*Inter vina fugam Stellæ mœrere protervæ*. And, again, in the year following, he remarks : " Your *Star* will probably hinder you from taking the journey." Not long before her death, he sends some fans to Swift, " to dispose of to the present 'Stella,' whoever she may be," (*Life of Jonathan Swift*, xv.). He himself seems to mention her name (in writing) only to his most intimate friend Sheridan. She lived, for the most part, in lodgings, not far from the Deanery; and at the dinners given by Swift, at which she assisted, as Johnson says, " she regulated the table, but appeared at it as a mere guest, like other ladies."

Vanhomrigh. A month before her end, Esther Johnson made a Will (she signed it with her maiden name), in which she scarcely makes mention of Swift, leaving all her small fortune to her mother and sister, with reversion to charitable institutions, with the exception of a legacy to a female cousin of Swift's, of which she appointed him trustee. To himself she bequeathed only certain papers, including, presumably, his own letters. This Will, it is of some significance to add, she seems to have drawn up with the knowledge and sanction of Swift, as he states in a letter to his friend Worrall (July 25, 1726). And from this fact, and from that of the trusteeship, it is, perhaps, a fair presumption that her alleged resentment was, at least, up to a late period, not so bitter as has been represented; whatever amount of truth or fiction there may be in the assertion of Sheridan (the biographer) of the angry refusal of Swift, at the last moment, to acknowledge the marriage, and her consequent bitter reproaches. She died on the evening of Sunday, January 28, 1728, at about the age of forty-six.[1]

[1] There is some doubt as to her exact age. In his *Birthday Poem* addressed to Stella, on March 13, 1719, Swift speaks of her vaguely as having attained her thirty-fourth year:—

"Stella this day is thirty-four,
(We shan't dispute a year or more).
However, Stella, be not troubled,
Although thy size and years are doubled
Since first I saw thee at sixteen,
The brightest virgin on the Green:
So little is thy form declined,
Made up so largely in thy mind."

In a succeeding one, six years later (1725), he represents her as forty-three :—

"Beauty and wit—too sad a truth!
Have always been confined to youth.
  * . * * * * *
No poet ever sweetly sung
Unless he were, like Phœbus, young.
Nor ever Nymph inspired to rhyme,
Unless like Venus, in her prime.
At fifty-six, if this be true,
Am I a poet fit for you?
Or, at the age of forty-three,
Are you a subject fit for me?
Adieu! bright wit and radiant eyes,
You must be grave, and I be wise."

According to these candid verses, Stella, like other mature *belles*, while losing much of her youthful charms, seems to have grown unpoetically stout. In the first of the series of six *Birthday Verses* (1719) her *embonpoint* is represented as already noticeable :—

"Oh! would it please the Gods to split
Thy beauty, size, and years, and wit,
No Age could furnish out a pair
Of Nymphs so graceful, wise, and fair—
With half the lustre of your eyes,
With half your wit, your years, your size."

Swift appeared neither at her last moments nor at the interment. It seems from the Paper he began to write on the night of her death,[1] that he was entertaining friends, on that Sunday evening, according to his custom, at the Deanery. "About eight o'clock at night," so he begins his eulogy, " a servant brought me a note, with an account of the death of the truest, most virtuous, and valuable friend that I, or perhaps any other person, was ever blessed with. She expired about six in the evening of this day; and [now] as soon as I am left alone, which is about eleven at night, I resolve, for my own satisfaction, to say something of her life and character." On the 30th of January she was buried in St. Patrick's Cathedral, according to the custom of the time, at night. Too ill to be present at the last ceremonies, or dreading the ordeal of the effort, Swift could not endure even the distant spectacle, and he caused himself to be removed to an apartment, where the gleam from the lights in the adjoining Cathedral did not penetrate and add to his mental tortures. When, seventeen years later, his own release from suffering came, his body was laid in the same grave, side by side, with the remains of Esther Johnson; and a recent examination has revealed that the remains of both were intermingled together. In a drawer of his cabinet a lock of her hair is said to have been found, and on the envelope is said to have been inscribed words of laconic brevity; but, however they may be interpreted, capable of the strongest meaning— "Only a woman's hair."

Henceforward, although he took part, with all his accustomed energy and controversial ability, in political, or rather social questions, a settled melancholy and gloom, increasing as time went on, took possession of him. Between the years 1727-37, pamphlets, tracts, satires, poems, or occasional verses came from him in astonishing number. In various pamphlets, relating to the miseries and misgovernment of Ireland, he returns again and again to the public questions uppermost in his thoughts. At the same time more and more evident become his despair of success, and *indignatio sæva*, at the prevailing indifference alike of governors and governed. With the same hand he deals out sound precepts, bitter sarcasm, and equally bitter scorn—sarcasm at English selfishness, and scorn at Irish supineness. Upon nothing did he insist oftener, or more strongly, than upon the disastrous folly of neglecting agriculture, and reverting to the barbarous stage of pastoral idleness :—"*Know*

---

[1] *The Character of Mrs. Johnson.*

that your strength is in the Plough, and not in the depopulated Pasture lands... Ajax was mad when he mistook a flock of sheep for his enemies; but we shall never be sober until *we* have the same way of thinking." [1]

His *Modest Proposal*,[2] 1729, proved him to have lost none of the secret of the "master-spell." Penetrated with the fierce indignation which perpetully gnawed at his heart, it is, as Mr. Stephen styles it, "one of the most terrific satires ever written." According even to the admissions of ecclesiastical dignitaries, and other authorities, least likely to exaggerate facts in such matters, in one of the frequently occurring famines that depopulated the land mothers and children by hundreds lay dying at the doors of actual starvation. In the *Modest Proposal* the English Voltaire ironically suggests his plan for utilising the starving children—by sending them with their fellow-slaves, the oxen and sheep, to the butcher. From this would follow a double gain—the getting rid of a starving and troublesome population, and adding considerably to the supplies of flesh meats:—" As to our city of Dublin, Shambles," he suggests, " may be appointed for this purpose in the most convenient parts of it, and butchers, we may be assured, will not be wanting; although I rather recommend buying the children alive than dressing them, hot from the knife, as we do roasting Pigs . . . . I grant that this food will

---

[1] Compare with this the remark of More in his *Utopia*, written some two hundred and twenty years previously :—

They [the Oxen and Sheep] consume, destroy, and devour whole fields, houses, and cities. These noblemen and gentlemen, yea, and certain Abbots—holy men, no doubt— not contenting themselves with the yearly profits and revenues that were wont to grow to their forefathers and predecessors of their land; nor being content that they live in rest and pleasure, nothing profiting, yea much annoying, the public weal, leave no land for tillage. They enclose all into pasture, they throw down houses, and leave nothing standing, but only the church to be made a Sheep-house; and, as though you lost no small quantity of ground by forests, chases, lands,and parks, these good, holy men turn dwelling-places and all glebe land into wilderness and desolation . . . For one shepherd or herdsman is enough to eat up that ground with cattle, to the occupying whereof about husbandry many hands would be requisite. And this is also the cause why victuals be now in many places dearer; yea, besides this, the price of wool is so risen, that poor folk, which were wont to work it and make cloth thereof, be now able to buy none at all, and by this means very many be forced to forsake work, and to give themselves to idleness. And after that so much land was enclosed for pasture, an infinite multitude of Sheep died of the *Rot*—such vengeance God took of their inordinate and insatiable covetousness, sending among the Sheep pestiferous morrain, which much more justly should have fallen on the Sheepmasters' own heads. And though the number of Sheep increase never so fast, yet the price falleth not one mite." *Utopia ii.* Translated by Ralph Robinson, London, 1556. It first appeared, in Latin, at Louvain, 1516. (It is a curious fact that no edition was published in England during the author's life, and that the first English version was made in 1551). For the ablest and most recent exposure of this sort of evils, see Professor Newman's *Essays on Diet.*

[2] In its full title : " *A Modest Proposal for Preventing the Children of the Poor People in Ireland from being a Burden to their Parents or Country, and making them Beneficial to the Country.*"

be somewhat dear, and, therefore, very proper for landlords who, as they have already devoured most of the parents, seem to have the best title to the children. Many other advantages might be enumerated. For instance, the addition of some thousand carcases in our exportation of barreled *beef*, the propagation of swine's flesh, and improvement in the art of making good *bacon*—so much wanted among us by the great destruction of Pigs, too frequent at our tables; which are in no way comparable, in taste and magnificence, to a well-grown, fat, yearly child, which, roasted whole, will make a considerable figure at a Lord Mayor's feast, or any other public entertainment. But this [detail] and many others I omit, being studious of brevity."

As for a proposition that had been made to the author by an American friend, "a very worthy person, a true lover of his country, and whose virtues I highly esteem," that it might, also, be possible to supply the deficiency of Deer, caused by the sporting landlords, with the bodies of young girls and boys, he considers it by no means so proper or feasible. Especially in regard to the females does he demur: for, besides other objections, "it is not improbable that some scrupulous persons might be apt to censure such a practice as a little bordering upon cruelty; which, I confess, has always been with me the strongest objection against any project, how well soever intended." For the rest, he protests the entire disinterestedness of his own plan. "I have no children," he declares, "by which I can propose to get a single penny; the youngest being nine years old, and my wife past child-bearing." Nothing seems to have been further from Swift's thoughts than (as he has been mistaken by some critics to mean) mere cynicism or unfeeling ridicule. "His sarcasm," justly remarks Mr. Craik, "was never applied with more thorough seriousness of purpose. With the grave and decent self-respect of a Reformer, who knows the value of the proposal he has to make, Swift propounds his scheme. There is no strain in the language with which the state of matters is described: but the very simplicity, and matter of fact tone, that are assumed, make the description all the more telling. Of a million and half inhabitants, about two hundred thousand may be the number of those who are bringing children into the world. Of these about thirty thousand can provide for their children. There remain one hundred and seventy thousand, whose case has to be met; and the Pamphlet assumes, as an admitted truth, that no method yet proposed can meet that case. Agricultural and handicraft employments there are not; and, though stealing may offer an employment, yet complete proficiency in that calling is not often attained under the age of six. What, then, has to be done? With the calm deliberation of a statistician, calculating the food supply of the country, Swift brings forward his suggestion. He has inquired into the facts; and finds that a well-grown child, of a year old, is a most delicious, nourishing, and wholesome food, whether stewed, roasted, baked, or boiled; and he makes no doubt that it will equally serve in a *fricassee* or a *ragout*. The charge for nourishing such a child, in the present scale, will be about two shillings *per annum*, "rags included"; and he believes no gentleman will repine to give ten shillings for the carcase of a good fat child. The mother will have eight shillings net profit. . . . The ridicule is but a thin disguise. From beginning to end it is laden with grave and tormenting bitterness. Each touch of calm and ghastly humour is added with the gravity of the surgeon, who probes a wound to the quick. Swift's clearness of vision laid the woes of Ireland bare to him; he has left them on record for all time."

Swift continued to hold communication, of a rather fitful kind, with his friends in England of whom, at least after Arbuthnot's death, Pope remained the most constant and the most esteemed correspondent. He writes to him (June, 1731), in a letter in which he mentions his recent publications in verse—*The Lady's Journal, The Lady's Dressing Room* (a stolen copy), and the *Plea of the Damned,* &c:—"I doubt, habit has little power to reconcile us with sickness attended by pain. With me the lowness of spirits has a most unhappy effect. I am grown less patient with solitude, and harder to be pleased with company; which I could formerly better digest, when I could be easier without it than at present." With Gay, who had found a pleasant asylum in the house of his patroness and protectress, the Duchess of Queensberry, at Aimsbury, he entered upon a lively correspondence, the Duchess taking a share in it; and his letters he addressed in part to Gay, and in part to his hostess. He had assisted the necessities of the amiable but thriftless Fabulist with a small loan; and he occasionally lectures him, parenthetically, on his careless extravagance. "I confess," he gently reminds him, "I begin to apprehend you will squander my money, because, I hope, you never less wanted it and if you go on with success two years longer, I fear I shall not have a farthing of it left." In the same letter he refers to his good relations with the late Lord Lieutenant, Carteret: "I believe my Lord Carteret, since he is no longer Lieutenant, may not wish me ill; and I have told him often that I only hated him as *Lieutenant*. I confess he had a genteeler manner of binding the chains of this kingdom than most of his predecessors, and I confess, at the same time, that he had, six times, a regard to my recommendation by preferring so many of my friends in the Church. The two best acts of his favour were to add to the dignities of Dr. Delany and Mr. Stopford." He then playfully alludes to the pressing invitations to Aimsbury; and excuses himself on the ground of his imperiousness of temper: "I now hate all people whom I cannot command, and consequently a Duchess is, at this time, the hatefullest lady in the world to me, one only excepted, and I beg her Grace's pardon for that exception: for, in the way I mean, her Grace is ten thousand times more hateful." As for himself and his prospects, he protests that since the Queen (Anne's) death, by which "all my hopes were cut off, I could have no ambition left, unless I would have been a greater rascal than happened to suit with my temper. I, therefore, sat down quietly at my morsel, adding only thereto a principle of hatred to all succeeding measures and Ministers, by way of sauce to my dish."

For Lord Bolingbroke his personal affection was mixed with some distrust of his principles (in politics), and dislike for his affectations of philosophy. In the ex-Statesman's letters these affectations figure conspicuously; yet he seems to have had a sincere regard for his former associate. Writing not long after Swift's final withdrawal from England, Bolingbroke assures him, in the most ardent terms, of his affection: "I know not whether the love of fame increases as we advance in age, sure I am that the force of friendship does. I loved you almost twenty years ago. I thought of you as well as I do now—*better* was beyond the power of conception—or, to avoid an equivoque, beyond the extent of my ideas. . . . Is it," he continues, "that we grow more tender as the moment of our great separation approaches? Or, is it that they who are to live together in another state (for *vera amicitia non nisi inter bonos*) begin to feel more strongly that divine sympathy which is to be the grand band of their future society? There is no one thought which soothes my mind like this. I encourage my imagination to pursue it, and am heartily afflicted when another faculty of the intellect comes boisterously in, and wakes me from so pleasing a dream, if it be a *dream*." Several papers, "of much curiosity and importance," he had been preparing for the press, had been lost, and "some of them in a manner which would surprise and anger you. However," he consoles himself, "I shall be able to convey several great truths to posterity, so clearly and so authentically, that the Burnets and the Oldmixons of another age may rail, but not be able to deceive."

A lady, with whom he maintained, in these years, a rather lively correspondence, was his old acquaintance at Dublin Castle, at that time a young girl, Lady Betty Germaine, who had since made for herself, with not a few of her contemporaries in the same rank, some renown in the world of scandal. She cannot quite compete with Lady M. W. Montagu in the epistolary style, but she sometimes amuses by her vivacity. She warns him, at the outset of their renewed epistolary communication. "do not flatter yourself: you began the correspondence. Set my pen a-going, and God knows when it will end : for I had it by inheritance from my father ever to please myself, when I could, and, though I do not just take the turn my mother did of fasting and praying, yet, to be sure, that was her pleasure, too, or else she would not have been so greedy of it. . . . I have not acquaintance enough," she professes, "with Mr. Pope, which I am sorry for; and expect you should come to England, in order to improve it. If it was the Queen [Caroline], and not the Duke of Grafton, that picked out such a laureat [Cibber], she deserves his poetry in her praise" (July, 1731). On one occasion, confidingly, she imparts to him her reason for her preference of country to town riding:—"Since I came out of the country," she announces, "my riding days are over; for I never was for your Hyde Park courses; although my courage serves me well at a hand gallop in the country for six or seven miles, with one horseman, and a ragged lad, a labourer's boy (that is to be clothed when he can run fast enough to to keep up with my horse), who has yet only proved his dexterity by escaping from school. But my courage fails me for riding in town, where I should have the happiness to meet with plenty of your very pretty fellows, that manage their own horses to show their art; or that think a postilion's cap, with a white frock, the most becoming dress. These and their grooms I am most bitterly afraid of; because, you must know, if my complaisant friend, your Presbyterian housekeeper [Mrs. Brent], can remember anything like such days with me, that is very good reason for me to remember that time is past, and your *toupees* would rejoice to see a horse throw an ancient gentlewoman." She incidentally adverts, in the same gossiping letter, to his proposal for the exclusive use of Irish manufactures. " I am sorry you are no wiser in Ireland than we English, for our [royal] birthday was as fine as hands could make us. But I question much whether we all paid *ready money*. I mightily approve of my Duchess [of Dorset, wife of the new Viceroy] being dressed in your manufacture. If your ladies will follow her example in all things, they cannot do amiss. . . . Why," she adjures him in conclusion, "do you tantalize me? Let me see you in England again, if you dare; and choose your residence, summer or winter, St. James's Square or Drayton. I defy you in all shapes—be it Dean of St. Patrick governing England or Ireland, or politician Drapier. But my choice should be the parson in Lady Betty's chamber. Make haste then." . . .

In Ireland he reckoned among his chief intimates Dr. Sheridan and Dr. Delany, both clerics. The latter, a Fellow of Trinity College, had some repute as a scholar. Sheridan, grandfather of the famous orator, became his more intimate friend and more frequent correspondent. He had kept a large school in Dublin, until the Dean procured for him from Lord Carteret, with whom Swift had a good understanding, a *Living* and Chaplaincy. But, of an easy and indolent temperament, Dr. Sheridan possessed little prudence or *savoir faire*.[1] He fell behind in the struggle for existence—or, rather, for office and emolument; and, at last, died impoverished and neglected. With Sheridan Swift was on more familiar and intimate terms than with any other of his friends; and their correspondence is the most free and easy in the entire Collection. Both, the latter especially, had fame as punsters; their letters contain enough evidence of their talent in this way. Among the published "Miscellanies in Prose," by Swift and Sheridan, the best is the *Ars Pun-ica: the Art of Punning*. Some of the most ingenious efforts of Swift, in this style, appear in his "Discourse to Prove the Antiquity of the English Tongue: shewing from various instances that Hebrew, Greek, and Latin, were derived from the English," in which, satirising the absurdities of the Etymology of his time, he wittily proves a number of names of the heroes of those peoples to have been derived, by corruption, from English names.[2] Another intimate friend, though not admitted

[1] He ruined his chances of preferment, it is said, by preaching a sermon, with the text, "Sufficient for the day is the evil thereof," on the anniversary of the Hanoverian Succession. "Poor Sheridan," said his friend, in his *Vindication of Lord Carteret*, "by mere chance medley, shot his own fortune dead with a single text."

[2] *E.G.*: "The next I shall mention is *Andromache*, the famous wife of Hector. Her father was a Scotch gentleman, of a noble family, still subsisting in that ancient kingdom. Being a foreigner in Troy, to which city he led some of his countrymen in the defence of Priam, as Dictys Cretensis learnedly observes, Hector fell in love with his daughter; and the father's name was Andrew Mackay. The young lady was called by the same name only a little softened to the Grecian accent.

"As to *Jupiter* himself, it is well known that the statues and pictures of this heathen God in Roman Catholic countries resemble those of *St. Peter*, and are often taken the one for the other. The reason is manifest; for when the Emperors established Christianity the heathen were afraid of acknowledging their heathen idols of their chief God, and pretended it was only a statue of the *Jew Peter*. And then the principal heathen God came to be called by the ancient Romans, with very little alteration, *Jupiter*."

into the same familiarity as Sheridan, Dr. Helsham, a Dublin physician, lived in the same house with Delany, where they received the selected circle of the Dean's friends. Others, of humbler position, among his acquaintance, were Alderman Faulkener, his eccentric Dublin publisher, a correspondent also of Chesterfield; and Ford, his publishing agent and editor of a Government newspaper. But more interesting as, by their reminiscences, they have helped to throw light upon his latter days, appear some of his women acquaintances: in particular, Mrs. Pilkington and Mrs. Pendarves; the former of whom has left *memoirs*, with interesting anecdotes of Swift's habits and conversation, and the latter many references, also of interest, in her *Autobiography* and *Letters*. More memorable for her extraordinary learning (exaggerations deducted), claims mention Mrs. Grierson, who died at the age of twenty-seven; not before she had exhausted, we are assured, all the treasures of literature, philosophy, and science. Mrs. Barber, another literary lady of his circle of friends, has deserved notice from the biographers of Swift, not from her eminence as a poetess, but for the reason that Swift good-naturedly wrote an *Introduction* to her volumes of commonplace poetic effusions. To her, too, he presented his manuscript of *Polite Conversation*. Of friends near, or not far distant from, the capital, for Lady Howth ("the blue-eyed nymph"), of Howth Castle, where he often visited, he entertained an especial regard. In Howth Castle remains one of the three paintings of him by Bindon, a full-length picture, in which William Wood, the unfortunate patentee of the halfpence coinage, is depicted in slavish attitude at the feet of his disdainful conqueror. Much less complacent than the portrait of Jervas (of (1711), the expression of the features reveals all the bitterness of his later life, the scorn and the cynical contempt of human littleness.

From the irksome routine of his ecclesiastical duties, and dissensions with ecclesiastical superiors or inferiors, Swift frequently took refuge with his acquaintances in the country. Yet, far from being a mere placeholder, or from deeming himself irresponsible for the miserable condition of the *proletariat* within his ecclesiastical domain, he constantly shewed the substantial benevolence of his disposition. Not content with mere chance-giving "charity," he sought out for himself, we are assured, the worse cases of the abundant wretchedness around him, to which, it is said, he gave up the third part of his official income. With all his beneficence, he assumed a certain contemptuousness

[1] See *Life of Jonathan Swift* by Henry Craik.

and arrogance of manner; but, at least, such demeanour he did not reserve for his dependants. It was equally exhibited towards his official superiors. Of this, his correspondence in general (and, in particular, with his ecclesiastical, superior Archbishop King) remains conspicuous proof. For the interest of his private friends he always cared more than for his own, as constant to his friends as he was a bitter hater of his enemies. Among his prose writings last prepared for the press, and which appeared after his death, are *Polite Conversation*[1] and *Direction to Servants.* In a letter to Gay (Aug. 28, 1731), he already mentions them:—"I have two great works in hand; one to reduce the whole politeness, wit, humour, and style of England into a short system, for the use of all persons of quality, and particularly of all Maids of Honour.[2] The other is of almost equal importance; I may call it the Whole Duty of Servants, in about twenty several stations, from the Steward and Waiting-Woman, down to the Scullion and Pantry Boy." The latter is too minute and monotonous, and the satire has too much of exaggeration, to be altogether a favourable specimen of his wit. On the other hand, his *Polite Conversation* may justly be reckoned among his wittiest productions. Its object is the ridicule of the style of drawing-room tittle-tattle—as Cowper puts it compendiously:

"Who danced with whom, and who are like to wed;
And who is hanged, and who is brought to bed."

A dramatic dialogue follows the ironical introduction. A number of fashionable persons assemble in a drawing-room, at various periods of the day, and engage in one of these "polite conversations," which, to the uninitiated, have but a slender appearance of *politeness*; but in which there shines a very considerable display of trifling talk and *doubles entendres.* The young lady, who represents the Maid of Honour, it may be remarked, in *persiflage* with her interlocutors of the privileged sex, quite holds her own.

Among his numerous poetic pieces foremost in merit or fame are:—*Cadenus and Vanessa* (1713), *The South Sea Project* (1721), *The Grand*

---

[1] In its full title—"A Complete Collection of Genteel and Ingenious Conversation, According to the most Polite Mode and Method, now used at Court, and in the best Companies of England. In three Dialogues by Simon Wagstaff, Esq."

[2] Of the virtues of *Maids of Honour* Swift had not formed a very complimentary estimate. His dislike for them seems to have been considerably influenced by his belief that his friend, Mrs. Howard, Maid of Honour to the Princess Caroline, had, from indifference or insincerity, neglected to promote his interests entrusted to her, at the Court at Leicester House.

Question Debated (1729),[1] *Verses on the Death of Dr. Swift* (1731), *Journal of a Modern Lady* (1728), *Poetry: A Rhapsody* (1733), in which, like Pope, he satirises royal neglect of the true poets; of later date, such pieces as *The Beasts' Confession*, (in which he drew parallels, with apologies to the "Beasts" for so uncomplimentary use of them, between members of the human and non-human species), the *Plea of the Damned*, and *On the Day of Judgment*. For the preservation of the last, a fragment of only a few lines, we are obliged to Lord Chesterfield, who sent them in a letter to Voltaire (in 1752), in which he says: "the piece has never been printed: you will easily guess the reason why; but it is authentic. I have the original written in his own hand."[2] To his latter days belong certain of his poems,

[1] With the alternative title: *Whether Hamilton's Bawn should be turned into a Barrack or Malt-house*. It is one of the series of verses written by him at Market Hill, while on a visit to Sir Arthur Acheson. Scott calls it an "inimitable poem." Hamilton's Bawn was an old building belonging to the Achesons, not far from Market Hill. The *poematis personæ* are Sir Arthur Acheson, Lady Acheson, and her waiting-woman Hannah. The first supports the Malt-house, the two women the Barrack. The whole piece is very lively and witty; the arguments of the waiting-woman and, in particular, her report of the (imaginary) Captain's dialogue with her mistress at the dinner-table on the "parsons," being very much in character:—

> " And ' Madam,' says he, ' if such dinners you give,
> You'll never want for parsons so long as you live.
> I ne'er knew a parson without a good nose,
> But the devil's as welcome wherever he goes :
> G— d— me! they bid us reform and repent,
> But, Zounds! by their looks they never keep Lent.
> Mister Curate, for all your grave looks, I'm afraid,
> You cast a sheep's look on her ladyship's maid ;
> I wish she would lend you her pretty white hand,
> In mending your cassock and smoothing your band.'
> (For the Dean was so shabby, and looked like a ninny
> That the Captain supposed he was curate to Jinny).
> ' Whenever you see a cassock or gown,
> A hundred to one but it covers a clown.
> Observe how a Parson comes into a room ;
> G— d— me, he hobbles as bad as my groom.
> A *Scholard*, when just from his college broke loose.
> Can hardly tell how to cry *bo* to a goose.
> Your Novels, and Bluturks, and Omars, and stuff,
> By G—, they don't signify this pinch of snuff.
> To give a young gentleman the right education,
> The Army's the only good school in the nation.
> My schoolmaster called me a dunce and a fool:
> But at cuffs I was always the cock of the school.' "

[2] It consists of some twenty lines :—

> " With a whirl of thought oppressed,
> I sank from reverie to rest.
> A horrid vision seized my head :
> I saw the graves give up their dead!

which rival the grossness of the grossest parts of Chaucer, and emulate almost Rabelais himself.[1] Scott has found the only excuse possible for the extreme cynicism, which could thus brave the commonest feeling of propriety, in the fact that their composition belongs to the time when the writer had become scarcely responsible for what he wrote; and, also, in the supposition that he never intended them for publication; but that the indiscretion of his friends, or the avarice of the booksellers, sent them abroad. In a letter to Pope (1731), when enumerating his poetical pieces, he adds that some of them were *stolen* copies. Of all his poems, the best of which are characterised by extraordinary correctness of versification, wit, and naturalness, almost unrivalled in their way, none exhibit finer wit than the verses on his own death. Nothing can be more felicitous than the representation of the manner in which the news of his illness, and lastly his death, is received by his various friends:—

> "And then their tenderness appears
> By adding largely to my years:
> 'He's older than he would be reckoned,
> And well remembers Charles the Second!
> He hardly drinks a pint of wine,
> And that, I doubt, is no good sign.
> His stomach, too, begins to fail—
> Last year we thought him strong and hale;
>
> Jove, armed with terrors, burst the skies,
> And thunder roars and lightning flies!
> Amazed, confused, its fate unknown,
> The world stands trembling at his throne!
> While each pale sinner hung his head,
> Jove, nodding, shook the heavens, and said:
> 'Offending race, of human kind,
> By nature, reason, *learning*, blind;
> You, who through frailty stepped aside,
> And you who never fell—*through pride*;
> You, who in different sects were shammed,
> And come to see each other damned—
> (So, some folks told you, but they knew
> No more of Jove's designs than you)—
> The World's mad business now is o'er,
> And I resent these pranks no more.
> —I to such blockheads set my wit!
> I damn such fools!—Go, go, you're bit.'"

[1] These Rabelaisian pieces are not many in number—the *Lady's Dressing Room, Strephon and Chloe* (the most coarse and offensive of all), and one or two others. Some of the poems have been too indiscriminately classed and condemned in the same category with these, such as *The Legion Club, The Plea of the Damned* (the latter published as a *broadsheet*, in Dublin, 1731), which have little or nothing to offend real delicacy of feeling.

But now he's quite another thing,
I wish he may hold out to Spring!'
They hug themselves, and reason thus :
'It is not yet so bad with us.'

"In such a case they talk in tropes,
And by their fears express their hopes
Some great misfortune to portend
No enemy can match a friend.
With all the kindness they profess,
The merit of a lucky guess
(When daily *how-d'yes* come of course,
And servants answer, worse and worse)
Would please them better than to tell
That, 'God be praised, the Dean is well.'
Then he, who prophesied the best,
Approves his foresight to the rest :
'You know I always feared the worst,
And often told you so at first.'
He'd rather choose that I should die
Than his prediction prove a lie.
Not one foretells I shall recover,
But all agree to give me over.

Yet should some neighbour feel a pain
Just in the parts where I complain,
How many a message would be send,
What hearty prayers that I should mend!
* * * * * * *
Before the passing-bell begun,
The news through half the town is run :
'Oh may we all for death prepare!
What has he left, and who's his heir?'
* * * * * * *
My female friends, whose tender hearts
Have better learned to act their parts,
Receive the news in doleful dumps :
'The Dean is dead (pray what is trumps?)
Then, Lord have mercy on his soul!
(Ladies, I'll venture for the vole.)
Six Deans, they say, must bear the pall—
(I wish I knew what king to call!)'
'Madam, your husband will attend
The funeral of so good a friend?'

> 'No, Madam, 'tis a shocking sight,
> And he's engaged to-morrow night:
> My Lady Club will take it ill,
> If he should fail her at quadrille.
> He loved the Dean—(I lead a heart),
> But dearest friends, they say, must part.
> His time was come: he ran his race—
> We hope he's in a better place.' "[1]

The year 1736 marks the beginning of that dark period in his life, which, in 1741, culminated in mental insanity. Recent scientific investigation goes to prove the peculiar disease, that at length eclipsed his reason, not to have been gradually developing, as generally inferred, but to have been the immediate consequence of paralysis. Until the paralysis came, while suffering often the greatest torture physically, and failing in memory, he still kept possession of his reason and of most of his mental faculties.[2] His last words, in writing, he addressed to his niece, Mrs. Whiteway, who superintended his household, and attended him during his illness:—"I have been very miserable all night, and to-day extremely deaf and full of pain. I am so stupid and confounded that I cannot express the mortification I am under, both in body and mind. All I can say is, I am not in torture; but I hourly expect it. . . . I hardly understand one word I write. I am sure my days

---

[1] To prevent further propagation of spurious copies of these *Verses* (in 1733 an unauthorised edition had appeared in London, of which Swift writes to Pope, hyperbolically, "not a single line, or bit of a line, or thought, anyway resembles the genuine copy"), the author entrusted, in 1738, the publication to his friend, Dr. King, Head of St. Mary Hall, Oxford. King, under date January, 1739, announces that they are at length in the press: "but I am in great fear," he adds, "lest you should dislike the liberties I have taken; although I have done nothing without the advice and approbation of those among your friends who love and esteem you most." He soon afterwards reports their extraordinary popularity. The liberty taken by his politic editor related to satirical lines in the MS., about the unfortunate medals (see Swift's letters to Mrs. Howard), and a reference to the death of Queen Anne.

The reference to the medals thus appeared in MS.:—

> "He's dead you say: *then let him rot*;
> I'm glad *the Medals were* forgot!
> I promised *him, I own : but* when?
> I only *was the Princess* then.
> But now, as consort of *the King*,
> You know 'tis quite a different thing."

(See *Notes and Queries*, Feb. 5, 1881).

[2] Dr. Wilde (*Closing Years of Swift's Life*) seems first to have disputed the commonly received belief in ordinary insanity; and to have attributed his mental disease to brain pressure, aggravated by gastric disorder. He shewed that it was paralysis that caused the *lethargy* (rather than *insanity*, in the ordinary sense of the word) of the brain. The latest theory assigns the deafness and giddiness to malformation of the ear.

will be very few—few and miserable they must be."—(July 26, 1740.) Five years more of acute disorders, and he at last obtained the final release from suffering he must so often have sighed for, on October 19, 1745, in his seventy-eighth year. His burial took place, according to his instructions, in the south aisle of his Cathedral, and in the same grave with Stella.[1] The inscription upon his monument, in Latin, written by himself, thus reads:—"Here is deposited the body of Jonathan Swift, S.T.P., Dean of the Cathedral Church, where Fierce Indignation can no longer lacerate the heart. Go, you who pass by, and imitate, if you can, a strenuous assertor of Freedom."

Mentally, morally, physically the character of the most famous of English prose Satirists forms one of the strangest compounds, of the most contradictory feelings and properties, to be found in all Literary history. Professing undisguised and unbounded contempt, and even hatred, for his own species, yet, in particular instances, he sometimes discovered much benevolence of disposition. An advocate of political freedom, and a hater of oppression and injustice, in general, yet, as a churchman, he exhibited bitter hostility towards nonconformity. Somers had been his political friend, while Atterbury (if not Sacheverell) seemed to be his ecclesiastical model. Himself using great freedom in allusions to theological creeds, he yet professed extreme aversion for free-thinkers or "infidels."[2] He was assiduous, however, in everything belonging to his ecclesiastical office. "In his [cathedral] church," says Johnson, "he restored the practice of weekly *communion*, and distributed the sacramental elements in the most solemn and devout manner, with his own hand. He came to church every morning, preached commonly in his turn, and attended the evening anthem, that it might not be negligently performed." Of his published *Sermons* (given by him in MS. to Sheridan) the ninth has the most merit—*On the Causes of the Wretched Condition of Ireland*—based on the *text*: "That there be no complaining in our streets, &c." A *Sermon* of a different style, in a somewhat serio-comic strain, is one "On Sleeping in Church"—from the *text* on Eutyches. "Some," laments the Dean,

---

[1] Dr. Wilde, in his *Closing Years of Swift's Life*, which was suggested by the disinterment of the skeletons of Swift and Stella in 1835, informs us that the skulls were the object of the greatest curiosity, and went the rounds of several drawing-rooms, where they were examined with the greatest eagerness.

[2] His well-known esoteric and conservative maxim, perhaps, best exhibits his attitude in regard to matters theological—viz., that "the mass of men are as capable of flying as of thinking."

"lie at catch to ridicule whatever they hear, and, with much wit and humour, provide a stock of laughter by furnishing themselves from the pulpit. But of all misbehaviour none is comparable to that of those who come here to sleep. Opium is not so stupifying to many persons as an afternoon *sermon*. Perpetual custom hath so brought it about, that the words of whatever preacher become only a sort of uniform sound at a distance, than which nothing is more effectual to lull the senses. For that it is the very sound of the sermon which bindeth up their faculties is manifest from hence, because they all awake so very regularly as soon as it ceaseth, and with much devotion receive the *blessing*, dozed and besotted with indecencies I am ashamed to repeat." Far from being a libertine in sexual morality, and severely repressive of all obscenity in private conversation (as we are assured), he yet, in his satires and poems, frequently transgressed the last bounds of decency and propriety. While extremely, sometimes unreasonably, parcimonious in regard to his personal expenses, he yet not seldom shewed the greatest generosity towards his friends, and gave ready assistance to the poor. And (to complete the antitheses in the entire personality of Swift), physically, of a strong and powerful frame, and capable of the most vigorous exercise, he, at the same time, suffered in body, as well as in mind, agonies of torture.

As a letter-writer Swift may claim a place, if not the foremost, at least, among the foremost in that species of writing. In the order of time, indeed, he may be said to stand at the head of the great English letter-writers. His epistolary correspondence (for the letters that have been preserved of his younger days are few and comparatively unimportant) begins with the opening of the Eighteenth Century, when the somewhat pedantic stiffness, which still adhered to the style of the older writers of the language, had given place to the greater ease and elegance of the more modern manner. The Seventeenth Century had, in England, produced no great models in the epistolary style, in the vernacular—with the exception, perhaps, of Howell (otherwise an obscure writer), who, in the earlier half of that century, seems to have anticipated, in a remarkable degree, the later ease and naturalness of manner, and unarchaic freedom. Of Swift's great literary contemporaries, who illustrated the two first decades of the new century, Addison and Steele, the former was not a letter-writer; and very few letters of his which have been preserved have any especial interest or importance. Those which we have of Steele are, chiefly, amatory missives. With the laboured and artificial manner of his friend, and younger contemporary, Pope, the freedom, ease, and unconventional naturalness of his style contrasts conspicuously. He used to say of himself that, when he began a letter, he never leaned on his elbows till he had finished it.[1]

Of his collected letters, as published in the ample, but incomplete, edition of Sir Walter Scott, next to the famous and voluminous letters to Esther Johnson, those written to his most familiar friends, Pope, Arbuthnot, Gay, and Sheridan, as might be expected, are among the best and most characteristic. The part of his Correspondence which would have had more attraction for the world in general—his letters to and from Esther Johnson—with the exception of his own in journal-form, has not come down to us, destroyed, it seems, by himself, with all the possible secrets it might have revealed. The last twenty-five letters of that series Dr. Hawkesworth, editor of *The Adventurer*, first published, depositing them in the British Museum. The earlier letters were published subsequently, and less faithfully, by Deane Swift. As for the letters to Hester Vanhomrigh, they possess more interest for the biographer than for the reader, being, for the most part, brief, and obscure in allusion. Swift was a prolific letter-writer, and his correspondence, in print or in manuscript, is voluminous. His most elaborate biographer (in intention—for the author's death prevented the completion of the biography) had access to a large number of unprinted letters (some one hundred and fifty)—to Knightly Chetwode of Woodbroke (1714-1731); to Archdeacon Wall; to Arbuthnot and others—which still remain in manuscript. Since the time of Scott (1824) very few additions have been made, *in extenso*, to the letters published up to that time. One of considerable curiosity has lately appeared, for the first time, in Mr. Craik's *Life*—to Arbuthnot (July 3, 1714), with references to *Scriblerus* and political matters. Two or three letters also, of interest, to Lord Orrery appear in the same work. Without doubt, the most important addition to the *bibliography* of Swift is, as Mr. Forster describes it, "the large paper copy of the first edition of *Gulliver*, which belonged to the friend (Charles Ford), who carried the MS., with so much mystery, to Benjamin Motte, the publisher, interleaved for alterations and additions by the author; and containing, besides all the changes, erasures, and substitutions adopted in the later editions, several interesting passages—mostly in the voyage

---

[1] See Scott's *Works of Swift*, Vol. xv.

to Laputa—which have never yet been given to the world."[1] A letter, of highly curious interest, to Motte, respecting his proposed illustrations to the *Travels*, is now printed (it is believed), for the first time, from the "Forster Collection" in the Museum at South Kensington.

The handwriting of Swift, differing from Pope's bold and legible hand, is cramped and minute. The legibility varies, presumably, with the pen, paper, and ink; but its minuteness and crampedness, its characteristics, often make a word here and there almost, if not altogether, undecypherable.

[1] Preface to the *Life of Swift*, by John Forster, 1876.

LETTERS OF SWIFT.

LETTERS.

To the Rev. John Kendall.[1]

Moor Park, February 11, 1691–2.

If anything made me wonder at your letter, it was your almost inviting me to do so in the beginning; which, indeed, grew less upon knowing the occasion, since it is what I have heard from more than one in and about Leicester. And for the friendship between us, as I suppose yours to be real, so I think it would be proper to imagine mine, until you find any cause to believe it pretended; though I might have some quarrel at you in three or four lines, which are very ill-bestowed in complimenting me. And as to that of my great prospects of making my fortune, on which as your kindness only looks on the best side, so my own cold temper, and unconfined humour, is a much greater hindrance than any fear of that which is the subject of your letter.

I shall speak plainly to you, that the very observations I made, with going half a mile beyond the University, have taught me experience enough not to think of marriage till I settle my fortune in the world, which I am sure will not be in some years; and even then itself [sic.], I am so hard to please, that I suppose I shall put it off to the other world. How all that suits with my behaviour to the woman in hand,[2] you may easily imagine, when you know there is something in me which must

---

[1] Vicar of Thornton, in Leicestershire.—Scott. He had written, it seems, a letter of advice in regard to Swift's love affair with Miss Jones.
[2] See *Life of Swift*.

be employed, and, when I am alone, turns all for want of practice into speculation and thought; insomuch that, these seven weeks I have been here, I have writ and burnt, and writ again, upon all manner of subjects—more, perhaps, than any man in England. And this is it which a great person of honour in Ireland [1] (who was pleased to stoop so low as to look into my mind) used to tell me, that my mind was like a conjured spirit, that would do mischief if I would not give it employment. It is this humour that makes me so busy, when I am in company, to turn all that way; and, since it commonly ends in talk, whether it be love or common conversation, it is all alike. This is so common, that I could remember twenty women in my life, to whom I have behaved myself just the same way; and, I profess, without any other design than that of entertaining myself when I am very idle, or when something goes amiss in my affairs. This I always have done as a man of the world,[2] when I had no design for anything grave in it, and what I thought, at worst, a harmless impertinence. But, whenever I begin to take sober resolutions, or, as now, to think of entering into the Church, I never found it would be hard to put off this kind of folly at the porch.

Besides, perhaps, in so general a conversation among that sex, I might pretend a little to understand where I am when I am going to choose for a wife; and though the cunning sharper of the town may have a cheat put upon him, yet it must be cleanlier carried than this, which you think I am going to top upon myself. And, truly, if you knew how metaphysical I am that way, you would little fear I should venture on one who has given so much occasion to tongues; for, though the people is a lying sort of beast (and, I think, in Leicester above all parts that I ever was in), yet they seldom talk without some glimpse of a

[1] His early patron, Lord Berkeley.

[2] Swift, it will be remembered, was now not more than twenty-three years of age.

reason, which I declare (so unpardonably jealous I am) to be a sufficient cause for me to hate any woman any farther than a bare acquaintance. Among all the young gentlemen that I have known, who have ruined themselves by marrying (which, I assure you, is a great number), I have made this general rule— that they are either young, raw, and ignorant scholars who, for want of knowing company, believe every silk petticoat includes an angel; or, else, these have been a sort of honest young men who, perhaps, are too literal in rather marrying than burning, and entail a misery on themselves and posterity by an overacting modesty. I think I am very far excluded from listing under either of these two heads. I confess I have known one or two men of sense enough who, inclined to frolics, have married and ruined themselves out of a maggot. But a thousand household thoughts, which always drive matrimony out of my mind whenever it chances to come there, will, I am sure, frighten me from that. Besides that I am naturally temperate, and never engaged in the contrary, which usually produces these effects.

Your hints at particular stories I do not understand; and, having never heard them but so hinted, thought it proper to give you this, to shew you how I thank you for your regard of me; and, I hope, my carriage will be so as my friends need not be ashamed of the name.[1] I should not have behaved myself after that manner I did in Leicester, if I had not valued my own entertainment beyond the obloquy of a parcel of very wretched fools, which I solemnly pronounce the inhabitants of Leicester to be, and so I contented myself with retaliation. I hope you

---

[1] "This sentence," observes Scott, "is very inaccurate"(grammatically). But it is singular that his principal editor should have thought it worth while to call attention to this particular sentence, which, by comparison with many other sentences of Swift, might almost escape the censure of a Lindley Murray or even Cobbett. In fact, some of the most admired English writers of the first half of the last century, not excepting Addison or Goldsmith, are remarkable more for ease of style than for grammatical correctness.

will forgive this trouble; and so, with my service to your good wife, I am, good cousin, your very affectionate friend and servant.

———

To Mr. William Swift.[1]

Moor Park, Nov. 29, 1692.

My sister has told me you was pleased (when she was here) to wonder I did so seldom write to you. I hope you have been so kind to impute it neither to ill-manners or disrespect. I have always thought that sufficient from one who has always been but too troublesome to you. Besides, I know your aversion to impertinence,[2] and God knows so very private a life as mine can furnish a letter with little else; for I often am two or three months without seeing anybody besides the family; and now my sister is gone, I am likely to be more solitary than before.

I am still to thank you for your care in my *testimonium*;[3] and it is to very good purpose, for I never was more satisfied than in the behaviour of the University of Oxford to me. I had all the civilities I could wish for, and so many substantial favours, that I am ashamed to have been more obliged in a few weeks to strangers than ever I was in seven years to Dublin College. I am not to take orders till the King gives me a prebend; and Sir William Temple, though he promises me the certainty of it, yet is less forward than I could wish,[4] because, I

[1] The uncle of the writer, living in Ireland.

[2] Used, of course, in its etymological and proper meaning—matter which is not to the purpose.

[3] For the certificate of his degree, in consequence of which he was admitted *ad eundem* at Oxford, June 14, 1692.—Deane Swift.

[4] Here are the grounds of a quarrel which happened between him and Sir W. Temple in 1694.—D. S.

suppose, he believes I shall leave him; and, upon some accounts, he thinks me a little necessary to him. If I were affording entertainment, or doing you any satisfaction by my letters, I should be very glad to perform it that way, as I am bound to do it by all others.

I am sorry my fortune should fling me so far from the best of my relations; but hope that I shall have the happiness to see you some time or other. Pay my humble service to my good aunt, and the rest of my relations, if you please.

To Mr. Deane Swift.[1]

Leicester, June 3, 1694.

I received your kind letter to-day from your sister, and am very glad to find you will spare time from business so far as to write a long letter to one you have none at all with but friendship, which, as the world passes, is, perhaps, one of the idlest things in it.

It is a pleasure to me to see you sally out of your road, and take notice of curiosities, of which I am very glad to have part, and desire you to set by some idle minutes for a commerce which shall ever be dear to me; and, from so good an observer as you may easily be, cannot fail of being useful. I am sorry to see so much superstition in a country so given to trade. I half used to think those two to be incompatible. Not that I utterly dislike your processions for rain or fair weather which, as trifling as they are, yet have good effects, to quiet common heads, and infuse a gaping devotion among the rabble. But your burning the old woman—unless she were a duenna—I shall

[1] A cousin of Dr. Swift, then at Lisbon.—S.

never be reconciled to;[1] though it is easily observed that nations, which have most gallantry to the young, are ever the severest upon the old.[2] I have not leisure to descant further upon your pleasing letter, nor anything to return you from so barren a scene as this, which I shall leave in four days toward my journey for Ireland. I had designed a letter to my cousin Willoughby;[3] and the last favour he has done me requires a great deal of acknowledgment. But the thought of my sending so many before has made me believe it enough to trust you with delivering my best thanks to him. My mother desires her best love to him and to you, with both our services to my cousin his wife.

I forgot to tell you I left Sir William Temple a month ago, just as I foretold it to you; and everything happened thereupon exactly as I guessed. He was extremely angry I left him; and yet would not oblige himself any farther than upon my good behaviour, nor would promise anything firmly to me at all, so that everybody judged I did best to leave him. I design to be ordained in September next, and make what endeavours I can for something in the Church. I wish it may ever lie in my cousin's way or yours to have interest to bring me in Chaplain of the Factory [at Lisbon]. If anything offers from Dublin, that may serve either to satisfy or divert you, I will not fail of contributing, and giving you constant intelligence from thence of whatever you shall desire.—I am your affectionate cousin and servant.

[1] Whether she were Jew, Protestant, or Witch does not appear—or, whether the burning happened in an *Auto-da-fé*, such as that so admirably described in the *Ingoldsby Legends*: the "receipt for a Prince of the Asturias" prescribed by the Archbishop, which, however, as is well-known, resulted in the production of two *Infantas*, in place of one *Infante*.

[2] Swift cannot have studied very attentively either the History of the Holy Office or the Annals of Diabolism and Witchcraft. Otherwise, he would have found that young as well as old women have been very numerous victims.

[3] A very considerable merchant at Lisbon.—D. S.

To the Rev. Dr. Tisdall.[1]

London, Dec. 16, 1703.

I put great violence on myself in abstaining all this while from treating you with politics. I wish you had been here for ten days, during the highest and warmest reign of party and faction that I ever knew or read of, upon the Bill against Occasional Conformity; which, two days ago, was upon the first reading rejected by the Lords.[2] It was so universal, that I observed the dogs in the streets much more contumelious and quarrelsome than usual; and, the very night before the Bill went up, a committee of Whig and Tory cats had a very warm and loud debate upon the roof of our house.

But why should we wonder at that, when the very ladies are split asunder into High-Church and Low,[3] and, out of zeal for religion, have hardly time to say their prayers... For the rest, the whole body of the Clergy, with a great majority of the House of Commons, were violent for this Bill. As great a majority of the Lords, among whom all the Bishops but four, were against it: the Court and the Rabble (as extremes often agree) were trimmers. I would be glad to know men's thoughts of it in Ireland. For myself, I am much at a loss, though I was

[1] An Irish Church dignitary (and a friend of Swift), a suitor of Esther Johnson's. This letter was written when Swift was unwilling to have the appearance of discountenancing addresses, which we cannot suppose him desirous should succeed. In a subsequent letter to the same person we shall find him vindicating himself from a charge of dissimulation in this particular.—S.

[2] The Bill against Occasional Conformity, a favourite measure with the Tories, as tending to enforce the Test Act against even those dissenters who were willing, occasionally, to take the *sacrament* according to the ritual of the Church, was revived with great keenness in 1703, and carried in the House of Commons, but thrown out by the Lords. The debates on both sides were conducted with great spirit and ability.—S.

[3] Or, in the language of the Liiliputian ladies and churchmen, *High-Heels* and *Low-Heels*.

mightily urged by some great people to publish my opinion. I cannot but think (if men's highest assurances are to be believed), that several, who were against this Bill, do love the Church and do hate and despise Presbytery. I put it close to my Lord Peterborough, just as the Bill was going up, who assured me, in the most solemn manner, that if he had the least suspicion the rejecting this Bill would hurt the Church, or do kindness to the Dissenters, he would lose his right hand rather than speak against it. The like profession I had from the Bishop of Salisbury,[1] my Lord Somers, and some others: so that I know not what to think, and, therefore, shall think no more—and you will forgive my saying so much on a matter that all our heads have been so full of, to a degree that, while it was on the anvil, nothing else was the subject of conversation. I shall return in two months, in spite of my heart. I have here the best friends in nature—only want that little circumstance of favour and power. But nothing is so civil as a cast courtier.

Pray, let the ladies[2] know I had their letter, and will answer it soon, and that I obeyed Mrs. Johnson's commands, and waited on her mother and other friend. You may add, if you please, that they advise her clearly to be governed by her friends there about the renewing her lease, and she may have her mortgage taken up here whenever she pleases, for the payment of her fine; and that we have a project for putting out her money in a certain lady's hands for annuities, if the Parliament goes on with them, and she likes it.

I'll teach you a way to outwit Mrs. Johnson. It is a new-fashioned way of being witty, and they call it a *bite*. You must ask a bantering question, or tell some damned lie in a

---

[1] The celebrated Gilbert Burnet. He headed the small majority of bishops who voted against the bill.—S.

[2] Miss Johnson and Mrs. Dingley, who were now in Ireland. In Swift's day unmarried as well as married women had the prefix *Mrs.*—*Miss*, at that time, bore an uncomplimentary meaning.

serious manner, and then she will answer or speak as if you were in earnest,—and then cry you, "Madam, there's *a bite*." I would not have you undervalue this, for it is the constant amusement in Court, and everywhere else among the great people; and I let you know it, in order to have it obtain among you, and teach you a new refinement.

To THE REV. DR. TISDALL.

London, Feb. 3, 1703-4.

I am content you should judge the order of friendship you are in with me by my writing to you; and, accordingly, you will find yourself the first after the ladies;[1] for I never write to any other, either friend or relation, till long after. I cannot imagine what paragraph you mean in my former, that was calculated for the Lord Primate,[2] or how you could shew it him without being afraid he might expect to see the rest.[3] But I will take better methods another time, and you shall never, while you live, receive a syllable from me fit to be shewn to a Lord Primate, unless it be yourself. Montaigne was angry to see his *Essays* lie in the parlour window, and therefore wrote a chapter that forced the ladies to keep it in their closets. After some such manner I shall henceforth use you in my letters, by making them fit to be seen by none but yourself.

[1] Miss Johnson and Mrs. Dingley.
[2] Dr. Narcissus Marsh—S.
[3] Tisdall probably alluded to the passage in Swift's letter, which mentioned the professions made by Lord Peterborough, the Bishop of Salisbury, Lord Somers, and others, of their zeal for the Church; and he might think the lightest part of the letter too jocular for the Primate's eye, the subject considered—S.

I am extremely concerned to find myself unable to persuade you into a true opinion of your own littleness, nor make you treat me with more distance and respect; and the rather, because I find all your little pretensions are owing to the credit you pretend with two ladies who came from England. I allow, indeed, the chambers in William Street[1] to be Little England by their influence; as an Ambassador's house, wherever it is, hath all the privileges of his master's dominions; and, therefore, if you wrote the letter in their room, or their company (for in this matter their room is as good as their company), I will indulge you a little. Then for the Irish legs you reproach me with, I defy you. I had one, indeed, when I left your island; but that which made it Irish is spent and evaporated, and I look upon myself now as upon a *new foot*.

You seem to talk with great security of your establishment near the ladies; though, perhaps, if you knew what they say of you in their letters to me, you would change your opinion both of them and yourself. A *bite*—and now you talk of a *bite*, I am ashamed of the ladies being caught by you, when I had betrayed you, and given them warning. I had heard before of the *choking*, but never of the *jest* in Church. You may find from thence that women's prayers are things perfectly by rote, as they put on one stocking after another, and no more.—But if she be good at blunders, she is as ready at come-offs; and to pretend her senses were gone was a very good argument she had them about her. You seem to be mighty proud (as you have reason, if it be true) of the part you have in the ladies' good graces—especially of her you call *the party*. I am very much concerned to know it: but, since it is an evil I cannot remedy, I will tell you a story. A cast mistress went to her rival, and expostulated with her for robbing her of her lover. After a long quarrel, finding no good to be done—" Well," says

---

[1] The street, in Dublin, in which the two ladies lived while in the Irish capital.

the abdicated lady, "keep him, and . . . " "No," says the other, "that will not be altogether so convenient. However, to oblige you, I will do something that is very near it."—*Dixi*.[1] I am mightily afraid the ladies are very idle, and do not mind their book. Pray, put them upon their reading; and be always teaching something to Mrs. Johnson, because she is good at comprehending, remembering, and retaining. I wonder she could be so wicked as to let the first word she could speak, after choking, be a pun. I differ from you; and believe the pun was just coming up, but met with the crumbs, and so, struggling for the wall, could neither of them get by, and, at last, came both out together. It is a pleasant thing to hear you talk of Mrs. Dingley's blunders, when she has sent me a list with above a dozen of yours, that have kept me alive, and I hope will do so till I have them again from the fountain-head. I desire Mrs. Johnson only to forbear punning after the Finglas rate, when Dilly [2] was at home. . . .

I will not buy you any pamphlets, unless you will be more particular in telling me their names or their natures, because they are usually the vilest things in Nature. Leslie has written several of late, violent against Presbyterians and Low-Churchmen. If I had credit enough with you, you should never write but upon some worthy subject, and with long thought. But I look upon you as under a terrible mistake, if you think you cannot be enough distinguished without writing for the public. Preach, preach, preach, preach, preach, preach: that is certainly your talent; and you will some years hence have time enough to be a writer. I tell you what I am content you should do. Choose any subject you please, and write for your private diversion, or by way of trial; but be not hasty to write for the world.

[1] In the indifference, affectedly expressed by this course humour, Swift was probably not more serious than Hamlet in the jests which he breaks upon Ophelia.—S.

[2] The Rev. Dillon Ashe, a celebrated punster. See the *Art of Punning*.—B

Besides, who that has a spirit would write in such a scene as Ireland? You and I will talk an hour on these matters. Pox on the Dissenters and Independents! I would as soon trouble my head to write against a louse or a flea. I tell you what: I wrote against the Bill that was against Occasional Conformity; but it came too late by a day, so I would not print it. But you may answer it if you please; for you know you and I are Whig and Tory: and, to cool your insolence a little, know that the Queen and Court, and House of Lords, and half the Commons almost, are Whigs; and the number daily increases. I desire my humble service to the Primate, whom I have not written to, having not had opportunity to perform that business he employed me in: but shall soon, now the days are longer. We are all here in great impatience at the King of Spain's [1] delay, who yet continues in the Isle of Wight. My humble service to Dean Ryves, Dilly, Jones, and other friends. And, I assure you, nobody can possibly be more, or I believe is half so entirely, yours as, &c.

To Archbishop King.[2]

London, Feb. 12, 1707-8.

Having written what I had of business about three posts ago (whereof I wait an answer), perhaps it may be some amuse-

[1] The Archduke Charles, who then assumed the title of King of Spain, and was wind-bound at the Isle of Wight, on his way to conquer that kingdom.—S.

[2] This letter narrates the result of the artful scheme laid by Robert Harley, afterwards Earl of Oxford, with the assistance of Mrs. Masham, Queen Anne's new favourite, who had succeeded to the ascendency over her mind possessed by the Duchess of Marlborough, to displace the Whig Ministry under which he was Secretary. It is worthy of observation with what coolness Swift writes of the failure of this project, which, when successfully renewed in 1711, formed the administration of which he was the warmest defender.—S. Harley had lately seceded from the Whigs.

ment to you for a few minutes to hear some particulars about the turns we have had at Court.

Yesterday the Seals were taken from Mr. Harley, and Sir Thomas Mansel gave up his Staff. They went to Kensington together for that purpose, and came back immediately, and went together into the House of Commons. Mr. St. John designs to lay down in a few days, as a friend of his told me, though he advised him to the contrary; and they talk that Mr. Bruges, and Mr. Coke, the Vice-Chamberlain, with some others, will do the like. Mr. Harley had been some time, with the greatest art imaginable, carrying on an intrigue to alter the Ministry, and began with no less an enterprise than that of removing the Lord Treasurer,[1] and had nearly affected it, by the help of Mrs. Masham, one of the Queen's Dressers, who was a great and a growing favourite of much industry and insinuation. It went so far, that the Queen told Mr. St. John, a week ago, that "she was resolved to part with Lord Treasurer," and sent him with a letter to the Duke of Marlborough, which she read to him, to that purpose: and she gave St. John leave to tell it about the town, which he did without any reserve; and Harley told a friend of mine a week ago, that he was never safer in favour or employment.

On Sunday evening last the Lord Treasurer and Duke of Marlborough went out of the [Privy] Council; and Harley delivered a memorial to the Queen, relating to the Emperor and the War,[2] upon which the Duke of Somerset rose, and said, "If her Majesty suffered that fellow (pointing to Harley) to treat affairs of the War, without advice of the General, he could not serve her," and so left the Council. The Earl of Pembroke, though in milder words, spoke to the same purpose. So did most of the Lords; and the next day the Queen was prevailed

[1] Lord Godolphin.

Then raging on the Continent between the allied English and Austrian armies and the French.

upon to turn him out, though the Seals were not delivered till yesterday. It was likewise said that Mrs. Masham is forbid the Court: but this I have no assurance of. Seven Lords of the Whig party are appointed to examine Gregg,[1] who lies condemned in Newgate; and a certain Lord of the Council told me yesterday that there are endeavours to bring in Harley as a party in that business, and to carry it as far as an impeachment. All this business has been much fomented by a Lord, whom Harley had been chiefly instrumental in impeaching some years ago. The Secretary always dreaded him, and made all imaginable advances to be reconciled, but could never prevail, which made him say yesterday to some one who told it to me, "that he had laid his neck under their feet, and they trod upon it."

I am just going this morning to visit that Lord, who has a very free way of telling what he cares not who hears; and, if I can learn any more particulars worth telling, you shall have them. I never in my life saw or heard such divisions and complications of parties as there have been for some time. You sometimes see the extremes of Whig and Tory driving on the same thing. I have heard the chief Whigs blamed by their own party for want of moderation, and I know a Whig Lord, in good employment, who voted with the highest Tories against the Court, and the Ministry with whom he is nearly allied. My Lord Peterborow's affair[2] is yet upon the anvil, and what they will beat it out to no man can tell. It is said that Harley had laid a scheme for an entire new Ministry, and the men are named to whom the several appointments were to be given. And, though his project has miscarried, it is reckoned the greatest piece of Court-skill that has been acted these many

[1] Gregg was an under clerk in Harley's office, who had carried on a traitorous correspondence with France, for which he was condemned and executed. Many attempts were made to fix some degree of connivance upon Harley himself.—S.

[2] A threatened impeachment for his conduct in Spain.

years. I have heard nothing since morning but that the Attorney[1] either has laid down, or will do it in a few days.

A MONSIEUR MONSIEUR HUNTER,[2]
Gentilhomme Anglois à Paris,
London, Jan. 12, 1708-9.

I know no people so ill-used by your men of business as their intimate friends. About a fortnight after Mr. Addison had received the letter you were pleased to send me, he first told me of it with an air of recollection, and, after ten days farther of grace, thought fit to give it me; so you know where to fix the whole blame that it was no sooner acknowledged. 'Tis a delicate expedient you prisoners have of diverting yourselves in an enemy's country, for which other men would be hanged. I am considering whether there be no way of disturbing your quiet by writing some dark matter, that may give the French Court a jealousy of you. I suppose Monsieur Chamillard, or some of his commissaries, must have this letter interpreted to them before it comes to your hands; and, therefore, I here think good to warn them, that, if they exchange you under six of their Lieutenant-Generals, they will be losers by the bargain. But that they may not mistake me, I do not mean as *Viceroy de Virginia*, mais comme le Colonel Hunter. I would advise you to be very tender of your honour, and not fall in love; because I have a scruple, whether you can keep your *parole*, if you become a prisoner to the ladies: at least, it

[1] Sir Simon Harcourt, afterwards Lord Harcourt, and Chancellor in Harley's Administration.—S.
[2] Colonel Hunter, then a prisoner of war in Paris.

will be scandalous for a free Briton to drag two chains at once.

I presume, you have the liberty of Paris and fifty miles round, and have a very light pair of fetters, contrived to ride or dance in, and see Versailles and every place else except St. Germain.[1] I hear the ladies call you already *nôtre prisonnier Hunter, le plus honnête garçon du monde.* Will you French yet own us Britons to be a brave people? Will they allow the Duke of Marlborough to be a great general? Or, are they all as partial as their Gazetteers? Have you yet met any French Colonel whom you remember to have formerly knocked from his horse, or shivered, at least, a lance against his breastplate? Do you know the wounds you have given, when you see the scars? Do you salute your old enemies with "Stetimus tela aspera contra, Contulimusque manus"?[2] *Vous savez que Monsieur d'Addison, nôtre bon ami, est fait Sécrétaire d'Etat d'Irlande;* and, unless you make haste over and get me my Virginian bishopric, he will persuade me to go with him, for the Vienna project is off;[3] which is a great disappointment to the design I had of displaying my politics at the Emperor's Court. I do not like the subject you have assigned me to entertain you with. Crowder is sick, to the comfort of all quiet people, and Frowde is *rêveur à peindre.*[4] Mr. Addison and I often drink your health, and this day I did it with Will Pate, a certain adorer of yours, who is both a *bel esprit* and a woollendraper. The Whigs carry all before them, and how far they will pursue their victories we underrate Whigs can hardly tell. I have not yet observed the Tories' noses—their number is not to be learnt by telling of noses; for every Tory has not a nose.

[1] Then the palace of the Queen Dowager of James II. and the Pretender.
[2] Æneis XI., 283.
[3] See *Life of Swift.*
[4] Philip Frowde held an inferior official post under the Government. He wrote a couple of tragedies. He was a friend of Addison's.

'Tis a loss, you are not here to partake of three weeks' frost, and eat gingerbread in a booth by a fire on the Thames. Mrs. Floyd[1] looked out with both her eyes, and we had one day's thaw: but she drew in her head, and it now freezes as hard as ever. As for the Convocation, the Queen thought fit to prorogue it, though at the expense of Dr. Atterbury's displeasure, who was designed their Prolocutor, and is now raving at the disappointment.

I amuse myself sometimes with writing verses to Mrs. Finch,[2] and sometimes with projects for the uniting of Parties, which I perfect over night, and burn in the morning. Sometimes Mr. Addison and I steal to a pint of bad wine, and wish for no third person but you, who, if you were with us, would never be satisfied without three more. You know, I believe, that poor Dr. Gregory is dead, and Keil solicits to be[3] his successor; but Party reaches even to lines and circles, and he will hardly carry it, being reputed a Tory, which yet he utterly denies. We are here nine times madder after operas than ever; and have got a new *castrato* from Italy called Nicolini, who exceeds Valentini I know not how many bars' length.

Lords Somers and Halifax are as well as busy statesmen can be in Parliament time. Lord Dorset[4] is nobody's favourite but yours and Mr. Prior's, who has lately dedicated his book of poems to him, which is all the Press has furnished us of any value since you went. Mr. Pringle, a gentleman of Scotland, succeeds Mr. Addison in the Secretary's office; Mr. Shute,[5] a

[1] The Biddy Floyd of his lively verses.—See Vol. xiv., page 73 [of Scott's Edition]—S.

[2] Afterwards Lady Winchelsea. A set of verses under the title of *Apollo Outwitted*, addressed to her as *Ardelia*, are printed in Scott, Vol. xiv.

[3] Two Mathematicians, who published several treatises on Mathematics and Astronomy.

[4] The father of Lady M. W. Montagu, afterwards Duke of Kingston.

[5] In a letter to Archbishop King, of November 30, 1708, Swift informs his correspondent that "Mr. Shute is named for secretary to Lord Wharton [Viceroy of Ireland]; he is a young man, but reckoned the shrewdest head in Europe; and the person in whom the Presbyterians chiefly confide... As to his principles, he is truly a moderate man, frequenting the Church and the Meeting indifferently."

notable young Presbyterian gentleman under thirty years old, is made a Commissioner of the Customs. This is all I can think of, either public or private, worth telling you. . .

P.S.—Mr. Steele presents his most humble service to you; and I cannot forbear telling you of your *méchanceté*, to impute the *Letter on Enthusiasm*[1] to me, when I have some good reasons to think the author is now at Paris.

To Dean Sterne.[2]

Laracor, April 17, 1710.

You have put me under the necessity of writing you a very scurvy letter, and in a very scurvy manner. It is the want of horses, and not of inclination, that hinders me from attending on you at the Chapter. But I would do it on foot to see you visit in your own right[3]; but, if I must be visited by proxy, by proxy I will appear. The ladies of St. Mary's delivered me your commands; but Mrs. Johnson had dropped half of them by the shaking of her horse. I have made a shift, by the assistance of two civilians and a book of precedents, to send you the jargon annexed, with a blank for the name and title of any Prebendary, who will have the charity

[1] The *Letter on Enthusiasm*, written by the third Earl of Shaftesbury, and published in 1708, was for a time pertinaciously ascribed to Swift, of which he complains in the *Apology* to the *Tale of a Tub*. It appears from what follows, that he suspected Colonel Hunter to be the author.—S.

[2] With a proxy for his appearance as Prebendary of Dunlavan, at the Archbishop's visitation. Sterne was Swift's predecessor in the Deanery of St. Patrick's.

[3] Dr. Sterne was then Vicar-General of the Diocese of Dublin, and was to visit the Clergy in the absence of the Archbishop.—S. The ladies of St. Mary's are Esther Johnson and Mrs. Dingley.

to answer for me. Those words *gravi incommodo* are to be translated, the want of a horse. In a few days I expect to hear the two ladies lamenting the flesh-pots of Cavan Street. I advise them, since they have given up their title and lodgings of St. Mary, to buy each of them a palfrey, and take a squire and seek adventures.

I am here quarrelling with the frosty weather for spoiling my poor half-dozen of blossoms. *Spes anni collapsa ruit.* Whether these words be mine or Virgil's, I cannot determine. I am this minute very busy, being to preach to-day before an audience of, at least, fifteen people—most of them gentle, and all simple. I can send you no news; only the employment of my parishioners may, for memory-sake, be reduced under these heads : Mr. Perceval is ditching ; Mrs. Perceval in her kitchen; Mr. Wesley switching; Mrs. Wesley stitching; Sir Arthur Longford *riching*, which is a new word for heaping up riches. I know no other rhyme but *bitching*, and that I hope we are all past. Well, Sir, long may you live the hospitable owner of good Bits, good Books, and good Buildings. The Bishop of Clogher would envy me for these three B's. I am your most obedient, humble servant.

ADDISON.[1]

Dublin, Aug. 22, 1710.

I looked long enough at the wind to set you safe at the other side, and then . . . our conduct, very unwilling for fear you [2] . . . up to a post-horse, and hazard your limbs to

[1] Published by Scott, from a letter communicated to him by Major Tickell, a descendant from the poet. Addison had just returned from Ireland to England.

[2] Two or three lines here effaced.

be made a member. I believe you had the displeasure of much ill news as soon as you landed. Even the moderate Tories are in pain at these revolutions, being what will certainly affect the Duke of Marlborough, and, consequently, the success of the war. My Lord Lieutenant asked me yesterday when I intended for England. I said I had no business there now, since I suppose in a little time I should not have one friend left that had any credit, and his Excellency was of my opinion. I never once began your [task?] since [you left?] this, being perpetually prevented by all the company I kept, and especially Captain Pratt, to whom I am almost a domestic upon your account. I am convinced that, what Government come over, you will find all marks of kindness from any Parliament here, with respect to your employment, the Tories contending with the Whigs which should speak best of you. Mr. Pratt says he has received such marks of your sincerity and friendship as he never can forget; and, in short, if you will come over again, when you are at leisure, we will raise an army, and make you King of Ireland. Can you think so meanly of a kingdom, as not to be pleased that every creature in it, who hath one grain of worth, has a veneration for you? I know there is nothing in this to make you add any value to yourself; but it ought to put you on valuing them, and to convince you that they are not an undistinguishing people.

On Thursday, the Bishop of Clogher, the two Pratts, and I are to be as happy as Ireland will give us leave. We are to dine with Mr. Paget at the Castle, and drink your health. The Bishop shewed me the first volume of the small edition of the *Tatler*, where there is a very handsome compliment to me. But I can never pardon the printing the news of every *Tatler*. I think he might as well have printed the advertisements. I know it was a bookseller's piece of craft, to increase the bulk and price of what he was sure would sell; but I utterly disapprove it.

I beg you would tell me freely whether it would be of any

account for me to come to England. I would not trouble you for advice if I knew where else to ask it. We expect every day to hear of my Lord President's removal. If he were to continue, I might, perhaps, hope for some of his good offices. You ordered me to give you a memorial of what I had in my thoughts. There were two things.[1] Dr. South's prebend and sinecure, or the place of Historiographer. But, if things go on in the train they are, now, I shall only beg you, when there is an account to be depended on for a new Government here, that you will give me early notice to procure an addition to my fortunes. And with saying so, I take my leave of troubling you with myself.

I do not desire to hear from you till you are out of hearing at Malmsbury.[2] I long till you have some good account of your Indian affairs, so as to make public business depend upon you, and not you upon that. I read your character in Mrs. Manly's noble [notable?] *Memoirs of Europe*. It seems to me as if she had about two thousand epithets and fine words packed up in a bag; and that she pulled them out by handfuls and strewed them on her paper, where about once in five hundred times they happen to be right. My Lord Lieutenant, we reckon, will leave us in a fortnight. I led him, by a question, to tell me he did not expect to continue in the Government, nor would, when all his friends were out. Pray, take some occasion to let my Lord Halifax know the sense I have of the favour he intended me.—I am, with great respect, &c.

[1] Places, *i.e.*, which Swift would be ready to accept.
[2] For which borough Addison was then a candidate, and afterwards member.—S.

To Dean Sterne.

London, September 26, 1710.

One would think this an admirable place from whence to fill a letter. Yet, when I come to examine particulars, I find they either consist of news, which you hear as soon by the public papers, or of persons and things to which you are a stranger, and are the wiser and happier for being so.

Here have been great men every day resigning their places; a resignation as sincere as that of a usurer on his death-bed. Here are some that fear being whipped because they have broken their rod [1]; and some that may be called to an account, because they could not cast one up. There are now not much above a dozen great employments to be disposed of; which, according to our computation, may be done in as many days. Patrick assures me his acquaintance are all very well satisfied without these changes, [2] which I take for no ill-symptom; and it is certain the Queen has never appeared so easy or so cheerful. I found my Lord Godolphin the worst dissembler of any of them that I have talked to; and no wonder, since his loss and danger are greater, besides the addition of age and complexion. My Lord-Lieutenant [Wharton] is gone to the country, to bustle about elections. He is not yet removed, because they say it will be requisite to supersede him by a successor, which the Queen has not fixed on; nor is it agreed whether the Duke of Shrewsbury, or Ormond, stands fairest. I speak only for this morning, because reports change every twenty-four hours.

Meantime the pamphlets and half-sheets grow so upon our

---

[1] Alluding to the forced resignation of Sidney Godolphin, the Lord Treasurer or Premier, the outward and visible sign of whose office was a *Staff*. Upon this fact Swift founded his political squib—*Sid Hamet's Rod*—brought out soon after this date.

[2] Compare his *Journal to Stella* under this date. Patrick was his Irish man-servant, who figures so frequently in that series of letters.

hands, it will very well employ a man every day from morning till night to read them; and so, out of perfect despair, I never read any at all. The Whigs, like an army beat three-quarters out of the field, begin to skirmish, but faintly; and deserters daily come over. We are amazed to find our mistakes, and how it was possible to see so much merit where there was none, and to overlook it where there was so much. When a great Minister has lost his place, immediately virtue, honour, and wit, fly over to his successor, with the other ensigns of his office. Since I left off writing, I received a letter from my Lord Archbishop of Dublin, or rather two letters, upon these memorials. I think immediately to begin my soliciting,[1] though they are not very perfect, for I would be glad to know whether my Lord Archbishop would have the same method taken here that has been done in England, and settle it by Parliament. But, however, that will be time enough thought of this good while. . . . .

I would much rather be now in Ireland drinking your good wine, looking over while you lost a crown at penny ombre. I am weary of the caresses of great men out of place. The Comptroller[2] expects every day the Queen's commands to break his staff. He is the best great Household Officer they intend to turn out. My Lord-Lieutenant is yet in, because they cannot agree about his successor.

To Miss Johnson.

London, September 21, 1710.

Here must I begin another letter on a whole sheet, for fear saucy little MD[3] should be angry, and think much that the

[1] On behalf of the Irish Church. See *Life and Writings of Swift*.
[2] Sir John Holland, Bart.
[3] Initials, apparently, of *My Dear*, or of some similar term of endearment.

paper is too little. I had your letter this night, as I told you just and no more in my last; for this must be taken up in answering yours, saucebox. I believe I told you where I dined to-day; and to-morrow I go out of town for two days to dine with the same company on Sunday, Molesworth, the Florence Envoy,[1] Stratford, and some others. I heard to-day that a gentleman from Lady Giffard's house had been at the coffee-house to enquire for me. It was Stella's mother, I suppose. I shall send her a penny post letter to-morrow, and contrive to see her without hazarding seeing Lady Giffard, which I will not do until she begs my pardon.[2]

September 23.

Here is such a stir and bustle with this little MD of ours, and I must be writing every night. I cannot go to bed without a word to them. I cannot put out my candle till I have bid them good-night. O Lord, O Lord! Well, I dined, the first time to-day, with Will Frankland[3] and his fortune; she is not very handsome. Did I not say I would go out of town to-day? I hate lying abroad and clutter. I go to-morrow in Frankland's chariot, and come back at night. Lady Berkeley[4] has invited me to Berkeley Castle, and Lady Betty Germaine to Drayton, in Northamptonshire, and I will go to neither. Let me alone; I

---

[1] Envoy-Extraordinary to the Gran Duca of Tuscany. He afterwards succeeded to the peerage as second Viscount Molesworth. Stratford, an old school and college friend of Swift, according to *The Spectator* (cccliii.), "with the abilities of a common scrivener," was worth £100,000. He lent the Government £40,000.

[2] With Sir William Temple's sister Swift had quarrelled, on the matter of his publication of Temple's posthumous writings. In his second letter (Sept. 9) he had reported: "I hear my Lady Giffard is much at Court, and Lady Wharton [the wife of the late Lord-Lieutenant] was ridiculing it the other day. So I have lost a friend there. I have not yet seen her, nor intend it; but I will contrive to see Stella's mother some other way." Mrs. Johnson still lived with Lady Giffard as her companion.

[3] Son of the Postmaster General.

[4] Wife of the late Lord-Lieutenant, to whom Swift had been Chaplain.

must finish my pamphlet. I have sent a long letter to Bikerstaff.[1] Let the Bishop of Clogher smoke it if he can. Well, I will write to the Bishop of Killala; but you might have told him how sudden and unexpected my journey was though. Deuce take Lady S——; and, if I know D——y, he is a raw-boned faced fellow, not handsome, nor visibly so young as you say. She sacrifices £2,000, and keeps only £600. Well, you have had all my land journey, and so much for that. So you have got into Presto's[2] lodgings—very fine truly. We have had a fortnight of the most glorious weather on earth, and it still

---

[1] Steele, the editor of the *Tatler*. The paper in question ridiculed the corruptions of the English language, and introduction of new-fangled words. "Some words," says the essayist, "are, hitherto, but fairly split, and, therefore, only in the way to perfection, as *Incog.* and *Plenipo.* But in a short time, 'tis to be hoped, they will be further docked to *Inc.* and *Plen.* This reflection has made me of late years very impatient for a Peace, which, I believe, would save the lives of many brave words as well as men. The War has introduced abundance of polysyllables, which will never be able to live many more campaigns—*Speculations, Operations, Preliminaries, Ambassadors, Pallisadoes, Communications, Circumvallation, Battalions....*" Among the new-fangled words he protests against, "invented by some pretty fellows," are: *Banter, Bamboozle, Kidney,* and *Mob.* In his *Proposal for Correcting the English Tongue,* addressed in the following year to Harley, he singles out for condemnation as "montrous productions," and "conceited appellations," *trip* and *amusement* (the orthodox equivalent for which was *diversion,* a word, by the way, which held its own to nearly the end of the century). In the *Tatler* he proceeds to administer castigation to "several young readers in our churches, who, coming up from our Universities, full fraught with admiration of our town politeness, will needs correct the style of their prayer-book. In reading the 'Absolution,' they are very careful to say *pardons* and *absolves* [in place of *pardoneth* and *absolveth*], and in the prayer for the Royal Family it must be *endue'um, enrich'um, prosper'um,* and *bring'um.* Then, in their sermons, they use all the modern terms of art—*sham, banter, mob, bubble, bully, cutting, shuffling,* and *palming*: all which, and many more of the like stamp, as I have heard them often in the pulpit from such young sophisters. so I have read them in some of *those sermons that have made most noise of late*."—[Sacheverell's, to wit.]

[2] *Presto,* like *Stella,* has been introduced into the printed copies by the editors, although it does not appear in the MS. until the twenty-seventh letter (August 2, 1711), when the Duchess of Shrewsbury, an Italian, so translated the English equivalent. In the MS. the initials P. D. F. R. (presumably, or, rather, conjecturally, doing duty for "poor, dear, foolish, rogue," or for some such expression) alone appear.

continues. I hope you have made the best of it. Balligal will be a pure good place for air, if Mrs. Ashe makes good her promise.[1] Stella writes like an Emperor. I am afraid it hurts your eyes: take care of that pray, pray, Mrs. Stella. Cannot you do what you will with your own horse? Pray do not let that puppy Parvisol sell him. Patrick[2] is drunk about three times a week, and I bear it, and he has got the better of me. But one of these days I will positively turn him off to the wide world, when none of you are by to intercede for him. Stuff, how can I get her husband into the Charter-house?[3] Get a —— into the Charter-house. Write constantly! Why, sirrah,[4] do not I write every day, and sometimes twice a day, to MD? Now, I have answered all your letter, and the rest must be as it can be. Send me my bill. Tell Mrs. Brent[5] what I say of the Charter-house. I think this enough for one night; and so farewell till this time to-morrow.

September 29.

I wish MD a merry Michaelmas. I dined with Mr. Addison, and Jervas, the painter, at Addison's country place, and then came home, and writ more to my lampoon.[6] I made a *Tatler* since I came. Guess which it is, and whether the Bishop of Clogher smokes it. I saw Mr. Sterne to-day; he will do as

---

[1] To invite Esther Johnson for change of air. Parvisol was his agent, a Frenchman by birth.

[2] His Irish man-servant, whom he brought over with him from Ireland, Swift frequently complains of his drunkenness and negligence.

[3] Swift is replying abruptly, as was his custom, to questions and remarks of his correspondent.

[4] The word, which the editors print *Sirrah*, in the MS. appears as *Sollah*, according to the Swift-Johnson style of converting *r* into *l*.

[5] His housekeeper in Dublin.

[6] *The Virtues of Sid Hamet the Magician's Rod*—a satire upon Lord Godolphin, the late Premier. *Sid* for Sidney, Godolphin's family name. The Rod is the Lord Treasurer's Staff, which he was forced to resign in the preceding August.

you order, and I will give him chocolate for Stella's health. He goes not these three weeks. I wish I could send it some other way. So now to your letter, brave boys. I do not like your way of saving shillings. Nothing vexes me, but that it does not make Stella a coward in a coach. I do not think any lady's advice about my ears signifies twopence; however, I will, in compliance to you, ask Dr. Cockburn. Radcliffe[1] I know not, and Bernard I never see. [Archdeacon] Walls will certainly be stingier for seven years, upon pretence of his robbery. So Stella puns again: why, it is well enough; but I will not second it, though I could make a dozen. I never thought of a pun since I left Ireland. Bishop of Clogher's bill! Why, he paid it me; do you think I was such a fool to go without it? . . . . To-morrow I go to Mr. Harley. Why small hopes from the Duke of Ormond? He loves me very well, I believe; and would, in my turn, give me something to make me easy; and I have good interest among his best friends. But I do not think of anything farther than the business I am upon. Yes, Mrs. Owl, Blighe's corpse came to Chester when I was there, and I told you so in my letter, or forgot it.

I lodge in Bury Street, where I removed a week ago. I have the first floor, a dining-room and bedchamber, at eight shillings a week—plaguy deep, but I spend nothing for eating, never go to a tavern,[2] and very seldom in a coach. Yet, after all, it will be expensive. Why do you trouble yourself, Mistress Stella, about my instrument?[3] I have the same the Archbishop

[1] The fashionable medical practitioner of the day. Dr. Radcliffe had been Court Physician to William III., but lost his place at Anne's succession by his singular candour in telling her that her ailments were due solely to the "vapours"; and not all the influence of the Premier (Godolphin) could procure him the post from the royal patent. He has given his name to the well known Library at Oxford.

[2] A good resolution too soon repented of, as sufficiently appears in succeeding letters.

[3] The document by which he was empowered, by the Irish clergy, to negociate for the restitution of the "first-fruits" by the Crown. Two of the Irish Bishops, originally, had been associated with him in the protracted business.

gave me; and it is as good, now the Bishops are away. The Dean[1] friendly! The Dean be p—t. A great piece of friendship, indeed, what you heard him tell the Bishop of Clogher. I wonder he had the face to talk so; but he lent me money, and that is enough. Faith, I would not send this these four days, only for writing to Joe and Parvisol. Tell the Dean, that when the Bishops send me any packets, they must not write to me at Mr. Steele's; but direct, For Steele, at his office at the Cockpit; and let the enclosed be directed for me: that mistake cost me eighteenpence the other day. . . .

To Miss Johnson.

London, October 19, 1710.

O Faith, I am undone! This paper is larger than the other, yet I am condemned to a sheet. . . To-day I went to Mr. Lewis,[2] at the Secretary's Office, to know when I might see Mr. Harley; and by-and-bye comes up Mr. Harley himself, and appoints me to dine with him to-morrow. I dined with Mrs. Vanhomrigh,[3] and went to wait on the two Lady Butlers;[4] but the porter answered they were not at home. The meaning was, the youngest, Lady Mary, is to be married to-morrow to Lord Ashburnham—the best match now in England, twelve thousand pounds a year, and abundance of money.

Tell me how my *Shower*[1] is liked in Ireland; I never knew

---

[1] Sterne, of St. Patrick's, an uncle probably of the Novelist.

[2] A great friend, and agent, of Harley, with whom Swift was on intimate terms of friendship, frequently mentioned in these letters.

[3] In the MS. always appears as *Mrs. Van.*

[4] Daughters of the Duke of Ormond; for Lady Ashburnham. who died two years later, Swift professed the greatest affection.

[5] *The City Shower*, No. ccxxxviii. of the *Tatler* (October 17, 1710). Steele introduces this short poem with the reflection that: "Virgil's Land-Shower [*Æn.* iv.] is the best in its kind. It is, indeed, a shower of consequence, and contributes to the main design of the Poem, by cutting off a tedious cere-

anything pass better here. I spent the evening with Wortley Montagu and Mr. Addison over a bottle of Irish wine. Do they know anything in Ireland of my greatness among the Tories? Everybody here reproaches me of it, but I value them not. Have you heard of the verses about the *Rod of Sid Hamet?* Say nothing of them for your life. Hardly anybody suspects me for them, only they think nobody but Prior or I could write them. But I doubt they have not reached you. There is, likewise, a Ballad, full of puns, on the Westminster Election, that cost me half an hour. It runs, though it be good for nothing. But this is likewise a secret to all but MD. If you have them not, I will bring them over.

October 21.

I got MD's fourth, to-day, at the Coffee-house. God Almighty bless poor Stella, and her eyes and head. What shall we do to cure them, poor dear life? Your disorders are a pull back for your good qualities. Would to heaven I were this minute shaving your poor dear head, either here or there. Pray do not write nor read this letter, nor anything else; and I will write plainer for Dingley to read, from henceforward, though my pen is apt to ramble when I think who I am writing to. I will not answer your letter until I tell you that I dined this day with Mr. Harley, who presented me to the Earl of Stirling, a Scotch Lord; and in the evening came in Lord

monial, and bringing matters to a speedy conclusion between two potentates of different sexes. My ingenious kinsman, Mr. Humphry Wagstaff, who treats of every subject after a manner that no other author has done, and better than any other can do, has sent me the description of a *City Shower.* I do not question but the reader remembers my cousin's description of the Morning as it breaks in town, which is printed in the ninth *Tatler,* and is another exquisite piece of this local poetry." It is hardly necessary to add that Humphrey Wagstaff, Isaac Wagstaff (the original one), and Swift are identical.

Peterborow. I staid till nine, before Mr. Harley would let me go, or tell me anything of my affair. He says the Queen has now granted the first-fruits and twentieth parts; but he will not yet give me leave to write to the Archbishop, because the Queen designs to signify it to the Bishops in Ireland in form, and to take notice it was done upon a Memorial from me, which Mr. Harley tells me he does to make it look more respectful to me, &c., and I am to see him on Tuesday. Pray, say nothing of the first-fruits being granted, unless I give leave at the bottom of this. I believe never anything was compassed so soon, and purely done by my personal credit with Mr. Harley, who is so excessively obliging, that I know not what to make of it, unless to show the rascals of the other Party that they used a man unworthily, who had deserved better.

The Memorial given to the Queen from me speaks with great plainness of Lord Wharton. I believe this business as important to you as the Convocation disputes from Tisdall.[1] I hope in a month or two all the forms of settling this matter will be over, and then I shall have nothing to do here. I will only add one foolish thing more, because it is just come into my head. When this thing is made known, tell me impartially whether they give any of the merit to me or no: for I am sure I have so much, that I will never take it upon me. Insolent sluts! Because I say *Dublin, Ireland,* therefore you must say *London, England:* that is Stella's malice. Well, for that, I will not answer your letter till to-morrow day; and so, and so, I will go

---

[1] The Rev. William Tisdall, the Vicar of a Dublin parish, the former suitor of Esther Johnson. He had first become known to her by having been employed by Swift himself as her adviser in some money matters, and also as an assistant in her studies. About the year 1704 he had sought Swift's good offices in promoting his suit, ignorant, presumably of the actual state of the case. Swift's reply seems to have been ambiguous and couched (as Tisdall puts it) "in a mystical strain," and to have reproached him with conduct "unfriendly, unkind, and unacccountable." The "Convocation disputes" refer to conversation held some years previously.—See *Life.*

write something else, and it will not be much, for it is late.

I was this morning with Mr. Lewis, the Under Secretary to Lord Dartmouth, two hours talking politics, and contriving to keep Steele in his office of Stamped Paper. He has lost his place of Gazetteer, three hundred pounds a year, for writing a *Tatler*, some months ago, against Mr. Harley,[1] who gave it him at first, and raised the salary from sixty to three hundred pounds. This was devilish ungrateful; and Lewis was telling me the particulars: but I had a hint given me that I might save him in the other employment, and leave was given me to clear matters with Steele. Well, I dined with Sir Matthew Dudley, and in the evening went to sit with Mr. Addison, and offer the matter at distance to him, as the discreeter person; but found that Party had so possessed him, that he talked as if he suspected me, and would not fall in with anything I said. So I stopped short in my overture, and we parted very dryly; and I say nothing to Steele, and let them do as they will. But, if things stand as they are, he will certainly lose it, unless I save him; and, therefore, I will not speak to him, that I may not report to his disadvantage. Is not this vexatious? And is there

---

[1] No. cxciii., in which Steele, comparing the Government and Ministers to a Theatre and its Actors, denounces the intrigues of the Tory party, and, in particular, of Harley, in the House of Commons. He wrote: "I have seen many changes, as well of scenes as of actors, and have known men, within my remembrance, arrive to the highest dignities of the Theatre, who made their entrance in the quality of mutes, joint-stools, flower-pots, and tapestry-hangings. It cannot be unknown to the nobility and gentry that a gentleman of the Inns of Court, and a deep intriguer, had some time since worked himself into the sole management and direction of the Theatre. Nor is it less notorious, that his restless ambition and subtle machinations did manifestly tend to the extirpation of the good old British Actors, and the introduction of foreign Pretenders—such as Harlequins, French Dancers, and Roman Singers, which, though they impoverished the proprietors, and imposed on the audience, were for a time tolerated, by reason of his dexterous insinuations, which prevailed upon a few deluded women, especially the vizard-masks, to believe that the Stage was in danger," &c. (July 4th, 1710). The *Examiner* accused the writer of having "violated the most solemn repeated promises, and that perfect neutrality which he had engaged to maintain."

so much in the proverb of *proffered service*? When shall I grow wise? I endeavour to act in the most exact points of honour and conscience, and my nearest friends will not understand it so.[1] What must a man expect from his enemies? This would vex me, but it shall not—and so I bid you good-night, &c.

I know it is neither wit nor diversion to tell you every day where I dine, neither do I write it to fill my letter; but I fancy I shall, some time or other, have the curiosity of seeing some particulars how I passed my life when I was absent from MD this time: and so I tell you now that I dined to-day at Molesworth's, the Florence Envoy; then went to the Coffeehouse, where I behaved myself coldly enough to Mr. Addison; and so came home to scribble. We dine together to-morrow and next day by invitation; but I shall alter my behaviour to him till he begs my pardon, or else we shall grow bare acquaintance. I am weary of friends, and friendships are all monsters but MD's.

October 25.

I was to-day to see the Duke of Ormond; and, coming out, met Lord Berkeley of Stratton, who told me that Mrs. Temple, the widow, died last Saturday—which, I suppose, is much to the outward grief and inward joy of the family. I dined to-day with Mr. Addison and Steele, and a sister of Mr. Addison, who is married to one Mons. Sartre, a Frenchman, Prebendary of Westminster, who has a delicious house and garden; yet I thought it was a sort of a monastic life in those cloisters, and I liked Laracor better. Addison's sister is a sort of a wit, very like him. I am not fond of her, &c.

---

[1] Swift's good intentions in Steele's behalf were misconstrued, to say the least, by that ardent Whig, and rather accelerated the breach which naturally they might have been expected to prevent.—S.

October 26.

I was to-day to see Mr. Congreve, who is almost blind with cataracts growing on his eyes; and his case is, that he must wait two or three years till the cataracts are ripe, and till he is quite blind, and then he must have them couched; and, besides, he is never rid of the gout. Yet he looks young and fresh, and is as cheerful as ever. He is younger by three years or more than I, and I am twenty years younger than he.[1] He gave me a pain in the great toe by mentioning the gout. I find such suspicions frequently, but they go off again. . . . What do I know whether China be dear or no? I once took a fancy of resolving to grow mad for it, but now it is off; I suppose I told you so in some former letter. And so you only want some salad-dishes, and plates, and &c. Yes, yes, you shall. I suppose you have named as much as will cost five pounds. Now to Stella's little postscript, and I am almost crazed that you vex yourself for not writing. Cannot you dictate to Dingley, and not strain your little dear eyes? I am sure it is the grief of my soul to think you are out of order. Pray be quiet, and if you *will* write, shut your eyes, and write just a line, and no more, thus: *How do you do, Mrs. Stella?* That was written with my eyes shut. Faith, I think it is better than when they are open; and then Dingley may stand by, and tell you when you go too high or too low. . . .

Is not this a terrible long piece for one evening? I dined to-day with Patty Rolt[2] at my cousin Leach's, with a pox, in the

---

[1] William Congreve was born in 1670. His comedies, *The Old Bachelor*, *The Double-Dealer*, *Love for Love*, *The Mourning Bride*, *The Way of the World*, were written between 1693 and 1700. He died in 1729. The conspicuous monument, at the entrance of Westminster Abbey, was put up to his memory by the Duchess of Marlborough.

[2] One of his many cousins. He mentions her more than once in these letters. Thompson, "my he-coz" as he calls him in another place, was, it seems (if the truth must be told), a butcher.

the city. He is a printer, and prints the *Postman*.¹ Oh! oh! and is my cousin, God knows how, and he married Mrs. Baby Aires, of Leicester; and my cousin Thompson was with us; and my cousin Leach offers to bring me acquainted with the author [editor] of the *Postman*, and says he does not doubt that the gentleman will be glad of my acquaintance, and that he is a very ingenious man, and a great scholar, and has been beyond sea. But I was modest, and said, May be the gentleman is shy, and not fond of new acquaintance; and so put it off, and I wish you could hear me repeating all I have said of this in its proper tone, just as I am writing it. It is all with the same cadence with *Oh hoo!* or, as when little girls say, "I have got an apple, Miss, and I won't give you some." It is plaguy twelvepenny weather this last week, and has cost me ten shillings in coach and chair hire. If the fellow that has your money will pay it, let me beg you to buy Bank Stock with it, which has fallen thirty *per cent.*, and pays eight pounds *per cent.*, and you have the principal when you please. It will certainly soon rise. I would to God Lady Giffard would put in the four hundred pounds she owes you, and take the five *per cent.* common interest, and give you the remainder. I will speak to your mother about it when I see her. I am resolved to buy three hundred pounds of it for myself, and take up what I have in Ireland. I have a contrivance for it that I hope will do, by making a friend of mine buy it as for himself, and I will pay him when I get in my money. I hope Stratford will do me that kindness. I will ask him to-morrow or next day.

October 27.

Mr. Rowe, the poet, desired me to dine with him to-day. I went to his office (he is Under-Secretary, in Mr. Addison's place

¹ A rabid Tory newspaper. Lady Giffard published in it, a few weeks later, an advertisement, accusing Swift of having mis-edited a part of her brother's Memoirs. Leach, upon his cousin's recommendation, for a short time published the *Tatler* for "little" Harrison.

that he had in England), and there was Mr. Prior; and they both fell commending my *Shower* beyond anything that has been written of the kind—"there never was such a Shower since Danae's," &c. You must tell me how it is liked among you. I dined with Rowe; Prior could not come; and after dinner we went to a blind tavern, where Congreve, Sir Richard Temple, Estcourt, and Charles Main, were over a bowl of bad punch. The knight sent for six flasks of his own wine for me, and we staid till twelve. But, now my head continues pretty well, I have left off my drinking, and only take a spoonful mixed with water, for fear of the gout, or some ugly distemper.

October 28.

Garth and Addison and I dined to-day at a hedge-tavern.[1] Then I went to Mr. Harley; but he was denied or not at home. So I fear that I shall not hear my business is done before this goes. Then I visited Lord Pembroke, who is just come to town, and we were very merry talking of old things, and I left him with one pun. Then I went to the Ladies Butler, and the son of a whore of a porter denied them [to be at home], so I sent them a threatening message by another lady, for not excepting me always to the porter. I was weary of the Coffee-house, and Ford[2] desired me to sit with him at next door, which I did, like a fool, chattering till twelve, and now am got into bed. I am afraid the new Ministry is at a terrible loss about money. The Whigs talk so, it would give one the spleen; and I am afraid of meeting Mr. Harley out of humour. They think he will never carry through this undertaking. God knows what will

[1] Low tavern. *Hedge*, formerly, did duty as an adjective of contempt or inferiority, as in the compounds, *hedge-priest*, *hedge-writer*, *hedge-marriage*. " Blind Tavern " seems to have much the same meaning.

[2] Charles Ford, a friend of Swift's, frequently mentioned in the letters. It was he who carried the MS. *Travels of Gulliver*, interleaved and revised by the author, to the publisher Motte, with so much mystery.

become of it. I should be terribly vexed to see things [*i.e.*, the Whig Government] come round again; it will ruin the Church and Clergy for ever. But I hope for better. . .

October 30-31.

I dined to-day at Mrs. Vanhomrigh's, and sent a letter to poor Mrs. Long,[1] who writes to us, but is God knows where, and will not tell anybody the place of her residence.

The month ends with a fine day; and I have been walking and visiting Lewis, and concerting where to see Mr. Harley. I have no news to send you. Aire, they say, is taken,[2] though the Whitehall letters this morning say quite the contrary; it is good, if it be true. I dined with Mr. Addison and Dick Stuart, Lord Mountjoy's brother—a treat of Addison's. They were half-fuddled, but not I, for I mixed water with my wine, and left them together between nine and ten, and I must send this by the bellman, which vexes me, but I will put it off no longer. Pray God it does not miscarry. I seldom do so, but I can put

[1] Mrs. Anne Long, for whom Swift had the highest admiration. In one of his note-books (formerly in the possession of Mr. Forster) he records that: "she was the most beautiful person in the age she lived in; of great honour and virtue, infinite sweetness and generosity of temper, and true good sense." (A eulogy, as far as the "good sense" is concerned, not quite consistent with his remark to "Stella," under date Dec. 11, 1710.) She was the especial "toast" at the not too respectable *Kit-cat Club*. She was sister of Sir James Long, and niece of Colonel Strangways. By her imprudence she fell into money difficulties, and, neglected by her former friends, she died in poverty and obscurity, under an assumed name, in Lynn, in Norfolk. Swift notices her death in his letter of Dec. 25, 1711:—"I never was more afflicted at any death. The poor creature had retired to Lynn two years ago to live cheap, and pay her debts. In her last letter she told me, she hoped to be easy by Christmas; and she kept her word, although she meant it otherwise. She had all sorts of amiable qualities, and no ill ones but the indiscretion of too much neglecting her own affairs. . . . I believe melancholy helped her on to her grave. I have ordered a paragraph to be put in the *Post-Boy*, giving an account of her death, and making honourable mention of her, which is all I can do to serve her memory: but one reason was spite; for her brother would fain have her death a secret, to save the charge of bringing her up here to bury her, or going in mourning."

[2] By the Allies. There are two towns of this name in France—the Aire here referred to lies near to St. Omer.

off little MD no longer. Pray give the under note to Mrs. Brent. I am a pretty gentleman; and you lose all your money at cards, sirrah Stella. I found you out, I did so. I am staying before I can fold up this letter, till that ugly D is dry in the last line but one. Do not you see it? O Lord, I am loth to leave you, faith—but it must be so till next time. Pox take that D! I will blot it to dry it.

To Miss Johnson.

Chelsea, May 24, 1711.

Morning.—Once in my life the number of my letters and of the month is the same; that's lucky, boys, that's a sign that things will meet and that we shall make a figure together. What, will you still have the impudence to say *London, England*, because I say *Dublin, Ireland*? Is there no difference between London and Dublin, saucyboxes? I have sealed up my letter, and am going to town. Morrow, sirrahs. *At night.*—I dined with the Secretary to-day, we sat down between five and six. Mr. Harley's patent passed this morning. He is now Earl of Oxford, Earl Mortimer, and Lord Harley of Wigmore Castle. My letter was sealed, or I would have told you this yesterday. but the public news may tell it you. The Queen, for all her favour, has kept a rod [the Treasurer's staff] for him in her closet this week. I suppose he will take it from her, though, in a day or two. At eight o'clock this evening it rained prodigiously, as it did from five. However, I set out, and in half way the rain lessened, and I got home, but tolerably wet; and this is the first wet walk I have had for a month's time that I am here.[1] But, however, I got to bed, after a short visit to Atterbury.

[1] An exceptional month. Almost throughout the three years' letters, Swift's records of the weather—either of extreme cold and rain or of extreme heat—instruct us that there was at least as much subject matter for weather-grumblers one hundred and eighty years ago as there can possibly be now. The superiority of the "old-fashioned" seasons, in fact, exists in the imagination of the *laudator temporis acti* rather than in the meteorological annals. Cf. Walpole's frequent lamentations over the weather.

May 25.

It rained this morning, and I went to town by water; and Ford and I dined with Mr. Lewis by appointment. I ordered Patrick to bring my gown and periwig to Mr. Lewis, because I designed to see Lord Oxford, and so I told the dog, but he never came; then I stayed a hour longer than I appointed. So I went in my old gown, and sat with him two hours, but could not talk over some business I had with him; so he has desired me to dine with him on Sunday, and I must disappoint the Secretary. My lord set me down at a coffee-house, where I waited for [Atterbury] the Dean of Carlisle's chariot to bring me to Chelsea; for the Dean did not come himself, but sent me his chariot, which has cost me two shillings to the coachman; and so I am got home, and Lord knows what is become of Patrick. I think I must send him over to you, for he is an intolerable rascal. If I had come without a gown, he would have served me so, though my life and preferment would have lain upon it; and I am making a livery for him will cost me four pounds; but I will order the tailor to stop till further orders. My Lord Oxford can't yet abide to be called "My Lord," and, when I called him "My Lord," he called me Dr. Thomas Swift,[1] which he always does when he has a mind to teaze me. By a second hand, he proposed my being his Chaplain, which I, by a second hand, excused. But we had no talk of it to-day; but I will be no man's Chaplain alive. But I must go, and be busy.

May 26.

I never saw Patrick till this morning, and that only once; for I dressed myself without him, and when I went to town he was

[1] Swift's little " parson-cousin," as he always termed him contemptuously, who had resided at the same time with himself at Moor Park, in quality of Chaplain. One cause of Swift's dislike for his cousin was his having audaciously laid claim to part-authorship in the *Tale of a Tub*.

out of the way. I immediately sent for the tailor, and ordered him to stop his hand in Patrick's clothes till further orders. Oh, if it were in Ireland, I should have turned him off ten times ago; and it is no regard to him, but myself, that has made me keep him so long. Now I am afraid to give the rogue his clothes. What shall I do? I wish MD were here to entreat for him, just here at the bed's side. Lady Ashburnham has been engaging me this long time to dine with her, and I set to-day apart for it; and, whatever was the mistake, she sent me word she was at dinner and undressed, but would be glad to see me in the afternoon. So I dined with Mrs. Vanhomrigh, and would not go to see her at all, in a huff. As I was coming home to-night, Sir Thomas Mansel and Tom Harley[1] met me in the Park, and made me walk with them till nine, like unreasonable whelps. So I got not here till ten; but it was a fine evening, and the footpath clean enough already after this hard rain.

May 29.

I was this morning in town by ten, though it was shaving day, and went to the Secretary about some affairs; then visited the Duke and Duchess of Ormond, but the latter was dressing to go out, and I could not see her. My Lord Oxford had the Staff given him this morning; so now I must call him Lord Oxford no more, but Lord Treasurer. I hope he will stick there; this is twice he has changed his name this week, and I heard to-day in the city (where I dined), that he will very soon have the Garter. Prithee, don't you observe how strangely I have changed my company and manner of living? I never go to a coffee-house. You hear no more of Addison, Steele, Henley, Lady Lucy,

[1] Son of the Premier. Mansel, according to Swift, was famous for bad dinners and a stingy wife, although he was enormously rich. He was a member of the *October Club*.

Mrs. Finch, Lord Somers, Lord Halifax, &c.[1] I think I have altered for the better. Did I tell you the Archbishop of Dublin has writ me a long letter of a squabble in your town about choosing a Mayor, and that he apprehended some censure for the share he had in it.[2] I have not heard anything of it here; but I shall not always be able to defend him. We hear your Bishop Hickman [of Derry] is dead; but nobody here will do anything for me in Ireland, so they may die as fast or slow as they please. . . .

May 30.

I am so hot and lazy after my morning's walk, that I loitered at Mrs. Vanhomrigh's, where my best gown and periwig was; and out of mere listlessness dine there very often—so I did to-day. But I got little MD's letter, No. 15 (you see, sirrahs, I remember to tell the number), from Mr. Lewis, and I read it in a closet they lend me at Mrs. Van's, and I find Stella is a saucy rogue and a great writer, and can write finely still when her hand's in, and her pen good. When I came here to-night, I had a mighty mind to go swim after I was cool; for my lodging is just by the river, and I went down with only my night gown and slippers on at eleven, but came up again. However, one of these nights I will venture.

May 31.

I was so hot this morning with my walk, that I resolved to do so no more during this violent burning weather. It is

[1] Anthony Henley, of the Grange, Hampshire, a contributor to Steele's *Tatler*, and the author of the paper which lost the editor his place of gazetteer. Garth dedicated his *Dispensary* to him. Lady Lucy Stanhope was one of Swift's greatest admirers (great Whig lady though she was).

[2] This "squabble" he refers to in a former letter (May 23). Four Tory mayors had been rejected by the Whig majority in the Dublin Corporation. The Whig Archbishop King's letter betrays anxiety as to the impression his part in the matter might produce in the London Cabinet.

comical that, now we happen to have such heat to ripen the fruit, there has been the greatest blast that ever was known, and almost all the fruit is despaired of. I dined with Lord Shelburne. Lady Kerry and Mrs. Pratt[1] are going to Ireland. I went this evening to Lord Treasurer's, and sat about two hours with him in mixed company. He left us and went to Court, and carried two staves with him, so I suppose we shall have a new Lord Steward or Comptroller to-morrow. I smoked that State-secret out by that accident. I won't answer your letter yet, sirrahs, no, I won't, madam. . . .

June 4.

When must we answer this letter, this No. 15 of our little MD? Heat, and laziness, and Sir Andrew Fountaine, made me dine to-day again at Mrs. Van's; and, in short, this weather is insupportable. How is it with you? Lady Betty Butler and Lady Ashburnham sat with me two or three hours this evening in my closet at Mrs. Van's. They are very good girls, and, if Lady Betty went to Ireland, you should let her be acquainted with you. How does Dingley do this hot weather? Stella, I think, never complains of it; she loves hot weather. There has not been a drop of rain since Friday se'ennight. Yes, you do love hot weather, naughty Stella, and Presto can't abide it. Be a good girl, then, and I'll love you; and love one another, and don't be quarrelling girls.

June 6.

I dined in the city to-day, and went hence early to town, and visited the Duke of Ormond and Mr. Secretary [St. John.] They

[1] Irish acquaintances. The former was one of his favourites. Under date of December 13, 1710, he records a round of sight seeing with a large party from Lord Shelburne's in three or four coaches, including the two ladies—the "lions," being the Tower, Bedlam, the Exchange, Gresham College, and, at night, the Puppet Show,—who all dined in the middle of the day at a "chop-house" behind the Exchange.

say my Lord Treasurer has a dead warrant in his pocket—they mean a list of those who are to be turned out of employment; and we every day now expect those changes. I passed by the Treasurer's to-day, and saw vast crowds waiting to give Lord Treasurer petitions as he passes by. He is now at the top of power and favour; he keeps no *levée* yet. I am cruel thirsty this hot weather. I am just this minute going to swim. I take Patrick down with me to hold my night-gown, shirt, and slippers, and borrow a napkin of my landlady for a cap. So farewell till I come up; but there's no danger, don't be frighted.—I have been swimming this half hour and more; and, when I was coming out, dived, to make my head and all through wet, like a cold bath; but, as I dived, the napkin fell off, and is lost, and I have that to pay for. O faith, the great stones were so sharp, I could hardly set my feet on them as I came out. It was pure and warm. I got to bed, and will now go sleep.

June 6.

Morning.—This letter shall go to-morrow; so I will answer yours when I come home to-night. I feel no hurt from last night's swimming. I lie with nothing but the sheet over me, and my feet quite bare. I must rise and go to town before the tide is against me. Morrow, sirrahs; dear sirrahs, morrow. *At night.*—I never felt so hot a day as this since I was born. I dined with Lady Betty Germaine, and there was the young Earl of Berkeley and his fine lady. I never saw her before, nor think her near so handsome as she passes for. After dinner Mr. Bertue would not let me put ice in my wine, but said my Lord Dorchester got the bloody flux with it, and that it was the worst thing in the world. Thus are we plagued, thus are we plagued; yet have I done it five or six times this summer, and was but the drier and hotter for it. Nothing makes me so excessively peevish as hot weather. Lady Berkeley, after dinner, clapped my hat on another lady's head, and she, in roguery, put it upon the rails. I minded them not, but in two minutes they called me to the window, and Lady Carteret showed me my hat out of her window five doors off, where I was forced to walk to it, and pay her and old Lady Weymouth a visit, with some more beldames. Then I went, and drank coffee, and made one or two puns with Lord Pembroke, and designed to go to Lord Treasurer; but it was too late, and besides I was half broiled, and broiled without butter, for I never sweat after dinner, if I drink any wine. Then I sat an hour with Lady Betty Butler at tea, and everything made me hotter and drier. Then I walked home, and was here by ten, so miserably hot that I was in as perfect a passion as ever I was in my life at the greatest affront or provocation. Then I sat an hour till I was quite dry and cool enough to go swim, which I did, but with so much vexation that I think I have given it over; for I was every moment disturbed by boats, rot them; and that puppy Patrick, standing ashore, would let them come within a yard or two, and then call sneakingly to them. The only comfort I proposed here in hot weather is gone, for there is no jesting with these boats after 'tis dark; I had none last night. I dived to dip my head, and held my cap on with both my hands, for fear of losing it. Pox take the boats! Amen. 'Tis near twelve, and so I'll answer your letter (it strikes twelve now) to-morrow morning.

June 7.

Morning. . . . Why, then, do you know in Ireland that Mr. St. John talked so in Parliament?[1] Your whigs are plaguily

[1] "I am heartily sorry," he writes on April 27, "to find my friend the Secretary [St. John] stands a little ticklish with the rest of the Ministry. There have been one or two disobliging things that have happened, too long to tell; and t'other day in Parliament, upon a debate of about thirty-five millions that have not been duly accounted for, Mr. Secretary, in his warmth of speech, and zeal for his friend Mr. Brydges [Paymaster-General of the Forces under the late Government], on whom part of the blame was falling

I

bit; for he is entirely for their being all out.—And are you as vicious in snuff as ever? I believe, as you say, it does neither hurt nor good; but I have left it off, and, when any body offers me their box, I take about a tenth part of what I used to do, and then just smell to it, and privately fling the rest away. I keep to my tobacco still,[1] as you say; but even much less of that than formerly, only mornings and evenings, and very seldom in the day. . . .

To Miss Johnson.

London, July 21, 22, 1711.

I dined yesterday with Lord Treasurer, who would needs take me along with him to Windsor, although I refused him several times, having no linen, &c. I had just time to desire Lord Forbes to call at my lodging, and order my man to send my things to-day to Windsor by his servant. I lay last night at the Secretary's [Bolingbroke's] lodgings at Windsor, and borrowed one of his shirts to go to Court in. The Queen is very well. I said, he did not know that either Mr. Brydges or the late Ministry were at all to blame in the matter; which was very desperately spoken, and giving up the whole cause. For the chief quarrel against the late Ministry was the ill-management of the Treasure, and was more than all the rest together. I had heard of this matter, but, Mr. Foley beginning to discourse to-day at table, without naming Mr. St. John, I turned to Mr. Harley, and said, if the late Ministry were not to blame in that article, he (Mr. Harley) ought to lose his head for putting the Queen upon changing them. He made it a jest; but, by some words dropped, I easily saw that they take things ill of Mr. St. John; and, by some hints given me from another hand that I deal with, I am afraid the Secretary will not stand long. This is the fate of Courts. I will, if I meet Mr. St. John alone on Sunday, tell him my opinion, and beg him to set himself right, else the consequences may be very bad. For I see not how they can well want [dispense with] him neither, and he would make a troublesome enemy."

[1] He does not mean smoking, which he never practised, but snuffing up cut and dry tobacco, which sometimes was just coloured with Spanish snuff; and this he used all his life, but would not own that he took snuff.—*Deane Swift.*

dined with Mr. Masham; and, not hearing anything of my things, I got Lord Winchelsea to bring me to town. Here I found that Patrick had broke open the closet to get my linen and night-gown, and sent them to Windsor, and there they are; and he, not thinking I would return so soon, is gone upon his rambles. So here I am left destitute, and forced to borrow a night-gown of my landlady, and have not a rag to put on to-morrow. Faith, it gives me the spleen.

July 23.

Morning.—It is a terrible rainy day, and rained prodigiously on Saturday night. Patrick lay out last night, and is not yet returned. Faith, poor Presto is a desolate creature—neither servant, nor linen, nor anything. *Night.*—Lord Forbes's man has brought back my portmantua, and Patrick is come; so I am in Christian circumstances. I shall hardly commit such a frolic again. I just crept out to Mrs. Van's and dined, and stayed there the afternoon. It has rained all this day. Windsor is a delicious place; I never saw it before, except for an hour, about seventeen years ago. Walls has been here in my absence —I suppose to take his leave, for he designed not to stay above five days in London. He says he and his wife will come here for some months next year; and, in short, he dares not stay now for fear of her.

July 24.

I dined to-day with a hedge-friend in the city, and Walls overtook me in the street, and told me he was just getting on horseback for Chester. He had as much curiosity as a cow; he lodged with his horse in Aldersgate Street. He has bought his wife a silk gown, and himself a hat. And what are you doing? What is poor MD doing now? How do you pass your time at Wexford? How do the waters agree with you? Let Presto know soon; for Presto longs to know, and must know. Is not Madame Proby curious company? I am afraid this rainy weather will spoil your waters. We have had a great deal of wet these three days. Tell me all the particulars of Wexford—the place, the company, the diversions, the victuals, the wants, the vexations. Poor Dingley never saw such a place in her life—sent all over the town for a little parsley, and it was not to be had! The butter is stark naught, except an old Englishwoman's! I am glad you carried down your sheets with you, else you must have lain in sackcloth. O Lord! . . .

July 26.

Mr. Addison and I have at last met again. I dined with him and Steele to-day at young Jacob Tonson's. The two Jacobs[1] think it is I who have made the Secretary take from them the printing of the *Gazette*, which they are going to lose, and Ben Tooke and another are to have it. Jacob came to me t'other day to make his court; but I told him it was too late, and that it was not my doing. I reckon they will lose it in a week or two. Mr. Addison and I talked as usual, and as if we had seen one another yesterday; and Steele and I were very easy, though I writ him a biting letter,[2] in answer to one of his, where he desired me to recommend a friend of his to Lord Treasurer. Go, get you gone to your waters, sirrah. Do they give you a stomach? Do you eat heartily? We had much rain to-day and yesterday.

July 28.

Morning.—Mr. Secretary sent me word he will call at my lodgings by two this afternoon, to take me to Windsor, so I

[1] Old Jacob was the celebrated bookseller of Dryden: he was a violent Whig, and secretary to the Kit-cat Club, which might seem a good reason to the Tory Ministers for taking the *Gazette* from him.—S.

[2] The old friendship between Steele and Swift had been interrupted by political differences; and, in the pages of the *Guardian* and *Examiner*, the quarrel was maintained with sufficient animosity on either side.

must dine nowhere, and I promised Lord Treasurer to dine with him to-day; but, I suppose, we shall dine at Windsor at five, for we make but three hours there. I am going abroad, but have left Patrick to put up my things, and to be sure to be at home half-an-hour before two.

Windsor, at night.—We did not leave London till three, and dined here betwixt six and seven; at nine I left the company, and went to see Lord Treasurer, who is just come. I chid him for coming so late: he chid me for not dining with him; said he staid an hour for me. Then I went and sat an hour with Mr. Lewis, till just now, and 'tis past eleven. I lie in the same house with the Secretary, one of the prebendaries' houses. The Secretary is not come from his apartment in the Castle. Do you think, that abominable dog Patrick was out after two to-day, and I in a fright every moment for fear the chariot should come; and, when he came in, he had not put up one rag of my things. I never was in a greater passion, and would certainly have cropped one of his ears, if I had not looked every moment for the Secretary, who sent his equipage to my lodging before, and came in a chair from Whitehall to me, and happened to stay half-an-hour later than he intended. One of Lord Treasurer's servants gave me a letter from —, with an offer of fifty pounds to be paid in what manner I pleased; because, he said, he desired to be well with me. I was in a rage, but my friend Lewis cooled me, and said it is what the best men sometimes meet with; and I have not seldom been served in the like manner, although not so grossly. In these cases I never demur a moment, nor ever found the least inclination to take anything. Well, I'll go try sleep in my new bed, and to dream of poor Wexford MD and Stella that drinks water, and Dingley that drinks ale.

July 29.

I was at Court and church to-day, as I was this day se'ennight. I generally am acquainted with about thirty in the drawing-room, and am so proud I make all the lords come up to me. One passes half-an-hour pleasant enough. We had a dunce to preach before the Queen to-day—which often happens. Windsor is a delicious situation, but the town is scoundrel. I dined with the Secretary; we were a dozen in all—three Scotch lords, and Lord Peterborow. Duke Hamilton would needs be witty, and hold up my train as I walked upstairs. It is an ill circumstance, that on Sundays much company meet always at the great tables. Lord Treasurer told at Court what I said to Mr. Secretary on this occasion. The Secretary showed me his bill of fare, to encourage me to dine with him. "Poh," said I, "show me a bill of company, for I value not your dinner." See how this is all blotted. I can write no more here, but to tell you I love MD dearly, and God bless them. . . .

August 2.

I have been now five days at Windsor, and Patrick has been drunk three times that I have seen, and oftener I believe. He has lately had clothes that have cost me five pounds, and the dog thinks he has the whip-hand of me. He begins to master me, so now I am resolved to part with him, and will use him without the least pity. The Secretary and I have been walking three or four hours to-day. The Duchess of Shrewsbury [1] asked him, was not that Dr.—Dr.—, and she could not say my name in English, but said Dr. Presto, which is Italian for *Swift*. Whimsical enough, as Billy Swift says. . . .

[1] The Duchess was daughter of the Marquis Paleotti, of Bologna, who descended, by the mother's side, from Robert, Earl of Leicester. She had been only a short time in England, since the Duke's appointment as Lord Chamberlain.—Purves.

August 4-5.

I dined yesterday at Buckleberry, where we lay two nights, and set out this morning at eight, and were here at twelve. In four hours we went twenty-six miles.[1] Mr. Secretary was a perfect country gentleman at Buckleberry; he smoked tobacco with one or two neighbours; he inquired after the wheat in such a field; he went to visit his hounds, and knew all their names. He and his lady saw me to my chamber, just in the country fashion. His house is in the midst of near three thousand pounds a-year he had by his lady, who is descended from Jack of Newbury,[2] of whom books and ballads are written; and there is an old picture of him in the house. She is a great favourite of mine. I lost church to-day; but I dressed and shaved and went to Court, and would not dine with the Secretary, but engaged myself to a private dinner with Mr. Lewis, and one friend more. We go to London to-morrow; for Lord Dartmouth, the other Secretary, is come, and they are here their weeks by turns.

August 6.

Lord Treasurer comes every Saturday to Windsor, and goes away on Monday or Tuesday. I was with him this morning at his *levée*, for one cannot see him otherwise here, he is so hurried. We had some talk, and I told him I would stay this week at Windsor by myself, where I can have more leisure to do some business that concerns them. Lord Treasurer and the Secretary thought to mortify me; for they told me they had been talking

[1] The frightful roads, and the heavy, lumbering coaches considered, by no means slow travelling.

[2] John Winchescombe, a clothier of Newbury, who kept a hundred looms at work. He marched to Flodden with one hundred of his workpeople, clothed and armed at his own cost; and then quietly returned to his own trade.—P. The lady, daughter and heiress of Sir H. Winchcomb, of Bucklersbury, in Berkshire, was Bolingbroke's first wife.

a great deal of me to-day to the Queen, and she said she had never heard of me. I told them that was their fault, and not hers, &c.; and so we laughed. . . .

August 8.

There was a Drawing-room to-day at Court; but so few company, that the Queen sent for us into her bedchamber, where we made our bows, and stood, about twenty of us, round the room, while she looked at us round with her fan in her mouth, and once a minute said about three words to some that were nearest her; and then she was told dinner was ready, and went out. I dined at the Green Cloth by Mr. Scarborow's invitation, who is in waiting. It is much the best table in England, and costs the Queen a thousand pounds a month, while she is at Windsor or Hampton Court; and is the only mark of magnificence or hospitality I can see in the Queen's family. It is designed to entertain foreign ministers, and people of quality, who come to see the Queen, and have no place to dine at. . . .

August 10.

Mr. Vice-Chamberlain [Coke] lent me his horses to ride about and see the country this morning. Dr. Arbuthnot, the Queen's physician and favourite, went out with me to shew me the places. We went a little after the Queen, and overtook Miss Forester, a maid of honour, on her palfrey, taking the air. We made her go along with us. We saw a place they have made for a famous horse-race to-morrow, where the Queen will come. We met the Queen coming back, and Miss Forester stood, like us, with her hat off, while the Queen went by. The doctor and I left the lady where we found her, but under other conductors. Much company is come to town this evening, to see to-morrow's race. I was tired with riding a trotting, mettlesome horse a dozen miles, having not been on horseback this twelvemonth. And Miss Forester did not make it easier. She is a silly, true maid of honour, and I did not like her, although she be a *toast*, and was dressed like a man.[1]

August 11.

I will send this letter to-day. I expect the Secretary by noon. I will not go to the race, unless I can get room in some coach. It is now morning. I must rise, and fold up and seal my letter. Farewell, and God preserve dearest MD. I believe I shall leave this town on Monday.

To Miss Johnson.

Windsor, August 11, 1711.

I sent away my twenty-seventh this morning in an express to London, and directed to Mr. Reading. This shall go to your lodgings, where, I reckon, you will be returned before it reaches you. I intended to go to the race to-day, but was hindered by a visit. I believe I told you so in my last. I dined to-day at the Green Cloth,[2] where everybody had been at the race but myself, and were twenty in all, and very noisy company; but I made [Coke] the Vice-Chamberlain, and two friends more, sit at a side-table to be a little quiet. At six I went to see the Secretary, who is returned [from his diplomatic mission to the Hague]; but Lord Keeper sent to desire I would sup with him, where I staid till just now. Lord Treasurer and Secretary were to come to us, but both failed. . . .

August 14.

We came to town this day in two hours and forty minutes; twenty miles are nothing here. I found a letter from the Arch-

[1] In a riding-habit, just then coming into fashion. Miss Forester had been married to Sir John Downing in 1701, when he was fifteen, and she but thirteen. They were divorced by mutual consent, springing from mutual aversion.—P.

[2] The table set apart for the guests at Windsor.

bishop of Dublin, sent me the Lord knows how. He says some of the [Irish] Bishops will hardly believe that Lord Treasurer got the Queen to remit the First-Fruits before the Duke of Ormond was declared Lord-Lieutenant, and that the Bishops have written a letter to Lord Treasurer to thank him. He has sent me the Address of Convocation ascribing, in good part, that affair to the Duke, who had less share in it than MD; for, if it had not been for MD, I should not have been so good a solicitor. I dined to-day in the City, about a little bit of mischief with a printer. I found Mrs. Vanhomrigh all in combustion, squabbling with her rogue of a landlord. She has left her house, and gone out of our neighbourhood a long way.[1] Her eldest daughter is come of age, and going to Ireland to look after her fortune, and get it in her own hands.[2]

August 15.

I dined to-day with Mrs. Van, who goes to-night to her new lodgings. . . He [Oxford] desired me to dine with him on Friday, because there would be a friend of his that I must see. My Lord Harley [3] told me, when he was gone, that it was Mrs. Masham his father meant, who is come to town to lie in, and whom I never saw, though her husband is one of our [October] Society. God send her a good time; her death would be a terrible thing. Do you know that I have ventured all my credit with these great Ministers, to clear some misunderstandings between them? And, if there be no breach, I ought to have

[1] Two months later he writes that Mrs. Vanhomrigh, who seems to have been peculiarly unfortunate in her choice of "landlord" and "landladies," had changed her lodgings again, having found her landlady to be a keeper of a house of "ill-fame." Swift already had suspected this Dame Quickly "by her eyebrows."

[2] Excepting once before, on the occasion of a birthday-feast, this is the only occasion on which Swift mentions the daughter who, under the name of Vanessa, was to be so closely connected with him.

[3] Lord Oxford's son.

the merit of it. 'Tis a plaguy ticklish sort of work, and a man hazards losing both sides. 'Tis a pity the world does not know my virtue. I thought the Clergy in Convocation, in Ireland, would have given me thanks for being their solicitor; but I hear of no such thing. Pray, talk occasionally on that subject, and let me know what you hear. Do you know the greatness of my spirit—that I value their thanks not a rush? but, at my return, shall freely let all people know that it was my Lord Treasurer's action, wherein the Duke of Ormond had no more share than a cat. And so they may go whistle, and I'll go sleep.

August 17.

I dined to-day at Lord Treasurer's with Mrs. Masham,[1] and she is extremely like one Mrs. Malolly, that was once my landlady in Trim. She was used with mighty kindness and respect, like a favourite. It signifies nothing, going to this Lord Treasurer about business, although it be his own. He was in haste, and desires I will come again, and dine with him to-morrow. His famous lying porter has fallen sick, and they think he will die. I wish I had all my half-crowns.[2] I believe I have told you he is an old Scotch fanatic, and the damn'dest liar in his office alive. I have a mind to recommend Patrick to succeed

---

[1] *Née* Abigail Hill, a relative, and formerly dependant, of Sarah, Duchess of Marlborough, whom she supplanted in the Queen's favour. She privately married (1707) Mr. Masham, groom of the bedchamber to the Queen's husband, Prince George, the Queen herself attending the ceremony. She shortly afterwards became Lady Masham, her husband having been made one of the Peers, who were created to balance against the Whig Lords, who happened, at that time, to be in the majority in the Upper House.

[2] Swift frequently laments his forced expenditure in the way of fees paid to the great man's great men, porters, and *hoc genus omne*. E.G.—On Dec. 26, 1710, he complains: "By the Lord Harry, I shall be undone here with Christmas boxes. The rogues at the coffee-house have raised their tax, every one giving a crown, and I gave mine for shame, besides a great many half-crowns to great men's porters, &c."

him. I have trained him up pretty well. I reckon for certain you are now in town. The weather now begins to alter to rain. . . .

August 19.

The Queen did not stir out to day; she is in a little fit of the gout. I dined at Mr. Masham's: we had none but our own society members, six in all, and I supped with Lord Treasurer. The Queen has ordered twenty thousand pounds to go on with the building of Blenheim, which has been starved till now, since the change of the Ministry. I suppose it is to reward his last action of getting into the French lines.[1] Lord Treasurer kept me till past twelve. . . .

To Miss Johnson.
London, October 3, 1711.

. . . Mr. Masham sent this morning to desire I would ride out with him, the weather growing again very fine. I was very busy, and sent my excuses, but desired he would provide me a dinner. I dined with him, his lady, and her sister, Mrs. Hill, who invites us to-morrow to dine with her, and we are to ride out in the morning. I sat with Lady Oglethorpe till eight this evening; then was going home to write—looked about for the woman who keeps the key of the house; she told me Patrick had it. I cooled my heels in the cloisters till nine, then went in to the music meeting, where I had been often desired to go; but was weary in half-an-hour of their fine stuff,[2] and stole out so

[1] Before Bouchain, a town in the north-east of France, not far from Cambrai. This affair was held to be one of Marlborough's greatest military achievements.

[2] Swift rather hated than loved music. Music and mathematics he made the two chief pursuits of the ridiculous Laputans —P. Possibly, his aversion was for *fashionable* music only.

privately that everybody saw me, and cooled my heels in the cloisters again till after ten. Then came in Patrick. I went up, shut the chamber door, and gave him two or three swinging cuffs on the ear, and I have strained the thumb of my left hand with pulling him, which I did not feel till he was gone. He was plaguily afraid and humbled.

October 4.

It was the finest day in the world, and we got out before eleven, a noble caravan of us. The Duchess of Shrewsbury in her own chaise with one horse, and Miss Touchet with her. Mrs. Masham and Mrs. Scarborow, one of the dressers, in one of the Queen's chaises; Miss Forester and Miss Scarborow, two maids of honour, and Mrs. Hill, on horseback. The Duke of Shrewsbury, Mr. Masham, George Fielding, Arbuthnot, and I, on horseback too. Mrs. Hill's horse was hired for Miss Scarborow, but she took it in civility: her own horse was galled, and could not be rid, but kicked and winced; the hired horse was not worth eighteenpence. I borrowed coat, boots, and horse, and, in short, we had all the difficulties, and more than we used to have, in making a party from Trim to Longfield's.[1] My coat was light camlet, faced with red velvet and silver buttons. We rode in the Great Park and the forest about a dozen miles, and the Duchess and I had much conversation. We got home by two, and Mr. Masham, his lady, Arbuthnot, and I dined with Mrs. Hill. Arbuthnot made us all melancholy; he expects a cruel fit of the stone in twelve hours. He says he is never mistaken, and he appears like a man that is to be racked to-morrow. I cannot but hope it will not be so bad; he is a perfectly honest man, and one I have much obligation to. . . '.

[1] At Killibride, about four miles from Trim. The roadless condition of Ireland must be remembered.—P.

To Archbishop King.

London, March 29, 1712.

I cannot ask pardon for not sooner acknowledging your Grace's letter, because that would look as if I thought mine were of consequence. Either I grow weary of politics, or am out of the way of them, or there is less stirring than usual, and, indeed, we are all in suspense at present; but I am told that, in ten or twelve days' time, we shall know what the issue will be at Utrecht. I can only tell your Grace that there are some unlucky circumstances, not proper to be trusted to a letter, which have hitherto retarded this great work. *Mihi ludibria rerum mortalium cunctis in negotiis observantur.*

Meantime, we are with great difficulty raising funds upon which to borrow *five millions*. One of these funds is a tax upon paper, and, I think, thirty *per cent.* upon imported books; and of such a nature as I could not yesterday forbear saying to my Lord Treasurer and the Chancellor of the Exchequer that, instead of preventing small papers and libels, it will leave nothing else for the Press. I have not talked to the Duke of Argyle upon the affairs of Spain since his return: but am told he affirms it impossible for us to carry on the loan there by our former methods. The Duke of Ormond is expected to go, in two or three days, for Flanders; and what I writ to your Grace, some months ago, of the Duke of Shrewsbury succeeding to govern Ireland, will, I suppose, be soon declared. I went the other day to see the Duchess, and reported your Grace's compliments, which she took very well, and I told her I was resolved your Grace and she should be very good acquaintance. I believe the spirit of your *Houghers* [1] has got into our *Mohawks*, who

---

[1] The horrible and barbarous cruelty of *houghing* thus seems to be of ancient date in Ireland.

are still very troublesome, and every night cut somebody or other over the face, aud commit a hundred insolent barbarities.

There was never the least design of any impeachment against the Duke of Marlborough; and it was his over-great weakness, or the folly of his friends, that the thing went so far as it did.

I know not whether it is that people have talked themselves hoarse; but, for some weeks past, we have heard less of the Pretender than formerly. I suppose it is, like a fashion, got into Ireland, when it is out here; but, in my conscience, I do not think any one person in the Court or Ministry here designs any more to bring in the Pretender than the Great Turk. I hope Mr. Harley, who is now on his journey to Hanover, will give that Court a truer opinion of persons and things than they have hitherto conceived. And, if your Grace knew the instrument through which these false opinions have been infused, you would allow it another instance of the *Ludibrium rerum mortalium*.[1] And your Grace cannot but agree that it is something singular for the Prince in possession to make perpetual advances, and the Presumptive heir to be standing off and suspicious.

I know not whether your Grace has considered the position that my Lord Treasurer is visibly in. The late Ministry and their adherents confess themselves fully resolved to have his head, whenever it is in their power; and were prepared, upon the beginning of the Sessions, when the vote was carried against any Peace without Spain, to move that he should be sent to the Tower. At the same time, his friends, and the Tories in general, are discontented at his slowness in the changing of commissions and employments, to which the weakness of the Court interest in the House of Lords is wholly imputed; neither do I find that those in the greatest stations, or most in the confidence of my

[1] M. Roberthon, the valet-de-chambre of the Elector of Hanover, was said to have considerable influence in prejudicing his m⸺er against Oxford's [Harley's] Administration.—S.

Lord Treasurer, are able to account for this proceeding, or seem satisfied with it. I have endeavoured to solve this difficulty another way; and I fancy I am in the right, from words I have heard let fall. But whatever be the cause, the consequences may be dangerous.

The Queen is in very good health, but does not use so much exercise as she ought. Pray God preserve her many years.

A projector has lately applied to me to recommend him to the Ministry about an invention for finding out the longitude. He has given in a petition to the Queen by Mr. Secretary St. John. I understand nothing of the mathematics, but I am told it is a thing as improbable as the *philosopher's stone* or *perpetual motion*. I lately writ a letter of about thirty pages to Lord Treasurer, by way of proposal for an Academy to correct, enlarge, and ascertain the English language. And he and I have named above twenty persons, of both parties, to be members. I will shortly print the letter, and I hope something will come of it. Your Grace sees I am something of a projector too. I am with great respect, &c.

To Miss Johnson.

Windsor, September 15, 1712.

I never was so long without writing to MD as now, since I left them,[1] nor ever will again, while I am able to write. I

[1] Swift's last letter is dated August 7. The last news of importance he had sent to Dublin had been the suppression of the anti-Ministerial papers by means of taxation :—" Do you know that Grub Street is dead and gone last week? No more ghosts or murders now for love or money. I plied it pretty close the past fortnight, and published at least seven penny Papers of

have expected, from one week to another, that something would be done in my own affairs; but nothing at all is, nor I don't know when anything will, or whether ever at all, so slow are people at doing favours. I have been much out of order of late, with the old giddiness in my head. I took a vomit for it two days ago, and will take another about a day or two hence. I have eaten mighty little fruit; yet I impute my disorder to that little, and shall henceforth wholly forbear it.[1]

I am engaged in a long work,[2] and have done all I can of it, and wait for some papers from the Ministry for materials for the rest; and they delay me, as if it were a favour I asked of them; so that I have been idle here this good while, and it happened in a right time, when I was too much out of order to study. One is kept constantly out of humour by a thousand unaccountable things in public proceedings; and, when I reason with some friends, we cannot conceive how affairs can last as they are. God only knows, but it is a very melancholy subject for those who have any near concern in it. I am again endeavouring, as I was last year, to prevent people from breaking to pieces upon a my own, besides some of other people's; but now every single half sheet pays a halfpenny to the Queen. The *Observator* is fallen; the *Medleys* are jumbled together with the *Flying Post*; the *Examiner* is deadly sick; the *Spectator* keeps up and doubles its price. I know not how long it will hold. Have you seen the red stamp the papers are marked with? Methinks it is worth a halfpenny, the stamping it." He also reports that: "Lord Bolingbroke [his friend the Secretary had just been made a Baron] and Prior set out for France last Saturday. My Lord's business is to hasten the Peace before the Dutch are too much mauled, and to hinder France from carrying the jest of beating them too far," and asks: "Have you seen the Fourth Part of *John Bull?* It is equal to the rest, and extremely good."

[1] Swift was strangely possessed of the prejudice that his peculiar maladies of giddiness and deafness, &c., had originated in a surfeit of fruit on one occasion in his youth. And this absured fancy has been gravely reported, as though credible, by some of his biographers. Dr. Johnson's way of dismissal of the story is one of the most sensible remarks in his *Life of Swift*:—" The original of diseases is commonly obscure; and almost every boy eats as much fruit as he can get, without any inconvenience."

[2] Apparently, the beginning of his contemporary History of Anne's reign. The *Conduct of the Allies* he had published in the preceding year.

hundred misunderstandings. One cannot withhold them from drawing different ways, while the enemy is watching to destroy them both. See how my style is altered by living, and thinking, and talking among these people, instead of my canal and rivers, walks and willows. I lose all my money here among the ladies, so that I never play when I can help it, being sure to lose. I have lost five pounds the five weeks I have been here. I hope Ppt. is luckier at picquet with the Dean and Mrs. Walls. The Dean never answered my letter, and I have clearly forgot whether I sent a bill for ME [1] in any of my last letters. I think I did: pray, let me know, and always give me timely notice. I wait here but to see what they will do for me; and whenever perferments are given from me, as hope saved, I will come over.

September 18.

I have taken a vomit to-day, and hope I shall be better. I have been very giddy since I wrote what is before, yet not as I used to be—more frequent, but not so violent. Yesterday we were alarmed with the Queen's being ill. She had an aguish and feverish fit; and you never saw such countenances as we all had, such dismal melancholy. Her physicians from town were sent for; but towards night she grew better. To-day she missed her fit, and was up; we are not now in any fear: it will be, at worst, but an ague, and we hope even that will not return. Lord Treasurer would not come here from London, because it would make a noise, if he came before his usual time, which is Saturday, and he goes away on Mondays. The Whigs have lost

---

[1] Initials, as Mr. Forster conjectures, for Madame Elderly (Mrs. Dingley). The words "as hope saved," a common expression of Swift in these letters, have been printed from the MS. by Mr. Forster, in place of the unintelligible "as — said" of the older editions. The full expression would be—"as I hope to be saved."

a great support in the Earl of Godolphin.[1] It is a good jest to hear the Ministers talk of him with humanity and pity, because he is dead and can do them no hurt. Lady Orkney,[2] the late King's Mistress (who lives at a fine place, five miles from hence, called Clifden), and I are grown mighty acquaintance. She is the wisest woman I ever saw; and Lord Treasurer made great use of her advice in the late change of affairs. I heard Lord Marlborough is growing ill of his *diabetes*, which, if it be true, may soon carry him off; and then the Ministry will be something more at ease.

MD has been a long time without writing to Presto, though they have not the same cause. It is seven weeks since your last came to my hands, which was No. 32, that you may not be mistaken. I hope Ppt. has not wanted her health. You were then drinking waters... My Lord Shrewsbury is certainly designed to be Governor of Ireland; and I believe the Duchess will please the people there mightily. The Irish Whig leaders promise great things to themselves from his Government; but

---

[1] The ex-Premier died on September 15.

[2] Lady Elizabeth Villiers. An estate in Ireland, of a rental of £20,000, had been settled upon her by her admirer, William III. Writing under date of October 30, of this year, he tells Esther Johnson: "Lady Orkney is making me a writing-table of her own contrivance, and a bed night-gown. She is perfectly kind, like a mother. I think the devil was in it the other day, that I should talk to her of an ugly squinting cousin of hers, and the poor lady herself, you know, squints like a dragon." She was sister-in-law of the Duchess of Hamilton, who, at the age of thirty-three, a fortnight later (Nov. 15), lost her husband, killed in a duel with Lord Mohun—not without suspicion of "foul play" at the hands of one of the Seconds, Mr. Macartney. The Duchess was inconsolable: nor did her sister-in-law's condolences (offered at the instance of Swift) effect the hoped-for good. In fact, "they have always been very ill together, and the poor Duchess could not have patience, when people told her I went often to Lady Orkney's. But I am resolved to make them friends." Two days afterwards (Nov. 17) he writes: "The Duchess told me Lady Orkney had been with her, and that she did not treat her as gently as she ought. They hate one another; but I will try to patch it up." The widowed Duchess he described as having "abundance of wit and spirit, handsome and airy, and seldom spared anybody that gave her the least provocation; by which she had many enemies and few friends."

care shall be taken, if possible, to prevent them. Mrs. Fenton[1] has writ to me that she has been forced to leave Lady Giffard, and come to town, for a rheumatism; that lady does not love to be troubled with sick people. Mrs. Fenton writes to me as one dying, and desires I would think of her son. I have not answered her letter. She is retired to Mrs. Povey's. Is my aunt alive yet, and do you ever see her? I suppose she has forgot the loss of her son. Is Raymond's new house quite finished? And does he squander as he used to do? Has he yet spent all his wife's fortune? I hear there are five or six people putting strongly in for my Livings. God help them! But, if ever the Court should give me anything, I would recommend Raymond to the Duke of Ormond—not for any particular friendship to him, but because it would be proper for the minister of Trim to have Laracor. You may keep the gold-studded snuff-box now; for my [Club] brother Hill, Governor of Dunkirk, has sent me the finest that ever you saw. It is allowed in Court that none in England comes near it, though it did not cost above twenty pounds. And the Duchess of Hamilton has made me a pocket for it, like a woman's, with a belt and buckle (for you know I wear no waistcoat in summer), and there are several divisions, and one on purpose for my box, oh, ho!

We have had most delightful weather this whole week; but illness and vomiting have hindered me from sharing in a great part of it. Lady Masham made the Queen send to Kensington for some of her preserved ginger for me, which I take in the morning, and hope it will do me good. I hope Parvisol has set

[1] Swift's only sister, who, against his wishes, had married, some ten or twelve years before, a currier, of Dublin, but a graduate of Trinity College. Upon the bankruptcy of her husband, she was allowed by her brother a small annuity, and she went to live with Lady Giffard at Moor Park. She died seven years before her brother, in 1739, in the house of Esther Johnson's mother, Mrs. Mose, at Farnham. The assertions of Lord Orrery and of Deane Swift, that Swift never saw or forgave his sister, after the marriage; or, that the cause of offence was the injury to his ambition, or a mercenary one, have been shown to be mere *hypotheses*.

my tithes well this year; he has writ nothing to me about it. Pray, talk to him of it when you see him, and let him give me an account how things are. I suppose the corn is now off the ground. I hope he has sold that great ugly horse. Why don't you talk to him ? He keeps me at charges for horses that I can never ride: yours is lame, and will never be good for anything. The Queen will stay here about a month longer, I suppose; but, Lady Masham will go in ten days to lie in at Kensington. Poor creature, she fell down in the Court here the other day. She would needs walk across it, upon some displeasure with her chairman, and was likely to be spoiled so near her time. But we hope all is over for a black eye and a sore side; though I shall not be at ease till she is brought to bed. I find I can fill up a letter, some way or other, without a journal. If I had not a spirit naturally cheerful, I should be very much discontented at a thousand things. Pray God preserve MD's health, and Pdfr's [1]; and that I may live far from the envy and discontent that attends those who are thought to have more favour at Court than they really possess.[2] Love Pdfr., who loves MD above all things. Farewell, deelest, ten thousand times deelest MD, MD, MD, FW, FW, ME, ME, ME, ME, Lele, Lele, Lele, Lele.

[1] Conjectured to stand for " Poor dear, foolish, rogues." The concluding sentences of this letter, as in many other instances, vary in the MS. from the printed editions. "Deelest," is Swift's usual way of writing dearest, according to the *little language*. "FW" may represent "Foolish, or Fond, Woman." "Lele" is supposed to represent "There." By analogy, *lele* ought rather to represent *really*. ME if applied to Stella, may represent "Mine Ever." But there is wide room for mere conjecture.

[2] A sort of prayer which we may take to have been far from unnecessary.

To Miss Vanhomrigh.[1]

Windsor, October, 1712.

I thought to have written to little Missessy by the Colonel, but at last I did not approve of him as a messenger. Mr. Ford began your health last night under the name of the *Jilt*, for which I desire you will reproach him. I do neither study nor exercise so much here as I do in town. The Colonel [2] will intercept all the news I have to tell you—of my fine snuff-box,[3] and my being at a ball, and my losing my money at Ombre with the Duke and Duchess of Shrewsbury.

I cannot imagine how you pass your time in our absence, unless by lying a-bed till twelve, and then having your followers about you till dinner. We have dispatches to-day from Lord Bolingbroke. All is admirably well, and a cessation of arms will be declared with France, in London, on Tuesday next. I dined with the Duke of Shrewsbury to-day, and sat an hour by Mrs. Warburton, teaching her when she played wrong at ombre, and I cannot see her defects. Either my eyes fail me, or they are partial. But Mrs. Touchet is an ugly, awkward slut. What do you do all the afternoon? How came you to make it a secret to me, that you all design to come to Windsor? If you were never here, I think you all cannot do better than come for

---

[1] Addressed, "At her lodgings, over against Park Place, in St. James's Street, London." This fatal correspondence seems to have commenced with Swift's residence in Windsor, in the autumn of 1712, while he was drawing together materials for his *History of the Peace of Utrecht*. It is, therefore, not wonderful that, about the same time, we find him apologising to Stella for the slackness of his correspondence.—S.

[2] Perhaps Vanessa's brother, who seems to have been in the army. He is sometimes called the Captain. Or more probably, Colonel Godfrey, mentioned in the Journal to Stella, an inhabitant of Windsor, whom Swift visited.—S.

[3] Presented to Swift by General Hill, Governor of Dunkirk, for his celebrated repartee to Lord Oxford, upon the subject of the snail and the goose, which were enchased on this snuff-box.—S.

three or four days. Five pounds will maintain you, and pay for your coach backwards and forwards. I suppose the Captain will go down with you now, for want of better company. I will steal to town one of these days, and catch you napping.

I desire you and Moll[1] will walk as often as you can in the Park, and do not sit moping at home, you that can neither work, nor read, nor play, nor care for company. I long to drink a dish of coffee in the Sluttery, and hear you dun me for *secrete*, and "Drink your coffee, why don't you drink your coffee?" My humble service to your mother, and Moll, and the Colonel. Adieu.[2]

To Miss Johnson.

London, April 1, 1713,

... The Swedish envoy told me to-day, at Court, that he was in great apprehensions about his master; and, indeed, we are afraid that Prince[3] is dead among those Turkish dogs. I prevailed on Lord Bolingbroke to invite Mr. Addison to dine with him on Good Friday. I suppose we shall be mighty mannerly. Addison is to have a Play on Friday in Easter week. 'Tis a tragedy called *Cato*. I saw it unfinished some years ago. Did I tell

[1] Miss Mary Vanhomrigh, whom he usually calls *Molkin*.

[2] A few weeks previously to this first of Swift's letters to her, that have been preserved, Hester Vanhomrigh had complained of his remissness in writing to her:—"Had I a correspondent in China," she reproaches him, "I might have had an answer by this time. I never could think till now that London was so far off in your thoughts; and that twenty miles were, by your computation, equal to some thousands."

[3] Charles XII., then a refugee at Bender, in Turkey, after the defeat at Poltava. The apprehensions as to the conduct of the Turks were groundless, as is well known. They, in fact, exhibited an astonishing degree of forbearance towards the expensive eccentricities and barbarisms of the northern hero.

you that Steele has begun a new daily paper, called the *Guardian* ?—they say good for nothing. I have not seen it. Night, dear MD. . . .

April 3.

I was at the Queen's Chapel to-day, but she was not there. Mr. St. John, Lord Bolingbroke's brother, came this day at noon with an express from Utrecht, that the Peace is signed by all the Ministers there but those of the Emperor, who, likewise, will sign in a few days ; so that now the great work is in effect done, and I believe it will appear a most excellent Peace for Europe, particularly for England. Addison and I, and some others, dined with Lord Bolingbroke, and sat with him till twelve. We were very civil, yet, when he grew warm, we talked in a friendly manner of Party. Addison raised his objections, and Lord Bolingbroke answered them with great complaisance. Addison began Lord Somer's health, which went about: but I bid him not name Lord Wharton's, for I would not pledge it, and I told Lord Bolingbroke frankly that Addison loved Lord Wharton as little as I did. So we laughed, &c. Well, but you are glad of the Peace, you Ppt. of a trimmer, are not you ? As for DD, I don't doubt her. Why now, if I did not think Ppt.[1] had been a violent Tory, and DD the greater Whig of the two ! It is late. Night, MD.

April 4.

This Passion week people are so demure, especially this last day, that I told Dilly, who called here, that I would dine with him. It rained all day. I came home at seven, and have never stirred out, but have been reading Sacheverell's long dull sermon, which

[1] Stands, perhaps, for *Poppet;* DD for Dear Dingley ?

he sent me.[1] It is his first sermon since his suspension has expired; but not a word in it upon the occasion, except two or three remote hints. . . .

April 6.

I was this morning, at ten, at the rehearsal of Mr. Addison's play called *Cato*, which is to be acted on Friday. There was not above half a score of us to see it. We stood on the stage, and it was foolish enough to see the actors prompted every moment, and the poet directing them; and the drab, that acts Cato's daughter,[2] out in the midst of a passionate part, and then calling out, "What's next?" The Bishop of Clogher was there too, but he stood privately in a gallery. I went to dine with Lord Treasurer, but he was gone to Wimbledon, his daughter Caermarthen's country seat, seven miles off. So I went back, and dined privately with Mr. Addison, whom I had left to go to Lord Treasurer. I keep fires yet; I am very extravagant. It is rainy weather again—never saw the like. This letter shall go to-morrow. Remember, young women, it is seven weeks since your last, and I allow you but five weeks; but you have been galloping in the country to Swanton's. . . .

[1] This sermon, the first preached after the expiration of the three years of silence imposed upon him by the House of Lords as part of his sentence, was entitled, *The Christian Triumph, on the Duty of Praying for our Enemies.* This clerical champion of the doctrine of "passive obedience," and "the right divine of kings to govern wrong," seems to have made a good speculation in the printing of his sermon—if the publisher did not. Swift writes to Stella, in the same letter: "I saw Dr. Sacheverell [at the Lord Treasurer's], who told us that the bookseller had given him £100 for his sermon, preached last Sunday, and intended to print 30,000. I believe he [the printer] will be confoundedly bit, and will hardly sell above half."

[2] Mrs. Oldfield—the famous actress, both tragic and comic, but especially comic. She was buried in Westminster Abbey. A portrait of her is in the National Gallery, at S. Kensington.

To Miss Johnson.

London, April 11, 1713.

. . . I dined at Lord Treasurer's with his Saturday company. We had ten at table, all lords but myself and the Chancellor of the Exchequer. Argyle went off at six, and was in very indifferent humour as usual. Duke of Ormond and Lord Bolingbroke were absent. I staid till near ten. Lord Treasurer showed us a small picture, enamelled work, and set in gold, worth about twenty pounds. A picture, I mean, of the Queen, which she gave to the Duchess of Marlborough, set in diamonds. When the Duchess was leaving England, she took off all the diamonds, and gave the picture to one Mrs. Higgins (an old intriguing woman, whom everybody knows), bidding her make the best of it she could. Lord Treasurer sent to Mrs. Higgins for this picture, and gave her a hundred pounds for it. Was ever such an ungrateful beast as that Duchess? Or did you ever hear such a story? I suppose the Whigs will not believe it. Pray, try them. She takes off the diamonds, and gives away the picture to an insignificant woman, as a thing of no consequence; and gives it to her to sell, like a piece of old-fashioned plate. Is she not a detestable slut? Night, dear MD.

April 12.

I went to Court to-day, on purpose to present Mr. Berkeley,[1] one of your fellows of Dublin College, to Lord Berkeley of Stratton. That Mr. Berkeley is a very ingenious man and great philosopher, and I have mentioned him to all the Ministers, and

[1] Afterwards the celebrated Bishop of Cloyne. Swift procured him the chaplaincy and secretaryship to Lord Peterborough, then going as Envoy to Sicily.—P.

have given them some of his writings; and I will favour him as much as I can. This I think I am bound to, in honour and conscience; to use all my little credit towards helping forward a man of worth in the world. The Queen was at chapel to-day, and looks well. I dined at Lord Orkney's, with the Duke of Ormond, and Sir Thomas Hanmer. Mr. St. John, secretary at Utrecht, expects every moment to return there with the ratification of the Peace. Did I tell you, in my last, of Addison's play called *Cato*, and that I was at the rehearsal of it? Night, MD.

April 13.

This morning my friend Mr. Lewis came to me, and showed me an order for a warrant for three Deaneries, but none of them to me. This is what I always foresaw, and received the notice of it better, I believe, than he expected. I bid Mr. Lewis tell my Lord Treasurer that I take nothing ill of him, but his not giving me timely notice, as he promised to do, if he found the Queen would do nothing for me. At noon Lord Treasurer, hearing I was in Mr. Lewis's office, came to me and said many things too long to repeat. I told him I had nothing to do but to go to Ireland immediately, for I could not, with any reputation, stay longer here, unless I had something honourable immediately given me. We dined together at the Duke of Ormond's. He there told me he had stopped the warrants for the Deans; that what was done for me might be at the same time, and he hoped to compass it to-night; but I believe him not. I told the Duke of Ormond my intentions. He is content Sterne should be a Bishop, and I have St. Patrick's; but I believe nothing will come of it—for stay I will not; and so I believe for all our. . . you may see me in Dublin before April ends. I am less out of humour than you would imagine; and if it were not that impertinent people will condole with me, as they used to give me joy, I would value it less. But I will avoid company, and muster up my baggage, and send them next Monday, by the carrier, to Chester, and come and see my willows, against the expectation of all the world. What care I? Night, dearest rogues, MD. . . .

April 16.

I was this noon at Lady Masham's, who was just come from Kensington, where her eldest son is sick. She said much to me of what she had talked to the Queen and Lord Treasurer. The poor lady fell a-shedding tears openly. She could not bear to think of my having St. Patrick's, &c. I was never more moved than to see so much friendship. I would not stay with her, but went and dined with Dr. Arbuthnot, with Mr. Berkeley, one of your fellows. Mr. Lewis tells me that the Duke of Ormond has been to-day with the Queen: and she was content that Dr. Sterne should be Bishop of Dromore, and I Dean of St. Patrick's; but then out came Lord Treasurer, and said he would not be satisfied, but that I must be prebendary of Windsor. Thus he perplexes things. I expect neither; but, I confess, as much as I love England, I am so angry at this treatment, that, if I had my choice, I would rather have St. Patrick's. Lady Masham says she will speak to the purpose to the Queen to-morrow. Night, dear MD.

April 17.

I went to dine at Lady Masham's to-day, and she was taken ill of a sore throat and aguish. She spoke to the Queen last night, but had not much time. The Queen says she will determine to-morrow with Lord Treasurer. The warrants for the Deaneries are still stopped, for fear I should be gone. Do you think anything will be done? I don't care whether it is or no. In the meantime, I prepare for my journey, and see no great people, nor will see Lord Treasurer any more, if I go. Lord Treasurer told Mr. Lewis it should be done to-night. So he said five nights ago. Night, MD.

April 21.

The Duke of Ormond has told the Queen he is satisfied Sterne should be Bishop, and she consents I should be Dean; and I suppose the warrants will be drawn in a day or two. I dined at an alehouse with Parnell and Berkeley, for I am not in humour to go among the Ministers, though Lord Dartmouth invited me to dine with him to-day, and Lord Treasurer was to be there. I said I would, if I were out of suspense.

April 22.

The Queen says warrants shall be drawn, but she will dispose of all in England and Ireland at once, to be teazed no more. This will delay it sometime, and, while it is delayed, I am not sure of the Queen, my enemies being busy. I hate this suspense. Night, dear MD.[1]

To MR. ADDISON.

May 13, 1713.

I was told yesterday, by several persons, that Mr. Steele had reflected upon me in his *Guardian*, which I could hardly believe, until, sending for the paper of the day, I found he had,

[1] The warrants were at length formally drawn, and the Deanery of St. Patrick's was granted to Swift, on the 25th of April. On the 6th of June the Dean elect writes to Esther Johnson, from Chester, that, after six days' riding on horseback, he has arrived at that city *en route* for Holyhead and Dublin.

in several parts of it, insinuated, with the utmost malice, that I was author [editor] of the *Examiner*, and abused me in the grossest manner he could possibly invent, and set his name to what he had written. Now, Sir, if I am not author of the *Examiner*, how will Mr. Steele be able to defend himself from the imputation of the highest degree of baseness, ingratitude, and injustice?

Is he so ignorant of my temper and of my style? Has he never heard that the author of the *Examiner*—to whom I am altogether a stranger—did, a month or two ago, vindicate me from having any concern in it? Should not Mr. Steele have first espostulated with me as a friend? Have I deserved this usage from Mr. Steele, who knows very well that my Lord Treasurer has kept him in his employment,[1] upon my entreaty and intercession? My Lord Chancellor and Lord Bolingbroke will be witnesses how I was reproached by my Lord Treasurer, upon the ill returns Mr. Steele made to his Lordship's indulgences.

To Mr. Steele.

London, May 27, 1713.

The reason I give you the trouble of this reply to your letter, is because I am going in a very few days to Ireland; and, although I intended to return toward winter, yet it may happen, from the common accidents of life, that I may never see you again.

In your yesterday's letter you are pleased to take the com-

[1] Of Commissioner in the Stamp Office.

plaining side, and think it hard I should write to Mr. Addison, as I did, only for an *allusion*.[1] This *allusion* was only calling a clergyman of some distinction an *infidel*—a clergyman who was your friend, who always loved you, who had endeavoured, at least, to serve you; and who, whenever he did write anything, made it sacred to himself never to fling out the least hint against you.

One thing you are pleased to fix on me, as what you are sure of : that the *Examiner* had talked after [at the bidding of] me, when he said, *Mr. Addison had bridled you in point of party*. I do not read one in six of those papers, nor ever knew he had such a passage; and I am so ignorant of this, that I cannot tell what it means—whether that Mr. Addison kept you close to a Party, or that he hindered you from writing about Party. I

[1] The former of the two letters from Steele to Swift, in regard to the remonstrance of the latter to Addison, is dated May 19. He writes: "Mr. Addison shewed me your letter wherein you mention me. They laugh at you, if they make you believe your interposition has kept me thus long in office. I am glad I have always treated you with respect, though I believe you an accomplice of the *Examiner's*. . . . You do not, in direct terms, say you are not concerned with him [the editor]; but make it an argument of your innocence that the *Examiner* has declared you have nothing to do with him. I believe I could prevail upon the *Guardian* to say there was a mistake in putting my name in his paper; but the English would laugh at us, should we argue in so Irish a manner. I am heartily glad," concludes Steele, "of your being made Dean of St. Patrick's."

Swift's reply to this letter is, in the MS., mutilated at the beginning and end. He reaffirms his interposition with the Ministry, and adds : "this is the history of what you think fit to call, in the spirit of insulting, *their laughing at me*, and you may do it securely ; for, by the most inhuman dealings, you have wholly put it out of my power, as a Christian, to do you the least ill-office. . . . I have several times assured Mr. Addison and fifty others, that I had not the least hand in writing any of these papers, and that I had never exchanged one syllable with the supposed author in my life, that I can remember. . . . I protest I never saw anything more liable to exception than every part of the letter you were pleased to write me. You plead : that I do not in mine to Mr. Addison, in direct terms, say I am not concerned in the *Examiner*. And is that an excuse for the most savage injuries in the world, a week before ? How far you can prevail with the *Guardian* I shall not trouble myself to inquire; and am more concerned how you will clear your own honour and conscience than my reputation."

never talked or writ to that author[1] in my life; so that he could not have learned it from me. And, in short, I solemnly affirm that, with relation to every friend I have, I am as innocent as it is possible for a human creature to be. And, whether you believe me or not, I think, with submission, you ought to act as if you believed me, till you have demonstration to the contrary. I have all the Ministry to be my witnesses, that there is hardly a man of wit of the adverse Party whom I have not been so bold as to recommend often, and with earnestness, to them. For I think principles, at present, are quite out of the case, and that we dispute wholly about persons. In these last you and I differ; but, in the other, I think we agree—for I have, in print, professed myself in *politics* to be what we formerly called a Whig.

As to the great man,[2] whose defence you undertake, though I do not think so well of him as you do, yet I have been the cause of preventing five hundred hard things being said against him.

I am sensible I have talked too much, when myself is the subject; therefore I conclude, with sincere wishes for your health and prosperity, and am, Sir, yours, &c.

You cannot but remember that, in the only thing I ever published with my name, I took care to celebrate you as much as I could, and in as handsome a manner, though it was in a letter to the present Lord Treasurer.[3]

[1] He means the then editor or conductor of the *Examiner*. Grammatically, Addison, is "that author;" but that, of course, is not so in fact.

[2] The Duke of Marlborough. Swift seems to have reserved to himself the right to vituperate the great Whig General; for the earlier *Examiners* contain a sufficient amount of strong language against him.

[3] *A Proposal for Correcting, Improving, and Ascertaining the English Tongue*, printed in May, 1712. Steele is "celebrated" in his character of editor of *The Spectator*. In a letter to Esther Johnson, May 31, of the same year, Swift writes: "Have you seen my *Letter* to the Lord Treasurer? There are two answers come out to it already, though it is no politics, but a harmless proposal about the improvement of the English tongue. I believe, if I writ an essay upon a straw, some fool would answer it."

To Mrs. Vanhomrigh.[1]

Chester, June 6, 1713.

You heard of me from Dunstable, by the way of Hessy. I have had a sad time since. If Moll's *even so* had been there, she would have none left. Now Hessy grumbles that I talk of Moll. I have resolved upon the direction of my letter already; for I reckon Hessy and Moll are widows as well as you, or at least half widows. Davila[2] goes off rarely now. I have often wished for a little of your ratsbane.[3] What I met on the road does not deserve the name of ratsbane.

I have told Mr. Lewis the circumstances of my journey, and the curious may consult him upon it. Who will Hessy get now to chide, or Moll to tell her stories, and bring her sugar-plums? We never know anything enough till we want it. I design to send Hessy a letter in print from Ireland, because she cannot read writing-hand, except from Mr. Partington. I hope you have heard again from the Colonel, and that he is fully cured of —, I don't know what, I forget. It was under cover to Mr. Lewis that I writ to you from Dunstable. I writ to Hessy, by Barber, from St. Albans. I left London without taking leave of Sir John. I fear a person of his civility will never pardon me.

[1] Addressed to "Madame Van. [the mother of Hester], at the sign of the Three Widows, in Pom-roy Alley. With care and speed."

[2] Hester Vanhomrigh and he, apparently, had been reading the Italian historian of *The Civil Wars of France* (1630), together. In a letter of the same date as this of Swift's to her mother, she wrote to him: "Pray why did you not remember me at Dunstable as well as Moll? Lord! what a monster is Moll grown since. But nothing of poor Hess, except that the mark will be in the same place of Davila where you left it. Indeed, it is not much advanced yet, for I have been studying of Rochefoucauld, to see if he described as much of love as I found in myself on Sunday; and I find he falls very short of it."

[3] Coffee, probably.—S.

I met no adventures in all my travels, only my horse fell under me, for which reason I will not ride him to Holyhead; I can assure him that. I could not see any marks in the chimney at Dunstable of the coffee Hessy spilt there, and I had no diamond-ring about me, to write any of your names in the windows. But I saw written, *Dearest Lady Betty Hamilton*, and hard by, *Middleton Walker*, whom I take to be an Irish man-midwife; which was a plain omen of her getting a husband. I hear Moor, the handsome parson, came over with the AB. of Dublin. Did he not marry one Mrs. Devenish? Lord Lanesborough has been here lately, in his way to Ireland, and has got the goodwill of all the folks in our town. He had something to say to every little boy he met in the streets. Well, he is the courteousest man, and nothing is so fine in the quality as to be courteous. Now Moll laughs, because I speak wisely, and now Hessy murmurs again.

Well, I had a charming handsome cousin here twenty years ago. I was to see her to-night, and, in my conscience, she is not handsome at all. I wonder how it comes about; but she is very good-natured, and you know, Moll, good-nature is better than beauty. I desire you will let me know what fellows Hessy has got to come to her bedside in a morning,[1] and when you design again to hobble to Chelsea; if you did not tell me a lie, as I must suspect. My head is something better, though not so well as I expected, by my journey. I think I have said enough for a poor weary traveller. I will conclude without ceremony, and go to bed. And, if you cannot guess who is the writer, consult your pillow, and the first fine gentleman you dream of is the man. So adieu.

[1] The French custom of ladies receiving visits at the toilette, or *ruette*, was then general.—S.

To Miss Vanhomrigh.

Laracor, July 8, 1713.

I stayed but a fortnight in Dublin, very sick, and returned not one visit of a hundred that were made me—but all to the Dean and none to the Doctor. I am riding here for life, and I think I am something better, and hate the thoughts of Dublin, and prefer a field-bed and an earthen floor before the great house there, which they say is mine. I had your last splenetic letter. I told you when I left England, I would endeavour to forget everything there, and would write as seldom as I could.[1] I did, indeed, design one general round of letters to my friends, but my health has not yet suffered me.

I design to pass the greatest part of the time, I stay in Ireland, here in the cabin where I am now writing; neither will I leave the kingdom till I am sent for, and, if they have no further service for me, I will never see England again. At my

---

[1] A fortnight before she received this letter Hester Vanhomrigh had written from London, impatiently : "Three long weeks have passed since you wrote to me. O happy Dublin that can occupy all your thoughts, and happy Mrs. Emerson that could hear from you the moment you landed! . . I really believe, before you leave Ireland, I shall give you just reason to wish I did not know my letters, or, at least, that I could not write : and I had rather you should wish so than entirely forget me. Confess—have you once thought of me since you wrote to my mother at Chester? Which letter, I assure you, I take very ill. My mother and I have counted the *Molls* and the *Hessys*. 'Tis true the number is equal; but you talk to Moll, and only say, *now Hessy grumbles*. How can you, indeed, possibly be so ill-natured to make me either quarrel or grumble, when you are at so great a distance that it is impossible for me to gain by doing so? Besides, you proposed the letter should be addressed to me; but I'll say no more of that, but keep my temper till we meet. Pray, have you received the letter I wrote you to Chester?" She concludes with telling him that: " Mr. Lewis has given me *Les Dialogues des Morts* [of Fontenelle]; and I am so charmed with them, that I am resolved to quit my body, let the consequence be what it will, except that *you* will talk to me: for I find no conversation on earth comparable but yours. So, if you care I should stay, do but *talk*, and you will keep me with pleasure."

first coming, I thought I should have died with discontent, and was horribly melancholy while they were *installing*; but it begins to wear off, and change to dulness. My river walk is extremely pretty, and my canal in great beauty, and I see trout playing in it. I know not anything in Dublin; but Mr. Ford is very kind, and writes to me constantly what passes among you. I find *you* are, likewise, a good politician, and I will say so much to you, that I verily think, if the thing you know of had been published just before the Peace,[1] the Ministry might have avoided what has since happened. But I am now fitter to look after willows, and to cut hedges, than to meddle with affairs of State. I must order one of the workmen to drive these cows out of my island, and make up the ditch again—a work much more proper for a country vicar than driving out factions and fencing against them. And I must go and take my bitter draught to ease my head, which is spoilt by the bitter draughts the public hath given me.

How does Davila go on? Johnny Clark is chosen *portreeve* of our town of Trim, and we shall have the assizes there next week, and fine doings; and I must go and borrow a horse to meet the Judges; and I and Beaumont, and all the boys that can get horses, will go too. Mr. Warburton[2] has but a thin school. Mr. Percival has built up the other side of his house, but people whisper it is but scurvily built. Mr. Steers is come to live in Mr. Melthorp's house, and 'tis thought the widow Melthorp will remove to Dublin. Nay, if you do not like this sort of news, I have no better; so go to your Dukes and Duchesses, and leave me to Goodman Bumford, and Patrick Dollan, of Glanduggan. Adieu.

[1] *The History of the Peace of Utrecht.*—S.
[2] His curate.

To Dr. Arbuthnot.

Letcombe, July 3, 1714.

I reckoned you would have held up for one letter, and so have given over—that is the usual way I treat my best absent friends, when I am in London. Did I describe myself in a happy state here? Upon my faith you read wrong. I have no happiness but being so far out of the way of the *Dragon*,[1] and the rest. Lewis reproaches me as one who has still an itch to the Court, only because I asked him how the *summa rerum* went. Was not that unjust? And quotes upon me, *Quæ lucis miseris tam dira Cupido!*[2] I do assert that living near a Court, with some circumstances, is a most happy life, and would be so still, if the *Dragon* did not spoil it.

I find the triumvirate of honest Counsellors is at an end. I am gone. Lewis says he lives in ignorance in his castle, and you meddle as little as you can. One thing still lies upon you, which is to be a constant adviser to Lady M[asham?] The game will, of course, be played into her hands. She has very good sense, but may be imposed upon, and I had a whisper that the Squire[3] plies there again. 'Tis as you say: if the *Dragon* speaks kindly of Parnell, he is gone. 'Tis the Ossorys that get the Derryes, and the Chesters the Yorks.[4] To talk of *Martin* [Scriblerus] in any hand but yours is a folly. You every day give better hints than all of us together could do in a twelvemonth. And to say the truth, Pope, who first thought of

---

[1] Robert Harley, Lord Oxford—the name by which he was known in the *Scriblerus* Club. He was now in retreat in Herefordshire, to which shire, at his urgent request, Swift soon followed him.

[2] "How can the wretched have so infatuated a longing for the light of day!" *Æneis* vi.

[3] Lord Bolingbroke. The familiar Scriblerus nickname.

[4] An obscure allusion to certain episcopal translations.

the hint, has no genius at all to it, in my mind. Gay is too young. Parnell has some ideas of it; but is idle. I could put together, and lard, and strike out well enough : but all that relates to the sciences must be from you. I am a vexed, unsettled vagabond, and my thoughts are turned towards some papers I have, and some other things I would fain get from you and Lady M——, and would have had from the *Dragon:* but that is impossible till he is out; and then I will go to him to Herefordshire, and make him give me hints. I have got my history[1] from Secretary Bromley; and they never shall have it again, and it shall be an altered thing, if I live.

The hints you mention relating to Medicine are admirable. I wonder how you can have a mind so *dégagé* in a Court, where there are so many millions of things to vex you. You must understand I have writ this post to the *Dragon*, but you must not take notice of it; nor I fancy will he, for what I writ is very odd and serious. I think to go and ramble for a month about Herefordshire and those parts. Ask the *Dragon* whether he will order his people at his Castle to receive me. Why do you not send your Parliament a-grazing ? What do you mean by your *Proclamation* and £5,000 ? Till I hear reasons, I dislike your politics. Why do I talk of it, say you? Why did that puppy, Barber, write of it to me? But the Commons offer £100,000. If I was the Pretender, I would come over myself, and take the money to help to pay my troops. They had better put out a Proclamation, that whoever discovers the Pretender or the Longitude shall have £100,000. This strain [?][2] is a sacrifice to Hanover, the Whigs, and the Queen's state of health. It will neither satisfy Hanover, silence the Whigs, nor cure the gout. Give him [the Pretender] a pension, and oblige him to live beyond the Alps. What is become of your project to make

---

[1] *History of the Peace of Utrecht.* It never appeared in his life-time.

[2] This word is illegible; indeed there are two or three other words in this minutely-written letter almost equally illegible.

it high treason to bring over foreign troops? I wish a little care was taken for securing the Kingdom as well as the Succession. But country politics are doubly insupportable, and so I have done, and retire to lament with my neighbours the want of rain, and the dearness of hay.

Farmer Tyler says the white mead at Chawdry has not been so bad in the memory of man, and the summer barley is quite dried up; but we hope to have a pretty good crop of wheat. Parson Hunsden, 'tis thought, must stick to his bargain; but all the neighbours say the attorney was an arrand rogue. We cannot get a bit of good butter for love or money. I could tell you more of the state of our affairs, but doubt your taste is not refined enough for it.

To Miss Vanhomrigh.
Letcombe, near Wantage.
August, 1714.

I have had two letters of yours to answer. I am pleased to see you piqued about my *dearness* to Ben and John.[1] They are worthy subjects. There are some words I never use to some people; let that satisfy. How many gentlemen, say you, and fine young gentlemen, truly, would be proud to have you desire so much of them.

Who told you I was going to Bath? No such thing. I had fixed to set out to-morrow for Ireland, but poor Lord Oxford

[1] It would seem that the Dean, in addressing his printer and bookseller, had styled them *dear Ben* and *dear John*. Vanessa appears to have been jealous of a distinction never paid to her in the course of their correspondence, and the Dean gaily justifies himself.—S.

desires I will go with him to Herefordshire, and I only expect his answer, whether I shall go there before, or meet him hereabouts, or go to Wimpole (his son's house), and go with him down. And I expect to leave this in two or three days, one way or other. I will stay with him till the Parliament meets again, if he desires it. I am not of your opinion about Lord Bolingbroke—perhaps he may get the Staff; but I cannot rely on his love to me. He knew I had a mind to be historiographer, although I valued it not but for the public service. Yet it is gone to a worthless rogue that nobody knows. I am writ to earnestly by somebody to come to town, and join with these people now in power, but I will not do it. Say nothing of this, but guess the person. I told Lord Oxford I would go with him when he was out; and now he begs it of me, and I cannot refuse him. I meddle not with his faults as he was a Minister of State; but you know his personal kindness to me was excessive. He distinguished and chose me above all other men while he was great, and his letter to me t'other day was the most moving imaginable.

The knife handles should surely be done up in silver, and strong. I believe Brandreth, my toy man, in Exchange Alley, would deal most honestly by me. Barber knows him. Where's your discretion in desiring to travel with that body, who,[1] I believe, would not do it for a thousand pounds, except it were to Italy. Pray God send you a good deliverance through your accounts. 'Tis well you have been a lawyer so long. You will be two hours reading this letter, it is writ so ill. When I am fixed anywhere, perhaps I may be so gracious as to let you know; but I will not promise. Service to Moll. Adieu.

[1] Barber seems to be indicated. He was a Jacobite, and to this the Dean probably alludes, in saying he would travel nowhere but to Italy.—S.

To Miss Vanhomrigh.

August 12, 1714.

I had your letter last post, and before you send me another I shall set out for Ireland. I must go and take the oaths; and the sooner the better. I think since I have known you, I have drawn an old house upon my head. You should not have come by Wantage for a thousand pounds.[1] You used to brag you were very discreet; where is it gone? It is probable I may not stay in Ireland long, but be back by the beginning of winter. When I am there, I will write to you as soon as I can conveniently, but it shall be always under a cover; and, if you write to me, let some other direct it, and I beg that you will write nothing that is particular, but what may be seen, for I apprehend letters may be opened and inconveniences will happen.

If you are in Ireland while I am there, I shall see you very seldom. It is not a place for any freedom, but where everything is known in a week, and magnified a hundred degrees. These are laws which must be passed through; but it is probable that we may meet in London in winter, or, if not, leave all to Fate that seldom cares to humour our inclinations. I say all this out of the perfect esteem and friendship I have for you. These public misfortunes have altered all my measures, and broke my spirits. I shall, I hope, be on horseback in a day after this comes to your hand. I would not answer your questions for a million, nor can I think of them with any ease of mind.[2] Adieu.

[1] In a subsequent letter he mentions the Berkshire surprise, which was, probably, an unexpected visit of Vanessa to Wantage.—S.

[2] The reference to these questions is a sort of cant expression, which repeatedly occurs afterwards. It would seem Vanessa subjected her admirer to a sort of regular catechism (it may be supposed to respect the state of his affection), which must have sometimes sufficiently embarrassed him.—S.

To Lord Bolingbroke.

Dublin, Sept. 14, 1714.

I hope your Lordship, who were always so kind to me while you were a servant, will not forget me now in your greatness. I give you this caution, because I really believe you will be apt to be exalted in your new station of retirement, which was the only honourable post that those who gave it you were capable of conferring. . . . I go on in writing, though I know not how to send you my letter. If I were sure it would be opened by the sealers of your Office, I would fill it with some terms of art that they would better deserve than relish.[1]

It is a point of wisdom too hard for me, not to look back with vexation upon past management. Divines tell us often from their pulpits, that "half the pains, which some men take to be damned, would have compassed their salvation." This, I am sure, was extremely our case. I know not what motions your Lordship intends: but, if I see the old Whig measures taken in the next elections, and that the Court, the Bank, East India, and South Sea [Companies] act strenuously, and procure a majority, I shall lie down, and beg of Jupiter to heave the cart out of the dirt. I would give all I am worth, for the sake of my country, that you had left your mantle with somebody in the House of Commons, or that a dozen honest men among them had only so many shreds of it. And so, having despatched all our friends in England, off flies a splinter, and knocks two Governors of Ireland dead. I remember, we never had leisure to think of that kingdom. The poor dead Queen is used like the giant Longaron in Rabelais. Pantagruel took Longaron by the heels, and made him his weapon to kill twenty

---

[1] The death of the Queen six weeks previously, and the expected advent of the Elector, had put to rout the Tory and Jacobite Ministry, in which Lord Bolingbroke had been Secretary of State.

other giants, then flung him over a river into the town, and killed two ducks and an old cat. I could talk very wisely to you; but you would regard me not. I could bid you *non desperare de republicâ*, and say, that *res nolunt diu male administrari*. But I will cut all short, and assure you, if *you* do not save us, I will not be at the pains of racking my invention to guess how we shall be saved, and yet I have read Polybius.¹

They tell me you have a very good crop of wheat, but the barley is bad. Hay will certainly be dear, unless we have an open winter. I hope you found your hounds in good condition [at Dawley], and that Bright has not made a stirrup-leather of your jockey-belt. I imagine you now smoking with your humdrum Squire (I forget his name), who can go home at midnight, and open a dozen gates, when he is drunk.

I beg your Lordship not to ask me to lend you any money. If you will come and live at the Deanery, and furnish up an apartment, I will find you in victuals and drink; which is more than ever you got by the Court. And, as proud as you are, I hope to see you accept a part of the offer before I die. The devil take this country. It has, in three weeks, spoiled two as good sixpenny pamphlets as ever a Proclamation was issued against. And since we talk of that, there will not be. . . .²

I shall be cured of loving England, as the fellow was of his ague by getting himself whipped through the town. I would retire too, if I could: but my country seat,³ where I have an acre of ground, is gone to ruin. The wall of my own apartment is fallen down, and I want mud to rebuild it, and straw to thatch it. Besides, a spiteful neighbour has seized on six feet of

---

¹ The *Pragmateia*, or *Practical History*, of the great Greek historian, the first attempt at a Science of History, consisted originally of forty books. Only five have come down to us entire.

² Here are two or three words in the MS. totally erased and illegible.—D. S.

³ At Laracor.

ground, carried off my trees, and I have not fortitude enough to go and see those devastations. But, in return, I live a country life in town, see nobody, and go every day once to prayers; and hope, in a few months, to grow as stupid as the present situation of affairs will require.

Well, after all, parsons are not such bad company, especially when they are under subjection; and I let none but such come near me. However, pray God forgive them by whose indolence, neglect, or want of friendship, I am reduced to live with twenty leagues of salt water between your Lordship and me.

To Miss Vanhomrigh.[1]

Philips-town, Nov. 5, 1714.

I met your servant when I was a mile from Trim, and could send him no other answer than I did, for I was going abroad by appointment; besides, I would not have gone to Kildrohod[2] to see you, for all the world. I ever told you, you wanted discretion. I am going to a friend upon a promise, and shall stay with him about a fortnight, and then come to town, and I will call on you as soon as I can, supposing you lodge at Turnstile Alley, as your servant told me, and that your neighbours can tell me its whereabouts. Your servant said you would be in town on Monday; so that I suppose this will be ready to welcome you there.

I fear you had a journey full of fatigues. Pray take care of your health in this Irish air, to which you are a stranger.[3] Does

[1] Addressed to "Mrs." Vanhomrigh, at her lodgings in Turnstile Alley, near College Green, Dublin.

[2] The Irish name for Cellbridge, where Vanessa had her country residence.—S.

[3] Miss Vanhomrigh had just now arrived in Ireland.

not Dublin look very dirty to you, and the country very miserable? Is Kildrohod as beautiful as Windsor, and as agreeable to you as the Prebend's lodgings there?[1] Is there any walk about you as pleasant as the Avenue and the Marlborough Lodge? I have rode a tedious journey to-day, and can say no more. Nor shall you know where I am till I come, and then I will see you. A fig for your letters and messages. Adieu.[2]

[1] Where Swift lodged when at Windsor. "My lodgings," he writes to Stella, Aug. 1712, "look upon Eton and the Thames. I wish I was owner of them: they belong to a Prebend."—S.

[2] The first and last sentence of this letter, which, taken apart from the rest, have almost an air of brutality, have found their way to the public. When the context is restored, it is merely an example of the Dean's playful rudeness.—S.

Writing from Dublin, sometime in the end of 1714, his fair devotee complains again:—"You cannot but be sensible, at least, in some degree, of the many uneasinesses I am slave to. . . . You fly me and give me no reason, but that we are among fools, and must submit. I am very well satisfied we are among such, but know no reason for having my happiness sacrificed to their caprice. You once had a maxim, which was—to act what was right, and not mind what the world said: I wish you would keep to it now. Pray, what can be wrong in seeing and advising an unhappy young woman?" And again, a few months later: "Well, now I plainly see how great a regard you have for me! You bid me be easy, and you'd see me as often as you could. You had better have said, as often as you could get the better of your inclinations so much; or, as often as you remembered there was such a person in the world. If you continue to treat me as you do, you will not be made uneasy by me long. 'Tis impossible to describe what I have suffered since I saw you last. I am sure I could have borne the rack much better than those killing, killing words of yours. Sometimes I have resolved to die without seeing you more; but those resolves, to your misfortune, did not last long: for there is something in human nature that prompts one so to find relief in this world, I must give way to it, and beg you'd see me, and speak kindly to me; for I am sure you would not condemn any one to suffer what I have done, could you but know it. The reason I *write* to you is, because I cannot *tell* it you, should I see you. For, when I begin to complain, then you are angry, and there is something in your look so awful that it strikes me dumb. Oh! that you may have but as much regard for me left, that this complaint may touch your soul with pity. I say as little as ever I can. Did you but know what I thought, I am sure it would move you!"

To Mr. Pope.

Dublin, June 28, 1715.

My Lord Bishop of Clogher[1] gave me your kind letter, full of reproaches for my not writing. I am naturally no very exact correspondent, and when I leave a country, without probability of returning, I think as seldom as I can of what I loved or esteemed in it, to avoid the *desiderium* which of all things makes life most uneasy. But you must give me leave to add one thing—that *you* talk at your ease, being wholly unconcerned in public events; for, if your friends the Whigs[2] continue, you may hope for some favour; if the Tories return, you are, at least, sure of quiet. You know how well I loved both Lord Oxford and Bolingbroke, and how dear the Duke of Ormond is to me. Do you imagine I can be easy, while their enemies are endeavouring to take off their heads?[3]

I nunc et versus tecum meditare canoros.—Do you imagine I can be easy, when I think of the probable consequences of these proceedings, perhaps upon the very peace of the nation, but certainly of the minds of so many hundred thousand good subjects? Upon the whole, you may truly attribute my silence to the eclipse, but it was that eclipse which happened on the first of August.[4] I borrowed your *Homer* from the bishop (mine is not

[1] Dr. Ashe, formerly Fellow of Trinity College, Cambridge, to whom the Dean was a pupil—afterwards Bishop of Clogher. It was he who married Swift to Mrs. [Miss] Johnson, 1716-17, and performed the ceremony in a garden.—Warton.

[2] Pope cannot, from his religion, be supposed to have had a violent partiality for the House of Hanover. But he had some powerful friends among the Whig party, and for some time seemed to preserve a sort of literary neutrality in politics.—S.

[3] These celebrated politicians were then under grave suspicion of conspiring to bring back the Stuarts. Lord Bolingbroke escaped to France, Lord Oxford was imprisoned in the Tower for two years.

[4] There was a great eclipse [of the sun] at this time. He alludes to the death of Queen Anne on the first of August.—Bowles.

yet landed), and read it out in two evenings. If it pleases others as well as me, you have got your end in profit and reputation. Yet I am angry at some bad rhymes and triplets; and pray, in your next, do not let me have so many unjustifiable rhymes to war and gods.[1] I tell you all the faults I know; only in one or two places, you are a little too obscure; but I expected you to be so in one or two and twenty. I have heard no foul talk of it here, for, indeed, it is not come over; nor do we very much abound in judges—at least, I have not the honour of being acquainted with them. Your notes are perfectly good, and so are your preface and essay.[2] You were pretty bold in mentioning Lord Bolingbroke in that preface.[3] I saw the Key to the [*Rape of the*] *Lock* but yesterday. I think you have changed it a good deal, to adapt it to the present times.

God be thanked, I have yet no Parliamentary business, and if they have none with me, I shall never seek their acquaintance. I have not been very fond of them for some years past—not when I thought them tolerably good; and, therefore, if I can get leave to be absent, I shall be much inclined to be on that side when there is a Parliament on this. But, truly, I must be a little easy in my mind before I can think of *Scriblerus*. You are to understand that I live in the corner of a vast unfurnished house. My family consists of a steward, a groom, a helper in the stable, a footman, and an old maid, who are all at board wages; and when I do not dine abroad, or make an entertainment (which last is very rare), I eat a mutton-pie, and

---

[1] He was frequently carping at Pope for bad rhymes in many other parts of his works. His own were remarkably exact.—W.

[2] Given to him by Parnell, and with which Pope told Mr. Spence he was never well satisfied, though he corrected it again and again.—W.

[3] The notice is brief though respectful. It barely intimates, that "such a genius as my Lord Bolingbroke, not more distinguished in the great scenes of business than in all the useful and entertaining parts of learning, has not refused to be the critic of these sheets, and the patron of their writer."— Preface to the *Iliad*.—S.

drink half a pint of wine. My amusements are defending my small dominions against the Archbishop, and endeavouring to reduce my rebellious choir. *Perditur hæc inter misero lux.* I desire you will present my humble service to Mr. Addison, Mr. Congreve, Mr. Rowe, and Gay. I am, and will be always, extremely yours, &c.

TO MR. POPE.

Dublin, Aug. 30, 1716.

I had the favour of yours by Mr. Ford of whom, before any other question relating to your health or fortune, or success as a poet, I inquired your principles in the common form, " Is he a Whig or a Tory ?" I am sorry to find they are not so well tallied to the present juncture as I could wish. I always thought the terms of *facto* and *jure* had been introduced by the poets, and that possession, in any sort, in kings was held an unexceptionable title in the Court of Parnassus.

If you do not grow a perfect good subject in your politics, in all its present latitudes, I shall conclude you are become rich, and able to live without Dedications to men in power; whereby one great inconvenience will follow—that, you, and the world, and posterity, will be utterly ignorant of their virtues. For, either your brethren have miserably deceived us these hundred years past, or power confers virtue, as naturally as five of your Popish sacraments do *grace*. You sleep less and drink more. But your master, Horace, was *vini somnique benignus*, and, as I take it, both are proper for your trade. As to wine, there are a thousand poetical texts to confirm the one,[1] and, as to the other,

[1] Not all the "tuneful tribe" have bowed the knee to Bacchus. Pindar, whatever may have been his practice, proclaimed the superiority of water— ἄοιστον τὸ ὕδωρ—water is best. Milton, in his elegiac verses addressed to his friend Diodati, declares that the poet who aspires to the highest flights of the Muse, must abjure the alcoholised juice of the grape, and, in fact, adopt the diet of the Samian Sage. Ovid, also, was a water-drinker.

I know it was anciently the custom to sleep in temples for those who would consult the Oracles. "Who dictates to me slumbering," &c.[1]

You are an ill Catholic, or a worse geographer—for I can assure you, Ireland is not Paradise, and I appeal even to any Spanish divine, whether Addresses were ever made to a friend in Hell or Purgatory. And who are all those enemies you hint at? I can only think of Curll, Gildon, Squire Burnet, Blackmore, and a few others, whose fame I have forgot—tools, in my opinion, as necessary for a good writer as pen, ink, and paper. And, besides, I would fain know whether every draper does not show you three or four damned pieces of stuff to set off his good one? However, I will grant that one thorough bookselling rogue is better qualified to vex an author than all his contemporary scribblers in critic or satire, not only by stolen copies of what was incorrect or unfit for the public, but by downright laying other men's dulness at your door.[2]

I had a long design upon the ears of that Curll, when I was in credit, but the rogue would never allow me a fair stroke at them, although my penknife was ready drawn and sharp. I can hardly believe the relation of his being poisoned, although the historian pretends to have been an eye-witness. But I beg pardon, sack might do it, although ratsbane would not.[3] I

---

[1] *Par. Lost*, ix., 23. On this passage Dr. Warton remarks that " this is the only time that Swift ever alludes to Milton, who was of an order of writers very different from what Swift admired and imitated;" an assertion which it may not be improper to controvert. To pass over an allusion to Milton's Prose Works, he twice mentions *Paradise Lost* with commendation.—Nichols. There was in existence, at the beginning of this century, a copy of the *Par. Lost*, annotated by Swift, in MS, for the use of "Stella," as appears from the information of one of Milton's commentators, Todd.

[2] Edmund Curll, the notorious pirate-bookseller of the day, had lately published a volume of *Town Eclogues*, with Pope's name on the title page, whereas it included but one of the poet's productions. He is gibbeted in the *Dunciad* as "shameless Curll," &c.

[3] This story originated in a practical joke, said to have been played off by Pope upon Curll, who gave him an emetic in a glass of sack. See the Account of the Poisoning of Edmund Curll, vol. xiii. [of Scott's Ed. of *Swift's Works*].—S.

never saw the thing you mention as falsely imputed to you, but I think the frolics of merry hours, even when we are guilty, should not be left to the mercy of our best friends, until Curll and his resemblers are hanged.

With submission to the better judgment of you and your friends, I take your project of an employment under Langallerie to be idle and unnecessary.[1] Have a little patience, and you will find more merit and encouragement at home, by the same methods. You are ungrateful to your country. Quit but your own religion and ridicule ours, and that will allow you a free choice for any other; or for none at all, and pay you well into the bargain. Therefore, pray do not run and disgrace us among the Turks, by telling them you were forced to leave your native home, because we would oblige you to be a Catholic; whereas we will make it appear to all the world, that we only compelled you to be a *Whig*. There is a young ingenious Quaker in this town, who writes verses to his mistress, not very correct, but in a strain purely what a poetical Quaker should do, commending her look and habit, &c. It gave me a hint that a set of Quaker Pastorals might succeed, if our friend Gay could fancy it,[2] and I think it a fruitful subject. Pray, hear what he says. I believe farther, the Pastoral ridicule is not exhausted, and that a porter, footman, or chairman's Pastoral might do well.[3] Or what think you of a Newgate Pastoral, among the whores and thieves there?[4]

Lastly, to conclude, I love thee never the worse for seldom writing to you. I am in an obscure scene, where you know

[1] The Marquis de Langallerie, who had distinguished himself in the French army, had renounced Catholicism, and was then engaged in raising troops for the Turks.

[2] Gay did write a Pastoral of this kind, which is published in his works.—Warburton.

[3] Swift himself wrote one of this kind, *Dermot and Sheelah*.—W.

[4] This hint is said to have suggested the *Beggar's Opera*.—S.

neither thing nor person. I can only answer yours, which I promise to do after a sort, whenever you think proper to employ me. But, I can assure you, the scene and the times have depressed me wonderfully; for I will impute no defect to those two paltry years which have slipped by since I had the happiness to see you. I am, with the truest esteem, yours, &c.

To Miss Vanhomrigh.

[Undated.]

I am now writing on Wednesday night, when you are hardly settled at home, and it is the first hour of leisure I have had, and it may be Saturday before you have it, and then there will be Governor Huff,[1] and to make you more so, I have enclosed a letter to poor Molkin, which I will command her not to shew you, because it is a love-letter.

I reckon by this time the groves and fields and purling streams have made Vanessa romantic, provided that poor Molkin be well. Your friend[2] sent me the verses he promised, which I here transcribe:—

> Nymph, would you learn the only art,
> To keep a worthy lover's heart—
> First to adorn your person well,
> In utmost cleanliness excel:

---

[1] This cant expression, which often occurs, and sometimes in very puzzling passages, refers to Vanessa's desire of having things her own way, in which she was but seldom indulged.—S.

[2] That is Swift himself, under the character of *Cadenus*. He often speaks, in his mysterious manner, of *Cadenus* as a different person from himself. The verses formed part of the published poem, *Cadenus to Vanessa.*—S.

> And though you must the fashions take,
> Observe them but for fashion's sake.
> The strongest reason will submit
> To virtue, honour, sense, and wit:
> To such a Nymph the wise and good
> Cannot be faithless if they would;
> For vices all have different ends,
> But virtue still to virtue tends;
> And when your lover is not true,
> 'Tis virtue fails in him or you:
> And either he deserves disdain,
> Or you without a cause complain—
> But here Vanessa cannot err,
> Nor are those rules applied to her—
> For who could such a Nymph forsake
> Except a blockhead or a rake?
> Or how could she her heart bestow,
> Except where wit and virtue grow?

In my opinion, these lines are too grave, and may therefore fit you who, I fear, are in the spleen. But that is not fit—either for yourself or the person you tend,[1] to whom you ought to read diverting things. Here is an epigram that concerns you not:—

> Dorinda dreams of dress a-bed:
> 'Tis all her thought and art.
> Her lace hath got within her head,
> Her stays stick to her heart.

If you do not like these things, what must I say? This town yields no better. The questions, which you were used to ask me, you may suppose to be all answered, just as they used to be after half-an-hour's debate. *Entendez-vous cela?*

You are to have a number of parsons in your neighbourhood,

---

[1] Her sister

but not one that you love—for your age of loving parsons is not yet arrived. What this letter wants in length, it will have in difficulty, for I believe you cannot read it. I will write plainer to Molkin, because she is not much used to my hand. I hold a wager there are some lines in this letter you will not understand, though you can read them. So drink your coffee, and remember you are a desperate chip, and that the lady who calls you bastard will be ready to answer all your questions. It is now Sunday night before I could finish this.

To Dr. King.

Trim, December 16, 1716.

I should be sorry to see my Lord Bolingbroke following the trade of an informer, because he is a person for whom I always had, and still continue, a very great love and esteem. For I think, as the rest of mankind do, that informers are a detestable race of people, although they may be sometimes necessary. Besides, I do not see whom his Lordship can inform against, except himself. He was three or four days at the Court of France, while he was Secretary, and it is barely possible he might then have entered into some deep negotiation with the Pretender; although I would not believe him, if he should swear it, because he protested to me, that he never saw him but once, and that was at a great distance, in public, at an opera.

As to any other of the Ministry at that time, I am confident he cannot accuse them, and that they will appear as innocent with relation to the Pretender as any who are now at the helm ; and as to myself, if I were of any importance, I should be very easy under such an accusation—much easier than I am to think your Grace imagines me to be in any danger, or that Lord Bolingbroke should have an ill story to tell of me. He knows, and loves, and thinks too well of me, to be capable of such an action. But I am surprised to think your Grace could talk, or act, or correspond with me for some years past, while you must needs believe me a most false and vile man—declaring to you, on all occasions, my abhorrence of the Pretender, and yet privately engaged with a Ministry to bring him in; and, therefore, warning me to look to myself, and prepare my defence against a false brother, coming over to discover such secrets as would hang me. Had there been even the least overture, or intent of bringing in the Pretender, during my acquaintance with the Ministry, I think I must have been very stupid not to have picked out some discoveries or suspicions. And, although I am not sure that I should have turned informer, yet I am certain I should have dropped some general cautions, and immediately have retired. When people say, things were not ripe at the Queen's death, they say they know not what. Things were rotten; and, had the Ministers any such thoughts, they should have begun three years before; and they who say otherwise understand nothing of the state of the Kingdom at that time.

But, whether I am mistaken or not in other men, I beg your Grace to believe that I am not mistaken in myself. I always professed to be against the Pretender, and am so still. And this is not to make my court (which I know is vain), for I own myself full of doubts, fears, and dissatisfactions, which I think on as seldom as I can; yet, if I were of any value, the public may safely rely on my loyalty, because I look upon the coming of the Pretender as a greater evil than any we are likely to suffer under the worst Whig Ministry than can be found.

I have not spoke or thought so much of Party these two

years, nor could anything have tempted me to it, but the grief I have in standing so ill in your Grace's opinion. I beg your Grace's blessing, and am, &c.

To Mr. Addison.[1]

Dublin, July 9, 1717.

I should be much concerned, if I did not think you were a little angry with me for not congratulating you upon being Secretary [of State]. But I choose my time, as I would to visit you, when all your company is gone. I am confident you have given ease of mind to many thousand people, who will never believe any ill can be intended to the Constitution in Church or State, while you are in so high a trust; and I should have been of the same opinion, though I had not the happiness to know you.

I am extremely obliged for your kind remembrance some months ago, by the Bishop of Derry, and for your generous intentions, if you had come to Ireland, to have made party give way to friendship by continuing your acquaintance. I examine my heart, and can find no other reason why I write to you now, besides that great love and esteem I have always had for you. I have nothing to ask you either for any friend or for myself. When I conversed among Ministers, I boasted of your acquaintance, but I feel no vanity from being known to a Secretary of State. I am only a little concerned to see you stand single; for it is a prodigious singularity in any Court to

---

[1] This curious and valuable letter was found among the papers of Mr. Tickell, the poet. There is a very kind letter from Addison, dated March 20, 1717-18.—S.

owe one's rise entirely to merit. I will venture to tell you a secret—that three or four more such choices would gain more hearts in three weeks than all the methods hitherto practised have been able to do in as many years.

It is now time for me to recollect that I am writing to a Secretary of State, who has little time allowed him for trifles. I therefore take my leave, with assurances of being ever, with the truest respect, &c.

To Miss Vanhomrigh.

May 12, 1719.

On vous a trompé en vous disant que je suis parti pour trois jours. Des affaires assez impertinentes m'ont tirée sitost, et je viens de quitter cette place pour aller voir quelques amis plus loin, purement pour le retablissement de ma santé.

Croyez-moi, s'il y a chose croyable au monde, que je pense tout ce que vous pouvez souhaiter de moy, et que tous vos desirs seront obéi, comme de commandemens qu'il sera impossible de violer. Je prétends de mettre cette lettre dans une ville de poste où je passerai. J'iray en peu de tems visiter un seigneur; mais je ne sçay encore le nom de sa maison, ni du pais où il demeure. Je vous conjure de prendre garde de votre santé. J'espère que vous passerez quelque part de cet èté dans votre maison de campagne, et que vous promenerez à cheval autant que vous pouvez. Vous aurez vos vers à revoir quand j'aurai mes pensées et mon tems libre : la Muse viendra. Faites mes complimens à la méchante votre compagnone, qui aime les contes et le Latin. J'espère que vos affaires de chicane sont en un bon train.

Je vous fais des complimens sur votre perfection dans la langue Françoise. Il fait vous connoître long-tems de connoître toutes vos perfections. Toujours en vous voyant et entendant, il en paroissent des nouvelles, qui estoient auparavant cachées. Il est honteux pour moy de ne savoir que le Gascon et la patois, au prix de vous. Il n'y rien à redire dans l'orthographie, la propriété, l'élégance, le douceur, et l'esprit, et que je suis sot moi de vous répondre en même langage, vous qui estes incapable d'aucune sottise, si ce n'est l'estime qu'il vous plaît d'avoir pour moy. Car il n'y a point de mérite, ni aucune preuve de mon bon goût, de trouver en vous tout ce que la nature a donnée à un mortel—je veux dire l'honneur, la vertu, le bons sens, l'esprit, la douceur, l'agrémen, et la fermeté d'âme. Mais en vous cachant, comme vous faites, le monde ne vous connoit pas, et vous perdez l'éloge des millions de gens. Depuis que j'avois l'honneur de vous connoître, j'ay tonjours remarqué que, ni en conversation particulière ni générale, aucun mot a échappé de votre bouche, qui pouvoit être mieux exprimé; et je vous jure, qu'en faisant souvent le plus severe critique, je ne pouvois jamais trouver aucun defaut en vos actions ni en vos parolles. Le coquetrie, l'affectation, la pruderie sont des imperfections que vous n'avois jamais connu.

Et avec tout cela, croyez-vous qu'il est possible de ne vous estimer au dessus du reste du genre humain? Quelles bestes en jûppes sont les plus excellentes de celles, que je vois semées dans le monde, au prix de vous. En les voyant, en les entendant, je dis cent fois le jour—ne parlez, ne regardez, ne pensez, ne faites rien comme ces misérables.—Sont-ce du même sexe—de même espèce de créatures? Quelle cruauté! de faire mepriser autant de gens qui, *sans songer de vous*, séroient assez supportables. Mais il est tems de vous délasser, et de vous dire *Adieu!*

Avec tout le respect, la sincerité, et l'estime de monde, je suis, et seray toujours [à vous].[1]

To Miss Vanhomrigh.
August 7, 1722.

I am this moment leaving my present residence, and, if I fix anywhere, shall let you know it, for I would fain wait till I got a little good weather for riding and walking, there never having been such a season as this remembered; though I doubt you know nothing of it, but what you learn by sometimes looking out at your back window to call your people.

I had your last, with a splendid account of your law affairs. You were once a better solicitor, when you could contrive to make others desire your consent to an Act of Parliament against their own interest, to advance yours. Yet, at present, you neither want power nor skill; but disdain to exercise either. When you are melancholy, read diverting or amusing books; it is my receipt and seldom fails.[2] Health, good humour, and fortune, are all that is valuable in this life, and the last contributes to the two former. I have not rode, in all, above a poor 400 miles since I saw you, nor do I believe I shall ride above 200

---

[1] Addressed, "For Madame Hester Vanhomri." The style of this French letter ("after the School of Stratford-atte-Bowe") is so hyperbolical, and so different from the somewhat cavalier-manner of his English letters, that we must suppose that the politeness of the language inspired the extravagance of the compliments. If Vanessa were at all accessible to flattery, this letter may have, in some measure, repaid her for some of the vexations which she had to endure.

[2] It is worth while to note Swift's use of the two *synonyms*. Not more than twelve years previously (in the *Tatler*) he had contemptuously condemned the latter as one of the "new-fangled" words, which were just then being imported into the language. *Diverting* and *diversion*, however, continued to be the usual and fashionable words down to the end of the century.

more till I see you again. But I desire you will not venture to shake me by the hand, for I am in mortal fear of the itch, and have no hope left but that some ugly vermin called *ticks* have got into my skin, of which I have pulled out some, and must scratch out the rest. Is not this enough to give me the spleen? For I doubt no Christian family will receive me; and this is all a man gets by a northern journey. It would be unhappy for me to be as nice in my conversation and company as you are, which is the only thing wherein you agree with Glassheel, who declares there is not a conversable creature in Ireland except *Cad.* What would you do in these parts, where politeness is as much a stranger as cleanliness? I am stopt, and this letter is intended to travel with me. So adieu till the next stage.

August 8.

Yesterday I rode twenty-nine miles without being weary, and I wish little *Heskinage*[1] could do as much. Here I leave this letter to travel on one way, while I go another, but where I do not know, nor what cabins or bogs are in my way. I see you this moment as you are visible at ten in the morning, and now you are asking your questions round, and I am answering them with a great deal of affected delays, and the same scene has passed forty times, as well as the other, from two till seven, longer than the first by two hours; yet each has *ses agrémens particuliers.*—A long Vacation. Law is asleep, and bad weather. How do you wear away the time? Is it among the fields and groves of your country-seat, or among your cousins in town, or thinking in a train that will be sure to vex you, and then reasoning, and forming teazing conclusions from mistaken thoughts? The best company for you is a philosopher, whom you would regard as much as a sermon. I have read more trash since I

---

[1] Another familiar form of his correspondent's name he uses is *Skinage.*

left you than would fill all your shelves, and am abundantly the better for it, though I scarce remember a syllable.

Go over the scenes of Windsor, Cleveland Row, Rider Street, St. James's Street, Kensington, the Sluttery, the Colonel in France, &c.[1] Cad thinks often of these, especially on horseback,[2] as I am assured. What a foolish thing is Time, and how foolish is Man, who would be as angry if Time stopt as if it passed! But I will not proceed at this rate; for I am writing and thinking myself fast into a spleen, which is the only thing that I would not compliment you by imitating. So adieu till the next place I fix in, if I fix at all till I return; and that I leave to fortune and the weather.[3]

---

[1] In a letter of Aug., 1720, Swift asks her—"What would you give to have the History of Cd—— and ——, exactly written, through all its steps, from the beginning to this time? I believe it would do well in verse, and be as long as the other [he refers to a possible Second Part of *Cadenus to Vanessa*, which was never accomplished]. It ought to be an exact chronicle of twelve years from ——, the time of spilling of coffee, to drinking of coffee; from Dunstable to Dublin, with every single passage since.—There would be the chapter of Madame going to Kensington; the chapter of the blister; the chapter of the wedding—with the adventures of the lost key; of the sham; of the joyful return; two hundred chapters of madness; the chapter of long walks; the Berkshire surprise; fifty chapters of little times; the chapter of Chelsey [Chelsea]; the chapter of swallow and cluster; a hundred whole books of myself, &c.; the chapter of hide and whisper; the chapter of who made it so; my sister's money." Upon which obscure and tantalising hints, Scott remarks—"They must be left chiefly to the charitable construction of the reader; a just penalty to the correspondents who wrap up an innocent meaning in innuendos. But, if any less than innocence were implied, it appears impossible that Vanessa should have received with rapture (as she does in the next letter) the proposal of *Cadenus* to immortalize these incidents of their interviews."

[2] *Cadenus* somewhat resembles *Hotspur* in this respect.—S

[3] In some undated letters, probably a year or two earlier than the date of this letter, Hester Vanhomrigh (who must have had some especial cause for anger) thus pours out her bitter complaints, mingled with something like threats to her strange lover, *e.g.*,—"Is it possible that again you will do the very same thing I warned you of so lately? I believe you thought I only rallied when I told you the other night that I would pester you with letters. Did I not know you very well I should think you knew but little of the world, to imagine that a woman would not keep her word, whenever she promised

To Mr. Cope.

Dublin, October 9, 1722.

I am just come to town, and therefore look upon myself to have just left Loughgall, and that this is the first opportunity I have of writing to you.

Strange revolutions since I left you. A Bishop of my old acquaintance [1] in the Tower for treason, and a doctor of my new

anything that was malicious. . . . Once more I advise you, if you have any regard for your own quiet, to alter your behaviour quickly: for I do assure you I have too much spirit to sit down contented with this treatment. Because I love frankness extremely, I here tell you now that I have determined to try all manner of human arts to reclaim you; and, if all these fail, I am resolved to have recourse to the black one, which [it] is said, never does. . . . Is it not better to come of yourself than to be brought by force, and that, perhaps, at a time when you have the most agreeable engagement in the world? For when I undertake anything, I don't love to do it by halves. . . ."

At another time she addresses him much more tenderly:—"We have had a vast deal of thunder and lightning. Where do you think I wished to be then? And do you think that was the only time I wished so since I saw you? I am sorry my jealousy should hinder you from writing more love-letters. . . I am now as happy as I can be without seeing—Cad. I beg you will continue happiness to your own *Skinage*."

In a later letter she reverts to his unaccountable neglect:—"I must either unload my heart, and tell you all its griefs, or sink under the inexpressible distress I now suffer by your prodigious neglect of me. 'Tis now ten weeks since I saw you; and, in all that time, I have never received but one letter from you, and a little note, with an excuse. Oh! how have you forgot me! You endeavour by severities to force me from you, nor can I blame you; for, with the utmost distress and confusion, I behold myself the cause of uneasy reflections to you. Yet I cannot comfort you; but here declare that 'tis not in the power of time or accident to lessen that inexpressible passion which I have for you. . . . For heaven's sake tell me what has caused this prodigious change on you, which I have found of late. If you have the least remains of pity for me left, tell me tenderly. No, don't tell it, so that it may cause my present death!" And again she assures him:—"Were I an *enthusiast*, still [always] you would be the deity I should worship."

[1] Dr. Atterbury, Bishop of Rochester, at this time imprisoned in the Tower for his share in what was called *Sayer's Plot*, or in favour of the Chevalier St. George, for which he was afterwards banished by Act of Attainder.—S.

acquaintance made a Bishop. Your new Bishop Bolton [of Clonfert] was born to be my tormentor; he ever opposed me as my subject,¹ and now has left me embroiled for want of him. The Government, in consideration of the many favours they have shown me, would fain have me give St. Bride's to some one of their hang-dogs, that Dr. Howard may come into St. Werburgh's; so that I must either disoblige Whig or Tory in my Chapter, or be ungrateful to my patrons in power.

When you come to town, you must be ready, at what time you hear the sound of tabret, harp, &c., to worship the brazen image set up, or else be cast into a cold watery furnace. I have not yet seen it, for it does not lie in my walks, and I want curiosity. The wicked Tories themselves begin to believe there was something of a plot; and every plot costs Ireland more than any plot can be worth. The Court has sent a demand here for more money, by three times, than is in the hands of the Treasury and all the Collectors put together. I escaped hanging very narrowly a month ago; for a letter from Preston, directed to me, was opened in the Post Office, and sealed again in a very slovenly manner, when Manley found it only contained a request from a poor curate. This hath determined me against writing treason; however, I am not certain that this letter may not be interpreted as comforting his most excellent Majesty's enemies, since *you* have been a State-prisoner. Pray God, keep all honest men out of the hands of lions and bears and uncircumcised Philistines! I hoped my brother Orrery ² had loved his land too much to hazard it on revolution principles. I am told that a lady of my acquaintance was the discoverer of this plot, having a lover among the true Whigs, whom she preferred before an old battered husband.

¹ Bolton had been Chancellor of St. Patrick's.

² Charles Boyle, Earl of Orrery, an accomplished and literary character, inventor of the philosophical instrument to which he bequeathed his name, was about this time committed to the Tower for some real or supposed accession to the plot which cost Atterbury so dear.—S.

You never saw anything so fine as my new Dublin plantations of elms. I wish you would come and visit them; and I am strong in wine, though not so liberal of it as you. It is said that Kelly the parson is admitted to Kelly the squire, and that they are cooking up a discovery between them, for the improvement of the hempen manufacture.[1] It is reckoned that the best trade in London this winter will be that of an evidence. As much as I hate the Tories, I cannot but pity them as fools. Some think, likewise, that the Pretender ought to have his choice of two caps, a red cap or a fool's cap. It is a wonderful thing to see the Tories provoking his present Majesty, whose clemency, mercy, and forgiving temper have been so signal, so extraordinary, so more than humane, during the whole course of his reign; which plainly appears, not only from his own speeches and declarations, but also from a most ingenious pamphlet just come over, relating to the wicked Bishop of Rochester.

But enough of politics. I have no town news; I have heard nothing. Old Rochfort has got a dead palsy. Lady Betty has been long ill. Dean Percivale has answered the other Dean's journal in Grub Street, justly taxing him for avarice and want of hospitality. Madam Percivale absolutely denies all the facts —insists that she never made candles of dripping, that Charley never had the chincough, &c. My most humble service to Mrs. Cope, who entertained that covetous, lampooning Dean much better than he deserved. Remember me to honest Nanty and boy Barclay. Ever yours, &c.

[1] George Kelly, an Irish clergyman, was apprehended by three messengers as an accessory to *Sayer's Plot*. He defended himself until he had burned a parcel of papers, and then surrendered. He was a non-juring clergyman, and is stated, in the Report of the Committee of the House of Commons, to have been the person principally trusted by the Bishop of Rochester. Captain Dennis Kelly, a gentleman of fortune in Ireland, was also seized as an active agent in Atterbury's plot.—S.

To Mr. Gay.

Dublin, Jan. 8, 1722-3.

Coming home after a short Christmas ramble, I found a letter upon my table, and little expected when I opened it to read your name at the bottom. The best and greatest part of my life, until these last eight years, I spent in England: there I made my friendships, and there I left my desires. I am condemned for ever to another country. What is in prudence to be done? I think to be *oblitusque meorum obliviscendus et illis*. What can be the design of your letter but malice, to wake me out of a scurvy sleep; which, however, is better than none! I am towards nine years older since I left you; yet that is the least of my alterations. My business, my diversions, my conversations, are all entirely changed for the worse; and so are my studies and my amusements in writing. Yet, after all, this humdrum way of life might be passable enough, if you would let me alone. I shall not be able to relish my wine, my parsons, my horses, nor my garden, for three months; until the spirit you have raised shall be dispossessed.

I have sometimes wondered that I have not visited you; but I have been stopped by too many reasons, besides years and laziness, and yet these are very good ones. Upon my return, after half-a-year among you, there would be to me *desiderio nec pudor nec modus*.[1] I was three years reconciling myself to the scene, and the business, to which fortune had condemned me, and stupidity was what I had recourse to. Besides, what a figure should I make in London, while my friends are in poverty, exile,

---

[1] " Quis desiderio sit pudor aut modus
    Tam cari capitis? Præcipe lugubres
    Cantus, Melpomene."

From the opening verses of the famous Ode addressed to Virgil—one of the best of the *Odes* of Horace.

distress, or imprisonment, and my enemies with rods of iron? Yet I often threatened myself with the journey; and am every summer practising to ride, and get health to bear it. The only inconvenience is, that I grow old in the experiment.

Although I care not to talk to you as a divine, yet I hope you have not been author of your colic. Do you drink bad wine, or keep bad company? Are not you as many years older as I? It will not be always *et tibi quos mihi dempserit apponet annos*. I am heartily sorry you have any dealings with that ugly distemper; and I believe our friend Arbuthnot will recommend you to temperance and exercise.[1] I wish they could have as good effect upon the giddiness I am subject to, and which this moment I am not free from. I should have been glad, if you had lengthened your letter by telling me the present condition of many of my old acquaintances, Congreve, Arbuthnot, Lewis, &c., but you mention only Mr. Pope who, I believe, is lazy; or else he might have added three lines of his own. I am extremely glad he is not in your case of needing great men's favour, and could heartily wish that you were in his. I have been considering why poets have such ill-success in making their court; since they are allowed to be the greatest and best of all flatterers. The defect is, that they flatter only in print or in writing, but not by word of mouth; they will give things under their hand which they make a conscience of speaking. Besides, they are too libertine to haunt ante-chambers, too poor to bribe the porters and footmen, and too proud to cringe to second-hand favourites in a great family.

Tell me, are you not under original sin by the dedication of your *Eclogues* to Lord Bolingbroke? I am an ill-judge at this distance; and, besides, am, for my ease, utterly ignorant of the commonest things that pass in the world. But, if all Courts

---

[1] He published a work on Diet Reform, entitled an *Essay Concerning Aliments.*

have a sameness in them (as the parsons phrase it), things may be as they were in my time, when all employments went to Parliament-men's friends, who had been useful in Elections; and there was always a huge list of names in arrears at the Treasury, which would at least take up your seven years' expedient to discharge even one half. I am of opinion, if you will not be offended, that the surest course would be, to get your friend, who lodges in your house, to recommend you to the next chief Governor, who comes over here, for a good civil employment, or to be one of his secretaries; which your Parliament-men are fond enough of, when there is no room at home. The wine is good and reasonable; you may dine twice a week at the Deanery-house; there is a set of company in this town sufficient for one man; folks will admire you, because they have read you and read of you; and a good employment will make you live tolerably in London, or sumptuously here; or, if you divide between both places, it will be for your health.

I wish I could do more than say, I love you. I left you in a good way, both for the late Court and the Successors; and, by the force of too much honesty, or too little sublunary wisdom, you fell between two stools. Take care of your health and money; be less modest and more active; or else turn parson, and get a Bishopric here. Would to God they would send us as good ones from your side! I am ever, &c.[1]

[1] Gay, replying to this letter, some three weeks later, writes:—" You made me happy in answering my last letter in so kind a manner; which, to common appearance, I did not deserve; but I believe you guessed my thoughts, and knew that I had not forgot you, and that I always loved you. . . . Mr. Congreve I see often; he always mentions you with the strongest expressions of esteem and friendship. He labours still under the same afflictions as to his sight and gout. I passed all the last season with him at the Bath. . . Pope has just now embarked himself in another great undertaking as an author; for, of late, he has talked only as a Gardener. He has engaged to translate the *Odyssey* in three years, I believe rather out of a prospect of gain than of inclination; for I am persuaded he bore his part in the loss of the South Sea [Bubble]. He lives mostly at Twickenham, and amuses himself in his house and garden. I supped about a fortnight ago with Lord Bathurst and Lewis at

To Lord Carteret.

Deanery House, April 17, 1725.

I have been so afflicted with a deafness, and, at present, with a giddiness in my head (both old distempers), that I have not been able to attend your Excellency and my Lady Carteret, as my inclination and duty oblige me; and I am now hastening into the country, to try what exercise and better air will do towards my recovery. Not knowing how long I may be absent, or how soon you may think fit to leave this kingdom,[1] I take this occasion of returning your Excellency and my Lady Carteret my most humble acknowledgments for your great civilities towards me, which I wish it was in my power to deserve.

I have only one humble request to make to your Excellency, which I had in my heart ever since you were nominated Lord-Lieutenant; and it is in favour of Mr. Sheridan. I beg you will take your time for bestowing on him some Church living, to the value of one hundred and fifty pounds *per annum*. He is agreed, on all hands, to have done more public service, by many degrees, in the education of lads, than any five of his vocation; and has much more learning than usually falls to the share of those who profess Teaching, being perfectly skilled in the Greek as well as Latin tongue, and acquainted with all the ancient writers in Poetry, Philosophy, and History. He is a man of good sense, modesty, and virtue. His greatest fault is a wife,[2]

Dr. Arbuthnot's. Whenever your old acquaintance meet, they never fail of expressing their want of you. I wish you would come, and be convinced that all I tell you is true.

"As for the reigning amusement of the town, it is entirely *music*—real fiddles, bass-viols and haut-boys; not poetical harps, lyres, and reeds. There's nobody allowed to say, I sing, but an eunuch, or an Italian woman. Everybody is grown now as great a judge of Music as they were, in your time, of Poetry; and folks, that could not distinguish one tune from another, now daily dispute about the different styles of Handel, Bononcini, and Attilio. . . ."

[1] Lord Carteret had been appointed to the Viceregal post in 1723.

[2] Mrs. Sheridan and Swift were not the best of friends. If report speak true, Sheridan suffered under the same misfortune as a much greater philosopher; for she seems to have been something of a Xanthippe.

and four children; for which there is no excuse, but that a wife is thought necessary to a schoolmaster. His constitution is so weak, that in a few years he must give up his business, and probably must starve, without some preferment, for which he is an ill solicitor. And I hope you will please to believe that it proceeds wholly from justice and humanity, for he is neither a relation nor dependant of mine.

I humbly take my leave, and remain with the utmost respect, &c.

To Dr. Sheridan.

Quilca,[1] June 29, 1725.

I wrote to you yesterday, and said as many things as I could then think on, and gave it to a boy of Kells, who brought me yours. It is strange that I, and Stella, and Mrs. Macfadin,[2] should light on the same thought—to advise you to make a great appearance of temperance while you are abroad. But Mrs. [Miss] Johnson and I go further, and say, you must needs observe all grave forms, for the want of which both you and I have suffered. On supposal that you are under the Bishop of Cork, I send you a letter enclosed to him, which I desire you will seal. Mrs. Johnson put me in mind to caution you not to drink or pledge any health in his company; for you know his weak side in that matter.[3] I hope Mr. Tickell has not compli-

[1] Sheridan had a house at Quilca, in Cavan, where Swift was now on a visit.

[2] Mrs. Macfadin was mother to Dr. Sheridan's wife.—Hawkesworth.

[3] He wrote a pamphlet against drinking to the memory of the dead.—H. This may be thought, at present, a very odd subject for a treatise: but the healths to the glorious and immortal memory of King William were, at that time, a party-signal, and occasioned many quarrels.—S. The Bishop's memory is thus sufficiently cleared from any suspicion of hostility to *Toasts* in general: or that his "weak side" was at all towards the Anti-Alcoholists.

mented you with what fees are due to him for your patent. I wish you would say to him (if he refuses them), that I told you it was Mr. Addison's maxim to excuse nobody: for here, says he, I may have forty friends, whose fees may be two guineas apiece; then I lose *eighty guineas*, and my friends save *but two apiece*. I must tell you Dan Jackson received his Living by huddling over the first year, and then hoping to mend it the next. Therefore, pray, take all the care you can to inquire into the value, and set it at the best rate to substantial people. I know not whether you are under the Bishop of Cork, or not: if not, you may burn the letter. I must desire that you will not think of enlarging your expenses, no, not for some years to come, much less at present; but rather retrench them. You might have lain destitute till Antichrist came, for anything you could have got from those you used to treat. Neither let me hear of one rag of better clothes for your wife or brats, but rather plainer than ever. This is positively Stella's advice as well as mine. She says, now you need not be ashamed to be thought poor.

We compute that you cannot be less than thirty days absent; and pray, do not employ your time in lolling a-bed till noon to read Homer; but mind your business effectually, and we think you ought to have no breaking up this August, but affect to adhere to your school closer than ever; because you will find that your ill-wishers will give out, you are now going to quit your school since you have got perferment, &c. Pray, send me a large bundle of Exercises, good as well as bad, for I want something to read. I would have you carry down three or four sermons, and preach every Sunday at your own church, and be very devout. . . .

Keep very regular hours for the sake of your health aud credit, and, wherever you lie a night within twenty miles of your Living, be sure call the family that evening to prayers. desire you will wet no commission with your old crew, nor with any but those who befriend you, as Mr. Tickell, &c.

To Dr. Sheridan.

Quilca, Sept. 11, 1725.

If you are, indeed, a discarded courtier,[1] you have reason to complain, but none at all to wonder. You are too young for many experiences to fall in your way; yet you have read enough to make you know the nature of Man. It is safer for a man's interest to blaspheme God than to be of a Party out of power, or even to be thought so. And, since the last was the case, how could you imagine that all mouths would not be open when you were received, and in some manner preferred, by the Government, though in a poor way? I tell you, there is hardly a Whig in Ireland who would allow a potato and butter-milk to a reputed Tory. Neither is there anything in your countrymen, upon this article, more than what is common to all other nations, only *quoad magis et minus*. Too much advertency is not your talent, or else you had fled from that text as from a rock. For as Don Quixote said to Sancho, What business had you to speak of a halter in a family, where one of it was hanged? And your innocence is a protection that wise men are ashamed to rely on, further than with God.

It is, indeed, against common sense to think that you should choose such a time, when you had received a favour from the Lord-Lieutenant, and had reason to expect more, to discover your disloyalty in the pulpit. But what will that avail? Therefore sit down and be quiet, and mind your business as you should do, and contract your friendships, and expect no more from men than such an animal is capable of, and you will every day find my description of *Yahoos* more resembling.[2] You

---

[1] On account of an unlucky sermon.—See *Life and Writings of Swift*.

[2] The *Travels of Gulliver* appeared in 1726-7: it appears Sheridan had seen the manuscript.—S.

should think and deal with every man as a villain, without calling him so, or flying from him, or valuing him less. This is an old true lesson. You believe that everyone will acquit you of any regard to temporal interest; and how came *you* to claim an exception from all mankind? I believe you value your temporal interest as much as anybody; but you have not the art of pursuing it. You are mistaken. Domestic evils are no more within a man than others; and he who cannot bear up against the first will sink under the second. And, in my conscience, I believe this is your case; for, being of a weak constitution, in an employment precarious and tiresome, loaden with children, *cum uxore neque leni neque commodâ*[1]; a man of intent and abstracted thinking, enslaved by mathematics and complaint of the world, this new weight of Party-malice had struck you down, like a feather on a horse's back, already loaden as far as he is able to bear. You ought to change the Apostle's expression and say, I will strive to learn in whatever state, &c.

I will hear none of your visions. You shall live at Quilca but three fortnights and a month in the year, and perhaps not so much. You shall make no entertainments but what are necesssary to your interests. . . All this you will do, *si mihi credis*, and not dream of printing your sermon,[2] which is a project abounding with objections unanswerable, and with which I could fill this letter. You say nothing of having preached before the Lord Lieutenant, nor whether he is altered towards you, for

[1] "With a wife not too mild and sweet-tempered," prudently expressed by Swift in a learned language.

[2] The unlucky discourse had no reference whatever to politics; which, perhaps, led Sheridan to hope printing it might be some sort of exculpation. It was in vain that he protested the text was chosen by mere inadvertence, that he had forgotten his engagement to preach for Archdeacon Russell of Cork (whose pulpit he occupied upon that unlucky day), and that, being suddenly called upon to fulfil his engagement, he seized the first old sermon he had by him, without even looking into it. All this profited nothing: Dr. Sheridan was disgraced at the Viceroy's Court, and his name struck out of the list of Chaplains.—S.

you speak nothing but generals. You think all the world has nothing to do but to pull Mr. Sheridan down; whereas it is nothing but a slap in your turn, and away. Lord Oxford once said to me on an occasion, "These fools, because they hear a noise about their ears of their own making, think the whole world is full of it." When I come to town, we will change all this scene, and act like men of the world. Grow rich, and you will have no enemies; go sometimes to the Castle; keep fast Mr. Tickell and Balaguer[1]; frequent those on the right side, friends to the present powers; drop those who are loud on the wrong Party, because they know they can suffer nothing by it.

To Mr. Pope.

Dublin, Sept. 29, 1725.

I am now returning to the noble scene of Dublin, into the *grand monde*, for fear of burying my parts, to signalise myself among curates and vicars, and correct all corruptions crept in, relating to the weight of bread and butter, through those dominions where I govern.[2] I have employed my time (beside ditching) in finishing, correcting, amending, and translating my [Gulliver's] *Travels*, in four parts complete, newly augmented, and intended for the press, when the world shall deserve them, or rather when a printer shall be found brave enough to venture his ears.

I like the scheme of our meeting after distresses and dispersions; but the chief end I propose to myself in all my labours is to vex the world rather than divert it; and, if I could

---

[1] Private Secretary to Lord Carteret.
[2] The liberties of St. Patrick's Cathedral.

compass that design without hurting my own person or fortune, I would be the most indefatigable writer you have ever seen, without reading. I am exceedingly pleased that you have done with translations. Lord Treasurer Oxford often lamented that a rascally world should lay you under a necessity of misemploying your genius for so long a time. But since now you will be so much better employed, when you think of the world, give it one lash the more, at my request. I have ever hated all nations, professions, and communities; and all my love is towards individuals. For instance, I hate the tribe of lawyers, but I love counsellor such a one, and judge such a one; it is so with physicians. I will not speak of my own trade, soldiers, English, Scotch, French, and the rest. But, principally, I hate and detest that animal called *Man*; although I heartily love John, Peter, Thomas, and so forth. This is the system upon which I have governed myself many years (but do not tell), and so I shall go on till I have done with them. I have got materials towards a treatise, proving the falsity of that definition *animal rationale*, and to show it should be only *rationis capax*.[1] Upon this great foundation of misanthropy (though not in Timon's manner) the whole building of my *Travels* is erected; and I never will have peace of mind till all honest men are of my opinion; by consequence, you are to embrace it immediately, and procure that all who deserve my esteem may do so too. The matter is so clear, that it will admit of no dispute; nay, I will hold a hundred pounds that you and I agree in this point.

I did not know your *Odyssey* was finished, being yet in the country, which I shall leave in three days. I thank you kindly for the present, but shall like it three-fourths the less, from the

[1] These and similar passages contain a great deal of wild and violent invective against mankind, which has been, perhaps, too hastily adopted as expressive of Swift's actual sentiments. It ought, however, to be remembered, that, if the Dean's principles were misanthropical, his character was benevolent. Few have written so much with so little view either to fame or to profit, or to aught but benefit the public.—S.

mixture you mention of other hands [in the translation]; however, I am glad you saved yourself so much drudgery. I have been long told by Mr. Ford of your great achievements in building and planting, and especially of your subterranean passage to your garden, whereby you turned a blunder into a beauty— which is a piece of *Ars Poetica*. I have almost done with harridans, and shall soon become old enough to fall in love with girls of fourteen. The lady[1], whom you describe to live at Court, to be deaf, and no Party-woman, I take to be mythology, but know not how to moralize it. She cannot be Mercy, for Mercy is neither deaf, nor lives at Court. Justice is blind, and perhaps deaf, but neither is she a Court lady. Fortune is both blind and deaf, and a Court lady; but then she is a most damnable Party-woman, and will never make me easy, as you promise. It must be Riches, which answers all your description. I am glad she visits you; but my voice is so weak, that I doubt she will never hear me.

Mr. Lewis sent me an account of Dr. Arbuthnot's illness, which is a very sensible affliction to me who, by living so long out of the world, have lost that hardness of heart contracted by years and long conversation. I am daily losing friends, and neither seeking nor getting others. Oh, if the world had but a dozen Arbuthnots in it, I would burn my *Travels*! but, however, he is not without fault. There is a passage in *Bede* highly commending the piety and learning of the Irish in that age where, after abundance of praises, he overthrows them all by lamenting that: Alas! *they kept Easter at a wrong time of the year.* So our doctor has every quality and virtue that can make a man amiable and useful; but, alas! he hath a sort of slouch in his walk. I pray God protect him, for he is an excellent Christian, though not a Catholic. I hear nothing of our friend Gay; but I find the Court keeps him at hard meat. I advised him to

---

Mrs. Howard.

come over here with a Lord Lieutenant. Philips[1] writes little *flams* (as Lord Leicester called those sort of verses) on Miss Carteret.[2] A Dublin blacksmith, a great poet, has imitated his manner in a poem to the same Miss. Philips is a complainer, and, on this occasion, I told Lord Carteret that complainers never succeed at Court, though railers do. Are you altogether a country gentleman, that I must address you out of London, to the hazard of your losing this precious letter, which I will now conclude, although so much paper is left. I have an ill-name, and therefore shall not subscribe it; but you will guess it comes from me, who esteem and love you about half as much as you deserve. I mean as much as he can.

I am in great concern at what I am just told is in some of the newpapers—that Lord Bolingbroke is much hurt by a fall in hunting. I am glad he has so much youth and vigour left—of which he has not been thrifty—but I wonder he has no more discretion.

To Mr. Worrall.[3]

Twickenham, July 15, 1726.

I wish you would send me a common bill in form, upon any banker, for one hundred pounds, and I will wait for it; and, in the meantime, borrow where I can. What you tell me of Mrs. Johnson I have long expected, with great oppression and heaviness of heart. We have been perfect friends these thirty-

---

[1] Ambrose Philips, an associate of Addison, Steele, and the Whig literary coterie, and the author of some tragedies, but most known as the rival, in Pastoral poetry, of Pope. He was a contributor to the *Free-Thinker*.

[2] Younger daughter of Lord Carteret, Lord-Lieutenant of Ireland.

[3] His agent in Ireland, to whom he frequently refers in his *Journal to Stella*.

five years. Upon my advice, they both came to Ireland, and have been ever since my constant companions; and the remainder of my life will be a very melancholy scene, when one of them is gone, whom I most esteemed, upon the score of every good quality that can possibly recommend a human creature.

I have these two months seen through Mrs. Dingley's disguises,[1] and, indeed, ever since I left you, my heart has been so sunk, that I have not been the same man, nor ever shall be again; but drag on a wretched life until it shall please God to call me away. I must tell you as a friend, that if you have reason to believe Mrs. Johnson cannot hold out till my return, I would not think of coming to Ireland; and, in that case, I would expect of you, in the beginning of September, to renew my licence [of absence] for another half-year; which time I will spend in some retirement far from London, till I can be in a disposition of appearing after an accident that must be so fatal to my quiet. I wish it could be brought about, that she might make her Will. Her intentions are to leave the interest of all her fortune to her mother and sister, during their lives, and afterwards to Dr. Stephen's Hospital, to purchase land for such uses there as she designs.

Think how I am disposed while I am writing this, and forgive the inconsistencies. I would not, for the universe, be present at such a trial of seeing her depart. She will be among friends, that, upon her own account and great worth, will tend her with all possible care, where I should be a trouble to her, and the greatest torment to myself. In case the matter should be desperate, I would have you advise, if they come to town, that they should be lodged in some airy healthy part, and not in the Deanery; which, besides, you know, cannot but be a very improper thing for that house to breathe her last in.[2] This I

[1] Probably endeavouring to conceal Mrs. Johnson's danger, in tenderness to the Dean.—Hawkesworth.

[2] This hint Swift repeated upon another occasion. Even during the extremity of distress, which he entertained at the apprehension of Stella's death, he remained stubbornly fixed that, living or dying, their marriage should remain concealed.—S.

leave to your discretion, and conjure you to burn this letter immediately, without telling the contents of it to any person alive. Pray, write to me every week, that I may know what steps to take; for I am determined not to go to Ireland, to find her just dead or dying. Nothing but extremity could make me so familiar with those terrible words, applied to such a dear friend. Let her know I have bought her a repeating gold watch, for her ease in winter nights. I designed to have surprised her with it; but now I would have her know it, that she may see how my thoughts are always to make her easy. I am of opinion that there is not a greater folly than to contract too great and intimate a friendship, which must always leave the survivor miserable. On the back of Burton's note there was written the account of Mrs. Johnson's sickness. Pray, in your next, avoid that mistake, and leave the back side blank. When you have read this letter twice, and retain what I desire, pray burn it; and let all I have said lie only in your breast.

Pray, write every week. I have (till I know further) fixed on August 15 to set out for Ireland. I shall continue or alter my measures according to your letters. Adieu.

Direct your letters still to Mrs. Rice, &c. Pray, tell Mr. Dobbs, of the College, that I received his letter, but cannot possibly answer it; which I certainly would, if I had materials. As to what you say about promotion, you will find it was given immediately to Maule,[1] as I am told; and I assure you I had no

---

[1] The Dean alludes to the general expectation that was entertained, that he would gain some promotion through the favour of the Princess of Wales. It was even reported that he had been offered the vacant Bishopric of Cloyne.—S. In a letter to Dr. Stopford, five days later, he reports his reception by "the people in power:"—"They have been civil enough to me. Many of them have visited me. I was not able to withstand seeing the Princess [a year later, Queen Caroline], because she had commanded that, whenever I came hither, as the news said I intended, that I should wait on her. I was latterly twice with the Chief Minister [Walpole]; the first time by invitation, and, the second time, at my desire, for an hour, wherein we differed in every point, but all this made a great noise, and soon got to Ireland," &c.

offers, nor would accept them. My behaviour to those in power has been directly contrary, since I came here. I would rather have good news from you than Canterbury, though it were given me upon my own terms.

To Dr. Sheridan.[1]

July 27, 1726.

I have yours just now of the 19th, and the account you give me [of the dangerous illness of Stella] is nothing but what I have some time expected with the utmost agonies; and there is one aggravation of constraint—that, where I am, I am forced to put on an easy countenance. It was, at this time, the best office your friendship could do—not to deceive me. I was violently bent all last year, as I believe you remember, that she should go to Montpelier, or Bath, or Tunbridge. I entreated, if there was no amendment, they might both come to London. But there was a fatality, although I indeed think her stamina could not last much longer, when I saw she could take no nourishment. I look upon this to be the greatest event that can ever happen to me; but all my preparations will not suffice to make me bear it like a philosopher, nor altogether like a Christian. There has been the most intimate friendship between us from our childhood, and the greatest merit on her side that ever was in one human creature toward another. Nay, if I were now near her,

---

[1] This was written from Mr. Pope's at Twickenham. But Swift's agony of mind, so forcibly expressed in the following letter, rendered him unable to bear the constraint which even Pope's society imposed on him ; and, shortly before his departure for Ireland, he left Twickenham, and went into lodgings in London.—S.

I would not see her; I could not behave myself tolerably, and should redouble her sorrow. Judge in what a temper of mind I write this. The very time I am writing, I conclude the fairest soul in the world hath left its body.

Confusion! that I am this moment called down to a visitor, when I am in the country, and not in my power to deny myself.—I have passed a very constrained hour, and now return to say I know not what. I have been long weary of the world, and shall for my small remainder of years be weary of life, having for ever lost that conversation which could only make it tolerable. I fear, while you are reading this, you will be shedding tears at her funeral. She loved you well, and a great share of the little merit I have with you is owing to her solicitations.[1]

I writ you about a week ago.

TO THE HON. MRS. HOWARD.[2]

Sept. 1, 1726.

Being perpetually teased with the remembrance of you, by the sight of your ring on my finger, my patience at last is at

[1] Stella rallied, and lived on to January, 1727-8.

[2] This celebrated, yet unhappy, lady was sister to the first Earl of Buckinghamshire, and wife of the Hon. Charles Howard, who succeeded to the Earldom of Suffolk by the death of his brother. She was Lady of the Bedchamber to the Princess of Wales, afterwards Queen Caroline, and had the misfortune to please the Prince, afterwards George II. Her situation must have been sufficiently uncomfortable; for her husband was worthless and brutal, her royal lover neither generous nor amiable, and her mistress too jealous of power to permit any share of it to the favourite, though she connived at her husband's gallantry. Mrs. Howard is said to have obtained the good graces of the Prince of Wales from being the *confidante* of his unsuccessful attachment to Miss Bellenden, afterwards Duchess of Argyll. As she had all the appearance of influence, many courtiers sought her favour, as a sure road to promotion. These were universally disappointed; for the influence of Queen Caroline, always most powerful with her husband, was secretly

an end; and, in order to be revenged, I have sent you a piece of Irish Plaid, made in imitation of the Indian, wherein our workmen are grown so expert, that, in this kind of stuff, they are said to excel that which comes from the Indies; and, because our ladies are too proud to wear what is made at home, the workman is forced to run a gold thread through the middle, and sell it as *Indian*. But I ordered him to leave out that circumstance, that you may be clad in Irish stuff, and in my livery.

But I beg you will not tell any Parliament-men from whence you had the Plaid; otherwise, out of malice, they will make a law to cut off all our weavers' fingers. I must likewise tell you, to prevent your pride, my intention is to use you very scurvily. For my real design is, that when the Princess asks you where you got that fine night-gown, you are to say that it is an Irish Plaid sent you by the Dean of St. Patrick's who, with his most humble duty to her Royal Highness, is ready to make her such another present, at the terrible expense of eight shillings and threepence per yard, if she will descend to honour Ireland with receiving and wearing it. And, in recompense, I, who govern the vulgar, will take care to have her Royal Highness's health drunk by five hundred weavers, as an encourager of the Irish manufactory. And I command you to add, that I am no courtier, nor have anything to ask. May all courtiers imitate me in that! . . . I hope the whole royal family about you is in health. Dr. Arbuthnot lately mortified me with an account of a great pain in your head. I believe that no head, that is good for anything, is long without some disorder—at least, that is the best argument *I* had for anything that is good in my own.

exerted against those who chose this contraband path to favour. The intercession in favour of Gay is supposed to have made shipwreck upon this concealed rock. Many curious anecdotes respecting Mrs. Howard, afterwards Lady Suffolk, are to be found in Horace Walpole's *Reminiscences*.—S. Swift had been one of these disappointed courtiers.—See *Life and Writings of Swift*.

I pray God preserve you, and entreat you to believe that I am, with great respect, Madam, you most obedient and most obliged servant.[1]

[1] Mrs. Howard, in her letter of acknowledgment, dated Nov. 1726, at the moment of the publication of *The Travels*, writes:—"I did not expect that the sight of my ring would produce the effect it has. I was in such a hurry to show your plaid to the Princess, that I could not stay to put it into the shape you desired. It pleased extremely, and I have orders to fit it up according to the first design. But, as this is not proper for the public, you are desired to send over, for the same Princess's use, the height of the Brobdingnag's dwarf multiplied by two-and-a-half. . . . If you want a more particular and better rule, I refer you to the *Academy of Lagado*. I am of opinion that many in this kingdom will soon appear in your plaid. . . . The Princess will take care that you shall have pumps sufficient to serve you till you return to England: but thinks you cannot, in common decency, appear in *heels* [High heels, presumably. High heels, as is well known, in Lilliput, were the badge of the High Church, Low heels of the Low Church Party], and, therefore, advises your keeping close till they arrive.

"Here are several Lilliputian mathematicians, so that the length of your head, or of your foot, is a sufficient measure. Send it by the first opportunity. Do not forget our good friends, the five hundred weavers. You may omit the gold thread. Many disputes have arisen here, whether the Big-Endians and Lesser-Endians ever differed in opinion about the breaking of eggs—when they were to be either buttered or poached, or whether this part of cookery was ever known in Lilliput. [The Big-Endians and their opponents representing the two great Christian sects.]

"I cannot conclude without telling you that our Island is in great joy: one of our Yahoos having been delivered of a creature, half ram and half Yahoo, and another has brought forth four perfect black rabbits. [An impostor, Mary Tofts, put some such trick upon the public at this time, and met with credit even among medical practioners.] May we not hope, and with some probability expect, that, in time, our female Yahoos will produce a race of Houyhnhnms?"

Mrs. Howard subscribes herself, "*Sieve Yahoo*, the Court lady." The prefix *Sieve* being derived from a passage in the *Voyage to Laputa*, where Gulliver informs his friend, the Laputan Professor, of certain forced interpretations given to words by official specialists—a *Sieve* becoming, in this distorted language, the synonym for a Court-lady. This letter of Mrs. Howard is one of many proofs that the MS. of the *Travels* was handed about pretty freely before its publication, for the Second Part did not appear until the next year.

TO THE HON. MRS. HOWARD.

Nov. 17, 1726.

When I received your letter, I thought it the most unaccountable one I ever saw in my life, and was not able to comprehend three words of it together. The perverseness of your lines astonished me, which tended downward to the right in one page, and upward in the two others. This I thought impossible to be done by any one who did not squint with both eyes—an infirmity I never observed in you. However, one thing I was pleased with, that after you had writ *down*, you repented, and writ *up* again.

But I continued four days at a loss for your meaning, till a bookseller sent me the Travels of one Captain Gulliver, who proved a very good explainer,[1] although, at the same time, I thought it hard to be forced to read a book of seven hundred pages, in order to understand a letter of fifty lines; especially, as those of our faculty are already but too much pestered with Commentators. The stuffs you require are making, because the weaver piques himself upon having them in perfection. But he has read Gulliver's book, and has no conception what you mean by returning money; for he has become a proselyte of the Houyhnhnms, whose great principle, if I remember right, is *benevolence*. And as to myself, I am so highly offended with such a base proposal, that I am determined to complain of you to her Royal Highness, that you are a mercenary Yahoo, fond of *shining pebbles*. What have I to do with you or your Court, further than to shew the esteem I have for your person, because you happen to deserve it; and my gratitude to her Royal Highness, who was pleased a little to distinguish me?

---

[1] In which it is said that the Lilliputians, like the ladies of England, write from one corner of the page to the other.—S.

Which, by the way, is the greatest compliment I ever paid, and may probably be the last; for I am not such a prostitute flatterer as Gulliver, whose chief study is to extenuate the vices, and magnify the virtues, of mankind, and perpetually dins our ears with the praises of his country, in the midst of corruption; and for that reason alone has found so many readers, and probably will have a pension, which, I suppose, was his chief design in writing. As for his compliments to the ladies, I can easily forgive him, as a natural effect of the devotion which our sex ought always to pay to yours.

You need not be in pain about the officers searching or seizing the plaids; for the silk has already paid duty in England, and there is no law against exporting silk manufacture from hence. I am sure the Princess and you have got the length of my foot, and Sir Robert Walpole says he has the length of my head,[1] so that I need not give you the trouble of sending you either. I shall only tell you, in general, that I never had a long head, and, for that reason, few people have thought it worth while to get the length of my foot. I cannot answer your queries about eggs buttered or poached; but I possess one talent which admirably qualifies me for *roasting* them. For as the world, with respect to eggs, is divided into *pelters* and *roasters*, it is my unhappiness to be one of the latter, and, consequently, to be persecuted by the former. I have been five days turning over old books to discover the meaning of those monstrous births you mention. That of the four black Rabbits seems to threaten some dark Court intrigue, and, perhaps, some change in the Administration; for the Rabbit is an undermining animal, that loves to walk in the dark. The blackness denotes the Bishops, whereof some of the last you have made are persons of such dangerous parts and profound abilities. But Rabbits, being clothed in furs, may,

---

[1] Swift had lately had an interview with the Premier —See *Life of Swift.*

perhaps, glance at the Judges.[1] However, the Ram, by which is meant the Ministry, butting with his two horns, one against the Church, and the other against the Law, shall obtain the victory. And, whereas the birth was a conjunction of Ram and Yahoo, this is easily explained by the story of Chiron governor, or, which is the same thing, chief minister to Achilles, who was half man and half brute; which, as Machiavel observes, all good governors of Princes ought to be.[2]

But I am at the end of my line, and my lines. This is without a cover, to save money; and plain paper, because the gilt is so thin, it will discover secrets between us. In a little room for

---

[1] Rabelais, it will be remembered, represents the interpreters of the Law as "Furred Cats"—*Chats Fourrés.*

[2] Lord Peterborough, in a letter to Swift, a week later, wittily notices this latest credulity of the time, after referring to the sensation produced by the Travels:—"The new language [of Gulliver] in fashion is much studied, and great pains taken about the pronunciation. Everybody (since a new turn) approves of it; but the women seem most satisfied. . . . . It suffices to let you know that there is a *neighing* duetto appointed for the next opera. Strange distempers rage in the nation, which your friend the doctor [Arbuthnot] takes no care of. In some, the imagination is struck with the apprehension of swelling to a giant, or dwindling to a pigmy. Others expect an oration, equal to any in Cicero's, from an eloquent bard, and some take the braying of an ass for the Emperor's speech in favour of the Vienna Alliance. The knowledge of the ancient world is of no use; men have lost their titles, continents and islands have got new names, just upon the appearance of a certain book. Women bring forth rabbits; and every man, whose wife has conceived, expects an heir with four legs. It was concluded not long ago that such confusion could only be brought about by the Black Art, and by the spells of a notorious Scribbling Magician, who was generally suspected, and was to be recommended to the mercy of the Inquisition. . . . They pretended to bring in certain proofs of his appearance in several shapes—at one time a drapier, at another a Wapping surgeon, sometimes a *nardac*, sometimes a reverend divine. This was the scene not many days ago, and burning was too good for the wizard! But what mutations among the Lilliputians! The greatest lady in the nation resolves to send a pair of shoes without heels to Captain Gulliver. She takes *vi et armis* the plaid from the lady it was sent to, which is soon to appear upon her royal person; and now who but Captain Gulliver? The Captain, indeed, has nothing more to do but to chalk his pumps, learn to dance upon the rope, and I may yet live to see him a Bishop. Verily, I believe he never was in such imminent danger of preferment.—Sir, your affect. Tar."

words I assure you of my being, with truest respect, Madam, your most obedient humble servant.

To Mr. Pope.

November 17, 1726.

I am just come from answering a letter of Mrs. Howard's, writ in such mystical turns, that I should never have found out the meaning, if a book had not been sent me called *Gulliver's Travels*, of which you say so much in yours. I read the book over, and, in the second volume, observed several passages which appeared to be patched and altered,[1] and the style of a different sort, unless I am mistaken. Dr. Arbuthnot likes the Projectors[2] least; others the Flying Island; some think it wrong to be so hard upon whole bodies or corporations. Yet the general opinion is that reflections on particular persons are most to be blamed; so that, in these cases, I think the best method is to let censure and opinion take their course. A bishop here said, That book was full of improbabilities, and, for his part, he hardly believed a word of it—and so much for Gulliver.

Going to England is a very good thing, if it were not attended with an ugly circumstance of returning to Ireland. It is a shame you do not persuade your Ministers to keep me on that side, if it were but by a Court expedient of keeping me in prison for a plotter. But, at the same time, I must tell you, that such journeys very much shorten my life; for a month here is longer than six at Twickenham. How comes friend Gay to be so tedious? Another man can publish fifty thousand lies sooner than he can publish fifty *fables*.

[1] See the introductory letter of Gulliver to his cousin Sympson.—S.
[2] Because he understood it to be a satire upon the Royal Society.—Warburton.

I am just going to perform a very good office. It is to assist with the Archbishop in degrading a parson who couples all our beggars, by which I shall make one happy man, and decide the great question, of an indelible character, in favour of the principles in fashion. This I hope you will represent to the Ministry, in my favour, as a point of merit.—I am come back, and have deprived the parson, who, by a law here, is to be hanged the next couple he marries. He declared to us that he resolved to be hanged; only desired that, when he was to go to the gallows, the Archbishop would take off his excommunication. Is not he a good Catholic? And yet he is but a Scotchman. This is the only Irish event I ever troubled you with, and I think it deserves notice. Let me add that, if I were Gulliver's friends, I would desire all my acquaintance to give out, that his copy was basely mangled and abused, and added to, and blotted out by the printer: for so to me it seems, in the second volume particularly.[1] Adieu.

To the Hon. Mrs. Howard.[2]

[December, 1726.?]

My correspondents have informed me that your Ladyship has done me the honour to answer several objections that ignorance, malice, and Party, have made to my Travels, and been so charitable as to justify the fidelity and veracity of the author.

This zeal you have shewn for truth calls for my particular thanks and, at the same time, encourages me to beg you would

[1] In the original copy the fourth part, on the Houyhnhmns and Yahoos, has, as already observed, two or three long paragraphs erased for alteration in ensuing editions.

[2] This letter must have been written about the end of the year 1726. It is in the character of Gulliver.—S.

continue your goodness to me by reconciling me to the Maids of Honour, whom they say I have most grievously offended. I am so stupid as not to find out how I have disobliged them. Is there any harm in a young lady's reading of romances? Or did I make use of an improper engine to extinguish a fire that was kindled by a Maid of Honour? And I will venture to affirm that, if ever the young ladies of your Court should meet with a man of as little consequence in this country as I was in Brobdingnag, they would use him with as much contempt. But I submit myself and my cause to your better judgment, and beg leave to lay the crown of Lilliput at your feet, as a small acknowledgment of your favour to my book and person.

I found it in the corner of my waistcoat pocket, into which I thrust most of the valuable furniture of the royal apartment, when the Palace was on fire, and, by mistake, brought it with me into England. For I very honestly restored to their Majesties all their goods that I knew were in my possession. May all Courtiers imitate me in that, and my being, Madam, &c.

To Miss Martha Blount.
Dublin, February 29, 1727-8.

I am told you have a mind to receive a letter from me, which is a very indecent declaration in a young lady, and almost a confession that you have a mind to write to me; for as to the fancy of looking on me as a man *sans consequence*, it is what I will never understand. I am told, likewise, you grow every day younger, and more a fool, which is directly contrary to me, who grow wiser and older, and at this rate we shall never agree. I long to see you a London lady, where you are forced to wear whole clothes, and visit in a chair; for which you must starve next summer at Petersham, with a mantua out at the sides,¹ and spunge once a week at our house, without ever nviting us in a whole season to a cow-heel at home.

I wish you would bring Mr. Pope over with you when you come; but we will leave Mr. Gay to his Beggars and his Operas till he is able to pay his Club. How will you pass this summer, for want of a squire to Ham Common and Walpole's Lodge; for as to Richmond Lodge and Marble Hill, they are abandoned as much as Sir Spencer Compton; and Mr. Schabe's coach, that used to give you so many a set down, is wheeled off to St. James's. You must be forced to get a horse, and gallop with Mrs. Jansen and Miss Bedier. Your greatest happiness is that you are out of the chiding of Mrs. Howard and the Dean; but I suppose Mr. Pope is so just as to pay our arrears, and that you edify as much by him as by us, unless you are so happy that he now looks upon you as reprobate and a cast-away, of which I think he hath given me some hints. However, I would advise you to pass this summer at Kensington, where you will be near the Court, and out of his jurisdiction, where you will be teased with no lectures of gravity and morality, and where you will have no other trouble than to get into the mercer's books, and take up a hundred pounds of your principal for quadrille. Monstrous indeed, that a fine lady, in the prime of life and gaiety, must take up with an antiquated Dean, an old gentlewoman of four-score,² and a sickly poet. I will stand by my dear Patty against the world, if Teresa beats you for your good, and I will buy her a fine whip for the purpose.

¹ "This confinement [from illness], together with the mourning [for George I.]" writes Miss M. Blount to Swift, "has enabled me to be very cosy in my chair here; for a dyed black gown and a scoured white one have done my business very well; and they are now just fit for Petersham, where we talk of going in three weeks; and I am not without hopes I shall have the same squire that I had last year. I am very unwilling to change, and, moreover, I begin to fear I have no great prospect of getting any new danglers."

² Pope's mother, who lived with him at Twickenham.

Tell me, have you been confined to your lodgings this winter for want of chair-hire? [Do you know that this unlucky Dr. Delany came last night to the Deanery, and, being denied without my knowledge, is gone to England this morning, and so I must send this by the post? I bought your *Opera* to-day for sixpence, so small-printed that it will spoil my eyes. I ordered you to send me your edition; but now you may keep it till you get an opportunity.] Patty, I will tell you a blunder: I am writing to Mr. Gay, and had almost finished the letter; but by mistake I took up this instead of it; and so the six lines in a hook are all to him, and therefore you must read them to him; for I will not be at the trouble to write them over again. My greatest concern in the matter is, that I am afraid I continue in love with you, which is hard after near six months' absence. I hope you have done with your *rash* and other little disorders, and that I shall see you a fine young, healthy, plump lady; and, if Mr. Pope chides you, threaten him that you will turn heretic.

Adieu, dear Patty, and believe me to be one of your truest friends and humblest servants; and that, since I can never live in England, my greatest happiness would be to have you and Mr. Pope condemned, during my life, to live in Ireland—he, at the Deanery, and you, for reputation's sake, just at next door, and I will give you eight dinners a week, and a whole half dozen of pint bottles of good French wines, at your lodgings, a thing you could never expect to arrive at, and every year a suit of fourteenpenny stuff, that should not be worn out at the right side; and a [sedan] chair costs but sixpence a job; and you shall have Catholicity as much as you please, and the Catholic Dean of St. Patrick's, as old again as I, for your confessor. Adieu, again, dear Patty.

To Dr. Sheridan.

London, May 13, 1727.

This goes by a private hand, for my writing is too much known, and my letters often stopped and opened. I had yours of the fourth instant, and it is the only one I have received out of Ireland since I left you.

I hardly thought our friend [1] would be in danger by a cold. I am of opinion she should be generally in the country, and only now and then visit the town. We are in a strange situation: a firm settled resolution to assault the present Administration, and break it if possible.[2] It is certain that Walpole is peevish and disconcerted, stoops to the vilest offices of hireling [hiring?] scoundrels to write Billingsgate of the lowest and most prostitute kind, and has none but beasts and blockheads for his penmen, whom he pays in ready guineas very liberally. I am in high displeasure with him and his partisans. A great man, who was very kind to me last year, doth not take the least notice of me at the Prince's Court, and there hath not been one of them to see me. I am advised by all my friends not to go to France (as I intended for two months), for fear of their vengeance in a manner which they cannot execute here. I reckon there will be a warm winter, wherein, my comfort is, I shall have no concern.

I desire you will read this letter to none but our two friends and Mr. P——. His cousin, with the red ribbon, inquired very kindly after him. I hear no news about your Bishops, farther than that the Lord Lieutenant stickles to have them of Ireland, which Walpole always is adverse from, but does not think it

---

[1] Esther Johnson, whom he rarely mentions *by name*. Writing to Walls from Dublin (April 8), desiring him to be his proxy at the Bishop's visitation, he informs him, "the ladies are with me, being now come to live at the Deanery for this summer"

[2] This alludes to the coalition of Bolingbroke and Pulteney.—S.

worth his trouble to exert his credit on such trifles. The dispute about a war, or no war, still continues, and the major part inclines to the latter, although ten thousand men are ordered to Holland. But this will bring such an addition to our debts, that it will give great advantages against those in power, in the next sessions. Walpole laughs at all this, but not so heartily as he used.

I have at last seen the Princess—twice this week, by her own command. She retains her old civility, and I my old freedom. She charges me, without ceremony, to be the author of a bad book; though I told her how angry the Ministry were. But she assures me that both she and the Prince were very well pleased with every particular. But I disown the whole affair, as you know I very well might; only gave her leave, since she liked the book, to suppose what author she pleased. You will wonder to find me say so much about politics, but I keep very bad company, who are full of nothing else. Pray be very careful of your charge,[1] or I shall order my lodgers the bulk of their glasses, and the number of their bottles. I stole this time to write you, having very little to spare. I go as soon as possible to the country, and shall rarely see this town. My service to all friends.

I desire you will send me six sets of the edition of the *Drapiers* by the first convenience of any friend or acquaintance that comes hither.

To Dr. Sheridan.

Twickenham, July 1, 1727.

I had yours of June 22. You complain of not hearing from me. I never was so constant a writer. I have writ six

[1] Esther Johnson and her friend, who were left at the Deanery, in the care of Sheridan.

times to our friends,[1] and as many to you. Mr. Pope is reading your Persius:[2] he is frequently sick, and so at this time. He has read it, but you must wait till next letter for his judgment. He would know whether it is designed for an elegant translation, or only to shew the meaning. I reckon it an explanation of a difficult author, not only for learners, but for those also who are not expert in Latin, because he is a very dark author. I would not have your book printed entire, till I treat with my bookseller for your advantage. There is a word *(Concacuus)*[3] which you have not explained, nor the reason of it. Where you are ignorant, you should confess you are ignorant.

I writ to Stella the day we heard the King was dead, and the circumstances of it. I hold you a guinea, I shall forget something. Worrall writ to me lately. In answer, I desire that when the Archbishop comes to a determination, an appeal be properly lodged, by which I will elude him till my return, which will be at Michaelmas. I have left London, and stay here a week, and then I shall go thither again, just to see the Queen, and so come back hither. Here are a thousand schemes, wherein they would have me engaged, which I embrace but coldly, because I like none of them. I have been this ten days inclined to my old disease of giddiness, a little tottering. Our friend [Stella] understands it; but I grow cautious, and am something better—cyder, and champagne, and fruit have been the cause. But now I am very regular, and I eat enough. I took Dr. Delany's Paper to the King when he was Prince. He and his Secretary [Molyneux] are discontented with the Provost,[4] but they find that he has law on his side. The King's death

---

[1] The two ladies at the Deanery.

[2] Sheridan had lately published an English version of this Latin satirist.

[3] No such word is found in the *Satires* of Persius, nor in any Latin classic writer. If the editor or printer have not blundered, Swift must have been playing off a joke.

[4] Of Trinity College, Dublin—Baldwin by name. Swift refers to some obscure dispute.

hath broke that measure. I proposed the Prince of Wales to be Chancellor [of Dublin University], and I believe so it will go.

Pray, copy out the verses I writ to Stella on her collecting my verses, and send them to me; for we want some to make our poetic Miscellany large enough, and I am not there to pick what should be added. Direct them and all other double papers to Lord Bathurst, in St. James's Square, London. I was in a fright about your verses on Stella's sickness; but glad when they were a month old.

Desire our friends to let me know what I should buy for them here of any kind. I had just now a long letter from Mrs. Dingley, and another from Mr. Synge. Pray, tell the latter that I return him great thanks, and will leave the visiting affair to his discretion. But all the lawyers in Europe shall never persuade me that it is in the Archbishop's power to take or refuse my proxy, when I have the King's leave of absence. If he be violent, I will appeal, and die two or three hundred pounds poorer, to defend the rights of the Dean. Pray, ask Mr. Synge whether his *fenocchio* be grown; it is now fit to eat here, and we eat it like celery, either with or without oil, &c. I design to pass my time wholly in the country, having some business to do and settle before I leave England for the last time. I will send you Mr. Pope's criticism and my own on your Work. Pray, forget nothing of what I desire you. Pray God bless you all. If the King [George I.] had but lived ten days longer, I should be now at Paris.

Simpleton! the Drapiers should have been sent unbound; but it is no great matter. Two or three would have been enough. I see Mrs. Fad but seldom; I never trouble them but when I am sent for. She expects me soon, and, after that, perhaps no more while I am here. I desire it may be told that I never go to Court; which I mention because of a passage in Mrs. Dingley's letter. She speaks mighty good things of your kindness.

I do not want that Poem to Stella to print it entire, but some passages out of it, if they deserve it, to lengthen the volume [of *Miscellanies*]. Read all this letter without hesitation, and I will give you a pot of ale. I intend to be with you at Michaelmas, bar impossibilities.

TO MR. WORRALL.

London, Sept. 12, 1727.

I have not writ to you this long time, nor would I now, if it were not necessary. By Dr. Sheridan's frequent letters, I am every day expecting the death of a friend, with [after] whose loss I shall have very little regard for the few years that nature may leave me. I desire to know where my two friends lodge. I gave a caution to Mrs. Brent[1] that it might not be *in domo decani, quoniam hoc minime decet uti manifestum est. Habeo enim malignos, qui sinistrè hoc interpretabuntur, si eveniet (quod Deus evertat) ut illic moriatur.*[2] I am in such a condition of health, that I cannot possibly travel. Dr. Sheridan, to whom I write this post, will be more particular, and spare my weak disordered head. Pray, answer all calls of money in your power to Mrs. Dingley, and desire her to ask it. I cannot come back at the time of my license, I am afraid. Therefore, two or three days before it expires, which will be the beginning of October (you will find by the date of the last), take out a new

[1] His housekeeper.
[2] "In the Dean's house, for that, as is manifest, is by no means becoming, forasmuch as I have malignant enemies who will put a bad interpretation upon it, if (which may heaven avert!) it should happen that she were to die there.

one for another half year, and let the same clause be in—of leave to go to Great Britain, or elsewhere, for the recovery of his health—for, very probably, if this unfortunate event should happen of the loss of our friend (and I have no probability or hopes to expect better), I will go to France, if my health will permit me, to forget myself.[1] I leave my whole little affairs with you; I hate to think of them.

If Mr. Deacon, or Alderman Pearson, come to pay rent, take it on account, unless they bring you their last acquittance to direct you. But Deacon owes me seventy-five pounds, and interest, upon his bond; so that you are to take care of giving him any receipt, in full, of all accounts. I hope you and Mrs. Worrall have your health. I can hold up my head no longer. I am sincerely yours, &c.

You need not trouble yourself to write till you have business; for it is uncertain where I shall be.

To Mr. Benjamin Motte.[2]

Dublin, Dec. 28, 1727.

I had yours of the 16th from Mr. Hyde, and desire that henceforth you write directly to me, without scrupling to load me with the postage. My head is so confused with the returns of my deafness to a very great degree (which left me after a

[1] Soon after the date of this letter the Dean went to Ireland; and Mrs. Johnson, after languishing about two months, died on the 28th of January, 1727-8.—Hawkesworth.

[2] From MS. letter, in the Forster Collection, South Kensington Museum. Motte was a bookseller at the Middle Temple Gate, Fleet Street, and publisher of *Gulliver*.

fortnight, and then returned with more violence), that I am in an ill way to answer a letter which requires some thinking.

As to having cuts in *Gulliver's Travels,* you will consider how much it will raise the price of the book. The world glutted itself with that book at first, and now it will go off but soberly; but I suppose will not soon be worn out. The Part of the *Little* men will bear cuts much better than that of the *Great.* I have not the book by me, but will speak by memory. Gulliver in his carriage to the metropolis; his extinguishing the fire; the ladies in their coaches driving about his [girdle]. His rising up out of his carriage, when he is fastened to his horse; his drawing the fleet; the troop upon his handkerchief; the army marching between his legs; his hat drawn by eight horses—seem the fittest to be represented, and perhaps two adventures may be sometimes put into one print.

It is difficult to do anything in the *Great* men, because Gulliver makes so diminutive a figure, and he is but one in the whole kingdom. Among some cuts I bought in London, he is shown taken out of the bowl of cream; but the hand that holds him hides the whole body. He would appear best wedged in the marrow-bone up to the middle, or in the monkey's arms upon the roof; or left upon the ridge, and the footman on the ladder going to relieve him; or fighting with the rats on the farmer's bed; or in the spaniel's mouth, which being described as a small dog he might look as large as a duck in one of ours. One of the best would be, I think, to see his chest just falling into the sea, while those eagles are quarrelling with one another; or the monkey haling him out of his box. Mr. Wotton, the painter, who draws landskips and horses, told Mr. Pope and me that the graver did wrong in not making the big folks [two words hopelessly illegible] and enormous; for, as drawn by those gravers, they look only like common human creatures. Gulliver being alone, and so little, cannot make the contrast appear.

The Flying Island might be drawn at large, as described in the book, and Gulliver drawing up into it, and some fellows with flappers. I know not what to do with the Projectors. Nor what figure the Island of Ghosts would make, or any passage related in it, because I do not well remember it.

The Country of Horses, I think, would furnish many. Gulliver brought to be compared with the Yahoos—the family at dinner, and he waiting; the Grand Council of Horses, assembled, sitting —one of them standing with a hoof extended, as if he were speaking; the she-Yahoos embracing Gulliver in the river, who turns away his head in disgust; the Yahoos got into a tree, to infest him under it; the Yahoos drawing carriages, and driven by a Horse with a whip in his hoof. I can think of no more. But Mr. Gay will advise you, and carry you to Mr. Wotton and some other skilful people.

As to the poetical volume of *Miscellany*,[1] I believe five parts in six, at least, are mine. Our two friends, you know, have printed their works already; and we could expect nothing but slight loose papers. There is all the poetry I writ worth printing. Mr. Pope rejected some I sent him, for I desired him to be as severe as possible, and I will take his judgment. He writ to me, that he intended a pleasant Discourse on the subject of Poetry should be printed later in the volume.[2] . . . not have let me suffer for my modesty, when I expected he could have done better. Others are more prudent, and cannot be blamed. I am as weary with writing as I fear you will be with reading. I am your, &c.

[1] The *Miscellanies*, the contributors to which were Swift, Pope, and Arbuthnot, was published by Pope during the visit of Swift to Twickenham in 1726. The principal contributor refused to share in the considerable pecuniary profits.

[2] A part of the letter here missing.

To Mr. Pope.

Dublin, Feb. 13, 1728-9.

I lived very easily in the country. Sir Arthur Acheson is a man of sense and a scholar, has a good voice, and my lady a better.[1] She is perfectly well-bred, and desirous to improve her understanding, which is very good, but cultivated too much like a fine lady.[2] She was my pupil there and severely chid, when she read wrong.[3] With that and walking, and making twenty little amusing improvements, and writing family-verses of mirth, by way of libels on my Lady, my time passed very well, and in very great order,—infinitely better than here, where I see no creature (but my servants, and my old Presbyterian housekeeper), denying myself to everybody, till I shall recover my ears.

The account of another Lord-Lieutenant was only in a common newspaper, when I was in the country;[4] and, if it should have happened to be true, I would have desired to have had access to him, as the situation I am in requires.[5] But this

---

[1] His difficulty in hearing rendered this important to him. "My duchess," he wrote to Mr. Worrall, Jan. 1729, "is not so extreme as you have known, when I have fretted at your mannerly voice. She is only relieved by Mrs. Worrall."—Elwin.

[2] See letter to Mrs. Pendarves (Jan. 1735).—Lady Acheson was not famous, it seems, for scholarship. In one of his poems Swift makes her say:

> "Poor I, a savage bred and born,
> By you instructed every morn,
> Already have improved so well
> That I have almost learned to spell."

[3] If Swift's verse is to be interpreted literally, she, the year after, grew impatient of his schooling:

> "Lest it may more quarrels breed,
> I will never hear you read."—E.

[4] It was a false report. Lord Carteret did not cease to be Lord Lieutenant of Ireland till May, 1730.—E.

[5] A passage seems to be missing here.

renews the grief for the death of our friend Mr. Congreve, whom I loved from my youth, and who surely, besides his other talents, was a very agreeable companion. He had the misfortune to squander away a very good constitution in his younger days; and, I think, a man of sense and merit like him is bound, in conscience, to preserve his health for the sake of his friends as well as of himself. Upon his own account, I could not much desire the continuance of his life under so much pain and so many infirmities. Years have not yet hardened me, and I have an addition of weight upon my spirits since we lost him, though I saw him so seldom; and possibly, if he had lived on, should never have seen him more.[1]

I do not only wish, as you ask me, that I was unacquainted with any deserving person, but almost that I never had a friend. Here is an ingenious, good-humoured physician, a fine gentleman, an excellent scholar,[2] easy in his fortunes, kind to everybody, has abundance of friends, entertains them often and liberally. They pass the evening with him at cards, with plenty of good [flesh] meat and wine, eight or a dozen together. He loves them all, and they him. He has twenty of these at command. If one of them dies, it is no more than poor Tom![3] He gets another, or takes up with the rest, and is no more moved than at the loss of his cat. He offends nobody, is easy with everybody. Is not this the true happy man? I was describing him to my Lady Acheson, who knows him too; but she hates him mortally by my character [of him], and will not drink his health. I would give half my fortune for the same temper, and yet I cannot say I love it; for I do not love my Lord —, who is much of the doctor's

[1] Swift was no admirer of his *Comedies.* "I looked into the volume," he remarks in one of his letters, " and, in mere loitering, read it till twelve, like an owl and a fool. If ever I do so again! Never saw the like." This *literary* indifference Congreve reciprocated, for he found nothing to admire in the *Tale of a Tub.*

[2] Dr. Helsham.

[3] A common term for poor and outcast. See *King Lear.*

nature. I hear Mr. Gay's second opera,¹ which you mention, is forbid, and then he will be once more fit to be advised, and reject your advice.—Adieu.

To Mr. Pope.

Dublin, March 6, 1728-9.

If I am not a good correspondent, I have bad health; and that is as good. I passed eight months in the country, with Sir Arthur and my Lady Acheson, and had, at least, half-a-dozen returns of my giddiness and deafness, which lasted me about three weeks apiece, and, among other inconveniences, hindered me from visiting my Chapter, and punishing enormities; but did not save me the charges of a Visitation Dinner.²

This disorder neither hinders my sleeping, nor much my walking; yet is the most mortifying malady I can suffer. I have been just a month, and have just got rid of it in a fortnight; and, when it is on me, I have neither spirits to write, or read, or think, or eat. But I drink as much as I like, which is a resource you cannot fly to, when you are ill. And I like it as

---

¹ *Polly.* The Lord Chamberlain, the Duke of the manager of the theatre that he would not permit it to be acted. Gay complained that he was persecuted for "writing in the cause of virtue," upon which Mr. Croker remarks:—Poor Gay must really have been, "in simplicity, a child," if he could persuade himself that the *Beggar's Opera* was written in the cause of virtue. He wrote it to make money, and to curry favour with the Prince, by assailing Walpole. . . . The Duke of Grafton's refusal to let it be produced on the stage enlisted party feeling on its side. The Duke and Duchess of Queensberry gave Gay an asylum in their house for the rest of his life; and from the subscriptions of the Opposition, and the sale of the printed play, he realized, as Pope told Spence, £1,100 or £1,200.—E.

² For a lively description of a *Visitation Dinner*, and of the inspired eloquence of the typical Dr. Marrowfat, see Goldsmith's *Citizen of the World*, lviii.

little as you; but I can bear a pint better than you can a spoonful. You were very kind in your care for Mr. Whaley; but I hope you remembered that Daniel is a damnable poet,[1] and consequently a public enemy to mankind. But I despise the Lords' decree, which is a jest upon common sense; for what did it signify to the merits of the Cause, whether George the Old, or the Young, were on the throne.

No. I intended to pass last winter in England, but my health said no; and I did design to live a gentleman, and, as Sancho's wife said, to go in my coach to Court. I know not whether you are in earnest to come hither in spring. If not, pray God, you may never be in jest! Dr. Delany shall attend you at Chester, and your apartment is ready; and I have a most excellent chaise, and about sixteen dozen of the best cider in the world; and you shall command the town and kingdom, and *digito monstrari*.[2] And, when *I* cannot hear, you shall have choice of the best people we can afford, to hear you, and nurses enough; and your apartment is on the sunny side.

The next paragraph strikes me dumb. You say, "I am to blame, if I refuse the opportunity of going with my Lady Bolingbroke to Aix la Chapelle." I must tell you that a foreign language is mortal to a deaf man. I must have good ears to catch up the words of so nimble a tongued race as the French, having been a dozen years without conversing among them. Mr. Gay is a scandal to all lusty young fellows with healthy countenances; and I think he is not intemperate in a physical sense. I am told he has an asthma, which is a disease I commiserate more than deafness, because it will not leave a man

---

[1] Richard Daniel, Dean of Armagh, attending as a witness in a lawsuit between Mr. Whaley and the Archbishop of Armagh on the one side, and the Crown on the other, which depended in the House of Lords on a writ of error, and in which the Dean greatly interested himself. Mr. Whaley was at length successful. The shape of the question resolved into a doubt, whether the death of George I. did not abate the writ.—S.

[2] "Et dicier, *Hic est*." Hor. Sat.

quiet either sleeping or waking. I hope he does not intend to print his Opera[1] before it is acted; for I defy all your subscriptions to amount to eight hundred pounds. And yet, I believe, he lost as much more for want of human prudence.

I told you some time ago, that I was dwindled to a writer of libels on the lady of the family where I lived,[2] and upon myself. But they never went further; and my Lady Acheson made me give her up all the foul copies, and never gave the fair ones out of her hands, or suffered them to be copied. They were sometimes shewn to intimate friends, to occasion mirth, and that was all. So that I am vexed at your thinking I had any hand in what could come to your eyes. I have some confused notion of seeing a paper called *Sir Ralph the Patriot*,[3] but am sure it was bad or indifferent; and as to the *Lady at Quadrille*, I never heard of it. Perhaps it may be the same with a paper of verses called *The Journal of a Dublin Lady*, which I writ at Sir Arthur Acheson's, and, leaving out what concerned the family, I sent it to be printed in a Paper which Dr. Sheridan had engaged in, called the *Intelligencer*, of which he made but sorry work, and then dropped it. But the verses were printed by themselves, and most horridly mangled in the press, and were very *mediocre* in themselves; but did well enough in the manner I mentioned, of a family jest.

I do sincerely assure you, that my frequent old disorders,

---

[1] The Second Part of the *Beggar's Opera*, which was excluded from the theatre by order of the Chamberlain.—S. It was entitled *Polly*.

[2] Lady Acheson, at whose request the "libels," in the shape of verse, were composed: although it was commonly said, or believed, that they were malicious verses, and a proof of his ingratitude. The most considerable of them is the piece on *Hamilton's Bawn*. See *Life, &c.* A far less creditable *jeu d'esprit*, as far as propriety was concerned, was his *Panegyric on the Dean*, which, to make matters worse, he attributed to his hostess.

[3] It appeared first in the *Country Journal*, Aug. 1728, and was transferred from thence to the 12th No. of the *Intelligencer*.—S. , The full title of this set of verses is *The Progress of Patriotism: a Tale*; a satire on Walpole. Scott evidently believes them to be Swift's.

and the scene where I am, and the humour I am in, and some other reasons which time has shewn, and will shew more if I live, have lowered my small talents with a vengeance, and cooled my disposition to put them in use. I want only to be rich, for I am hard to be pleased; and, for want of riches, people grow every day less solicitous to please me. Therefore I keep humble company, who are happy to come where they can get a bottle of wine, without paying for it. I give my vicar a supper, and his wife a shilling, to play with me at home at backgammon once a fortnight. To all people of quality, and especially of titles, I am not within; or, at least, am deaf a week or two after I am well. But, on Sunday evenings, it costs me six bottles of wine to people whom I cannot keep out. Pray, come over in April, if it be only to convince you that I tell no lies; and the journey will certainly be for your health. Mrs. Brent, my housekeeper, famous in print for digging out the great bottle, says, "she will be your nurse," and the best physicians we have shall attend you without fees: although, I believe, you will have no occasion but to converse with one or two of them, to make them proud. Your letter came but last post, and you see my punctuality. I am unlucky at everything I send to England. Two bottles of Usquebaugh were broken.

Well, my humble services to my Lord Bolingbroke, Lord Bathurst, Lord Masham and his lady, my dear friend, and Mr. Pulteney, and the Doctor, and Mr. Lewis, and our sickly friend Gay, and my Lady Bolingbroke; and very much to Patty [Blount], who, I hope, will learn to love the world less, before the world leaves off to love her. I am much concerned to hear of my Lord Peterborough being ill. I am exceedingly his servant, and pray God recover his health. As for your courtier, Mrs. Howard, and her mistress, I have nothing to say, but that they have neither memory nor manners; else I should have some mark of the former from the latter, which I was promised about two years ago. But, since I made them a present,[1] it would be mean to remind them. I am told poor Mrs. Pope is ill: pray God preserve her to you, or raise you up as useful a friend!

This letter is in answer to Mr. Ford, whose hand I mistook for yours, having not heard from him this twelvemonth. Therefore, you are not to stare; and it must not be lost, for it talks to you only. Again, forgive my blunders; for, reading the letter by candle-light, and not dreaming of a letter from Mr. Ford, I thought it must be yours, because it talks of our friends. The letter talks of Gay, and Mr. Whaley, and Lord Bolingbroke; which made me conclude it must be yours. So all the answering part must go for nothing.

To Lord Bolingbroke.

Dublin, Oct. 31, 1729.

I received your Lordship's travelling letters of several dates at several stages, and from different nations, languages, and religions. Neither could anything be more obliging than your kind remembrance of me in so many places. As to your ten *lustres*. I remember when I complained in a letter to Prior, that I was fifty years old, he was half angry in jest, and answered me out of Terence, *ista commemoratio est quasi exprobatio*. How then ought I to rattle you, when I have a dozen years more to answer for, all monastically passed in this country of liberty, and delight, and money, and good company!

I go on answering your letter.—It is you were my hero, but

---

[1] Of Irish plaid. Swift expected a present of Medals from the Queen, which he never received.

the other [1] never was. Yet if he were, it was your own fault, who taught me to love him, and often vindicated him, in the beginning of your Ministry, from my accusations. But I granted that he had the greatest inequalities of any man alive, and his whole scene was fifty times more a *what-d'ye-call-it* than yours, for I declare yours was *unie;* and I wish you would so order it, that the world may be as wise as I upon that article. Mr. Pope wishes it too, and I believe there is not a more honest man in England, even without wit. But you regard us not. I was forty-seven years old when I began to think of death;[2] and the reflections upon it now begin when I wake in the morning, and end when I am going to sleep.

My birth, although from a family not undistinguished in its time, is many degrees inferior to yours; all my pretensions from person and parts infinitely so. I a younger son of younger sons, you born to a great fortune. Yet I see you, with all your advantages, sunk to a degree that you could not have been, without them. But yet I see you as much esteemed, as much beloved, as much and perhaps more (though it be almost

---

[1] Lord Oxford.—Warburton. This passage has been founded upon by the late ingenious Mr. Warton, as inconsistent with Swift's preference of Oxford to Bolingbroke. But to those who look narrowly into Swift's writings it will, perhaps, appear that he preferred Lord Oxford as a private friend, yet believed that much of the ruin of Queen Anne's Administration was owing, on the one hand, to his indolence, and, on the other, to his jealousy of Bolingbroke, whose active spirit was more fitted to meet the events of that critical period.—S. In his letter to Swift, from Aix-la-Chapelle and Brussels, Bolingbroke had thus referred to his old rival, Oxford:—" Both of us [Lady Bolingbroke was with him] have closed the tenth *lustre,* and it is high time to determine how we shall play the last act of the farce. Might not my life be entitled much more properly a *What-d'ye-Call-It* than a Farce? Some comedy, a great deal of tragedy, and the whole interspersed with scenes of Harlequin, Scaramouch, and Dr. Balvardo, the prototype of your hero, Oxford." In the same letter he speaks of "your old prating friend, Montaigne." The *What-d'ye-Call-It* is a farce of Gay's.

[2] The year of Queen Anne's death.—Warburton. The remark arises in reference to his correspondent's quasi-philosophical platitudes, which are at once so common and so unreal.

impossible) than ever you were in your highest exultation—only I grieve, like an Alderman, that you are not so rich. And yet, my Lord, I pretend to value money as little as you, and I will call five hundred witnesses (if you will take Irish witnesses) to prove it. I renounce your whole philosophy, because it is not your practice. By the *figure* of living—if I used that expression to Mr. Pope—I do not mean the parade, but a suitableness to your mind; and, as for the pleasure of giving, I know your soul suffers, when you are debarred of it.

Could you, when your own generosity and contempt of outward things (be not offended, it is no ecclesiastical, but an Epictetian, phrase) could you, when these have brought you to it, come over and live with Mr. Pope and me at the Deanery? I could almost wish the experiment were tried. No, God forbid that ever such a scoundrel as Want should desire to approach me.[1] But, in the meantime, do not brag — retrenchments are not your talent. But, as old Weymouth said to me in his lordly Latin, *philosopha verba, ignava opera.* I wish you could learn arithmetic, that three and two make five, and will never make more. My philosophical spectacles, which you advise me to, will tell me that I can live upon fifty pounds a year (wine excluded, which my bad health forces me to); but I cannot endure that *otium* should be *sine dignitate.* My Lord, what I would have said of fame is meant of fame which a man enjoys in this life. Because I cannot be a great lord, I would acquire what

[1] Bolingbroke had, in joke or earnest, asked him to "come over and live with Pope and me. I will show you in an instant, why these two things ["the figure of living and the pleasure of giving"] should not *aller de pair*, and that forced retrenchments on both may be made, without making us uneasy. You know I am too expensive, and all mankind knows that I have been cruelly plundered; and yet I feel, in my mind, the power of descending, without anxiety, two or three stages more. In short, Mr. Dean, if you will come to a certain farm [Dawley] in Middlesex, you shall find that I can live frugally, without growling at the world, or being peevish with those whom Fortune has appointed to eat my bread, instead of appointing me to eat theirs; and yet I have," he reminds his friend, unnecessarily, "naturally, as little disposition to frugality as any man alive."

is a kind of *subsidium*. I would endeavour that my betters should seek me by the merit of something distinguishable, instead of my seeking them. The desire of enjoying it, in after times, is owing to the spirit and folly of youth. But with age we learn to know the house is so full, that there is no room for above one or two at most in an Age, through the whole world.[1]

My Lord, I hate and love to write you. It gives me pleasure, and kills me with melancholy. The devil take stupidity [stupor], that it will not come to supply the want of philosophy.

To Mr. Gay.

Dublin, November 20, 1729.

In answer to your kind reproaches of the 9th instant, I declare myself to have not received above two letters from you at most since I left England. I have every letter by me that you writ since I first knew you, although neither those, nor of some other friends, are in such order as I have long intended them. But one thing you are to consider, because it is an old compact, that when I write to you or Mr. Pope, I write to both; and, if you are such a vagabond and truant as not to see your friends above once a quarter, who is to blame? Who could write to you in Scotland? Yet I am glad you were in a country nine times worse than this, wherein I speak very favourably of the soil, the

---

[1] When Lord Bolingbroke was very old, in his retirement at Battersea, it was customary for many people to pay their respects to him, chiefly with the view of seeing and conversing with a character so distinguished. Among others, Lord Chatham, then a young man, called on him: but found him pedantic, fretful, angry with his wife, &c. Such is the melancholy picture of the last stage of existence! (Communicated by Lord Chatham to the late Marquis of Lansdowne.)—S.

climate, and the language. But you were among a brave people and defenders of their liberty, which out-balances all our advantages of Nature. Here I will define Ireland a region of good eating and drinking, of tolerable company, where a man from England may sojourn some years with pleasure, make a fortune, and then return home with the spoils he has got by doing us all the mischief he can, and by that make a merit at Court. Pray, tell Mr. Pope what a wise thing he has done. He gave my Lord Allen's lady a commission to buy him here a bed of Irish stuff. Like a right Englishman, he did not imagine any nation of human creatures were deprived of sending their own goods abroad. But we cannot send an inch of wrought woollen to any foreign place without the penalty of 500*l.*, and forfeiture of the stuff, and the English sea-publicans [1] grumble if we carry our own night gowns, unless they be old. Lady Allen used all endeavours, but found it impossible, and I told her she was a fool to attempt it. But, if he will come over, he shall lie in one of mine.

I have heard of the *Wife of Bath*,[2] I think in Shakespeare. If you wrote one, it is out of my head. I had not the cant word *damned* in my head; but if it were acted, and damned, and printed, I should not be your counsellor to new lick it. I wonder you will doubt of your genius. The world is wider to a poet than to any other man, and new follies and vices will never be wanting, any more than new fashions. *Je donne au diable* the wrong notion that matter is exhausted; for, as poets, in their Greek name, are called *creators*, so in one circumstance they resemble the great Creator by having an infinity of space to work in.

Mr. Pope has been teased ten times to pay your five guineas,

---

[1] Custom-house officers.

[2] Gay's first comedy, acted unsuccessfully at Drury Lane, in 1713. It was altered by the author, and again put on the stage in 1730—again without success. In his letter to Swift, Gay tells him that—"the ridicule turns upon superstition, and I have avoided the very words bribery and corruption."

and in his last letter he says it is done. But you say otherwise. However, I do not understand Lord Bathurst to be my cashier, but my cully and creditor upon interest; else you are a bad manager, and our money had better have been in the funds. I assure you, I will give Lord Carteret a note on him for nine guineas, which his Excellency has squeezed from many of us for a job to Buckley, the Gazetteer, who, in conjunction with a jacobite parson, is publishing a most monstrous, unreasonable edition of Thuanus. I understand the parson is only to be paid as a corrector of the press; but Buckley is to have all the profit. The parson's name is Carte.[1] I wish you would occasionally inquire into this matter, for the subscribers on your side are many and glorious.

I cannot be angry enough with my Lord Burlington. I sent him an order of the Chapter of St. Patrick's, desiring the Dean would write to his Lordship about his ancestor's monument in my Cathedral. The gentlemen are all persons of dignity and consequence, of birth and fortune, not like those of your hedge-chapters[2] in England; and it became him to send an answer to such a body, on an occasion where only the honour of his family is concerned. I desired in England that he would order the monument to be repaired, which may be done for 50*l*., and that he would bestow a bit of land not exceeding 5*l*. a year, to repair it for ever, which I would have ordered to be entered in our

---

[1] Carte, in 1722, was accused of high treason, and a reward of a £1,000 was offered for his apprehension. He fled to France, where he resided under the name of Phillips, and employed his leisure in collecting the manuscripts and printed copies of the (Latin) History of his own time by the President De Thou, and in writing an explanatory comment, without which much of the context could no longer be understood. He sold his materials to Dr. Mead, and it was agreed that Buckley should be the nominal editor. . . His valuable and laborious edition is in seven vols. folio, and was far more exact and complete, as well as more intelligible, than any which had appeared in France itself. The whole of the merit belonged to Carte.—E. De Thou's celebrated book, in question, is entitled *History of My Own Times* (1545-1607). Carte, his translator, was the Jacobite author of *The History of England*.

[2] On meaning of *hedge* see letter of Swift, *ante*, to Esther Johnson, page 105.

records in the most solemn manner. This he promised me. I believe the Dean and Chapter are worth, in preferments and real estates, above ten thousand pounds a year, they being twenty-five and the Dean, and he cannot imagine they would cheat his posterity to get about 3s. 6d. a man. Pray, tell him this in the severest manner, and charge it all upon me, and so let the monument perish.

So they have taken away your lodgings [in Whitehall]. This is a sample of Walpole's magnanimity. When princes have a private quarrel with their subjects, they have always the worst of the fray. You have sent us over such a cargo of violent colds, that the well are not sufficient to attend the sick, nor have we servants left to deliver our orders. I apprehend myself to be this moment seized, for I have coughed more these three minutes past than I have done in as many years. I wish, for her own sake, that I had known the Duchess of Queensberry, because I should be a more impartial judge than you. But it was her own fault, because she never made me any advances. However, as to you, I think the obligation lies on her side, by giving her an opportunity of acting so generous and honourable a part, and so well becoming her dignity and spirit. Pray, tell her Grace that the fault was in Mr. Pope's poetical forks, and not in my want of manners[1]; and that I will rob Neptune of his trident rather than commit such solecism in good breeding again; and that when I return to England I will see her at the tenth message, which is one fewer than I had from another of her sex.[2] With my humble respects to her Grace, I beg she will be your guardian,

---

[1] Gay, in his letter, to which this is a reply, had jokingly noticed one of Swift's *solecisms* in eating, and exhorted him to the use of orthodox forks (as to which Swift, it seems, had been twitted by the Duchess): "never more despise a fork with three prongs; I wish, too, you would not eat from the point of your knife."

[2] The Queen Caroline, then Princess of Wales.

take care to have your money well put out, and not suffer you to run in debt or encroach on the principal. And so God continue to you the felicity of thriving by the displeasure of Courts and Ministries; and to your goddess many disgraces that may equally redound to her honour with the last.[1] My most humble service to my Lord Peterborough, Lord Oxford, Lord Bolingbroke, Lord Masham, Lord Bathurst, Mr. Pulteney, the Doctor, Mr. Pope and Mr. Lewis. Alas! poor Alderman Barber! I doubt he has left me nothing.[2]

TO MR. POPE.

Dublin, Feb. 6, 1729-30.

There are three citizens' wives in this town. One of them, whose name is Grierson, a Scotch bookseller's wife. She is a very good Latin and Greek scholar, and has lately published a fine edition of Tacitus, with a Latin dedication to the Lord-Lieutenant, and she writes *carmina anglicana non contem*

---

[1] The Duchess seized the opportunity of the suppression of *Polly* to display her dissatisfaction [at some slight to her husband from the Government or Court] by soliciting subscriptions for the printed Play in the drawing-room at St. James's, and she made, says Lord Hervey, "even the King's servants contribute to the printing of a thing which the King had forbid being acted." The King asked her what she was doing, and she answered, "what must be agreeable, she was sure, to anybody so humane as his Majesty; for it was an act of charity, and a charity to which she did not despair of bringing his Majesty to contribute. . ." The Vice-Chamberlain was sent the next day to desire she would keep away. Upon this she wrote a note in which she said that she was "well-pleased the King had given her so agreeable a command as forbidding her the Court, where she never came for diversion, but to bestow a very great civility on the King and Queen."—E.

[2] A false alarm. Alderman Barber survived to 1741, and left £200 to Swift.

nenda.¹ The second is one Mrs. Barber, wife to a woollen-draper, who is our chief poetess, and, upon the whole, has no ill genius. I fancy I have mentioned her to you formerly. The last is the bearer hereof, and the wife of a surly, rich husband, who cheeks her vein; whereas Mrs. Grierson is only well to pass; and Mrs. Barber, as it becomes the chief poetess, is but poor. The bearer's [maiden?] name is Sykins. She has a very good taste of poetry, has read much, and, as I hear, has writ one or two things with applause, which I never saw, except about six lines she sent me unknown, with a piece of sturgeon, some years ago, on my birthday. Can you show such a triumfeminate in London? They are all three great friends and favourites of Dr. Delany, and, at his desire, as well as from my own inclination, I gave her this passport to have the honour and happiness of seeing you; because she has already seen the estrich [ostrich?], which is the only rarity, at present, in this town, and her ambition is to boast of having been well received by you, upon her return; and I do not see how you can well refuse to gratify her, for if a Christian will be an estrich, and the only estrich in a kingdom, he must suffer himself to be seen, and, what is worse, without money.

I writ this day to Mr. Lewis, to settle that scrub affair with Motte. It is now at an end, and I have all the money or receipts for it except 20*l*., which is in Mr. Lewis's hands, so that I have come off better than you.² I am enquiring an opportunity to send

¹ She afterwards published an edition of Terence. Mrs. Barber affirms that she was not merely a Greek and Latin scholar, but was well read in History, Philosophy, and Mathematics. Mrs. Pilkington endows her with fresh accomplishments, and declares that she was a proficient in Hebrew, French, and Midwifery. To complete the wonder, she was the daughter of poor, illiterate peasants, who kept her close at needlework as long as she remained at home. The whole of her reported acquisitions had been made before she was twenty-seven, at which age she died, in 1733.—E.

² Motte purchased the copyright of *Gulliver* and the *Miscellanies*. He had been backward in his payments, and had now come to a final settlement. Swift got the full sum agreed upon for *Gulliver*, and therefore says he had

you four bottles of usquebaugh. May God bless Mrs. Pope. I despair of seeing her in this world; and I believe the most pious person alive would be glad to share with her in the next.

You will see eighteen lines relating to yourself in the most whimsical paper that ever was writ, and which was never intended for the public.[1]

I do not call this a letter, for I know I long owe you one. I protest you must allow for the climate, and for my disposition from the sad prospect of affairs here, and the prostitute slavery of the representers of this wretched country. I have not been deaf this ten months, but my head is an ill second to my feet in the night.

To The Countess of Suffolk.

Nov. 31, 1730.

I do now pity the leisure you have to read a letter from me—and this letter shall be a history.

"come off better" than Pope, who had to give up £25 of the price he was to have received for the *Miscellanies*, which had been less successful than was anticipated.—E.

[1] The lines are in the poem entitled *A Libel on Dr. Delany and Lord Carteret:*

> Hail! happy Pope, whose generous mind,
> Detesting all the Statesmen kind,
> Condemning Courts, at Courts unseen,
> Refused the visits of a Queen, &c.

A few months after the date of Swift's letter Pope went to Windsor, and Mrs. Howard wrote to Gay, Aug. 22, 1730: "Mr. Pope has been to see me, Lord Burlington brought him. He dined and supped with my lady all the time he stayed. He was heartily tired, and I not much pleased, though I thought myself exceedingly obliged to him for the visit." My "lady" was Lady Burlington, and from Pope's tone on the occasion to Gay it would seem that he was rather annoyed at not being admitted to the Queen. "I shall certainly," he said, "make as little Court to others as they do to me, and that will be none at all."—E.

First, therefore, I call you to witness, that I did not attend on the Queen till I had received her own repeated messages; which, of course, occasioned my being introduced to you. I never asked anything till, upon leaving England the first time, I desired from you a present worth a guinea, and from her Majesty one worth ten pounds, by way of a memorial. Yours I received; and the Queen, upon my taking leave of her, made an excuse that she intended a medal for me, which, not being ready, she would send to me the Christmas following. Yet this was never done, nor at all remembered when I went back to England the next year, and, by her commands, attended her as I had done before. I must now tell you, Madam, that I will receive no medal from her Majesty, nor anything less than her picture, at half length, drawn by Jervas; and, if he takes it from another original, the Queen shall sit, at least, twice for him to touch it up. I desire you will let her Majesty know this in plain words; although I have heard that I am under her displeasure. But this is an usual thing with Princes as well as Ministers, upon every false representation. And so I took occasion to tell the Queen, upon the quarrel Mr. Walpole had with our friend Gay, the first time I ever had the honour to attend her.

Against you I have but one reproach—that when I was last in England, and just after the present King's accession, I resolved to pass that summer in France, for which I had then a most lucky opportunity; from which those who seemed to love me well dissuaded me, by your advice. And, when I sent you a note, conjuring you to lay aside the character of a courtier and a favourite, upon that occasion, your answer positively directed me not to go in that juncture; and you said the same things to my friends, who seemed to have power of giving me hints that I might reasonably hope for a settlement in England: which God knows, was no very great ambition, considering the station I should leave here of greater dignity, and which might easily have been managed to be disposed of as the Queen pleased. If these hints came from you, I affirm you then acted too much like a courtier. But I forgive you, and esteem you as much as ever. You had your reasons, which I shall not enquire into; because I always believed you had some virtues, besides all the accomplishments of mind and person that can adorn a lady.

I am angry with the Queen for sacrificing my friend Gay to the mistaken piques of Sir Robert Walpole, about a libel written against him; although he were convinced, at the same time, of Mr. Gay's innocence, and although, as I said before, I told her Majesty the whole story. Mr. Gay deserved better treatment among you, upon all accounts, and particularly for his excellent unregarded *Fables*, dedicated to Prince William,[1] which I hope his Royal Highness will often read for his instruction. I wish her Majesty would a little remember what I largely said to her about Ireland, when, before a witness, she gave me leave, and commanded me, to tell here what she spoke to me upon that subject; and ordered me, if I lived, to see her in her present station, to send her our grievances, promising to read any letter, and do all good offices in her power for this miserable and most loyal kingdom, now at the brink of ruin, and never so near as now. As to myself, I repeat again, that I never asked anything more than a trifle, as a memorial of some distinction which her Majesty graciously seemed to make between me and every common clergyman; but that trifle was forgotten, according to the usual method of Princes, although I was taught to think myself upon a foot of pretending to some little exception.

As to yourself, Madam, I most heartily congratulate with you for being delivered from the toil, the envy, the slavery, and vexation of a favourite; where you could not always answer

[1] Then a youth, afterwards known as the Duke of Cumberland, and the hero of Culloden. The *Fables* were "unregarded," it is evident, in a sense more important than that intended by Swift.

the good intentions that I hope you had.[1] You will now be less teazed with solicitations, one of the greatest evils in life. You possess an easy employment, with quiet of mind, although it be by no means equal to your merit; and, if it shall please God to establish your health, I believe you are too wise to hope for more. Mr. Pope has always been an advocate for your sincerity; and even I, in the character I gave you of yourself, allowed you as much of that virtue as could be expected in a lady, a courtier, and a favourite. Yet, I confess, I never heartily pledged your health as a toast upon any other regard than beauty, wit, good sense, and an unblemished character. For as to friendship, truth, sincerity, and other trifles of that kind, I never concerned myself about them, because I know them to be only parts of the lower morals, which are altogether useless at Courts. I am content that you should tell the Queen all I have said of her, and in my own words, if you please.

[1] If we may believe Lord Hervey's account, Mrs. Howard's position, as attendant on the Queen, was not more pleasant than was Miss Burney's, in the next reign. The Queen (Caroline), delighted in annoying her rival as much as possible—in particular, in the offices of the toilet. "It seems," explains Mr. Croker, "that Mrs. Howard consulted, through Dr. Arbuthnot, Lady Masham, the celebrated Bedchamber-woman to Queen Anne, on this point of etiquette [the manner of presenting the washing-basin]." Her answer was: "When the Queen washed her hands, the Page of the Back-stairs brought and set down upon a side table the basin and ewer, then the Bedchamber-woman set it before the Queen, the Bedchamber-lady only looking on. The Bedchamber-woman brought the chocolate, and gave it kneeling. In general the Bedchamber-woman had no dependence upon the Lady of the Bedchamber. (*Suffolk Cor.*, i., 293.) We shall see, by-and-bye, that the Lady of the Bedchamber (though a Countess) presented the basin for the Queen *kneeling*."— *Memoirs of the Reign of George II.* By John, Lord Hervey. Edited by the Rt. Hon. W. Croker, 1848. The Toilet of the French Queen and, still more, of the French King (Louis XVI., *e.g.*), demanded an even greater amount of minute ceremonialism and servility from the Maids of Honour and Gentlemen-in-Waiting—so oriental in their character as to be incredible, were we not assured of the facts in the histories and memoirs of the last century. Of the character of Lady Suffolk, Thackeray has expressed a high opinion:—" Of all the Court of George and Caroline," he says, "I find no one but Lady Suffolk with whom it seems pleasant to hold converse," and he extols her "sweet graciousness," which attracted the good-will of nearly all who knew her.— *Lectures on the Four Georges.*

I could have been a better prophet, in the character I gave you of yourself, if it had been good manners, in the height of your credit, to put you in mind of its mortality; for you are not the first, by at least three ladies, whom I have known to undergo the same turn of fortune.[1] It is allowed that ladies are often very good scaffoldings; and I need not tell you the use that scaffoldings are put to by all builders, as well political as mechanic. I should have begun this letter by telling you, that I was encouraged to write it by my best friend, and one of your great admirers, who told me, "that from something that passed between you, he thought you would not receive it ill." After all, I know no person of your sex, for whom I have so great an esteem, as I do, and believe I shall always continue to, bear for you. I mean a private person, for I must except the Queen, and it is not an exception of form; because I have really a very great veneration for her great qualities, although I have reason to complain of her conduct to me, which I could not excuse, although she had fifty kingdoms to govern. I have but room to conclude with my sincere professions of being, with true respect, &c.

TO MR. POPE.

Dublin, June 12, 1731.

I doubt, habit has little power to reconcile us with sickness attended by pain. With me, the lowness of spirits has a most unhappy effect. I am grown less patient with solitude, and harder to be pleased with company; which I could formerly

---

[1] The dean probably alludes to the Duchess of Marlborough, Lady Masham, and the Duchess of Somerset, all of whom had been favourites of Queen Anne.—S. The character of Mrs. Howard, to which Swift refers, had been drawn three years before the date of this letter.

better digest, when I could be easier without it than at present. As to sending you anything that I have written since I left you (either verse or prose), I can only say, that I have ordered by my Will that all my papers, of any kind, shall be delivered you to dispose of as you please.

I have several things that I have had schemes to finish, or to attempt, but I very foolishly put off the trouble, as sinners do their repentance; for I grow every day more averse from writing, which is very natural, and, when I take a pen, say to myself a thousand times—*non est tanti*. As to those papers of four or five years past, that you are pleased to require soon, they consist of little accidental things writ in the country—family amusements, never intended farther than to divert ourselves and some neighbours; or some effects of anger on public grievances here, which would be insignificant out of this kingdom. Two or three of us had a fancy, three years ago, to write a weekly paper, and call it an *Intelligencer*. But it continued not long: for the whole volume—it was reprinted in London, and I find you have seen it—was the work only of two, myself and Dr. Sheridan. If we could have got some ingenious young man to have been the manager, who should have published all that might be sent to him, it might have continued longer, for there were hints enough. But the printer here could not afford such a young man one farthing for his trouble, the sale being so small, and the price one half-penny. And so it dropped. In the volume you saw—to answer your questions—the 1st, 3rd, 5th, 7th, were mine. Of the 8th I writ only the verses (very incorrect, but against a fellow we all hated); the 9th mine; the 10th only the verses, and of those not the four last slovenly lines; the 15th is a pamphlet of mine printed before, with Dr. Sheridan's preface, merely for laziness, not to disappoint the town; and so was the 19th, which contained only a parcel of facts relating purely to the miseries of Ireland, and wholly useless and unentertaining.

As to other things of mine, since I left you, there are, in prose: *A View of the State of Ireland, A Project for Eating Children,*[1] and a *Defence of Lord Carteret.* In verse: a *Libel on Dr. Delany and Lord Carteret, a Letter to Dr. Delany on the Libels Writ Against Him, The Barrack* (a stolen copy), *The Lady's Journal, The Lady's Dressing Room* (a stolen copy), the *Plea of the Damned* (a stolen copy). All these have been printed in London. (I forgot to tell you that the *Tale of Sir Ralph* was sent from England.) Besides these, there are five or six (perhaps more) papers of verse writ in the North, but perfect *family things,*[2] two or three of which may be tolerable, the rest but indifferent, and the humour only local, and some that would give offence to the times. Such as they are, I will bring them, tolerable or bad, if I recover this lameness, and live long enough to see you either here or there.

I forgot again to tell you that the *Scheme of Paying Debts by a Tax on Vices* is not one syllable mine, but of a young clergyman whom I countenance. He told me it was built upon a passage in *Gulliver,* where a Projector hath something upon the same thought. This young man [3] is the most hopeful we have. A book of his poems was printed in London. Dr. Delany is one of his patrons. He is married and has children, and makes up about £100, on which he lives decently. The utmost stretch of his ambition is, to gather up as much superfluous money as will give him a sight of you, and half-an-hour of your

---

[1] In its full title: *A Modest Proposal for Preventing the Children of Poor People in Ireland from being a Burden to their Parents or Country, and for making them Beneficial to the Public,* 1729. In this highly original and witty piece Swift proposes that the starving children of the poor should, at once, be put out of their misery and utilised as "butchers' meat."

[2] A very excellent, because perfect, sort of primitive verses, which never rose above daily topics, and the *chat* of the times. The greatest part of Swift's poetry is of this kind.—Warton.

[3] His name was Pilkington, and he was husband of the lady who wrote *Memoirs of her Own Life.*—W.

presence, after which he will return home in full satisfaction, and, in proper time, die in peace.

My poetical fountain is drained, and I profess I grow gradually so dry that a rhyme with me is almost as hard to find as a guinea, and even prose speculations tire me almost as much. Yet I have a thing in prose,[1] begun above twenty-eight years ago, and almost finished. It will make a four shilling volume, and is such a perfection of folly that you shall never hear of it till it is printed, and then you shall be left to guess. Nay, I have another of the same age,[2] which will require a long time to perfect, and is worse than the former, in which I will serve you the same way. I heard lately from Mr. ——, who promises to be less lazy in order to mend his fortune. But women who live by their beauty, and men by their wit, are seldom provident enough to consider that both wit and beauty will go off with years, and there is no living upon the credit of what is past.

I am in great concern to hear of my Lady Bolingbroke's[3] ill health returned upon her, and, I doubt, my Lord will find Dawley too solitary without her. In that neither he nor you are companions young enough for me; and, I believe, the best part of the reason why men are said to grow children when they are old is, because they cannot entertain themselves with thinking, which is the very case with little boys and girls, who love to be noisy among their play-fellows. I am told Mrs. Pope is without pain, and I have not heard of a more gentle decay, without uneasiness to herself or friends. Yet I cannot but pity you, who are ten times the greater sufferer, by having the person you most love so long before you, and dying daily; and, I pray God, it may not affect your mind or your health.

---

[1] *Polite Conversation.*

[2] *Directions to Servants.* An ironical piece, which seems to have suggested similar things in the comic periodicals of the present day.

[3] Lord Bolingbroke married as his second wife, in 1720, the Marquise de Villette (a niece of Mde. de Maintenon), eighteen months after the death of his first wife. She had been during the three years before the marriage living under his "protection." She was a devoted wife.

To Lord Orrery.¹

March 22, 1733.

I had this minute a letter from England, telling me that excise on Tobacco is passed, 265 against 204, which was a greater number of sitters than I can remember. It is concluded they will go on, in another Session, to further articles, and then you will have the honour to be a slave in two kingdoms. Here is a pamphlet just come out in defence of the Excise; it was reprinted here by a rascal from England, in a great office and at his own charge, to pave the way for the same proceeding here, but I hope our Members will think they are slaves enough already, and, perhaps, somebody or other may be tempted to open folks' eyes.

I sent the Epitaph on Mr. Gay² to Mrs. B——, to be copied for your Lordship, and I think there are some lines that might and should be corrected. I am going to write to the author, and shall tell him my opinion. I agree with your Lordship that his imitation of Horace is one of the best things he hath lately writ, and he tells me himself, that he never took more pains than in his Poem to Lord Bathurst upon the use of riches; nor less than in this which, however, his friends call his *chef-d'œuvre*, although he writ it in two mornings, and this may happen when a poet lights upon a fruitful hint, and becomes fond of it. I have often thought that hints were owing as much to good fortune as to invention. And I have sometimes chid poor Mr. Gay for dwelling too long upon a hint (as he did in the Sequel of the *Beggar's Opera*, and this unlucky posthumous production).³ He hath like-

[1] Printed in Mr. Craik's *Life of Swift*, in extracts, from MSS. in possession of Lord Cork.

[2] By Pope in Westminster Abbey: "Of manners gentle," &c.—C.

[3] The "Sequel" was *Polly*. The "posthumous production," the opera of *Achilles*.—C.

wise left a Second Part of *Fables*, of which I prophesy no good. I have been told that few painters can copy their own originals to perfection. And I believe the first thoughts on a subject, that occur to a poet's imagination, are usually the most natural. . . .

A stupid beast in London, one Alexander Burnet (I suppose the Bishop's son), has parodied Mr. Pope's satirical Imitation in a manner that makes me envy Mr. Pope for having such an adversary, than whose performance nothing can be more low and scurrilous.

To Mr. Pope.

Dublin, July 8, 1733.

I must condole with you for the loss of Mrs. Pope, of whose death the papers have been full. But I would rather rejoice with you, because, if any circumstances can make the death of a dear parent and friend a subject for joy, you have them all. She died in an extreme old age, without pain, under the care of the most dutiful son that I have ever known or heard of; which is a felicity not happening to one in a million. The worst effect of her death falls upon me; and so much the worse because I expected *aliquis damno usus in illo*—that it would be followed by making me and this kingdom happy with your presence. But I am told, to my great misfortune, that a very convenient offer happening, you waived the invitation pressed on you, alleging the fear you had of being killed here with eating and drinking. By which I find that you have given some credit to a notion of our great plenty and hospitality. It is true our meat and wine is cheaper here, as it is always in the poorest countries, because there is no money to pay for them. I believe there are not, in this whole city, three gentlemen out of employment, who are able to give entertainments once a month.

Those who are in employments of Church or State are three parts in four from England, and amount to little more than a dozen; those, indeed, may once or twice invite their friends, or any person of distinction who makes a voyage hither. All my acquaintance tell me, they know not above three families where they can occasionally dine in a whole year.[1] Dr. Delany is the only gentleman I know, who keeps one certain day in the week to entertain seven or eight friends at dinner and to pass the evening, where there is nothing of excess either in eating or drinking. Our old friend Southern, who has just left us, was invited once or twice by a Judge, a Bishop, or a Commissioner of the Revenues; but most frequented a few particular friends, and chiefly the Doctor [Delany], who is easy in his fortune, and very hospitable.

The conveniences of taking the air, winter or summer, do far exceed those in London. For the two large Strands, just at two edges of the town, are as firm and dry in winter as in summer. There are, at least, six or eight gentlemen of sense, learning, good-humour, and taste, able and desirous to please you, and orderly females—some of the better sort—to take care of you. These were the motives that I have frequently made use of to entice you hither. And there would be no failure, among the best people here, of any honours that could be done you. As to myself, I declare my health is so uncertain, that I dare not venture among you at present. I hate the thoughts of London,

---

[1] The Dean who (unfortunately for himself), little more than his correspondents, could sympathize with the pythagorean feeling embodied (*e.g.*) in the regrets of the poet for the *noctes cœnæque deûm*, here repeats his complaints poured forth in a letter to Gay, of July 10, 1732, in which he assures him: "I have a large house, yet I should hardly prevail to find one visitor, if I were not able to hire him with a bottle of wine: so that when I am not abroad on horseback, I generally dine alone, and am thankful if a friend will pass the evening with me."

where I am not rich enough to live otherwise than by shifting, which is now too late. Neither can I have conveniences in the country for three horses and two servants, and many others which I have here at hand. I am one of the governors of all the hackney coaches, carts, and carriages, round this town, who dare not insult me like your rascally waggoners or coachmen, but give me the way; nor is there one lord or squire, for a hundred of yours, to turn me out of the road, or run over me with their coaches and six.[1]

Thus I make some advantage of the public poverty, and give you the reasons for what I once writ—why I choose to be a freeman among slaves, rather than a slave among freemen. Then, I walk the streets in peace, without being jostled, nor even without a thousand blessings from my friends, the vulgar. I am Lord Mayor of one hundred and twenty houses. I am absolute lord of the greatest cathedral in the kingdom, am at peace with the neighbouring princes—the Lord Mayor of the city, and the Archbishop of Dublin. Only the latter, like the King of France, sometimes attempts encroachments on my dominions, as old Louis [XIV.] did upon Lorraine. In the midst of this raillery I can tell you with seriousness, that these advantages contribute to my ease, and therefore I value them. And in one part of your letter, relating to Lord Bolingbroke and yourself, you agree with me entirely, about the indifference, the love of quiet, the care of health, &c., that grow upon men in years. And, if you discover those inclinations in my Lord and yourself, what can you expect from me, whose health is so precarious? Yet, at your or his time of life, I could have leaped over the moon.

[1] It is remarkable, however, that Swift had occasion, literally, to complain of this insult in Ireland to the House of Peers, in the case of Lord Blaney; and to the Public, in the second number of the *Intelligencer*, against Squire Ram of Gory, by whose carriage he was nearly ridden down.—S.

TO MRS. PENDARVES.[1]

Oct. 7, 1734.

When I received the honour and happiness of your last letter (dated Sept. 9), I was afflicted with a pair of disorders that usually seize me once a year, and with which I have been acquainted from my youth; but it is only of late years that they have begun to come together, although I should have been better contented with one at a time—these are *giddiness and deafness*, which usually last a month: the first tormenting my body, and the other making me incapable of conversing.

In this juncture your letter found me, but I was able to read, though *not to hear;* neither did I value my deafness for three days, because your letter was my constant entertainment during that time. After which, I grew sensibly better, and, although I was not abroad till yesterday, I find myself well enough to acknowledge the great favour you have done me, but cannot guess your motive for so much goodness.[2] I guess that *your* good genius, accidentally meeting *mine*, was prevailed on to solicit your pity! Or did you happen to be at leisure by the summer

[1] Better known as Mary Granville and Mrs. Delany. She was the daughter of Mr. Bernard Granville, and great granddaughter of the more famous Sir Bevil Granville; and was born in the year 1700, at Coulston, in Wiltshire. She was remarkable for her beauty and accomplishments. Her *Autobiography* and *Correspondence* first appeared in 1861-2. This seems to be the first of the two or three letters of Swift to her that have been preserved. It is addressed to her "in Little Brook Street, near Grosvenor Square, London."

[2] Mrs. Pendarves had begun her letter in terms, which could not well be more flattering to Swift's *epistolary* ambition:—"I find," she writes, "your correspondence is like the singing of the nightingale—no bird sings so sweetly; but the pleasure is quickly past. A month or two of harmony, and then we lose it till next spring. I wish your favours may as certainly return. . . . The last letter I writ to you," she reminds him, "was from Gloucester, about a twelvemonth ago. After that I went to Longleat [in Somerset] to my lady Weymouth: came to town in January, where I have remained ever since, except a few weeks I spent at Sir John Stanley's, at Northend (the Delville of this part of the world)."

absence of your friends? Or would you appear a constant nymph, when all my goddesses of much longer acquaintance have forsaken me, as it is reasonable they should? But the men are almost as bad as the ladies, and I cannot but think them in the right: for I cannot make shifts, and lie rough, and be undone by starving in scanty lodgings, without horses, servants, or conveniences, as I used to do in London, with port wine, or, perhaps, Porter's ale to save charges!

You dare not pretend to say that your town equals ours in hospitable evenings, with your *deep play* and no entertainment but a cup of chocolate, unless you have mended your manners. I will not declare your reasons for not taking a second trip over hither, because you have offered none but your royal will and pleasure; but, if I were in the case of your friends here, with more life before me and better health, I would solicit an Act of Parliament to prevent your coming among us or, at least, to make it high treason in you ever to leave us. In the meantime, I wish you were forced over by debts or want, because we would gladly agree to a contribution for life, dinners and suppers excluded, that are to go for nothing. I speak for the public good of this country; because a pernicious heresy prevails here among the men, that it is the duty of your sex to be fools in every article, except what is merely domestic; and, to do the ladies justice, there are very few of them without a good share of that heresy, except upon one article—that they have as little regard for family business as for the improvement of their minds!

I have had for some time a design to write against this heresy; but have now laid those thoughts aside, for fear of making both sexes my enemies. However, if you will come over to my assistance, I will carry you about among our adversaries, and dare them to produce *one instance* where your *want of ignorance* makes you affected, pretending, conceited, disdainful, endeavouring to speak like a scholar, with twenty more faults objected by themselves, their lovers, or their husbands. But I fear your case is desperate; for I know you never laugh at a jest before you understand it, and I much question whether you *understand a fa'z*, or have so good a fancy *at silks* as others;[1] and your way of *spelling* would *not be intelligible*. Therefore, upon your arrival hither (which I expect in three packets at furthest), I will give you a license to be as silly as you can possibly afford, one half-hour every week, to the heretics of each sex; to atone for which you are to keep one fasting day at Dr. Delany's or Dr. Helsham's, and one at the Deanery.

I think my Lord Carteret is the most happy, in all circumstances of life, that I ever have known; and, as he well deserves it, so I hope he is sensible of it. All my fear is, that he will be too rich. I am no cause of my Lord Bathurst's forsaking you. He hath long done the same with me; and, to say the truth, Madam, it is a very cold scent to continue a correspondence with one whom we never expect to see. I never knew it long practised, except among the learned of different nations. Mr. Pope and my Lord Bolingbroke themselves begin to fail me, in seven years. Nothing vexes me so much with relation to you as that, with all my disposition to find faults, I was never once able to fix upon anything that I could find amiss, although I watched you narrowly. For, when I found we were to lose you soon, I kept my eyes and ears always upon you, in hopes that you would make some *boutade*. It is, you know, a French word, and signifies a sudden jerk from a horse's hinder feet which you did not expect, because you thought him for some months a sober animal; and this hath been my case with several ladies whom I chose for friends. In a week, a month, or a year, hardly one of them failed to give me a *boutade*; therefore, I command you will obey my orders, in coming over

---

[1] An allusion to Gay's satirical pieces in verse.

hither for one whole year: after which, upon the first *boutade* you make, I will give you my pass to be gone.

Are you acquainted with the Duke of Chandois?[1] I know your cozen Lansdown and he were intimate friends. I have known the Duke long and well, and thought I had a share in his common favour; but he hath lately given me great cause of complaint. I was pressed by many persons of learning here to write to his Grace, that, having some old Records relating to this Kingdom, which were taken from hence by the Earl of Clarendon, who was Lieutenant here, and purchased them from private owners, and are now in the Duke's possession, that his Grace would please to bestow them to the University here; because Irish antiquities are of little value or curiosity to any other nation. I writ with all the civility in my power, and with compliments on the fame of his generosity, and in a style very different from what I use to my friends with titles. But he hath pleased to be silent for above six weeks, which is the first treatment I ever met with of that kind from any English person of quality, and what would better become a *little* Irish Baron than a *great* English Duke. But whether *grandeur* or *party* be the cause I shall not enquire, but leave it to you, and expect you will employ *my brother Lansdown* (his Lordship will tell you why I give him that title), if he still converses with the Duke, to know the reason of this treatment, and you shall be my instrument to find it out, although it shall cost you two shillings for a chair!

If I have tired you, it is the effect of the great esteem I have for you. Do but lessen your own merits, and I will shorten my letters in proportion. If you will come among us, I engage your dreadful old beggarly western parson[2] to residence.

---

[1] James Brydges, created Marquis of Carnarvon and Duke of Chandos in 1719.—*Your cozen Lansdown* is a mistake for *your uncle Lansdown.*—Lady Llanover.

[2] Swift himself.

Otherwise, we all resolve to send him over, which is, in our opinion, the surest way to drive you hither: for you will be in more haste to fly from than to follow *even* Mrs. Donellan, when you keep out of sight. If she be among you, I desire she may know I am her true admirer and most humble servant. I am, with true respect and high esteem, &c.

To Mrs. Pendarves.

Dublin, Jan. 29, 1735.

I had, indeed, some intention to go to Bath,[1] but I had neither health nor leisure for such a journey. Those times are past with me, and I am older by fourscore years since the first time I had the honour to see you. I got a giddiness by raw fruit when I was a lad in England, which I never could be wholly rid of, and it is now too late; so that I confine myself entirely to a domestic life. I am visited seldom, but visit much seldomer. I dine alone, like a king, having few acquaintance, and those lessening daily. This town is not what you left it, and I impute the cause altogether to your absence. I fear, if your sister mends, as I pray God she will, it is rather due to the journey than the Bath water.

It was impossible to answer your letter from *Paradise*

---

[1] Of this even then fashionably-crowded resort, Mrs. Pendarves writes to Swift somewhat more than a year later (April, 1736) :—" I left the Bath last Sunday se'night, very full and gay. I think Bath a *more comfortable* place to live in than London. All the entertainments of the place lie in a small compass, and you are *at your liberty* to partake of them, and let them alone, just as it suits your humour. This town [London] is grown to *such an enormous size*, that *above half the day* must be spent in the streets, going from one place to another. I like it every year less and less."

R

—the old Grecians of Asia called every fine garden by that name—and besides, when I consulted some friends, they conceived that wherever *you* resided, that must needs be a *paradise*. Yet this was too general a distinction, if you were in a humour of rambling, unless the Post Office had constant intelligence of your stages. With great submission, I am sorry to find a lady make use of the word Paradise, from which *you* turned *us out* as well as yourselves. And, pray, tell me freely, how many of your sex bring it along with them to their husbands' houses? I was still at a loss where this *Paradise*[1] of yours might be, when Mrs. Donellan discovered the secret. She said it was a place (I forget in what shire) where King Charles 1st, in his troubles, used to ride, because he found good watering for his horse! If *that be all*, we have ten thousand such paradises in this kingdom, of which you may have your choice, as my *bay mare* is ready to depose.

It is either a very low way of thinking, or as great a failure of education in either sex, to imagine that any man increases in his critical faculty in proportion to his wit[2] or learning. It falls out always directly contrary. A common carpenter will work more cheerfully for a gentleman, skilled in his trade, than for a conceited fool who knows nothing of it. I must despise a lady who takes me for a pedant, and you have made me half angry with so many lines in your letter, which look like a kind of apology for writing to me. Besides, to say the truth, the ladies, in general, are *extremely mended* both in writing and reading since I was young. Only it is to be hoped that, in proper time, *Gaming* and *Dressing*, with some other accomplishments, may reduce them to their native ignorance. A woman of quality, who had excellent good sense, was formerly my corres-

---

[1] Sir John Stanley's villa at North End was called "Paradise"; but there was also another place, where Mrs. Perdarves was staying with her mother, which was also called "Paradise."—Lady L'anover.

[2] Used in its first sense of *knowledge*.

pondent; but she scrawled and spelt like a Wapping wench, having been brought up at a Court at a time before reading was thought of any use to a female; and I know *several* others of *very high quality* with the same defect.

I am very glad to find that poor Mrs. Barber hath the honour to be in your favour. I fear she is in no very good way either as to health or fortune. The first must be left to God's mercy, the other to the generosity of some wealthy friends; and I do not know the reason why she is not more at ease in the latter. Her sickness hath made her more expensive than her prudence or nature inclined her. I think she hath every kind virtue, and only one defect—which is too much bashfulness. Dr. Delany hath long ago given up his house in town. His Dublin friends seldom visit him till the swallows come in. He is too far from town for a winter visit, and too near for staying a night, in the country manner: neither is his house [Delville] large enough. It minds me of what I have heard the late Duchess[1] complain—that Sion House was a "hobble-de-hoy, neither town nor country."

I believe, Madam, I am mistaken, and think myself to be in your company, where I could never be weary. No, it is otherwise: for, in such a case, I would rather choose to be your silent hearer and looker-on. But whether you may not be tired for the three minutes past, is a different question. The surest way is to put an end to the debate by concluding by assuring you that I am, with the truest respect and esteem, &c.

[1] Lady Elizabeth Percy, who married, as her third husband, Charles Seymour, Duke of Somerset. Her first husband, to whom she was married at the age of fourteen, was Henry Cavendish, Earl of Ogle (son and heir of Henry, Duke of Newcastle); her second, in a marriage only in name, Thomas Thynne, of Longleat, who was assassinated in 1682.

To Mr. Thomas Beach.[1]

Dublin, April 12, 1735.

After the fate of all poets, you are no favourite of Fortune; for your letter of March 31st did not come to my hands till two days after Sir William Fowne's death, who, having been so long afflicted with the stone and other disorders, besides great old age, died about nine days ago. If he had recovered, I should certainly have waited on him with your Poem, and recommended it and the author very heartily to his favour. I have seen fewer good panegyrics than any other sort of writing, especially in verse, and therefore, I much approve the method you have taken. . . . I read your Poem several times, and shewed it to three or four judicious friends, who all approved it, but agreed with me, that it wanted some corrections.

Upon which I took a number of lines, which are, in all, 299, the odd number being occasioned by what they call a *triplet*, which was a vicious way of rhyming, wherewith Dryden abounded, and was imitated by all the bad versifiers in Charles the Second's reign. Dryden, though my near relation, is one I have often blamed as well as pitied. He was poor, and in great haste to finish his plays, because by them he chiefly supported his family, and this made him so very incorrect; he likewise brought in the Alexandrine verse at the end of his triplets. I was so angry at these corruptions, that about twenty-four years ago I banished them all by one triplet, with the Alexandrine, upon a very ridiculous subject.[2] I absolutely did prevail with Mr.

---

[1] Addressed, "Merchant in Wrexham, Denbighshire." Author of a poem entitled *Eugenio; or a Virtuous and Happy Life*, to which this letter alludes. It is dedicated to Mr. Pope. The unfortunate author committed suicide a few weeks after publication of his poem, in 1737.—S.

[2] These lines, to which Swift imputes greater influence than they possessed, concluded the *City Shower*:—

Pope, and Gay, and Dr. Young, and one or two more, to reject them. Mr. Pope never used them till he translated Homer, which was too long a work to be very exact in; and I think in one or two of his last poems, he has, out of laziness, done the same thing, though very seldom.

I now proceed to what I would have corrected in your Poem: line 6, for *han't* read *want*. I abhor those *han'ts* and *won'ts*, &c., &c., they are detestable in verse as well as prose; line 46, for *whilst* put *while*; line 83, *derives*. I doubt there is no verb deponent, but always active. Line 106, "If *Noll* usurps on James"—*Noll* is too much a cant word for a grave poem, and as to *James*, he was a weak, bigoted papist, desirous, like other kings, of absolute power, but not properly a tyrant. Line 109, *And midst*, harsh and rough, the elision unluckily placed; line 115, 116, I cannot suffer an ill-rhyme such as *seen* and *scene* (I forgot the triplet in line 108, which I wish were clipped of one of its three wings). . . . . . You will do right to read over your poem carefully, and observe where there be any more oversights of the same kind with those I have noted, and to be corrected; which you can do better than any other person. A friend can only see what is amiss, but the writer can mend it more easily. All you desire in relation to Sir William Fowne's is at an end by his death; otherwise, I should gladly have performed it in the best and most effectual manner I was able.

As to the publishing it here, I utterly differ from you. No printer in this beggarly town, and enslaved starving kingdom, would print it without being paid his full charge of his labour; nor would he be able to sell two dozen, unless he could afford it for a penny. I would rather advise you to have it published in

"Sweepings from butchers' stalls, dung, guts, and blood,
Drowned puppies, stinking sprats, all drenched in mud,
Dead rats, and turnip tops, come tumbling down the flood."—S.
The *City Shower*, which made a considerable "sensation" at its publication, appeared first in *The Tatler*.

London by Motte or Lintot, or any other bookseller there, who deals in poetry. It would bear a shilling price; but, as I presume you are not much known as a poet in that great city, you should get some person of consequence to recommend it.

As to what things were printed here, on supposition they were mine, the thing was done against my inclinations—out of the disdain I had of their being published in so obscure and wretched a country.[1] But I could have been well enough satisfied, if the booksellers in London could have agreed among themselves to print them there. And I believe they now repent they did not, because every printer there hath a property in their copy; and what things are mine belonged to several booksellers, who might have shared equally, according to what copies they held. I have been called away till evening. However, my paper could have afforded me but little more room, if I had staid. I am, with true esteem, &c

---

To Lady Betty Germaine.

June 8, 1735.

I trouble you sooner than usual, in acknowledging your letter of May 27th, because there are some passages in it

[1] Swift often complains of the Dublin publishers printing his unacknowledged as well as pirating his confessed writings, without his consent. Writing to Pulteney the year before, he remarks: "You will hear, perhaps, that one Faulkner has printed four volumes, which are called my works. He has only prefixed the first letters of my name—it was done utterly against my will: for there is no property in printers or booksellers here, and I was not able to hinder it. I did imagine that, after my death, the several London booksellers would agree among themselves to print what each of them had, by common consent. But the man here has prevented it, much to my vexation: for I would as willingly have it done even in Scotland. All this has vexed me not a little, as done in so obscure a place. I have never yet looked into them, nor, I believe, I ever shall."

that seem to require a quick answer.¹ If I forgot the date of mine, you must impute it to my ill head; and, if I live two years longer, I shall first forget my own name, and last your ladyship's. I gave my Lady Kelly an account of what you said in relation to her son, with which she is fully satisfied. I detest the House of Lords for their indulgence to such a profligate, prostitute villain as Curll,² but am at loss how he could procure any letters written to Mr. Pope; although, by the vanity or indiscretion of correspondents, the rogue might have picked up some that went from him. Those letters have not yet been sent hither; therefore I can form no judgment on them. When I was leaving England, upon the Queen's death, I burnt all the letters I could find that I had received from Ministers for several years before.

[1] The passage in Lady B. Germaine's letter, to which her correspondent alludes, is the following:—

"I must recommend to you an affair, which has given me some small palpitations of the heart, which is, that you would not wrap up old shoes, or neglected sermons, in my letters: but that what of them have been spared from going towards making gin for the ladies may henceforth be committed instantly to the flames—for, you being stigmatised with the name of a wit, Mr. Curll will rake to the dung-hill for your correspondence. And, as to my part, I am satisfied with having been honoured in print by your amorous, satirical, and gallant letters." The famous Curll mystification was now engaging the talk of the town, and, of course, unaware of the real facts of the case, the quondam *belle,* who had been well known for her *affaires de cœur,* feared, or affected to fear, that some of them might be divulged in the manner she hints at.

[2] Curll was summoned before the House of Lords for breach of privilege, by publishing the letters of Peers in his pirated *Correspondence.* But he used to boast that he had more friends in the House than Pope; or, as he has elegantly expressed it in poetry:—

> He undeceived the nobles all:
> More could he wish or hope?
> When Pope had thus contrived his fall,
> He triumphed over Pope.

The Dean appears not to have suspected what has been since made tolerably plain, that Pope himself had contrived to put a part of his *correspondence* into Curll's hands, in order that the surreptitious edition, which he foresaw would be the consequence of his doing so, might make an accurate publication a matter of apparent necessity.—S. See Pope's *Life and Writings.*

But as to the letters I received from your Ladyship, I neither ever did, or ever will burn any of them, take it as you please; for I never burn a letter that is entertaining, and consequently will give me new pleasure, when it is forgotten.[1] It is true I have kept some letters, merely out of friendship; although they sometimes wanted true spelling and good sense, and some others, whose writers are dead; for I live like a monk, and hate to forget my departed friends. Yet I am sometimes too nice; for I burnt all my Lord —'s letters,[2] upon receiving one where he had used these words to me:—" All I pretend to is a great deal of sincerity," which, indeed, was the chief virtue he wanted. Of those from my Lord Halifax I burnt all but one, which I keep as a most admirable original of Court promises and professions. I confess, also, that I have read some passages, in many of your letters, to a friend (but without naming you—only that "the writer was a lady"), which had such marks of good sense that often the hearers would not believe me. And yet I never had a letter of mine printed, nor of any others to me.

Your Ladyship very much surprises me with one passage in your letter which, however, I do not in the least understand; where you say, you "have been honoured in print by amorous, satirical, and gallant letters," where there was no word but your bare name mentioned.[3] I can assure you, this is to me altogether a riddle, and what I never heard the least syllable of;

[1] It is to be regretted, perhaps, that Lady Betty Germaine, had not formed the same resolution in regard to her letters from Swift, which, apparently, were for the most part destroyed.

[2] Probably those of Lord Somers.—S.

[3] Lady Betty Germain explains her allusion in a later letter: "In this hurry of matrimony [the marriage of her brother to the Countess of Suffolk] I had like to forget to answer that part of your letter, where you say, you never heard of our being in print together. I believe it was about twenty years ago Mr. Curll set forth 'Letters, Amorous, Satirical, and Gallant between Dr. Swift, Lady Mary Chambre, Lady Betty Germain, and Mrs. Anne Long, and several other persons.' I am afraid," she adds, "some of my people used them according to their desert, for they have not appeared above ground this great while."

and wish you would explain it. No, Madam, I will never forgive your insolent niece,[1] without a most humble submission under her own hands; which if she will not comply with, I shall draw up letters between us, and send them to Curll.

I will tell your Ladyship a cause I have of complaint against the Duke of Dorset. I have written to him about four times since he was Lieutenant, and three of my letters were upon subjects that concerned him much more than it did any friend of mine, and not at all myself. But he was never pleased to return me an answer; which omission (for I disdain to call it contempt) I can only account for by some of the following reasons. He is either extremely busy in the affairs of the highest importance; or he is a Duke with a Garter; or he is a Lieutenant of Ireland; or he is of a very ancient noble extraction; or so obscure a man as I am is not worth his remembrance; or, like the Duke of Chandos, he is an utter stranger to me,[2] and it would grieve me to the soul to put them together upon any one article. . . . I do assure you, Madam, that I have not been troublesome to my Lord Duke in any particular. Since he has been Governor, my letters have been, at most, but once a year, and my personal requests not so many; nor any of them for the least interest that regarded myself. And, although it be true that I do not much approve the conduct of affairs in either kingdom, wherein I agree with vast numbers of both parties, yet I have utterly waived intermeddling even in this enslaved kingdom, where, perhaps, I might have some influence to be troublesome. Yet I

[1] Mary, eldest daughter of Mr. Chambers, of Hanworth, in Middlesex, by Lady Mary Berkeley, sister to Lady B. Germain. She married, 1736, Lord Vere Beauclerc, afterwards Lord Vere.—B. She was in the habit of calling Swift, *parson Swift.*

[2] See the Epigram beginning:—

"James Bridges and the Dean had long been friends:
James is be-duked, and so their friendship ends.
And sure the Dean deserves a sharp rebuke,
From knowing James to boast he knows the Duke," &c.

(Scott's *Swift*, xiv., 373.)

have long quitted all such thoughts out of perfect despair; although I have sometimes wished that the true loyal Whigs here might be a little more considered in the disposition of employments, notwithstanding their misfortune of being born on this side of the Channel, which would gain abundance of hearts both to the Crown and his Grace. My paper is so full, that I have not room to excuse its length.

To LORD ORRERY.[1]

Dublin, July 17, 1735.

I am like a desperate debtor, who keeps out of the way as much as he can; and want of health, in my case, is equal to want of money or of honesty in the other. I have been some months settling my perplexed affairs, like a dying man, and, like the dying man, pestered with continual interruptions as well as difficulties. I have now finished my *Will* in form, wherein I have settled my whole fortune on the city, in trust for building and maintaining an Hospital for idiots and lunatics, by which I save the expense of a chaplain, and almost of a physician; so that I now want only the circumstances of health to be very idle, and a constant correspondent, but no further than upon trifles.

As to writing in verse or prose, I am a real king, for I never had so many good *subjects* in my life; and the more a king, because, like all the rest of my rank (except K. George), I am so bad a governor of them, that I do not regard what becomes of them; nor hath any single one among them thrived under me

---

[1] Printed in Mr. Craik's *Life of Swift* (in part), from MSS. in Lord Cork's possession.

these three years past. My greatest loss is that of my Viceroy, Trifler Sheridan. . . . Our Bishop Rundle is not yet come over, and I believe his Chaplain, Philips, is in a reasonable fright that his patron may fall sooner than any living in the diocese. I suppose it is Trim Tram betwixt both, for neither of them have threepenny worth of stamina. If there be any merry company in this town, I am an utter stranger to the persons and places, except when half a score come to sponge on me every Sunday evening. Dr. Helsham is as arrogant as ever, and Dr. Delany costs two *thirteens* to be visited in wet weather, by which I should be out of pocket ninepence when I dine with him.

This moment (Wednesday, six o'clock, evening, July 6th) Mr. Philips sent me word that he landed with his bishop this morning, and hath sent me two volumes of poetry just reeking, by one John Hughes, Esq. . . . I have been turning over Squire Hughes's poem, and his puppy publisher, one Duncomb's preface and life of the author. This is all your fault. I am put out of all patience to the present set of *Whifflers*, and their new fangled politeness. Duncomb's preface is fifty pages upon celebrating a fellow I never once heard of in my life, though I lived in London most of the time that Duncomb makes him flourish. Duncomb put a short note in loose paper, to make me a present of the two volumes, and desired my pardon for putting my name among the subscribers. I was in a rage when I looked and found my name; but was a little in countenance when I saw your Lordship's there too. The verses and prose are suc¹ our Dublin third-rate rhymers might write just the same, nine hours a day, till the coming of Antichrist. I wish I could send them to you by post for your punishment. Pray, my Lord, as you ride along, compute how much the desolation and poverty of the people have increased since your last travels through your dominions; although, I fancy, we suffer a great deal more twenty miles round Dublin than in the remoter parts, except your city of Cork, who are starving (I hope) by their own villainy.

Since you left the town there hath not been one riot, either in the University, nor among the Cavan Bail,[1] which causes a great dearth of news, nay, not so much as a Review, and but two or three bloody murders. . . . I called at my Lady Acheson's, and in came Philips very hearty, and has some excellent stories piping hot from London, which I have entreated him to send you. His Bishop is full of disease; but Philips pronounces him the best man alive, and he does not value the Chaplainship the thousandth part so much as the agreeable manner that it was given. This you will agree to be a compliment perfectly new, as new as any of my *Polite Conversation*. I will hold you no longer, but remain, my dear Lord, with more expression than the remainder of this paper will hold, ever yours.

To Dr. Sheridan.[2]

September 12, 1735.

Here is a very ingenious observation upon the days of the week and in rhyme, worth your observation—and very proper for the information of boys and girls, that they may not forget to reckon them :—

Sunday's a pun day, Monday is a dun day, Tuesday is a news day, Wednesday's a friend's day, Thursday's a cursed day, Friday's a dry day, Saturday's the latter day. I intend something of equal use upon the months : as—January, women vary. I shall, likewise, in due time make some observation upon each year as it passes. So for the present year :

[1] The mob in St. Patrick's Liberty.—C.

[2] This and the following letters are given as examples of jocular trifling, in which Swift often indulged in writing to Sheridan.

One thousand seven hundred and thirty-five,
When only the devil and bishops will thrive.
And for the next :—
One thousand seven hundred and thirty-six,
When the devil will carry the bishops to Styx.
Perge :—
One thousand seven hundred and thirty seven,
When the Whigs are so blind they mistake hell for heaven.

I will carry these predictions no farther than to year 2001, when the learned think the world will be at an end, or the *fine-all cat-a-straw-fee :*

The last is the period two thousand and one,
When M— and B— to hell are all gone.
When that time comes, pray remember the discovery came from me.

It is now time I should begin my letter. I hope you got safe to Cavan, and have got no cold in those two terrible days. All your friends are well, and I as I used to be. I received yours. My humble service to your lady, and love to your children. I suppose you have all the news sent to you. I hear of no marriages going on. One Dean Cross, an eminent divine, we hear is to be Bishop of Cork. Stay, till I ask a servant what Patrick's bells ring for so late at night.—You fellow, is it for joy or sorrow ?—I believe it is some of our Royal Birthdays. Oh, they tell me it is for joy a new Master is chosen for the Corporation of Butchers. So farewell.

To Dr. Sheridan.[1]

April 24, 1736.

. . . Your friend, Mrs. Whiteway, who is upon all occasions so zealous to vindicate you, is one whom I desire you to chide; for, during my whole sickness, she was perpetually plaguing and sponging on me; and, though she would drink no wine herself, yet she increased the expense by making me force it down her throat. . . .

[Every syllable, that is worth reading in this letter, you are to suppose I writ. The Dean only took the hints from me; but he has put them so ill together, that I am forced to tell you this in my own justification. Had you been worth hanging, you would have come to town this Vacation, and I would have shown you a poem on the *Legion Club*. I do not doubt but that a certain person will pretend he writ it, because there is a copy of it in his hand lying on his table. But do not mind that, for there are some people in the world will say anything. I wish you could give some account of poor Dr. Sheridan. I hear the reason he did not come to town this Easter is, that he waited to see a neighbour of his hanged.]

Whatever is said in this page by Goody Whiteway I have not read, nor will read; but assure you, if it relates to me, it is all a lie; for she says *you* have taught her that art. And, as the world goes, and she takes you for a wise man, she ought to follow your practice. To be serious, I am sorry you said so little of your own affairs, and of your health. And when will you pay me any money? for, upon my conscience, you have half starved me.

[1] Written alternately by Swift and his cousin Mrs. Whiteway, who so long acted as his nurse. The parts written by Mrs. Whiteway are marked by brackets.

[The plover eggs were admirable, and the worsted for the Dean's stockings so fine, that not one knitter here can knit them.]

We neither of us know what the other hath writ. So one answer will serve, if you write to us both, provided you justly give us both our share; and each of us will read our own part. Pray, tell me how you breathe, and whether that disorder be better.

[If the Dean should give you any hint about money, you need not mind him; for, to my knowledge, he borrowed twenty pounds a month ago to keep himself alive.]

I am sorry to tell you that poor Mrs. Whiteway is to be hanged on Tuesday next, for stealing a piece of Indian silk out of Bradshaw's shop, and did not set the house on fire as I advised her. I have writ a very masterly poem on the *Legion Club*; which, if the printer should be condemned to be hanged for it, you will see in a threepenny book; for it is two hundred and forty lines. Mrs. Whiteway is to have half the profit and half the hanging.

[The Drapier went this day to the Tholsel as a *Merchant*, to sign a petition to the Government against lowering the gold; where we hear he made a long speech, for which he will be reckoned a Jacobite. God send hanging does not go round.] Yours, &c.

To Dr. Sheridan.

1736.

I received your letter which began with *lings*.[1] You have, thirteen in all, and I have got but a hundred and sixty—a trifle!

---
[1] In one of his letters to Sheridan, of this time, Swift takes up a large part of it with a number of words all so ending. The correspondence of the two intimate friends abound in trifling of this or a similar kind.

Find me ten more than mine, and I will give you ten guineas for the eleventh. Mine are all down, and only twelve which are not entered in a letter, which I will send you when health permits, and I have nothing else to do, and that may be a twelvemonth hence, if my disorder will let me hold out so long.

You were born to be happy, for you take the least piece of good fortune cheerfully. I suppose that your arithmetic is, that three boys a week are a hundred and fifty-nine in a year; and seven guineas a week are three hundred and sixty-five *per annum*. Can you reckon that the county, and the next, and Dublin, will provide you with thirty lads in all, and good pay, of which a dozen shall be lodgers? Does the cheapness of things answer your expectation? Have you sent away your late younger married daughter? And will you send away the other? Let me desire you will be very regular in your accounts: because a very honest friend of mine and yours tells me, that, with all your honesty, it is an uneasy thing to have any dealings with you that relate to accounts, by your frequent forgetfulness and confusion. For you have no notion of regularity; and I do not wonder at it, considering the scattered, confused manner in which you have lived. Mrs. Whiteway thanks you for the good opinion you have of her, and I know she always loved and defended you. I cannot tell when I shall be able to travel; I have three other engagements on my hands, but the principal is to see the Bishop of Ossory. Yet I dread the lying abroad above five miles. I am never well. Some sudden turns are every day threatening me with a giddy fit; and my affairs are terribly embroiled. I have a scheme of living with you, when the College Green Club[1] is to meet; for, in those times, I detest the town, and hearing the follies, corruptions, and slavish

---

[1] The Irish Parliament, for the political proceedings of which he expresses contempt equal, at least, to his dislike for those of the Parliament of Great Britain. His *Legion Club* is a severe satire upon it.

practices of those misrepresentative brutes; and resolve, if I can stir, to pass that whole time at Bath or Cavan.

I say again, keep very regular accounts, in large books, and a fair hand—not like me, who, to save paper, confuse everything. Your mind is honest, but your memory a knave; and, therefore, the Scotch mean the same thing by "minding" that we do by "remembering." "Sirrah," said I, to a Scotch footman, "why did not you go that errand?" "Because I did not *mind* it," quoth Sawny. A curse on those twenty soldiers drumming through my Liberty twice a day, and going to a Barrack [1] the Government hath placed just under my nose. I think of a line in *Virgil Travesty*:—"The devil cut their yelping weasons."

We expect Lord Orrery and Bishop Rundle next week. This letter was intended for last post, but interruptions and horses hindered it. Poor Mrs. Acheson is relapsed at Grange, and worse than ever. I was there yesterday, and met Dr. Helsham, who hopes she was a little better.—16th. Here has nobody been hanged, married, or dead, that I hear of. Dr. Grattan is confined by a boil—if you ask him where, he will sell you a bargain. My chief country-companion now is Philosopher Webster: for the Grattans and Jacksons are neither to be found at home or abroad, except Robin, who cannot stir a foot.

To Mr. John Temple.[2]

Dublin, Feb. 1736-7.

The letter which I had the favour to receive from you I read to your cousin Mrs. Dingley, who lodges in my neighbourhood.

[1] Afterwards called the *Piddle-Guard*, and kept within the Liberties of St. Patrick's, to suppress riots.—Faulkner.

[2] John Temple, Esq., was the nephew, and his wife the granddaughter of Sir William Temple, by his only son, John Temple, who died before his father in 1689. Mr. Temple was Solicitor and Attorney-General in Ireland, and esteemed an excellent lawyer. He died at Moor Park in 1752.—N.

She was very well pleased to hear of your welfare, but a little mortified that you did not mention or inquire after her. She is quite sunk with age and unwieldiness, as well as with a very scanty support. I sometimes make her a small present, as my abilities can reach: for I do not find that her nearest relations consider her in the least.

Jervas told me that your aunt's picture[1] is in Sir Peter Lely's best manner, and the drapery all in the same hand. I shall think myself very well paid for it, if you will be so good as to order some mark of your favour to Mrs. Dingley. I do not mean a pension, but a small sum to put her for once out of debt; and, if I live any time, I shall see that she keeps herself clear of the world; for she is a woman of as much piety and discretion as I have known.

I am sorry to have been so much a stranger to the state of your family. I know nothing of your lady, or what children you have, or any other circumstances; neither do I find that Mr. Hatch can inform me in any one point. I very much approve of your keeping up your family-house at Moor Park. I have heard it is very much changed for the better as well as the Gardens. The tree on which I carved those words—*factura nepotibus umbram*—is one of those elms that stand in the hollow ground just before the house: but I suppose the letters are widened and grown shapeless by time.

I know nothing more of your brother than that he has an Irish title (I should be sorry to see you with such a feather), and that some reason or other drew us into a correspondence, which was very rough.[2] But I have forgot what was the quarrel. This letter goes by my Lord Castledurrow, who is a gentleman of very good sense and wit. I suspect, by taking

---

[1] Picture of Lady Giffard, sister of Sir W. Temple.—S. It will be remembered that Swift and she had been on not the best terms.

[2] See the correspondence with Lord Palmerston.—S.

his son with him, that he designs to see us no more. I desire to present my most humble service to your lady, with hearty thanks for her remembrance of me.

To Mr. Pope.

Feb. 9, 1736-7.

I cannot properly call you my best friend, because I have not another left who deserves the name—such a havoc have time, death, exile, and oblivion made. Perhaps you would have fewer complaints of my ill health and lowness of spirits, if they were not some excuse for my delay of writing even to you. It is perfectly right what you say of the indifference in common friends—whether we are sick or well, happy or miserable. The very maid-servants in a family have the same notion. I have often heard them say, Ah! I am very sick, *if anybody cared for it!* I am vexed when my visitors come with the compliment usual here—Mr. Dean, I hope you are very well. My popularity that you mention is wholly confined to the common people, who are more constant than those we miscall their *betters*. I walk the streets, and so do my lower friends, from whom, and from whom alone, I have a thousand hats and blessings upon old scores, which those we call the *gentry* have forgot. But I have not the love, or hardly the civility, of any one man in power or station; and I can boast that I neither visit nor am acquainted with any lord, temporal or spiritual, in the whole Kingdom; nor am able to do the least good office to the most deserving man, except what I can dispose of in my own Cathedral upon a vacancy. What has sunk my spirits more than even years and sickness, is reflecting on the most execrable corruptions that run through every branch of public management.

I heartily thank you for those lines translated, *singula de nobis anni*.[1] You have put them into a strong and admirable light: but, however, I am so partial as to be more delighted with those which are to do me the greatest honour I shall ever receive from Posterity, and will outweigh the malignity of ten thousand enemies. I never saw them before, by which it is plain that the letter you sent me miscarried. I do not doubt that you have choice of new acquaintances,[2] and some of them may be deserving, for youth is the season of virtue; corruptions grow with years, and I believe the oldest rogue in England is the greatest. You have years enough before you to watch whether these new acquaintances will keep their virtue, when they leave you and go into the world: how long their spirit of independency will last against the temptations of future ministers and future kings. As to the new Lord-Lieutenant, I never knew any of the family; so that I shall not be able to get any job done by him for any deserving friend.

To Mr. Pulteney.

March 7, 1736-7.

. . . I did not receive the letter you mentioned from Bath; and yet I have imagined, for some months past, that the meddlers of the Post-Offices here and in London have grown

---

[1] "The circling years on human pleasures prey:
They steal my humour and my mirth away."—S.

[2] His new acquaintances were, probably, Lyttelton, Murray, Lord Cornbury, &c.—Bowles.

weary of their curiosity by finding the little satisfaction it gave them. I agree heartily in your opinion of physicians. I have esteemed many of them as learned, ingenious men: but I never received the least benefit from their advice or prescriptions. And poor Dr. Arbuthnot was the only man of the faculty who seemed to understand my case; but could not remedy it. But to conquer five physicians, all eminent in their way, was a victory that Alexander and Cæsar could never pretend to. I desire that my prescription of living may be published, which you design to follow, for the benefit of mankind;[1] which, however, I do not value a rush, nor the animal itself, as it now acts: neither will I ever value myself as a *philanthropus*, because it is now a creature (taking a vast majority) that I hate more than a toad, a viper, a wasp, a stork, a fox, or any other that you will please to add.

Since the date of your letter, we understand there is another Duke to govern here. Mr. Stoplond was with me last night. He is as well provided for, and to his own satisfaction, as any private clergyman. He engaged me to present his best respects and acknowledgments by you. Your modesty in refusing to take a *motto* goes too far. The sentence is not a boast, because it is every man's duty in morals and religion.[2]

[1] "Rising early, eating little, drinking less, and riding daily."—Pulteney to Swift—Dec. 31, 1736.

[2] "There is a sentence," writes Mr. Pulteney, Dec. 31, 1736, "I think it is in Tully's *Offices*, which I admire extremely, and should be tempted to take it for a *motto*, if ever I took one, *Amicis prodesse, nemini nocere*. It is a noble sentiment, and shall be my rule, though, perhaps, never my *motto*." He adds, in the same letter, "Pope shewed me a letter he had lately from you. We grieved extremely to find you so full of complaints, and we wished heartily you might be well enough to make a trip here in spring. Shifting the scene was of great service to me: perhaps it might be so to you. I mended from the moment I had crossed the seas, and sensibly felt the benefit of changing air. His Majesty is still on the other side. He has escaped being at sea in the tempestuous weather we have had—but when the wind will let him come, God knows. Lord Chesterfield says, if he does not come by *Twelfth-day*, the people will *King and Queen* without him.—I must tell you a ridiculous incident, perhaps you have not heard it. One Mrs.

Indeed, we differ here from what you have been told of the Duke of Dorset's having given great satisfaction the last time he was with us—particularly, in his disposal of two bishoprics, and other Church as well as Civil preferments. I wrote to a lady in London, his Grace's near relation and intimate,[1] that she would no more continue the office of a go-between (as she called herself) betwixt the Duke and me; because I never design to attend him [at the Castle], and yet I allow him to be as agreeable a person in conversation as I have almost anywhere met. I sent my letter to that lady under a cover addressed to the Duke; and in it I made many complaints against some proceedings, which I suppose he has seen. I never made him one request for myself; and, if I spoke for another, he was always upon his guard—which was but twice, and for trifles—but failed in both.

The father of our friend[2] in France may outlive the son; for I would venture a wager, that if you pick out twenty of the oldest men in England, nineteen of them have been the most worthless fellows in the kingdom. You tell me with great kindness as well as gravity, that I ought this spring to make a trip to England; and your motive is admirable—that shifting the scene was of great service to you, and, therefore, it may be so to me. I answer as an Academic, *nego consequentiam*. And, besides, comparisons are odious. You are what the French

---

Mapp, a famous she bone-setter and mountebank, coming to town with a coach and six horses, on the Kentish road, was met by a rabble of people, who, seeing her very oddly and tawdrily dressed, took her for a foreigner, and concluded she must be a certain great person's mistress. Upon this they followed the coach, bawling out, 'No Hanover whore! No Hanover whore!' The lady within the coach was much offended, let down the glass, and screamed louder than any of them,—'She was no Hanover whore! She was an English one!' Upon which they cried out, God bless your Ladyship, quitted the pursuit, and wished her a good journey."

[1] Lady Betty Germaine, Jan. 29.

[2] Bolingbroke, whose father, Sir Henry St. John (Bart.), had been created Baron St. John, of Battersea, and Viscount St. John.

call *plein de vie*. As you are much younger, so I am a dozen years older than my age makes me, by infirmities of mind and body: to which I add the perpetual detestation of all public persons and affairs in both kingdoms.

I spread the story of Mrs. Mapp, while it was new to us. There was something humorous in it throughout that pleased everybody here. Will you engage for your friend Carteret that he will oppose any step toward arbitrary power? He has promised me, under a penalty, that he will continue firm; and yet some reports go here of him that have a little disconcerted me. Learning and good sense he has to a great degree, if the love of power and riches do not overbalance.

Pray God long continue the gifts he has bestowed you, to be the chief support of liberty to your country, and let all the people say *Amen*. I am, with the truest respect, and highest esteem, &c.

To The Earl Of Oxford.[1]

June 14, 1737.

I had the honour of a letter from your Lordship, dated April the 7th, which I was not prepared to answer till this time. Your Lordship must needs have known that the *History* you mention, of the Four Last Years of the Queen's Reign,[2] was

---

[1] Son of Robert Harley, first Lord Oxford.

[2] Lord Oxford had heard of Swift's purpose to publish this well-known narrative, and fearing some inconvenient revelations, it seems, in regard to his father's political conduct, had written to Swift deprecating immediate publication:—" As I am most truly sensible of your constant regard and sincere friendship for my father—even to partiality, if I may say so—I am very sensible of the share and part he must bear in such a History. As I remember when I read over that History of yours, I can recollect that there seemed to

written at Windsor, just upon finishing the Peace; at which time your father and my Lord Bolingbroke had a misunderstanding with each other, that was attended with very bad consequences.

When I came to Ireland to take this Deanery (after the Peace was made) I could not stay here above a fortnight, being recalled by a hundred letters to hasten back, and to use my endeavours in reconciling those Ministers. I left them the *History* you mention, which I finished at Windsor, to the time of the Peace. When I returned to England I found their quarrels and coldness increased. I laboured to reconcile them as much as I was able. I contrived to bring them to my Lord Masham's, at St. James's. My Lord and Lady Masham left us together. I expostulated with them both, but could not find any good consequences. I was to go to Windsor next day with my Lord Treasurer; I pretended business that prevented me, expecting that they would come to some.[1] . . But I followed them to Windsor, where my Lord Bolingbroke told me that my scheme had come to nothing. Things went on all the same rate; they grew more estranged every day. My Lord Treasurer found his credit daily declining. In May, before the Queen died, I had my last meeting with them at my Lord Masham's. He left us together,

be a want of some papers to make it more complete, which was not in our power to obtain: besides, there were some severe things said, which might have been very currently talked of, but now will waut a proper evidence to support. For these reasons it is that I do entreat the favour of you, and make it my earnest request, that you will give your positive directions, that this History be not printed and published, until I have had an opportunity of seeing it, with a liberty of shewing it to some family friends, whom I would consult upon this occasion. I beg pardon for this: I hope you will be so good as to grant my request. I do it with great deference to you. If I had the pleasure of seeing you, I could soon say something to you that would convince you I am not wrong: they are not proper for a letter, as you will easily guess." He again protests, with equal deference, against the publication, in a letter dated July 4. This renewed application, it seems, had the desired effect: for the MS. was sent to England, and submitted to Lord Oxford and his friends.

[1] Here is a blank left for some word or other, such as *agreement, reconciliation*, or the like.—S.

and therefore I spoke very freely to them both, and told them, "I would retire, for I found all was gone." Lord Bolingbroke whispered me, I was in the right, Your father said, "All would do well." I told him that I would go to Oxford on Monday, since I found it was impossible to be of any use. I took coach to Oxford on Monday; went to a friend in Berkshire; there staid until the Queen's death; and then to my station here, where I staid twelve years, and never saw my Lord, your father, afterward.

They could not agree about printing the *History of the Four Last Years;* and therefore I have kept it to this time, when I determine to publish it in London, to the confusion of all those rascals who have accused the Queen and that Ministry of making a bad Peace—to which that [Whig] Party entirely owes the Protestant Succession. I was then in the greatest trust and confidence with your father, the Lord Treasurer, as well as with my Lord Bolingbroke, and all others who had part in the Administration. I had all the Letters from the Secretary's Office during the Treaty of Peace. Out of those, and what I learned from the Ministry, I formed that History, which I am now going to publish for the information of Posterity, and to control the most impudent falsehoods which have been published since. I wanted no kind of materials. I knew your father better than you could at that time; and I do impartially think him the most virtuous Minister, and the most able, that ever I remember to have read of.

If your Lordship has any particular circumstances that may fortify what I have said in the *History*, such as letters or materials, I am content they should be printed at the end, by way of appendix. I loved my Lord, your father, better than any other man in the world, although I had no obligation to him on the score of preferment, having been driven to this wretched kingdom, to which I was almost a stranger, by his want of power to keep me in what I ought to call my own country, although I happened to be dropped here, and was a year old before I left it, and, to my sorrow, did not die before I came back to it again. I am extremely glad of the felicity you have in your alliances, and desire to present my most humble respects to my Lady Oxford, and your daughter, the Duchess.

As to the *History* it is only of affairs which I know very well, and had all the advantages possible to know, when you were, in some sort, but a lad. One great design of it is, to do justice to the Ministry at that time, and to refute all objections against them, as if they had a design of bringing in Popery and the Pretender; and, farther, to demonstrate that the present Settlement of the Crown was chiefly owing to my Lord, your father.[1] I can never expect to see England; I am now too old and too sickly, added to almost a perpetual deafness and giddiness. I live a most domestic life. I want nothing that is necessary; but I am in a cursed, factious, oppressed, miserable country, not made so by Nature, but by the slavish, hellish, principles of an execrable, prevailing faction in it.

Farewell, my Lord. I have tired you and myself. I desire again to present my most humble respects to my Lady Oxford, and the Duchess, your daughter. Pray God preserve you long and happy! I shall diligently inquire into your conduct from those who will tell me. You have hitherto continued right; let me hear that you persevere so. Your task will not be long, for I am not in a condition of health or time to trouble this world [long], and I am heartily weary of it already; and so should be in England, which I hear is full as corrupt as this poor enslaved country. I am, with the truest love and respect, &c.

---

[1] In reply to all this confident assertion, it can only be answered, that Swift, in this case, could not have been admitted into the secret counsels of the Ministry.

TO MR. LEWIS.[1]

July 23, 1737.

While any of those who used to write to me were alive, I always inquired after you. But, since your Secretaryship in the Queen's time, I believed you were so glutted with the office, that you had not patience to venture on a letter to an absent, useless acquaintance; and I find I owe yours to my Lord Oxford.

The *History* you mention was written above a year before the Queen's death. I left it with the Treasurer and Lord Bolingbroke, when I first came over to take the Deanery. I returned in less than a month; but the Ministry could not agree about printing it. It was to conclude with the Peace. I staid in London above nine months; but, not being able to reconcile the quarrels between these two, I went to a friend in Berkshire, and, on the Queen's death, came here for good and all. I am confident you read that History, as this Lord Oxford did, as he owns in his two letters, the last of which reached me not above ten days ago. You know, on the Queen's death, how the Peace and all proceedings were universally condemned. This I knew would be done, and the chief cause of my writing was, not to let such a Queen and Ministry be under such a load of infamy, or posterity be so ill-informed, &c.

Lord Oxford is in the wrong to be in pain about his father's character, or his proceedings in his Ministry; which is so drawn that his greatest admirers will rather censure me for partiality. Neither can he tell me anything material out of his Papers, which I was not then informed of; nor do I know anybody but yourself who could give me more light than what I then

[1] A great favourite of Harley's, and intimate friend of Swift during the period 1710-14.

received. For I remember I often consulted with you, and took memorials of many important particulars which you told me, as I did of others, for four years together. I can find no way to have the original delivered to Lord Oxford or to you; for the person who has it will not part it out of his hands, but, I believe, would be contented to let it be read to either of you, if it could be done without letting it out of his hands,[1] although, perhaps, that may be too late. If my health would have permitted me, for some years past, to have ventured as far as London, I would have satisfied both my Lord and you. I believe you know that Lord Bolingbroke is now busy in France, writing the History of his Own Time; and how much he grew to hate the Treasurer you know too well, and I know how much Lord Bolingbroke hates his very memory. This is what the present Lord Oxford should be in most pain at, not about me.

I have had my share of affliction sufficient, in the loss of Dr. Arbuthnot, and poor Gay, and others[2]; and I heartily pity poor Lord Masham. I would fain know whether his son be a valuable young man; because I much dislike his education. When I was last among you, Sir William Wyndham was in a bad state of health. I always loved him, and I rejoice to hear from you the figure he makes. But I know so little of what passes, that I never heard of Lady Blandford, his present wife. Lord Bathurst used to write to me, but has dropped it some years. Pray, is Charles Ford yet alive? for he has dropped me, too; or, perhaps, my illness has hindered me from provoking his remembrance, for I have been long in a very bad condition. My deafness, which used to be occasional, and for a short time, has

---

[1] As a little before this period the great abilities of Dr. Swift had begun to fail, he had, in order to gratify some of his acquaintances, called for the *History* once or twice out of his friend's hands, and lent it abroad: by which means parts of the contents were whispered about the town, and several had pretended to have read it, who, perhaps, had not seen one line of it.—Deane Swift.

[2] Arbuthnot died in Feb., 1735, Gay in Dec., 1732.

stuck by me now several months, without intermission; so that I am unfit for any conversation, except one or two Stentors of either sex, and my old giddiness is likewise become chronical, although not in equal violence with my former short fits.

I was never so much deceived in any Scot as that execrable Lord K——,[1] whom I loved extremely, and now detest beyond expression. You say so little of yourself, that I know not whether you are in health or in sickness, only that you lead a mere animal life, which, with nine parts in ten, is a sign of health. I find you have not, like me, lost your memory; nor, I hope, your sense of hearing, which is the greatest loss of any, and more comfortless than even being blind. I mean, in the article of company. Writing no longer amuses me, for I cannot think. I dine constantly at home, in my chamber, with a grave houskeeper, whom I call *Sir Robert*, and sometimes receive one or two friends, and a female cousin, with strong, high, tenor voices.[2]

---

[1] Lord Kinnoul, whose pecuniary embarrassments had involved, it would seem, Lord Oxford. He is often mentioned with regard in the *Journal*.—S.

[2] In an interesting letter of Lewis, of April, 1738, first published by Scott, Harley's old confidant sends his friend the criticisms of Lord Oxford and two or three other Tory friends (unnamed), upon the *History*. As for the part relating to the negociations for Peace, in London and Utrecht, " they admire it exceedingly, and declare they never saw that, or any other transaction, drawn up with so much perspicuity, or in a style so entertaining and instructive to the reader, in every respect. . . . . But I should be wanting in the sincerity of a friend," he adds, "if I did not tell you plainly, that it was the unanimous opinion of the company a great deal of the first part should be retracted, and many things altered." Objections, severally, are raised to the account of the establishment of the South Sea Company—"for no part of the debt, then unprovided for, was paid; however, the advantages arising to the public," they think, "were very considerable : for, instead of paying for all provisions *cent. per cent.* dearer than the common market price, as we did in Lord Godolphin's times, the credit of the public was immediately restored ; and, by means of this scheme, put upon as good a footing as the best private security";—to the disparagement of the Duke of Marlborough's personal courage and bravery, upon which the brief comment is: "The D—— of M——'s courage not to be called in question";—and the *mere* report of a plot on the part of Prince Eugene to assassinate Harley. "The projected design of an assassination they believe true, but that a matter of so high a nature

To Mr. Alderman Barber.

August 8, 1738.

I have received yours of July 27th; and two days ago had a letter from Mr. Pope, with a dozen lines from my Lord Bolingbroke, who tells me he is just going to France and, I suppose, designs to continue there as long as he lives. I am sorry he is under the necessity of selling Dawley. Pray let me know whether he be tolerably easy in his fortunes; for he has these several years lived very expensively. Is his lady still alive? And has he still a country-house, and an estate of hers to live on? I should be glad to live so long as to see his History of His Own Times, which would be a work very worthy of his Lordship, and will be a defence of that Ministry, and a justification of our late glorious Queen, against the malice, ignorance, falsehood, and stupidity of our present times and managers.

I very much like Mr. Pope's last poem, entitled "MDCCXXXVIII.," called Dialogue II.[1] But I live so obscurely, and know so little of what passes in London, that I cannot know the names of persons and things by initial letters. I am very glad to hear that the Duke of Ormond lives so well at ease and

ought not to be asserted without exhibiting the proofs." The Committee of Censors, also, strongly advise modification of the *characters* of the enemy who figure in the *History*—for "nothing could save the author's printer and publishers from some grievous punishment." Lewis adds:—"What I have to say from myself is, that there were persons in the company, to whose judgment I should pay entire deference. . . . I concurred in the same opinion with them from the bottom of my heart; and therefore conjure you, as you value your fame as an author, and the honour of those who were the actors in the important affairs that make the subject of your *History*, and as you would preserve the liberty of your person, and enjoyment of your fortune, you will not suffer this work to go to the Press without making some, or all, of the amendments proposed. I am, my dear Dean, most sincerely and affectionately your, E. L."

Whether from infirmity, or from not being shaken in his own convictions, or from whatever reason, none of these criticisms induced Swift to make any alterations; and, when the Narrative came out, after his death, it was found to have beem unrevised.

[1] Epilogue to the *Satires*.

in so good health, as well as with so valuable a companion. His Grace has an excellent constitution at so near to fourscore. Mr. Dunkin is not in town, but I will send to him, when I hear he is come. I extremely love my Lord and Lady Oxford; but his way of managing his fortune is not to be endured. I remember a rascally butcher, one Morley, a great land-jobber and knave, who was his Lordship's manager, and has been the principal cause of my Lord's wrong conduct, in which you agree with me in blaming his weakness and credulity. I desire you will please, upon occasion, to present my humble service to my Lord and Lady Oxford, and to my Lord Bathurst. I just expected the character you give of young ——. I hated him from a boy. I wonder Mr. Ford is alive—perhaps walking preserves him. I very much lament your asthma. I believe temperance and exercise have preserved me from it. I seldom walk less than four miles, sometimes six, eight, ten, or more—never beyond my own limits; or, if it rains, I walk as much through the house, up and down stairs. And, if it were not for the cruel deafness, I would ride through the kingdom, and half through England—pox on the modern phrase *Great Britain*, which is only to distinguish it from *Little Britain*, where old clothes and old books are to be bought and sold. However, I will put Dr. Sheridan (the best scholar in both kingdoms) upon taking your receipt for a terrible asthma. I wish you were rich enough to buy and keep a horse, and to ride every tolerable day twenty miles.

Mr. Richardson is, I think, still in London. I have not written as much this many a day. I have tired myself much; but, in revenge, I will tire you.

Nature or their Office.

— It is a Maxim among these Lawyers, that whatever hath been done before, may legally be done again: and therefore they take special Care to record all the Decisions formerly made against common Justice and the general Reason of Mankind. These under the Name of Precedents they produce as Authoritys to justify the most iniquitous Opinions; and the Judges never fail of decreeing accordingly.

In pleading, &c. to — three hundred miles off.

P. 77.

In the Tryal of Persons accused for Crimes against the State the Method is much more short and commendable: The Judge first sends to sound the Disposition of those in Power, after which he can easily hang or save the Criminal, strictly preserving all due Forms of Law.

Here my Master interposing, said it was a Pity, that Creatures endowed with such prodigious Abilities of Mind as these Lawyers by the Description I gave of them must certainly be, were not rather encouraged to be Instructors of others in Wisdom and Knowledge. — In answer to which I assured his Honour, that in

From original interleaved copy of "Gulliver's Travels," in the Forster Collection in the South Kensington Museum.

The Life and Writings of Pope.

Autotype.

MARTHA BLOUNT.

FROM AN ORIGINAL PICTURE IN THE COLLECTION OF
MICHAEL BLOUNT, ESQ., AT
MAPLE DURHAM.

THE LIFE AND WRITINGS OF POPE.

THE conspicuous place of the first of the English poets of the eighteenth century, among Letter-Writers, depends more upon extrinsic than intrinsic merits—upon his pre-eminent fame, with his contemporaries, as poet and critic, the consequent literary and historic interest attaching to his prose productions, and the number and celebrity of his correspondents. That the letters of Pope, unlike those of Swift, and, still more, of Cowper, are not "emanations of the heart," as he himself wished them to be considered, but laborious compositions is sufficiently apparent; that a large part of his collected Correspondence was the product of the most extraordinary artifice as well as labour can adequately be known only to those who have carefully studied the results of the minute investigations of (comparatively) recent research. As the poet of Art and Epigram, *par excellence,* whatever rank may be assigned to him in the national literature, at least he has the singular honour of being, next to Shakspeare, the most often quoted of all its contributors.

Of the lower middle rank on the side of his father, whose parentage has not been clearly ascertained,[1] on his mother's side (as is alleged), of the higher middle class, his place in the social scale was a little ambiguous. His father followed the trade of a linen draper in Lombard Street; his

---

[1] When Lady M. Wortley Montagu and Lord Hervey, resenting the innuendos of his gross satire, retaliated in some equally satirical verses, taunting him with his "birth obscure," he took great pains (in a *Letter to a Noble Lord,* and in a note to his *Epistle to Arbuthnot*) to clear himself in the eyes of his numerous aristocratic friends, and represents himself as of an old Oxfordshire family, who derived their chief honours from an Earl of Downe, an Irish peer. Not content with these declarations, he sent to Curll, the bookseller, on the eve of the publication of the Letters, under a fictitious signature ("P. T."), an elaborate claim of the same kind. The genealogy seems to be imaginary. The name of Pope, in the sixteenth and seventeenth centuries, was curiously common throughout the country Even his mother's lineage, if not social position, has been matter of dispute. As for his creed, his father seems to have been a convert.

mother, for whom he always retained a strong affection, and for whose sake chiefly he seems to have adhered to the creed she professed, belonged (as it is commonly described) to an old Yorkshire family of the name of Turner. Both parents professed faithful allegiance to the Papal Church; and it is curious to note that the author of the *Essay on Man* owed all his education to, and in early youth mixed exclusively with, adherents of that religion. From his father, Alexander Pope, an only son,[1] born in the Revolution year, 1688, inherited a deformed as well as feeble body. In his childhood, by his sensibility and by the sweetness of his voice, which gained for him the distinguishing name of *the Nightingale*, he is said to have charmed all about him; "but the mildness of his disposition," as his biographer, Johnson, puts it, "perhaps ended with his childhood." His first instruction he received from a neighbouring priest, who taught him the elements of the Greek and Latin grammars. From the two Catholic schools—where he acquired his next experiences in learning—over one of which presided an ex-Fellow of Oxford and a convert of James II. (whose controversial zeal and party intrigues placed him frequently in jail and once in the pillory), he derived, apparently, very little more of *secular* knowledge. For such as he then obtained, he declares himself to have been mainly or entirely indebted, like many other eminent writers, to his own efforts. Soon after the Revolution, so adverse to his co-religionists, his father gave up his business, having secured in trade a fortune of ten or twenty thousand pounds. He bought a small house, with twenty acres of land, at Binfield, on the borders of Windsor Forest, investing a part of his wealth in the French funds. In this quiet home, to which he returned after leaving his school, and after some two years given to learning French and Italian, in London, young Pope formed for himself a course of desultory literary study. "I followed everywhere," as he describes it himself, "as my fancy led me, and was like a boy gathering flowers in the fields and woods, just as they fell in the way."

From a very early age he discovered an extraordinary aptitude for versifying. But he does not stand alone in this repect. Almost all the greatest poets have, as he expresses it of himself, "lisped in numbers," —Milton, Chatterton, Shelley, Byron, among Englishmen. When only eight years old, he had already indulged his poetic instincts by trans-

---

[1] He had a half-sister, named Magdalen, who married a Mr. Rickett, and lived at Staines. Of this only sister and her children little has been reported.

lating, or attempts at translating, in verse, some of the Latin poets; and (according to the information of his anecdotist biographer, Spence) at the age of twelve he composed a large part of an epic poem, an experiment in the styles of various poets—Homer, Virgil, Ovid, Statius, Claudian, Spenser, Milton, Cowley; also a tragedy on the legend of St. Geneviève. From Sandy's *Ovid*, and Ogilby's *Homer*, he obtained his earliest acqaintance with those two poets; to one of whom, especially, he was to devote so much labour, and to owe so much of his contemporary fame. Of English poets, he made Dryden his chief favourite and study. His first attempt at original composition is said to be the short *Ode on Solitude*; but great uncertainty attaches to the bibliography of Pope's juvenile attempts; nor can it be proved how far they remained untouched before publication in later years. "My first taking to imitating," he confided to his friend Spence, "was not out of vanity, but humility. I saw how defective my own things were, and endeavoured to mend my manner by copying good strokes from others. My epic was about two years in hand, from thirteen to fifteen."[1]

Composed, or rather, probably, sketched out, when he was of the age of sixteen, in 1709 appeared his first published poem, the *Pastorals*. An ex-Secretary of State, Sir William Trumbull, "a learned civilian and an experienced diplomatist" (as Macaulay styles him), who now lived in retirement near Binfield, acted as his first literary sponsor, and became his intimate friend. To him Pope shewed his manuscript four or five years before its publication. Impressed by its remarkable merits, he welcomed the young poet in terms of high eulogy. To Wycherley, the dramatist, also, the manuscript had been confided. From him it passed into the hands of Walsh, who, upon Dryden's *ex cathedrâ* sentence, passed for being the "best critic of the nation," but who occupies only a page of Johnson's *Lives*. Walsh, a man of large property, resided at Abberley, in Worcestershire, to which place he invited his *protégé* in the summer of 1705. In a letter to the author of *The Plain Dealer* he professes, "it is not flattery at all to say that Virgil had written nothing so good at his age." The manuscript passed from hand to hand in the circles of letters and fashion, and had the honour of criticism, or rather of enthusiastic praise, from some of the principal statesmen as well as

---

[1] Spence's *Observations, Anecdotes,* &c. Spence has not the reputation of a Boswell in accuracy; nor Pope the reputation of Boswell's hero in candour. The Anecdotist's representations, therefore, in minuter particulars, have to be read with some caution. The *Observations, Anecdotes, and Characters of Books and Men* of the Oxford Professor of Poetry did not see the light until the year 1820.

most approved *littérateurs* of the day—Somers, Halifax, Lansdowne, Congreve, and others.

When, at the end of four years, it emerged in print, in the *Poetic Miscellanies* of Jacob Tonson (a periodical originally started by Dryden, under whose editorship four or five volumes had been published), the applause of its readers entirely responded to the encomiums of the friendly critics. In a letter to Walsh (July 1706), Pope requests his correspondent's opinion upon the liberty of borrowing, and adds: "I have sometimes defended it by saying that it seems not so much the perfection of sense to say things that had never been said before, as to express those best that have been said oftenest." Imitations of the *Idylls* of Theocritus, the *Eclogues* of Virgil, and the *Aminta* of Tasso, in which conventional shepherds, in alternate verse, sing their highly idealised labours and their loves, the *Pastorals*, artificial and open to criticism as they are upon other grounds, have, at least, deserved the praises given to them for extraordinarily correct and harmonious verse. Prefixed to the poem is a *Discourse on Pastoral Poetry*. "This sensible and judicious Discourse," according to Warton, one of the most considerable of the critics of Pope, "written at so early an age, is a more wonderful production than the poem that follows it"—an expression of opinion, the not surprising want of originality of the Essay considered, scarcely to be endorsed. In the opening pages of the same volume of *Miscellanies* appeared the *Pastorals* of Ambrose Philips, those of Pope concluding it. This proved to be the beginning of a quarrel little creditable to the candour of Pope. At first (in a letter to his friend Cromwell, October, 1710), he had assented to the praise of Philips in the *Tatler*—that "we had no better Eclogues in our language"; —but, when the repeated eulogies of his rival appeared in the *Guardian* (xxii., xxiii., xxx., xxxii., in the last of which Philips is exalted to the fourth place among idyllic poets, and next to Spenser), written probably by Tickell, his own poem being but slightly noticed, his jealousy declared itself. He sent a paper to that lately started periodical (which Steele, with whom he had not yet quarrelled, edited) in which, under disguise of admiration of Philips and depreciation of himself, with remarkable skill and ingenuity, he produced, or attempted to produce, in his readers an entirely opposite feeling. So adroitly did he manage his language as even to deceive his editor.

"As simplicity," he writes, "is the distinguishing characteristic of *Pastoral*, Virgil has been thought guilty of too courtly a style. His language is perfectly pure, and he often forgets he is among peasants. I have frequently wondered that, since he was so conversant with the writings of Ennius, he had not imitated the rusticity of the Doric as well by the help of the old obsolete Roman language as Philips has by the antiquated English. For example, might he not have said *quoi* instead of *cui; quoijum* for *cujum; volt* for *vult,* &c., as well as our modern has *welladay* for *alas; whilome* for *old; make mock* for *deride;* and *witless younglings* for *simple lambs,* &c.; by which means he had attained as much of the air of Theocritus, as Philips has of Spenser. Mr. Pope has fallen into the same error with Virgil. His clowns do not converse in all the simplicity proper to the country. His names are borrowed from Theocritus and Virgil, which are improper to the scene of his *Pastorals*. He introduces *Daphnis, Alexis,* and *Thyrsis* on British plains, as Virgil had done before him on the Mantuan. Whereas Philips, who has the strictest regard to propriety, makes choice of names peculiar to the country, and more agreeable to a reader of delicacy—such as *Hobbinol, Lobbin, Cuddy,* and *Colin Clout.* . . .

"But," he proceeds, "the better to discover the merits of our two contemporary *Pastoral* writers, I shall endeavour to draw a parallel of them, by setting several of their particular thoughts in the same light, whereby it will be obvious how much Philips has the advantage. With what simplicity he introduces two shepherds singing alternately:—

> *Hobb.* Come, Rosalind, O come, for without thee
> What pleasure can the country have for me?
> Come, Rosalind, O come. My brindled kine,
> My snowy sheep, my farm, and all is thine.
>
> *Lanq.* Come Rosalind, O come. Here shady bowers,
> Here are cool fountains, and here springing flowers.
> Come, Rosalind; here ever let us stay,
> And sweetly waste our live-long time away.

Our other Pastoral writer, in expressing the same thought, deviates into downright poetry:—

> *Streph.* In Spring the fields, in Autumn hills I love,
> At morn the plains, at noon the shady grove,
> But Delia always. Forced from Delia's sight,
> Nor plains at morn, nor groves at noon delight.
>
> *Daph.* Sylvia's like Autumn ripe, yet mild as May,
> More bright than noon, yet fresh as early day.
> E'en Spring displeases, when she shines not here:
> But blest with her, 'tis Spring thoughout the year."

To further provoke the ridicule of his fashionable readers for the *rustic* idyll, the essayist ironically introduces specimens from a pretended Somersetshire ballad, which would, perhaps, have delighted the old poet of the *Owl and the Nightingale*—the Dorsetshire Philips, or rather Barnes, of the thirteenth century:—"But the most beautiful example of this kind that I ever met with is a very valuable piece, which I chanced to find among some old manuscripts, entitled *A Pastoral Ballad*; which I think, for its nature and simplicity, may (notwithstanding the modesty of the title) be allowed a perfect *Pastoral*. It is composed in the Somersetshire dialect, and the names such as are proper to the country people. It may be observed, as a farther beauty of this *Pastoral*, the words *Nymph, Dryad, Naiad, Faun, Cupid*, or *Satyr*, are not once mentioned through the whole. I shall make no apology for inserting ome few lines of this excellent piece."[1]

Byron, the most distinguished eulogist of Pope, while deeming it vain to attempt "to match the youthful eclogues of our Pope," perhaps fairly characterises the styles of the two *Pastorals*:—

> "Yet his and Philip's faults of different kind—
> For Art too rude, for Nature too refined—
> Instruct how hard the medium 'tis to hit
> 'Twixt too much polish and too coarse a wit."

Pope was sure of the suffrages of almost all the critics of his own time at least; but, correctness and conventionalism apart, the superior propriety and *naturalness*, if less *elegance*, in manners and language of the associate of Addison and Steele, and, still more, of the Somerset Eclogue will, perhaps, be allowed by most readers of the present day.

---

[1] Pope goes on to quote from the extemporised idyll, first explaining that "Cicily breaks thus into the subject, as she is going a-milking:—

> *Cicily.* Rager, go vetch tha Kee, or else the Zun
> Will quite bego bevore c'have half adon.
> *Roger.* Thou shouldst not ax me tweece, but I've a be
> To dreave our bull to bull the parson's kee.

"It is to be observed that this whole dialogue is formed upon the passion of jealousy; and his mentioning the parson's kine naturally revives the jealousy of the Shepherdess Cicily, which she expresses as follows:—

> *Cicily.* Ah, Rager, Rager, chez was zore avaid
> When in yond vield you kissed the parson's maid;
> Is this the love that once to me you zed,
> When from the wake thou broughtst me ginger bread?
> *Roger.* Cicily, thou charg'st me false. I'll zwear to thee,
> The parson's maid is still a maid for me.

"In which answer of his are expressed at once that spirit of religion, and that innocence of the Golden Age, so necessary to be observed by all writers of *Pastoral*." (*Guardian, XL.*) The irony was continued by Gay, in his *Shepherd's Week*.

At the outset of his paper Pope had represented himself as a writer "whose character it is, that he takes the greatest care of his works before they are published, and has the least concern for them afterwards." Read in the light of recent researches, this character of himself, as far as the latter part of it is concerned, may seem to be written in the same spirit of irony with the rest. At the same time with the principal contribution appeared, in Tonson's *Miscellany*, an imitation of Chaucer's *January and May*, and a (verse) translation of an episode in the *Iliad* (xii, xvi). All earlier efforts he eclipsed in the *Essay on Criticism*, published anonymously in 1711, but written (as generally accepted) in his twentieth year. As a production of early and original genius it is surpassed by Milton's *Hymn on the Nativity*, and, much more, by Shelley's *Queen Mab*; in brilliancy and wit by Byron's *English Bards and Scotch Reviewers*; but its generally acute, if not very profound criticism, superior, though not by any means perfect, versification, and, still more, its promise of future excellence, have received the admiration, sometimes extravagant, of most of his critics.

Its most conspicuous fault is the large number of defective rhymes, which is the more surprising that, above all poets, he has exercised the *labor limæ*. He took for his models the *Ars Poetica* of Horace, and *L'Art Poétique* of Boileau, deriving some hints from the now almost forgotten verse-essays of Roscommon and Mulgrave. Leading off with the principle that, "It is as great a fault to judge ill as to write ill, and a more dangerous one to the public," and with the postulates that, "a true taste is as rare to be found as a true genius," that "most men are born with some taste, but are spoiled by false education," it proceeds to consider the causes hindering a true judgment. Prejudices and partisanship, so generally prevalent, he thus exposes:—

> "Some foreign writers, some our own despise,
> The Ancients only or the Moderns prize.
> Thus Wit, like Faith, by each man is applied
> To one small sect, and all are damned beside.
> Meanly they seek the blessing to confine,
> And force the Sun but on a part to shine.
>   *   *   *   *   *   *
> Regard not, then, if Wit be new or old,
> But blame the False, and value still the True."

In a well-known passage (like a still more famous critic, in his equally celebrated and still bolder verse[1]) he seems to challenge, but, unlike his great contemporary, he had not equally to fear, the hostility of a powerful Order:—

> "Learning and Rome alike in empire grew,
> And Arts still followed where her Eagles flew.
> From the same foes, at last, both felt their doom,
> And the same Age saw Learning fall and Rome.[2]
> With Tyranny then Superstition joined,
> As that the Body, this enslaved the Mind.
> Much was believed, but little understood;
> And to be dull was construed to be good.
> A second deluge Learning thus o'er-run,
> And the Monks finished what the Goths begun!
> At length Erasmus, that great injured name,
> (The Glory of the Priesthood and the Shame!)
> Stemmed the wild torrent of a barbarous Age,
> And drove those holy Vandals off the Stage."

One life-long enemy, among the Zoiluses of the day, he provoked and immortalised by his satire. Dennis, a writer of turgid plays, and of ferocious but not always wholly unjust *critiques*, three years before had brought out a tragedy on the story of Appius and Virginia; and Pope, in two or three sarcastic lines, took upon himself to revenge the sufferings of former victims of "Sir Tremendous" (as he styles him in a later production), under the name of the Roman tyrant of his own drama. The enraged critic retaliated in a strongly vituperative pamphlet, not without an occasionally successful hit; and thus began a war *à outrance*, to end only with the death of a principal hero of the first *Dunciad*, in 1734. Addison's laudatory notice in the *Spectator*, who pronounced the Essay to be "a masterpiece of its kind," more than sufficiently compensated the young poet for the censure of his hostile critic. Later, as well as contemporary, writers of authority have lavished praises upon it, which now appear a little hyperbolical. Johnson pronounces it " a work which displays such extent of comprehension, such nicety of distinction, such acquaintance with mankind, and such knowledge, both

---

[1] In the Tragedy of *Œdipe*:—

"*Nos prêtres ne sont pas ce qu'un vain peuple pense:
Nôtre crédulité fait toute leur science.*"

[2] In Pope's, as in Shakspeare's day, Rome had the same pronunciation as the word with which it here rhymes. In the following couplet, what has now become a vulgarism was also in the first half of the last century, apparently, the fashionable pronunciation. Many

of ancient and modern learning, as are not often attained by the maturest age and longest experience," and, in another place, he repeats his eulogy in still stronger terms : " If he had written nothing else," he holds, " it would have placed him among the first critics and the first poets, as he exhibits every mode of excellence that can embellish or dignify didactic composition.—selection of matter, novelty of arrangement, justness of precept, splendour of illustration, and propriety of digression." [1] Among admiring recent critics, Sainte-Beuve, disputing Taine's rather depreciatory judgment (*Hist. de la Lit. Anglaise*) on the general character of Pope and his poetic style, thinks the poem " well worth the *Epistle to the Pisos* (which is called the *Art of Poetry*) of Horace, and that of Boileau." [2]

Windsor Forest and the *Messiah*, both of which poems Pope ranked among his Pastorals, came out about the same time, the latter in the *Spectator* (May 14, 1712) ; and Steele, the editor, who seems to have undertaken to revise it, wrote to the author in terms of high eulogy, complimenting him on his having " preserved the sublime, heavenly spirit, throughout the whole," and declaring it to be " better than the *Pollio.*" As is well-known, the *Messiah* derived its inspiration from that *Eclogue* of the Roman poet, and from the sublimest of the Jewish prophets, in their magnificent prophecies of a Golden Age of Innocence to be. By most of the critics of Pope it has been almost unreservedly praised for its sublimity of idea, beauty of expression, and faithful-

similar instances might be cited from Pope, and other poets, of the truth of the observation of the Roman critic, upon the equal force and fickleness of fashion in orthoepy :— *Quem penes arbitrium est et jus et norma loquendi.*—*Ars Poet.*

[1] *Life of Pope. En revanche,* the Coryphæus of English criticism of the last Age, it may here be added, severely attacks the philosophy, though not the poetry, of the yet more famous essay—the *Essay on Man.* In the matter of the *Essay on Criticism,* Dennis, among other charges, after complaining of having been " attacked without any sort of provocation on his side, and attacked in his person instead of his writings, by one who was wholly a stranger to him, at a time when all the world knew he was persecuted by fortune " and " in a clandestine manner, with the utmost falsehood and calumny. . . by a little affected hypocrite, who had nothing in his mouth, at the same time, but truth, candour, friendship, good-nature, humanity and magnanimity," objects that, " his caluminator, while he pretends to give laws to others, is a pedantic slave to authority and opinion." Among other choice comparisons, in his *critique,* we find the following :— "Inquire between Sunning-hill and Oakingham, for a young, short, squat, gentleman, the very bow of the God of Love ; and tell me whether he be a proper author to make reflections. He may extol the Ancients, but he has reason to thank the gods that he was born a Modern, for had he been born of Grecian parents, and his father, consequently, had by law had the absolute disposal of him, his life would have been no longer than that of one of his poems—the life of half a day."

[2] *Causeries de Lundi.* In France it was soon in high repute. Anthony Hamilton, of *Mémoires du Comte de Grammont* celebrity, translated it into French, but, for some reason, did not publish his version. Two French translations appeared not long afterwards.

ness to the spirit of the originals. Wordsworth first ventured to call in question the justness of these panegyrics, and objected to the affectation of certain of the epithets. But, upon the whole, most readers will, probably, approve the awards, in the present instance, of Johnson, Warton, and Bowles. In the same year came out in Lintot's *Miscellany* (who had taken the idea of the periodical from Tonson) the First Book of the *Thebaid*, the Fable of *Vertumnus and Pomona* and of *Dryope* from the *Metamorphoses*, and the *Sappho to Phaon* from the *Epistles of the Heroines*, of Ovid. A more celebrated contribution was the first edition of his *Rape of the Lock*, without his name. *Windsor Forest*, sometimes included in the *Pastorals*, but not published till 1713, modelled upon Denham's *Cooper's Hill* (1642), has the merit of being one of the earliest attempts, in more modern English poetry, to give some place to the celebration of the natural beauties of landscape; nor is it without something of the same spirit which, fifteen years later, inspired the author of the *Seasons*. Picturing the utterly barbarous Ages of forest laws and other ferocious tyrannies, when the country became—

> " To savage beasts and savage laws a prey,
> And Kings more furious and severe than they,
> Who claimed the skies, dispeopled air and floods—
> The lonely lords of empty wilds and woods,"

the poet proceeds to celebrate the (comparative) peacefulness and cultivation, in his own time, of the scenes lying before him: the partialness of the civilisation of the modern Age being visible to his eyes in such relics of barbarism as the "Sports" of the neighbouring squires and their followers, where:

> " Beasts, urged by them, their fellow-beasts pursue,
> And learn of men each other to undo."

That *Windsor Forest* lies open to the objection of a certain artificiality of sentiment and expression in landscape description, and to point out its inferiority, in this respect, to the manner of Thomson and, still more, of Cowper, is obvious; but to expect a taste and inspiration scarcely known to Pope's time, and foreign to his mental constitution and training is, perhaps, equally useless and unreasonable.

Next came from the same publisher, Lintot, his *Ode for Music on St. Cecilia's Day*; and in the same year he inserted in the *Guardian* his *Prologue* to Addison's *Cato*, and a number of papers on various subjects.[1]

---

[1] *Nos.* iv., xi., xl., lxi., lxxviii., xci., xcii., clxxiii.

Of these none does so much credit to him as the admirable Essay upon some of the various atrocities—in particular, the atrocities of the Slaughter-House—of which the subject species have always been the victims. In Pope's day, it is scarcely necessary to remark, not even the slender provisions of Law, which now partially protect them, interposed any sort of barrier against the various selfishness and brutality of their tyrants. After quoting Montaigne, and pointing out the early and fatal initiation of children in cruelty, the Essayist goes on to denounce (as far as he could venture to do so), the selfishness and barbarism of Hunting :

"When we grow to men, we have another succession of sanguinary sports, in particular, Hunting. I dare not attack a diversion [he cautiously adds] which has such authority and custom to support it ; but must have leave to be of opinion, that the agitation of that exercise, with the example and number of the chasers, not a little contributes to resist those checks which compassion would naturally suggest in behalf of the animal pursued. Nor shall I say with M. Fleury that this sport is a remain of the Gothic barbarity; but I must animadvert upon a certain custom yet in use with us, and barbarous enough to be derived from the Goths, or even the Scythians. I mean that savage compliment our huntsmen pass upon ladies of quality, who are present at the death of a Stag, when they put the knife in their hands to cut the throat of a helpless, trembling, and weeping creature :

Questuque cruentus atque imploranti similis.[1]

Who lies beneath the knife,
Looks up, and from her butcher begs her life.

"But if our *Sports* are destructive, our *Gluttony* is more so, and in a more inhuman manner. Lobsters roasted alive, Pigs whipt to death, Fowls sewed up [and he might have added, among other culinary atrocities, Calves bled slowly to death], are testimonies of our outrageous luxury. Those, who (as Seneca expresses it) divide their lives betwixt an anxious conscience and a nauseated stomach, have a just reward of their gluttony in the diseases it brings with it. For human savages, like other wild beasts, find snares and poison in the provisions of life, and are allured by their appetite to their destruction. I know nothing more shocking or horrid than the prospect of one of their kitchens covered with blood, and filled with the cries of creatures expiring in tortures. It gives one an image of a giant's den in a romance, bestrewed with the

[1] See the Story of Silvia and her murdered Fawn, one of the most charming episodes in the whole of the *Æneis.*

scattered heads and mangled limbs of those who were slain by his cruelty. The excellent Plutarch (who has more strokes of good nature in his writings than I remember in any author) cites a saying of Cato to this effect—that *'tis no easy task to preach to the belly which has no ears.* 'Yet if,' says he, 'we are ashamed to be so out of fashion as not to offend, let us, at least, offend with some discretion and measure. If we kill an animal for our provision, let us do it with the meltings of compassion, and without tormenting it. Let us consider that 'tis, in its own nature, cruelty to put a living creature to death—we, at least, destroy a soul that has sense and perception.' In the life of Cato the Censor he takes occasion, from the severe disposition of that man, to discourse in this manner :—'It ought to be esteemed a happiness to mankind that our Humanity has a wider sphere to exert itself in than bare justice [*i.e.*, of mere legal obligation]. It is no more than the obligation of our very birth to practice equity to our own kind; but humanity may be extended through the whole order of Beings, even to the meanest. It is certainly the part of a well-natured man to take care of his horses and dogs, not only in expectation of their labour, while they are foals and whelps, but even when their old age has made them incapable of all service. History tells us of a wise and polite nation that rejected a person of the first quality, who stood for a judiciary office, only because he had been observed, in his youth, to take pleasure in tearing and murdering of birds; and of another that expelled a man out of the Senate for dashing a bird against the ground who had taken shelter in his bosom.'[1] Every one knows how remarkable the Turks are for their humanity in this kind. I remember an Arabian author, who has written a Treatise to shew how far a man supposed to have subsisted on a desert island, without any instruction, or so much as the sight of any other man, may by the pure light of nature attain the knowledge of philosophy and virtue. The first act of virtue he thinks a self-taught philosopher would, of course, fall into is, to relieve and assist all the animals about him in their wants and distresses."[2] One who could write thus strongly and

---

[1] Plutarch's *Essay on Flesh-Eating*. Probably the translation is that of the version of the *Morals* made in 1684-94 "by several hands, based on Holland's. It is not a very accurate or faithful one. Plutarch's *Essay* (one of the most remarkable productions of Greek or Latin Antiquity, little known or noticed though it be), has been quoted, in part, by two of the most eloquent writers in all Literature—Rousseau (in the *Emile*) and Shelley (in his Note to *Queen Mab*).

[2] The *Guardian*, lxi., May 21, 1713. This paper deserves the more remark and the greater praise that it stands almost alone in the periodical literature of the day. A protest against the prevalent savagery of bull-baiting and cock-fighting by Steele in the *Tatler* (Feb.,

feelingly on behalf of the most helpless, and least considered, of his fellow-beings, it is impossible to believe to have been without real virtues or real feeling, whatever his regretable weaknesses in other respects.

Pope had now achieved a distinguished place among the writers of his time. The most prominent personages of both parties, in politics, literature, and society, hastened to express for him their admiration and their friendship—Swift, Addison, Steele, Halifax, Somers, Bolingbroke, Harley, Arbuthnot, Congreve, and lesser celebrities, such as Gay, Parnell, and Garth. To Swift he first became known when the former returned to England, after three months' possession of his Deanery, to mediate between the rival Tory chiefs; their correspondence began, at the end of the same year (1713), with the ironical, but friendly, letter of Swift, inviting the poet to change his religion, and offering him a bribe of twenty guineas, and the equally ironical reply of Pope. He had then commenced to canvass for subscriptions for his translation of the *Iliad*.

"I believe," he rejoins, "it will be better worth my while to propose a change of my faith by subscription than a translation of Homer..... I am afraid there is no being at once a poet and a good Christian; and I am very much straitened between the two, while the Whigs seem willing to contribute as much to continue me the one as you would to make me the other. But, if you can move every man in the Government, who has above ten thousand pounds a year, to subscribe as much as yourself, I shall become a convert, as most men do, when the Lord turns it to my interest. I know they have the truth of religion so much at heart, that they would certainly give more to have one good subject translated from Popery to the Church of England than twenty heathenish authors out of any unknown tongue into ours. I therefore commission you, Mr. Dean, with full authority, to transact this affair in my name." The correspondence, thus begun between the two most distinguished men of letters of their day, ended only with the virtual death of Swift in 1739. With Addison and Steele his acquaintance originated in the publication of the *Essay*

1739) excepted, scarcely any earnest denunciation of cruelty to the lower animals appears in the periodicals of the time, until about the middle of the century, when an admirable paper was inserted in the *World* (Aug., 1756), which has been attributed to Lord Chesterfield, inveighing against the atrocities of butchering. A few years later Hawkesworth, in his *Adventurer* raised an almost solitary voice against the cruelties of " Sport," and Johnson, in the *Rambler*, had, somewhat earlier, stigmatised the cold-blooded barbarity of the physiological torture dens. These appear to be almost the only protests on behalf of the unprotected non-human species, in the periodical literature of the century. Among the poets, Thomson has deserved the honour of being the first earnestly to insist upon this all-important, but neglected department of Ethics.

on Criticism. In a letter, in most of the editions of his Correspondence, addressed to Addison, but actually written to Steele (under date Dec. 30, 1711), he excuses himself for delay in acknowledging the encomiums of Addison (in the *Spectator*) by saying that the "honest country gentlemen," with whom he was celebrating Christmas, having "no relish for polite writing," did not take in that tri-weekly paper, and proceeds to express his gratification at finding himself "commended by a person whom all the world commends. Yet I am not the more obliged to you [he supposed Steele to be the writer of the *critique*] for that than for your candour and frankness in acquainting me with the error I have been guilty of, in speaking too freely of my brother moderns." He promises, if his poem reach a second edition, to correct this fault. The contribution of the *Messiah* to the *Spectator*, in the spring of the next year, and his papers in the *Guardian* brought him still more into acquaintance with the great Whig essayists. His *Prologue* to *Cato*, the typical

"Brave man struggling in the storms of Fate,
And greatly falling with a falling State,"

added to the obligation of Addison. It happened, however, that the irrepressible Dennis had published a minute and severe examination of that celebrated but somewhat too "classical" tragedy, in which, as Johnson admits, the critic had exposed some real faults.[1] Pope, eager to seize the opportunity of another attack upon his antagonist, and not displeased, perhaps, to take part in so public a controversy. sent to the press, without his name, a vehement satire upon Dennis. It bore the sensational title of the *Narrative of Dr. Robert Norris on the Frenzy of J. D.*—Norris being the name of a popular apothecary or doctor, who pretended to the discovery of a short and sure method of curing the insane—in the manner of Swift's *Predictions*. Addison, conscious, perhaps, that he had laid himself open to severe criticism, and, at all events, not much pleased to be championed in so violent a way, did not

---

[1] His remarks upon the inconsistencies of some of the *dramatis personæ* have much more reason than his cardinal objection of the violation of "poetic justice." Johnson has justly exposed the hollowness of this form of the popular optimism :—"Whatever pleasure there may be in seeing crimes punished and virtue rewarded, yet since wickedness often prospers in real life, the poet is entirely at liberty to give it prosperity on the Stage. For if poetry has an imitation of reality, how are its laws broken by exhibiting the world in its true form? The Stage may sometimes gratify our wishes; but if it be truly the *mirror of life*, it ought to show us sometimes what we are to expect."—*Life of Addison.* The finest verse of the *Prologue* is the epigram on the character of the typical despot :—
"Ignobly vain, and impotently great."

welcome the pamphlet with all the enthusiasm its author expected. He intimated, in fact, to the publisher, Lintot, through Steele, his disapproval. Upon this Pope addressed what purports to be an original letter to Addison—the first of the two or three letters which appear in the Correspondence of Pope, as written to Addison, but which have marks of later composition—assuring him that "it was never in my thoughts to offer you my poor pen in any direct reply to such a scoundrel (who, like Hudibras, needs fear no blows but such as bruise) but only in some little raillery."[1]

Another difference served to create a coldness of feeling between the two, the masked attack on Philips (a friend of Addison) in the *Guardian*, already noticed. But the chief *casus belli* occurred two years later, in the preference given by Addison to his friend Tickell's version of the first book of the *Iliad*: for which Pope afterwards revenged himself by his famous allusion to "Atticus," in the *Epistle to Arbuthnot* (1735); but which first appeared, in a rather different shape, so early as 1723, where Addison figures under his proper name:—

> "Should such a one, resolved to reign alone,
> Bear, like the Turk, no brother near the throne,
> View him with jealous, yet with scornful eyes,
> Hate him for arts that caused himself to rise,
> Damn with faint praise, assent with civil leer,
> And, without sneering, teach the rest to sneer;
> Alike reserved to blame or to commend,
> A timorous foe and a suspicious friend;
> Fearing e'en fools, by flatterers besieged,
> And so obliging that he ne'er obliged:
> Willing to wound, and yet afraid to strike,
> Just hint the fault, and hesitate dislike—
> Who, when two wits on rival themes contest,
> Approves of both, but likes the worse the best—
> Like Cato, give his little Senate laws,
> And sit attentive to his own applause,

---

[1] The original and published letters, slightly differing, have been printed, at length, in the *Athenæum* (July 8, 1854). Besides internal evidence, proving the letters, in the first instance, to have been written to his friend, Caryll; the fact that only one letter (of earlier date, in reference to the *Essay on Criticism*) of Pope was found among the papers of Addison—that letter itself, too, apparently intended for Steele—forces the conviction that this Addisonian Correspondence is not authentic. See Carruthers' *Life of Pope*, and Elwin's *Introduction* to the *Works of Pope*.

> While Wits and Templars every sentence raise,
> And wonder with a foolish face of praise :—
> Who would not smile, if such a man there be ?
> Who would not laugh, if *Addison* were he ?" [1]

A quarrel with Addison, at this period, almost necessarily involved one with his chief colleagues ; and the Pope and Steele correspondence is as brief, as well as uncertain, as the Addisonian. Friendship with Swift brought him, as a matter of course, that of the intimate associates of Swift, their acknowledged chief,—of Arbuthnot, Gay, Prior, Parnell, and the flattering notice of the leading Tory politicians, Bolingbroke, Harley, and the rest. Partly owing to his quarrel with the great Whig writers, partly, and principally perhaps, influenced by his surroundings, he now, for the most part, associated himself to that party without, however, mixing, like Swift, in the fierce political and party strife to which, by natural temperament, he little inclined. Until his literary celebrity, Pope's circle of friends almost entirely had consisted of Catholic families, living in the neighbourhood of Binfield—the Carylls, Stonors, Englefields, Fermors, and Blounts. John Caryll, the principal correspondent of his youth, and with whom he kept up correspondence to the time of the death of his friend, in 1736, was the nephew of the Caryll who had been high in the confidence of the last Stuart King, had been secretary to the Queen, and, accompanying the fugitive King to France, had received the reward of the empty title of a Stuart peer; dying in 1711. In that year the *Essay on Criticism* had surprised the world of letters and, as already noticed, its rather free allusion to Superstition and Intolerance had excited some suspicions of anti-papal heresy. To allay these suspicions, and the resentment of the Catholic authorities, or, perhaps, rather to take the opportunity of displaying his philosophic tolerance to his friend, who seems to have been a somewhat

---

[1] The last couplet went through two or three revisions—" smile " being exchanged for " grieve," and " laugh " for " weep." *Cato* and *his little Senate* is quoted by Pope from his *Prologue*. He had already given expression to these sarcasms in a letter to Secretary Craggs, or rather to Caryll (July, 1715). His friend Atterbury (now Bishop of Rochester), who had seen it in manuscript, thus writes to Pope, requesting a complete copy of the verses :—" No small piece of your writing has ever been sought after so much. It has pleased every man, without exception, to whom it has been read. Since you now, therefore, know (adds Dr. Atterbury, significantly), *where* your real strength lies, I hope you will not suffer that talent to lie unemployed." The Bishop's Christian charity hardly balanced his ecclesiastical, or rather political, zeal. The insinuation of Pope (or Tonson according to Spence), that his rival's *Defence of the Christian Religion* was inspired by hopes of a bishopric, upon his resignation of the Secretaryship of State, we must suppose to be only a cynical *on dit :* but Tonson imparted to Pope that he " always thought him [Addison] a priest in his heart."—Spence's *Observations*, &c.

indifferent zealot, he sent to him a letter of apology. "Nothing," he professes, "has been so much a scarecrow to them [their Protestant enemies] as that too peremptory and uncharitable assertion of an utter impossibilty of salvation to all but ourselves, invincible ignorance excepted ; which, indeed, some people define under so great limitations, and with such exclusions, that it seems as if that word were rather invented as a *salvo*, or expedient, not to be thought too bold with the thunderbolts of God (which are hurled about so freely on almost all mankind by the hands of ecclesiastics) than as a real exception to almost universal damnation. For, besides the small number of the truly faithful in our Church, we must again sub-divide; the Jansenist is damned by the Jesuit, the Jesuit by the Jansenist, the Scotist by the Thomist, and so forth. . . . I hoped a slight insinuation, introduced so easily by a casual similitude only, could never have given offence, but, on the contrary, must needs have done good in a nation and time, wherein we are the smaller party, and consequently most misrepresented, and most in need of vindication." Pope's heretical freedom of opinion does not appear to have called down upon him now, or afterwards, any special or public ecclesiastical anathemas ; but the interests of the Papal Church, in the last century, lay, perhaps, more in the region of Politics than in that of Faith.

His connexion with Steele and the *Guardian*, also, gave some offence to the Tory party. In a letter to Caryll (June, 1713), he refers to this scandal, and remarks, "This, I know, you will laugh at, as well as myself ; yet I doubt not but many little calumniators and persons of soured disposition will take occasion hence to bespatter me. I confess I scorn narrow souls of all parties; and, *if* I renounce my reason in religious matters, I will never do it in any other affair." In an interesting notice of *Cato*, sent to his friend about the same time, we learn that " the town is so fond of it, that the orange-wenches and fruit-women in the park offer the books at the side of the coaches, and the prologue and epilogue are cried about the streets by the common hawkers." But of all his Catholic friends, most prominent in the biography of Pope figure the Blounts, and especially the two ladies of that family, of Mapledurham, on the Thames, not far from Reading. The occupants of Mapledurham consisted, upon Pope's first introduction to them, of Mr. Lister Blount, his wife, a son, and two daughters, Teresa and Martha ; the elder being of exactly the same age as Pope, the other two years younger. The brother, heir to the estate, married, in 1715, the daughter of Sir J. Tichborne, of Tichborne, in Hampshire. Accounts as to the date of the first meeting of Pope and the two sisters do not agree; but it happened some time before 1712, when they had reached the age of twenty. Their natural charms of manner had been heightened by a French education.[1] In 1715, after the marriage of their brother, the sisters, with their mother, settled in London, in Bolton and afterwards in Welbeck Street; but they made frequent visits to Berkshire. Among their town acquaintance they numbered Mrs. Howard. One of their admirers and correspondents was James Moore Smythe (a son of Arthur Moore, a subordinate member of the Harley Government), a Fellow of All Souls, and, also, a place-holder under the Government. He figures as one of the less prominent subjects of the Goddess of Dulness.

Both Teresa and Martha Blount received the homage of Pope, and he constantly corresponded with either of them, sometimes addressing his letters to them conjointly. To the younger he especially paid court, and he professed for her, in later years, the greatest ardour of affection. According to his own account of himself, in these letters, he seems to have been ambitious of the reputation, as Mr. Carruthers expresses it, "of a Don Juan in miniature." But it is to be observed that he addressed very free expressions of admiration to Lady M. W. Montagu and, less strongly, to Miss Judith Cowper. Scandal, however, attributed a more intimate connexion with the lady of Mapledurham; and, unless we interpret very liberally some parts of the correspondence, it must be admitted, not without some appearance of reason. The reports of an irregular connexion he indignantly repudiated; but that, at least, a remarkably strong attachment existed between them sufficiently appears from various proofs; and he left her, at his death, the greater part of his property. Among critics, who professed to believe in the common rumour, appear Lady Hervey, Warburton, and the Allens of Bath. So persistent, indeed, became the reports of this kind, that, in a letter to

---

[1] A large picture at Mapledurham represents them together, gathering flowers. It is usually assigned to Kneller; but Mr. Carruthers conjectures it, with much reason, to be the portrait-picture alluded to by Jervas, in a letter to Parnell. "I have just [1716] set the last hand," he reports, "to a couplet; for so I may call two nymphs in one piece. They are Pope's favourites; and—though few, you will guess, have cost me more pains than any nymphs can be worth—he is so unreasonable as to expect that I should have made them as beautiful upon canvas as he has done upon paper." These (engraved) portraits adorn the edition of Pope by Bowles—not as in the picture, but separated; the effect, Mr. Carruthers remarks, being thus injured.—*Life of Pope.* A supposed portrait of Martha Blount appears in the picture of Pope by Jervas: she is represented reaching a book from a shelf. This picture is now in the National Gallery at South Kensington. Gay describes the sisters as "fair-haired Martha, and Teresa brown."

Caryll (Miss M. Blount's godfather), Dec. 25, 1725, he takes much pains to discredit the *on dit*, and expresses much indignation against the scandalmongers :—" Falsehood is folly (says Homer), and liars, and calumniators, at last, hurt none but themselves, even in this world. In the next, 'tis charity to say, God have mercy on them! They were the devil's vicegerents upon earth, who is the father of lies, and I fear has a right to dispose of his children. I've had an occasion to make these reflections of late much juster than from anything that concerns my morals, and (which I ought to be as tender of as my own) the good character of another very innocent person; who, I am sure, shares your friendship no less than I do. You, too, are brought into the story so falsely, that I think it but just to appeal against the injustice to yourself singly, as a full and worthy judge and evidence too. A very confident asseveration has been made, which has spread over the town, that your god-daughter, Miss Patty, and I lived two or three years since in a manner that was reported to you as giving scandal to many; that, upon your writing to me upon it, I consulted with her, and sent you an excusive, alleviating answer; but did, after that, privately, and of myself, write to you a full confession—how much I myself disapproved the way of life, and owning the prejudice done her, charging it on herself, and declaring that I wished to break off what I acted against my conscience, &c.; and that she, being at the same time spoken to by a lady of your acquaintance, at your instigation, did absolutely deny to alter any part of her conduct, were it ever so disreputable or exceptionable. Upon this villanous lying tale it is further added, by the same hand, that I brought her acquainted with a noble lord, and into an intimacy with some others, merely to get quit of her myself. . . . God knows upon what motives any one should malign a sincere and virtuous friendship. . . ."[1]

In the Blount-Pope correspondence, Teresa seems to have been, at first, the most favoured. So early as 1712 he addressed to her (through Lintot's *Miscellany*) an Epistle in the form of verse, accompanying a copy of the Works of Voiture, the popular French poet and letter-writer of the preceding century, in which he dissuades her from submission to conjugal bonds, and reminds her :—

[1] *Athenæum*, July, 1854, quoted by Carruthers, who prints from the Mapledurham MSS. a letter from Mrs. Caryll to Miss M. Blount, expressing her pleasure at what she considers the satisfactory exculpation of their mutual friend, and adding :—" I am so far convinced of his honour and worth, joined with his good understanding, that should all the peevish ill-will or passionate malice in the world invent all that lay in them [*i.e.* in their power], it would in no kind ever make me have the least thought of what I could wish otherwise as to your friendship."

> "Still in constraint your suffering Sex remains,
> Or bound in formal, or in real chains,
> Whole years neglected, for some months adored:
> The fawning servant turns a haughty lord.
> Ah! quit not the free innocence of life,
> For the dull glory of a virtuous wife;
> Nor let false shows or empty titles please,
> Aim not at joy, but rest content with ease."

Again, on the occasion of her visit to London to be present at the coronation of the new King (in Sept. 1714), he dedicates to her another poetical epistle, under the name of Zephalinda. It wittily pictures the ennui of country life for the London *belle*, bored to death by country dulnesses, and drunken, sporting, squires:—

> "As some fond virgin, whom her mother's care
> Drags from the Town to wholesome country air,
> Just when she learns to roll a melting eye,
> And hear a spark, yet think no danger nigh:
> From the dear man unwilling she must sever,
> Yet takes one kiss before she parts for ever!
> Thus from the world fair Zephalinda flew,
> Saw others happy, and with sighs withdrew.
> Not that their pleasures caused her discontent—
> She sighed not that they stayed, but that she went.
>
> "She went to plain-work, and to purling brooks,
> Old fashioned halls, dull aunts, and croaking rooks:
> She went from Opera, Park, Assembly, Play,
> To morning walks, and prayers three hours a day:
> To pass her time 'twixt reading and bohea,
> To muse, and spill her solitary tea,
> Count the slow clock, and dine exact at noon,
> Divert her eyes with pictures in the fire,
> Hum half a tune, tell stories to the squire,
> Up to her godly garret after seven,
> There starve, and pray, for that's the way to heaven."

Such routine was to be exchanged only for:—

> "Some squire, perhaps, you take delight to rack,
> Whose game is whisk, whose treat 'a toast in sack;
> Who visits with a gun, presents you birds,
> Then gives a smacking *buss*, and cries—'no words!'"

> Or with his hound comes halloing from the stable,
> Makes love with nods, and knees beneath a table;
> Whose laughs are hearty, though his jests are coarse,
> And loves you best of all things—but his horse."

To Martha Blount, who had remained at home, and had written, it seems, to him in flattering strains, he replies ecstatically:—" Most divine! . . . In these overflowings of my heart I pay you my thanks for those two obliging letters you favoured me with of the 18th and 24th instant. That which begins with 'Dear creature,' and ' My charming Mr. Pope,' was a delight to me beyond all expression. You have, at last, entirely gained the conquest over your fair sister. 'Tis true you are not handsome, for you are a woman, and think you are not. But this good humour and tenderness for me has a charm that cannot be resisted. That face must needs be irresistible which was adorned with smiles, even when it could not see a *coronation*. I must own I have long been shocked at your sister on several accounts, but, above all things, at her prudery. I am resolved to break with her for ever; and, therefore, tell her I shall take the first opportunity of sending back all her letters.[1]" The concluding threat we may take to have been merely a hyperbole. At least, they remained friends long after this date. Mr. Carruthers (it may here be stated), with most of the biographers of Pope, maintains his innocence of undue intimacy with her sister, with which the scandal of the drawing-rooms charged him. Besides that the fashion of the time allowed much greater freedom of expression than now, "the license, in which Pope occasionally indulged, would be the more readily tolerated, or, at least, forgiven, on account equally of his genius and his person."

Among other correspondents of this earlier period figure, especially, Wycherley the dramatist and Henry Cromwell. The letters to Wycherley (the earliest in the collected Correspondence), for whom Pope undertook the hazardous task of correcting or polishing his verses, cannot be received as genuine *effusions*, for they have undergone the "improvements" of so many other of Pope's productions. But we can collect pretty certainly the history of the unequal partnership, and the inevitable *finale* of such a compact. In the beginning of this Gil Blas and Archbishop of Granada situation Wycherley compliments, or appears as complimenting, his *protégé-critic*, in highly flattering terms. "You have," he protests, "pruned my falling laurels of some super-

[1] Roscoe (Ed. of Pope, viii., 390), collated with the original, and quoted, by Carruthers

fluous, sapless, and dead branches, to make the remainder live the longer; and thus, like your master, Apollo, you are at once a poet and a physician." Not to be outdone in this *amœbean* contest of mutual compliments, Pope rejoins that he contracts some of the pieces, " as we do sunbeams, to improve their energy and force;" but he soon adds a less flattering assurance, that others he had "entirely new expressed and turned more into poetry." He goes on, indeed, in a still more critical mood, and, mixing bitter with sweet, remarks that, " the greatest dealers in wit, like those in trade, take least pains to set off their goods; while the haberdashers of small wit spare for no decorations or ornaments. You have commissioned me to paint your shop, and I have done my best to brush you up like your neighbours." When, emboldened by impunity, the young reviser ventured actually to propose a complete alteration and reduction of his friend's poems, the *amour-propre* of Wycherley, not unnaturally, took serious alarm; and he hastened to demand back his manuscripts. A period of coolness between the boy of sixteen and the old man of seventy followed; but, before the death of the dramatist, at which Pope was present, five years afterwards, a reconciliation had been effected. About Henry Cromwell (whom Pope, who now frequented the great meeting-place of the wits of the day, Will's coffee-house, used to meet there), little more is known than what Johnson and Gay record of his eccentric style of dress and manner. He affected the character of a beau, and Pope, who knew how to adapt his style to his correspondents' capacity or prejudices, did not throw away upon him too many pearls. The Cromwell correspondence has little more of interest than as having been the first published (in 1726) of the Pope letters. They were published, without authority, for her own profit, by Mrs. Thomas, Cromwell's mistress, who sold the manuscripts to Curll.

Revised and greatly enlarged, the *Rape of the Lock* astonished and delighted the world of fashion and of literature at the beginning of 1714. Its origin has been often told. Miss Fermor, of the Catholic family of that name, had quarrelled with her lover (Lord Petre), who had jestingly stolen a lock of her hair. To appease the indignant beauty, and to effect " the renewal of love," at the suggestion of Caryll, Pope composed this mock-heroic, or, as he himself styles it, *heroi-comical* poem. At first, the lady, with whom he seems to have been not then acquainted, accepted this novel sort of mediation with approval, or, at least, acquiescence: but afterwards her family, or herself, thinking her reputation to be endangered by the rather free treatment of Belinda (a name borrowed from one of the heroines of the *Epigrams* of Martial), professed displeasure. Her resentment the offending poet appeased by this second "improved" edition, in which, in a dedication to Miss Fermor, he assures her "the human persons are as fictitious as the airy ones, and the character of Belinda, as it is now managed, resembles you in nothing but in the beauty." Its chief improvement consisted in the introduction of the fairy machinery of *Sylphs* and *Gnomes;* an addition of which Addison, with a failure of his usual taste, professed disapproval, and which formed one of the many causes of quarrel between Pope and him. The improved edition was, in reality, almost a new poem. As it first appeared, in the *Miscellany*, it had not more than 190 verses: in the new edition it numbered 800. Its original models are to be found in the *Lutrin* of Boileau (in which two ecclesiastics contend about a reading-desk), the *Secchia Rapita* of Tassoni, and the *Comte de Gabalis* of the Abbé de Villars,[1] from whom he partly borrowed the idea of his *machinery;* but it surpasses all its predecessors in the poetic excellences. Not its least interest lies in its skilful parody of the epic style, in particular, of the *Iliad* and *Æneid*. All Pope's critics unite, with one consent, to extol its pre-eminent merits. "The most exquisite example of ludicrous poetry," pronounces Johnson. "In this composition," thinks Warton, "Pope principally appears as a poet, in which he has displayed more imagination than in all his other works put together." "A composition," says Bowles, "to which it will be in vain to compare anything of the kind: it stands alone unrivalled, and, possibly, never to be rivalled." "The most exquisite monument of playful fancy," admits De Quincey, "that universal literature offers." In France, Marmontel's version, *La Boucle de Cheveux enlevée*, a tolerably good one, though far inferior to the original, was, as may be imagined, greatly in demand.

Although, unlike an Olivia or a Lavinia, the heroine can hardly be said to owe everything to "Nature's own sweet and cunning hand," yet,

---

[1] The author "of this diverting work," as Warton describes it, "came from Toulouse to Paris to make his fortune by preaching. The five Dialogues, of which it consists, are the results of those gay conversations in which the Abbé was engaged with a small circle of men of fine wit and humour like himself. When this work first appeared it was universally read, as innocent and amusing. But, at length, its consequences were perceived, and reckoned dangerous, at a time when this sort of conversation began to gain credit. Our devout preacher was denied the Chair, and his work forbidden to be read." To the Abbé de Villars the story of *Undine* owes, also, its origin. Tassoni's *Rape of the Bucket* appeared at the beginning of the Seventeenth Century.

if any art might be supposed to be able to atone for a rather free eulogy, and use, of feminine charms, the skilful painting and flattery of the portrait were not unfitted to make such atonement:—

> "Every eye was fixed on her alone :
> On her white breast a sparkling cross she wore,
> Which Jews might kiss and Infidels adore.
> Her lively looks a sprightly mind disclose,
> Quick as her eyes, and as unfixed as those.
> Favours to none, to all she smiles extends:
> Oft she rejects, but never once offends—
> Bright as the Sun, her eyes the gazers strike,
> And, like the Sun, they shine on all alike.
> Yet graceful ease, and sweetness void of pride,
> Might hide her faults, if belles had faults to hide.
> If to her share some female errors fall,
> Look on her face, and you'll forget them all." [1]

A Key to the Lock, by "Esdras Barnevelt, Apoth.," one of the many *aliases* of Pope, came out in the next year, pretending—in order to draw the greater attention to the mock-epic, and also to ridicule its blind critics, of whom Dennis was a chief offender—to be a true explanation of its hidden meaning, as a concealed satire on the late "Barrier Treaty." According to the *Key*, Belinda represents Queen Anne, Clarissa, Lady Masham, Thalestris, the Duchess of Marlborough, the "bold Lord," whom Belinda "with one finger and a thumb subdued," Lord Oxford, &c. "Sir Plume" was the real portrait of a Sir George Brown, who, according to Warburton, felt aggrieved at his presentation as the typical fop, and, especially, at the expletives put into his mouth on the memorable occasion.[2] The *Rape of the Lock*, in its enlarged form, brought the

---

[1] Wakefield remarks that the last verse is marred by the abbreviation, and suggests that a better reading would be,—
"Look on her face, and you forget them all."—Elwin.
Miss Arabella, or Belle Fermor, thus immortalised, married in the same year, not the original cause of her immortality, but a Mr. Perkins. Her portrait is preserved at Tusmore, the first place of residence of her father. According to the engraving, the poetical picture of Belinda was not all flattery. It gives the impression of a distinguished beauty. According to Mrs. Piozzi's report, Miss Fermor's niece, a Prioress of an English Convent at Paris, "remembered that Mr. Pope's praise made her aunt very troublesome and conceited. She believed there was but little comfort to be found in a house that harboured *poets*."

[2] Dennis, in his *Letters* (of criticism), denounced, among other violations of probability, the *hyperbole* of Belinda's screams when she discovers the loss of her lock of hair,—
"Then flashed the living lightning from her eyes,
And screams of horror rend the affrighted skies,"
ignoring that the poet is parodying the manner of the heroes of the epics. In a copy

poet from the publisher Lintot, the modest sum of fifteen pounds. It was adorned with engravings after Du Guernier, in no very high style of art.

In the same year he published more translations and adaptations (in a volume of *Miscellanies*, edited by Steele) from the *Odyssey*, and Chaucer's *Wife of Bath*, which even Dryden had pretended to be shy of putting into a modern dress, followed, in the next year, by another adaptation from Chaucer, the *Temple of Fame*. A more memorable, or, at least, laborious work than any he had yet undertaken, he had now almost ready for the press, a translation of the *Iliad* ; for which he sought and obtained subscriptions from friends in both political parties. He set to work on it in earnest, in 1714, having already printed specimens of his poetical translations in the *Miscellanies*. The first volume, containing the four first books, came out in June of 1715. In Swift he found his most active supporter and canvasser. But a matter of greater solicitude to him than raising subscriptions was the vastness of the labour he had imposed upon himself, the more severe, that he had little knowledge of the original language. His letters reveal his intense anxiety about it. In a letter to Edward Blount, recounting his difficulties with his engraver, in bringing out his illustrative maps, he affects to laugh at this lesser incidental trouble, but more often he expresses serious concern. Of living aids he had the help, especially, of his friend Dr. Parnell, to whom he writes in terms of grateful recognition: also, of Fenton and Broome (the former a Cambridge man, and tutor in the family of the Trumballs); but their chief assistance was given in the *Odyssey* translation. His correspondence with them appears in the collected Correspondence. Of books, his chief aids were the English versions of Chapman, Hobbes, and Ogilby, and the French of Dacier and La Valterie. To Chapman, the sixteenth century dramatist, he owed the greatest obligation. For each of the six volumes, which formed the completed *Iliad*, he received from the publisher, Lintot, two hundred pounds. Besides this, he had the amount of the payments of his six hundred and fifty subscribers. Altogether, he made by the *Iliad* between five and six thousand pounds. The volumes came out successively in 1715, 1717, 1718, and 1720. The *Odyssey*, of which Broome and Fenton translated half, begun in 1723, he finished in 1725. By the

of the poem, on the margin, Pope has inscribed, in reply to Dennis (as a summary of his objections in *Letter* III): " Where it appears to demonstration, that no handsome lady ought to dress herself, and no modest one to cry out or be angry." Quoted in Elwin's *Works of Pope*, II.

lesser Homeric poem he acquired between three and four thousand pounds. His Homer thus brought him, altogether, the sum of about nine thousand pounds; by far the largest amount of money ever gained by any writer up to that time. From the first his work found an enthusiastic welcome from his friends, in particular from Swift, Berkeley, Arburthnot, and Gay.[1] Addison, alone, seemed doubtful, or inclined to "damn with faint praise." His friend and colleague Tickell had brought out, contemporaneously, a version of the first book of the *Iliad*; in his preface, however, deprecating suspicion of rivalry with Pope, and announcing that he had "the pleasure of being diverted from that design [of translating the whole poem] by finding the work had fallen into a much abler hand." Addison none the less expressed his preference, on the whole, for Tickell; and Pope, unfairly interpreting it as an intended insult, became furious. He wrote to Craggs (or to Caryll), in the terms of indignation afterwards versified in his Arbuthnot *Epistle*, denouncing the "great Turk in poetry who can never bear a brother on the throne," and the "little Senate of Cato." In fact, the quarrel had become a sort of party-question between the rival Whig and Tory clubs, or coffee-houses, of Button's and Will's. From this moment the two leading men of letters in England (for Swift had now become an exile) ceased to be on terms of cordial amity. Pope's version of the Homeric epics had no sort of rival until the publication of

[1] Of all the congratulations of his friends the most interesting as well as most considerable are Gay's verses: "To Alexander Pope on his Safe Return from Troy." He assembles and describes, in their appropriate characters, all the numerous and various acquaintances of the poet, "in the manner of the beginning of the last canto of Ariosto [*Orlando Furioso*]." The piece consists of twenty-one stanzas. Gay thus introduces the principal ladies:

"What lady's that to whom he gently bends?
Who knows not her? Ah! those are Wortley's eyes!
How art thou honoured, numbered with her friends!
For she distinguishes the good and wise.
The sweet-tongued Murray near her side attends—
Now to my heart the glance of Howard flies;
Now Hervey, fair of face, I mark full well
With thee, Youth's youngest daughter, sweet Lepell.

I see two lovely sisters, hand in hand,
— The fair-haired Martha and Teresa brown,
Madge Bellenden, the tallest of the land,
And smiling Mary, soft and fair as down," &c., &c.

In the MS., in the British Museum, *Howard* occupies the place of *Wortley*. Mary Bellenden, youngest daughter of Lord Bellenden, one of the Maids of Honour to the Princess of Wales, was the rival of Lady Mary W. Montagu in fame for beauty. Horace Walpole speaks of her as of the most perfect beauty possible to imagine. Lord Hervey describes her as "incontestably the most agreeable, the most insinuating, and the most likeable woman of her time. Made up of every ingredient likely to engage or attach a lover." She married Col. Campbell, afterwards Duke of Argyll.

Cowper's in 1791. In spite of the much superior faithfulness of the latter, it never came near the popularity of Pope's, which, at least, until quite recent times, still bore away the palm of *classical* fame from all its many later rivals.¹

In the year 1715 Pope made the acquaintance of the portrait-painter Jervas. The poet, in his childhood, had shewn a taste and aptitude for drawing; and his father entertained some purpose of apprenticing him to that art. A few of his early sketches in India-ink still remain. He now placed himself under the tuition of Jervas, but, if ever he had a serious purpose of following the profession of a painter, his defective sight stood in the way of it. He produced, however, some portraits to which he refers in his letters to Jervas and Gay. The only specimens of his powers, in this art, existing are a copy from Kneller's portrait of Betterton, the actor, formerly belonging to his friend Murray, Lord Mansfield, and a satirical picture of the "Prodigal Son."² Among the "plays of wit," thrown off in this year, is *A Farewell to London*, in which he sketches his friends and others with a light and skilful touch, one of the best of his trifles in this kind.³ At some time in 1716 Pope migrated from Binfield (his father being now dead) to Chiswick, where he occupied a house in a newly-erected terrace close to the river, called "Mawson's Buildings," which still exists. For some reason— perhaps thinking his more obscure abode there to be unfitting the future owner of the Twickenham Villa—he seems industriously to have tried to obliterate this period from the public memory; in spite of the

---

¹ Johnson, who has printed specimens of Pope's *Iliad*, with the variations, from the manuscript in the British Museum, considers it as "certainly the noblest version of poetry which the world has ever seen," and thinks it idle to attempt to supersede it. But Gibbon's characteristic remark that, "it has every merit but that of likeness to its— original," is much nearer the judgment of the present day. It may be added here that, of all attempts at representing the form and meaning of the Greek epic, the most successful is, perhaps, that of Professor Newman, *The Iliad of Homer*: *Faithfully Translated into Unrhymed English Metre*.

² A picture in water-colours about 3 × 4 feet in size, representing the Prodigal Son, with other allegorical designs and descriptions, as a death's head crowned with laurel, a philosopher blowing bubbles in the air, a fallen statue, ruined columns, &c. An engraving was made from this picture, though not containing all the figures, as a frontispiece to an edition of the *Essay on Man*, with Warburton's Commentary, published by the Knaptons in 1748. The original has long been in the family of its present owner, Mr. Stoneham. —Carruthers' *Life of Pope*.

³ He thus apostrophises "the town":—
  "Why should I stay? Both parties rage,
    My vixen Mistress squalls,
  The Wits in envious feuds engage,
    And Homer (damn him!) calls."

His "vixen mistress" being the Muse who so often involved him in literary brawls.

malicious reminder of Dennis, who takes care that he shall not forget it, in an answer to the *Dunciad*. Yet during his Chiswick life he frequently visited the Court of the Princess of Wales, and received and returned the visits of his aristocratic intimates, Lord Peterborough, Lord Burlington, and others. While at Chiswick he wrote what is, in some respects, the finest of all his poems, the *Eloisa to Abelard*, dedicated, in the first instance, to Miss Martha Blount, but afterwards to Lady M. W. Montagu; and his *Elegy to the Memory of an Unfortunate Lady*, the history and identity of whom so long remained unknown. Warburton's confident assertions long misled the biographers and editors, from Johnson onwards; until Mr. Dilke identified the mysterious lady with a Mrs. Weston ("Mrs. W.," of the letters) eldest daughter of Mr. Gage, the owner of Sherbourne Castle, and sister of the Gage of the *Epistle of Bathurst*.[1] Composed during the absence of Lady M. W. Montagu in the East of Europe, and dedicated to her, the *Epistle of Eloisa to Abelard* appeared at some time in the year 1717. Seldom have the passions of love, devotion, and despair, alternatingly predominating, been so exquisitely painted as in the representation of the distracted Eloisa; and nothing in Pope's poetry surpasses, in its way, the description of the various rapture and conflicting emotions of the nun:—

> " How happy is the blameless Vestal's lot!
> The World forgetting, by the World forgot:
> Eternal sunshine of the spotless mind!
> Each prayer accepted, and each wish resigned;
> Labour and rest that equal periods keep,
> ' Obedient slumbers that can wake and weep,'
> Desires composed, affections ever even,

[1] Her father died in 1700 and left Sir W. Goring, of Burton in Sussex, executor and guardian of his children ["the false guardian of a charge too good" of the *Elegy*.] Miss Gage married John Weston, of Sutton, in the county of Surrey. They lived unhappily, and were soon separated. (*Athenæum*, July 15, 1854.) By Pope's mediation they were reconciled, and Mrs. Weston lived with her husband till her death in 1724, which happened, not in the violent and tragic way of the *Elegy*, but much more prosaically, In fact, Pope seems to have indulged poetic license to a large extent in his version of the story, which has excited so much fictitious sensation and interest. He did not, at the time, derive much applause or sympathy from his intervention in their quarrel, either from his family or from his friends, who suspected, it seems, some intrigue. Nor did the heroine herself accept his tribute with excessive pleasure. See Carruthers' *Life of Pope*. Whatever may have been the original inspiration of the poem as a whole, that of the following sentiment, at least, is of an unquestionable kind :—

> " Thus unlamented pass the Proud away,
> The gaze of fools, and pageant of a day!
> So perish all, whose breast ne'er learnt to glow
> For others' good, or melt at others' woe."

Tears that delight, and sighs that waft to heaven.
Grace shines around her with serenest beams,
And whispering Angels prompt her golden dreams.
For her the unfading rose of Eden blooms,
And wings of Seraphs shed divine perfumes.
For her the Spouse prepares the bridal ring,
For her white Virgins hymeneals sing :
To sounds of heavenly harps she dies away,
And melts in visions of eternal day.

" Far other dreams my erring soul employ,
Far other raptures of unholy joy ;
When, at the close of each sad, sorrowing day,
Fancy restores what Vengeance snatched away,
Then Conscience sleeps, and leaving Nature free,
All my loose soul unbounded springs to thee.

* * * * * *

" Thy voice I seem in every hymn to hear,
With every bead I drop too soft a tear.
When from the censer clouds of fragrance roll,
And swelling organs lift the rising soul,
One thought of thee puts all the pomp to flight—
Priests, tapers, temples, swim before my sight.
In seas of flame my plunging soul is drowned,
While altars blaze, and angels tremble round."

The *Eloisa* has received enthusiastic eulogy from almost all the critics, even from Wordsworth. Pope derived it from the celebrated *Letters* (whether forged or authentic, most probably forged) of the famous lovers. The original *Letters,* alleged to have been written by Abelard and Heloisa, in Latin, in the twelfth century, had been very freely translated and "improved" in 1693, in a French version, which has often been reprinted. In 1714 Hughes, author of the *Siege of Damascus*, published this "adulterate French concoction" in an English dress.[1] From the English versions of Hughes, or Rawlinson,

[1] The Latin *Letters* have been generally received as authentic ; but, as Mr. Elwin shews, there are good reasons for believing them to be of later composition. Apart from the improbability that Heloisa, or any other woman, could publish, in so unreserved a fashion, the confessions of her ardent passion, the whole series bears too much the character of a romancer's style to leave much reasonable doubt that they form one of those numerous forgeries which have been received with too easy faith. Some eminent French critics, however, have assumed the reality of the Heloisa of the *Letters,* and have exalted her to a high place among French heroines ; and Mde. Guizot thinks the exceedingly unreserved confessions of the involuntary *réligieuse* to be only in keeping with the

it was that Pope derived the prose material for his verse. But, as to form, he adopted as his model Ovid's *Letters of the Heroines*, and he, probably, had in mind also the same poet's romantic episode of Byblis and Ianthe in the *Metamorphoses*. Not long before her departure from England, he had made the acquaintance of the greatest beauty and wit of her time, when she had left her Yorkshire home to dazzle the *habitués* of the Court and the Society of the metropolis. At Chiswick, too, he mixed in familiar intercourse with other beauties, with Maids of Honour and favourites of the Court, the Duchesses of Queensberry, Hamilton, and Kingston, Mrs. Howard, Miss Lepell, Miss Bellenden, who took him "into their protection, contrary to the law against harbouring papists." He joined in their parties of various pleasure and diversion: some of the "diversions," as he reports them, in a letter to Miss Teresa Blount—"to eat Westphalia ham in a morning, ride over hedges and ditches (hunting in Windsor Forest), come home in the heat of the day, with a fever and a red mark on the forehead from a beaver hat, simper an hour and catch cold in the Princess's apartment; then to dinner, with what appetite they may, and after that, till midnight, walk, work, or think, which they please"—being sufficiently characteristic. In the same letter he rather maliciously tells her, "Mrs. [Miss] Lepell walked with me three or four hours by moonlight, and we met no creature of quality but the King, who gave audience to the Vice-Chamberlain all alone under the garden wall."[1]

manners of the age "in which educated and even delicate sentiments, in a distinguished and naturally modest woman, might be allied to the strongest forms of language." (*Essai Hist.*). Elwin's *Works of Pope*, II. Mr. A. W. Ward thinks that Pope used the edition of Rawlinson, printed in 1717. "Mr. Hallam," remarks Professor Ward, "charges Pope with injustice to Eloisa in substituting for the real motive of her refusal to marry him (unwillingness to interfere with the prospects of his career) 'an abstract predilection for the name of mistress above that of wife.' A poet, however, has undoubtedly the right to make such a change. The ordinary objection, that the effect of the whole poem is immoral, is obviously inapplicable to a distinctly dramatic piece. Most readers of the poem will be inclined to consider that its language is appropriate to passion, but not the language of passion itself. From this point of view should be contrasted with it, not Ovid's *Heroides*, of which it is a most felicitous imitation, but such an epistle as that of Julia in the first canto of Byron's *Don Juan*" (*Works of Pope*). The verse in inverted commas, "Obedient slumbers," &c., Pope, as he tell us, borrowed from Crashaw.

[1] From one of the lively duchesses he received the following invitation, the original of which is in the British Museum. It is addressed to 'Alex. Pope, Esq., at Mr. Jervas's house in Cleveland Court.'—' Sir, my lady duchess being drunk at this present, so not able to write herself, has commanded me to acquaint you, that there is to be music on the water on Thursday next; therefore desires you to be that evening at her house in Bond Street, by six o'clock at farthest; and her grace will call of you there to take you to her barge, which she ordered to be ready at that time, at Whitehall, with provisions, and shall land you on the wished-for shore.—I am, sir, your most humble servant, G. Maddison. East Acton, Tuesday Night.'

Bath had lately been brought into fashion by Queen Anne; and to that city, from about the beginning of the century, flocked all the world of triflers, loungers, rank, wealth, and leisure, and the diseased and enfeebled, for the most part, by their own various excesses. With the rest of the world, alone or in company with his friends, Pope made periodical visits to this principal resort of pleasure or health-seeking. Its fashionable amusements, under the despotic control of the great *arbiter elegantiarum*,[1] and the manner of taking the bath *à la mode*, he very graphically describes to Miss Teresa Blount.

After the publication of his first volume of the *Iliad*, with the purpose of consulting the manuscripts of the University Library, he made a journey to Oxford. In reporting it to the sisters of Mapledurham, he indulges in an unaccustomed strain of romantic description. This visit gave occasion to the most humorous of his letters, addressed to Lord Burlington, but, as Mr. Carruthers observes, evidently intended for public perusal. Riding through Windsor Forest, he fell in with his old publisher, Lintot, also mounted on horseback, and the dialogue, which followed upon the encounter, forms the point of the narrative:—" Mr.

(In another hand [the duchess's?]) 'Out of the abundance of the heart the mouth speaketh. So Pope is the word. A disappointment is not to be endured.'

Acton, near London, was the residence of the Pierrepoint family, and Pope's acquaintance must have been Isabella Bentinck—a celebrated beauty—then recently married to the first Duke of Kingston, father of Lady Mary Wortley Montagu. —Carruthers. In a lively and rather free "Court Ballad," which he calls *The Challenge*, he offers his tribute of admiration to some of these Court ladies—in particular:

> "To one fair lady out of Court,
> And two fair ladies in,
> Who think the Turk and Pope a sport,
> And wit and love no sin,
> Come these soft lines, with nothing stiff in,
> To Bellenden, Lepell, and Griffin."

The Turk, it seems, was a negro page of one of the Maids of Honour.

[1] The Queen visited Bath in the year 1703. The reign of Nash began in 1710 (his predecessor having been a Captain Webster), and lasted some fifty years. During the visit of Pope, in 1738, Nash preferred a request to him to write a set of verses for an obelisk, in commemoration of the high honour done to the city by the presence of the Prince of Wales, the father of George III. To which Pope is said to have replied, " whether the Prince most loves poetry or prose, I protest I do not know; but this I dare venture to affirm, that *you* can give him as much satisfaction in either as I can." To Nash and the architect, Wood, Bath owed its pre-eminence in fashion, among the *Spas*, in the last century. In his *Life of Richard Nash*, Goldsmith, who assures his readers that he has " chosen to describe the man as he was, not such as imagination could have helped in completing his picture," adds justly enough in regard, at least, to the " subjects," that he " will be found to have been a weak man governing weaker subjects, and may be considered as resembling a monarch of Cappadocia whom Cicero somewhere calls, ' the little king of a little people.'" Tunbridge Wells, the lesser rival of Bath, also may claim the honour of having received its first ceremonial laws from the same omnipotent legislator.

Lintot began in this manner: 'Now, damn them! what if they should put into the newspaper, how you and I went together to Oxford? What would I care? If I should go down into Sussex, they would say I was gone to the Speaker. But what of that? If my son were big enough to go on with the business, by God, I would keep as good company as old Jacob [Tonson.]' Hereupon I enquired of his son. 'The lad' (says he) 'has fine parts, but is somewhat sickly, much as you are. I spare for nothing in his education at Westminster. Pray, don't you think Westminster to be the best school in England? Most of the late Ministry came out of it, so did many of this Ministry. I hope the boy will make his fortune.' 'Do you not design to let him pass a year at Oxford?' 'To what purpose' (said he), 'the universities do but make pedants, and I intend to breed him a man of business.'"

By way of passing the time, during a halt on the road, the publisher proposes to his companion to "turn" an Ode of Horace:—

"Silence ensued for a full hour, after which Mr. Lintot lugged the reins, stopped short, and broke out, 'Well, sir, how far have you gone?' I answered, 'Seven miles.' 'Zounds, sir,' said Lintot, 'I thought you had done seven stanzas. Oldsworth, in a ramble round Wimbledon Hill, would translate a whole Ode in half this time. I will say that for Oldsworth, though I lost by his *Timothys* [a certain controversial book], he translates an Ode of Horace the quickest of any man in England. I remember Dr. King would write verses in a tavern three hours after he could not speak; and there is Sir Richard [Blackmore], in that rumbling old chariot of his, between Fleet Ditch and St. Giles's Pond, shall make you half a *Job*.' 'Pray, Mr. Lintot,' said I, 'now you talk of translators, what is your method of managing them?' 'Sir,' replied he, 'those are the saddest rogues in the world; in a hungry fit they will swear they understand all the languages in the universe. I have known one of them take down a Greek book upon my counter, and cry, Ah! this is Hebrew, I must read it from the latter end. By the Lord, I can never be sure in these fellows, for I neither understand Greek, Latin, French, nor Italian myself. But this is my way: I agree with them for ten shillings per sheet, with a proviso, that I will have their doings corrected by whom I please. So by one or other they are led, at last, to the true sense of an author: my judgment giving the negative to all my translators.' 'But how are you so sure those correctors may not impose upon you?' 'Why, I get any civil gentleman (especially any Scotsman) that comes into my shop, to read the original to me in English.

By this I know whether my first translator be deficient, and whether my corrector merits his money or not.'"

This exhibits the *pleasant* side of Pope's dealings with the bookselling tribe, with whom he was not in the habit of interchanging the *amenities* of intercourse. During his whole literary life he waged almost incessant war with publishers as well as authors. Two quarrels of this kind, the most conspicuously prominent in his career, began in the first month of his life at Chiswick. With the notorious publisher Edmund Curll, he first came into collision in 1716.[1]

On the eve of setting out with her husband's embassy, Lady M. W. Montagu sent to the press her satirical sketches, the *Town Eclogues*, one of which (the *Basset-Table*) Pope had the credit of contributing. They soon became the talk of the whole town. Curll, according to his custom of assigning anything famous or popular to some eminent writer, brought out these "Court Poems," with the name of Pope attached as principal author. An interview, by appointment, took place between the indignant poet and the offending publisher in a tavern in Fleet Street. Failing to obtain satisfaction, or not content with the explanation, Pope at once launched against him satirical pamphlets, full of coarse vituperation. Most famous of these remains the burlesque he entitled an *Account of the Poisoning of Edmund Curll*, an absurdly grotesque narrative of the pretended death of his enemy.[2] In return, Curll printed every sort of scurrilous and offensive writing he could purchase or pick up against the principal offender and his friends. Hence the conspicuous place of the publisher in the *Dunciad*, ten years later.

[1] This immortal publisher—"one of the new terrors of death," as Arbuthnot styled him, with a double allusion to his odd figure, and his piracies, had a great reputation for impudence. For his enemy, Pope, he affected great contempt. "He has a knack of versifying," he gave it as his opinion at the bar of the Lords, before whom he had been summoned to answer for his (alleged) fraudulent publication of the Letters, "but, in prose, I think myself a match for him;" and, as for patronage, he could boast, "where Pope has one lord I have twenty." He frequently fell into the clutches of the Law (more deservedly than very many of its victims), and suffered not a few indignities at the hands of injured and insulted authors. But, to the last, he deserved the epithet of his arch-enemy—"the dauntless Curll," and, in some sort, his motto, *Nemo me impune lacesset*. But, as far as Pope was concerned, it must be admitted, the proprietor of the "Chaste Press," in Covent Garden, was, at least, as sinned against as sinning.

[2] The pamphlet bears as the complete title, on its first page, *A full and true Account of a horrid and barbarous Revenge by Poison on the Body of Mr. Edmund Curll, Bookseller, with a faithful Copy of his latest Will and Testament*, in evident imitation of Swift's *Predictions*. Other pamphlets followed purporting to give *A further Account of the most deplorable Condition of Mr. Edmund Curll, Bookseller*, and *A Strange but true Relation, how Mr. Edmund Curll, of Fleet Street, Stationer, out of an extraordinary desire of lucre, went into Change Alley, and was converted from the Christian Religion by certain eminent Jews, &c.*

Not less prominent, if conducted with less disregard of the *convénances*, is the history of the commencement and progress of the quarrel with Colley Cibber, the laureate. Gay, in Jan., 1717, brought out his comedy, or rather farce, *Three Hours after Marriage;* Pope and Arbuthnot having some share in it. It contained copious satire on contemporary writers, critics, and certain eminent persons in society. Pope contributed the character of Dennis as " Sir Tremendous," and the Duchess of Monmouth, the early patroness of Gay (to whom succeeded the Duchess of Queensberry), figures as the "Countess of Hippokekoana." In the course of the farce —in ridicule of a Dr. Woodward, physician, and professor at Gresham College, and author of a *Natural Theory of the Earth*, and his antiquarian researches—a mummy and crocodile appear on the stage, out of which odd disguises emerge a pair of lovers. The absurdity of the scene raised a storm of hisses. Another war of pamphlets ensued; but the only noteworthy incident of this squabble is the part taken in it by Cibber. Accounting for Pope's persistent hostility, he states that it originated in an interpolation, by himself, while acting in the *Rehearsal*, of an *ex tempore* speech, ridiculing the mummy scene. The audience took the hint, and roared applause. Pope, one of the spectators, imagined himself to have been particularly aimed at and his dignity to be in danger. According to Cibber, he became furious with resentment, and, at the fall of the curtain, attacked him for the insult in vehement language. To this offence Cibber added another which, Pope's own expressions considered, can scarcely appear an actual *casus belli*—his holding up to ridicule, in his play of the *Nonjuror* (an imitation of *Tartuffe*), the Jacobites and Papists who took part in the rising of 1715. However, for these insults, as he chose to consider them, although he had previously eulogised the author of the *Careless Husband*, Pope, in bringing out his complete *Dunciad*, took elaborate pains to instal the laureate-poet in the place of Theobald, on the throne of Dulness—not to the better intelligibility of the numerous allusive parts of the poem.

Early in 1718 Pope moved from Chiswick to Twickenham. With the famed villa he rented, on a long lease, five acres of land. The house itself had nothing pretentious about it, and Pope's improvements were confined chiefly to the grounds. These occupy a considerable space in his letters: for he expended much time on his various ornamentations, as to the merits of which the estimates of his critics have not been entirely unanimous. His enemies, indeed, did not scruple to indulge in some sneers at his Grotto and shells. His Twitenham villa (as he usually spells the name) consisted of "a small body, with a small hall, paved with stone, and two small parlours on each side: the upper story being disposed on the same plan. The wings at the sides, which figure in most of the engravings, and which contained handsome rooms, with bay windows, were added, after Pope's death, by his successor in the villa, Sir William Stanhope, brother of the Earl of Chesterfield."[1] As the outcome of the united horticultural genius of himself, Kent, the landscape gardener, and his friends, Peterborough, Bathurst, Burlington, Bolingbroke, and the rest, his small estate "ultimately boasted, amidst their winding walks and recesses, a shell temple, a large mount (the work of Kent), a vineyard, two small mounts, a bowling-green, a wilderness, a grove, an orangery, a garden house, and kitchen garden." Like many other amateur gardeners and architects, the poet and his visitors seem to have derived almost as much satisfaction in destruction and re-construction as in the original work of laying out and planting. Many of his friends contributed to the decoration of the Grotto, and from all parts of the world. To the end of his life he continued to indulge this, at least, innocent amusement. Mr. Carruthers has printed a letter (dated Oct. 1740) sent to a Dr. Oliver, of Bath, in which Pope represents himself as still expecting contributions.[2]

---

[1] Writing in the year 1760 Horace Walpole reports, " Sir William Stanhope has bought Pope's house and garden. The former was so small and bad, one could not avoid pardoning his hollowing out that fragment of the rock Parnassus into habitable chambers—but would you believe it? he has cut down the sacred groves themselves. In short, it was a little bit of ground of five acres, enclosed with three lanes, and seeing nothing. Pope had twisted and twirled, and rhymed and harmonized this, till it appeared two or three sweet little lawns, opening and opening beyond one another, and the whole surrounded with thick impenetrable woods. Sir William, by advice of his son-in-law, Mr. Ellis, has hacked and hewed these groves, wriggled a winding gravel walk through them with an edging of shrubs, in what they call the modern taste; and, in short, has desired the three lanes to walk in again—and now is forced to shut them out again by a wall; for there was not a muse could walk there but she was spied by every country fellow that went by with a pipe in his mouth." Walpole was an authority upon the subject, and he wrote towards the end of his life, an *Essay on Gardening*. The Grotto still exists, but " divested of the glittering spars and mirrors with which he had decorated it. The spring, for which the poet desired a guardian nymph, in sculpture, had for years disappeared, when about 1842 it was discovered and made to flow into a stone cistern" (quoted from *Gent. Mag.*, 1842). Many of the trees planted by Pope still exist. " The old prints represent the villa as having several low, mean, houses in its neighbourhood, close to the river."—See Carruthers. Johnson's remark on the *Grotto* is characteristic:—" A grotto is not often the wish or pleasure of an Englishman, who has more frequent need to solicit than exclude the sun: but Pope's excavation was requisite as an entrance to his garden; and, as some men try to be proud of their defects, he extracted an ornament from an inconvenience, and vanity produced a *grotto* where necessity enforced a *passage*."

[2] Formerly in possession of Mr. H. G. Bohn. Mr. Carruthers also prints from a fragment of a letter, formerly in the possession of this same well-known publisher, an outline-sketch by Pope of the front of the grounds towards the river.

A letter to Edward Blount (June, 1725), founded on the model style of the younger Pliny, gives a detailed account of the Twitenham Grotto. "I have put," he writes, " the last hand to my works of this kind, in happily finishing the subterraneous way and Grotto. I there found a spring of the clearest water, which falls in a perpetual rill, that echoes through the cavern day and night. From the river Thames you see through my Arch up a walk of the wilderness, to a kind of open temple, wholly composed of shells, in the rustic manner; and from that distance, under the temple, you look down through a sloping arcade of trees, and see the sails on the river passing suddenly and vanishing, as through a perspective glass. When you shut the doors of the Grotto, it becomes, in the instant, from a luminous room a *camera obscura*; on the walls of which all objects of the river—hills, woods, and boats—are forming a moving picture in their visible radiations; and, when you have a mind to light it up, it affords you a very different scene. It is finished with shells, interspersed with pieces of looking-glass in angular forms; and, in the ceiling is a star of the same material, at which, when a lamp (of an orbicular figure of thin alabastar) is hung in the middle, a thousand pointed rays glitter, and are reflected over the place." He gallantly desires "the young ladies" (the daughters of his friend, and cousins of the Mapledurham ladies) to be assured that he makes nothing new in his Gardens, " without wishing to see the print of their fairy steps in every part of them."

Whatever his gardening, in practice, may have been, in *theory* it was superior to the ordinary taste of his contemporaries. In his paper in the *Guardian* (September 29, 1713), quite in the Addisonian style, he wittily ridicules the prevailing absurdly formal and artificial fashion:—
" I believe it is no wrong observation, that persons of genius, and those who are most capable of Art, are always most fond of Nature, as such are chiefly sensible that all Art consists in the imitation and study of Nature. . . . A citizen is no sooner proprietor of a couple of yews, but he entertains thoughts of erecting them into giants, like those of Guildhall. I knew an eminent cook, who beautified his country-seat with a Coronation-dinner in Greens, where you see the Champion flourishing on horseback at one end of the table, and the Queen, in perpetual youth, at the other. For the benefit of all my loving countrymen, of this curious taste, I shall here publish a catalogue of Greens to be disposed of by an eminent Town-Gardener, who has lately applied to me on this head. He represents that, for a politer sort of ornament in

the Villas and Gardens adjacent to this great city, and in order to distinguish those places from the more barbarous countries of gross nature, the world stands much in need of a *virtuoso* Gardener, who has a turn to sculpture, and is thereby capable of improving upon the Ancients of his profession in the imagery of ever-greens. My correspondent is arrived to such perfection, that he cuts family-pieces of men, women, or children. Any ladies that please may have their own effigies in Myrtle, or their husbands in Horn-beam. He is a Puritan wag, and never fails, when he shows his garden, to repeat that passage in the *Psalms*—" *Thy wife shall be as the fruitful Vine, and thy children as Olive-branches round about thy table.*" Then follows a catalogue of specimens of approved designs —*e.g.,* " Adam and Eve in Yew. Adam a little sheltered by the fall of the Tree of Knowledge in the great storm [of Nov. 26-27, 1703]. Eve and the Serpent very flourishing." " The Tower of Babel not yet finished." " Edward, the Black Prince, in Cypress." " Queen Elizabeth in Myrtle, which was very forward, but mis-carried by being too near a Savine." " An old Maid of Honour, in Wormwood." " Divers eminent Poets in Bays, somewhat blighted, to be disposed of—a pennyworth." " Noah's Ark, in Holly, standing on the Mount, the ribs a little damaged for want of water."

That Pope, in fact, in spite of the few signs of it in his poetry, was not without the faculty for appreciating the charms of natural landscape, and Nature unadorned, his letters give some proof. His description of his experiences on an excursion to Oxford, and many years later to Bristol and Clifton, in letters to the Blounts, unless indeed they are taken as mere *façons de parler,* shew that, if he had not altogether the taste or, at all events, the enthusiasm of Gray or Cowper, he possessed, at least, something of the kind. " Our river glitters beneath an unclouded sun," he writes of Twickenham (*e.g.*), to his friend, Robert Digby, " at the same time that its banks retain the verdure of showers ; our gardens are offering their first nosegays ; our trees, like new acquaintance brought happily together, are stretching their arms to meet each other, and growing nearer and nearer every hour ; the birds are paying their thanksgiving songs for the new habitations I have made them. . . . . Do not talk of the decay of the year ; the season is good when the people are so. It is the best time in the year for a painter. There is more variety of colours," &c.

Pope's relations with Lady M. Wortley Montagu, the Sappho of his poems, will be recounted in her *Life.* Another lady, of his correspondents, whom he celebrated under the name of Erinna (the famous Lesbian poetess, and friend of Sappho), whose identity has been discovered in recent times, has a double interest—both on her own account, and as a near relative of the second greatest poet of the century. Until Mr. Dilke's investigations, all that had been publicly known of "Erinna" was, that she had remarkable talents, had some title to the name of poetess, was a friend of Mrs. Howard, and had her home somewhere in Hertfordshire. With this lady, who proved to be Miss Judith Cowper, daughter of Spencer Cowper, a Judge of the Common Pleas, niece of the Lord Chancellor of that name, and (a much more illustrious relationship) aunt of the poet, Pope began correspondence in the autumn of 1722. Her eulogy of him, in some verses entitled *The Progress of Poetry*, written at the age of eighteen, seems to have been the first cause of their acquaintance. To Judith Cowper Pope sent, in return, a copy of his verses *To a Lady on her Birthday* (1723), addressed to Martha Blount, in a more serious strain than usual with him. He begs her to "alter it to her own wish," and supplies her, at the same time, with hints for a more ambitious poetical attempt. "This beautiful season [September]," her tells her, "will raise up so many rural images and descriptions in a poetical mind, that I expect you, and all such as you (if there be any such), at least all who are not downright dull translators like your servant, must necessarily be productive of verses. I lately saw a sketch this way of the *Bower of Beddington*. I could wish you tried something in the descriptive way on any subject you please, mixed with vision and moral, like pieces of the old Provençal poets, which abound with fancy, and are the most amusing scenes in Nature. There are three or four of this kind in Chaucer admirable. I have long had an inclination to tell a Fairy Tale, the more wild and exotic the better; therefore, a *vision*, which is confined to no rules of probability, will take in all the variety and luxuriancy of description you will—provided there be an apparent moral to it. I think one or two of the *Persian Tales* would give one hints for such an invention; and, perhaps, if the scenes were taken from real places that are known, in order to compliment particular Gardens and Buildings of a fine taste (as I believe, several of Chaucer's descriptions do, though it is what nobody has observed), it would add great beauty to the whole." In the same year Miss Cowper married Mr. Madan, and, at the same time, the twelve months' correspondence came to an end.

The unprecedented success of the *Iliad*, and the fame of its translator, induced Tonson to engage him upon an edition of Shakspeare. It came out in 1725, in six quarto volumes, at a guinea the volume to the subscribers. At first the sale proceeded fairly well; but, whether owing to indifference to Shakspeare in the admirers of Homer, or to Theobald's *critique*, the sale sank so low, as Johnson tell us, that many copies remained on the booksellers' hands, and at last were sold off at a reduced price. Pope's pecuniary profits little exceeded two hundred pounds. The year following its appearance, Theobald, a translator of Greek Plays, who, in *Mist's Journal* (according to Pope), "crucified Shakspeare once a week," and a writer, as Johnson expresses it, of "heavy diligence," published his criticism, *Shakspeare Restored*.[1] Seven years later he aggravated his offence by bringing out, with the aid of some men of letters, not backward to assist at wounding their common enemy, an edition of his own, in which "he detected his [rival's] deficiencies with all the insolence of victory. . . . From this time Pope became an enemy to editors, collators, commentators, and verbal critics; and hoped to be able to persuade the world that he miscarried in this undertaking only by having a mind too great for such minute employment." Johnson's remarks sum up fairly enough the merits and demerits of the *Shakspeare*: "Pope, in his edition, undoutedly did many things wrong, and left many things undone; but let him not be defrauded of his due praise. He was the first that knew, at least the first that told, by what helps the text might be improved. If he inspected the early editions negligently, he taught others to be more accurate." In this year came out the *Odyssey*, in five volumes. Only half of the work was Pope's, and on his unwillingness to own his obligations to his *collaborateurs* (Fenton and Broome) the hostile critics took care to be sufficiently sarcastic. One life-long friend, however, he acquired among the critics of the *Odyssey*. Joseph Spence, Prelector of Poetry at Oxford, had examined the translation with candour, but in no unfavourable spirit. Pope sought his acquaintance, and from that moment he shines in ardour, if not in fame, a rival with Warburton (who later attached himself as a revolving *satellite*) in reflecting the light of the sun of their poetic heaven.

[1] In its full title—*Shakespeare Restored; or a Specimen of the many Errors as well Committed and Unamended by Mr. Pope in his late Edition.* In the *duodecimo* edition, brought out by Tonson, Pope announces: "Since the publication of our first edition, there having been some attempts upon Shakspeare by Lewis Theobald (which he would not communicate during the time wherein that edition was preparing for the press, when we, by public advertisements, did request the assistance of all lovers of this author), we have inserted in this impression as many of them as are judged of any the least advantage to the poet; *the Whole amounting to about Twenty-five Words*." Johnson, the next considerable editor of Shakspeare, it may be remarked, criticises his subject more severely than Pope had done.

Among the guests entertained at Twickenham the most celebrated, and one of the most welcome, was Swift. In the year 1727 he made a prolonged visit of four months, and the two friends (Swift taking the larger share) prepared conjointly three volumes of their *Miscellanies*, to which also Gay and Arbuthnot contributed.[1] Pope's part included his *Treatise on the Bathos : or Art of Sinking in Poetry ; Memoirs of P. P. Clerk of the Parish* (a satire on Bishop Burnet, in his *History of the Reformation) ;* a reprint of the *Key to the Lock ;* and a *Debate upon Black and White Horses* (a parody of legal absurdities, supervised, it is said, by his friend Fortescue, the future Master of the Rolls). Of all the contents of these volumes, most considerable and important in its consequences is the *Treatise on the Bathos ;* for it gave birth, as he himself relates, to the most famous of all his Satires. With much wit, and in an ironical commentary, he quotes and parodies passages from his enemies of the tuneful tribe; in particular, from Philips, Theobald, Broome (of *Odyssey* fame, with whom he had quarrelled), and Blackmore. He classifies the "confined and less copious geniuses" under the designation of various kinds of the non-human species, appended to each of which are the initials of the writers who exemplify the special class. "It happened," explains Pope, in a *Dedication* to one of his titled friends, "that in a chapter of this piece the several species of bad poets were ranged in classes, to which were prefixed almost all the letters of the alphabet (the greatest part of them at random). But such was the number of poets eminent in that art, that some one or other took every letter to himself. All fell into so violent a fury, that for half a year or more the common newspapers, in most of which they had some property, as being hired writers, were filled with the most abusive falsehoods and scurrilities they could possibly devise." Such was the original of the *Dunciad,* and the war with "the Dunces" and the "Journals, Medleys, Mercuries, Magazines."

Nothing of Pope's in the volumes has more humour than the *jeux d'esprit* suggested by the *Travels of Lemuel Gulliver,* or, as he called them, "poems, occasioned by reading the Travels of Captain Lemuel Gulliver, explanatory and commendatory." There are four of these

[1] A final and fourth volume of *Miscellanies* was published by Pope in 1728. In a letter to his publisher, Motte (1732), Swift assures him that he never acquired pecuniary profit from any one of the four volumes, and he repeats the same statement to Pulteney, in 1735. Swift, in fact, with rare exceptions, neither secured nor sought pecuniary advantage from his writings. A fact the more surprising, that he was very far from being indifferent to the acquisition or, as least, to the care of money. Pope, on the contrary, as is well known, made a considerable fortune by means of his publishers.

Gulliverian pieces. In the second, the *Lamentation of Glumdalclitch for the loss of Grildrig: a Pastoral*, is represented the despair of the Brobdingnagian Maid of Honour (at the flight of her pigmy Æneas), to whom he was known by the name of *Grildrig*:—

> "Soon as Glumdalclitch missed her pleasing care,
> She wept and blubbered, and she tore her hair—
> No British Miss sincerer grief has known,
> Her Squirrel missing, or her Sparrow [1] flown.
> She furled her samplers, and hauled in her thread,
> And stuck her needle into Grildrig's bed:
> Then spread her hands, and with a bounce let fall
> Her baby, like the giant in Guildhall—
> In peals of thunder now she roars, and now
> She gently whimpers like a lowing cow—
> Yet lovely in her sorrow still appears,
> Her locks dishevelled. . . . . . .
>
> "Vain is thy courage, Grilly, vain thy boast—
> But little creatures enterprise the most.
> Trembling I have seen thee dare the kitten's paw,
> Nay, mix with children as they played at taw:
> Nor fear the marbles as they bounding flew—
> Marbles to them, but rolling rocks to you.
>
> "Why did I trust thee with that giddy youth?
> Who from a page can ever learn the truth?
> Versed in Court-tricks, that money-loving boy
> To some lord's daughter sold the living toy;
> Or rent him limb from limb in cruel play,
> As children tear the wings of flies away—
> From place to place o'er Brobdingnag I'll roam,
> And never will return, or bring thee home.
>
> * * * * *
>
> "But, ah! I fear thy little fancy roves
> On little females, and on little loves:
> Thy pigmy children, and thy tiny spouse—

---

[1] The "Sparrow" is the conventional modern representative of the *Passer* of Catullus, in his charming *Ode to Lesbia*:—

> "Lugete, O Veneres, Cupidinesque,
> Et quantum est hominum venustiorum!
> Passer mortuus est meæ Puellæ, &c."

But it is not so easy to explain why translators and poets have chosen to metamorphose the Latin *Passer* (any bird of the Finch tribe) into the English "Sparrow."

> Thy baby-playthings that adorn thy house,
> Doors, windows, chimneys, and the spacious rooms,
> Equal in size to cells of honeycombs.
> Hast thou for these now ventured from the shore,
> Thy bark a bean-shell, and a straw thy oar?
> Or in the box, now bounding o'er the main,
> Shall I ne'er bear thyself and house again?
> And shall I set thee on my hand no more,
> To see thee leap the lines, and traverse o'er
> My spacious palm? Of stature scarce a span,
> Mimic the actions of a real man?
> No more behold thee turn my watch's key,
> As seamen at a capstan anchors weigh?
> How wert thou wont to walk with cautious tread,
> A dish of tea, like milk-pail, on thy head!
> How chase the mite that bore thy cheese away!
> And keep the rolling maggot at a bay!"

Not less in keeping with the original is the *Epistle of Mary Gulliver* (a parody of Ovid's *Epistles of the Heroines*), when, upon her lord's return from his wanderings in Lilliput and elsewhere, that illustrious discoverer (after a brief visit to his spouse) leaves her for retirement in the country, and strangely prolongs his absence:—

> "Welcome, thrice welcome to thy native place!
> What, touch me not? What shun a wife's embrace!
> Have I for this thy tedious absence borne,
> And waked and wished whole nights for thy return?
> In five long years I took no second spouse,
> What Redriff[1] wife so long has kept her vows?
>
> *   *   *   *   *
>
> Not touch me! Never neighbour called me slut—
> Was Flimnap's dame more sweet in Lilliput?
>
> *   *   *   *   *
>
> When folks might see thee all the country round
> For sixpence, I'd have given a thousand pound.
> Lord! when the giant-babe that head of thine
> Got in his mouth, my heart was up in mine.
> When in the marrow-bone I see thee rammed,
> Or on the housetop by the monkey crammed,

[1] The birthplace, or at least, residence, of Captain Gulliver

The piteous images renew my pain,
And all thy dangers I weep o'er again.

    *   *   *   *   *

"Glumdalclitch too—with thee I mourn her case,
Heaven guard the gentle girl from all disgrace!
Oh, may the King that one neglect forgive,
And pardon her the fault by which I live!
Was there no other way to set him free?
My life, alas! I fear, proved death to thee!"

The third set of verses, in a graver key, commemorate *The Grateful Address of the Unhappy Houyhnhnms, now in Slavery and Bondage in England, to Mr. Lemuel Gulliver.* They thus apostrophise the late guest of their race:—

"To thee we wretches of the *Houyhnhnm* band,
Condemned to labour in a barbarous land,
Return our thanks. Accept our humble lays,
And let each grateful *Houyhnhnm* neigh thy praise!
O, happy Yahoo! purged from human crimes
By thy sweet sojourn in those virtuous climes,
Where reign our sires. There—to thy country's shame—
Reason you found and virtue were the same.
Their precepts razed the prejudice of youth,
And e'en a Yahoo learned the love of Truth.
Art thou the first who did the coast explore?
Did never Yahoo tread that ground before?
Yes, thousands! But, in pity to their land,
Or swayed by envy, or through pride of mind,
They hid their knowledge of a nobler Race,
Which, owned, would all their sires and sons disgrace.

"You, like the Samian, visit lands unknown,
And by their wiser morals mend your own.
Thus Orpheus travelled to reform his kind,
Came back, and tamed the brutes he left behind.
You went, you saw, you heard, with virtue fought,
Then spread those morals which the *Houyhnhnms* taught.
Our labours *here* must touch thy generous heart—
To see us strain before the coach and cart,
Compelled to run each knavish jockey's heat!
Subservient to Newmarket's annual cheat!"

A few weeks after Swift's departure for Ireland, Pope nearly lost his life by drowning. On a return journey from Bolingbroke's house, at Dawley, his coach and six, lent to him by his friend, upset in a stream, and, before the driver could bring help, the water had almost covered him; as it happened, he escaped with no very serious injury. It was this accident that called forth the letter of condolence from Voltaire, then on a visit at Dawley; and, if the English poet could have foreseen the towering eminence to which the French poet (who then had fame only as such) was to reach, forty or fifty years later, he would probably have thought himself sufficiently compensated for his mishap by the compliment paid to his *Essay on Criticism* and *Rape of the Lock* by the first of French writers. Pope, it has been stated, disliked Voltaire, for reasons which may be regarded as mythical as the alleged dislike, perhaps, itself. Nor does it seem probable that the guest of Bolingbroke, and the admired of the Princess Caroline, would be received by him with indifference.

Of the bibliography of the first editions of the *Dunciad* information, accessible to the public, long remained uncertain and contradictory. More recent investigation has, for the most part, cleared up the mystification. Its earliest conception has been traced back, by internal evidence, to the year 1720 or 1721, and between that date and its publication the idea of a satire to be called *Dulness,* or the *Progress of Dulness,* or by some such title, appears in letters of Pope to Lord Bolingbroke. Swift and, more slightly, Atterbury have the credit of the suggestion of the new *Mac Flecknoe.* But, obviously, the immediate inspiration came from the ardour for revenge upon the critics in general, and upon Theobald, in particular, increased since the furious attacks provoked by the *Treatise on the Bathos.* In May, 1728, appeared, anonymously, the first ascertained edition of the satire, with the title of " *The Dunciad, an Heroic Poem in Three Books. Dublin Printed: London Reprinted.* For A. Dodd, 1728, 12mo." A frontispiece represented an Owl (with a label in its beak, inscribed *The Dunciad*), perched on a pile of books.[1] None the less, London, not Dublin, seems to have given birth to it. During 1728 four incorrect and imperfect editions issued from the Press: a "shadowy progeny," proceeding from himself, which served at once as further advertisement and as a pretext for a perfect edition. This

[1] This first edition was advertised in the *Daily Post* of May 18. Ten days later came out "*A Complete Key to the Dunciad, with a Character of Mr. Pope and his Profane Writings,* by Sir Richard Blackmore, Knight, M.D." Those who knew Pope's methods and style of advertising could hardly fail to recognise the real author. All the circumstances, says Mr. Carruthers, connected with the publication of the *Dunciad* have been ably and fully elucidated in *Notes and Queries* for 1854.

came out in the spring of the next year, thus announced to Swift, June 28: "The *Dunciad* is going to be printed, in all pomp, with the inscription which makes me proudest. It will be attended with *proeme, prolegomena, testimonia scriptorum, index authorum,* and notes *variorum*": the inscription being the well-known apostrophe to Swift—"O thou! whatever title please thine ear, Dean, Drapier, Bickerstaff, or Gulliver," &c. Many of the notes were supplied by Arbuthnot. Pirate-publishers, an appeal to the Court of Chancery, a formal consignment of the copyright to Lords Oxford, Bathurst, and Burlington, and other ingenious means of acquiring notoriety, roused still further the public curiosity. On the day of publication, according to the account of Pope, who prefixed to his narrative (dedicated to Lord Middlesex) the name of the notorious Richard Savage—his trusted agent, and the friend of Johnson—" a crowd of authors besieged the shop [of the publisher]. Entreaties, advices, threats of law and battery,—nay, cries of treason, were all employed to hinder the coming out of the *Dunciad*. On the other hand, the booksellers and hawkers made as great efforts to procure it. What could a few poor authors do against so great a majority as the public? There was no stopping a torrent with a finger. So, out it came." Many "ludicrous circumstances," we are told, attended it. " The 'Dunces' (for by this name they were called) held weekly clubs to consult of hostilities against the author. . . . Some false editions of the book having an Owl in their frontispiece, the true one—to distinguish it—fixed in its stead an Ass laden with authors. Then another surreptitious one being printed with the same Ass, the new edition in *octavo* returned, for distinction, to the Owl again. Hence arose a great contest of booksellers against booksellers, and advertisements against advertisements—some recommending the edition of the Owl, and others the edition of the Ass: by which names they came to be distinguished, to the great honour, also, of the gentlemen of the *Dunciad*." Walpole, the Premier, presented a copy to the King (George II.) and the Queen (Caroline), who had seen, it seems, the earlier, imperfect, editions; and, "some days after, the whole impression was taken and dispersed by several noblemen and persons of the first distinction." A whole army of insulted authors hurled itself against the common enemy. Chief among them marched Theobald, Dennis, and Smedley, Dean of Clogher (the last with a collection of lampoons, entitled *Alexandriana*). Next to Theobald, or Tibbald, as Pope writes his name, Cibber, Dennis, Curll (or as he is spelled Curl), Ambrose Philips, *Sappho* (Lady M. W. Montagu), *Sporus*

(Lord Hervey), Moore Smythe, the admirer of the Blounts, Aaron Hill (a dramatic writer, at one time Manager of Drury Lane Theatre, at another Secretary to Lord Peterborough, and who had turned his hand to almost everything), Edward Howard (author of the *British Princes*), Sir Richard Blackmore (MD., author of certain epics, having some popularity at the time, and who suffered much from the Wits), Elkanah Settle (the Lord Mayor—and—City Laureate), and others of more or less celebrity, occupy places of different degrees of exaltation. Fourteen years later (in 1742), at Warburton's instigation, a Fourth Book was added. In this latest development of the satire Theobald is made to abdicate the throne in favour of Cibber, who could never understand why he had been selected to fill the unenviable position, preferably to so many more illustrious claimants.[1] The choice of the new monarch of the realms of Dulness, indeed, was not a happy one: for, whatever his demerits may or may not have been, dulness did not happen to be one of them. As a writer of plays he exhibited considerable skill, and his adaptations of Shakspeare had no little merit.

Of the Four Books, as well from the less personal character of the satire as from the greater care bestowed upon it, the last holds the highest place. Some of the finest of his epigrammatic verses occur in this Part. For instance:—

> "Morality by her false guardians drawn—
> Chicane in furs, and Casuistry in lawn.
> * * * *
> Words are Man's province, Words we teach alone ;
> When Reason doubtful, like the Samian letter,[2]
> Points him two ways, the narrower is the better.
> Placed at the door of Learning, youth to guide,
> We never suffer it to stand too wide.
> * * * *
> Confine the thought to exercise the breath,
> And keep them in the pale of words till death.
> * * * *
> May you, may Cam and Isis preach it long!—

[1] Cibber's *Apology for his Life* Mr. Carruthers considers to be " one of the most delightful, gossiping, works in the language." Some of the alterations in the *Dunciad*, necessary upon the substitution of the laureate for Theobald, are skilfully done. But in many cases the adaptations did not fit the new hero, nor make the satire more intelligible for its readers.

[2] The letter Y used by Pythagoras as an emblem of the different roads of Virtue and Vice—*Et tibi quæ Samios diduxit litera ramos* (Persius, *Sat*).—Warburton.

> The Right Divine of Kings to govern wrong.
> * * * * *
> Ah! think not, Mistress, more true dulness lies
> In Folly's cap than Wisdom's grave disguise.
> * * * * *
> Princes are but things
> Born for First Ministers, as Slaves for Kings.
> * * * * *
> See skulking Truth to her old Cavern fled,—
> Mountains of Casuistry heaped o'er her head." &c.

But, in spite of the extraordinary wit and skilful versification of the greater part of the Satire, for most readers, not versed in the obscure histories of the literary squabbles of the day, the constant need of a running commentary may seem, perhaps, hardly to be compensated by the excellence and epigrammatic force of particular passages. But what most must be deplored, is an indiscriminateness of censure which tends to vitiate the whole criticism—a demerit which too often attaches to the satire of Pope; and we cannot but be conscious that, in many instances, they are rather the enemies of Pope (or of Warburton) than of right reason and of truth who are assailed. Yet where his own, or his commentator's, animosity did not intervene, it must be admitted that a just and sincere aversion from falsehood and prejudice, as well as from pretentious dulness and pedantry, in no small measure inspires the satirist; and that, if they are his personal foes who first and pre-eminently animate his Archilochian rage, he none the less holds up to deserved ridicule or detestation the follies of the world in general.

Not content with lashing his enemies in the *Dunciad*, for eight years he maintained the combat, *à outrance*, in the pages of the *Grub Street Journal*, 1730-37. In this notorious paper, "an imaginary *junto* of critics, named 'Knights of the Bathos,' sat in judgment on contemporary writers, affecting to condemn Pope and his friends as enemies of their order, but, in reality, espousing all the poet's quarrels, and attacking the objects of his poetical satire and his supposed enemies with the keenest irony and invective." Its reputed editors were Dr. John Martyn, who had held a Professorship at Cambridge, and Dr. Richard Russell, author of a medical treatise.[1] In the years 1731-5 appeared his *Epistles*, addressed to various eminent personages. The epistle, *Of Taste*, or as afterwards entitled, *Of False Taste*, and (in the latest alteration), *Of the Use of Riches*, he dedicated to his friend Burlington, and another, with

[1] See Carruthers' *Life of Pope*.

the same title and subject, to Bathurst Both contain some admirable strokes of wit and satire; but the optimistic fatalism, which underlies his chief moral poem, appeared also in these. The Moral Essay, placed as the first in the series, *Of the Knowledge and Characters of Men* and, especially, the second, *Of the Characters of Women* (dedicated "To a Lady," supposed to be Martha Blount), Pope, according to his custom, used as a vehicle for attacks (some of them gross enough) upon his enemies among the other sex, Sappho (Lady M. W. Montagu), *Narcissa* (the Duchess of Hamilton) and, in particular, *Atossa* (the Duchess of Marlborough), and *Chloe* (Lady Suffolk). Of the "great Duchess," Sarah, he sums up the character in a comprehensive couplet. She:—

> "Shines in exposing knaves and painting fools,
> Yet is whate'er she hates and ridicules."

His character of the celebrated Maid of Honour, who so greatly disappointed the expectations of Swift of preferment by her influence, is more ambiguous, but little more flattering:—

> "'With every pleasing, every prudent part,
> Say, what can Chloe want?'—She wants a heart.
> She speaks, behaves, and acts just as she ought:
> But never, never, reached one generous thought.
> Virtue she finds too painful an endeavour,
> Content to dwell in Decencies for ever."

To the *Characters* Johnson gives high praise as "the product of diligent speculation upon human life. Much labour has been bestowed upon them, and Pope very seldom laboured in vain. That his excellence may be properly estimated, I recommend," he continues, "a comparison of his *Characters of Women* with Boileau's Satire; it will then be seen with how much more perspicacity female nature is investigated, and female excellence selected. The *Characters of Men*, however, are written with more, if not with deeper thought, and exhibit many passages exquisitely beautiful. The *Gem and the Flower* will not easily be equalled." The Essay, last in the series but written at a much earlier age, dedicated to Addison and occasioned by his *Dialogue on Medals*, contains a witty epigram at the expense of the coin-collectors, who:—

> "The Inscription value, but the Rust adore."

Why these *Epistles* have been classed as Moral Essays rather than as Satires does not very evidently appear. In the year of the publication of the Essay *Of Taste*, 1732, Pope visited Lord Peterborough at Bevis Mount, near Southampton; accompanying that military hero to Winchester, to assist at the annual distribution of prizes at the school.

Of all his connexions, his alliances with Lord Bolingbroke and with Warburton most influenced his didactic poetry, the former philosophically, the latter theologically. With Bolingbroke he had formed acquaintance at the time of his introduction to Swift; and, in later years, the acquaintance developed into intimacy. At the moment when the Jacobite Bishop of Rochester, Atterbury, after a narrow escape from the executioner's axe, landed an exile at Calais, Bolingbroke returned from his banishment (1723) to supply the Bishop's place in the Councils of Twickenham. He had acted, until his abrupt dismissal in 1716, as Secretary to the ex-King, at Versailles, and had married (as his second wife) the Marquise de Villette, a French lady of fortune, a niece of Mde. de Maintenon; from whom he derived the ten thousand pounds' bribe that procured for him, through the Duchess of Kendal, permission to return to England, without, however, reinstating him in his title and place in the House of Lords, or in immediate possession of his estate. For his political disfranchisement and incapacity he took revenge in joining himself to the heterogeneous array of enemies of Walpole, and harassing the Whig Government to the best of his power, through pamphlets and newspapers; in particular, in his famous *Letters to the Craftsman*, entitled *Remarks on the History of England*. In the course of the ten next years of his life, chiefly passed in England, Bolingbroke resided at Dawley, near Uxbridge; when, tired of vain opposition to the all-powerful Minister, he went back to alternate dissipation and philosphical studies at Paris and at La Source. In the highest degree indignant at his abrupt dismissal from the Councils of the Pretender, after the failure of 1715, he had from that time withdrawn from active co-operation with the Jacobite party in France. He was one of the very few speculators in the Mississippi Bubble Company, who had escaped in time from the general crash; and with the fortune thus acquired he purchased the Château, near Orléans, where he lived in philosophical, but forced, retirement, and where he entertained his friends, among whom Voltaire received the highest honour. His father's death, in 1742, put him in possession of the family mansion at Battersea (where he had been brought up under the opposite influences of his cavalier father and puritan grandmother), from which time he lived mostly in England. Dawley he had sold three years previously. At Twickenham and at

Dawley, in the earlier period, the poet and the ex-Secretary of State, with such members of the *October* or *Scriblerus Club* as survived, philosophised in literature and politics—occupations which did not hinder them in indulging in the ordinary trifling and frivolities of Society; nor, we have too good reason to lament, did the "feast of reason" invariably accompany "the flow of soul."

The correspondence of Pope with his so distinguished intimate friend and counsellor would, reasonably, be regarded with especial interest. But the style, on the part of Bolingbroke, has too much of the rhetorical art in which he excelled, and, on both sides, there appears too much of the affectation of *philosophising* upon the vanity of the world; a sort of cynicism at once so common and so unreal with public men, when the world (of politics and publicity) has ceased, through disappointed ambition, satiety, or disabling years, to present the old attractions. It is, indeed, astonishing that two men of the world, equally devoured with ambition, in different ways, and equally restless, could think to deceive themselves and others by such affectations. "I have no very strong faith," protested Swift (who did not suffer himself to be deceived by such platitudes) to Pope, "in your pretenders to retirement."

For us, now, the interest of the friendship of the satirist-poet and the rhetorical philosopher depends chiefly upon the part taken by the latter in the scheme of the *Moral Essays*, and, in particular, of the *Essay on Man*. That the influence of Lord Bolingbroke was positive and considerable we have internal and external evidence. Internal evidence, from the coincidence of the deistic optimism of the author of the *Fragments* and *Minutes of Essays* with the pervading principle of the poem; external proof from the assertions of witnesses who had seen outlines of its main propositions in the handwriting of Bolingbroke. Spence, his intimate confidant, declares that Pope "at several times mentioned how much, or rather how wholly, he was obliged to Lord Bolingbroke for the thoughts and reasonings in his moral work; and once, in particular, said that, besides their frequent talking over that subject together, he had received (I think) seven or eight sheets from Lord Bolingbroke in relation to it (as I apprehended, by way of letters), both to direct the plan in general, and to supply the matter for the particular *Epistles*," and Lord Bathurst assured Drs. Warton and Blair that he had himself seen the prose sketch in question. The conception of the poem Bolingbroke seems to have been the first to note, in a letter to Swift (1729).

Like most of Pope's productions it appeared originally without his name (1732); and the authorship remained a secret for some time to many even of his intimate friends. The fourth and last part he gave to the world two years later, with a complete edition of the poem, and an avowal of its authorship; until then, says Warburton, ascribed " to every man except him who could write it." Its reception, at first, seemed doubtful, but the sale gradually increased and new editions came out. At the outset of the *Essay*, the poet had invited his " guide, philosopher, and friend " to,

> " Expatiate freely o'er this scene of Man—
> A mighty maze of walks *without a plan.*"

By a very radical alteration, in following editions, this appears (probably at Warburton's suggestion) as,

> " Expatiate free o'er all this scene of Man—
> A mighty maze! *but not without a Plan!*"

An almost equally significant substitution was *from* for *at* in a verse in the same *Epistle:*—

> " The soul uneasy and confined from home."

In France it had been early translated, and it fell into the hands of De Crousaz, a Professor of Logic at Lausanne, author of *Examen de Pyrrhonisme.* Persuaded that it was an insidious attack upon orthodox Christianity, and a scheme "to represent," as Johnson expresses it, " the whole course of things as a necessary concatenation of indissoluble fatality," the Swiss professor assailed it with all the vigour of a theologian. At a critical moment for the orthodox reputation of Pope, there now stepped forward a voluntary and redoubtable champion —redoubtable by his arrogant self-assertion no less than by his formidable erudition. Warburton, who began life in an attorney's office, and was now a beneficed cleric, had not then attained the grand object of his ambition—a Bishopric; but he had already achieved a reputation for extraordinary learning, if not for profound wisdom, by the first volumes of his *Divine Legation of Moses.* He now sent to a periodical of the day, called the *Works of the Learned,* a series of vindications of the orthodoxy of the most distinguished poet of the age, who could not but reflect some lustre upon his advocate. Pope, pleased at being thus extricated from what he perceived, with his accustomed caution, might become a disagreeable position, wrote to his apologist in terms of high satisfaction: "I have just received," he announces (April, 1739), "two more of your *Letters* [to the magazine]. It is in the greatest hurry imaginable that I write this; but I cannot help thanking you, in particular, for you third *Letter*, which is so extremely clear, short, and full, that I think Mr. Crousaz ought never to have another answer, and deserved not so good an one. I can only say you do him too much honour, and me too much right, so odd as the expression seems; for you have made my system as clear as I ought to have done and could not. It is, indeed, the same system as mine, but illustrated with a ray of your own, as they say our natural body is the same still when it is *glorified*. I am sure I like it better than I did before, and so will every man else. . . . Pray accept the sincerest acknowledgments."

The poet and the theologian first met at Twickenham, at Lord Radnor's house; and the alliance was confirmed at Pope's villa, where Warburton lingered a couple of weeks, in the spring of 1740. Warburton was a deserter from the enemy's camp. When Theobald brought out his *Shakspeare*, he had been one of the chief contributors of the critical notes; and, according to our sympathy or antipathy, we may lament, or rejoice, that the commentator on the *Essay of Man* so fortuitously escaped from having a place among "the Dunces." From this time Pope and Warburton continued to be on terms of ostentatious and, apparently, cordial friendship. To Warburton, as Mr. Carruthers summarises it, this desirable alliance brought "fame, fortune, a wife, an estate, and a bishopric." The wife was the niece and heiress of Ralph Allen, of Prior Park, the friend and frequent host of Pope. Nor does this end the history of the good things falling to the fortunate apologist of the *Works of the Learned*. At his death, Pope left him the sole copyright of his writings, valued at four thousand pounds. Meanwhile, in proportion as Warburton grew into the favour of Pope, the influence of Bolingbroke declined—for the two rival counsellors had no liking one for the other. After Pope's death, the violence of their mutual hostility reappeared in the attack upon and defence of his memory, caused by the publication of the statesman's writings—the fierceness of this controversial warfare culminating in the latter's *Familiar Epistle to the Most Impudent Man Living*. The correspondence of Pope and Warburton has little more of interest or edification, regarded as "emanations from the heart," than the Pope-Bolingbroke letters. Mutual admiration, and equal affectation of contempt for the rest of the world, who happened not to please them, forms the staple of their epistolary productions.

The leading principle of the *Essay on Man* is a quasi-philosophic Optimism, which undertakes to vindicate and explain the moral and physical constitution of the Universe in general, and of our world in particular, and the author strikes the key-note of the whole system of his Metaphysics and Theology at the conclusion of the first *Epistle* in the apophthegm—"Whatever is, is Right." It is, in fact, a terse, vigorous, and brilliant epigrammatic versification of the prose essays of King's *Origin of Evil* (1702), of Shaftesbury's *Moralists* (1709), and of the *Théodikee*, or "Vindication of Divine Government," of Leibnitz (1710), and other similar Apologies, called forth, in part, by Bayle's *Dictionnaire Philosophique* (1695) and criticism of the *Tout Est Bien* philosophy. Leibnitz (as he informs Warburton, in one of his letters) Pope knew only through the presentation of him by Bolingbroke, whose own *Fragments* correspond so exactly with the poet's *Essay*. Other principal authorities to whom they were indebted are Pascal (*Pensées*), Mandeville (the *Fable of the Bees*) and, apparently, Hobbes. That the fundamental principle of the poem logically leads to Fatalism, and involves the mind in "endless mazes" of contradiction, must be sufficiently obvious. If, however, the false Optimism deserves all the onslaught and ridicule to which it has been subjected, there is another and a true Optimism, at once reasonable and beneficent, the Optimism which regards not the Present or the Past, but the Future: which teaches the possibility of the ultimate elimination of Evil, the ultimate triumph of the Best—in fine, the *perfectibility* of Man, and the proportionate, consequent, improvement and happiness of the rest of the World. As for the "All is Good" deductions of the poem, they fail to follow from the poet's predicate since, as has been remarked by a recent editor, "the perfection of the entire system of the Universe is merely generalised out of a few phenomena, which man may misjudge as utterly as, according to the poet, he misjudges extraordinary occurrences which seem evil to him."[1]

De Crousaz had denounced, and Warburton denied, not the *Optimism* but the *Deism* of its principles. That the latter could have even thought of attempting so impossible an enterprise must appear astonishing. If any *external* proof were needed, in the face of so much internal evidence, we have the clear testimony of Pope's most distinguished associates,

[1] *The Poetical Works of Alexander Pope*, ed. by Professor A. W. Ward, 1873. As for the heterodox theology of the poem, it seems to have escaped the penetration of ordinary orthodox readers; and, as Johnson, who altogether disliked the principles of the *Essay*, informs us, "many read it for a manual of piety."

Chesterfield, Lyttelton, Middleton, and others. Warburton himself, indeed, while he still adhered to the anti-Pope party, had gone so far as to maintain the teaching of the *Essay* to be " rank atheism " and actually read papers, at a literary club at Newark, expressly in denunciation of it.[1]

As for Pope himself, it was only when the *Examen* of De Crousaz excited attention, and Warburton's apology brought the subject still more prominently to notice, that he began to take alarm, and to be anxious to shelter himself behind the ingenious interpretations of his advocate. To produce the same impressions of his orthodoxy upon the Continent, in counteraction to the influence of De Crousaz, he caused Warburton's Reply to be translated into French (as he tells Warburton, writing September, 1739), and sent a letter, through a friend, to Louis Racine, author of a poem called *La Religion*, to assure the orthodox Frenchman that he was not so heretical as he had been represented, and of his real belief in "original sin."[2] "He is a very good Catholic," writes Ramsay, his interpreter, to Racine, "and has always kept to the religion of his forefathers, in a country where he had many temptations to abandon it." Racine seems to have been hard to convince. He declares that he is "obliged to confess that we seem to detect it [his "infidelity"] in the midst of all his abstract reasonings, and that it even presents itself so naturally, that we may attribute to it the rapid spread of the poem in France." Pope wished, especially, to soften matters to his Catholic friends. Hence his anxiety in his letter to Caryll, of March 8, 1733, to make it appear that the (unknown) author of the *Essay*, in spite of appearances, professed belief in continued existence. "I believe," he writes a few months later, "the author will end his poem in such a manner as will satisfy your scruple. . . . . To the best of my judgment the author shows himself a Christian, at last, in the assertion, that all earthly happiness, as well as future felicity, depends upon the doctrine of the *Gospel*—love of God and Man—and that the whole aim of our being is to attain happiness here and hereafter, by the practice of universal charity to man and entire resignation to God. More particular than this

---

[1] Commonly orthodox, Warburton nevertheless seems to have perceived the essential weakness of Optimism. "If only those beings had been brought into existence who would not have abused their freedom," he maintained, "Evil had been prevented, without intrenching upon Free-will," and he thinks it difficult to hold that existence, with so large an admixture of evil, is preferable to non-existence.—Quoted by Elwin, *Works*, &c.

[2] Racine, in his poem, had thrown out the sarcasm:—

" Sans doute qu'à ces mots, des bords de la Tamise
Quelque abstrait raisonneur, qui ne se plait de rien,
Dans son flegme Anglican repondra, *Tout est bien*."—E.

he could not be with any regard to the subject, or manner in which he treated it."[1]

If the optimistic fatalism, and consequent (necessary) inconsistency of the philosophy of the poem, make it faulty as a whole, the merit and beauty of particular parts need no insistance. No single work in the English language, two or three of Shakspeare's dramas and the *Paradise Lost* excepted, is so often quoted. Its peculiarly concentrated condensed, and incisive expressions eminently lend themselves to proverbial phraseology. Nor, apart from its metaphysics, are its ethics less deserving of praise. None of Pope's verse contains so much of a truer philosophy as those parts of the poem which satirise the arrogant assumption, that all living beings have been brought into existence for the sole use and enjoyment of the human species, in so large part (as Montaigne and, indeed, Plutarch and Porphyry long before, had eloquently insisted) really less noble than the highest of the non-human races; a most mischievous, as well as absurd, assumption, since it necessarily leads to attempts to justify and excuse the selfishness of human tyranny over all the subject species, regardless at once of their innocence, their rights, and their sufferings:—

> "Has God, thou fool, worked solely for thy good—
> Thy joy, thy pastime, thy attire, thy food?"

The concluding verses of the poem represent the philosophy of a true Cosmopolitanism, and prefigure the "Golden Age" to be:—

> Self-love, thus pushed to Social, to Divine,
> Gives thee to make thy neighbour's blessing thine—
> * * * * * * *
> Grasp the whole worlds of Reason, Life, and Sense,
> In one close system of Benevolence.
> * * * * * * *
> Self-love but serves the virtuous mind to wake,
> As the small pebble stirs the peaceful lake;
> The centre moved, a circle straight succeeds,
> Another still, and still another spreads.
> Friend, parent, neighbour first it will embrace,
> His country next, and next all human race:
> Wide, and more wide, the overflowings of the mind
> Take every being in of every kind—

[1] Quoted in Mr. Elwin's Ed. of Pope, Vol. ii., where is collected a large amount of external evidence of the real theological beliefs of Pope.

> Earth smiles around, with boundless bounty blest,
> And heaven beholds its image in his breast."[1]

The last edition, during the author's life, came out in 1743, with the Commentary and Notes of Warburton: dedicated to H. St. John Bolingbroke, and published by Bowyer, at the Globe, Paternoster Row. How much Pope revised, may be seen by comparing the final with preceding editions. He did not always improve his earlier verse, which sometimes is more elegant or, at least, less elliptical than in the latest form. As an example may be cited one of the best known couplets in the poem :—

> "Who, foe to Nature, hears the general groan,
> Murders their species, and betrays his own."

which he substituted for :—

> "Who, deaf to Nature's universal groan,
> Murders all other kinds, betrays his own."

Attached to the *Essay* (in 1738), is one of Pope's most generally known productions—the *Universal Prayer*; and this after-thought of the poem forms one of the finest parts of it.

Of the "Moral Essays," already noticed—in the shape of five *Epistles* dedicated to various personages—with the *Essay on Man* designed to form part of an entire System of Ethics, which he did not live to complete, the chronological order is confused; the central poem having been brought out at intervals between the appearance of the several lesser *Epistles*. For the most part, the same criticism applies to them as to the principal work. Their interest and merit lie in particular parts rather than in the philosophy of the whole. In polish and easiness of versification, in liveliness and wit combined, the masterpieces of Pope are the *Satires* in imitation of Horace and of one or two of Donne, the satirist-Dean of St. Paul's. They came from the press in the period 1733-8. Dedicated to his friend Arbuthnot, the *Prologue* has an especial significance as being, in some sort, an "Apology for his Life;" but the personal feeling, which reappears in this piece, is too freely indulged; as

---

[1] *Ep.* iv. This true, comprehensive, Benevolence he illustrates by particular instances, in *Ep.* i. and iii., where he stigmatises the selfish cruelty and gluttony of Man which,

> "Destroy all creatures for thy Sport or Gust,"

and which make him,

> "Of half that live the butcher and the tomb."

But, it must be confessed, like that of some of his successors, his philosophy, in this most important department of Ethics, is not so consistent with itself as it might have been.

also in the First Satire of the Second Book of Horace. Of the latter he writes to Caryll, March, 1732-3 : " You may have seen my last piece of Song, which has met with such a flood of favour that my ears need no more flattery for a twelvemonth. However, it was a light thing—the work of two days ; whereas that to Lord Bathurst was the work of two years, by intervals." Among the best of the Imitations of the Latin Satirist is *Sat.* ii. 2, and *Ep.* ii. 1, in which the original dedication to Augustus is retained and transferred, in a transparent disguise, to George II., whom he ironically eulogises. Besides all this, in the intervals of severer labour, Pope threw off an immense number of *parerga*, lighter and occasional pieces of wit or epigram. The most considerable of these have already been noticed. The old friends of his youth, Trumbull, Cromwell, Caryll, Digby, Harcourt, Craggs, Peterborough, Gay, Arbuthnot, Atterbury, Garth, Prior, Rowe, died long before him, and many of them he commemorated in Epitaphs; of which the best known is the eulogy of Gay, for whom he sincerely laments in his letter to Swift. Some of the *apotheoses*, it must be admitted, although not to be classed exactly with the "sepulchral lies," composed "our holy walls to grace" (as he satirises them in his *Dunciad*, and of which the inscription to the memory of the immortal Captain Blifil is a notable specimen), yet hardly escape suspicion of the accustomed *hyperbole* of the species. His cynical epitaph, "For One who would not be buried in Westminster Abbey," Warburton, contrary to Pope's expressed wish to have no sepulchral commemoration but the dates of his birth and death, placed in the Twickenham Church.[1]

Lord Hervey, provoked by the continued attacks upon himself and Lady M. Wortley Montagu, published, in verse "An Epistle to a Doctor of Divinity from a Nobleman at Hampton Court, Aug. 1733," in which, besides stigmatising the moral character of his adversary's writings, he ridiculed his physical defects and, worse offence than all, his obscurity of birth. Pope's reply came out, in the November following, as *A Letter to a Noble Lord: On Occasion of some Libels Written and Propagated at Court*. In respect of vigour and style, it is one of his best attempts in prose satire, although not without some grossness; and the "tedious malignity" (in Johnson's sentence upon it), as far the epithet, at least,

---

[1] The epitaph is as follows:—

"Heroes and Kings ! your distance keep;
In peace let one poor Poet sleep,
Who never flattered folks like you ;
Let Horace blush and Virgil too."

is concerned, does not do it justice. In one passage he answers, not very happily, the ungenerous charge of obscurity of origin. Lord Hervey enjoyed a high post and high favour at the Court, and Pope prudently suppressed this piece of personal satire—as he informs Swift in a letter of Jan. 6, 1734: "There is a woman's war declared against me by a certain Lord. His weapons are the same which women and children use: a pin to scratch, and a squirt to bespatter. I writ a sort of answer, but [he disingenuously adds] was ashamed to enter the lists with him, and, after shewing it to some people, suppressed it; otherwise it was such as was worthy of him and worthy of me." None the less he held up the "noble Lord" to ridicule in his *Grub Street Journal*; in one ironical piece adopting the character of the "Doctor of Divinity" (a Dr. Sherwin), and making free use of that divine's presumed acquaintance with the biblical style and lauguage. While these more ephemeral displays of wit (sometimes sufficiently forced) attracted attention from a few readers, his more concentrated and polished invective in verse, in his *Epistle to Arbuthnot*, soon afterwards gave greater permanence and prominence to the quarrel; and, as far as poetical superiority was in question, gained for him a not very difficult victory over his otherwise powerful antagonists.

From these quarrels, so little creditable to himself or edifying for the public, we turn with some relief to his relations with his intimate friends. One of his most eloquently descriptive letters of natural scenery he sent to the Blounts from Bristol. He had been on one of his visits to Allen at Prior Park, Bath, and he went on to the Hot Wells of what was then the small village of Clifton. He writes in a strain of appreciation of the landscape, if not with all the simplicity, with some of the enthusiasm of a Cowper. At Bristol, Savage, the poet, at length deserted by friends and fortune, who had so remarkably and so long tolerated his extraordinary follies, was now in the extremities of poverty. Pope, whom he had formerly assisted in his literary intrigues, while refusing an interview with so impracticable an ally and so disreputable an acquaintance, undertook to raise subscriptions among his friends, to offer him another chance of social salvation. Long experience and self-incurred misery could do nothing to teach the aristocratic outcast the commonest wisdom or prudence, and soon afterwards he died in the Bristol jail, owing even his burial to the charity of his keeper.[1] One of Pope's places

---

[1] The extraordinary career of this literary bohemian has been traced with great minuteness by Johnson in the *Life* of his quondam associate. See *Lives of the Poets*.

of frequent resort was Lord Bathurst's estate at Cirencester. During the life of Peterborough he often visited, also, Bevis Mount, near Southampton. In the year of the completion of the *Dunciad* we find him, in company with Lord Chesterfield, entertained by the old Duchess of Marlborough, "Atossa," who lately had begun to pay court to the dreaded epigrammatist (as he informs Swift, writing in 1739), and by Lord Cobham at Stowe. Next summer he went to Bath, where he found Chesterfield, and where he was again the guest of Allen, with Martha Blount and Warburton. During this visit, some (apparently sectarian) difference or disagreement arose between the hostess and her lady-guest, ending in the abrupt departure of Pope, and an indignant letter to him from Miss Blount, who remained behind. "I hope you are well—I am not," she complains bitterly. "My spirits are quite down, though they should not, for these people deserve so much to be despised. One should do nothing but laugh. I packed up my things yesterday; the servants knew it; Mr. and Mrs. Allen never said a word, nor so much as asked me how I went, where, or when. In short [I experienced] from everyone of them much greater inhumanity than I could conceive anybody could show. Mr. Warburton took no notice of me. 'Tis most wonderful: they have not one of them named your name, nor drunk your health since you went. They talk to one another without putting me at all in the conversation. Lord Archibald [Hamilton] is come to Lincoln [Lincombe]. I was to have gone this morning in his coach but, unluckily, he keeps it here. I shall go and contrive something with them to-day; for I really do think these people would shove me out, if I did not go soon. I would run all inconveniences, and drink the waters, if I thought they would do me good. My present state is deplorable. I'll get out of it as soon as I can. Adieu."[1] We may hope that the lady somewhat exaggerated the hardship of her situation: but Pope responded with equal bitterness, and a little incoherently: "So strange a disappointment as I met with," he exclaims, "the extreme sensibility, which I know is in your nature, of such monstrous treatment, and the bitter reflection that I was wholly the unhappy cause of it,[2] did really so distract me, while with you, that I could neither speak, nor move, nor act, nor think. I was like a man stunned or stabbed, where he expected an embrace; and I was dejected to death, seeing I could do or say nothing to comfort but everything rather to hurt you.

[1] In the Mapledurham Collection, quoted by Mr. Carruthers.
[2] This remark does not seem to favour the supposition of a *religious* quarrel.

But, for God's sake, know that I understood it was goodness and generosity you showed me under the appearance of anger itself. When you first bid me go to Lord B[athurst?] from them and hasten thither, I was sensible it was resentment of their conduct to me, and to remove me from such treatment, though you stayed alone to suffer it yourself. But I depended you would not have been a day longer in the house after I left you last; and, of all I have endured, nothing gave me so much pain of heart as to find, by your letters, you were still under their roof. I dread their provoking you to any expression unworthy of you. Even *laughter* would be taking too much notice. But I more dread your spirits, and falling under such dejection as renders you incapable of resolving on the means of getting out of all this. If you would go directly to London," he suggests, " you may, without the least danger, go in a coach and six of King's horses (with a servant on horseback as far as Marlborough, writing to John [Searle, his gardener] to meet you there) for six pounds or seven pounds, as safe, no doubt, as in any nobleman's or gentleman's coach." He encloses this letter under cover to a friend, for, he adds, " I should not wonder if listeners at doors should open letters. W. is a sneaking parson, and I told him he flattered."[1]

Pope's last visits were made to Battersea: his last letters written to Bolingbroke, Martha Blount, and Warburton. To the woman whom he most loved he thus writes, on Easter day, March 25, 1744, two months only before his death:—" I assure you I don't think half so much what will become of me, as of you; and when I grow worse, I find the anxiety for you doubled. Would to God you would quicken your haste to settle,[2] by reflecting what a pleasure it would be to me just to see it, and to see you at ease; and then I could contentedly leave you to the providence of God in this life and resign myself to it in the other. I have little to say to you, when we meet, but I love you upon unalterable principles, which makes me feel my heart the same to you as if I saw you every hour.

[1] Roscoe's *Life and Works of Pope*, viii., 508. Collated with the original.—Carruthers. The " sneaking parson" (however startling the expression), evidently, is Warburton, who was on a visit to Allen at the same time. The quarrel, whatever its origin, did not last very long either with Allen or Warburton.

[2] By *settling* Pope evidently means that she should take up housekeeping, and have an establishment of her own. She seems, at this time, to have been much with Lady Gerard, alluded to in the postscript to the above letter. This lady seems to have been of the Catholic family of Gerard, of New Hall, Lancashire, the widow of Sir William Gerard, the sixth baronet, who was married to Elizabeth, daughter of Thomas Clifton of Lytham, Lancashire. Martha Blount, after Pope's decease, moved from Welbeck Street to Berkeley Street, and occupied till her death the house which Pope had taken on lease— " the last house on the end next Berkeley Square,"—which, apparently, still remains.—C. She died in 1763: Teresa, her elder sister, in 1759.

Adieu." He died on May 30, at the age of fifty-six, "so easily and imperceptibly, that his attendants did not know the exact time of his departure," solicitously watched, to the end, by Bolingbroke, Marchmont, and Spence. Almost to the last he retained energy enough to be taken out, for some hours, into his garden each day; and the day before his decease he was carried for "an airing" into Bushy Park. To the question of Hooke, the historian, "a zealous Catholic," who asked whether he would not die as his parents had done, and send for a priest, he is said to have replied: "I do not suppose that is essential, but it will look right; and I thank you for putting me in mind of it."[1] He was buried in the Twickenham Church, by his own request, near his parents, and, according to a special provision in his Will, was borne to his burial "by six of the poorest men of the parish, to each of whom I order a suit of grey coarse cloth as mourning." A number of various epitaph or epigram-verses upon him, by friends and foes, appeared in the newspapers and magazines.

By the terms of his will Pope left his manuscripts to Lord Bolingbroke, "either to be preserved or destroyed;" to Miss Martha Blount, "younger daughter of Mrs. Martha Blount, late of Welbeck Street, Cavendish Square, the sum of one thousand pounds, immediately on my decease, and all the furniture of my grotto, urns in my garden, household goods, chattels, plate, or whatever is not otherwise disposed of in this my will, I give and devise [to her] out of a sincere regard and long friendship for her." As a permanent income he settled upon her all his personal property, in money, after deduction of debts and other legacies. To Warburton and Allen he bequeathed his library of printed books, and, what was of more importance to the former, "the property of all such of my works already printed, as he has written, or shall write, commentaries or notes upon, and all the profits which shall arise after my death from such editions as he shall publish without future alterations." The most memorable event connected with the death of Pope is the furious controversy waged between his two counsellors. Bolingbroke, some years before the death of his friend, had confided to him the printing of a few copies of his political Treatises, *Letters on the Spirit*

---

[1] Warton relates that the priest had scarcely departed from Pope's house, when Bolingbroke, coming over from Battersea, flew into a great fit of passion and indignation at his being called in. Lord Chesterfield's comment on the incident is of a similar complexion: "He [Pope] was a Deist, believing in a future state. This he has often owned to me; but when he died, he sacrificed a cock to Æsculapius, and suffered the priests who got about him to perform all their absurd ceremonies on his body."—Carruthers.

of Patriotism, &c., for private circulation among his acquaintance. In place of this limited number, Pope secretly printed as many as fifteen hundred copies, keeping them in his possession. A few months after Pope's death (Oct., 1744), informed of this breach of confidence, Bolingbroke wrote to Marchmont, one of the executors, requesting the instant destruction of the whole impression. Next year, Warburton meditating a biography, his rival wrote to Mallet: "they say that War[burton] talks very indecently of your humble servant, and threatens him with the terrible things he shall throw out in a *Life* he is writing of our poor deceased friend Pope. I value neither the good nor the ill-will of the man: but, if he has any regard for the man he flattered living and thinks himself obliged to flatter dead, he ought to let a certain proceeding die away in silence as I endeavour it should."

Neither antagonist fulfilled his promise. Warburton did not write the *Life*,[1] nor did Bolingbroke refrain from publishing a furious attack upon his late bosom-friend. Four years afterwards the latter gave to the world, through Mallet, a revised edition of his Treatises, to which he prefixed a preface denouncing the (fancied) treachery of Pope in vehement and offensive language. What had greatly aggravated, or, perhaps, had really provoked the resentment of the aggrieved author was, as he expresses it, that "the man who had been guilty of this breach of trust had taken upon him further to divide the subject, and *to alter and omit passages*, according to the suggestions of his own fancy;" and, at least, an equal cause of offence, doubtless, may be found in the preference of his detested rival as a depository of the copyright and control of the poet's works. To the coarse and unjustifiable language of Bolingbroke Warburton replied, in "A Letter to the Editor of the *Letters on the Spirit of Patriotism*," in which, with more justice and success than usual in his controversial productions, the writer defends the conduct of Pope, and with much show of reason undertakes to clear it, in the matter in question, from the suspicion of avarice on the one hand or of treachery on the other. From that of avarice, for the poet, in his exceedingly feeble health, could hardly have hoped to be the survivor; from treachery, for he must have known that the dispersed copies could not but come into the hands of their author. His motive

---

[1] He left the work to Ruffhead, a barrister, who brought out his *Life* in 1769, having obtained information and documents from Warburton, then a Bishop. It was the first Life of Pope of any value. It had been preceded by two almost worthless biographies—that of Ayre, in 1745, and Dilworth's, in 1759. Warburton's Edition and Commentaries came out in 1751.

may, probably, be traced partly to his innate and invincible love of mystifying, and partly to the hope of persuading his friend to publish for the benefit of the world. Bolingbroke, however, put forth anonymously an equally strongly-worded rejoinder, of which the title was perhaps the least exceptionable part—*A Familiar Epistle to the most Impudent Man Living*. A war of winged words ensued, long carried on by the friends of either party in newspapers and pamphlets.

Shakspeare (and perhaps Byron) excepted, no English Poet has had so many biographers and editors as Pope. Of no Poet has the (literary) character, or relative place in literature been more hotly contested. No Poet has had so many (more or less) eulogistic admirers, or so many (more or less) adverse critics, from his own time down to the present day: among others on the one side, Warburton, Hurd, Spence, Voltaire, Johnson, Wakefield, Warton, Byron, Campbell, Dugald Stewart, Roscoe, Hallam, Sainte-Beuve, Carruthers, Thackeray, Ward; on the other, Bowles, De Quincey, Wordsworth, Hazlitt, Macaulay, Croker, Taine, Lowell, Elwin. Of all the eulogists, Voltaire and Byron stand out pre-eminently (the one as poet, the other as critic) at once by the greatness of their genius and the extravagance of their panegyric. As Warburton quotes him (in an unpublished letter so early as 1726), Voltaire already proclaims the author of *Eloisa to Abelard* and *The Rape of the Lock* as "the best poet of England, and, at present, of all the world." Again, at a later period, he maintains that he had "carried the torch into the abyss of being, and the art of Poetry, sometimes frivolous and sometimes divine, was in him useful to the human race." Of the *Essay on Man* he declares, "It appears to me the most beautiful, the most useful, the most sublime, didactic poem that ever has been written in any language."[1] Byron's estimate, often repeated by him, was equally eulogistic: "He is the most perfect of our poets; the only poet whose faultlessness has been made his reproach."[2]

---

[1] *Œuvres* xxxvii. 260, and xii. 156, quoted by Mr. Elwin, who remarks that "Voltaire had a twofold reason for his admiration. As a hater of Christianity he hailed, in the *Essay*, the championship of natural religion against revealed; and, as an author, he delighted in the rhymed philosophy which was the staple of his own prosaic verse." (Vol. II.) But if there was one thing Voltaire hated and (in his later period) ridiculed more than any other, it was the *Optimistic* creed—that "everything is for the best in this best of all possible Worlds"—and, as this is the key-note of the *Essay*, it seems scarcely probable that, unless he had a genuine admiration for what he conceived to be its *poetic* excellence, he would have forgiven this cardinal error, from any consideration of the *deism* of the poet. His bitterest feuds were by no means with orthodox theologians only.

[2] *Life and Letters of Byron*, by Moore. His *Letters to John Murray on the Rev. W. L. Bowles's Strictures on the Life and Writings of Pope* (1821), his most eloquent and most considerable

Dr. Warburton's edition of Pope appeared in 1751. How much his forced interpretations, and indiscriminating panegyric, obscured and injured his subject is well-known. "A diseased ambition," justly observes Pope's latest editor, "rendered his talents and opportunities useless. Without originality, he aspired to be original, and imagined that to fabricate hollow paradoxes, and torture language into undesigned meanings, was the surest evidence of a fertile, penetrating genius. . . . Lord Marchmont said laughingly to Pope, that "he must be the vainest man alive, and must want to show Posterity what a quantity of dulness he could carry down on his back, without sinking under the load." His absurd arrogance and self-conceit he displayed conspicuously in his frontispiece to his Edition, in which not only does his portrait appear with that of his hero, but it intentionally occupies the principal place. It has been sarcastically observed that the heads are appropriately drawn, looking in opposite directions. Next in order of time (1759) came Ruffhead's *Life*, based on materials supplied by Warburton. Its value, such as it has, is biographical rather than critical. Johnson's *Life* (forming one of the series of *Lives of the Poets*, written for an edition of the English Poets, of the xvii. and xviii. centuries, 1779-81), the best of all those famous biographies and criticisms, although containing some few errors arising from want of complete information obtainable only at a later time, and occasionally questionable criticism, is characterised by the common sense and judicious observation which, when not obscured by his well-known prejudices, usually appear in his literary judgments. On the whole, it remains the best *literary*, as Carruthers' *Life* is the best *personal* biography of Pope. Wakefield's unfinished Edition came out in 1794. Upon learning that Warton had undertaken the same work, he abandoned the field to him. His panegyric, in which he maintains that an inculpable perfection pervades the whole body of Pope's compositions, it hardly need be observed, does not

prose writing, is conceived in the highest strain of eulogy. That his admiration, sincere as in great measure it undoubtedly was, had been intensified by dislike for Wordsworth and the Lake School, seems to be sufficiently obvious. Byron's profession of faith as to the highest office of Poetry (in his panegyric upon Pope), whatever may be thought of his particular instance, must recommend itself as unexceptionable. "In my mind," he declares, " the highest of all poetry is *Ethical* Poetry, as the highest of all earthly objects must be Moral Truth. Ethical or Didactic Poetry requires more mind, more wisdom, more power, than all the descriptions of natural scenery that ever were penned, and all the epics that were ever founded upon fields of battle."—*Life and Letters*. Only, in place of descriptions of natural scenery, Byron might more properly have instanced, or, at least, a critic of the present day might instance, a much more fashionable and prevalent, as well as less edifying species of verse—the morbidly introspective and egoistic kind whose principal, if not sole, object seems to be the *Self*.

err on the side of moderation. His notes and illustrations, however, did much to lighten the labour of succeeding editors.[1]

The edition of Warton appeared in 1797,[2] with the announcement that "the universal complaint, that Dr. Warburton had disfigured and disgraced his edition with many forced and far-sought interpretations, totally unsupported," had necessitated, and suggested to him, the production of a new one. His notes abound, Mr. Elwin observes, in just remarks and comparisons, but, for the most part, have more of elegance and taste than of profoundness. But a more remarkable presentation of Pope—remarkable by reason of its consequences—was that of Bowles (who had been a pupil of Warton, at Winchester) ten years later. "His taste," according to Mr. Elwin, who has formed a more favourable estimate of his criticism than some of his predecessors have done, "was exquisite, and he was well read, shrewd, and candid. His failing was a hurry of mind, which disqualified him for a painstaking commentator. . . The chief merit of his Edition is his excellent literary criticism, which is truer, deeper, and more refined than that of his old Winchester master."[3] Bowles, while also freely criticising his poetic faults, directed his assaults chiefly upon the moral character of the poetry of Pope. But he had not a perspicuous style; his method was confused, and his judgments were inconsistent. His Edition was published in 1806, and excited much attention and occasional controversy. Thirteen years afterwards, Campbell, in his *Specimens of the British Poets*, disputed the judgments of Bowles, both moral and literary, and replaced his client upon his high pedestal. Bowles replied in a *Letter* to Campbell, taking up his position upon what he called "the invariable principles of Poetry." A *Quarterly* reviewer came to the rescue of Campbell. Bowles sharply retorted, with a good deal of personal acrimony; and soon the Pope controversy increased in extent and vehemence, the chief combatants, after Byron,

---

[1] Gilbert Wakefield, a Fellow of Jesus College, Cambridge, and a scholar of considerable repute in his time, is chiefly known now by his *Tragædiarum Græcarum Delectus*. But his heterodox pamphlet, entitled *An Inquiry into the Expediency and Propriety of Public or Social Worship* (1792), was the one, perhaps, of his numerous productions which caused the most sensation among his contemporaries. It was left, it seems, to the (orthodox) dissenters to answer. In other respects, he ranged himself on the side of the orthodox world, and put forth several controversial works—among others, two *Replies* to Paine's *Age of Reason*. In 1798 he published "A Reply to Some Parts of the Bishop of Llandaff's Address to the People of Great Britain," for which he was sentenced to be incarcerated in the Dorchester jail for two years. He had left the Established Church some years previously, and joined a Nonconformist body. He died in 1801.

[2] Dr. Joseph Warton was son of Thomas Warton, Professor of Poetry, at Oxford, and brother of the author of the *History of English Poetry*, also Poetry Professor at Oxford.

[3] *Works of Alexander Pope*, Introduction, Vol. I. 1871.

being Gilchrist, editor of the *Quarterly*, Roscoe, and the elder Disraeli. Little of this, one of the most famous "quarrels of Authors," (1819-27), is now remembered; and the contributions of Byron, vitiated though they are by partiality, remain, probably, the only *critiques* on the subject that are still occasionally read, for the sake of their author still more than for their brilliant style.

The next Edition (1824) was superintended by Wm. Roscoe.[1] Wilson Croker, Secretary to the Admiralty, the subject of the well-known *critique* of Macaulay (in his article in the *Edinburgh Review* on Croker's Edition of Boswell's *Life of Johnson*), made preparations for a new Edition of Pope, which he did not live to publish; but he collected a large mass of notes, chiefly upon the *Satires*. These came into the hands of Mr. Elwin, the editor of the latest and the most comprehensive Edition of Pope yet produced. It forms an almost complete repertory of all that had hitherto been written upon the Poet—with much searching, and, apart from metaphysical opinions, often very just original criticism. But, if Voltaire, Johnson, Byron, and others have erred on the side of excessive praise, with De Quincey (who somewhat contradicted himself) the bias of his latest editor inclines too much in the opposite direction. His most adverse critics, however, while denying to Pope, in almost every other of his productions, the praises generally lavished upon him, unite in extolling the merits of his two happiest achievements, the *Rape of the Lock* and the *Eloisa*. De Quincey holds the former poem to be "the most exquisite movement of playful fancy that universal Literature offers," and Mr. Elwin admits that "few masterpieces have more originality in the aggregate. . . They [the two poems] have the merit of being masterpieces in opposite styles; the first is remarkable for its delicious fancy and sportive satire; the second for its fervid passion and tender melancholy. Two poems of such rare, and such different excellence, would alone entitle Pope to his fame." The *Eloisa* even Wordsworth, who classes it (as a sort of monodrama) in the dramatic species of poetry, spoke of in terms of high appreciation. Pope himself strangely considered, or affected to consider, that in the way of versification he had never surpassed his *Essay on Criticism*. He would, with more justness and reason, have instanced his *Rape of the Lock*.

[1] Chiefly known as the author of the *Life of Lorenzo de' Medici*. But his best title to fame is the part he took in the *Slavery* question and his *Wrongs of Africa*, 1788 (a pamphlet). He composed two popular Revolutionary Songs, at the time of the French Uprising. His *Pope* errs on the side of too little scepticism.

Between Roscoe's and Elwin's Editions, an acute and laborious investigator, Mr. C. W. Dilke, applied himself, with more penetration and success than up to that time characterised the criticism of Pope, especially to ascertaining the chronology and genuineness of the Correspondence. The results of his labours he left in copious and minute manuscript notes, on interleaved pages, in the edition of 1735, and, especially, in that of Roscoe; and in some important remarks in the *Athenæum* (1854). In the preceding year appeared the first Edition of Mr. Carruthers—of which the most valuable part was the *Life*, illustrated by numerous portraits and other woodcuts. Some errors appeared in the 1853 Edition, and a revised presentation of the *Life* came out in 1859.

In estimating Pope's character, whether literary or moral, his adverse critics have seemed to judge him without taking quite enough into account his age, his education, and the society in which he chiefly mixed. In an examination, however, of two of his most considerable poems, the *Essay on Criticism* and the *Essay on Man*, his latest editor has pointed out, in detail, some faults which had been passed over too easily, for the most part, by former critics. In particular, he has remarked, with much justness, upon the harsh inversions and obscurity of many of the verses in the *Essay on Man*, arising from an extremely elliptical and condensed style; and upon the philosophical contradictions and inconsistencies in that most ambitious but, upon the whole, least satisfactory of all Pope's works. But, if we wish to fix the place of Pope among English poets, it is necessary first carefully to distinguish the class to which he belongs. To compare him with the poets of a period of time very different from his own—with Chaucer, Milton, Shelley,— to measure him by the dimensions of the great master-spirits, who drew their inspiration, more or less, from the whole of Nature, not from artificial Society alone, is to compare two quite distinct things. He is, above everything, the poet of Art and Society ; and in this province he must be acknowledged to be the first. His greatest power and merit lie in terseness and force of expression, in the neat incisiveness of his satire, in his judgment and good taste, in general, and in the rapidity and vigour of his verse. That the first named of these qualities have been gained sometimes at the expense of clearness and meaning, and even of grammatical correctness, must be obvious to most of his readers. It is surprising, indeed, that with all his practice of his well-known principle —" the first, the greatest art, the art to blot"—after all his many careful revisions, there should survive so many harsh and awkward lines, and even imperfect rhymes. Some of the latter, which have been taken to be originally defective, in Pope's day were, in fact, legitimate—so much has fashion changed pronunciation; but, in spite of this deduction, there still remain a large number which have been always illegitimate, and for which Swift himself, very careful in this respect, found fault with him.

As for the metaphysical and the moral character of some of his principal poems, unfortunately he adopted a system of metaphysics (in his *Essay on Man*) radically unsound, and self-contradictory, which betrayed him into a number of obvious inconsistencies in attempting to justify it. But, in the strictly ethical parts, he has given phrase and currency to many neglected but highly important moral truths, some of which, by their incisive expression, have become incorporated in the national proverbial language. His satirical genius (most conspicuously employed against his personal enemies) places him, among the poets, in the first rank, and even above his models Horace or Boileau. "His imagery, wit, and sense," says Mr. Carruthers, "his critical rules, and moral reflections have made us rich in expression. His maxims on life and manners form part of our daily speech and involuntary thought; nor have the most profound or acute of our Moralists enunciated finer axioms than are to be found in his *Essays* and *Epistles*."

It is as a Letter-Writer that the character of Pope claims especial attention here, and, in this respect, he has lately been subjected to a severe and searching criticism. No correspondence—certainly none of so distinguished a writer—has caused so much perplexity to biographer or editor as Pope's. The intricate maze began, in 1735, with the mysterious publication of his correspondence with various personages, for which he sought to make the bookseller, Curll, responsible and brought him before a House of Lords' Committee. Bowles was the first to draw attention to the *composition* of some of the letters, but the first minutely to investigate their history was Mr. C. W. Dilke, the father of the present Cabinet Minister, who, by his knowledge of the periodical and ephemeral literature of the time, and by his freedom from prejudice, was well prepared for the task. An unexpected discovery put him upon the right track, and revealed the first certain proof of the epistolary insincerity of Pope. Manuscript copies of the letters of Caryll—one of Pope's earliest and principal correspondents—which had been prudently taken by the writer (when, at last, he yielded to the earnest solicitations of his friend for the originals), accidently turned up in an old lumber-room belonging to the Caryll family. Compared with the correspondence published by Pope himself in 1735,[1] they incontestably proved that, altered and revised, they had served him as material for other epistolary compositions, addressed to personages more considerable than the obscure country-gentleman of Sussex. Further careful examination discovered correspondence with other persons—with Wycherley, Blount, Lady M. W. Montagu, and even with Swift—to have been also revised or *adapted*. Worst of all for his reputation for sincerity, has been the difficult unravelling of his tortuous proceedings in regard to the friend, for whom he had constantly professed the highest affection and esteem; and his tampering with the letters of Swift, when the unconscious agent in the fraud was no longer in a condition to expose it, forms, perhaps, the worst part of the entangled web of this epistolary history.

It is not possible, in these pages, to do more than trace the principal steps in the narrative of this series of extraordinary frauds. The first of the letters of Pope to see the light were surreptitiously published, it has already been noticed, in 1726. They were followed by the Wycherley correspondence in 1729. Theobald, the rival editor of *Shakspeare*, had brought out an edition of Wycherley's unpublished writings. Pope seized the opportunity, under the pretext of vindicating the reputation of his friend, of giving to the world, by the unsuspected medium of Curll, his own letters, with the real purpose of exalting his own fame. Pope's *correct* Edition (as he advertised it) of his correspondence up to that date, he printed in 1735. It begins with the year 1704, with his letters to Walsh and Wycherley. His chief and early correspondent, Caryll, died in 1736, and he was now more free to "revise" at his pleasure. He circulated a proposal to publish, by subscription, and his friend Allen came forward, engaging to take the whole expense upon himself. Eventually Allen and the public shared it between them. The volume appeared in 1737, in *folio* and *quarto*, and, later, in *octavo* form, at a guinea to subscribers for the *quarto*. A Preface announces the reasons which forced him to place the *genuine* edition before the world. He asserts that "several letters have been attributed to him which he did not write, that the piratical editions contain various passages, which 'no man of common sense would have printed himself,' that he had not authorised any of the surreptitious impressions, laments the need which

[1] "It had filled the nation," Johnson tells us, "with praises of his candour, tenderness, and benevolence, the purity of his purpose, and the fidelity of his friendship." Warburton professes that it had caused him to change his opinion of his character.

exists for his own volume, and indulges in general declamation upon the enormity of procuring letters by disreputable contrivances, assures us that his genuine letters are 'emanations of the heart, and not efforts of genius,' and feels confident that this alone may induce any candid reader to believe their publication an act of necessity rather than vanity."

In this volume first appeared the Atterbury Correspondence. Pope "omitted as well as added, and left out some of the letters to and from Wycherley, some of the letters to and from Cromwell, some of the letters to ladies, and a few scattered letters from the remaining groups. In the letters he republished he here and there erased a sentence, which had appeared in the volume of 1735, or inserted a sentence which was new. The minuter verbal alterations are numerous; but many of them are only corrections of errors of the press. . . . He set aside the portions of his Correspondence which were condemned, he endeavoured to rectify the imconsistencies into which he had been betrayed, and he sometimes altered a word or a phrase in the final revision to which he subjected the work. The changes leave it apparent that the Pope text and the P.T. [the assumed initials under which he had already mystified Curll and the public] are identical in their origin; and neither of them are the text of the actual letters of the poet."[1] The Swift Correspondence appeared in 1741, in an edition of the Prose Works of Pope, whose letters to Swift are stated to have been "copied from an impression sent from Dublin, and said to have been printed by the Dean's direction," and "begun without our author's knowledge, and continued without his consent." Until the researches of Mr. Dilke this account received general credit. Pope affected the greatest anxiety about the Correspondence, and, in a letter to Allen, he expresses the hope that, at least, "they are castigated in some degree."

They are the Caryll Letters which form the original source of so many later manufactured ones. Out of them Pope composed four to Blount, four to Addison, two to Congreve, and one each to Wycherley, Steele, Trumbull, and Digby. Only six letters were assigned to Caryll, the remaining sixteen having been adapted and addressed to more distinguished names. The letters to Lady M. Wortley Montagu, being "in hostile

---

[1] *The Works of Alexander Pope.* New Edition. Collected in part by the late Right Hon. John Wilson Croker. With Introduction and Notes by the Rev. Whitwell Elwin. Vol. I. 1871.

hands," were inaccessible to him, and he could not venture to make any great perversions; but on a smaller scale, here and there, he erased and altered significant phrases. Inordinate literary vanity or ambition, an extraordinary propensity for mystification, even (as we are assured by his friends) in the most ordinary affairs of life, which became at last a monomania with him, and the habit from his youth, which constantly grew more inveterate, of touching and re-touching, altering and re-altering everything in the shape of writing in his possession, lay at the foundation of all these astonishing and otherwise unaccountable deceptions. To this vain ambition, and to this monomania of mystifying, and of "improving" his writings, he was ready to sacrifice not only his enemies, but the reputation even of his best friends. Where these predominant influences did not come into operation, his devotion and affection for his friends, to whom he remained constant in bad as in good fortune, appear to have been disinterested and sincere. His affection for his mother, over whom he watched, in her extreme old age, with the greatest solicitude, is the private virtue which does him most honour. In public life, his independence of Party, in an Age especially characterised by political corruption and self-seeking, and his devotion to Literature for its own sake, instead of using it as a means for mere pecuniary or political gain; and, above all, a certain humaneness of philosophy—although not so prominent as in his contemporary Thomson —form together, it must be allowed, no inconsiderable balance against his deplorable literary vanity and epistolary meannesses.[1]

[1] Some of the panegyrics of his eulogists have already been quoted. But, of all who have written upon Pope, none has assigned him so exalted a character, as a moral Satirist, as the great English prose-satirist of our time:—"The silver-trumpet ringing defiance to falsehood and tyranny, deceit, dulness, superstition. It is Truth, the champion, shining, and intrepid, and fronting the great World-tyrant with armies of slaves at his back. It is a wonderful and victorious single combat, in that great battle which has always been waging since Society began." Such are some of the expressions of the author of *Lectures on the Humourists*. The following is the opinion of him of a contemporary, one well acquainted with him, although of an opposite political party:—"He was as great an instance as any he quotes," writes Lord Chesterfield, "of the contradictions and inconsistencies of human nature; for, notwithstanding the malignancy of his satires, and some blameable passages in his life, he was charitable, to his power, active in doing good offices, and piously attentive to an old bed-ridden mother, who died but a little time before him. His poor, crazy, deformed body was a mere Pandora's box, containing all the physical ills that ever afflicted humanity. This, perhaps, whetted the edge of his satire, and may, in some degree, excuse it." As for conversational talent, he did not shine among his contemporaries:—"Pope, in conversation, was below himself: he was seldom easy and natural, and seemed afraid that the man should degrade the poet, which made him always attempt wit and humour, often unsuccessfully, and too often, unreasonably. I have been with him a week at a time," adds Chesterfield, " at his house, at Twickenham, where I necessarily saw his mind in its undress, when he was both an agreeable and instructive companion."

The Bolingbroke Correspondence has already been characterised. The letters to and from Warburton, sufficiently numerous, are vitiated by the same affectations. They contain, however, some interesting references to the poet's accomplished or contemplated enterprises. The same remark applies to the Atterbury Correspondence, and, in fact, to a large proportion of the letters addressed to conspicuous personages. Of the few which are addressed to Addison, the value, as *letters*, has been, by recent investigation, reduced to the vanishing point. Besides being but slightly modified second editions of the earlier Caryll letters, they seem never to have come into Addison's hands ; written, apparently, with the sole purpose of imposing upon the world a belief in the high deference for him of his Whig rival. As for the Wortley Montagu Correspondence, while he could not venture to tamper much with his own letters, there seems to be no room for doubt that, in preparing her letters for publication, he interpolated words, or, more than once, even whole passages, to justify his insinuations, in his poems, of the character of "Sappho." Apart, however, from the particular motive to such inexcusable baseness, it was the habit of Pope, in common with his fashionable contemporaries, to address women in terms of the most high flown "gallantry," which, in his case, could scarcely be anything more than the language of affectation. His letters to the Blount sisters, and, in a less degree, those to Miss Cowper, contain similar expressions of gallantry and compliment, meaning anything or nothing. Among the best specimens of his epistolary style, as might be expected, are the letters which he wrote, apparently without intention of publication, such as some of those to his friends Digby and Fortescue. Many of the letters to Swift, Gay, Arbuthnot, Jervas, and others of his intimate friends, have considerable interest, either literary or personal.[1] But of the voluminous mass of Pope's Letters, filling three or four large octavo volumes, a large proportion has interest only for the biographer ; and for the general reader a careful and judicious selection is especially desirable. One of the best of his correspondents, in the way of picturesque writing, was

---

Upon his poetical merits the same authority declares : "I will say nothing of his Works. They speak sufficiently for themselves. They will live as long as Letters and Taste shall r main in the country, and be more and more admired as envy and resentment shall subside. But I will venture the *classical* blasphemy, which is, that, however he may be supposed to be obliged to Horace, Horace is more obliged to him."—*Characters.*

[1] Pope's latest biographer, Mr. Leslie Stephen, while admitting all that has been said of his *artificiality* in the Letters, thinks that there is "scarcely a more interesting volume in the Language than that which contains the correspondence of Swift, Bolingbroke, and Pope."—*Life of Pope,* 1880.

David Mallet (the legatee and publisher of Bolingbroke's Works), two of whose letters, from Wales and from Geneva, may rank, for descriptive and humorous power, with some of Cowper's. But, with the exception of Swift, Gay, and Arbuthnot, and one or two others, perhaps, the letters of his friends are not distinguished by any special merit.

Pope's manner of life, his habits, and his physical infirmities, have been often sketched, from Johnson onwards. His enemies, and Dennis in particular, did not lose the opportunity of assailing him with ridicule upon the side of his well-known physical defects. Apparently to deprive them of the merit of originality, Pope published, early in his career, a caricature picture of himself, under the thin disguise of "Dick Distich," the president of the Little Club (in the *Guardian*, 91-92), "half as tall as an ordinary man." "The most eminent persons of our Assembly," he humorously proclaims, "are a little poet, a little lover, a little politician, and a little hero. The first of these, Dick Distich by name, we have elected President, not only as he is the shortest of us all, but because he has entertained so just a sense of his stature as to go generally in black, that he may appear yet less. Nay, to that perfection is he arrived, that he stoops as he walks. The figure of the man is odd enough—he is a lively little creature, with long arms and legs. A spider is no ill emblem of him. He has been taken at a distance for a small windmill. But, indeed, what principally moved us in his favour was his talent in poetry; for he hath promised to undertake a long work in *short verse*, to celebrate the heroes of our size. He has entertained so great a respect for Statius, on the score of that line,

> *Major in exiguo regnabat corpore virtus,*
> "A larger portion of heroic fire
> Did his small limbs and little breast inspire,"

that he once designed to translate the whole *Thebaid*, for the sake of little Tydeus." But, if he chose himself thus to ridicule his deformed and diminutive person, he did not tolerate that freedom in others, and nothing excited his resentment so much as any satire upon him of that kind. For such physical defects, the remarkable intellectual character of his thin and pale countenance, and, in particular, his fine and piercing eyes, may well have seemed (in the estimate of his friends, at least) to have been some compensation. The earliest portrait of him, by Jervas (now in the National Portrait Gallery), represents him as a young man of not more than twenty, full length, seated in an arm chair, in a musing attitude, and with dark vivacious eyes. He is dressed in a plain grey suit, black silk stockings, white cravat, with long ends overhanging in front, and ruffles. In the back ground the figure of a young woman, who is supposed to be Martha Blount, is seen reaching a book from a shelf. In the same Gallery is a portrait of him in crayons, by William Hoare, a half-figure, age about thirty. The face has a somewhat worn and eager expression: the eyes are represented as of a dark blue colour, lips full and of a pale red. He is dressed in a blue dressing gown, on his head a blue turban cap, in large folds. It is said to resemble a portrait attributed to Richardson, formerly belonging to Sir Robert Peel. It was engraved by Warren, 1821. From one by Pond there is a very fine engraving by Houbraken, made for the *Heads of Illustrious Persons*, Ed. by Th. Birch, 1747. Other portraits of him are those of Hudson, Kneller, and of Jervas, at Mapledurham, painted for Martha Blount.[1]

His handwriting, in his epistolary correspondence, is large, firm, and legible. In his manuscripts for the press, from which Johnson seems to have formed his opinion of it, it is usually minute, and, being full of erasures, is much less legible.

---

[1] A bust, by Roubiliac, taken in the year 1741, also is, or was, in the Peel Gallery. A *fac-simile* of a rough sketch of a full-length portrait of Pope is given by Mr. Carruthers as the only full-length representation of him, apparently forgetful of the early portrait of Jervas.

Letters of Pope.

LETTERS.

To Mr. William Walsh.

July 2, 1706.

I cannot omit the first opportunity of making you my acknowledgments for revising those papers of mine. You have no less right to correct me than the same hand that raised a tree has to prune it. I am convinced, as well as you, that one may correct too much: for in Poetry, as in Painting, a man may lay colours one upon another till they stiffen and deaden the piece. Besides, to bestow heightening on every part is monstrous: some parts ought to be lower than the rest; and nothing looks more ridiculous than a work where the thoughts, however different they are in their own nature, seem all on a level. It is like a meadow newly mown, where weeds, grasses, and flowers are all laid even, and appear undistinguished. I believe, too, that sometimes our first thoughts are the best, as the first squeezing of the grapes makes the finest and richest wine.

I have not attempted anything of a pastoral comedy,[1] because I think the taste of our Age will not relish a poem of that sort. People seek for what they call *wit* on all subjects and in all places; not considering that Nature loves truth so well that it hardly ever admits of flourishing. Conceit is to Nature what paint is to Beauty: it is not only needless, but impairs what it would improve. There is a certain majesty in simplicity, which

---

[1] Pope refers to his first published verses—the *Pastorals*, a copy of which he had sent to Walsh. They were not published until the year 1709.

is above all the quaintness of wit; insomuch that the critics have excluded wit from the loftiest Poetry as well as the lowest, and forbid it to the Epic no less than the Pastoral. It should certainly displease all those who are charmed with Guarini and Bonarelli,[1] and imitate Tasso not only in the simplicity of his thoughts, but in that of the fable too. If surprising discoveries should have place in the story of a Pastoral Comedy, I believe it would be more agreeable to probability to make them the effects of chance than of design—intrigue not being very consistent with that innocence which ought to constitute a shepherd's character. There is nothing in all the *Aminta*, as I remember, but happens by mere accident, unless it be the meeting of Aminta with Silvia at the fountain, which is the contrivance of Daphne,—and even that is the most simple in the world. The contrary is observable in *Pastor Fido*, where Corisca is so perfect a mistress of intrigue, that the plot could not have been brought to pass without her. I am inclined to think the Pastoral Comedy has another disadvantage as to the manners. Its general design is to make us in love with the innocence of rural life, so that to introduce shepherds of vicious character must, in some measure, debase it;[2] and hence it may come to pass that even the virtuous characters will not shine so much, for want of being opposed to their contraries. These thoughts are purely my own, and, therefore, I have reason to doubt them: but I hope your judgment will set me right.

I would beg your opinion, too, as to another point. It is,

[1] Italian pastoral poets of the sixteenth century. *Il Pastor Fido*, the celebrated pastoral drama of Guarini, is most famous in this country as, with the *Aminta* of Tasso, having been the store-house from which English poets, during the period 1570-1640, borrowed many of their ideas in this species of poetry.

[2] The *Pastoral* character, in spite of its having always been, with the poets, the type of innocence no less than of simplicity of manners is, as Gibbon has remarked (*Decline and Fall*, xxv., writing of the Tartars), " much better adapted to the fierce and cruel habits of a military life." Such, in fact, has been the teaching of History.

how far the liberty of *borrowing* may extend? I have defended it sometimes by saying, that it seems not so much the perfection of sense to say things that had never been said before as to express those best that have been said oftenest—and that writers, in the case of borrowing from others, are like trees which, of themselves, would produce only one sort of fruit, but by being grafted upon others may yield variety. A mutual commerce makes Poetry flourish: but then poets, like merchants, should repay with something of their own what they take from others: not, like pirates, make prize of all they meet. I desire you to tell me sincerely, if I have not stretched this license too far in these *Pastorals*. I hope to become a critic by your precepts, and a poet by your example. Since I have seen your *Eclogues*[1] I cannot be much pleased with my own. However, you have not taken away all my vanity so long as you give me leave to profess myself yours, &c.

To the Rev. Ralph Bridges.

1708.

The favour of your letter, with your remarks, can never be enough acknowledged; and the speed, with which you discharged so troublesome a task, doubles the obligation.

I must own you have pleased me very much by the commendations so ill-bestowed upon me; but, I assure you, much more

[1] In the single page which he allots to Walsh, Johnson enumerates among his few writings (in prose), *Eugenia, a Defence of Women; Æsculapius, or the Hospital of Fools; A Collection of Letters and Poems;* and *The Golden Age Restored.* This earliest of Pope's literary correspondents, the son of a Worcestershire squire, sat in the House of Commons and in several Parliaments. He began to correspond with Pope in 1705. He died sometime before the year 1711.

z

by the frankness of your censure, which I ought to take the more kindly of the two, as it is more advantageous to a scribbler to be improved in his judgment than to be soothed in his vanity. The greater part of those deviations from the Greek, which you have observed, I was led into by Chapman and Hobbes, who are, it seems, as much celebrated for their knowledge of the original as they are decried for the badness of their translations. Chapman[1] pretends to have restored the genuine sense of the author, from the mistakes of all former explainers, in several hundred places; and the Cambridge editors of the large Homer, in Greek and Latin, attributed so much to Hobbes, that they confess they have corrected the old Latin interpretation very often by his version. For my part, I generally took the author's meaning to be as you have explained it: yet their authority, joined to the knowledge of my own imperfectness in the language, overruled me. However, Sir, you may be confident I think you in the right, because you happen to be of my opinion: for men—let them say what they will—never approve any other's sense but as it squares with their own. But you have made me much more proud of and positive in my judgment, since it is strengthened by yours. I think your criticisms, which regard the expression, very just, and shall make my profit of them. To give you some proof that I am in earnest, I will alter three verses on your bare objection, though I have Mr. Dryden's example for each of them. And this, I hope, you will account no small piece of obedience, from one who values the authority of one true poet above that of twenty critics or commentators.

But, though I speak thus of commentators, I will continue to read carefully all I can procure, to make up, that way, for my own want of critical underlanding in the original beauties of Homer, though the greatest of them are certainly those of in-

[1] The translation of George Chapman appeared in 1596. He was the author of seventeen dramas. It is his *Homer* which has given him his principal fame. Hobbes (of Malmesbury) published his version about 1670.

vention and design, which are not at all confined to the language; for the distinguishing excellences of Homer are, by the consent of the best critics of all nations, first in the manners (which include all the speeches, as being no other than the representations of each person's manners by his words), and then in that rapture and fire, which carries you away with him with that wonderful force that no man, who has a true poetical spirit, is master of himself while he reads him. Homer makes you interested and concerned before you are aware, all at once, whereas Virgil does it by soft degrees. This, I believe, is what a translator of Homer ought principally to imitate; and it is very hard for any translator to come up to it, because the chief reason why all translations fall short of their originals is, that the very constraint they are obliged to renders them heavy and dispirited [spiritless]. The great beauty of Homer's language, as I take it, consists in that noble simplicity which runs through all his works; and yet his diction, contrary to what one would imagine consistent with simplicity, is, at the same time, very copious.[1]

I do not know how I have run into this pedantry in a letter: but I find I have said too much as well as spoken too inconsiderately. What further thoughts I have upon this subject I shall be glad to communicate to you, for my own improvement, when we meet, which is a happiness I very earnestly desire; as I do likewise some opportunity of proving how much I think myself obliged to your friendship, and how truly I am, Sir, your most faithful and humble servant.

[1] The poetical translations of the *Iliad*, which Pope had submitted to the criticism of Bridges, were first essays published in the *Miscellany*. The *Iliad* (first volume) appeared in 1715.— See his *Life and Writings.*

To Mr. Henry Cromwell.

May 7, 1709.

You had long before this been troubled with a letter from me, but that I deferred it till I could send you either the *Miscellany*,[1] or my continuation of the version of Statius. The first I imagine you might have had before now, but, since the contrary has happened, you may draw this moral from it, that authors in general are more ready to write nonsense than booksellers are to publish it. I had I know not what extraordinary flux of rhyme upon me for three days together, in which time all the verses you see added have been added; which I tell you, that you may more freely be severe upon them.

It is a mercy that I do not assault you with a number of original sonnets and epigrams, which our modern bards put forth in the Spring-time in as great abundance as trees do blossoms, a very few whereof can come to be fruit, and please no longer than just in their birth. So that they make no less haste to bring their flowers of wit to the Press than gardeners to bring their other flowers to the market, which, if they cannot get off their hands in the morning, are sure to die before night. Thus the same reason, that furnishes Common [Covent] Garden with those nosegays you so delight in, supplies the *Muses' Mercury*, and *British Apollo*, not to say Jacob's *Miscellanies*, with verses. And it is the happiness of this Age, that the modern invention of printing poems for pence a-piece has brought the nosegays of Parnassus to bear the same price; whereby the public-spirited Mr. Henry Hills,[2] of Blackfriars,

[1] Jacob Tonson's sixth volume of *Poetical Miscellanies*, in which Mr. Pope's *Pastorals*, and some versions of Homer and Chaucer, were first printed.—Pope, 1735. Henry Cromwell seems to have been some remote cousin of the Protector.

[2] An account of this " notorious printer " will be found in Nichols's *Literary Anecdotes*. He is said to have " regularly pirated every good poem or sermon that was published," generally reproducing it on rough paper, and selling it

has been the cause of great ease and singular comfort to all the learned, who, never over-abounding in transitory coin, should not be discontented, methinks, even though poems were distributed *gratis* about the streets, like Bunyan's sermons, and other pious treatises, usually published in a like volume and character.

The time now drawing nigh, when you use with Sappho[1] to cross the water in an evening to Spring Garden, I hope you will have a fair opportunity of ravishing her—I mean only as Oldfox, in the *Plain-Dealer* [of Wycherley], says of ravishing her through the ear with your well-penned verses. I have been told of a lucky compliment of an officer to his mistress in the same place, which I cannot but set down (and desire you, at present to take it in good part, instead of a Latin quotation), that it may some time or other be improved by your pronunciation, while you walk *solus cum solâ* in those amorous shades:—

When at Spring Garden Sappho deigns t'appear, &c.

I wish you all the pleasures which the season and the nymph can afford, the best company, and the best coffee, and the best news you can desire. And what more to wish you than this I do not know, unless it be a great deal of patience to read and examine the verses I send you, and I promise you in return a great deal of deference to your judgment, and an extraordinary obedience to your sentiments for the future, to which you know I have been sometimes a little refractory. If you will please to begin where you left off last, and mark the margins, as you have done in the pages immediately before (which you will find corrected to your sense since your last perusal), you will extremely oblige me, and improve my translation. Besides those

---

for a penny. The poem entitled *Wine*, which Aaron Hill asserts was written by Gay, was treated by Hills in this manner, which may account for the attack upon him in Gay's verses to Lintot, the bookseller:—

"While neat old Elzevir is reckoned better
Than pirate Hills' brown sheets and scurvy letter."—Elwin.

[1] Mrs. Thomas, Cromwell's "mistress."

places which may deviate from the sense of the author, it would be very kind in you to observe any deficiences in the diction or numbers. The *hiatus*, in particular, I would avoid as much as possible, which you are certainly in the right to be a professed enemy to; though, I confess, I could not think it possible at all times to be avoided by any writer, till I found by reading the famous French poet Malherbe,[1] lately, that there is but one throughout all his poems. I thought your observation true enough to be passed into a rule, but not a rule without exceptions, nor that ever it had been reduced to practice. But this example of one of the correctest and best of their poets has undeceived me, and confirms your opinion very strongly, and much more than Mr. Dryden's authority, who, though he made it a rule, seldom observed it. Sir, I shall be very proud of a line or two from you sometimes during the summer, which always will be very welcome and very obliging to, Sir, your most humble and most obedient servant.

I desire you will be so kind to me as not to show what I send to anybody. I am not certain whether Mr. Wycherley be yet in London or no; if he be, I desire you to give him my most hearty service, and to let him know that I writ him this very day: for I find our letters sometimes miscarry of late. If he be not in town now, you will favour me by letting me know if he was in good health when last you saw him.

---

[1] **François de Malherbe**, the Father of French Poetry, 1555-1628. Balzac, his disciple, thus wittily describes his well-known *Grammatical* tyranny.—" Vous vous souvenez," he writes to a friend, " du vieux pedagogue de la Cour [of Henri IV.] qu'on appeloit autrefois le tyran des mots et des syllables, et qui s'appeloit lui-même, lorsqu' il étoit en bonne humeur, 'le grammairien en lunettes et en cheveux gris.' J'ai pitié d'un homme, qui fait de si grandes différences entre *pas* et *point*, qui traite l'affaire des *gérondifs* et des *participes* comme si c'étoit celle de deux peuples voisins l'un de l'autre, et jaloux de leurs frontières."

He wrote Odes and Sonnets. The *Ode à Du Perrier Sur la Mort de sa Fille* is one of his best productions. Boileau gives him high praise as the refiner of French Poetry. Malherbe also translated some of Seneca's *Letters*.

To Mr. Henry Cromwell.

July 17, 1709.

The morning after I parted with you I found myself, as I had prophesied, all alone, in an uneasy stage-coach—a doleful change from that agreeable company I enjoyed the night before—without the least hope of entertainment but from my last recourse in such cases, a book. I then began to enter into acquaintance with the Moralists, and had just received from them some cold consolation for the inconveniences of this life, and the uncertainty of human affairs, when I perceived my vehicle to stop, and heard from the side of it the dreadful news of a sick woman preparing to enter it. It is not very easy to guess at my mortification, but, being so well fortified with philosophy, I stood resigned with a stoical constancy to endure the worst of evils, a sick woman. I was, indeed, a little comforted to find by her voice and dress that she was young and a gentlewoman; but no sooner was her hood removed, but I saw one of the finest faces I ever beheld and, to increase my surprise, heard her salute me by my name.

I had never more reason to accuse Nature for making me short-sighted than now, when I could not recollect I had ever seen those fair eyes which knew me so well; and was utterly at a loss how to address myself, till, with a great deal of simplicity and innocence, she let me know (even before I discovered my ignorance) that she was the daughter of one in our neighbourhood, lately married, who, having been consulting her physicians in town, was returning into the country to try what good air and a new husband could do to recover her. My father, you must know, has sometimes recommended the study of physic to me, but the devil take me if ever I had any ambition to be a doctor till this instant. I ventured to prescribe her some fruit, which I happened to have in the coach, which, being forbidden by her damned doctors, she had the more inclination to. In short, I tempted and she ate; nor was I more like the devil than she like Eve. Having the good success of the foresaid gentleman before my eyes, I put on the gallantry of the old serpent, and, in spite of my evil form, accosted her with all the gaiety I was master of, which had so good effect that in less than an hour she grew pleasant, her colour returned, and she was pleased to say my prescription had wrought an immediate cure. In a word, I had the pleasantest journey imaginable. . . .

TO MR. STEELE.[1]

December 30, 1711.

I have passed part of this Christmas with some honest country gentlemen, who have wit enough to be good-natured but no manner of relish for criticism or polite writing, as you may easily conclude, when I tell you they never read the *Spectator*. This was the reason I did not not see that of the 20th till yesterday at my return home, wherein, though it be the highest satisfaction to find oneself commended by a person whom all the world commends, yet I am not more obliged to you for that than for your candour and frankness in acquainting me with the error I have been guilty of, in speaking too freely of my brother moderns.[2]

[1] Formerly wrongly printed with superscription to Addison. The letter has no address, and was handed on to Addison by Steele, to whom it is especially addressed.

[2] In his *Essay on Criticism* published this year. "I am sorry to find," says the *Spectator* (Dec. 20), "that an author, who is very justly esteemed among the best judges, has admitted some strokes of this nature into a very fine poem, I mean the *Art of Criticism*, which was published some months since, and is a masterpiece of its kind."

It is, indeed, the common method of all counterfeits in wit, as well as in physic, to begin with warning us of others' cheats in order to make the more way for their own. But, if ever this Essay be thought worth a second edition, I shall be very glad to strike out all such strokes which you shall be so kind as to point out to me. I shall really be proud of being corrected, for I believe it is with the errors of the mind as with the weeds of a field, which, if they are consumed upon the place, enrich and improve it more than if none had ever grown there. Some of the faults of that book I have myself found, and more, I am confident, others have—enough, at least, to have made me very humble had not you given this public approbation of it, which I can look upon only as the effect of that benevolence you have ever been so ready to show to any who but make it their endeavour to do well. But, as a little rain revives a flower, which too much over-charges and depresses, so moderate praise encourages a young writer; but a great deal may injure him. And you have been so lavish in this point, that I almost hope— not to call in question your judgment of the piece—that it was some particular partial inclination to the author which carried you so far. This would please me more than I can express, for I should, in good earnest, be fonder of your friendship than the world's applause. I might hope, too, to deserve it better, since a man may more easily answer for his own sincerity than his own wit. And, if the highest esteem built on the justest ground in the world, together with gratitude for an obligation so unexpectedly conferred, can oblige a man to be ever yours, I beg you to believe no one is more so than, Sir, your most faithful and obedient humble servant.[1]

[1] To this letter Steele briefly replied, Jan. 20, 1711-12: "I have received your very kind letter. That part, which is grounded upon your belief that I have much affection and friendship for you, I receive with great pleasure. That, which acknowledges the honour done to your *Essay*, I have no pretence to. The paper was written by one with whom I will make you acquainted, which is the best return I can make to you for your favour to, Sir, &c."

To the Hon. James Craggs.[1]

May 20, 1712.

It is not only the disposition I always have of conversing with you, that makes me so speedily answer your obliging letter, but the apprehension lest your charitable intent of writing to my Lady A. on Mrs. W's affair[2] should be frustrated by the short stay she makes there. She went thither on the 25th, with that mixture of expectation and anxiety with which people usually go into unknown or half-discovered countries, utterly ignorant of the disposition of the inhabitants, and the treatment they are to meet with. The unfortunate, of all people, are the most unfit to be left alone. Yet, we see, the world generally takes care they shall be so; whereas, if we took a considerate prospect of the world, the business and study of the happy and easy should be to divert and humour as well as comfort and pity the distressed.

I cannot, therefore, excuse some near allies of mine for their conduct of late towards this lady, which has given me a great deal of anger as well as sorrow. All I shall say to you of them at present is, that they have not been my *relations* these two months. The consent of opinions, in our minds, is certainly a nearer tie than can be contracted by all the blood in our bodies; and I am proud of finding I have something congenial with you. Will you permit me to confess to you, that all the favours

[1] Few persons appear to have enjoyed a greater share of the confidence and friendship of Pope than the younger Craggs. . . . After filling several confidential employments, and being sent to Hanover in 1714, he was appointed Secretary of State, and died in the year 1720. He was buried in Westminster Abbey. See his Epitaph by Pope.—Roscoe.

[2] Mrs. Weston. She was the "Unfortunate Lady," over whose story so much mystery has hung; for Pope himself refused to answer the question which was put to him *twice* by his friend, Caryll, respecting her name. She was related to the Duke of Buckingham, and, possibly, Craggs means the Duchess by "my Lady A."—Bowles.

and kind offices, you have shewn towards me, have not so strongly cemented me yours as the discovery of that generous and manly compassion you manifested in the case of this unhappy lady? I am afraid to insinuate to you how much I esteem you. Flatterers have taken up the style which was once peculiar to friends, and an honest man has now no way left to express himself, besides the common one of knaves. . . . Yours, &c.[1]

TO MR. STEELE.

Nov. 16, 1712.

You oblige me by the indulgence you have shown to the poem I sent you,[2] but will oblige me much more by the kind severity I hope for from you. No errors are so trivial, but they deserve to be mended; but, since you say you see nothing that may be called a fault, can you not think it so—that I have confined the

---

[1] "I have," writes Craggs rather enigmatically, a few days earlier, "since I saw you, corresponded with Mrs. W. I hope she is now with her aunt, and that her journey thither was something facilitated by my writing to that lady as pressingly as possible, not to let anything whatever obstruct it. I sent her obliging answer to the party it most concerned; and, when I hear Mrs. W. is certainly there, I will write again to my Lady, to urge as much as possible the effecting the only thing that, in my opinion, can make her niece easy." As to the identity of the "Unfortunate Lady" with Mrs. Weston, see *Life and Writings of Pope*.

[2] A few days previously (Nov. 12), Steele had written to Pope a highly complimentary and friendly note: "I have read over your *Temple of Fame* twice, and cannot find anything amiss, of weight enough to call a fault, but see in it a thousand, thousand beauties. Mr. Addison shall see it to-morrow. After his perusal of it, I will let you know his thoughts." He adds: "I desire you would let me know whether you are at leisure or not. I have a design [to bring out the *Guardian*, which first appeared March 12, 1713], which I shall open a month or two hence, with the assistance of the few like yourself. If your thoughts are unengaged, I shall explain myself further."

attendance of guardian spirits to Heaven's favourites only?[1] I could point you to several; but it is my business to be informed of those faults I do not know, and, as for those I do, not to talk of them but to correct them. You speak of that poem in a style I neither merit nor expect; but, I assure you, if you freely mark or dash out, I shall look upon your blots to be its greatest beauties. I mean, if Mr. Addison and yourself should like it in the whole. Otherwise, the trouble of correction is what I would not take; for I was really so diffident of it, as to let it lie by me these two years; just as you now see it. I am afraid of nothing so much as to impose anything on the world, which is unworthy of its acceptance.

As to the last period of your letter, I shall be very ready and glad to contribute to any design that tends to the advantage of mankind which, I am sure, all yours do. I wish I had but as much capacity as leisure, for I am perfectly idle—a sign I have not much capacity.

If you will entertain the best opinion of me, be pleased to think me your friend. Assure Mr. Addison of my most faithful service. Of every one's esteem he must be assured already.

To Mr. John Caryll.

London, April 30, 1713.

I think it very happy for me that the circumstances of our friendship are so much changed since I first knew you, as it now requires an excuse when I do not write to you, no less than

[1] This is not now to be found in the *Temple of Fame*, of which poem he speaks here.—Pope, 1735. *Gil Blas* was not yet published, otherwise we might fancy Steele to have had in memory the Archbishop of Granada.

it once required one when I did. I can assure you nothing less
than the pardon you freely promised me when last I saw you, in
case of such omission on my part, could have made me satisfied
so long without accosting you by way of letter. I have been
almost every day employed in following your advice in learning
to paint, in which I am most particularly obliged to Mr. Jervas,[1]
who gives me daily instructions and examples. As to poetical
affairs, I am content at present to be a bare looker on, and from
a practitioner turn an admirer, which is, as the world goes, not
very usual. Cato was not so much the wonder of Rome itself,
in his days, as he is of Britain in ours; and, though all the
foolish industry has been used to make it a party play,[2] yet, what
the author once said of another may be the most properly in the
world applied to him on this occasion:—

"Envy itself is dumb, in wonder lost,
And factions strive who shall applaud him most." [3]

The numerous and violent claps of the Whig party, on the one
side the theatre, were echoed back by the Tories on the other,
while the author sweated behind the scenes with concern to find
their applause proceeded more from the hand than the head.
This was the case too of the prologue-writer, who was clapped
into a staunch Whig, sore against his will, at almost every two
lines. I believe you have heard that, after all the applause of
the opposite factions, my Lord Bolingbroke sent for Booth, who
played *Cato*, into the box, between one of the Acts, and presented
him with fifty guineas in acknowledgment, as he expressed it,
for his defending the cause of Liberty so well against a perpetual
dictator. The Whigs are unwilling to be distanced this way, as

---

[1] The fashionable portrait painter of the time, a pupil of Kneller, died in 1739. He was, also, a translator of *Don Quixote*.—See *Life and Writings of Pope*.

[2] Addison's *Cato* had just been put upon the stage, where it had a run of thirty-five nights.

[3] Addison's *Campaign*.

it is said, and therefore design a present to the said Cato very speedily. In the meantime, they are getting ready as good a sentence as the former on their side. So betwixt them it is probable that Cato, as Dr. Garth expressed it, may have something to live upon after he dies.

The Play was published but this Monday, and Mr. Lewis tells me it is not possible to convey it to you before Friday next. The town is so fond of it, that the orange wenches and fruit-women in the park offer the books at the side of the coaches, and the prologue and epilogue are cried about the streets by the common hawkers. But, of all the world, none have been in so peculiar a manner enamoured with *Cato* as a young gentleman of Oxford, who makes it the sole guide of all his actions and subject of all his discourse. He dates everything from the first or third night, &c., of *Cato:* he goes out of town every day it is not played, and fell in love with Mrs. Oldfield for no other reason than because she acted Cato's daughter.

But I find myself just at the end of my paper, and have only room to assure you that I should write with more ceremony and care if I loved and esteemed you less, and to entreat the continuance of your obliging letters and wonted favours to, dear Sir, your ever obliged, affectionate, humble servant.

To Mr. John Caryll.

London, June 12, 1713.

I have been prevented in the design of writing to you by several, who have told me you would certainly be here in a few days. But I find this happiness, like most others, still farther off the nearer we fancy we approach them. I therefore resolved no longer to delay the pleasure

I always take in assuring you how faithfully I am yours.

As I hope, and would flatter myself, that you know me and my thoughts so entirely as never to be mistaken in either, so it is a pleasure to me that you guessed so right in regard to the author of that *Guardian* you mentioned, but am sorry to find it has taken air that I have some hand in those papers; because I write so very few as neither to deserve the credit of such a report with some people, nor the disrepute of it with others. An honest Jacobite, that we met on the 10th of June, spoke to me the sense, or nonsense, of the weak part of his party very fairly and innocently—that the good people took it very ill of me that I write with Steele, though upon never so indifferent subjects. This I know you will laugh at, as well as myself; yet I doubt not but many little calumniators and persons of soured dispositions will take occasion hence to bespatter me. I confess I scorn narrow souls of all parties; and if I renounce my reason in religious matters, I will never do it in any other affair. But enough of this trifle. One word, however, of a private trifle. Honest Mr. Englefield has not shown the least common civility to my father and mother by sending, or inquiring of them from our nearest neighbours, his visitants, or any otherwise, these five months. I take the hint as I ought, in respect to those who gave me being, and he shall be as much a stranger to me as he desires. I ought to prepare myself by such small trials for those numerous friendships of this sort which, in all probability, I shall meet with in the course of my life.

I shall stay in town yet this afternoon, or thereabouts, in which time, if you come, you will find me in the close pursuit of the advice you gave me three months since, painting at Mr. Jervas's in Cleveland Court by St. James's. I generally employ the mornings this way, and the evenings in the conversation of such as I think can most improve my mind, of whatever party or denomination they are. . . .

Adriani Morientis ad Animam.[1]

Poor, little, pretty fluttering thing!
  Must we no longer live together?
And dost thou prune thy doubtful wing,
  To take thy flight thou know'st not whither?

Thy humorous vein, thy pleasing folly,
  Lies all neglected, all forgot,
And pensive, wavering, melancholy,
  Thou dread'st, and hop'st, thou know'st not what!

The same by another hand—

Ah, fleeting spirit! wandering fire,
  That long hast warmed my tender breast,
Must thou no more this frame inspire?
  No more a pleasing, cheerful guest?

Whither, ah whither, art thou flying?
  To what dark, undiscovered shore?
Thou seem'st all trembling, shivering, dying,
  And wit and humour are no more.

Christiani Morientis Ad Animam.

Vital spark of heavenly flame,
Dost thou quit this mortal frame?
Trembling, hoping, ling'ring, flying,
Oh! the pain, the bliss of dying!
Cease, fond Nature, cease thy strife,
And let me languish into life![2] &c.

[1] The first version of this well-known epigram of the Emperor Hadrian (*Animula, Vagula, Blandula,* &c.,) is by Prior. These stanzas appear thus abruptly in the MS.

[2] The only variation, in the final edition of this stanza, is in the second line, where the imperative takes the place of the interrogative form.

I desire your opinion of these verses, and which are best written. They are of three different hands.¹

TO MR GAY.

August 23, 1713.

Just as I received yours I was set down to write to you, with some shame that I had so long deferred it. But I can hardly repent my neglect when it gives me the knowledge how little you insist upon ceremony, and how much a greater share in your memory I have than I deserve. I have been near a week in London, where I am like to remain, till I become, by Mr. Jervas's help, *elegans formarum spectator*.² I begin to discover beauties that were till now imperceptible to me. Every corner of an eye, or turn of a nose or ear, the smallest degree of light or shade on a cheek, or in a dimple, have charms to distract me. I no longer look upon Lord Plausible as ridiculous for admiring a lady's fine tip of an ear, and pretty elbows, as the Plain Dealer³ has it, but am in some danger even from the ugly and disagreeable, since they may have their retired beauties in one trait or other about them.

You may guess in how uneasy a state I am, when every day the performances of others appear more beautiful and excellent,

---

¹ Pope's version, or rather imitation, "Vital spark of heavenly flame, &c.," in spite of his disingenuous attempts, in his correspondence, to make it appear quite otherwise, "as just warm from the brain," underwent two or three revisions, the last of which was made in 1736, and appeared in Lintot's edition of his works. A letter to Steele, on these verses, appears in the various editions of Pope's Correspondence. It seems, however, to be one of Pope's numerous "adaptations."

² See Letter to Caryll, April 30, 1713, in which he tells him that he has been following his advice in learning to paint.

³ A Comedy of his friend Wycherley (1677).

and my own more despicable. I have thrown away three Dr. Swifts, each of which was once my vanity, two Lady Bridgewaters,[1] a Duchess of Montague, besides half-a-dozen Earls, and one Knight of the Garter.[2] I have crucified Christ over again in effigy, and made a Madonna as old as her mother St. Anne. Nay, what is yet more miraculous, I have rivalled St. Luke himself in painting; and, as it is said an angel came and finished his piece, so you would swear a devil put the last hand to mine, it is so begrimed and smutted. However, I comfort myself with a Christian reflection, that I have not broken the commandment, for my pictures are not the likeness of anything in heaven above, or the earth below, or in the waters under the earth.[3] Neither will anybody adore or worship them, except the Indians should have a sight of them, who, they tell us, worship certain pagods and idols purely for their ugliness.

I am very much recreated and refreshed with the news of the advancement of the *Fan*,[4] which, I doubt not, will delight the eye and sense of the fair, as long as that agreeable machine shall play in the hands of Posterity. I am glad your *Fan* is mounted so soon; but I would have you varnish and glaze it at your leisure, and polish the sticks as much as you can. You may then cause it to be borne in the hands of both sexes, no less in Britain than it is in China, where it is ordinary for a Mandarin to fan himself cool after a debate, and a Statesman to hide his face with it when he tells a grave lie.

[1] Daughters of the first Duke of Marlborough. Jervas, according to Horace Walpole, transferred the charms of Lady Bridgewater "to many a homely dame."

[2] They were no doubt copies. Lord Mansfield possesses a copy of Kneller's portrait of Betterton [the Actor], which is reputed to have been done by Pope.—E.

[3] This is a repetition of Arbuthnot's sarcasm on Pope's master, Jervas. As he was talking [as a free thinker], Arbuthnot said to him: "You are a *practical* believer. You strictly observe the second commandment, for, in your pictures, you make not the 'likeness,' &c."—E.

[4] *The Fan*, a somewhat feeble production of Gay, was published at the beginning of 1714.

To Mr. Gay.

Oct. 23, 1713.

I have been perpetually troubled with sickness of late, which has made me so melancholy, that the immortality of the soul has been my constant speculation, as the mortality of the body my constant plague. In good earnest, Seneca is nothing to a fit of illness.

Dr. Parnell will honour Tonson's *Miscellany*[1] with some very beautiful copies, at my request. He enters heartily into our design. I only fear his stay in town may chance to be but short. Dr. Swift much approves what I proposed, even to the very title, which I design shall be *The Works of the Unlearned*, published monthly, in which whatever book appears that deserves praise shall be depreciated ironically, and in the same manner that modern critics take to undervalue works of value and to commend the high productions of Grub Street.[2]

I shall go into the country about a month hence, and shall then desire to take along with me your poem of the *Fan*, to consider it at full leisure. I am deeply engaged in poetry,[3] the particulars whereof shall be deferred till we meet. I am very desirous of seeing Mr. Fortescue[4] when he comes to town, before his journey. If you can, in any way, acquaint him of my desire, I believe his good nature will contrive a way for our meeting. I am ever, with all sincerity, &c.

---

[1] Edited by Steele, and published by Tonson, in 1714.—E.

[2] This project came to nothing, and could not have been long continued with effect. The irony would have lost its relish by repetition.—E.

[3] In revising the *Rape of the Lock*, among other things.

[4] Afterwards Master of the Rolls.

To Dean Swift.[1]

Binfield, Dec. 8, 1713.

Not to trouble you at present with a recital of all my obligations to you, I shall only mention two things, which I take particularly kind of you—your desire that I should write to you, and your proposal of giving me twenty guineas to change my religion; which last you must please to give me leave to make the subject of this letter.

Sure no clergyman ever offered so much out of his own purse for the sake of any religion. It is almost as many pieces of gold as an Apostle could get of silver, from the priests of old, on a much more valuable consideration. I believe it will be better worth my while to propose a change of my faith by subscription than a translation of Homer. And, to convince you how well disposed I am to the Reformation, I shall be content, if you will prevail with my Lord Treasurer and the Ministry to rise to the same sum each of them, on this pious account, as my Lord Halifax has done on the profane one. I am afraid there is no being at once a poet and a good Christian; and I am very much straitened between the two, while the Whigs seem willing to contribute as much to continue me the one as you would to make me the other. But, if you can move every man in the Government, who has above ten thousand pounds a year, to subscribe as much as yourself, I should become a convert, as most men do, when the Lord turns it to my interest. I know they have the truth of religion so much at heart, that they would certainly give more to have one good subject translated from Popery o the Church of England than twenty heathenish authors out of any unknown tongue into ours. I, therefore, commission

[1] This is the opening of the correspondence between these celebrated men, which began in favours on Swift's part, and gratitude on that part of Pope, and ended in the most strict friendship on both.—Scott.

you, Mr. Dean, with full authority to transact this affair in my name, and to propose as follows:—

First, that as to the head of our Church, the Pope, I may engage to renounce his power, whensoever I shall receive any particular indulgences from the head of your Church, the Queen. As to Communion in one kind, I shall also promise to change it for Communion in both, as soon as the Ministry will allow me. For Invocation to Saints, mine shall be turned to Dedications to Sinners, when I shall find the great ones of this world as willing to do me any good as I believe those of the other are.

You see I shall not be obstinate in the main points: but there is one article I must reserve, and which you seemed not unwilling to allow me, Prayer for the Dead. There are people to whose souls I wish as well as to my own; and I must crave leave humbly to lay before them that, though the subscriptions above mentioned will suffice for myself, there are necessary perquisites and additions which I must demand on the score of this charitable article. It is, also, to be considered, that the greater part of those whose souls I am most concerned for were, unfortunately, heretics, schismatics, poets, painters, or persons of such lives and manners as few or no churches are willing to save. The expense will, therefore, be the greater to make an effectual provision for the said souls. Old Dryden, though a Roman Catholic, was a poet; and it is revealed in the visions of some ancient saints, that no poet was ever saved under some hundreds of masses. I cannot set his delivery from Purgatory at less than fifty pounds sterling. Walsh was not only a Socinian but (what *you* will own is harder to be saved) a Whig. He cannot, modestly, be rated at less than a hundred. L'Estrange, being a Tory, we compute him but at twenty pounds; which, I hope, no friend of the party can deny to give, to keep him from damning in the next life, considering they never gave him sixpence to keep him from starving in this.

All this together amounts to one hundred and seventy pounds.

In the next place, I must desire you to represent that there are several of my friends, yet living, whom I design, God willing, to outlive, in consideration of legacies; out of which it is a doctrine, in the Reformed Church, that not a farthing shall be allowed to save their souls who gave them. There is one * * who will die within these few months with * * one Mr. Jervas, who hath grievously offended, in making the likeness of almost all things in heaven above and earth below. And one Mr. Gay, an unhappy youth, who writes Pastorals during the time of divine service; whose case is the more deplorable, as he hath miserably lavished away all that silver he should have reserved for his soul's health, in buttons and hoops for his coat.

I cannot pretend to have these people honestly saved under some hundred pounds, whether you consider the difficulty of such a work, or the extreme love and tenderness I bear them, which will infallibly make me push this charity as far as I am able.

There is but one more whose salvation I insist upon, and then I have done; but, indeed, it may prove of so much greater charge than all the rest, that I will only lay the case before you and the Ministry, and leave to their prudence and generosity what sum they shall think fit to bestow on it. The person I mean is Dr. Swift : a dignified clergyman, but one who, by his own confession, has composed more libels than sermons. If it be true, what I have heard often affirmed by innocent people, that too much wit is dangerous to salvation, this unfortunate gentleman must certainly be damned to all eternity. But I hope his long experience in the world, and frequent conversation with great men, will cause him (as it has some others) to have less and less wit every day. Be it as it will, I should not think my own soul deserved to be saved, if I did not endeavour to save his; for I have all the obligations in nature to him. He has brought me into better company than I cared for, made me merrier when I was sick than I had a mind to be, and put me on making poems on purpose that he might alter them.

I once thought I never could have discharged my debt to his kindness; but have lately been informed, to my unspeakable comfort, that I have more than paid all. For Monsieur de Montaigne has assured me, "That the person who receives a benefit obliges the giver," for, since the chief endeavour of one friend is to do good to the other, he who administers both the matter and occasion is the man who is liberal. At this rate, it is impossible that Dr. Swift should ever be out of my debt, as matters stand already; and, for the future, he may expect daily more obligations from his most faithful, affectionate, humble servant.

I have finished the *Rape of the Lock*, but I believe I may stay here till Christmas without hindrance of business.

To Mr. John Caryll.

London, Jan. 9, 1713-14.

Though I believe I am one of the last who have congratulated yourself and Mr. Caryll upon the birth of his first-born, yet this I dare assure you both, that no man is more rejoiced at that blessing, except the father, unless you will require me to speak more correctly, and say, except the grandfather too. I ought also to felicitate you, in particular, that you are so early arrived to the dignity of a patriarch, and that you can bear that venerable name without the stooping in the shoulders, and that length of beard, which I have observed to denote one of those sires in all the representations of them hitherto. I cannot flatter your son so far as to say anything fine upon the beauty of the babe, or the near resemblance it has to his own lineaments, not having yet the pleasure of conversing with the nurse upon that agreeable subject. But I am told here, that few statues of Phidias or Praxiteles themselves made so good a figure the first month of their appearing.

I am thoroughly sensible of your most righteous endeavours to serve me in my new capacity of a Greek translator, and I hope, by the assistance of such solicitors as Mr. Caryll, to make Homer's works of more value and benefit to me than ever they were to himself. What I have, in particular, to desire further is, that you will send me the subscriptions by the first sitting of the Parliament,[1] at which time it will be necessary for me to know exactly what number we have secure,—there being then to be printed a list of those who already have subscribed, or shall, to that time, upon the credit and figure of which persons a great part of the success with the town will inevitably depend. I now think it pretty certain that I shall be warmly supported on all sides in this undertaking.

As to the *Rape of the Lock*, I believe I have managed the dedication so nicely, that it can neither hurt the lady nor the author.[2] I writ it very lately, and upon great deliberation. The young lady approves of it, and the best advice in the kingdom, of the men of sense, has been made use of in it, even to the Treasurer's [Lord Oxford's]. A preface, which salved the lady's honour, without affixing her name, was also prepared, but by herself superseded in favour of the dedication. Not but that, after all, fools will talk, and fools will hear them.

I wish you could inform me, by the most convenient opportunity, how the matter stands as to the foreign affair. I suppose you had no concern in the *rentes viagères*. This misfortune

---

[1] Pope's proposals for the translation of the *Iliad* were issued in October, 1713. Parliament met on the 18th of February.—E.

[2] The revised, or "full edition," as it was called, of the *Rape of the Lock* came out on the 2nd of March.

will go near to ruin me, it being more especially my concern than my father's.[1] I shall revenge myself on the mighty monarch by giving the more spirit to what Homer says of the injustice of kings. I was beginning to think I would go and live upon Mr. John Caryll [the younger], but have lost all my hopes since he has a child, unless he will maintain me as his huntsman. Believe me, dear Sir, under all circumstances whatever, and in all respects whatever, with the last sincerity and deference, your most obliged and most faithful friend and servant.

My most humble service attend all your good family, even from the grandsire to the grandson. I shall be in London all the winter.

To Mr. John Caryll.

May 1, 1714.

Your letter found me at Binfield, very busy in my grand undertaking,[2] to which I must wholly give myself up for some time, unless when I snatch an hour to please myself with a distant conversation with you and one or two more, by writing a line or two. I am much afraid I ought not to trust myself at Ladyholt so soon as you mention. The pleasures of that place

---

[1] The elder Pope, in July, 1707, had invested 5,220 livres in an annuity on his son's life, at 10 per cent., which is what makes the poet say that it was more his concern than his father's. His notion that the loss [caused by the reduction in the rate of interest by the French Government] would go far to ruin him arose from a report that the annuities posterior to 1706 were to be reduced one-half, whereas this provision applied only to those which were granted since 1710. As some compensation for so arbitrary a measure, the creditors were promised more punctual payment, and a remission of the *dîme* or income-tax.—E.

[2] The translation of the *Iliad*.

will take up my head too much to suffer even poetry to enter into competition with them, and Homer himself will have too powerful a rival in Mr. Caryll. If I knew your time of returning to Grinstead, I believe I could be more easy for a month after the heat of the work was over, though not more happy. It is no comfortable prospect to be reflecting, as else I must, that so long a siege as that of Troy lies upon my hands, and the campaign above half over before I have made any progress. I must confess the Greek fortification does not appear so formidable as it did, upon a nearer approach; and I am almost apt to flatter myself that Homer secretly seems inclined to correspond with me, in letting me into a good part of his designs. There are, indeed, a sort of underling auxiliars to the difficulty of the work, called commentators and critics, who would frighten many people by their number and bulk. These lie entrenched in the ditches, and are secure only in the dirt they have heaped about them, with the great pains in the collecting it. But, I think, we have found a method of coming at the main works by a more speedy and gallant way than by mining under ground; that is, by using the poetical engines, wings, and flying thither over their heads.

While I am engaged in the fight, I find you are concerned how I shall be paid,[1] and are soliciting with all your might that I may not have the ill-fate of many discarded generals, to be first envied and maligned, then perhaps praised, and, lastly, neglected. The former, the constant attendant upon all great and laudable enterprises, I have already experienced. Some have said I am not a master in the Greek, who either are so themselves or are not. If they are not, they cannot tell; and if they are, they cannot without having catechised me. But if they can read (for I know some critics can, and others cannot),

---

[1] For the *Iliad*, completed in 1720, Pope received about £5,000; for the *Odyssey*, finished in 1725, he received between £3,000 and £4,000, exclusive of the sums he paid to Fenton and Broome, who had largely assisted him.

there are fairly lying before them and all the world some specimens of my translation from this author in the *Miscellanies*,[1] which they are heartily welcome to. I have also encountered much malignity on the score of religion, some calling me a papist and a Tory; the latter, because the heads of the Party have been distinguishingly favourable to me; but why the former, I cannot imagine, but that Mr. Caryll and Mr. E. Blount have laboured to serve me. Others have styled me a Whig, because I have been honoured with Mr. Addison's good word, and Mr. Jervas's good deeds,[2] and, of late, with my Lord Halifax's patronage. How much more rational a conclusion would it be, to any good-natured man, to think a person, who has been favoured by all sides, has been inoffensive to all.

This miserable Age is so sunk between animosities of party and those of religion, that I begin to fear most men have politics enough to make the best scheme of government a bad one, through their extremity of violence, and faith enough to hinder their salvation. I hope, for my own part, never to have more of either than is consistent with common justice and charity, and always so much as becomes a Christian and honest man—that is, just as much as you. Though I find it an unfortunate thing to be bred a papist, when one is obnoxious to four parts in five as being so too much, and to the fifth part for being so too little, I shall yet be easy under both their mistakes, and be what I more than seem to be, for I suffer for it. God is my witness, that I no more envy the Protestants their places and possessions than I do our priests their charity or learning. I

[1] The arrival of Ulysses in Ithaca, and the Garden of Alcinous, from the *Odyssey*, in Steele's *Miscellany*, 1714; and the episode of Sarpedon, in Tonson's *Miscellanies*, 1709.—E.

[2] In the edition of his Letters of 1735 Pope omitted the names of his catholic friends, Caryll and Blount, and substituted Congreve and Craggs for Addison and Jervas.—E. Pope, as is abundantly evident from his correspondence, knew sufficiently well how to be "all things to all men," and his letters to his free-thinking friends such as Lord Bolingbroke are in a different (theological) strain from his letters to his papist correspondents.

am ambitious of nothing but the good opinion of all good men of all sides, for I know that one virtue of a free spirit is more worth than all the virtues put together of all the narrow-souled people in the world. If they promise me all the good offices they ever did, or could do, I would not change for them all one kind word of yours. I am entirely, dear Sir, your obliged and faithful friend and servant.[1]

TO MR. GAY.[2]

Binfield, May 4, 1714.

Above all other news send us the best—that of your good health, if you enjoy it, which Mr. Harcourt made us very much fear. If you have any design either to amend your health or your life, I know no better expedient than to come hither, where you should not want room, though I lay, myself, on a truckle bed under the doctor [Parnell]. You might here converse with the old Greeks, be initiated into all their customs, and learn their prayers by heart as we have done.[3] The doctor last Sunday, intending to say *Our Father*, was got half-way in Chryses' prayer to Apollo. The ill effects of contention and squabbling, so lively described in the first *Iliad*, make Dr. Parnell and myself continue in the most exemplary union in everything. We deserve to be worshipped by all the poor, divided, factious, interested, poets of this world.

As we rise in our speculations daily, we are grown so grave,

[1] The greater part of this letter is published in the edition of 1735 as addressed to Addison, and is dated January 30, 1713-14.

[2] This letter [written jointly by Pope and Dr. Parnell] first appeared in the P. T. volume, and was omitted by Pope from his later Collections.—E.

[3] Pope was then engaged upon his translation, or rather paraphrase, of the *Iliad*.

that we have not condescended to laugh at any of the idle things about us this week. I have contracted a severity of aspect from deep meditation on high subjects, equal to the formidable front of black-browed Jupiter, and become an awful nod as well, when I assent to some grave and weighty proposition of the doctor or enforce a criticism of my own. In a word, Young himself has not acquired more tragic majesty in his aspect by reading his own verses than I by Homer's. In this state, I cannot consent to your publication of that ludicrous trifling burlesque you write about. Dr. Parnell, also, joins in my opinion that it will by no means be well to print it.

Pray give, with the utmost fidelity and esteem, my hearty service to the Dean, Dr. Arbuthnot, Mr. Ford, and Mr. Fortescue. Let them also know at Button's that I am mindful of them. I am, divine Bucoliast! thy loving countryman.[1]

To Miss Arabella Fermor.[2]

1714.

It will be in vain to deny that I have some regard for this Piece, since I dedicate it to you. Yet you may bear me witness, it was intended only to divert a few young ladies, who have good sense and good humour enough to laugh not only at their sex's little unguarded follies but at their own. But, as it was communicated with the air of a secret, it soon found its way into the world. An imperfect copy having been offered to a bookseller, you had the good nature, for my sake, to consent to the publication of one more correct. This I was forced to

[1] This refers to the Address to the reader in the *Shepherd's Week*, which is signed "Thy loving countryman, John Gay."—E.
[2] This letter was prefixed to the 1714 ed. of the *Rape of the Lock*.

before I had executed half my design; for the machinery was entirely wanting to complete it.

The *machinery*, Madam, is a term invented by the critics to signify that part which the deities, angels, or demons are made to act in a poem. For the ancient poets are, in one respect, like many modern young ladies. Let an action be never so trivial in itself, they always make it appear of the utmost importance.[1] These *machines* I determined to raise on a very new and odd foundation, the Rosicrucian doctrine of Spirits. I know how disagreeable it is to make use of hard words before a lady, but 'tis so much the concern of a poet to have his works understood, and particularly by your sex, that you must give me leave to explain two or three difficult terms.

The Rosicrucians [2] are a people I must bring you acquainted with. The best account I know of them is in a French book called *Le Comte de Gabalis*, which, both in its title and size, is so like a novel that many of the fair sex have read it for one by mistake. According to these gentlemen, the four elements are inhabited by Spirits, which they call Sylphs, Gnomes, Nymphs, and Salamanders. The Gnomes, or demons of Earth, delight in mischief; but the Sylphs, whose habitation is in the Air, are the best conditioned creatures imaginable. For they say any mortals may enjoy the most intimate familiarities with these gentle spirits, upon a condition very easy to all true Adepts—an inviolable preservation of chastity.

As to the following Cantos, all the passages of them are as fabulous as the Vision at the beginning, or the Transformation

---

[1] This, we may, with some probability, take to be a sort of sly revenge, skilfully contrived, on Miss Fermor for her resentment at the part she was made to play in the *Rape of the Lock* as it first appeared.

[2] Literally the *Dew-Cross* (Ros-Crux) alchymists, or searchers after the "philosopher's stone;" so styled because they held dew to be the most powerful solvent of the *Cross*, their cabalistic term for the grosser part of the atmosphere, by the proper solution of which they expected to find the grand object of all their vain labours—Gold.

at the end (except the loss of your hair, which I always mention with reverence). All the human persons are as fictitious as the airy ones; and the character of Belinda, as it is now managed, resembles you in nothing but in beauty. If this poem had as many graces as there are in your person or in your mind, yet I could never hope it should pass through the world half so uncensured as you have done. But let its fortune be what it will, mine is happy enough to have given me this occasion of assuring you that I am, with the truest esteem, Madam, your most obedient, humble servant.

TO MISS ARABELLA FERMOR.[1]

1714.

You are by this time satisfied how much the tenderness of one man of merit is to be preferred to the addresses of a thousand. And, by this time, the gentleman you have made choice of is sensible how great is the joy of having all those charms and good qualities, which have pleased so many, now applied to please one only. It was but just that the same virtues, which give you reputation, should give you happiness; and I can wish you no greater than that you may receive it in as high a degree yourself, as so much good humour must infallibly give it to your husband.

It may be expected, perhaps, that one who has the title of poet should say something more polite on this occasion; but I am really more a well-wisher to your felicity than a celebrator of your beauty. Besides, you are now a married woman, and in a

[1] On her marriage. This letter was prefixed to the 1714 edition of the *Rape of the Lock*, and was published with the consent of the lady. See letter to Caryll, January 9, 1713-14.—C. W. D.

way to be a great many better things than a fine lady; such as an excellent wife, a faithful friend, a tender parent, and at last, as a consequence of them all, a saint in heaven. You ought now to hear nothing but that which was all you ever desired to hear (whatever others may have spoken to you)—I mean, truth. And it is with the utmost that I assure you, no friend you have can more rejoice in any good that befalls you, is more sincerely delighted with the prospect of your future happiness, or more unfeignedly desires a long continuance of it.

I hope you will think it but just that a man, who will certainly be spoken of as your admirer after he is dead, may have the happiness to be esteemed one while he is living.

To Dr. Parnell.[1]

Binfield near Oakingham, Tuesday. [May ?], 1714.

I believe the hurry you were in hindered your giving me a word by the last post, so that I am yet to learn whether you got well to town, or continue so there. I very much fear both for your health and your quiet—and no man living can be more truly concerned in anything that touches either than myself. I would comfort myself, however, with hoping that your business may not be unsuccessful, for your sake; and that, at least, it may soon be put into other proper hands. For my own, I beg earnestly of you to return to us as soon as possible. You know how very much I want you, and that, however *your* business may depend upon any other, *my* business depends entirely upon you, and yet still I hope you will find your man even though I lose you the meanwhile. At this time, the more I love

---

[1] Published by Goldsmith in his *Life of Parnell*.

you, the more I can spare you, which alone will, I dare say, be a reason to you to let me have you back the sooner.[1]

The minute I lost you, Eustathius, with nine hundred pages, and nine hundred contractions of the Greek character,[2] arose to my view, Spondanus, with all his auxiliaries, in number a thousand pages (value three shillings), and Dacier's three volumes, Barnes's two, Valterie's three, Cuperus (half in Greek), Leo Allatius (three parts in Greek), Scaliger, Macrobius, and (worse than them all) Aulus Gellius! All these rushed on my soul at once, and whelmed me under a fit of the headache. I cursed them all religiously, damned my best friends among the rest, and even blasphemed Homer himself. Dear Sir, not only as you are a friend, and a good-natured man, but as you are a Christian and a divine, come back speedily, and prevent the increase of my sins; for, at the rate I have to rave, I shall not only damn all the poets and commentators who have gone before me, but be damned myself by all who come after me. To be serious, you have not only left me to the last degree impatient for your return, who at all times should have been so (though never so much as since I knew you in best health here), but you have wrought several miracles upon our family. You have made old people [his parents] fond of a young and gay person, and inveterate papists [fond] of a clergyman of the Church of England. Even nurse[3] herself is in danger of being in love in her old age,

[1] He may mean that he was too much occupied with the Homer to have leisure for friendly society, which was yet a reason for Parnell's speedy return, because his help was essential.—E.

[2] Eustathius, the most considerable scholiast or commentator on Homer, Archbishop of Thessalonica, lived in the XII. century. Aulus Gellius, of the second century, was the author of the famous miscellany of extracts from Greek and Latin writers, *Noctes Atticæ* ("Nights at Athens")—The *Saturnalia* of Macrobius (of the fifth century) is also a miscellany of antiquarian (Greek and Latin) literature and criticism. Of the modern commentators mentioned, the most learned and famous is Scaliger (the elder), author of *De Arte Poeticâ*, d. 1558.

[3] Pope's nurse, Mary Beach, to whom he always showed great kindness.— Dennis was, no doubt, an Irish servant of Parnell's.—Croker.

and (for all I know) would even marry Dennis for your sake, because he is your man, and loves his master.

In short, come down forthwith, or give me good reasons for delaying, though but for a day or two, by the next post. If I find them just, I will come up to you, though you know how precious my time is at present. My hours were never worth so much money before : but, perhaps, *you* are not sensible of this, who give away your own works.[1] You are a generous author, I a hackney scribbler; you are a Grecian and bred at a University, I a poor Englishman of my own educating; you are a reverend parson, I a wag. In short, you are Dr. Parnelle (with an *e* at the end of your name), and I your most obliged and affectionate friend, and faithful servant.

My hearty service to the Dean, Dr. Arbuthnot, Mr. Ford, and the true genuine "Shepherd," J. Gay of Devon. I expect him down with you.

To Dr. Arbuthnot.

Binfield, July 11, 1714.

I have been so much afflicted with the headache, in the hot weather, that I have had perpetual opportunities of reflecting on those elegant verses of Dr. Scriblerus, which you favoured us with.[2] This is not a time for us to make others live, when we

---

[1] He made Pope a present of the Essay on the Life and Writings of Homer, prefixed to the translation of the *Iliad*. Parnell was a man of private fortune, and had considerable landed property in Ireland, and at Congleton in Cheshire. He lived expensively, and sometimes beyond his means.—E. The present M P. for Cork, it is believed, derives his descent from the poet.

[2] The same (on the dust-plague) which Arbuthnot sent to Swift, June 26, 1714. The Satire of *Martin Scriblerus* was principally the work of Arbuthnot. See *Life and Writings of Swift*.

can hardly live ourselves. So Scriblerus, contrary to other maggots, must lie dead all the summer, and wait till winter shall revive him. This, I hope, will be no disadvantage to him; for mankind will be playing the fool in all weathers, and affording us materials for that life, which every mortal contributes his quota to, and which I hope to see the grand receptacle of all the addresses of the world.

We have paid a visit to the Dean at thirty miles' distance, with whom we stayed, and are but just returned hither. As I fancy you will be somewhat inquisitive after the manner of his life, and our reception, I will couch the particulars in the way of a news-letter:

From Letcombe, near Wantage, July 4.[1]

This day the envoys, deputed to Dean Swift on the part of his late confidants, arrived here during the time of divine service. They were received at the back door, and having paid the usual compliments on their part, and received the usual chidings on that of the Dean, were introduced to his landlady,[2] and entertained with a pint of the Lord Bolingbroke's *Florence*. The health of that great Minister was drunk in this, partly, together with the Lord Treasurer's, whose wine we also wished for; after which were commemorated Dr. Arbuthnot and Mr. Lewis, in a sort of cider, plentiful in these parts, and not altogether unknown in the taverns of London. There was likewise a sideboard of coffee,

---

[1] Swift had left London for that seclusion, in disgust with the dissensions of his Tory friends at the head of the Government. See his *Life*, &c.

[2] Mrs. Gery. "I am at a clergyman's house, whom I love very well," Swift writes to Miss Vanhomrigh, June 8, "but he is such a melancholy, thoughtful, man, partly from nature, and partly by a solitary life, that I shall soon catch the spleen from him. His wife has been this month twenty miles off, at her father's, and will not return these ten days, and, perhaps, the house will be worse when she comes. I read all day, or walk, and do not speak so many words as I have now writ, in three days." Swift had an old friend, named Molly Gery, who was a mantua-maker at Farnham, and he probably became intimate with the family when he lived at Moor Park.—E.

which the dean roasted with his own hands in an engine for the purpose, his landlady attending all the while that office was performing.

He talked of politics over coffee with the air and style of an old statesman, who had known something formerly, but was shamefully ignorant of the last three weeks. When we mentioned the welfare of England he laughed at us, and said Muscovy would become a flourishing empire very shortly. He seems to have wrong notions of the British Court, but gave us a hint as if he had a correspondence with the King of Sweden. As for the methods of passing his time, I must tell you one which constantly employs an hour about noon. He has, in his windows, an orbicular glass which, by contraction of the solar beams into a proper focus, doth burn, singe, or speckle white or printed paper, in curious little holes, or various figures. We chanced to find some experiments of this nature upon the votes of the House of Commons. The name of Thomas Hanmer, Speaker,[1] was much singed, and that of John Barber.[2] There was a large gap at the edge of the bill of Schism,[3] and several specks upon the proclamation for the Pretender.[4] I doubt not

---

[1] A section of the Tories, who had little faith in his [Oxford's] policy or integrity, was led by Hanmer, and, in the hope of conciliating him, Lord Oxford supported his election to the Speakership. Hanmer remained true to his own band, and his opposition to the Ministry was annoying to Swift.—E.

[2] Printer of the votes of the House of Commons. He had been taken up in the course of the Session, by order of the House of Lords, for printing Swift's pamphlet, *The Public Spirit of the Whigs*: but he had not betrayed his employer, nor otherwise offended him; and it is not apparent why his name should have been burnt out.—E.

[3] This was the Bill which prohibited any person from being a teacher of youth, who had not subscribed a declaration of conformity to the Church of England, received the sacrament in some parish church, and obtained a licence from the bishop of the diocese. The Bill was advocated by Lord Bolingbroke, with a view to win the favour of the high church party, and supersede Lord Oxford, who had existed by trimming. . . . Swift, though a zealot for the high church treatment of dissenters, did not relish a Schism Bill which fostered schism in the Government.—E.

[4] A Proclamation was issued on June 21, offering a reward of £5000 to any

but these marks of his are mystical, and that the figures he makes this way are a significant cypher to those who have the skill to explain them.

That I may not conclude this letter without some verses, take the following epigram, which Dr. Parnell and I composed as we rode towards the Dean, in the mist of the morning, and is after the Scriblerian manner:

> How foolish men on expeditions go!
> Unweeting wantons of their wetting woe.
> For drizzling damps descend adown the plain,
> And seem a thicker dew or thinner rain.
> Yet, dew or rain may wet us to the shift,
> We'll not be slow to visit Dr. Swift.

I am, with the truest esteem, Sir, your most obliged servant.

TO MR. JERVAS.

Aug. 27, 1714.

I am just arrived from Oxford, very well diverted and entertained there. All very honest fellows, much concerned for the Queen's death; no panegyrics ready yet for the King. I admire your Whig principles of resistance exceedingly, in the spirit of the Barcelonians: I join in your wish for them. Mr. Addison's verses on Liberty, in his letter from Italy, would be a good form of prayer in my opinion: *O Liberty! thou goddess heavenly bright*, &c.

---

one who should apprehend the Pretender, whenever he should land in Great Britain. The precaution was forced upon the Government, and no proceedings would be agreeable to Swift, which were symptomatic of the increasing power of the Opposition.—E.

What you mentioned of the friendly office you endeavoured to do, betwixt Mr. Addison and me, deserves acknowledgments on my part. You thoroughly know my regard to his character, and my propensity to testify it by all ways in my power. You as thoroughly know the scandalous meanness of that proceeding which was used by Philips,[1] to make a man I so highly value suspect my dispositions towards him. But as, after all, Mr. Addison must be the judge in what regards himself, and has seemed to be no very just one to me, so I must own to you, I expect nothing but *civility* from him, how much soever I wish for his friendship. As for any offices of real kindness or service, which it is in his power to do me, I should be ashamed to receive them from any man who had no better opinion of my morals than to think me a party man, nor of my temper than to believe me capable of maligning or envying another's reputation as a poet. So I leave it to time to convince him as to both, to show him the shallow depths of those half-witted creatures who misinformed him, and to prove that I am incapable of endeavouring to lessen a person whom I would be proud to imitate, and therefore ashamed to flatter. In a word, Mr. Addison is sure of my respect at all times, and of my real friendship, whenever he shall think fit to know me for what I am.

For all that passed betwixt Dr. Swift and me, you know the whole, without reserve, of our correspondence. The engagements I had to him were such as the actual services he had done me, in relation to the subscription for Homer, obliged me. I must have leave to be grateful to him, and to any one who serves me, let him be never so obnoxious to any party: nor did the Tory party ever put me to the hardship of asking this

---

[1] Pope, in his letter to Caryll, June 8, 1714, says that Philips accused him of having entered into a cabal with Swift and others to write against the Whig interest, and to undermine the interests of Addison, Steele, and Philips himself.—E.

leave, which is the greatest obligation I owe to it; and I expect no greater from the Whig party than the same liberty. A curse on the word *Party*, which I have been forced to use so often in this period! I wish the present reign [1] may put an end to the distinction, that there may be no other for the future than that of honest and knave, fool and man of sense.[2] These two sorts must always be enemies, but, for the rest, may all people do as you and I—believe what they please, and be friends.

To Mr. Edward Blount.

Oxford, August 27, 1714.

Whatever studies on the one hand, or amusements on the other, it shall be my fortune to fall into, I shall be equally incapable of forgetting you in any of them. The task [of Homer] I undertook, though of a weight enough in itself, has had a voluntary increase by the enlarging my design of the Notes; and the necessity of consulting a number of books has carried me to Oxford. But, I fear, through my Lord Harcourt's and Dr. Clarke's [3] means, I shall be more conversant with the pleasures

---

[1] Or rather, the future; for the Elector of Hanover had not yet arrived, or been crowned.

[2] A sentiment which Pope expresses in the well-known verses of his *Essay on Man*:—

> For forms of Government let fools contest:
> Whate'er is best administered is best.

[3] Of All Soul's College, a *virtuoso* and a man of taste.—Warton. In the course of conversation he showed some desire to enter into a discussion with Pope upon the Roman Catholic tenets, and Pope replied: "It is but a little while I can enjoy your improving company here in Oxford, which we will not so misspend, as it would be doing, should we let it pass in talking of divinity. Neither would there be time for either of us half to explain ourselves, and at last you would be protestant Clarke, and I papist Pope."—E.

and company of the place than with the books and manuscripts of it.

I find still more reason to complain of the negligence of the geographers in their maps of old Greece, since I looked upon two or three more noted names in the public libraries here. But, with all the care I am capable of, I have some cause to fear the engraver will prejudice me in a few situations. I have been forced to write to him in so high a style that, were my epistles intercepted, it would raise no small admiration in an ordinary man. There is scarce an order in it of less importance than to remove such and such mountains, alter the course of such and such rivers, place a large city on such a coast, and raze another in another country. I have set bounds to the sea, and said to the land, "Thus far shalt thou advance, and no further."[1]

In the meantime, I, who talk and command at this rate, am in danger of losing my horse, and stand in some fear of a country justice.[2] To disarm me, indeed, may be but prudential, considering what armies I have, at present, on foot and in my service. A hundred thousand Grecians are no contemptible body. For all that I can tell, they may be as formidable as four thousand priests; and they seem proper forces to send against those in Barcelona. That siege deserves as fine a poem as the *Iliad*, and the machining part of poetry would be the juster in it, as they say the inhabitants expect angels from heaven to their assistance.[3]

---

[1] This relates to the Map of Ancient Greece, laid down by our author in his Observations on the second *Iliad*..—Pope, 1735.

[2] Some of the laws were at this time put in force against the papists.—Warburton. The enactment, which prohibited a Roman Catholic from keeping a horse above the value of 5*l*., does not seem to have been pressed.—E.

[3] The siege of Barcelona by Philip V. had been going on since July, 1713. At the peace of Utrecht Louis XIV. sent an army to his assistance, under the Duke of Berwick. Notwithstanding the overwhelming forces brought against them, amounting to 40,000 men, the inhabitants determined not to surrender, and hoisted a black flag with a death's-head upon it. On August 12, 1714, they repulsed two assaults with great slaughter, but the town was at last taken on September 11, after an obstinate resistance and dreadful carnage.

May I venture to say, who am a papist, and say to you who are a papist, that nothing is more astonishing to me than that people, so greatly warmed with a sense of liberty, should be capable of harbouring such weak superstition, and that so much bravery and so much folly can inhabit the same breasts?

I could not but take a trip to London on the death of the Queen,[1] moved by the common curiosity of mankind, who leave their own business to be looking upon other men's. I thank God that, as for myself, I am below all the accidents of State changes by my circumstances, and above them by my philosophy. Common charity of man to man, and universal goodwill to all, are the points I have most at heart; and I am sure those are not to be broken for the sake of any Governors or Government. I am willing to hope the best, and what I more wish than my own or any particular man's advancement is, that this turn may put an end entirely to the divisions of Whig and Tory; that the parties may love each other as well as I love them both, or at least hurt each other as little as I would either; and that our own people may live as quietly as we shall certainly let theirs—that is to say, that want of power itself in us may not be a surer prevention of harm than want of will in them. I am sure, if all Whigs and all Tories had the spirit of one Roman Catholic that I know, it would be well for all Roman Catholics; and if all Roman Catholics had always had that spirit, it had been well for all others, and we had never been charged with so wicked a spirit as that of persecution.

I agree with you in my sentiments of the state of our nation since this change. I find myself just in the same situation of

---

Pope speaks of four thousand priests being engaged in the defence of the place, and it is a fact that five hundred and forty-three monks and clergy fell in the course of the siege.—E. The city was defended in the interests of the Austrian claimant to the Spanish throne.

[1] Lord Bathurst says, in one of his letters, that Pope was as sure to be in London at any crisis as a porpoise was to appear in a storm.—E.

mind you describe as your own, heartily wishing the good, that is, the quiet of my country, and hoping a total end of all the unhappy divisions of mankind by party-spirit, which, at best, is but the madness of many for the gain of a few.

To Mr. William Fortescue.[1]

Bath, [1714?]

The gaiety of your letter proves you not so studious of wealth as many of your profession are, since you can derive matter of mirth from want of business. You are none of those lawyers who deserve the motto of the devil, *circuit quærens quem devoret*. But your *circuit* will at least procure you one of the greatest of temporal blessings, *health*. What an advantageous circumstance is it, for one that loves rambling so well, to be a grave and reputable rambler; while (like your fellow-circuiter, the Sun) you travel the round of the Earth, and behold all the iniquities under the heavens! You are much a superior genius to me in rambling. You, like a pigeon (to whom I would sooner compare a lawyer than to a hawk), can fly some hundred leagues at a pitch. I, like a poor squirrel, am continually in

---

[1] An eminent barrister, afterwards a judge, and finally Master of the Rolls. He was one of the early and intimate friends of Pope, whose attachment to him remained uninterrupted through life. To him Pope has addressed the First Satire of the Second Book of Horace.—Roscoe. These letters are valuable in one point of view, as they prove, clearer than a thousand arguments, that the letters which Pope published were published and laboured for the press. It may be amusing to compare these unvarnished and unaffected effusions of friendship with his elegant and more elaborate epistolary compositions.— Bowles. The first portion of them were first published in Polwhele's *Hist. of Devon*, and republished by Bowles: the second part by Miss Warner, from the papers of Mr. Reynolds of Bristol, in her Collection of Original Letters, 1817. They are, for the most part, without dates.

motion, indeed, but it is about a cage of three foot. My little excursions are like those of a shop-keeper, who walks every day a mile or two before his own door, but minds his business [all the while].

Your letter, of the cause lately before you, I could not but communicate to some ladies of your acquaintance. I am of opinion, that if you continued a correspondence of the same sort, during a whole circuit, it could not fail to please the sex better than half the novels they read. There would be in them what they love above all things—a most happy union of truth and scandal. I assure you the Bath affords nothing equal to it. It is, on the contrary, full of *grave* and *sad* men; Mr. Baron S., Lord Chief Justice A., Judge P., and Counsellor B., who has a large pimple on the top of his nose, but thinks it inconsistent with his gravity to wear a patch, notwithstanding the precedent of an eminent Judge.

To Miss Teresa Blount.

Bath, 1714.

You are to understand, Madam, that my passion for your fair self and your sister has been divided with the most wonderful regularity in the world. Even from my infancy I have been in love with one after the other of you, week by week, and my journey to Bath fell out in the three hundred seventy sixth week of the reign of my sovereign Lady, Sylvia. At the present writing hereof, it is the three hundred eighty-ninth week of the reign of your most serene Majesty, in whose service I was listed some weeks before I beheld your sister [Martha]. This information will account for my writing to either of you, hereafter, as either shall happen to be queen-regent at the time.

Pray tell your sister, all the good qualities and virtuous inclinations she has never gave me so much pleasure in her conversation, as that one vice of her obstinacy will give me mortification this month. Radcliffe [1] commands her to the Bath, and she refuses! Indeed, if I were in Berkshire I should honour her for this obstinacy, and magnify her no less for disobedience than we do the Barcelonians.[2] But people change with the change of places (as we see of late), and virtues become vices when they cease to be for one's interest, with me, as with others. Yet let me tell her, she will never look so finely, while she is upon earth, as she would here in the water. It is not here, as in most other instances; for those ladies, that would please extremely, must go out of their own element. She does not make half so good a figure on horseback as Christina, Queen of Sweden; but, were she once seen in the Bath, no man would part with her for the best mermaid in Christendom. You know, I have seen you often; I perfectly know how you look in black and in white.[3] I have experienced the utmost you can do in colours; but all your movements, all your graceful steps, deserve not half the glory you might here attain, of a moving and easy behaviour in buckram; something between swimming and walking —free enough, and more modestly half-naked than you can appear anywhere else. You have conquered enough already by land. Show your ambition, and vanquish, also, by water. The *buckram*, I mention, is a dress peculiarly useful at this time, when we are told they are bringing over the fashion of German *ruffs*. You ought to use yourself to some degree of stiffness beforehand, and, when our ladies' chins have been tickled awhile

---

[1] See Letters of Swift, page 97, *note*.

[2] See Letters of Pope, *ante*.

[3] Such is the superior decency and propriety of public manners, that the strange circumstance of ladies appearing in the Bath, *pro bono publico*, seems, at this time, scarcely credible. These very letters may further tend to prove the great superiority of the present period, in this respect.—Bowles.

with starch muslin and wire, they may possibly bear the brush of a German beard and whiskers.

I could tell you a delightful story of Dr. P., but want room to display it in all its shining circumstances. He had heard it was an excellent cure for love to kiss the aunt of the person beloved, who is generally of years and experience enough to damp the fiercest flame. He tried this course, in his passion, and kissed Mrs. E— at Mr. D's, but he says it will not do, and that he loves you as much as ever. Yours, &c.

To Dr. Arbuthnot.

Binfield, Sept. 2, 1714.

Though Dr. Parnell has preoccupied the first part of this paper, and so seems to lead the way in this address to you, yet I must tell you I have several times been inspiriting him to join with me in a letter to you, and been prevented, by his delays, for some posts. And, though he mentions the name of Scriblerus to avoid my reproaching him, yet is he conscious to himself how much the memory of that learned phantom, which is to be immortal, is neglected by him at present. But I hope the revolutions of State will not affect Learning so much as to deprive mankind of the lucubrations of Martin, to the increase of which I will watch all next winter, and grow pale over the midnight candle.

Homer's image begins already to vanish from before me, the season of the campaign before Troy is near over, and I rejoice at the prospect of my amusements in winter quarters with you in London. Our friend Gay will still continue secretary to Martin, at least,[1] though I could be more glad he had a better master for his profit—for his glory he can have no better. You must not wonder I enlarge upon this head. The remembrance of our agreeable conferences, as well as our occasional honours on your account,[2] will ever dwell upon my thoughts with that pleasure, which I think one honest and cheerful man ought to take in being obliged to another. That we may again enjoy those satisfactions is heartily my wish, and it is my request to you, in the meantime, that you will continue to think me what I so sincerely am, your most affectionate and most faithful humble servant.[3]

[1] Having lost his office of Secretary to the Hanoverian Embassy.—E. Martin is Arbuthnot.

[2] As physician to the Queen he had occupied apartments in St. James's Palace, where the Scriblerus Club used to meet.

[3] Arbuthnot, who had just lost his post at Court, by the Queen's death, replies to Pope (September 7): "I am extremely obliged to you for taking notice of a poor old distressed courtier, commonly the most despicable thing in the world. This blow has so roused Scriblerus that he has recovered his senses, and thinks and talks like other men. From being frolicsome and gay he is turned grave and morose. His lucubrations lie neglected amongst old newspapers, cases, petitions, and abundance of unanswerable letters. I wish to God they had been amongst the papers of a noble lord [Bolingbroke] sealed up, then might Scriblerus have passed for the Pretender, and it would have been a most excellent and laborious work for the Flying Post, or some such author, to have allegorised all his adventures into a plot, and found out mysteries somewhat like the Key to the Lock. Martin's office is now the second door on the left hand in Dover Street, where he will be glad to see Dr. Parnell, Mr. Pope, and his old friends, to whom he can still afford a half-pint of claret. It is with some pleasure that he contemplates the world still busy, and all mankind at work for him," &c.

To Mr. Gay.

September 23, 1714.

Welcome to your native soil!¹ Welcome to your friends; thrice welcome to me! Whether returned in glory, blessed with Court-interest, the love and familiarity of the great, and filled with agreeable hopes; or melancholy with dejection, contemplative of the changes of fortune, and doubtful for the future; whether returned a triumphant Whig, or a desponding Tory, equally all hail! Equally beloved and welcome to me! If happy, I am to share in your elevation; if unhappy, you have still a warm corner in my heart, and a retreat at Binfield, in the worst of times, at your service. If you are a Tory, or thought so by any man, I know it can proceed from nothing but your gratitude to a few people, who endeavoured to serve you, and whose politics were never your concern. If you are a Whig, as I rather hope (and, as I think, your principles and mine, as brother poets, had ever a bias to the side of Liberty), I know you will be an honest man, and an inoffensive one. Upon the whole, I know you are incapable of being so much of either party as to be good for nothing. Therefore, once more, whatever you are, or in whatever state you are, all hail!

One or two of your own friends complained they had heard nothing from you since the Queen's death. I told them no man living loved Mr. Gay better than I, yet I had not once written to him in all his voyage. This I thought a convincing proof, how truly one may be a friend to another, without telling him so every month. But they had reasons, too, themselves to allege in your excuse, as men, who really value one another, will never want such as make their friends and themselves easy. The late universal

---

¹ The letter of welcome to Gay was addressed to him on his return from Hanover, after the Embassy of Lord Clarendon had been brought to a sudden termination by the death of Queen Anne.—E.

concern in public affairs threw us all into a hurry of spirits. Even I, who am more a philosopher than to expect anything from any reign, was borne away with the current, and full of expectation of the successor.

During your journeys I knew not whither to aim a letter after you—that was a sort of shooting flying: add to this, the demand Homer had upon me, to write fifty verses a day, besides learned notes, all which are at a conclusion for this year. Rejoice with me, O my friend, that my labour is over. Come and make merry with me in much feasting, for I to thee and thou to me [sic]. We will feed among the lilies. By the *lilies* I mean the ladies, with whom I hope you have fed to a satiety. Hast thou past through many countries, and not tasted the delights thereof? Hast thou not left of thy issue in divers lands, that German Gays and Dutch Gays may arise to write *pastorals* and sing their songs in strange countries? Are not the Blouzelindas of the Hague as charming as the Rosalindas of Britain?[1] Or have the two great pastoral poets of our nation renounced love at the same time? For Philips, immortal Philips, Hanover Philips,[2] has deserted, yea, and in a rustic manner, kicked his Rosalind. Dr. Parnell and I have been inseparable ever since you went. We are now at the Bath, where—if you are not, as I heartily hope, better engaged—your coming would be the greatest pleasure to us in the world. Talk not of expenses. Homer shall support his children. I beg a line from you directed to the post-house in Bath. Poor Parnell is in an ill-state of health.

Pardon me, if I add a word of advice in the poetical way. Write something on the king, or prince, or princess.[3] On what-

---

[1] Blouzelinda is the name of a shepherdess in the *Pastorals* of Gay, and Rosalinda figures in the *Pastorals* of Pope.—E.

[2] He was Secretary to the Hanover Club.—E. His Pastorals are much more true to nature than those of his rival. They appeared in 1708, and were ironically eulogised by Pope himself in the *Tatler*.—See *Life* &c.

[3] Arbuthnot gave the same counsel. "Poor Gay," he wrote to Swift, October, 1714, "is much where he was, only out of the Duchess [of Mon-

soever foot you may be with the Court, this can do no harm. I shall never know where to end, and am confounded in the many things I have to say to you, though they all amount but to this, that I am entirely, as ever, yours, &c.

To Miss Martha Blount.[1]

Bath, Oct., 1714.

If I may ever be allowed to tell you the thoughts I have so often of you in your absence, it is at this time, when I neglect the company of a great number of ladies to write this letter. From the window where I am seated I command the prospect of twenty or thirty, in one of the finest promenades in the world, every moment that I take my eye off from the paper.

If variety of diversions and new objects be capable of driving our friends out of their minds, I have the best excuse imaginable for forgetting you; for I have slid, I cannot tell how, into all the amusements of this place. My whole day is shared by the pump-assemblies, the walks, the chocolate-houses, raffling shops, plays, medleys, &c. We have no ladies who have the face, though some of them may have the impudence, to expect a lampoon. The prettiest is one I had the luck to travel with, who has found out, so far as to tell me that, whatever pretences

---

mouth's] family and service. I advised him to make a poem on the Princess before she came over, describing to her the English ladies; but he was in such a grovelling condition, as to the affairs of the world, that his muse would not stoop to visit him." Gay, after all, took the hint, and addressed an *Epistle to a Lady*, "occasioned by the arrival of her Royal Highness." He did not affect to disguise the object of his poetical offering:

    Places, I found, were daily given away,
    And yet no friendly Gazette mentioned Gay.—E.

[1] With the former, first published by Bowles from MS. at Mapledurham.

I make to gaiety, my heart is not at Bath. Mrs. Gage came hither the other day, and did me a double honour in speaking to me and asking publicly, when I saw you last. I endeavour (like all awkward fellows) to become agreeable by imitation; observing who are most in favour with the fair. I sometimes copy the civil air of Gascoin, sometimes the impudent one of Nash,[1] and, sometimes for vanity, the silly one of a neighbour of yours, who has lost to the gamesters here that money, of which the ladies only deserve to rob a man of his age. This mistaken youth is so ignorant as to imagine himself as agreeable in the eyes of the sex to-day as he was yesterday, when he was worth three or four hundred pounds more. Alas! he knows not, that just as much is left of a mistress's heart as is emptied from one's own pocket.

My chief acquaintance, of my own sex, are the aforesaid Mr. Gascoin and Mr. Nash; of the other, Dame Lindsey and Jenny Man. I am so much a rake as to be ashamed to be seen with Dr. Parnelle. I ask people abroad, who that parson is? We expect better company here next week; and then a certain Earl shall know what ladies drink his health every day since his disgrace, that you may be in the public pamphlets as well as your humble servant. They say, here are Cabals held, under pretence of drinking waters; and this scandal, like others, refreshes me and elevates my spirits. I think no man deserves a monument, that could not be wrapped in a winding-sheet of papers writ against

[1] Richard Nash—beau Nash, as he was called—the celebrated Master of the Ceremonies at Bath. Nash was so far "impudent" as not only to establish, but to enforce, laws for the regulation of the assemblies, which he refused to allow a deviation from, even at the request of the Princess Amelia. He was very strict in regard to dress. "I have known him," says Goldsmith, who wrote his life, "on a ball night strip even the Duchess of Queensberry, and throw her apron at one of the wenches among the ladies' women, observing 'that none but abigails appeared in white aprons.' This, from another, would be an insult: in him it was considered a just reprimand, and the good-natured Duchess acquiesced in his censure."—C. W. D. (MS. note) in Roscoe's edition of Pope, 1847.

him. If women could digest scandal as well as I, there are two that might be the happiest creatures in the universe. I have in one week run through whatever they call diverting here, and I should be ashamed to pass two just in the same track. I will therefore take but a trip to Longleat, which is twelve miles hence, to visit my Lord Lansdown, and return to London.

I must tell you a truth, which is not, however, much to my credit. I never thought so much of yourself and your fair sister as since I have been fourscore miles distant from you. At Binfield I look upon you as good neighbours; at London as pretty kind of women; and here as divinities, angels, goddesses, or what you will. In like manner, I never knew at what a rate I valued your life, till you were upon the point of dying. If Mrs. Teresa and you will but fall sick every season, I shall certainly die for you. Seriously, I value you both so much that I esteem others much the less for your sakes. You have robbed me of the pleasure of esteeming a thousand fine qualities in them, by showing me so many in a superior degree in yourselves. There are but two things in the world which can make you indifferent to me, which I believe you are not capable of: I mean ill-nature and malice. I have seen enough of you not to resent any frailty you could have; and nothing less than a vice can make me like you less. . . . Your faithful, obliged humble servant.

To Mr. John Caryll.

[1715.]

The calamity of your gout is what all your friends, that is to say, all that know you, must share in.[1] Mr. Gay and myself have

---

[1] If the frequency of the mention of "gout," in the correspondence of the last century, be any measure of its prevalence throughout the richer sections

often wished ourselves with you, in the capacity of comforters, or Merry Andrews,[1] which you should like best—a task we are the fitter for, as we have, since you left town, been employed in that way by a fellow-sufferer of yours, Mr. Harcourt, who is now laid up with your distemper. We desire you, in your turn, to condole with us, who are under a persecution, and much afflicted with a distemper which proves mortal to many poets—a criticism. We have, indeed, some relieving intervals of laughter, as you know there are in some diseases; but the attacks are renewed, and it is the opinion of divers good guessers that the last fit will not be more violent than advantageous to us; for poets, assailed by critics, are much like men bitten by tarantulas—they dance on the faster, the deeper they are stung, till the very violence and sweating makes them recover.

Mr. Thomas Burnet hath played the precursor to the coming of Homer, in a treatise called *Homerides*.[2] He has since risen very much in his criticisms, and, after assaulting Homer, made a daring attack upon *What-D'ye-Call-It*.[3] Yet is there not a proclamation issued forth for the burning of Homer and the Pope by the common hangman, nor is *What-D'ye-Call-It* yet silenced by the Lord Chamberlain. They shall survive the conflagration of his father's works, and live after his father is damned; for

of the community, that disease must have been exceedingly prevalent. Gay, in his Fable of the *Court of Death*, assigns it a distinguished place. Whether the " good living " of the present time be equally productive of it or no, may be an open question.

[1] The origin of this popular character has been traced to the name and peculiarities of a physician in repute with Henry VIII., a Dr. Andrew Borde (1500-1549), who was accustomed, it is said, to frequent fairs and other popular places of resort, for the purpose of fleecing the gaping crowds. It seems he gained the attention and favour of his audience by his excellence in buffoonery. There is a poem by Prior on *Merry Andrew*.

[2] *Homerides ; or, a Letter to Mr. Pope, occasioned by his intended Translation of Homer*. By Sir Iliad Doggrel, March 7, 1715.—E.

[3] A Farce by Gay, in which he parodies certain passages in Addison's *Cato*, and which, on that account, would not meet with much favour from Steele, who, at this time, had official control of the Stage at Drury Lane.

that the Bishop of Salisbury is so already, is the opinion of Dr. Sacheverell and the Church of Rome.¹

It remains that I should, in a brief and perspicuous manner, acquaint you with the news of this place. The Bishop of Oxford expects the Bishopric of Sarum; Mr. Gay expects a present from the Princess [of Wales]; we are invited this day to dinner at my Lord Lansdown's; we are invited to see the lions at the Tower *gratis* by a lord, who expects to have a new lodge given him by the Parliament.² Mr. Steele declares the farce should not have been acted, if he had been in town. The new theatre in Lincoln's Inn Fields have thoughts of acting it without his consent.³ The rest is no news, being that we are everlastingly your most obliged, and most faithful, and affectionate servant.

To Dr. Parnell.

London, March 18, 1715.

I must own I have long owed you a letter, but you must own you have owed me one a good deal longer. Besides, I have but two people in the whole Kingdom of Ireland to take care of—the Dean and you, but you have several who complain of your

---

¹ Dr. Burnet, Bishop of Salisbury, died March 17, 1715.

² The lord, whose name is suppressed by Pope from caution, may have been Lord Lansdowne himself, who was committed to the Tower in the September following.—E.

³ When Rich was turned out of Drury Lane, he built a theatre in Lincoln's Inn Fields, which was completed about the time that George I. ascended the throne, and the new King, at the intercession of the younger Craggs, granted the proprietor a patent to act plays.—E.

⁴ Published by Goldsmith.

neglect in England. Mr. Gay complains, Mr. Harcourt complains, Mr. Jervas complains, Dr. Arbuthnot complains, my Lord [Bolingbroke] complains, I complain. (Take notice of this figure of iteration when you make your next sermon.)

Some say, you are in deep discontent at the new turn of affairs; others, that you are so much in the Archbishop's good graces,[1] that you will not correspond with any that have seen the last Ministry. Some affirm you have quarrelled with Pope (whose friends they observe daily fall from him, on account of his satirical and comical disposition); others, that you are insinuating yourself into the opinion of the ingenious Mr. What-d'ye-Call-Him.[2] Some think you are preparing your sermons for the Press, and others that you will transform them into essays and moral discourses. But the only excuse that I will allow you is, your attention to the Life of Zoilus. The frogs already seem to croak for their transportation to England,[3] and are sensible how much that doctor is cursed and hated, who introduced their species into your nation.[4] Therefore, as you

---

[1] Dr. King, the Archbishop of Dublin, was a Whig. Parnell was certainly in his "good graces," for the Archbishop had given him a prebend in 1713, and presented him in 1716, to the vicarage of Finglass. "Such notice," says Johnson, "from such a man, inclines me to believe that the vice of which he has been accused, was not gross, or not notorious," and, undoubtedly, the promotion discredits Pope's statements to Spence that Parnell "was extremely open and scandalous in his debaucheries."—E.

[2] An allusion to Gay's *What-d'ye-Call-It* which was first acted in Feb., 1715.—E.

[3] Parnell had undertaken to translate the *Batrachomyomachia*, the "Battle of the Frogs and Mice." This amusing earliest, serio-comic epic, commonly assigned to the author of the *Iliad*, is much more probably the work of a parodist of that very military poem, in which the high-sounding names, the long genealogies, and the various fortunes of the combatants, and the intervention of the Olympian divinities, amusingly remind one of the *heroic* strains of the *Iliad*. It was not the only parody of the Homeric epic. Two of the most interesting of these comic-heroic poems bear the names of the *Kerkopes*, and the *Seven Times Shorn Goat*.

[4] Frogs were unknown in Ireland till they were introduced at the beginning of the XVIIIth century. Pope's allusions are to Parnell and his poem: and either the real frogs had not yet made their appearance, or the news had not yet reached Twickenham.—E.

dread the wrath of St. Patrick, send them hither, and rid your kingdom of those pernicious [pertinacious?] and loquacious animals.

I have, at length, received your poem out of Mr. Addison's hands, which shall be sent as soon as you order it, and in what manner you shall appoint. I shall, in the meantime, give Mr. Tooke[1] a packet for you, consisting of divers merry pieces—Mr. Gay's new Farce, Mr. Burnet's letter to Mr. Pope,[2] Mr. Pope's Temple of Fame, Mr. Burnet's Grumbler on Mr. Gay,[3] and the Bishop of Ailsbury's Elegy,[4] written either by Mr. Cary or some other hand.

TO MR. JOHN CARYLL.

Bath, Sept. 25, 1715.

I deferred my returning an answer to your kind letter till I came to this place, which I thought would have been before this time; but my companion, Dr. Parnell, retarded my journey till now. I am this evening arrived extremely weary, and new to all the wonders of the place. I have stared at the Bath, and sneaked along the walks with that astonished and diffident air which is natural to a modest and ignorant foreigner. We have scarce any company of figure, no lampoons dispersed, and not a face that promises any. As for my own part, my genius was

[1] A bookseller. The poem received by Pope was probably some piece in MS., which Addison had been asked to revise.—E.

[2] Homerides, or a letter to Mr. Pope, occasioned by his intended translation of Homer.—E.

[3] The *Grumbler* was a weekly publication. The first number appeared on February 14, 1715.—E.

[4] Bishop of Salisbury, Burnet's. He had died the previous day. From its title, the Elegy seems to have been satirical.—E.

never turned to that sort of satire, and, if I had never so much natural malice, a laborious translation would extinguish all such impetuous emotions. I should be in Dryden's case, of whom it was said,

> " He turned the malice of a spiteful satire
> To the safe innocence of a dull translator." [1]

So that, upon the whole, I walk about here as innocently, and as little dreaded, as that old lion in satire, Mr. Wycherley, who now goes tame about this town. I named you to him, and he speaks such things of you—to give him his due—as may be heard by your friend with satisfaction. He that dares to despise the great ones of this Age, to deny common sense to Ministers of State, their small portion of wit to the poets who live by it, and honesty to the maids of fourteen, dares not refuse Mr. Caryll his due.

How well the manner of life, which all people are obliged to here, will agree with my disposition I cannot tell. How far the necessary care of my health may coincide with a duty as indispensable to me at this time—that of finishing my year's task—or how far Homer may be the worse for my being better, are things I am under some doubt about. I hope to give a more reasonable account of myself when I pass a week or two at Ladyholt, where I propose to contrive it so as to meet you rather than at Grinstead, on account of the fear I have of that air in the winter. I see I scarce write common English or grammar at this time, and therefore ought to conclude. I have ten people round me at a tavern table, and more noise than will agree with my brains, especially when my head aches, as it does after this day's journey. But I would not longer omit to

---

[1] The "malice" was that of *Mac-Flecknoe;* the "innocence" that of his translation of the *Æneis*. Pope reversed this order: his *Homer* preceded his principal satire, the *Dunciad*, the first part of which he published in 1727, the fourth and concluding book in 1742, at the suggestion of Dr. Warburton.

take the occasion of assuring you of the old story, which will be a true one as long as I live, that I am unfeignedly, dear Sir, your most faithful, obedient, affectionate servant.

To Miss Martha Blount.[1]
Stanton Harcourt?. 1716.

Nothing could have more of that melancholy which once used to please me than my last day's journey; for, after having passed through my favourite woods in the forests, with a thousand reveries of past pleasures, I rid over hanging hills, whose tops were edged with groves, and whose feet watered with winding rivers, listening to the falls of cataracts below, and the murmuring of the winds above. The gloomy verdure of Stonor succeeded to these, and then the shades of the evening overtook me. The moon rose in the clearest sky I ever saw, by whose solemn light I paced on slowly, without company, or any interruption to the range of my thoughts. About a mile before I reached Oxford all the bells tolled in different notes, the clocks of every College answered one another, and sounded forth (some in deeper, some a softer tone) that it was eleven at night. All this was no ill preparation to the life I have led since, among those old walls, venerable galleries, stone porticoes, studious walks, and solitary scenes of the University. I wanted nothing but a black gown and a salary, to be as mere a bookworm as any there. I conformed myself to the college hours, was rolled up in books, lay in one of the most ancient, dusty, parts of the

---

[1] First in edition 1735. There are some unimportant alterations in *Quarto*. The original is at Mapledurham.—C. W. D. (MS. note.) The date from Stanton Harcourt (given by Roscoe) is doubtful.

University, and was as dead to the world as any hermit of the desert. If anything was alive or awake in me, it was a little vanity, such as even those good men used to entertain, when the monks *of their own order* extolled their piety and abstraction. For I found myself received with a sort of respect, which this idle part of mankind, the learned, pay to their own species, who are as considerable here as the busy, the gay, and the ambitious are in your world.

Indeed, I was treated in such a manner, that I could not but sometimes ask myself, in my mind, what College I was founder of, or what Library I had built. Methinks I do very ill, to return to the world again, to leave the only place where I make a figure, and, from seeing myself seated with dignity on the most conspicuous shelves of a library, put myself in the abject posture of lying at a lady's feet in St. James's Square.[1] I will not deny but that, like Alexander, in the midst of my glory, I am wounded, and find myself a mere man. To tell you from whence the dart comes is to no purpose, since neither of you will take the tender care to draw it out of my heart, and suck the poison with your lips.

Here, at my Lord Harcourt's, I see a creature nearer an angel than a woman (though a woman be very near as good as an angel): I think you have formerly heard me mention Mrs. T,[2] as a credit to the Maker of angels. She is a relation of his Lordship's, and he gravely proposed her to me for a wife, being tender of her interest, and knowing (what is a shame to Providence) that she is less indebted to fortune than I. I told him it was what he never could have thought of, if it had not been his misfortune to be blind, and what I never could think of, while I had eyes to see both her and myself.

I must not conclude without telling you that I will do the

---

[1] Bolton Street, in original. The Blounts, at this time, resided in that part of London.

[2] Mrs. Jennings, in the original.—C.

utmost in the affair you desire.¹ It would be an inexpressible joy to me, if I could serve you, and I will always do all I can to give myself pleasure. I wish as well for you as for myself. I am in love with you both as much as I am with myself: for I find myself most so with either when I least suspect it.

To DEAN SWIFT.

June 20, 1716.

I cannot suffer a friend to cross the Irish sea,² without bearing a testimony from me of the constant esteem and affection I am both obliged and inclined to have for you. It is better he should tell you than I, how often you are in our thoughts and in our cups, and how I learn to sleep less and drink more whenever you are named among us. I look upon a friend in Ireland as upon a friend in the other world, whom (popishly speaking) I believe constantly well-disposed towards me, and ready to do me all the good he can, in that state of separation, though I hear nothing from him, and make addresses to him but very rarely. A Protestant divine cannot take it amiss that I treat him in the same manner with my patron saint.

I can tell you no news but what you will not sufficiently wonder at, that I suffer many things as an author militant: whereof, in your days of probation, you have been a sharer, or you had not arrived in that triumphant state you now deservedly enjoy in the Church. As for me, I have not the least hopes of the Cardinalate, though I suffer for my religion in almost every

---

¹ This last paragraph is considerably altered from the original, but it is not worth transcription. The affair here mentioned, in which he promises to do his utmost, was the purchase of an annuity for his fair correspondent.—C.

² Mr. Jervas, who paid a visit to Ireland soon after the date of this letter.—R.

weekly paper. I have begun to take a pique at the *Psalms of David*, if the wicked may be credited, who have printed a scandalous one in my name.[1]

This report I dare not discourage too much, in a prospect I have, at present, of a post under the Marquis de Langallerie; wherein, if I can do but some signal service against the Pope, I may be considerably advanced by the Turks, the only religious people I dare confide in. If it should happen hereafter that I should write for the Holy Law of Mahomet, I hope it may make no breach between you and me. Every one must live, and I beg you will not be the man to manage the controversy against me. The Church of Rome I judge (from many modern symptoms as well as ancient prophecies) to be in a declining condition. That of England will, in a short time, be scarce able to maintain her own family. So Churches sink as generally as Banks in Europe, and for the same reason—that religion and trade, which at first were open and free, have been reduced into the management of Companies and the roguery of Directors.

I do not know why I tell you all this, but that I always loved to talk to you. But this is not a time for any man to talk to the purpose. Truth is a kind of contraband commodity, which I would not venture to export, and, therefore, the only thing tending that dangerous way which I shall say is, that I am, and always will be, with the utmost sincerity, yours, &c.

[1] "It is observable," says Warton, "that he does not deny being the writer of it." I have little doubt that he was so. The *Psalm* is printed in the *Additions to Pope's Works.*—Bowles. It is a parody on *Ps. I.*

To LADY MARY WORTLEY MONTAGU.[1]

Oct. 1716 ?

After having dreamed of you several nights, besides a hundred reveries by day, I find it necessary to relieve myself by writing, though this is the fourth letter I have sent—two by Mr. Methuen,[2] and one by Lord James Hay, who was to be your convoy from Leghorn. In all I can say, I only make you a present in many words of what can do you no manner of good, but only raises my own opinion of myself—all the good wishes and hearty dispositions I am capable of forming or feeling for a deserving object. But mine are, indeed, so warm, that I fear they can proceed from nothing but what I cannot very decently own to you, much less to any other—yet what, if a man, he cannot help it. For God's sake, Madam, let not my correspondence be like a traffic with the grave, from whence there is no return. Unless you write to me, my wishes must be like a poor papist's devotions to separate[d] spirits who, for all they know or hear from them, either may or may not be sensible of their addresses. None but your guardian angels can have you more constantly in mind than I; and, if they have, it is only because they can see you always. If ever you think of those fine young *beaux* of heaven, I beg you to reflect that you have just as much consolation from them as I, at present, have from you.

While all people here are exercising their speculations upon

---

[1] First published by Warton, from the original. This is, no doubt, the letter forwarded by Mr. Stanyan mentioned in a later letter. It appears from the *London Gazette*, of December 4-8, 1716, that Mr. Stanyan arrived in Vienna on the 17th November (O.S.) a few days after Lady Mary and her husband had started thence for Hanover. This letter, therefore, was, probably, written in October, 1716.—C. W. D. (MS. note), in Roscoe's edition of Pope's *Letters*.

[2] The Secretary of State, who corresponded with Mr. Wortley on the affairs of the Embassy.—C. W. D.

the affairs of the Turks,[1] I am only considering them as they may concern a particular person; and, instead of forming prospects as to the general tranquility of Europe, am hoping for some effect that may contribute to your greater ease. Above all, I would fain indulge an imagination that the nearer view of the unquiet scene you are approaching to may put a stop to your further progress. I can hardly yet relinquish a faint hope I have ever had, that Providence will take some uncommon care of one who so generously gives herself up to it; and I cannot imagine God Almighty so like some of his vicegerents as absolutely to neglect those who surrender to his mercy. May I thus tell you the truth of my heart? or must I put on a more unconcerned person, and tell you gaily, that there is some difference between the Court of Vienna and the Camps in Hungary: that scarce a Basha living is so offensive a creature as Count Volkra: that the wives of Ambassadors are as subject to human accidents, and as tender as their skins: that it is not more natural for glass to cut than for Turks and Tartars to plunder (not to mention ravishing, against which, I am told, beauty is no defence in those parts): that you are strangely in the wrong to forsake a nation, that but last year toasted Mrs. Walpole, for one that has no taste of beauty after twenty, and where the finest women in England would be almost superannuated? Would to God, Madam, all this might move either Mr. Wortley or you; and that I may soon apply to you both what I have read in one of Harlequin's Comedies. He sees Constantinople in a raree-show, vows it is the finest thing upon earth, and protests it is prodigiously like. "Ay, sir," says the man of the Show, "you have been at Constantinople, I perceive." "No, indeed," says Harlequin, "I was never there myself, but I had a brother I loved dearly, who had the greatest mind in the world to have gone thither."

[1] A war was then being waged between the Turks and Imperialists, under Eugéne, the old associate of Marlborough.

This is what I really wish from my soul, though it would ruin the best project I ever laid, that of obtaining, through your means, my fair Circassian slave; she whom my imagination had drawn more amiable than angels, as beautiful as the lady as was to choose her by a resemblance to so divine a face; she whom my hopes had already transported over so many seas and lands, and whom my eager wishes have already lodged in my arms and heart. She, I say, upon this condition, may remain under the cedars of Asia, and weave a garland of palms for the brows of a Turkish tyrant with those hands which I had destined for the soft offices of love, or, at worst, for transcribing amorous madrigals. Let that breast, I say, be now joined to some savage heart.—— I cannot go on in this style. I am not able to think of you without the utmost seriousness; and, if I did not take a particular care to disguise it, my letters would be the most melancholy things in the world. I believe you see my concern through all this affectation of gaiety, which is but like a fit of laughing in the deepest spleen or vapours. I am just alarmed with a piece of news, that Mr. Wortley thinks of passing through Hungary, notwithstanding the war there.

If ever any man loved his wife, or any mother her child, this offers you the strongest reason imaginable for staying at Vienna, at least this winter. For God's sake, value yourself a little more, and do not give us cause to imagine that such extravagant virtue can exist anywhere else than in a romance. I tremble for you the more, because (whether you believe it or not) I am capable myself of following one I love, not only to Constantinople, but to those parts of India where they tell us the women best like the ugliest fellows, as the most admirable productions of Nature, and look upon deformities as the signatures of divine favour. But (so romantic as I am) I should scarce take these rambles, without greater encouragement than I fancy any one who has been long married can expect. You see what danger I shall be in, if I ever find a fair one born under the same planet with Astolfo's [1] wife. If, instead of Hungary, you passed through Italy, and I had any hopes that lady's climate might give a turn to your inclinations, it is but your sending me the least notice, and I will certainly meet you in Lombardy, the scene of those celebrated amours between the fair princess and her dwarf.[2] From thence how far you might draw me, and I might run after you, I no more know than the spouse in the *Song of Solomon*—this I know, that I could be so very glad of being with you in any pleasure, that I could be content to be with you in any danger. Since I am not to partake either, adieu! But may God, by hearing my prayers and preserving you, make me a better Christian than any modern poet is at present. I am Madam, yours, &c.

To Lady Mary Wortley Montagu.

Nov. 10, 1716.

The more I examine my own mind, the more romantic I find myself. Methinks it is a noble spirit of contradiction to Fate and Fortune not to give up those that are snatched from us; but to follow them the more, the farther they are removed from

---

[1] One of the heroes of *Orlando Furioso*. His fate in the palace of Alcina, and his journey to the Moon, are well known.

[2] Alluding to the Tale in verse entitled *Woman* published in Tonson's *Miscellany*, in 1709, to which Pope contributed some of his early poems.—C. W. D.

[3] This garbled copy was first published in Cooper's edition, 1737. The letter is addressed to Lady M. W. Montagu at Constantinople.—C. W. D. (MS. Note).—Mr. Bowles has asserted that Pope has left out some very exceptionable passages, by which we are to understand that he corrected for publication. But the fact is, that any passages (exceptionable or not, on which different opinions may be entertained), which appear in the copy as sent, and not in the sketch retained, were *added* by Pope in copying it, and

the sense of it. Sure, flattery never travelled so far as three thousand miles. It is now only for truth, which overtakes all things, to reach you at this distance. 'Tis a generous piece of popery, that pursues even those that are to be eternally absent into another world. Whether you think it right or wrong, you will own the very extravagance a sort of piety. I cannot be satisfied with strewing flowers over you, and barely honouring you as a thing lost; but consider you as a glorious though remote being, and be sending addresses and prayers after you. You have carried away so much of me, that what remains is daily languishing and dying over my acquaintance here; and, I believe, in three or four months more, I shall think *Auratbazar* as good a place as *Covent Garden*. You may imagine this is raillery, but I am really so far gone as to take pleasure in reveries of this kind. Let them say that I am romantic—so is every one said to be that either admires a fine thing or does one. On my conscience, as the world goes, it is hardly worth any one's while to do one for the honour of it. Glory, the only pay of generous actions, is now as ill-paid as other just debts; and neither Mrs. Macfarland, for immolating her lover, nor you, for constancy to your lord, must ever hope to be compared to Lucretia or Portia.

I write this in some anger; for having, since you went, frequented those people most, who seemed most in your favour, I heard nothing that concerned you talked of so often as—that you went away in a black full-bottomed wig which I did but assert to be a *bob*, and was answered *Love is blind*. I am persuaded your

---

considerable additions made to the letter, as may appear by comparing them together. This comparison will further show that the theories, which Mr. Bowles has attempted to raise on the variations of these letters, both as to Pope's having suppressed the exceptionable passages, and his having participated with Curll in the surreptitious edition of his works, and even corrected his letters for him, are equally void of foundation.—Roscoe, 1847. It has, however, been too clearly proved that Pope did publish *garbled* copies of these letters.

2 D

wig had never suffered this criticism, but on the score of your head, and the two eyes that are in it. Pray, when you write to me, talk of yourself; there is nothing I so desire to hear of—talk a great deal of yourself, that she, who I always thought talked best, may speak upon the best subject. The shrines and relics you tell me of no way engage my curiosity. I had ten times rather go on pilgrimages to see one such a face as yours than both St. John Baptist's heads. I wish (since you are grown so covetous of golden things) you had not only all the fine statues you talk of, but even the golden image which Nebuchadnezzar set up, provided you were to travel no further than you could carry it.

The Court of Vienna is very edifying. The ladies, with respect to their husbands, seem to understand that text literally, that commands to *bear one another's burdens;* but, I fancy, many a man there is like *Issachar*—an *ass* between *two burthens.* I shall look upon you no more as a Christian, when you pass from that charitable Court to the land of jealousy. I expect to hear an exact account how, and at what places, you leave one of the Thirty-nine *Articles* after another, as you approach to the lands of Infidelity. Pray, how far are you got already? Amidst the pomp of a High Mass and the ravishing trills of a Sunday Opera, what did you think of the doctrine and discipline of the Church of England? Had you, from your heart, a reverence for Sternhold and Hopkins?[1] How did your Christian virtues hold out in so long a voyage? You have, it seems—without passing the bounds of Christendom—out-travelled the sin of fornication; in a little time, you will look upon some others with more patience than the ladies here are capable of. I reckon you will time it so well, as to make your

---

[1] Sternhold, Groom of the Robes to Henry VIII. and Edward VI., was responsible for the versification of some fifty of the *Psalms.* The rest were achieved by Hopkins and others. They retained their reputation and place in the Anglican Liturgy until superseded by Tate and Brady about 1690.

religion last to the verge of Christendom, that you may discharge your chaplain (as humanity requires) in a place where he may find some business.

I doubt not but I shall be told—when I come to follow you through those countries—in how pretty a manner you accommodated yourself to the customs of the true Musselmen. They will tell me at what town you practised to sit on the sopha; at what village you learned to fold a turban; where you was bathed and anointed; and where you parted with your black *full-bottom*. How happy it must be, for a gay young woman, to live in a country where it is part of religious worship to be *giddy-headed*. I shall hear, at Belgrade, how the good Basha received you with tears of joy; how he was charmed with your agreeable manner of pronouncing the words *Allah* and *Muhammed*; and how earnestly you joined with him in exhorting your friend to embrace that religion. But I think his objection was a just one—that it was attended with some circumstances, under which he could not properly represent his Britannic Majesty. Lastly, I shall hear how, the first night you lay at Pera, you had a vision of Mahomet's Paradise, and happily awaked without a soul; from which blessed moment the beautiful body was left at full liberty to perform all the agreeable functions it was made for.

I see I have done in this letter as I have often done in your company—talked myself into a good humour, when I begun in an ill one. The pleasure of addressing you makes me run on, and it is in your own power to shorten this letter as much as you please, by giving over when you please. So I will make it no longer by apologies.

To Mr. Jervas.

Nov. 29, 1716.

That you have not heard from me of late ascribe not to the usual laziness of your correspondent, but to a ramble to Oxford, where your name is mentioned with honour, even in a land flowing with Tories. I had the good fortune there to be often in the conversation of Dr. Clarke.[1] He entertained me with several drawings, and particularly the original designs of Inigo Jones's Whitehall. I there saw and reverenced some of your first pieces,[2] which future painters are to look upon as we poets do on the Culex of Virgil and Batrachom of Homer.

Having named this latter piece, give me leave to ask what is become of Dr. Parnell and his Frogs? *Oblitusque meorum obliviscendus et illis*, might be Horace's wish, but will never be mine, while I have such *meorums* as Dr. Parnell and Dr. Swift. I hope the Spring will restore you to us, and with you all the beauties and colours of Nature. Not but I congratulate you on the pleasure you must take in being admired in your own country [Ireland], which so seldom happens to prophets and poets. But in this you have the advantage of poets—you are master of an Art that must prosper and grow rich, as long as people love or are proud of themselves or their own persons. However, you have stayed long enough, methinks, to have painted all the numberless histories of old Ogygia.[3] If you

---

[1] Dr. George Clarke had been Secretary at War under William III., a Lord of the Admiralty under Anne, and Judge Advocate under George I. He represented his University in Parliament from Nov. 1717 to his death.

[2] Jervas copied, says Horace Walpole, Raphael's "Cartoons in little, and sold them to Dr. Clarke, who became his protector and furnished him with money to visit Paris and Italy."—E.

[3] The island of Kalypso, placed by the author of the *Odyssey* in mid-ocean. It was this enchanted palace and the immortal charms of the Greek Alcina that Ulysses, according to the poet, abandoned for his old wife—*Vetulam prætulit immortalitati*.

have begun to be *historical*, I recommend to your hand the story which every pious Irishman ought to begin with, that of St. Patrick, to the end you may be obliged (as Dr. Parnell was when he translated the Batrachomuomachia) to come into England to copy the frogs, and such other vermin as were never seen in that land since the time of that confessor. I long to see you a history painter. You have already done enough for the private; do something for the public, and be not confined, like the rest, to draw only such silly stories as our own faces tell of us. The Ancients, too, expect you should do them right. Those statues, from which you learned your beautiful and noble ideas, demand it as a piece of gratitude from you, to make them truly known to all nations, in the account you intend to write of their characters.[1] I hope you think more warmly than ever of that design.

As to your inquiry about your house, when I come within the walls they put me in mind of those of Carthage, where your friend, like the wandering Trojan,

animum picturâ pascit inani.

For the spacious mansion, like a Turkish caravanserah, entertains the vagabond with only bare lodging. I rule the family very ill, keep bad hours, and lend out your pictures about the town. See what it is to have a poet in your house. Frank,[2] indeed, does all he can in such a circumstance; for, considering he has a wild beast in it, he constantly keeps the door chained. Every time it is opened, the links rattle, the rusty hinges roar. The house seems so sensible that you are its support, that it is ready to drop in your absence: but I still trust myself under its roof, as depending that Providence will preserve so many Raphaels, Titians, and Guidos, as are lodged in your cabinet.

---

[1] The projected treatise of Jervas upon ancient statues was never written.—E.
[2] Jervas's man-servant.

Surely the sins of one poet can hardly be so heavy as to bring an old house over the heads of so many painters. In a word, your house is falling; but what of that? I am only a lodger.[1]

TO THE HON. ROBERT DIGBY.[2]

June 2, 1717.

I had pleased myself sooner in writing to you, but that I have been your successor in a fit of sickness, and am not so much recovered but that I have thoughts of using your physicians.[3] They are as grave persons as any of the Faculty, and (like the Ancients) carry their own medicaments about with them. But, indeed, the Moderns are such lovers of raillery, that nothing is grave enough to escape them. Let them laugh, but people will still have their opinions. As they think our doctors asses to them, we will think them asses to our doctors. I am glad you are so much in a better state of health as to allow me to jest about it. My concern when I heard of your danger was so very serious, that I almost take it ill Dr. Evans[4] should tell you of it, or you mention it. I tell you fairly,

---

[1] Alluding to the story of the Irishman.—Warburton.

[2] Mr. Digby, the second son of Lord Digby, of about the same age as Pope, was born at Sherborne, in Dorsetshire, and educated at Magdalen College, Oxford—the College of the family, it seems. He represented Warwick in the House of Commons during ten years. He was of a very feeble constitution, and, after long lingering, he died in 1732, and was buried at Sherborne, where an epitaph, in memory of himself and his sister, by his friend, was placed in the Abbey.

[3] Asses [whose milk Digby used].—Roscoe. Pope seems not to have held with his friend Homer; or Idomeneus:

"Ιητρὸς γαρ ἄνηρ πολλῶν ἀντάξιος ἄλλων,"

which may be translated: "The physician is worth fifty laymen."

[4] The well-known Epigrammatist, of St. John's College, Oxford. It appears from the letters in the British Museum, that Evans was much in the confidence of Pope, as, indeed, were all who *looked up* to him.—Bowles.

if you and a few more such people were to leave the world, I would not give sixpence to stay in it. I am not so much concerned as to the point, whether you are to live fat or lean. Most men of wit or honesty are usually decreed to live *very lean.* So I am inclined to the opinion it is decreed *you* shall. However, be comforted, and reflect that you will make the better *busto* for it.

It is something particular in you, not to be satisfied with sending me your own books, but to make your acquaintance continue the frolic. Mr. Warton forced me to take *Gorboduc*,[1] who has since done me great credit with several people, as it has done Dryden and Oldham some diskindness, in showing there is as much difference between their *Gorboduc* and this as between Queen Anne and King George. It is truly a scandal, that men should write with contempt of a piece which they never once saw as those two poets did, who were ignorant even of the sex, as well as sense, of *Gorboduc.*

Adieu! I am going to forget you. This minute you took up all my mind; the next I shall think of nothing but the reconciliation with Agamemnon, and the recovery of Briseis. I shall be Achilles's humble servant these two months (with the good leave of all my friends). I have no ambition so strong at present as that noble one of Sir Salathiel Lovel, Recorder of London,[2] to furnish out a decent and plentiful execution of

---

[1] *Gorboduc* was the first drama in our language that was like a regular tragedy. It was first exhibited in the Hall of the Temple, and afterwards before Queen Elizabeth, 1561. It was written by Thomas Sackville, Lord Buckhurst, the original contriver of the *Mirror of Magistrates*. He was assisted in it by Thomas, a translator of some of the *Psalms*. Mr. Spence, who succeeded my father as Professor of Poetry at Oxford, printed an edition of *Gorborduc* from this very copy of Pope, 1736. . . . For a full account of *Gorborduc* see the *History of English Poetry* (III., 536), by Mr. Thomas Warton.—Warton. It is alluded to by Shakspeare in *Twelfth Night.*

[2] This allusion, whether in jest or earnest, is obscure. Sir Salathiel Lovel was made Recorder in 1692, and held that office till 1708, when he was promoted to be a Baron of the Exchequer. During his time the laws against the Papists were frequently enforced.—B.

Greeks and Trojans. It is not to be expressed how heartily I wish the death of all Homer's heroes, one after another. The Lord preserve me in the day of battle, which is just approaching! Join in your prayers for me, and know me to be always yours, &c.

To Lady Mary Wortley Montagu.

June, 171*.

If to live in the memory of others have anything desirable in it, it is what you possess with regard to me in the highest sense of the words. There is not a day in which your figure does not appear before me, your conversation return to my thoughts, and every scene, place, or occasion, where I have enjoyed them, are as vividly painted as an imagination, equally warm and tender, can be capable to represent them. Yet how little accrues to you from all this, when not only my wishes, but the very expressions of them, can hardly ever arrive to be known to you! I cannot tell whether you have seen half the letters I have writ, but, if you have, I have not said in them half what I designed to say; and you have seen but a faint, slight, timorous *échantillon* of what my spirit suggests, and my hand follows slowly and imperfectly, indeed unjustly, because discreetly and reservedly. When you told me there was no way left for our correspondence but by merchant ships, I watched ever since for any that set out, and this is the first I could learn of. I owe the knowledge of it to Mr. Congreve (whose letters, with my Lady Rich's, accompany this). However, I was impatient enough to venture to enquire from Mr. Methuen's office. If they have miscarried, you have lost nothing but such words and wishes as I repeat every day in your memory and for your welfare. I have had thoughts of causing what I write for the future to be transcribed, and to send copies by more ways than one, that one at least might have a chance to reach you.

My eyesight is grown so bad, that I have left off all correspondence, except with yourself; in which, methinks, I am like those people who abandon and abstract themselves from all that are about them (with whom they might have business and intercourse), to employ their address as only to invisible and distant beings, whose good offices and favours cannot reach them in a long time, if at all. If I hear from you, I look upon it as little less than a miracle, an extraordinary visitation from another world; it is a sort of dream of an agreeable thing, which subsists no more to me. But, however, it is such a dream as exceeds most of the dull realities of my life. Indeed, what with ill-health and ill-fortune, I am grown so stupidly philosophical as to have no thought about me that deserves the name of *warm* or *lively*, but that which sometimes awakens me into an imagination that I may yet see you again. Compassionate a poet, who has lost all manner of romantic ideas, except a few that hover about the Bosphorus and Hellespont—not so much for the fine sound of their names as to raise up images of Leander, who was drowned in crossing the sea to kiss the hand of fair Hero.[1] This were a destiny less to be lamented than what we are told of the poor Jew, one of your interpreters, who was beheaded at Belgrade as a spy.[2] I confess such a

---

[1] See the charming poem of *Hero and Leander*, of Musæus, and Ovid's *Epistle*.

[2] Mr. Wortley, in a letter dated Pera, 2 August, 1716 (O.S.), among the Official papers of the Embassy in the State-Paper Office, alludes to this circumstance as follows : "It is said, in a Dutch Gazette, that a Jew, who came with me to Belgrade, was there hanged as a spy. The Jew was not only very well with the Basha of Belgrade that knew him, but at Adrianople, where he lived. He went often to the houses of those that were in the greatest employments, and was well received by them."—C. W. D.

death would have been a great disappointment to me; and believe Jacob Tonson will hardly venture to visit you, after this news. . . .

I make not the least question but you could give me great *éclaircissements* upon many passages in Homer, since you have been enlightened by the same sun that inspired the father of poetry. You are now glowing under the climate that animated him: you may see his images rising more boldly about you, in the very scenes of his story and action: you may lay the immortal work on some broken column of a hero's sepulchre, and read the Fall of Troy in the shade of a Trojan ruin. But if, to visit the tomb of so many heroes, you have not the heart to pass over that sea where once a lover perished, you may, at least, at ease in your own window contemplate the fields of Asia, in such a dim and remote prospect as you have of Homer in my translation. I send you, therefore, with this the third volume of the *Iliad*, and as many other things as fill a wooden box, directed to Mr. Wortley. Among the rest, you have all I am worth—that is, my Works. There are few things in them but what you have already seen, except the Epistle of *Eloisa to Abelard*, in which you will find one passage that I cannot tell whether to wish you should understand or not.

For the news in London, I will sum it up in short. We have masquerades in the theatre in the Haymarket, of Mr. Heideker's institution.[1] They are very frequent, yet the adventures are not so numerous but that of my Lady Mohun[2] still makes the chief figure. Her marriage to young Mordaunt, and all its circumstances, I suppose you will have from Lady Rich or Miss Griffith. The political state is under great divisions—the

---

[1] Heydegger, the celebrated introducer of *Masquerades*. He is alluded to in the *Dunciad*.—C. W. D.

[2] Widow of Lord Mohun, who was killed in a duel with the Duke of Hamilton in 1712. [See Letters of Swift to Esther Johnson.] She married Colonel Charles Mordaunt, a nephew of Pope's friend, Lord Peterborough. Mordaunt was her third husband, and was much younger than his wife.—C. W. D.

parties of Walpole and Stanhope as violent as Whig and Tory. The K. and P.[1] continue two [opposed] names. There is nothing like a coalition, but at the masquerade. However, the Princess is a dissenter from it, and has a very small party in so unmodish a separation.

The last I received from your hands was from Peterwaradin. It gave me the joy of thinking you in good health and humour. One or two expressions in it are too generous ever to be forgotten by me. I writ a very melancholy one just before, which was sent to Mr. Stanyan, to be forwarded through Hungary. It would have informed you, how meanly I thought of the pleasures of Italy, without the qualification of your company, and that mere statues and pictures are not more cold to me than I to them. I have had but four of your letters: I have sent several, and wish I knew how many you have received. For God's sake, Madam, send to me as often as you can, in the dependence that there is no man breathing more constantly, or more anxiously, mindful of you. Tell me that you are well, tell me that your little son is well, tell me that your dog (if you have one) is well. Defraud me of no one thing that pleases you: for, whatever that is, it will please me better than anything else can do. I am always yours.

To Dr. Parnell,[2]

July 6, 1717.

I write to you as a friend, without apology or study, without intending to appear anything but what I am, and without so much as thinking I stand in need of any excuses or ceremonies for doing so. If it were otherwise, how many pretty things

[1] George the First and his son, the Prince of Wales, who were at this time at open rupture.—C. W. D.

[2] From the original, in the possession of Mr. Murray.—E.

might be said for my silence, and what ingenious turns might be given to yours,—that, as soon as you have obliged a man, you quite forget it, and that I know nothing is so ungrateful to you as thanks. To tell you that your translation of the Batrachomuomachia is an excellent piece is no more than everybody now knows, and to say that I like it still the better, and am more in your debt than the rest of the world, because it was done at my desire, is no more than you know already; and to acquaint you that there is not one man of any taste who does not approve the whole, verse and prose, is (after all that modesty may fancy it thinks) no more than what you must needs give a good guess at.

The other pieces you entrusted to my care lie preserved with the same veneration as relics, but I look upon them with greater pleasure when I reflect that the owner of them is yet living, though, indeed, you live to me but as a saint or separated spirit, whose sight I must never enjoy, though I am always sure of his good offices. It is through your mediation that Homer is to be saved,—I mean my Homer, and, if you could yet throw some hours away rather upon me than him, in suggesting some remarks upon his 13th, 14th, 15th, and 16th books, it would be charitable beyond expression; for I am very backward in this year's task, through the interruption of many different cares and distractions, to which none but as intimate and tender a friend as you ought to be privy. I could unload upon you with much comfort and confidence; but the very things I complain of prevent my seeing you in Ireland, which else I had done this summer.

I have, before I was aware, run into my own affairs too far, when I only meant to have told you the reason that your poems are not published. The present violent bent to politics and earnest animosities of parties, which grow within one another so fast, that one would think even every single heart was breeding a worm to destroy itself—these have left no room for any thought but those of mischief to one another. The Muses are all run mad and turned bacchanals, and a poet now may be like Amphion, and sing with the stones about his ears. This is my case, whose Works my bookseller would publish at such a juncture that I take it to be tempting Providence. I send them you all, and I think them but a poor return for those fine lines you allowed me to print in the front of them.

I must never forget my obligations to the Dean of St. Patrick's, and I hope you never omit to acquaint him with all that esteem, affection, and remembrance, which there is no putting upon paper, and which can only be felt in the heart. You will also put Dr. Ellwood and Mr. Ward in mind of me, each of whom I have desired, by Mr. Jervas, to accept of all I am worth—that is to say, my poems.

Gay is going for France next week in company with the late Secretary, Pulteney. I remain within four miles of London, a man of business and poetry,[1] from both of which I pray to be delivered. I am always the same in one respect— that is, always yours most sincerely.

To the Misses Teresa and Martha Blount.[2]

Sep. 13, 1717.

You cannot be surprised to find him a dull correspondent, whom you have known so long for a dull companion. And though I am pretty sensible that, if I have any wit, I may as

[1] At Chiswick.

[2] Published in ed. of 1735, not reproduced in *Quarto*. Reappeared in Cooper (1737). Mr. Carruthers gives extracts from the original, which is, he says, dated 13th Sept., 1717. But the reader must remember that there were not only omissions and alterations, but interpolations, in the letter when published: for example, the account of the death of Radcliffe, which took place in 1714, and which was here inserted from a suppressed letter written in 1714, is proof how Pope altered the letters on publication.—C.W.D.

well write to show it as not; yet I will content myself with giving you as plain a history of my pilgrimage as Purchas[1] himself, or as John Bunyan could do of his *walking through the wilderness of this world*, &c.

First, then, I went by water to Hampton Court, unattended by all but my own virtues, which were not of so modest a nature as to keep themselves or me concealed: for I met the Prince, with all his ladies, on horseback, coming from hunting. Mrs. B—— and Mrs. L——[2] took me into protection (contrary to the laws against harbouring papists), and gave me a dinner, with something I like better—an opportunity of conversing with Mrs. H. We all agreed that the life of a Maid of Honour was, of all things, the most miserable; and wished that every woman, who envied it, had a specimen of it. To eat Westphalia ham in a morning, ride over hedges and ditches on borrowed hacks, come home in the heat of the day with a fever, and (what is worse a hundred times) with a red mark in the forehead from an uneasy hat,[3] all this may qualify them to make excellent wives for foxhunters, and bear abundance of ruddy-complexioned children. As soon as they can wipe off the sweat of the day, they must simper an hour, and catch cold, in the Princess's apartment: from thence (as Shakspeare has it) to *dinner with what appetite they may*—and, after that, till midnight, walk, work, or think, which they please. I can easily believe no lone house in Wales, with a mountain and a rookery, is more contemplative than this Court; and, as a proof of it, I need only tell you, Mrs. L[epell] walked with me three or four hours by moonlight, and we met no creature of any quality but the King,

---

[1] Author of *Purchas his Pilgrimage; or Relations of the World*, &c.; and of *Haklytus Posthumus: or Purchas his Pilgrimes, Containing a History of the World in Sea Voyages and Land Travels*. Died 1626.

[2] Mary Bellenden and Mary Lepell, Maids of Honour to the Princess (of Wales). Mrs. H. is Mrs. Howard. The Prince was the future George II.

[3] "Beaver hat" in orig.—C. W. D.

who gave audience to the Vice-Chamberlain, all alone, under the garden wall.[1]

In short, I heard of no ball, assembly, basset-table, or any place where two or three were gathered together, except Madam Kilmansegg's: to which I had the honour of being invited, and the grace to stay away. I was heartily tired, and posted to —— park. There we had an excellent discourse of quackery. Dr. S—— [Shadwell?] was mentioned with honour. Lady —— walked a whole hour abroad without dying after it, at least in the time I stayed, though she seemed to be fainting, and had convulsive motions several times in her head. I arrived in the Forest by Tuesday noon, having fled from the face (I wish I could say the horned face) of Moses, who dined in the midway thither. I passed the rest of the day in those woods, where I have so often enjoyed a book and a friend. I made a hymn as I passed through, which ended with a sigh, that I will not tell you the meaning of.

Your doctor is gone the way of all his patients, and was hard put to it, how to dispose of an estate miserably unwieldly and splendidly unuseful to him. Sir Samuel Garth says, that for Radcliffe to leave a library was as if an eunuch should found a seraglio.[2] Dr. S—— lately told a lady, he wondered she could be alive after him. She made answer, she wondered at it for two reasons—because Dr. Radcliffe was dead, and because Dr. S. was living. I am, &c.

---

[1] This [the last sentence], I am assured, exists in the MS. : otherwise it is very like a passage in a letter to Lady M. W. Montagu (summer of 1718).— C. W. D.

[2] Because it was notorious that he had little learning : but he possessed what was better—wonderful sagacity and penetration in judging of diseases. Dr. Young has the same *simile* in his second Satire :—

"Unlearned men of books assume the care,
As Eunuchs are the Guardians of the Fair."—Warton.

To the Duchess of Hamilton.[1]

London, Oct. [1717?]

Mrs. Whitworth (who, as her epitaph on Twitnam Highway assures us, had attained to as much perfection and purity as any since the Apostles) [2] is now deposited, according to her own orders, between a fig tree and a vine, there to be found at the last resurrection. I am just come from seeing your Grace in much the like situation—between a honeysuckle and a rose-bush; where you are to continue as long as canvas can last. I suppose the painter by those emblems intended to intimate, on the one hand, your Grace's sweet disposition to your friends, and, on the other, to show you are near enough related to the Thistle of Scotland to deserve the same motto with regard to your enemies: *Nemo me impune lacesset.* Lord William will *conster* this Latine, if you send it to Thistleworth.

The two foregoing periods, methinks, are so mystical, learned, and perplexed, that if you have any statesmen or divines about you, they cannot choose but be pleased with them. One divine you cannot be without, as a good Christian, and a statesman you have lately had, for I hear my Lord Selkirk has been with you. But (that I may not be unintelligible quite to the bottom of this page) I must tell your Grace, in English, that I have made a painter bestow the aforesaid ornaments round about you

---

[1] So far as I know, this letter first appeared in the *Annual Register*, 1764, p. 222 : but most probably copied from a newspaper or magazine : but I have never seen the original. I believe 1717 to be the date.—C.W.D. The Duchess of Hamilton was the widow of the Duke who was killed in a duel with Lord Mohun. See Letters of Swift to Esther Johnson.

[2] This epitaph is thus referred to in Theobald's *Censor*, No. 27, for June 10, 1717 :—"I cannot dismiss this subject without taking notice of a monument, which has more ostentation in it than is decent on these occasions. It is erected on the side of a garden wall, on the entrance to the town of Twickenham, under which are laid the ashes of Mrs. Whitson [so he spells the name], a Quaker, and over which the inscription is engraved in stone."—C.W.D.

(for *upon* you there needs none), and I am, upon the whole, pleased with my picture beyond expression. I may now say of your picture, it is the thing in the world the likest you, except yourself; as a cautious person once said of an elephant— it was the biggest in the world, except itself.

You see, Madam, it is not impossible for you to be compared to an elephant, and you must give me leave to show you one may carry on the simile. An elephant never bends his knees, and I am told your Grace says no prayers. An elephant has a most remarkable command of his snout, and so has your Grace when you imitate my Lady Orkney.[1] An elephant is a great lover of men, and so is your Grace for all I know; though, from your partiality to myself, I should rather think you loved little children. . . . .

I beg Mr. Blondel may know Dr. Logg[2] has received ordination, and enters upon his function this winter at Mrs. Blount's. They have chosen this innocent man for their confessor: and I believe most Roman Catholic ladies, that have any sins, will follow their example. This good priest will be of the order of Melchizedec, a priest for ever, and serve a family from generation to generation. He will stand in a corner as quietly as a clock, and, being wound up once a week, strike up a loud alarum to sin, on a Sunday morning. Nay, if the Christian religion should be abolished (as, indeed, there is great reason to expect it from the wisdom of the Legislature), he might, at worst, make an excellent bonfire, which is all that (upon a change of religion) can be desired from a heretic. I do not hope your Grace should be converted; but, however, I wish you would call at Mrs. B's out of curiosity. To meet people one likes is thought by some the best reason for going to church, and I dare promise you will

---

[1] See Letters of Swift, page 131.

[2] A joke may here be intended, for, in what I believe to be the answer of the Duchess, she speaks of "father Legg."—C. W. D.

like one another. They [1] are extremely your servants, or else I should not think them my friends.

I ought to keep up the custom, and ask you to send me something. Therefore, pray, Madam, send me yourself, that is, a letter, and pray make haste to bring up yourself, that is, all I value, to town. I am, with the truest respect, the least ceremony, and the most zeal, &c.

To Dr. Atterbury.[2]

Nov. 20, 1717.

I am truly obliged by your kind condolence on my father's death, and the desire you express that I should improve this incident to my advantage.[3] I know your Lordship's friendship to me is so extensive, that you include in that wish both my spiritual and my temporal advantage; and it is what I owe to that friendship to open my mind unreservedly to you on this head.

It is true I have lost a parent for whom no gains I could make would be any equivalent. But that was not my only tie; I thank God, another still remains (and long may it remain) of the same tender nature. *Genetrix est mihi*, and excuse me, if

---

[1] The Blounts of Mapledurham.

[2] Bishop of Rochester. By his zeal in the Tory and High Church interest he had rapidly attained, in succession, the posts of Canon, Dean, and Bishop.

[3] Atterbury had written: "When you have paid the debt of tenderness you owe to the memory of a father, I doubt not but you will turn your thoughts towards improving that accident to your own ease and happiness. You have it now in your power to pursue that method of thinking and living which you like best." The Bishop suggests the secession of Pope from the Church to which he only nominally, but constantly, adhered.

say with Euryalus:

> *Nequeam lachrymas perferre parentis.*[1]

A rigid divine may call it a carnal tie, but sure it is a virtuous one. At least, I am more certain that it is a duty of nature to preserve a good parent's life and happiness than I am of any speculative point whatever:

> *Ignaram hujus quodcunque pericli
> Hanc ego nunc linquam?*

For she, my Lord, would think this separation more grievous than any other, and I, for my part, know as little as poor Euryalus did of the success of such an adventure: for an adventure it is, and no small one, in spite of the most positive divinity! Whether the change would be to my spiritual advantage, God only knows. This I know, that I mean as well in the religion I now profess as I can possibly ever do in another. Can a man, who thinks so, justify a change, even if he thought both equally good? To such an one the part of *joining* with any one body of Christians might, perhaps, be easy: but I think it would not be so, to *renounce* the other.

Your Lordship has, formerly, advised me to read the best controversies between the Churches. Shall I tell you a secret? I did so at fourteen years old, for I loved reading, and my father had no other books: there was a Collection of all that had been written, on both sides, in the reign of King James the Second. I warmed my head with them, and the consequence was, that I found myself a papist and a protestant by turns, *according to the last book I read.* I am afraid most seekers are in the same case, and, when they stop, they are not so properly converted as *outwitted*.[2] You see how little glory you would gain by my

---

[1] See *Æneis* IX. for the episode of Euryalus and Nisus. The next allusion is to Creüsa, wife of Æneas, at the burning of Troy.—(*Æn.* II.)

[2] Compare the account of Gibbon's temporary conversion to Catholicism as given by himself in his *Memoirs*. Gibbon was sixteen years of age at the time of his *conversion*.

conversion. And, after all, I verily believe your Lordship and I are both of the same religion, if we were thoroughly understood by one another, and that all honest and reasonable Christians would be so, if they did but talk enough together every day, and had nothing to do together but to serve God, and live in peace with their neighbour.

As to the *temporal* side of the question, I can have no dispute with you. It is certain all the beneficial circumstances of life, and all the shining ones, lie on the part you would invite me to.[1] But, if I could bring myself to fancy, what I think you do but fancy, that I have any talents for active life, I want health for it, and, besides, it is a real truth, I have less inclination (if possible) than ability. Contemplative life is not only my scene, but it is my habit too. I begun my life where most people end theirs, with a disrelish of all that the world call ambition. I do not know why it is called so, for to me it always seemed to be rather *stooping* than *climbing*. I will tell you my political and religious sentiments in a few words. In my politics, I think no further than how to preserve the peace of my life, in any Government under which I live, nor in my religion, than to preserve the peace of my conscience in any Church with which I communicate. I hope all Churches and all Governments are so far of God, as they are rightly understood and rightly administered;[2] and, where they are, or may be, wrong, I leave it to God alone to mend or reform them; which, whenever He does, it must be by greater instruments than I am.

I am not a *papist*, for I renounce the temporal invasions of the papal power, and detest their arrogated authority over

---

[1] The Catholics, it is scarcely necessary to observe, at this time, and for another century, lay under political disabilities.

[2] A sort of theological indifferentism which he has embodied in his *Essay on Man*:—

"For modes of Faith let graceless zealots fight :
His can't be wrong whose life is in the right," &c.

princes and states. I am a Catholic,[1] in the strictest sense of the word. If I was born under an absolute prince, I would be a quiet subject: but I thank God I was not. I have a *due* sense of the excellence of the British Constitution. In a word, the things I have always wished to see are, not a Roman Catholic, or a French Catholic, or a Spanish Catholic, but a true Catholic: not a King of Whigs, or a King of Tories, but a King of England: which God of His mercy grant his present Majesty may be, and all future Majesties. You see, my Lord, I end like a preacher. This is *Sermo ad clerum* not *ad populum*.[2] Believe me, with infinite obligation and sincere thanks, ever yours, &c.

TO THE HON. ROBERT DIGBY.

London, March 31, 1718.

To convince you how little pain I give myself in corresponding with men of good nature and good understanding, you see I omit to answer your letters till a time when another man would be ashamed to own he had received them. If, therefore, you are ever moved, on my account, by that spirit which I take to be as familiar to you as a quotidian ague, I mean the spirit of goodness, pray never stint it in any fear of obliging me to a civility beyond my natural inclination. I dare trust you, Sir, not only with my folly when I write, but with my negligence when I do not; and expect equally your pardon for either.

If I knew how to entertain you through this paper, it should

[1] Were words and names used grammatically and reasonably, he seems to imply, a *Catholic* would be employed to mean a person of *cosmopolitan* and *eclectic* sympathies.

[2] He means (but, perhaps, did not expect to be too literally interpreted) that he does not wish his opinion here expressed to be divulged.

be spotted and diversified with conceits all over. You should be put out of breath with laughter at each sentence, and pause at each period, to look back over how much wit you have passed. But I have found by experience that people now-a-days regard Writing as little as they do Preaching: the most we can hope, is to be heard just with decency and patience, once a week, by folks in the country. Here in town we hum over a piece of fine writing, and we whistle at a sermon. The Stage is the only place we seem alive at. There, indeed, we stare, and roar, and clap hands for King George and the Government. As for all other virtues but this loyalty, they are an absolute train, so ill-dressed that men, women, and children hiss them out of all good company. Humility knocks so sneakingly at the door, that every footman outraps it, and makes it give way to the free entrance of Pride, Prodigality, and Vain-Glory.

My Lady Scudamore,[1] from having rusticated in your company too long, really behaves herself scandalously among us. She pretends to open her eyes for the sake of seeing the sun, and to sleep because it is night; drinks tea at nine in the morning, and is thought to have said her prayers before; talks, without any manner of shame, of good books, and has not seen Cibber's play of the *Non-Juror*.[2] I rejoiced the other day to see a libel on her toilet, which gives me some hope that you have, at least, a taste of scandal left you, in defect of all other vices.

Upon the whole matter, I heartily wish you well: but as I cannot entirely desire the ruin of all the joys of this city, so all that remains is to wish you would keep your happiness to yourselves, that the happiest here may not die with envy at a bliss which they cannot attain to.

[1] Lady Scudamore was connected with the Digbys by marriage.—Bowles.

[2] Cibber always insisted that this comedy, founded on the admirable *Tartuffe* of Molière, was the chief cause of our author's resentment against him. It met with great success on the stage.—Warton. It came out in the winter of 1717.

To the Hon. Robert Digby.

July 20, 1720.

Your kind desire to know the state of my health had not been unsatisfied so long, had not that ill state been the impediment. Nor should I have seemed an unconcerned party in the joys of your family, which I heard of from Lady Scudamore, whose short *échantillon* of a letter (of a quarter of a page) I value as the short glimpse of a vision afforded to some devout hermit: for it includes (as those revelations do) a promise of a better life in the Elysian groves of Cirencester, whither, I could say almost in the style of a sermon, the Lord bring us all, &c. Thither may we tend by various ways to one blissful bower; thither may health, peace, and good humour wait upon us as associates; thither may whole cargoes of nectar-liquor of life and longevity—by mortals called Spa-waters—be conveyed; and there, as Milton has it, may we, like the deities:

" On flowers reposed, and with fresh garlands crowned,
    Quaff immortality and joy!"[1]

When I speak of garlands, I should not forget the green vest-

---

[1] The exquisite verses of Milton, in which Raphael describes the celestial dinner of the Immortals (imitated from Homer, with improvement), are as follow :—

" On flowers reposed. and with fresh flowerets crowned,
  They eat, they drink, and in communion sweet
  Quaff immortality and joy, secure
  Of surfeit."

A sort of feast which his terrestrial hostess, who had just before
                  " Prepared
  For dinner savoury fruits, of taste to please
  True appetite, and not disrelish thirst
  Of nectarous draughts between, from milky stream,
  Berry, or grape,"

could appreciate, we may imagine, more easily than her degenerate and carnivorous sons and daughters.

ments and scarfs, which your sisters promised to make for this purpose. I expect you, too, in green, with a hunting-horn by your side and a green hat, the model of which you may take from Osborne's description of King James the First. What words, what numbers, what oratory, or what poetry can suffice to express how infinitely I esteem, value, love, and desire you all, above all the great ones of this part of the world—above all the Jews, Jobbers, Bubblers, Subscribers, Projectors, Directors, Governors, Treasurers, &c., &c., &c., *in sœcula sœculorum*.[1]

Turn your eyes and attention from this miserable, mercenary, period; and turn yourself, in a just contempt of these sons of Mammon, to the contemplation of books, gardens, and marriage; in which I now leave you, and return (wretch that I am!) to water-gruel, and Palladio.[2]

---

[1] The "South Sea Bubble," supported by Harley (under political necessities), was, at this moment, the rage of the town, and blown up to its fullest extent. "I congratulate you, dear sir," says Digby, replying a few days later, "on the return of the Golden Age: for sure this must be such, in which money is showered down in such abundance upon us. I hope," he goes on ironically, "the overflowing will produce great and good fruits, and bring back the figurative moral Golden Age to us. . . . You seem to intimate in yours another face of things from this inundation of wealth. . . . If so, and if monsters only, as various as those of Nile, arise from this abundance, who that has any spleen about him will not haste to town to laugh? What will become of the Play-house? Who will go thither while there is such entertainment in the streets? I hope we shall neither want good satire nor comedy. If we do, the Age may well be thought barren of geniuses, for none has ever produced better subjects." At least, one immortal satire and comedy (combined) was inspired by this eager scramble of all classes, including Dukes, Duchesses, Generals, Judges, Bishops, Lord Mayors, &c., in a print (1721) of Hogarth. There is, also, a well-known painting by Ward upon the same promising subject. Pope himself was, to some extent, a speculator and loser—as he intimates in the next letters to Atterbury and to Caryll. The Bubble burst in 1720, and with it the reputations of not a few eminent people.

[2] Andrea Palladio, the great Italian Architect of the *Renaissance*. He designed a large number of the public and private palaces in Italy. His best-known writing is his *Trattato Dell' Architectura*. 1518—1580.

To Dr. Atterbury.

Sept. 28, 1720.

I hope you have some time ago received the sulphur, and the two volumes of Mr. Gay, as instances (how small ones soever) that I wish you both health and diversion.[1]

What I now send you for your perusal I shall say nothing of—not to forestall by a single word what you promised to say

[1] The volumes of Gay, in question, contained, his *Shepherd's Week*, *Trivia*, and the Farce of *What-D'ye-Call-It*—which had been published five years before. Pope had, also, sent to the Bishop of Rochester a copy of the *Arabian Tales* which had been translated by the French Orientalist, Antoine Galland (1646—1715), under the well-known title of the *Mille-et-un-Nuits*. It is scarcely necessary to remark that the popular title does not accurately describe this collection of Eastern Tales, derived as they are from the Persians, and even from Mohammedan India, much more than from the Arabs. The Bishop did not find them at all to his *classical* taste. "Ill as I have been almost ever since they came to hand," writes Atterbury, " I have read as much of them as ever I shall read while I live. Indeed, they do not please my taste. They are writ with so romantic an air, and, allowing for the difference of Eastern manners, are yet, upon any supposition that can be made, of so wild and absurd a contrivance (at least to my Northern understanding), that I have not only no pleasure, but no patience, in perusing them. They are to me like the odd paintings on Indian screens, which, at first glance, may surprise and please a little; but, when you fix your eye intently upon them, they appear so extravagant, disproportioned, and monstrous, that they give a judicious eye pain, and make him seek relief from some other object. They may furnish the mind with some new images: but I think the purchase is made at too great an expense. For to read those two volumes through, liking them as little as I do, would be a terrible penance; and to read them with pleasure would be dangerous, on the other side, because of the infection. I will never believe that you have any keen relish of them, till I find you write worse than you do, which, I dare say, I never shall. Who that Petit de la Croise is, the pretended author of them, I cannot tell : but observing how dull they are in the descriptions of dress, furniture, &c., I cannot help thinking them the product of some woman's imagination ; and, believe me, I would do anything, but break with you, rather than be bound to read them over with attention."—Petis de la Croix, whom Atterbury so much contemns, was a contemporary of Galland, and, like him, an eminent Oriental scholar, and author of several works on Mohammedan history. He was professor of Arabic in the College of Louis XIV., about the time that Ockley occupied the same position at Oxford. His *Persian Tales* appeared in 1720, in five volumes.

upon that subject. Your Lordship may criticise from Virgil to these Tales, as Solomon wrote of everything from the Cedar to the Hyssop. I have some cause, since I last waited on you at Bromley, to look upon you as a prophet in that retreat, from whom oracles are to be had, were mankind wise enough to go thither to consult you.

The fate of the South Sea scheme has, much sooner than I expected, verified what you told me. Most people thought the time would come, but no man prepared for it; no one considered it would come *like a thief in the night*. Methinks God has punished the avaricious, as he often punishes sinners, in their own way—in the very sin itself. The thirst of gain was their crime, that thirst continued became their punishment and ruin. As for the few, who have the good fortune to remain with half what they imagined they had (among whom is your humble servant), I would have them sensible of their felicity, and convinced of the truth of old Hesiod's maxim, who, after half his estate was swallowed by the directors of those days, resolved that Half to be more than the Whole.[1]

Does not the fate of these people put you in mind of two passages, one in *Job*, the other from the *Psalmist?*—

"Men shall groan out of the city, and hiss them out of their place."

"They have dreamed out their dream, and awakening have found nothing in their hands."

Indeed, the universal poverty, which is the consequence of universal avarice, and which will fall hardest upon the guiltless and industrious part of mankind, is truly lamentable. The universal deluge of the South Sea, contrary to the old deluge, has drowned all except a few unrighteous men: but it is some

---

[1] "Oh fools! they know not in their selfish soul,
How far the Half is better than the Whole—
The good that Asphodels and Mallows yield,
The feast of herbs, the dainties of the field."—*Works and Days*.

comfort to me that I am not one of them, even though I were to survive, and rule the world by it. I am much pleased with the thought of Dr. Arbuthnot's. He says, the Government and the South Sea Company have only locked up the money of the people, upon conviction of their lunacy (as is usual in the case of lunatics), and intend to restore them as much as may be fit for such people, as fast as they shall see them return to their senses.

TO MR. JOHN CARYLL.

Dec. 12, 1720.

I had epistolised you long ago but in the expectation of your coming to town, which was given me by several hands. I was lately very happy in an evening's conference with your son who, like all the rest of the world, has an undoubted right to me; though I took it a little ill he did not make use of it, in making my cottage his habitation during his stay at Twitenham. I was, unfortunately, at London all but one day, and I cannot express how concerned I am to have missed the satisfaction of both Lady Mary's and his neighbourhood. Nothing can make it up but your own coming, which your last letter gave me some hopes of: but Mr. Caryll tells me you do not as yet intend to leave the country.

My present situation very much resembles Noah's Ark, not only on account of the wide watery prospect of all the face of the earth overflowed round about me,[1] but, also, because I find myself and little family in a manner separated from all the

---

[1] Pope, in a letter to Teresa Blount, says that the Thames had risen so high that the tops of the walls which flanked his grass-plot were only just visible, an opposite meadow was covered with sails, and gudgeons were pumped up through a pipe in the kitchen.—C.

world, without commerce or society, and what makes society or commerce—money. The vast inundation of the South Sea [Bubble] has drowned all, except a few unrighteous men, contrary to the Deluge; and it is some comfort to me I am not one of those, even in my afflictions. It is a serious satisfaction to me to reflect that I am not the richer for the calamities of others which, as the world has gone, must have been the case nine times in ten. I protest to you I speak in earnest[1] . . . than to have been the greatest gainers with that reflection; and to convince you how much I am in earnest, I am really forced to desire you to order me the little you owe me, if you can, to even it to Christmas, being in more necessity for present money than I ever yet was. I am much pleased with a thought of Dr. Arbuthnot, who says the Government and South Sea Company have only locked up the money of the people upon conviction of their lunacy, as is usual in the case of lunatics, and intend to restore them as much as is fit for such people, as they see them return more and more to their senses.

I am got to the bottom of my letter before I was aware. There is a pleasure in writing or talking to you, which I could indulge, but must have mercy on you. I am constantly and faithfully yours.

To Lord Oxford.[2]

From my Lord Harley's in Dover Street, Oct. 21, 1721.

Your Lordship may be surprised at the liberty I take in writing to you, though you will allow me always to remember

---

[1] The transcriber appears here to have missed a line.

[2] Published by Pope in the Quarto of 1737, and printed here from the original letter in the Oxford papers, which is nearly the same with the Quarto text.—E. When the intimacy of the late Minister with Pope is considered, it may seem strange that this is the only existing (or at least published) letter to him from the poet. Lord Harley was Lord Oxford's eldest son.

that you once permitted me that honour, in conjunction with some others who better deserved it. Yet I hope you will not wonder I am still desirous to have you think me your grateful and faithful servant. But I own I have an ambition yet farther, to have others think me so, which is the occasion I give your Lordship the trouble of this.

Poor Parnell, before he died, left me the charge of publishing those few remains of his. I have a strong desire to make them, their author, and their publisher more considerable by addressing and dedicating them all to you. There is a pleasure in bearing testimony to truth, and a vanity, perhaps, which at least is as excusable as any vanity can be. I beg you, my Lord, to allow me to gratify it, in prefixing this paper of honest verses to the book. I send the book itself, which, I dare say, you will receive more satisfaction from perusing than you can from anything written upon the subject of yourself. Therefore I am a good deal in doubt whether you will care for such an addition to it. I will only say for it, that it is the only dedication I ever writ,[1] and shall be, whether you permit it or not, for I will not bow the knee to a less man than my Lord Oxford, and I expect to see no greater in my time.[2]

[1] This is a strange assertion. The dedication is dated Sept. 25, 1721, and, in 1714, Pope had formally dedicated the *Rape of the Lock* to Miss Fermor, and, in 1720, the translation of the *Iliad* to Congreve. Each of his *Pastorals* and *Windsor Forest* were inscribed to particular persons, and he afterwards continued the practice in his *Dunciad, Moral Essays*, and *Imitations of Horace*. Few poets have turned their pieces to more account, in paying tribute to individuals.—E.

[2] Either Pope descended to flattery, or he subsequently formed a juster estimate of Lord Oxford. Pope told Spence :—" He was not a very capable Minister, and had a good deal of negligence into the bargain. He used to send trifling verses from the Court to the Scriblerus Club almost every day, and would come and talk idly with them almost every night, even when his All was at stake. He was huddled [*sic*] in his thoughts, and obscure in his manner of delivering them. He talked of business in so confused a manner, that you did not know what he was about, and everything he went to tell you was in the epic way: for he always began in the middle." He had been brought up a dissenter, and he used to keep

After all, if your Lordship will tell my Lord Harley that I must not do this, you may depend upon a total suppression of the verses, the only copy whereof I send you. But you never shall suppress that great, sincere, and entire admiration and respect with which I am, &c.[1]

chaplains of various sects at his table, and among them a clergyman of the Established Church.

Erasmus Lewis wrote to Swift (July 27, 1714), after the dismissal of Lord Oxford, "the Queen has told all the lords the reasons for her parting with him, viz., that he neglected all business; that he was seldom to be understood; that when he did explain himself she could not depend upon the truth of what he said; that he never came to her at the time she appointed; that he often came drunk; lastly, to crown all, he behaved himself towards her with bad manners, indecency, and disrespect."—E. None the less, in some of his political views he seems to have been superior to many of his Tory successors. He was opposed to engaging the country in foreign and useless wars. See a notice of him in *Bolingbroke: a Political Study*, 1884.

[1] In reply to this flattering letter Lord Oxford, a fortnight later, writes from Brampton Castle an equally flattering one:—"Sir,—I received your packet, which could not but give me great pleasure, to see you preserve an old friend in your memory: for it must needs be very agreeable to be remembered by those we highly value. But, then, how much shame did it cause me, when I read your very fine verses enclosed? My mind reproached me, how far short I came of what your great friendship and delicate pen would partially describe me. You ask my consent to publish it. To what straits does this reduce me. I look back, indeed, to those evenings I have usefully and pleasantly spent with Mr. Pope, Mr. Parnell, Dr. Swift, the doctor [Arbuthnot], &c. I should be glad the world knew you admitted me to your friend, and, since your affection is too hard for your judgment, I am contented to let the world know how well Mr. Pope can write upon a barren subject. I return you an exact copy of the verses, that I may keep the original, as a testimony of the only error you have been guilty of. I hope very speedily to embrace you in London, and to assure you of the particular esteem and friendship, wherewith I am, &c."

To Dr. Atterbury.

March 19, 1721-22.

I am extremely sensible of the repeated favour of your kind letters,[1] and your thoughts of me in absence, even among thoughts of much nearer concern to yourself on the one hand, and of much more importance to the world on the other, which cannot but engage you at this juncture. I am very certain of your goodwill, and of the warmth which is in you inseparable from it.

Your remembrance of Twitenham is a fresh instance of that partiality. I hope the advance of the fine season will set you upon your legs, enough to enable you to get into my garden, where I will carry you up a mount, in a point of view to shew you the glory of my little kingdom. If you approve it, I shall be in danger to boast, like Nebuchadnezzar, of the things I have made, and be turned to converse, not with the beasts of the field, but with the birds of the grove, which I shall take to be no great punishment. For, indeed, I heartily despise the ways of the world, and most of the great ones of it.

Oh! keep me innocent, make others great!

---

[1] In one of his more recent letters, the Bishop had written:—"I will bring your small volume of *Pastorals* along with me [from Bromley to town], that you may not be discouraged from lending me books, when you find me so punctual in returning them. *Shakspeare* shall bear it company, and be put into your hands as clean and as fair as it came out of them, though you, I think, have been dabbling here and there with the text. I have had more reverence for the writer and the printer, and left everything standing just as I found it. However, I thank you for the pleasure you have given me, in putting me upon reading him once more before I die." In a postscript he adds:—"Addison's works came to my hand yesterday. I cannot but think it a very odd set of incidents that the book should be dedicated by a dead man to a dead man [Secretary Craggs], and even that the new patron [Lord Warwick], to whom Tickell chose to inscribe his verses, should be dead also before they were published. Had I been in the editor's place, I should have been a little apprehensive for myself, under a thought that every one who had any hand in that work was to die before the publication of it. You see, when I am conversing with you, I know not how to give over, till the very bottom of the paper admonishes me once more to bid you adieu!"

And you may judge how comfortably I am strengthened in this opinion, when such as your Lordship bear testimony to its vanity and emptiness. *Tinnit, inane est,* with the picture of one ringing on the globe with his fingers, is the best thing I have the luck to remember in that great poet Quarles—not that I forget the Devil at bowls, which I know to be your Lordship's favourite cut, as well as favourite diversion.¹ The situation here is pleasant, and the views rural enough to humour the most retired, and agree with the most contemplative, good air, solitary groves, and sparing diet, sufficient to make you fancy yourself (what you are in temperance, though elevated into a greater figure by your station) one of the Fathers of the desert. Here you may think—to use an author's words, whom you so justly prefer to all his followers that you will receive them kindly, though taken from his worst work :—

"That in Elijah's banquet you partake,
Or sit a guest with Daniel, at his pulse." ²

I am sincerely free with you, as you desire I should, and approve of you not having your coach here; for, if you would see Lord C——, or anybody else, I have another chariot besides that little one you laughed at, when you compared me to Homer in a nutshell. But, if you would be entirely private, nobody

---

¹ In the *Emblems, Divine and Moral* (1635.) Quarles who was "cup-bearer" to the sister of Charles I., and afterwards Secretary to Usher, Archbishop of Armagh, left behind him, besides the *Emblems*, a number of more or less quaint and eccentric quasi-religious and moral poems, somewhat in the spirit of Diogenes of Sinope—*A Feast for Wormes, Hieroglyphics of the Life of Man,* &c. Died in 1644.

² *Paradise Regained,* ii. Compare the sentiments of Milton, expressed through the Young Lady in *Comus,* in reply to that sophistical sorcerer :—

"If every just man, that now pines with want," &c.

and Shelley's eloquent description of the Reformed Banquets, inaugurated by Laone :—

"Their feast was such as Earth, the general mother,
Pours from her fairest bosom . . ." &c.—*Revolt of Islam V.*

shall know anything of the matter. Believe me, my Lord, no man is with more perfect acquiescence, nay, with more willing acquiescence—not even any of your own sons of the Church— your obedient, humble, servant.

To the Hon. Robert Digby.

1722.

Your making a sort of apology for your not writing is a very genteel reproof to me. I know I was to blame, but I know I did not intend to be so, and (what is the happiest knowledge in the world) I know you will forgive me: for sure, nothing is more satisfactory than to be certain of such a friend as will overlook one's failings, since every such instance is a conviction of his kindness.

If I am all my life to dwell in intentions, and never to rise to actions, I have but too much need of that gentle disposition which I experience in you. But I hope better things of myself, and fully purpose to make you a visit this summer at Sherborne. I am told you are all upon removal very speedily, and that Mrs. Mary Digby talks, in a letter to Lady Scudamore, of seeing my Lord Bathurst's Wood in her way. How much I wish to be her guide through that enchanted forest is not to be expressed. I look upon myself as the magician appropriated to the place, without whom no mortal can penetrate into the recesses of those sacred glades. I could pass whole days in only describing to her the future, and as yet visionary, beauties that are to rise in those scenes—the palace that is to be built, the pavilions that are to glitter, the colonnades that are to adorn them. Nay, more, the meeting of the Thames and the Severn,[1] which (when the noble owner has finer dreams than ordinary) are to be led into each other's embraces, through secret caverns of not above twelve or fifteen miles, till they rise and celebrate their marriage in the midst of an immense amphitheatre, which is to be the admiration of posterity a hundred years hence. But, till the destined time shall arrive that is to manifest these wonders, Mrs. Digby must content herself with seeing what is, at present, no more than the finest Wood in England.

The objects that attract this part of the world are of a quite different nature. Women of quality are all turned followers of the camp in Hyde Park this year, whither all the town resort to magnificent entertainments given by the officers, &c. The Scythian ladies, that dwelt in the waggons of war, were not more closely attached to the luggage. The matrons, like those of Sparta, attend their sons to the field, to be the witnesses of their glorious deeds; and the maidens, with all their charms displayed, provoke the spirit of the soldiers. Tea and coffee supply the place of Lacedemonian black broth. This camp seems crowned with perpetual victory, for every sun that rises in the thunder of cannon sets in the music of violins. Nothing is yet wanting, but the constant presence of the Princess, to represent the *Mater Exercitûs*.

At Twickenham the world goes otherwise. There are certain old people who take up all my time,[2] and will hardly allow me to keep any other company. They were introduced here by a man of their own sort, who has made me perfectly rude to all contemporaries, and would not so much as suffer me to look

---

[1] Such has been the rapid [?] improvement in everything relating to general and public utility in the course of much less than a hundred years, that what Pope and Bathurst considered as "such things as dreams are made of"—the junction of the Thames and Severn—has actually taken place [1806]; and the "admiration" is, that it could be so long before it was effected.—Bowles.

[2] Pope means Homer, and his Greek or Latin Critics.

upon them. The person I complain of is the Bishop of Rochester. Yet he allows me (from something he has heard of your character and that of your family, as if you were of the old sett of moralists) to write three or four sides of paper to you, and to tell you (what these sort of people never tell but with truth and religious sincerity) that I am, and ever will be, Yours, &c.

To Mr. Hugh Bethel.[1]

July, 1723.

I assure you, unfeignedly, any memorial of your good-nature and friendliness is most welcome to me, who know those tenders of affection from you are not like the common traffic of compliments and professions, which most people only give that they may receive, and is, at least, a commerce of vanity, if not of falsehood. I am happy in not immediately wanting the good offices you offer: but, if I did want them, I should not think myself unhappy in receiving them at your hands. This really is some compliment, for I would rather most men did me a small injury than a kindness.

I know your humanity, and, allow me to say, I love and value you for it. It is a much better growth of love and value than all the qualities I see the world so fond of: they generally advise in the wrong place, and generally most advise the things they do not comprehend, or the things one never can be the better for. Very few can receive pleasure or advantage from wit, which they seldom taste, or learning which they seldom understand, much less from the quality, high birth, or shining cir-

[1] A gentleman of good fortune in Yorkshire, with whom Pope maintained an uninterrupted intercourse to the close of his life.—Roscoe.

cumstances of those to whom they profess esteem, and who will always remember how much they are their inferiors. But humanity and sociable virtues are what every creature wants every day, and still wants more the longer he lives, and most the moment he dies. It is ill travelling either in a ditch or on a terrace. We should walk in the common way, where others are continually passing on the same level, to make the journey of life supportable by bearing one another company in the same circumstances.

Let me know how I may convey over the *Odysseys* for your amusement in your journey, that you may compare your own travels with those of Ulysses. I am sure yours are undertaken upon a more disinterested, and, therefore, a more heroic motive. Far be the omen from you of returning as he did, alone, without saving a friend. There is lately printed a book,[1] wherein all human virtue is reduced to one lesson—that of truth; and branched out in every instance of our duty to God and Man. If you have not seen it, you must, and I will send it together with the *Odyssey*. The very women read it, and pretend to be charmed with that beauty which they generally think the least of. They make as much ado about *Truth*, since the book appeared, as they did about *Health*, when Dr. Cheyne's came out,[2] and will doubtless be as constant in the pursuit of one as of the other. Adieu.

[1] Mr. Wollaston's excellent book of the *Religion of Nature Delineated*. The Queen was fond of it, and that made the reading of it, and the talking of it, fashionable.—Warburton. Pope also read it attentively, as appears by many passages taken from it, in the *Essay of Man*.—Warton.

[2] *Essay of Health and a Long Life*, published about a year previously. It went through several editions. Haller gave it high praise. In 1740 appeared his *Essay on Regimen*, and, in 1742, his *Natural Method of Curing the Diseases of the Body and the Disorders of the Mind Depending on the Body*. Dr. George Cheyne was the leading, and much-esteemed, Medical Reformer of the first half of the last century. He advocated strongly the adoption of a radically-reformed Diet. See Horace Walpole's Letters.

To Miss Judith Cowper.

Twitenham, Oct. 18 [1723].

We are indebted to heaven for all things, and, above all, for our sense and genius (in whatever degree we have it): but to fancy yourself indebted to anything else moves my anger at your modesty. The regard I must bear you, seriously, proceeds from myself alone; and I will not suffer even one I like so much as Mrs. H[oward] to have a share in causing it. I challenge a kind of relation to you on the soul's side, which I take to be better than either on a father's or mother's; and, if you can overlook an ugly *body* (that stands much in the way of any friendship, when it is between different sexes), I shall hope to find you a true and constant kinswoman in Apollo.

Not that I would place all my pretensions upon that poetical foot, much less confine them to it. I am far more desirous to be admitted as yours, on the more meritorious title of friendship. I have ever believed this as a sacred maxim: that the most ingenious natures were the most sincere, and the most knowing and sensible minds make the best friends. Of all those that I have thought it the felicity of my life to know, I have ever found the most distinguished in capacity the most distinguished in morality; and those the most to be depended on whom one esteemed so much as to desire they should be so. I beg you to make me no more compliments. I could make *you* a great many; but I know you neither need them, nor can like them: be so good as to think *I* do not. In one word, your writings are very good, and very entertaining: but not so good, nor so entertaining, as your life and conversation. One is but the effect and emanation of the other. It will be always a greater pleasure to me to know you are well than that you write well, though, every time you tell me the one, I must know the other.

I am willing to spare your modesty; and, therefore, as to your writing, may, perhaps, never say more (directly to yourself) than the few verses I send here; which (as a proof of my own modesty too) I made so long ago as the day you sate for your picture, and yet never till now durst confess to you:

> Though sprightly Sappho force our love and praise,
> A softer wonder my pleased soul surveys,
> The mild Erinna, blushing in her bays.
> So, while the Sun's broad beam yet strikes the sight,
> All mild appears the Moon's more sober light—
> Serene, in virgin majesty, she shines,
> And, unobserved, the glaring Sun declines.

The brightest wit in the world, without the better qualities of the heart, must meet with this fate; and tends only to endear such a character as I take yours to be. In the better discovery, and fuller conviction, of which I have a strong opinion I shall grow more and more happy the longer I have your acquaintance, and (if you will indulge me in so much pleasure), your faithful friend, and most obliged servant.

To Miss Judith Cowper.

Twitenham, Nov. 5 [1723].

Though I am extremely obliged by your agreeable letter, I will avoid the mention of the pleasure you give me, that we may have no more words about compliments; which I have often observed people talk themselves into, while they endeavour to talk themselves out of [them]. It is no more the diet of friendship and esteem than a few thin wafers and marmalade were to so hearty a stomach as Sancho's. In a word, I am very proud of my new relation, and like Parnassus much the better since I found I had so good a neighbour there. Mrs. Howard, who lives at Court, shall teach the country-folks sincerity; and, when I am so happy as to meet you, she shall settle the proportions of that regard or good-nature, which she can allow you to spare me, from a heart which is so much known as yours is.

That lady is the most trusty of friends, if the imitation of Shakspeare be yours,[1] for she made me give my opinion of it with the assurance it was none of Mrs. — [Miss Cowper's]. I honestly liked and praised it, whosesoever it was. There is in it a sensible melancholy, and too true a picture of human life; so true an one, that I can scarce wish the verses yours at the expense of your thinking that way, so early. I rather wish you may love the town (which the author of those lines cannot *immoderately* do) these many years. It is time enough to like, or affect to like, the country, when one is out of love with all but oneself, and, therefore, studies to become agreeable or easy to oneself. Retiring into oneself is generally the *pis-aller* of mankind.

Would you have me describe my solitude and Grotto to you? What if, after a long and painted description of them in verse (which the writer I have just been speaking of could better make, if I can guess by that line—*No noise but water, ever friend to thought*), what, if it ended thus:—[2]

> What are the falling rills, the pendant shades,
> The morning bowers, the evening colonnades,
> But soft recesses for the uneasy mind,
> To sigh unheard in, to the passing wind!

[1] *A Fit of the Spleen*, inserted afterwards in the *London Magazine*, 1737.

[2] These verses form the concluding part of those addressed to Gay, with some variations. In the earlier part are the well-known lines to Lady M. W. Montagu:

> "Joy lives not here—to happier seats it flies,
> And only dwells where Wortley casts her eyes."

> So the struck Deer, in some sequestered part,
> Lies down to die (the arrow in his heart):
> There hid in shades, and wasting day by day,
> Inly he bleeds, and pants his soul away.[1]

If these lines want poetry, they do not want sense. God Almighty long preserve you from a feeling of them! The book you mention, Bruyère's *Characters*, will make anyone know the world, and, I believe, at the same time, despise it; which is a sign it will make one know it thoroughly. It is certainly the proof of a master hand, that can give such striking likenesses, in such slight sketches, and in so few strokes in each subject.[2]

In answer to your question about *Shakspeare*, the book is about a quarter printed, and the number of emendations very great. I have never indulged my own conjectures,[3] but kept merely to such amendments as are authorised by old editions, in the author's lifetime: but I think it will be a year, at least, before the whole Work will be finished. In reply to your very handsome (I wish it were a very true) compliment upon this head, I only desire you to observe, by what natural, gentle, degrees I have sunk to the humble thing I now am: first from a pretending poet to a critic; then, to a low translator; lastly, to a mere publisher. I am apprehensive I shall be nothing that is of any value long, except, Madam, your most obliged, &c.

I long for your return to town—a place I am unfit for, but shall not be long out of as soon as I know I may be permitted to wait on you there.

---

[1] This is a merely illustrative *simile:* but the reader may see a touching description of this sort of spectacle in *As You Like It*, where the philosophic Jaques, or rather Shakspeare, denounces the selfish cruelty of Deer-hunting.

[2] La Bruyère's *Caractères* is an (improved) imitation of the *Characters* of Theophrastus. The author died in 1696.

[3] A too modest estimate of his Shaksperian labours: but some of his conjectures have more ingenuity than probability: *e.g.*, the well-known substitution of *South* for *Sound* in *Twelfth Night*, Act I., 1.

To Miss Judith Cowper.
[1723.]

I could not play the impertinent so far as to write to you [again], till I was encouraged to it by a piece of news Mrs. Howard tells me, which ought to be the most agreeable in the world to any author—that you are determined to write no more. It is now the time, then, not for me only, but for everybody, to write without fear, or wit; and I shall give you the first example here. But for this assurance, it would be every way too dangerous to correspond with a lady whose very first sight, and very first writings, had such an effect upon a man used to what they call fine sights, and what they call fine writings. Yet he has been dull enough to sleep quietly, after all he has seen, and all he has read, till yours broke in upon his stupidity and indolence, and totally destroyed it. But, God be thanked, you will write no more: so I am in no danger of increasing my admiration of you one way, and, as to the other, you will never (I have too much reason to fear) open these eyes again with one glimpse of you.

I am told you named lately, in a letter, a place called Twitenham with particular distinction.[1] That you may not be misconstrued, and have your meaning mistaken for the future, I must acquaint you, Madam, that the name of the place where Mrs. Howard is, is not Twitenham, but Richmond; which your ignorance in the geography of these parts has made you confound together. You will, unthinkingly, do honour to a paltry hermitage (while you speak of Twitenham), where lives a creature altogether unworthy your memory or notice, because he really wishes he had never beheld you nor yours. You have spoiled

---

[1] In her *Progress of Poetry*. She had eulogised Pope himself in the most flattering terms, in whom :—
"Nature and Art in bright conjunction shine," &c.

him for a *solitaire* and a book, all the days of his life, and put him in such a condition, that he thinks of nothing, and enquires of nothing, but after a person who has nothing to say to him, and has left him for ever without hope of ever again regarding, or pleasing, or entertaining him, much less of seeing him. He has been so mad with the idea of her, as to steal her picture, and passes whole days in sitting before it, talking to himself, and (as some people imagine) making verses. But it is no such matter, for, as long as he can get any of hers, he can never turn his head to his own—it is so much better entertainment.

To Miss Judith Cowper.

[1723.]

I am touched with shame when I look on the date of your letter. I have answered it a hundred times in my own mind, which I assure you has few thoughts, either so frequent or so lively, as those relating to you. I am sensibly obliged by you, in the comfort you endeavour to give me upon the loss of a friend. It is like the shower we have had this morning, that just makes the drooping trees hold up their heads, but they remain checked and withered at the root: the benediction is but a short relief, though it comes from heaven itself. The loss of a friend is the loss of life. After that is gone from us, it is all but a gentler decay, and wasting and lingering a little longer.

I was the other day forming a wish for a lady's happiness, upon her birthday, and thinking of the greatest climax of felicity I could raise, step by step, to end in this—a *friend*. I fancy I have succeeded in the gradation, and send you the whole copy, to ask your opinion, or (what is much the better reason) to desire you to alter it to your own wish: for I believe you are a woman that can wish for yourself more reasonably than I can for you. Mrs. Howard made me promise her a copy; and, to the end she may value it, I beg it may be transcribed, and sent her by you:—

To a Lady on her Birthday.[1]

Oh! be thou blest with all that heaven can send:
Long life, long youth, long pleasure—and a friend!
Not with those toys the women-world admire,
Riches that vex, and vanities that tire.
Let joy or ease, let affluence or content,
And the gay conscience of a life well-spent,
Calm every thought, inspirit every grace,
Glow in thy heart, and smile upon thy face!
Let day improve on day, and year on year,
Without a pain, a trouble, or a fear!
And ah! (since death must that dear form destroy)
Die by some sudden ecstasy of joy—
In some soft dream may thy mild soul remove,
And be thy latest gasp a sigh of love!

Pray, Madam, let me see this mended in your copy to Mrs. Howard, and let it be an exact scheme of happiness drawn and, I hope, enjoyed by yourself, to whom, I assure you, I wish it all, as much as you wish it her. I am always, with true respect, &c.

To Lord Bolingbroke.[2]

April 9, 1724.

You will think me very indolent till I tell you I have been very sick, the only reason that has left your letter unacknow-

---

[1] Another copy of these verses, with variations, was sent to Martha Blount, about the same time. Some of them had been sent to Gay, in the preceding year; and they were also adapted, with additions, for an epitaph on Henry Mordaunt, nephew of Lord Peterborough, who put an end to himself in 1724.

[2] From the copy in the Oxford MSS.—E.

ledged so long by words, which has every day been acknowledged in my heart. A severe fit of illness, a sort of intermitting fever, has made me unfit for all sorts of writing and application. You will see, I fear, the effects of it in this letter, which will be almost enough to convince you that all those mighty hopes of improvement of the English language, and the glory of its poetry, must rest upon some abler prop than your servant.

To answer first to your Lordship's charge against me as a translator *convict*. I do confess, I do not translate Homer as a great work, but as an easy one; which I really find less difficult than it seems Mr. de Sacy does to write Pliny into French prose. Whatever expectations my own vanity, or your partiality, might give me of a better fate than my predecessors in poetry, I own I am already arrived to an age which more awakens my diligence to live satisfactorily than to write unsatisfactorily to myself— more to consult my happiness than my fame; or, in defect of happiness, my quiet. Methinks quiet serves instead of happiness to philosophers, as vanity serves instead of fame to authors, for in either case the art of contentment is all. But, when men grow too nice and too knowing, the *succedaneum* will not do to such delicate constitutions; and the author becomes miserable to himself in the degree that he grows acceptable to others. What you call a happy author is the unhappiest man, and from the same cause that men are generally miserable —from aiming at a state more perfect than man is capable of. *Victor virûm volitare per ora* may indeed sound nobly in the ears of the ambitious, whether in the field, the State, or the study. But sure that consideration, to a man's self, is not of such weight as to sacrifice to that alone all the more attainable, and the more reasonable aims of our being. To write well, lastingly well, immortally well, must not one leave father and mother and cleave unto the Muse? Must not one be prepared to endure the reproaches of men, want, and much fasting, nay martyrdom, in its cause? It is such a taste as scarce leaves a man time to be a good neighbour, an useful friend, nay to plant a tree, much less to save his soul. Pray, my Lord, may not one ask this question of so just, so grateful, and so deserving a thing as the present Age,—*Tanti est, ut placeam tibi, perire?*—that present Age which you charge me as so much in debt to, and which you rank with my two other great creditors—Posterity and my Country. To the two first truly I think I am indebted just equally: for one of them has done exactly as much for me as the other. But to my Country, sure, my Lord, I owe nothing, for it has driven away my best friends. I shall owe it something when it calls them back again. This general reflection makes me shake my head at all encouragements you muster up, to induce me to write.

I own your observations, as to the possibility of fixing a Language, and as to the necessity of good original Works, to perpetuate it, to be just, and of a much greater strength and solidity than the usual arguments on that head. I admire your remark, that it is not always a consequence that Languages must decay as Governments fall: and it is very truly, as well as finely, said, that Greek, like Christianity, spread by persecution—as much as Latin, like Mahometanism, by victory. But allow me to say, that for an Englishman to ground an opinion of the immortality of his language from that of Homer, because the States of Greece were then inferior to what our nation is at present, would be just such a way of reasoning as if five or six hundred *Rapparees*, getting together to plunder a few villages, should hope to lay the foundations of an Empire, because that of the Ottomans began much in the same manner. Neither do I think the examples of the best writers in our time and nation would have that prevalence over the bad ones, which your Lordship observes them to have had in the Roman times. A State, constantly divided into various factions and interests, occasions an eternal swarm of bad writers. Some of these will be encouraged by the Government equally, if not superiorly, to the good ones; because the latter will rarely, if ever, dip their pens for such ends. And they are sure to be cried up and followed by one half of the Kingdom, and consequently possessed of no small degree of reputation. Our English style is more corrupted by the party-writers than by any other cause whatever. They are universally read, and will be read, and approved, in proportion to their degree of merit, much more than any other set of authors in any science, as men's passions and interests are stronger than their tastes and judgments.

It is but this week that I have been well enough in my head to read the poem of the *League*,[1] with the attention it deserves. Next to my obligation to Mr. de Voltaire for writing it, is that I owe to you for sending it. I cannot pretend to judge, with any exactness, of the beauties of a foreign language, which I understand but imperfectly. I can only tell my thoughts in relation to the design and conduct of the poem, or the sentiments. I think the forming the *machines* upon the allegorical persons of Virtues and Vices very reasonable, it being proper to ancient and modern subjects, and to all religions and times. Nor do we look upon them so much as heathen divinities as natural passions. This is not the case when Jupiter,

---

[1] The *Henriade* was originally published, in 1723, under the title of *La Ligue: ou Henri-le-Grand*. While Voltaire was in England, he collected a large subscription for a quarto edition of his Epic. . . . On Nov. 17, 1727, Young announced that the work had appeared, and said, "We have had no attempts of any note but Mr. Voltaire's Epic, which is thought to have considerable merit. The author I know well. He is a gentleman, and of great vivacity and industry, and has a good deal of knowledge out of the poetical way." (Letter to Tickell.)—E. In a letter of Feb. 24, 1724, Lord Bolingbroke writes to Pope that he was much interested in the genius of Voltaire (who had been his guest two years before, at La Source)," who says that he will introduce himself to you, and that the Muses shall answer for him. I am reading a tragedy which he has just finished, and which will be played this Lent. The subject is the *Death of Mariamne*. You will, I believe, find in it that art which Racine put into the conduct of his pieces, and that delicacy which appears in his diction, with a spirit of poetry which he never had, and which flags often in the best of Corneille's tragedies. But I will say no it, since he intends to send it to you."

Juno, &c., are introduced, who, though sometimes considered as physical powers, yet that sort of allegory lies not open enough to the apprehension. We care not to study or anatomise a poem, but only to read it for our entertainment. It should certainly be a sort of machinery, for the meaning of which one is not at a loss for a moment. Without something of this nature, his poem would too much resemble Lucan or Silius; and, indeed, the subject being so modern, a more violent or remote kind of fable or fiction would not suit it.

If I have anything to wish on this head, it were to have a little more of the fictitious, I dare not say the wonderful, for the reason just now given. Yet that would give it a greater resemblance to the ancient epic poem. He has helped it much, in my opinion, by throwing so much of the story into narration, and entering at once into the middle of the subject as well as by making the action single—viz., the Siege of Paris. This brings it nearer the model of Homer and Virgil. Yet I cannot help fancying, if the fabulous part were a little more extended into descriptions and speeches, &c., it would be of service; and for this very cause, methinks, that book which treats of the King's love to Madame Gabrielle appears more of a poem than the rest. Discord and Policy might certainly do and say something more; and so I judge of some other occasions for invention and description, which, methinks, are dropped too suddenly.

As to all the parts of the Work, which relate to the actions or sentiments of men, or to characters and manners, they are undoubtedly excellent, and the *forte* of the poem. His characters and sentences are not, like Lucan's, too professed, or formal, and particularised; but full, short, and judicious, and seem naturally to rise from an occasion, either of telling what the man was, or what he thought. It seems to me that his judgment of mankind, and his description of human actions in a lofty and philosophical view, is one of the principal characteristics of the writer, who, however, is not less a poet for being a man of sense, as Seneca and his nephew were.

Do not smile when I add that I esteem him for that honest-principled spirit of true religion which shines through the whole, and from whence, unknown as I am to Mr. de Voltaire, I conclude him at once a freethinker, and a lover of quiet; no bigot, but yet no heretic; one who honours authority and national sanctions, without prejudice to truth or charity; one who has studied controversy less than reason, and the Fathers less than mankind—in a word, one worthy, from his rational temper, of that share of friendship and intimacy with which you honour him.[1] Notwithstanding you tell me the oracles of our Lady of La Source are ceased, and that she returns no more answers, I shall expect the favour she promises to a poor hermit on the banks of the Thames. In the meantime, I see visions of her and of La Source.

> " An me ludit amabilis
> Insania? Audire et videor pios
> Errare per lucos, amœnæ
> Quos et aquæ subeunt et auræ."

What pleasing frenzy steals away my soul?
   Through thy blest shades, La Source, I seem to rove:
I see thy fountains fall, thy waters roll,
   And breathe the Zephyrs that refresh thy grove.
I hear whatever can delight inspire—
Villette's soft voice, and St. John's silver lyre.

> "Seu voce nunc mavis acutâ,
> Seu fidibus, citharâve Phœbi."

I cannot subscribe myself better than as Horace did—
> "Vestris amicum fontibus et choris." [2]

---

[1] These remarks appear to have occasioned a direct correspondence with Voltaire; for Pope, in a letter to Caryll, Dec. 25, 1725, says that he "formerly had some correspondence about the poem on the *League* with its author."—E. If this be so, we have greatly to regret that it is not now in existence.

[2] Hor. *Carm* III. 4. La Source, near Orléans, was the residence of Bolingbroke.

To Mr. William Fortescue.
Twitnam, Sept. 17, 1724.

Your friendly and kind letter I received with real joy and gladness; to hear, after a long silence, of the welfare of a whole family which I shall ever unfeignedly wish well to in all regards. I knew not in what part of the land to level a letter at you, or else you would have heard first from me. My mother, indeed, is very ill; but, as it seems only the effects of a cold, which always handles her severely, I hope not in any danger. I am in the old way —this day well, however, and the past and future are not in my power, so not much in my care.

Gay is at the Bath, with Dr. Arbuthnot. Mrs. Howard returns your services, and Marble-hill[1] waits only for its roof — the rest finished. The little Prince William wants Miss Fortescue, or, to say truth, anybody else that will play with him. You say nothing at what time we may expect you here; I wish it soon, and thought you talked of Michaelmas. I am grieved to tell you that there is one Devonshire man not honest: for my man Robert proves a vile fellow, and I have discarded him. *Auri sacra fames* is his crime—a crime common to the greatest and meanest, if any way in power, or too much in trust!

I am going upon a short ramble to my Lord Oxford's and Lord Cobham's, for a fortnight, this Michaelmas; and the hurry I am at present in, with preparing to be idle (a common case), makes it difficult for me to continue this letter, though I truly desire to say many things to you. Homer [*Odyssey*] is advanced to the Eighth book—I mean printed so far. My gardens improve more than my writing. My head is still more upon Mrs. Hd., and her works, than upon my own. Adieu! God bless you; an ancient and christian, therefore an unmodish, and unusual salutation. I am, ever sincerely and affectionately, yours.

---

[1] The residence of Mrs. Howard. Prince William was the second son of the Prince of Wales (George II.), and the future hero of Culloden.

To Mr. William Fortescue.

[Twickenham] Sept. 23, 1725.

"Blessed is the man who expects nothing, for he shall never be disappointed," was the ninth *beatitude*, which a man of wit (who, like a man of wit, was a long time in gaol) added to the eighth. I have long ago preached this to our friend:[1] I have *preached* it, but the world and his other friends *held it forth*, and exemplified it. They say, Mr. Walpole has friendship and keeps his word. I wish he were our friend's friend, or had ever promised him anything.

You seem inquisitive of what passed when Lord Peterborough spirited him hither, without any suspicion of mine. Nothing extraordinary, for the most extraordinary men are nothing before their masters; and nothing, but that Mr. Walpole swore by God Mrs. Howard should have the grounds she wanted from V——n. Nothing would be more extraordinary, except a Statesman made good his promise or oath, as very probably he will. If I have any other very extraordinary thing to tell you, it is this—that I have never since returned Sir R. W.'s visit. The truth is, I have nothing to ask of him; and I believe he knows that nobody follows him *for nothing*. Besides, I have been very sick, and sickness (let me tell you) makes one above a Minister, who cannot cure a fit of a fever or ague. Let me also tell you that no man who is lame, and cannot stir, will wait upon the greatest man upon earth; and lame I was, and still

[1] Gay, who had written the preceding part of this joint-letter. "I know," he writes to Fortescue, "I have sincerely your good wishes upon all occasions. One would think that my friends use me to disappointments, to try how many I could bear. If they do so, they are mistaken: for I dare not expect much, and I can never be much disappointed. I am in hopes of seeing you in town," he adds, "the beginning of October, by what you writ to Mr. Pope, and, sure, your father will think it reasonable that Miss Fortescue should not forget her French and dancing."

am, by an accident which it will be time enough to tell you when we meet, for I hope it will be suddenly [quickly]. Adieu, dear Sir, and believe me a true well-wisher to all yours, &c.[1]

To Mr. Edward Blount.

Twickenham, June 2, 1725.

You show yourself a just man and a friend in those guesses and suppositions you make at the possible reasons of my silence, every one of which is a true one. As to forgetfulness of you and yours, I assure you the promiscuous conversations of the town serve only to put me in mind of better, and more, quiet to be had in a corner of the world, undisturbed, innocent, serene, and sensible, with such as you.[2] Let no access of any distrust make you think of me differently in a cloudy day from what you do in the most sunshiny weather.

Let the young ladies[3] be assured I make nothing new in my gardens, without wishing to see the print of their fairy steps in every part of them. I have put the last hand to my works of this kind, in happily finishing the subterraneous way and Grotto. I there found a spring of the clearest water, which falls in a

---

[1] In a letter (dated April, 1726) Pope reports to Fortescue that "Dr. Swift is come into England, who is now with me, and with whom I am to ramble again to Lord Oxford's and Lord Bathurst's, and other places. Dr. Arbuthnot has led him a course through the town, with Lord Chesterfield, Mr. Pulteney, &c. Lord Peterborough and Lord Harcourt propose to carry him to Sir R. Walpole, and I to Mrs. Howard, &c. I wish you were here [at Twitnam] to know him."

[2] Edward Blount, who had an estate in Devonshire, resided at Blaydon House, at Paignton, Torbay.

[3] Blount had four daughters. One of them became Lady Clifford, another Duchess of Norfolk, and a brother of the Duke married a third when she was a widow. Her first husband was a Dutch merchant.—E.

perpetual rill that echoes through the cavern day and night. From the river Thames you see through my arch, up a walk of the wilderness, to a kind of open temple, wholly composed of shells in the rustic manner; and, from that distance, under the temple you look down through a sloping arcade of trees, and see the sails on the river passing suddenly and vanishing as through a perspective glass. When you shut the doors of this Grotto, it becomes on the instant, from a luminous room, a *camera obscura*, on the walls of which all the objects of the river, hills, woods, and boats are forming a moving picture in their visible radiations; and, when you have a mind to light it up, it affords you a very different scene. It is finished with shells, interspersed with pieces of looking-glass in angular forms; and in the ceiling is a star of the same material, at which, when a lamp, of an orbicular figure of thin alabaster, is hung in the middle, a thousand pointed rays glitter, and are reflected over the place.

There are connected to this Grotto by a narrower passage two porches with niches and seats—one towards the river, of smooth stones, full of light, and open; the other towards the arch of trees, rough with shells, flints, and iron-ore. The bottom is paved with simple pebbles, as the adjoining walk up the wilderness to the temple is to be cockle-shells, in the natural taste, agreeing not ill with the little dripping murmurs, and the aquatic idea of the whole place.[1] It wants nothing to complete it but a good statue with an inscription, like that beautiful antique one which you know I am so fond of:—

[1] He had greatly enlarged and improved this grotto not long before his death, and, by encrusting it about with a great number of ores and minerals of the richest and rarest kinds, it was become one of the most elegant and romantic retirements anywhere to be seen.—Warburton. Dr. Johnson speaks with an unreasonable contempt of this romantic grotto. Our poet's good taste in gardening was unquestionable.—Warton.

The taste of Pope was, perhaps, the best of the age; but nothing can appear more puerile and affected, at this time [about 1810], than what Warton calls his "romantic grotto." Warton spoke of an art of which he knew very little, and which, as exemplified by Pope's *Camera Obscura*, Johnson's strong inherent sense taught him to despise.—Bowles.

> "*Hujus Nympha loci, sacri custodia fontis,*
>   *Dormio, dum blandæ sentio murmur aquæ.*
> *Parce meum, quisquis tangis cava marmora, somnum*
>   *Rumpere: sive bibas, sive lavare, tace.*"

Nymph of the grot, these sacred springs I keep,
And to the murmurs of these waters sleep:
Ah, spare my slumbers, gently tread the Cave!
And drink in silence, or in silence lave!

You will think I have been very poetical in this description, but it is pretty near the truth. I wish you were here to bear testimony how little it owes to art, either the place itself or the image I give of it. I am, &c.

To Dean Swift.

March 8, 1726-7.

Mr. Stopford will be the bearer of this letter, for whose acquaintance I am, among many other favours, obliged to you; and I think the acquaintance of so valuable, ingenious, and unaffected a man to be none of the least obligations.

Our Miscellany[1] is now quite printed. I am prodigiously pleased with this joint volume, in which, methinks, we look like friends, side by side, serious and merry by turns, conversing interchangeably, and walking down hand in hand to Posterity—not in the stiff forms of learned authors, flattering each other, and setting the rest of mankind at nought; but in a free, un-

---

[1] The volume was an ill-arranged medley, and excites something of the feeling which Ford expressed to Swift, November 6, 1733:—"I have long had it at heart to see your works collected and published with care. It is become absolutely necessary since that jumble with Pope, &c., in three volumes, which put me in a rage whenever I meet them."—E.

important, natural, easy, manner, diverting others just as we diverted ourselves. The third volume consists of Verses; but I would choose to print none but such as have some peculiarity, and may be distinguished for ours from other writers. There is no end of making books, Solomon said; and, above all, of making *Miscellanies*, which all men can make. For, unless there be a character in every piece, like the mark of the Elect, I should not care to be one of the Twelve Thousand signed.

You received, I hope, some commendatory verses from a Horse,[1] and a Lilliputian, to Gulliver; and an heroic Epistle to Mrs. Gulliver. The bookseller would fain have printed them before the second edition of the book, but I would not permit it without your approbation: nor do I much like them. You see how much like a poet I write, and yet, if you were with us, you would be deep in politics. People are very warm and very angry, very little to the purpose; but, therefore, the more warm and the more angry. *Non nostrûm est tantas componere lites.*[2] I stay at Twit'nam without so much as reading newspapers, votes, or any other paltry pamphlets. Mr. Stopford will carry you a whole parcel of them, which are sent for your diversion but not imitation. For my own part, methinks I am at Glubbdubdrib,[3] with none but ancients and spirits about me. I am rather better than I used to be at this season: but my hand (though, as you see,

[1] Entitled, *The Grateful Address of the Unhappy Houyhnhnms now in Slavery and Bondage in England.* For this, and the "heroic Epistle," see *Life and Writings of Pope.*

[2] The words of the umpire shepherd, in the Third *Eclogue* of Virgil, a little altered.

[3] The island of Glubbdubdrib, meaning the island of Sorcerers or Magicians, visited by Gulliver. As every reader of the *Travels* is aware, it was here that Gulliver had the good fortune, by the courtesy of the Governor, to interview the ghosts or spirits of some of the most famous Ancients. From one of them he learns, among other interesting facts, that their interpreters and commentators are kept in the shades below, or rather keep themselves, at a proper distance from their principals, "through a consciousness of shame and guilt, because they had so terribly misrepresented the meaning of their Authors to posterity."

it has not lost its cunning) is frequently in very awkward sensations rather than pain. But to convince you it is pretty well, it has done some mischief already, and just been strong enough to cut the other hand, while it was aiming to prune a fruit tree. Lady Bolingbroke has writ you a long lively letter, which will attend this. She has very bad health, he very good. Lord Peterborough has writ twice to you. We fancy some letters have been intercepted, or lost by accident. About ten thousand things I want to tell you. I wish you were as impatient to hear them: for, if you were so, you would—you must—come early this spring. Adieu. Let me have a line from you. I am vexed at losing Mr. Stopford as soon as I knew him: but I thank God I have known him no longer. If every man one begins to value must settle in Ireland, pray make me know no more of them, and I forgive you this one.

To Lord Bathurst.

Bath, Sept. 15 [1726?].

Plato says a man in anger should not take the lash, that is the pen, in his hand; and a certain emperor, as I learn from Don Antonio de Guevara,[1] used to count over the four-and-twenty letters in such case before he spake. I have, therefore, thought it fit to count four-and-twenty days before I would mention to your Lordship what has passed between us. I will keep my temper, and now only acquaint you that I went, according to

---

[1] A Spanish bishop, historiographer to Charles V. [Emperor of Germany and King of Spain]. He died in 1544. His most popular work, *Marco-Aurelio*, was translated into English, but in Pope's day its credit had fallen to nothing.—E. The "certain emperor," it hardly needs to be added, was not the German but the Roman one.

your order (though I received no further invitation, as you were pleased to promise, by a letter to Stow), to Cirencester in full and certain hopes of attending you to Bath. I staid to the last day I could, namely, the second of September. I found you not, nor any letter from you, so that, had not Mr. Howe received me in my wanderings, I had been cast out on the common, and reduced to feed, like Nebuchadnezzar, among the beasts, and to travel on afterwards in the manner of John Coryate.[1]

However, my visit to your house was not wholly void of all comfort to me, for I saw the steeple of Cirencester stand on one side over it, and the great vista in Oakley wood to the said steeple, by being widened beyond its former hedges, bordered now only with some low thing, which I took to be a box-edging, on either side. Moreover, I beheld with singular consolation the back of the high wood pierced through, and every tree that bore the least pretence to be timber totally cut down and done away.[2] Whereby I see with delight not only the bare prospect you have made, but also another of the necessity you are now reduced to of raising some building there. And I form to myself yet a third prospect—that you will so unwillingly and grudgingly undertake the said building, that it will be so small and inconsiderable as to oblige you to pull it down again another year to erect a bigger and more adequate. Nevertheless, my Lord (to prove I am not angry, but, with a mixture of charity,

[1] On foot. In 1608 Coryate walked a thousand miles on the continent in the same pair of shoes, and on his return hung them up in the village church of Odcombe in Somersetshire, where the despicable memorial of his trampings was suffered to remain till the beginning of the reign of Queen Anne, or for nearly one hundred years. "He carried folly," says Fuller, "on his very face."—E. Coryate was son of the vicar of Odcombe. Upon his return from his thousand miles' peregrination he published (about 1620) an account of his experiences which he entitled, not unfitly, *Coryate's Crudities*. It is well printed and curiously illustrated. There are, it seems, not more than two or three copies of this eccentric book now in existence.

[2] If this letter had been designed for the purpose, it could not illustrate more completely Lord Bathurst's account of Pope's propensity for disparaging alterations he did not himself suggest.—E.

inclined to rectify what I disapprove), I could not advise you to an obelisk, which can bear no diameter to fill so vast a gap, unless it literally touched the skies, but rather to a solid pyramid of a hundred feet square, to the end there may be something solid and lasting of your works.

As to the church steeple, I am truly sorry for it: yet I would not, however, pull down the house. I would rather the reformation began, as reformations always ought, at the church itself. Not that I would wish the body of it entirely taken away, but only the steeple lowered. This would bring matters to some uniformity, and the dissenters and quakers be greatly obliged, as it is the high tower itself which, above all, they hold in abomination;[1] whereby your Lordship's interest in the next Elections might vastly be strengthened. Certain it is, that something extraordinary and *éclatant* must be done, if you would render yourself agreeable to the present Administration, which may be a convincing proof to all the world of the conversion of one who has been so long, and so distinguished, a patron of the Church of England.[2] It would not be amiss, I further think, if your Lordship would also give some other evidence of your capacity for a Statesman, and pretensions to make a greater figure in another house[3] than you yet have done, by breaking

[1] George Fox gave to churches the contemptuous title of "steeple-houses," which may have deceived Pope into fancying that "dissenters and quakers" had an especial hostility to the steeple. Every part of the edifice was equally under a ban, as may be seen from the *Journal* of Fox, who only named a church a "steeple-house" to denote that he denied it to be "God's house." "The steeple-houses and pulpits," he says, "were offensive to my mind, because both priests and people called them the *House of God*, and idolised them, reckoning that God dwelt there in the outward house, whereas they should have looked for God and Christ to dwell in their hearts, and their bodies to be made the temples; for the apostle said: 'God dwelleth not in temples made with hands.' But, by reason of the people's idolising those places, it was counted a heinous thing to declare against them."—E.

[2] Walpole favoured the toleration of Dissenters to the extent of his power, and the Opposition sometimes taunted him with his good-will towards them.—E.

[3] House of Lords.

your word with your friends, &c.,[1] which, though I never perceived it but by one late instance, I was exceedingly rejoiced to find was not entirely out of your power.

Mr. Lewis is offended by your letters, for he is a serious man. But Mrs. Lewis is the youngest and gayest lady here, and would be an excellent match for your Lordship, if my Lady cares to part with you. Pray tell my Lady that either Mr. Lewis or I have that opinion of her steadiness and sobriety, that we will take a lodging for her here the moment she appoints, provided she pleases to write to us in her own hand, by the young ladies your daughters, who are also sober persons; and provided it be not wrapped up, countersigned, or superscribed by your Lordship, in which case we shall suspect some fraud or insincere practices.

We shall both leave this place for Cirencester on the last day of this month, and be with you by dinner-time on the first of October punctually. In the meantime, believe me, my Lord, to forget all that is passed, and to be with the very same sincerity, affection, and esteem, which I have always felt in your regard, my Lord, your most faithful, and most hearty, humble servant.

To Mr. John Knight.

Twitenham, Nov. 24 [1727?].

I had some view of seeing you in the country; but the weather proved so cold, that the Duchess of Bucks came back

[1] The letter was probably written at some period when Lord Bathurst had declared to his friends that he would not take part in the debates, from despair of producing the least result. "I have attended Parliament many years," he said on a subsequent occasion to Swift, Dec. 6, 1737, " and never found that I could do any good. I have therefore entered upon a new scheme of life, and am determined to look after my own affairs a little."—E.

to town before I was ready to go to Lees. I am forced now to content myself with such informations of Mrs. Knight's state of health as your people gave me in Dover Street. If these be true, she is pretty well; and I hope the cheerfulness you two can give one another will make all that bad seasons, ill air, and uncomfortable prospects can do ineffectual to molest or cloud you.

Here the most unhappy, gay, people are reduced to mere children's play, and childish sights to divert them. They go every day to stare at a mock Coronation [1] on the stage, which is to be succeeded by a more ridiculous one of the Harlequins (almost as ridiculous a farce as the real State one of a Coronation itself). After that, they hope for it again in a puppet show, which is to recommend itself by another qualification—of having the exact portraits of the most conspicuous faces of our nobility in wax-work, so as to be known at sight, without Punch's help, or the master's pointing to each with his wand as they pass. So much for news. It is what passes most material in this metropolis, till you, Sir, with your fellow-Members [of the Legislature], come to find us greater business after Christmas.

At last I have seen the statue up,[2] and the statuary down, at the same time. The poor man has not been out of bed since. I sent part of the money to him, and offered him more, which he refused till he has been at the Abbey, to do some little more matter to the hair (as I understand) and feet. The inscription on the Urn is not done yet, though they promised it two months ago, and had the draught—but yesterday they sent to me again

---

[1] The Coronation of George II., which nearly ascertains the date of this letter.—C.

[2] Of Mr. Secretary Craggs, brother of Mrs. Knight. It was the work of Guelfi, an Italian sculptor, who executed several commissions for Lord Burlington. The memorial, in question, to Craggs, was placed in Westminster Abbey. It is the subject of more than one letter of Pope's to Mrs. Knight or, rather, Mrs. Newsham.

for it, which I cannot conceive the meaning of, for I saw it scored on in the Abbey. I have sent it over again to Mr. Bird this day, however.

I shall think it a favour to hear of you both, when your leisure permits. Believe me a sincere well-wisher to you both, and (if you will allow me a higher title), dear Sir, a faithful friend and affectionate servant.

My mother is well, and very much yours and Mrs. Knight's.

To Lord Peterborough.[1]

August 24, 1728.

I presume you may before this time be returned from the contemplation of many beauties, animal and vegetable, in gardens, and, possibly, some rational in ladies—to the better enjoyment of your own at Bevis Mount. I hope, and believe, all you have seen will only contribute to it. I am not so fond of making compliments to ladies as I was twenty years ago, or I would say there are some very reasonable [ladies] and one, in particular, there.

[1] Horace Walpole describes this famous knight-errant of the first quarter of the XVIII century, as "of an advantageous figure and enterprising spirit, as gallant as Amadis [de Gaul] and as brave, but a little more expeditions in his journeys; for he is said to have 'seen more kings and postilions than any man in Europe.' His enmity to the Duke of Marlborough, and his friendship with Pope, will preserve his name, when his genius, too romantic to have laid a solid foundation for fame, and his politics, too disinterested for his age and country, shall be equally forgotten. He was a man, as his friend said, 'who could neither live nor die like any other mortal.' [Swift hit off his two especial peculiarities, in his verses cited above. See page 27.] He married Mrs. Anastasia Robinson, the celebrated Singer, a woman of irreproachable character. After his death she found his *Memoirs*, written by himself, in which, it is said, he boasted he had committed three capital crimes before he was twenty. In consequence of this she committed them to the flames."—R.

I think you happy, my Lord, in being at least half the year almost as much your own master as I am mine the whole year; and, with all the disadvantageous incumbrances of quality, parts, and honour, as mere a gardener, loiterer, and labourer as he who never had titles, or from whom they are taken. I have an eye, in the last of these glorious appellations, to the style of a Lord degraded or attainted.[1] Methinks, they give him a better title than they deprive him of, in calling him "labourer." *Agricultura*, says Tully, *proxima sapientiæ*, which is more than can be said, by most modern nobility, of *Grace* or *Right Honourable*, which are often *proxima stultitiæ*. The Great Turk, you know, is often a gardener, or of a meaner trade; and are there not some circumstances in which you would resemble the Great Turk? The two paradises are not ill connected—of gardens and gallantry; and some there are (not to name my Lord Bolingbroke), who pretend they are both to be had, without turning Mussulmen.

We have as little politics here, within a few miles of the Court (nay, perhaps, at the Court), as you at Southampton; and our Ministers, I dare say, have less to do. Our weekly histories are only full of the feasts given to the Queen and Royal Family by their servants, and the *long* and *laborious* walks her Majesty takes every morning. Yet, if the graver historians hereafter shall be silent of this year's events, the amorous and anecdotical may make Posterity some amends, by being furnished with the gallantries of the Great at home; and it is some comfort, that, if the men of the next Age do not read of us, the women may.

From the time you have been absent I have not been to wait on a certain great man, through modesty, through idleness, and

---

[1] An allusion to Lord Bolingbroke, who used somewhat ostentatiously to boast, after his fall, of his delight in agricultural or (more accurately) *bucolical* occupations. As for the Grand Turk's gardening, it must be less arduous even than that of his imperial brother at Pekin.

through respect.¹ But, for my comfort, I fancy that any great man will as soon forget one that does him no harm as he can one that has done him any good. Believe me, &c.²

To Mr. John Knight.³

Stowe, Aug. 23, 1731.

The place from which I write to you will be a proof alone, how incapable I am of forgetting you and your Gosfield: for, if anything, under Paradise, could set me beyond all earthly cogitations, Stowe might do it. It is much more beautiful this year than when I saw it before, and much enlarged, and with variety. Yet I shall not stay in it, by a fortnight, so long as I did (with pleasure) with you. You must tell Mrs. Knight she has been spoken of, and her health toasted here; and that Lord Cobham sends his services, with a *memorandum* to perform her promise of seeing this place. If she keeps it, I do not despair to live (partly by my exemplary temperance, and partly by the

---

¹ Probably Sir Robert Walpole.—Bowles.

² To this letter Peterborough replies :—I must confess that in going to Lord Cobham's [at Stowe], I was not led by curiosity : I went thither to see what I had seen and what I was sure to like. I had the idea of those gardens so fixed in my imagination, by many descriptions, that nothing surprised me— immensity and Van Brugh appear in the whole, and in every part. Your joining in your letter "animal and vegetable" beauty makes me use this expression : I confess the stately Sacharissa at Stow, but am content with my little Amoret." [Alluding to Waller's *Sacharissa and Amoret.*—R. His "little Amoret" was Bevis Mount, overlooking Itchin Ferry and the Southampton River, where Pope spent many days, and where a Walk is still called by his name.—B.]

³ Of Bellowes, or Bellhouse, and Gosfield-hall, was M.P. for St. Germains, in Cornwall, in 1710-13-14, and for Spalding in 1727. He married, as his second wife, Mrs. Newsham [to whom Pope addressed several letters, first as Mrs. Newsham, secondly as Mrs. Knight, and thirdly as Mrs. Nugent, husband of Mr., afterwards Lord, Nugent].—Roscoe.

assistance of Mother Vincent) to meet you both here another season. I shall yet think it a diminution of my happiness, to miss of half our companions and compotators of syllabub, and not to have Mr. Newsham,[1] and his dogs, and his preceptors, and his dearly-beloved cousin, and his mathematics, and his Greek, and his horses. Without a compliment to all or any of them, I never passed an easier or more agreeable month, in spite of some ill-health, and some melancholy, than that of July last: I hope you will long enjoy that tranquility and that satisfaction, which you spread over all that is about you. I often wish Mr. Mallet[2] joy, in my own heart, of his having exchanged such a whining, valetudinary, cloudy, *journalier* companion as myself for the good humour, and serenity, and indulgence of your family. I am pretty sure he will deserve it all.

Mrs. Patty [Blount] languishes in town, and diets there on fools, in defect of friends. I am sorry to forsake her at such a time; and she is more sorry you live at such a distance. Her sister affirms nobody of sense can live six miles out of London; and, indeed, I know nothing that can set her right but the free use of the cane you bestowed upon me. I cannot say my rambles contribute much to my health. Yet I take no corporeal *medicaments*, but wholly apply to remedies of the mind. If human philosophy will not do, I must desire Mrs. Elliot to pray for me. My next journey is to Southampton, to my Lord Peterborough, where, also, I have a Catholic friend, who will take care of my soul; and shall dine with a Jesuit thrice a week, worth all the priests in Essex, if you except Mr. Tripsack. I desire you all to accept of my faithful services, and to know no man is more mindful of you than, &c.

[1] Mrs. Knight's son, by her first husband.—C.
[2] He appears to have been tutor to young Newsham.—C.

TO MR. RICHARDSON.[1]

Jan. 13, 1732-3.

I have at last got my mother so well, as to allow myself to be absent from her for three days. As Sunday is one of them, I do not know whether I may propose to you to employ it in the manner you mentioned to me once.[2] Sir Godfrey [Kneller] called employing the pencil the prayer of a painter, and affirmed it to be his proper way of serving God, by the talent he gave him.[3] I am sure, in this instance, it is serving your friend, and you know that we are allowed to do that (nay even to help a neighbour's ox or ass) on the Sabbath: which, though it may

---

[1] Jonathan Richardson (1664-1745), a pupil of Riley, the portrait painter, was after the death of Kneller at the head of his profession. As an artist it was allowed that "no one drew a better head than Richardson," and he was moreover a very worthy and excellent man. His essays on *The Art of Criticism in Painting*, and *On the Science of a Connoisseur*, abound with judicious and solid observations, and are well calculated to inspire a knowledge and love of Art; qualities which he himself possessed in an eminent degree, as was shown by his fine Collection of Drawings by the ancient Masters, which was sold after his death, in 1748, and produced upwards of £2,000, a large sum for that period, although greatly below their value. These drawings he had carefully mounted, and wrote the name of the artist, frequently with his own observations, in a neat and correct hand, at the back, in which state we often meet with them in Collections. In the use of the needle Richardson particularly excelled. Of Pope he has etched many striking and characteristic likenesses in different attitudes; some of them with verses testifying his admiration of and respect for him. He also etched those of several of their common friends, and particularly of Swift and of Bolingbroke. Hudson, the son-in-law and successor to Richardson, as an artist, was the master of Sir Joshua Reynolds.—R.

[2] Probably in painting or etching his portrait.—R.

[3] One or two notes from Kneller have been preserved. From the following specimen we may infer that Sir Godfrey's English was not learned in fashionable circles:—" Dear friend,—I find them pictures are very fresh, being painted in three collers, and ought to be near a fier several days; for, as they are, it is impracticall to put them where you intend. It would be pitty they should take dust. Jenny stays here eight or ten days, and will not fail of sending them when reddy; and I am, giving my hearty and humble service to your dear mother, dear Mr. Pope, yours, &c."

seem a general precept, yet in one sense particularly applies to you, who have helped many a human ox, and many a human ass, to the likeness of man, not to say of God.

Believe me, dear Sir, with all good wishes for yourself and your family (the happiness of which ties I know by experience, and have learned to value from the late danger of losing the best of mine), Your, &c.

TO MR. JOHN CARYLL.

March 8, 1732-3.

You will excuse my delay in answering yours, if you know how I have been employed. I am now building a portico, in which I hope you will sit, like Nestor, on a stone at the gate, and converse delightfully with us one of these days. Poetry has given place for the present, as it always does with me, to the beauties of Nature, and the pleasures of the Spring advancing every day. I do not sing with birds—I love better to hear them. You may have seen my last piece of song, which has met with such a flood of favours, that my ears need no more flattery for this twelvemonth. However, it was a slight thing, the work of two days,[1] whereas that to Lord Bathurst was the work of two years by intervals.

I have not forgot your questions in relation to the scrivener, Sir J. Blunt; and can assure you Morgan is a fictitious name. You will smile to hear that one or two good priests were gravelled at my saying, in the last thing, "Term me what you will, papist or protestant," &c., not seeing so plain a meaning as that an

---

[1] *The First Satire of the Second Book of Horace Imitated*, Feb. 14, 1733.

honest man, and a good catholic, might be indifferent what the world called him, while he knew his own religion, and his own integrity.[1] A man, that *can* write in this Age, *may*: but he really will find that he writes to fools, and it is now a most unreasonable demand to cry *Qui legit intelligat.*

The town is now very full of a new poem entitled an *Essay on Man*, attributed I think with reason, to a divine.[2] It has merit in my opinion, but not so much as they give it. At least, it is incorrect, and has some inaccuracies in the expressions,— one or two of an unhappy kind, for they may cause the author's sense to be turned, contrary to what I think his intention, a little unorthodoxically. Nothing is so plain as that he quits his proper subject, this present world, to assert his belief of a future state, and yet there is an *if*, instead of a *since*, that would overthrow his meaning;[3] and, at the end, he uses the words " God, the soul of the world," which, at the first glance, may be taken

> [1] " My head and heart thus flowing through my quill,
> Verseman or proseman, term me what you will;
> Papist or Protestant, or both between;
> Like good Erasmus, in an honest mean,
> In moderation placing all my glory,
> While tories call me whig, and whigs a tory."
> —*Im. Hor. Sat. ii.* 1.

[2] The first part of the *Essay on Man* was published anonymously in February; and Pope, who was accustomed to say what was convenient without much regard to what was true, has here, by implication, disclaimed the authorship.—E.

> [3] " If to be perfect in a certain state,
> What matter here or there, or soon or late?"

Pope omitted the lines in several editions subsequent to the first, but he afterwards restored them. No one could have interpreted them as suggesting a doubt of the immortality of man, if the belief in a future state had not been spoken of in the context rather as a hope given to satisfy us here than as the assurance of a reality. The studied ambiguity of the passage was probably adopted by Pope to please his prompter, Bolingbroke; while, on the other hand, he was anxious to vindicate the orthodoxy of the poem to his christian friend, Caryll.—E.

for heathenism; while his whole paragraph proves him quite christian in his System, from man up to seraphim.[1]

I want to know your opinion of it after twice or thrice reading. I give you my thoughts very candidly of it, though I find there is a sort of faction to set up the author and his piece in opposition to me and my little things, which, I confess, are not of so much importance as to the subject, but I hope they conduce to morality in their way; which way is, at least, more generally to be understood, and the seasoning of satire makes it more palatable to the generality. Adieu.

TO MR. RICHARDSON.

Twickenham, June 10, 1733.

As I know you and I naturally desire to see one another, I hoped that this day our wishes would have met, and brought you hither. And this for the very reason which, possibly, might hinder you coming—that my poor mother is dead.[2] I thank God, her death was as easy as her life was innocent, and, as it cost her not a groan, or even a sigh, there is yet upon her countenance such an expression of tranquility, nay, almost of pleasure, that it is even amiable to behold it. It would afford the finest image of a saint expired that ever painting drew; and it would be the greatest obligation that ever that obliging Art

---

[1] "All are but parts of one stupendous Whole,
Whose body Nature is, and God the soul."

The reader will look in the paragraph in vain for any of those vindications of the christian system to which Pope refers. The passage might have been written by a Greek or Roman philosopher.—E.

[2] Mrs. Pope died the 7th of June, 1733, aged ninety-three.—Warburton.

could ever bestow on a friend, if you would come and sketch it for me.¹

I am sure, if there be no very prevalent obstacle, you will leave any common business to do this, and I hope to see you this evening, as late as you will, or to-morrow morning as early, before this winter-flower is faded. I will defer her interment till to-morrow night. I know you love me, or I could not have written this—I could not, at this time, have written at all. Adieu! May you die as happily!

TO MR. HUGH BETHEL.

Aug. 9, 1733.

You might well think me negligent or forgetful of you, if true friendship and sincere esteem were to be measured by common favours and compliments. The truth is, I could not write then, without saying something of my own condition, and of my loss of so old and so deserving a parent, which really would have troubled you; or I must have kept a silence on that head, which would not have suited that freedom and sincere opening of the heart, which is due to you from me.

I am now pretty well: but my home is uneasy to me still, and I am therefore wandering about all this summer. I was but four days at Twickenham since the occasion that made it so melancholy. I have been a fortnight in Essex, and am now at Dawley (whose master is your servant), and going to Cirencester to Lord Bathurst. I shall also see Southampton with Lord

¹ A drawing was accordingly made, and a print has been engraved from it, in which she is called, by mistake, "daughter of Sam. Cooper, painter."—R. This etching appears in Mr. Elwin's *Works of Pope*, ed. 1872.

Peterborough. The Court and Twitenham I shall forsake together. I wish I did not leave our friend,[1] who deserves more quiet, and more health and happiness than can be found in such a family. The rest of my acquaintances are tolerably happy in their various ways of life—whether Court, Country, or Town—and Mr. Cleland is as well in the Park as if he were in Paradise. I heartily hope Yorkshire is the same to you; and that no evil, moral or physical, may come near you.

I have now but too much melancholy leisure, and no other care but to finish my *Essay on Man*. There may be in it one line[2] that may offend you, I fear; and yet I will not alter or omit it, unless you come to town and prevent me before I print it, which will be in a fortnight in all probability. In plain truth, I will not deny myself the greatest pleasure I am capable of receiving, because another may have the modesty not to share it. It is all a poor poet can do—to bear testimony to the virtues he cannot reach: besides that, in this Age, I see too few good examples, not to lay hold on any I can find. You see what an interested man I am. Adieu.

To Mr. Aaron Hill.

Twickenham, Nov. 13, 1733.

I writ to you a very hasty letter, being warmed in the cause of an old acquaintance, in which I was sure you would concur. I mean John Dennis, whose circumstances were described to me in the most moving manner. I went next day with the lord, to

---

[1] Martha Blount, apparently. Who the "such a family" was, does not appear.

[2] In which Pope apostrophises him as the "blameless Bethel."—*Epistle* IV.

whom you directed your letter and Play, which, at my return home, I received but yesterday.

I thank you for your agreeable present to my Grotto, for your more agreeable letter, and your most excellent translation of Voltaire,[1] to whom you have presented all the beauty he had, and added the nerves he wanted. This short acknowledgment is all I can make just now: I am just taken up by Mr. Thomson, in the perusal of a new Poem he has brought me.[2] I wish you were with us. The first day I see London I will wait on you, on many accounts, but on none more than my being affectionately, and with true esteem, &c.

I desire Miss Uranie[3] will know me for her servant.

[1] The tragedy of *Zaïre*. If Pope spoke before contemptuously of Hill, he now makes ample amends by flattery.—Bowles. In his letter, accompanying the tragedy, Hill writes:

"Though I have really no skill in the French, and am (perhaps, for that reason) not over fond of the language, yet I have seldom been more strongly delighted than with the tragedy of *Zaïre*. I had seen nothing of M. Voltaire's before, except the *Henriade*; and, whether it was from my own want of taste, or the poem's want of fire, I found it too cold for an epic spirit, so conceived but a moderate opinion as to the dramatic attempts of the same author. But genius being limited, we act too rash and unreasonable a part, when we judge after so general a manner. Having been agreeably disappointed in *Zaïre*, it was due, as an atonement, that I should contribute to widen his applause, whom I had thought of too narrowly. . . . I should be vexed to have it miscarry, because it is certainly an excellent piece, and has not suffered, I hope, so much in the translation as to justify a cold reception at London, after having run into the most general esteem at Paris. I will do all in my power to prepare the town to receive it, . . . and your good taste and good nature assure me of your willing concurrence so far as not only to say of it what it deserves, but to say it at such times, and in such manner, as you know best how to choose, in order to give your recommendation the intended good consequence." Voltaire, it is to be noted, was yet only at the beginning of his extraordinary literary career. The *Zaïre* appeared in 1731.

[2] Probably his *Liberty*, published in the next year. His great Poem, the *Seasons*, on the score of moral sentiment, the most meritorious poem of the century, in which Pope has the credit of having assisted, appeared, complete, in 1730.

[3] Miss Hill—a daughter of his correspondent.

To Mr. Richardson.

Nov. 31, [1733?].

Every thing was welcome to me in your kind letter, except the occasion of it, the confinement you are under. I am glad you count the days when I do not see you: but it was but half an one that I was in town upon business with Dr. Mead, and returned to render an account of it.

I shall in the course of the winter, probably, be an evening visitant to you, if you sit at home, though I hope it will not be by compulsion or lameness. We may take a cup of sack together, and chatter like two parrots, which are, at least, more reputable and menlike animals than the grasshoppers, to which Homer likens old men. I am glad you sleep better. I sleep in company, and wake at night, which is vexatious. If you did so, you, at your age, would make verses. As to my health, it will never mend; but I will complain less of it, when I find it incorrigible.

But for the news of my quitting Twit'nam for Bath—inquire into my years, if they are past the bounds of dotage? Ask my eyes if they can see, and my nostrils if they can smell? To prefer rocks and dirt to flowery meads and silver Thames, and brimstone and fogs to roses and sunshine! When I arrive at these sensations I may settle at Bath, of which I never yet dreamt further then to live just out of the sulphurous pit, and at the edge of the fogs, at Mr. Allen's, for a month or so. I like the place so little, that health itself should not draw me thither, though friendship has twice or thrice.

Having answered your questions, I desire to hear if you have any commands. If the first be to come to you, it is probable I shall, before you can send them so round about as to Twit'nam, for I have lived of late at Battersea.

To Mrs. Knight.[1]

Southampton, Aug. 5, 1734.

If I did not know you must take it for granted that I am always mindful of you, I should have been earlier in telling you such a piece of news. But the truth is, that all I ever think letters good for is to convey to those who love one another the news of their welfare, and the knowledge that they continue in each other's memory. The first of these I heard by enquiries in London, which have been transmitted to me; and the last I think so well both of you and myself as to think unnecessary. It was very certain Mrs. Elliott's company would be an equivalent to you for all you could leave in town, and yours would be so to her. Indeed, I had a wish to make you a short visit by surprise, and see this with my own eyes: but the account given me at Stowe (where I had but one week to stay), and given me after I had been half-jumbled to death, and just before I was to be jumbled again, on the abominable stony roads thereabouts, gave me a terror I could not overcome; especially when, chancing to see a clergyman who lives by you, and whose name I have forgot, he told me the way was further and worse than even my fears had imagined.

I have been but in a poor state of health ever since I set out from home; and can scarce say I have found rest till (where you would least expect it) under my Lord Peterborough. This place [Bevis Mount] is beautiful beyond imagination, and as easy as it is beautiful. I wish you and Mrs. Elliott saw it. Here is a very good catholic lady in the house, and she and I might pray together for you. One motive, which perhaps may one time or other draw you is, that the Duchess of Montague is

---

[1] She was now a second time a widow.—R. Not long afterwards she married Mr. Nugent.

within ten miles of us, at Bewley, which, I am told, is a fine situation on the sea, and I shall see it to-morrow. Lord Peterborough carries me thither. I had the satisfaction to hear this week from Mrs. Patty Blount that you were well. She is got into Surrey to another papist lady, and stays some time with her. I design to steer towards London before the end of this month. We expect here Mr. and Mrs. Poyntz. What else can I say to you? I wish you very happy. I wish Mr. Newsham [the Younger] all that you wish him to have and to be. Where is he and Mr. Mallet? When shall you return to town? I desire you to be very kind to me, and very just to me: that is, to let me know you continue well, now, when I can no other way be sure of it than by a line hither; and to believe me sincerely ever, with all esteem, Madam, yours, &c.

I think I need not send Mrs. E. my services, for they will do her no good; but desire her prayers, which may do *me* some good.

To Mr. Ralph Allen.

Twit'nam, Ap. 30, 1736.

I saw Mr. M. yesterday, who has readily allowed Mr. V[anloo?] to copy the picture. I have inquired for the lost originals of these two subjects, which, I found, were favourite ones with you, and well deserve to be so—the Discovery of Joseph to his Brethren, and the Resignation of the Captive by Scipio. Of the latter my Lord Burlington has a fine one done by Ricci, and I am promised the other, in a good print, from one of the chief Italian painters. That of Scipio is of the exact size one would wish for a *basso relievo*, in which manner, in my opinion, you would best ornament your Hall, done in *chiaro obscuro*.

A man not only shows his taste but his virtue in the choice of such ornaments: and whatever example most strikes us, we may reasonably imagine, may have an influence upon others. So that the history itself, if well chosen, upon a rich man's walls, is very often a better lesson than any he could teach by conversation. In this sense, the stones may be said to speak when men cannot or will not. I cannot help thinking (I know you will join with me, you who have been making an altarpiece) that the zeal of the first [ecclesiastical] Reformers was ill-placed in removing *pictures* (that is to say, examples) out of churches, and yet suffering *epitaphs* (that is to say, flatteries, and false history) to be the burden of church walls, and the shame, as well as the derision, of all honest men.

I have heard little yet of the Subscription.[1] I intend to make a visit for a fortnight from home to Lady Peterborough, at Southampton, about the middle of May. After my return I will inquire what has been done; and I really believe what I told you will prove true, and I shall be honourably acquitted of a task I am not fond of. I have run out my leaf, and will only add my sincere wishes for your happiness of all kinds.

To Mr. AARON HILL.[2]

June 9, 1738.

The favour of yours, of May 11, had not been unacknowledged so long, but it reached me not till my return from

---

[1] For his own edition of the first volume of his Letters, undertaken at Mr. Allen's request.—Warburton. The "task" he is "not fond of," is the publishing his Letters by subscription. The present letter to Allen first appeared in Warburton's Edition of 1751.

[2] This letter from Pope to Hill is an answer to a very long epistle from Hill, May 11, 1738, in which he renews the correspondence by informing Pope that it was his intention to publish *An Essay on Propriety in the Thought and*

Bathos from the Play, which I never supposed to be his. He gave it as Shakspeare's, and I take it to be of that Age; and, indeed, the collection of those, and many more of the thoughts censured there, was not made by me but Dr. Arbuthnot. I have had two or three occasions to lament, that you seem to know me much better as a poet than as a man. You can hardly conceive how little either pique or contempt I bear to any creature, unless for immoral or dirty actions. Any mortal is at full liberty, unanswered, to write and print of me as a poet—to praise me one year and blame me another: only I desire him to spare my character as an honest man, over which he can have no private, much less any public right, without some personal knowledge of my heart, or the motives of my conduct. Nor is it a sufficient excuse to allege he was so and so informed, which was the case with those men.

I am sincere in all I say to you, and have no vanity in saying it. You really overvalue me greatly in my poetical capacity; I am sure your Work would do me infinitely too much honour, even if it blamed me oftener than it commended: for the first you will do with lenity, the last with excess. But I could be glad to part with some share of any good man's admiration for some of his affection, and his belief that I am not wholly undeserving to be thought what I am to you, Sir, a most faithful, affectionate servant.

TO DEAN SWIFT.

May 27, 1739.

Every time I see your hand, it is the greatest satisfaction any writing can give me; and I am, in proportion, grieved to find that several of my letters to testify it to you miscarry; and you

a journey, which had carried me from scene to scene, *where Gods might wander with delight.*

I am sorry yours was attended with any thoughts less pleasing, either from the conduct towards you of the world in general, or of any one else in particular. As to the subject matter of the letter, I have found what I have often done in receiving letters from those I most esteemed, and most wished to be esteemed by—a great pleasure in reading it, and a great inability to answer it. I can only say, you oblige me in seeming so well to know me again, as one extremely willing that the free exercise of criticism should extend over my own Writings, as well as those of others, whenever the public may receive the least benefit from it, as I question not they will a great deal when exerted by you. I am sensible of the honour you do me in proposing to send me your Work before it appears: if you do, I must insist that no use, in my favour, be made of this distinction by the alteration or softening of any censure of yours on any line of mine.

What you have observed in your letter I think just: only I would acquit myself in one point. I could not have the least pique to Mr. Theobald, in what is cited in the Treatise of the

Expression of Poetry, in which he intended to take his examples from the Works of Pope, and, at the same time, offering to send the manuscript to Twickenham for Pope's correction, being resolved, he says, "to carry no example of his to the press in a manner against which he has any just cause of exception." In the same letter we find a vindication of some passages cited by Pope from Theobald, in the Treatise on the Bathos, and, particularly, of the expression,

"None but himself can be his parallel,"

and of the lines,

"—— The obscureness of her birth
Cannot eclipse the lustre of her eyes,
Which make her all one light."

The criticisms upon which by Pope he considers as "rash, unweighed censure." This letter which, as the writer justly observes, "had grown to *an unmerciful long one*," extending to nearly twenty pages, may be found in the *Works* of Aaron Hill, I., 341.—Roscoe.

ask me the same questions again, which I prolixly have answered before. Your last, indeed, which was delivered to me by Mr. Swift, inquires where and how is Lord Bolingbroke, who, in a paragraph in my last, under his own hand, gave you an account of himself; and I employed almost a whole letter on his affairs afterwards. He has sold Dawley for twenty-six thousand pounds, much to his own satisfaction.[1] His plan of life now is a very agreeable one, in the finest country of France, divided between study and exercise; for he still reads or writes five or six hours a day, and generally hunts twice a week. He has the whole Forest of Fontainebleau at his command, with the King's stables and dogs, &c., his lady's son-in-law being Governor of that place.[2] She resides most part of the year with my Lord, at a large house they have hired, and the rest with her daughter, who is Abbess of a royal Convent in the neighbourhood.

I never saw him in stronger health, or in better humour with his friends, or more indifferent and dispassionate to his enemies. He is seriously set upon writing some parts of the history of his times, which he has began by a noble Introduction, presenting a view of the whole state of Europe, from the Pyrenees Treaty. He has hence deduced a summary sketch of the natural and incidental interests of each kingdom, and how they have varied from, or approached to, the true politics of each in the several Administrations to this time. The history itself will be particular only on such anecdotes and facts as he personally knew, or produces vouchers for, both from home and abroad. This puts me in mind to tell you a fear he expressed lately to me—that some facts in your *History*[3] of the Queen's last years

[1] Dawley is in Kent. In Coxe's *Memoirs*, the fact is mentioned of Bolingbroke's introduction to George II. It was supposed that Walpole was obliged to *retire*, and that Bolingbroke had at last succeeded to that station, for which all his life he had panted: This was his *last effort*. He retired soon after to France again.—Bowles.

[2] Bolingbroke's second wife was the Marquise de Villette.

[3] *History of the Four Last Years of Queen Anne.*

(which he read here with me in 1727), are not exactly stated, and that he may be obliged to vary from them, in relation, I believe, to the conduct of the Earl of Oxford, of which great care, surely, should be taken.[1] And he told me that, when he saw you in 1727, he made you observe them, and that you promised you would take care.

We very often commemorated you during the five months we lived together at Twickenham. At which place could I see you again, as I may hope to see him, I would envy no country in the world; and think not Dublin only, but France and Italy, not worth the visiting once more in my life.[2] The mention of travelling introduces your old acquaintance Mr. Jervas, who went to Rome and Naples purely in search of health. An asthma has reduced his body, but his spirit retains all its vigour; and he is returned, declaring life itself is not worth a day's journey, at the expense of parting with one's friends. Mr. Lewis every day remembers you. I lie at his house in town. Dr. Arbuthnot's daughter does not degenerate from the humour and goodness of her father. I love her much. She is like Gay, very idle, very ingenious, and inflexibly honest. Mrs. Patty Blount is one of the most considerate and mindful women in the world towards others, the least so in regard to herself. She speaks of you constantly. I scarce know two more women worth naming to you. The rest are ladies, run after music, and play at cards.

I always make your compliments to Lord Oxford and Lord Masham, when I see them. I see John Barber seldom; but always find him proud of some letter from you. I did my best with him on behalf of one of your friends, and spoke to Mr. Lyttelton for the other, who was more prompt to catch than I to

---

[1] It may be easily supposed that Swift and Bolingbroke would have differed widely in their account of that Statesman's conduct, whom the former honoured, and the latter detested beyond all men living.—Scott.

[2] The meaning of this is not clear, for Pope never crossed either Channel.

give fire, and flew to the Prince that instant, who was as pleased to please me. You ask me how I am at Court. The Prince [Frederick] shows me a distinction beyond any pretence or merit on my part; and I have received a present from him of some marble heads of poets for my Library, and some urns for my Garden. The Ministerial writers rail at me; yet I have no quarrel with their masters, nor think it of weight enough to complain of them. I am very well with the courtiers I ever was or would be acquainted with. At least, they are civil to me; which is all I ask from courtiers, and all a wise man will expect from them. The Duchess of Marlborough makes great court to me : but I am too old for her, mind and body. Yet I cultivate some young people's friendship, because they may be honest men: whereas the old ones experience too often proves not to be so—I having dropped ten where I have taken up one, and I hope to play the better, with fewer in my hand.

You compliment me in vain upon retaining my poetical spirit. I am sinking fast into prose; and, if I ever write more, it ought (at these years, and in these times) to be something, the matter of which will give a value to the work, not merely the manner. . . . Having nothing to tell you of my poetry, I come to what is now my chief care—my health and amusement. The first is better as to headaches; worse as to weakness and nerves. The changes of weather affect me much: otherwise I want not spirits, except when indigestions prevail. The mornings are my life; in the evenings I am not dead, indeed, but sleep, and am stupid enough. I love reading still better than conversation: but my eyes fail, and, at the hours when most people indulge in company, I am tired, and find the labours of the past day sufficient to weigh me down. So I hide myself in bed, as a bird in his nest, much about the same time, and rise and chirp the earlier in the morning. I often vary the scene (indeed, at every friend's call) from London to Twickenham, or the contrary, to receive them, or be received by them.

Lord Bathurst is still my constant friend and yours: but his country-seat is now always in Gloucestershire, not in this neighbourhood. Mr. Pulteney has no country-seat; and in town I see him seldom: but he always asks after you. In the summer I generally ramble for a month to Lord Cobham's, the Bath, or elsewhere. In all these rambles, my mind is full of you and poor Gay, with whom I travelled so delightfully two summers. Why cannot I cross the sea? The unhappiest malady I have to complain of, the unhappiest accident of my whole life, is that weakness of the breast, which makes the physicians of opinion that a strong vomit would kill me. I have never taken one, nor had a natural motion that way in fifteen years. I went, some years ago, with Lord Peterborough about ten leagues at sea, purely to try if I could sail without sea-sickness, and with no other view than to make yourself and Lord Bolingbroke a visit before I died. But the experiment, though almost all the way near the coast, had almost ended all my views at once. Well, then, I must submit to live at the distance which fortune has set us at. But my memory, my affections, my esteem, are inseparable from you, and will, my dear friend, be for ever yours.[1]

P.S.—This I end at Lord Orrery's, in company with Dr. King. Wherever I can find two or three that are yours, I adhere to them naturally, and by that title they become mine. I thank you for sending Mr. Swift to me. He can tell you more of me.

[1] This letter from Pope to Swift, in which he enumerates their living friends, and commemorates so many of those they had lost, seems to have been intended by him as the winding up of the drama and the close of their long correspondence, which it, accordingly, proved to be.—R.

To Miss Martha Blount.

Stowe, July 4 [1739?].

The post after I writ to you I received, with great pleasure, one from you; and it increased that pleasure to hope you would be in a little time in the country, which you love so well, and when the weather is so good. I hope it will not be your fate, though it commonly proves that of others, to be deserted by *all* your friends at Court. I direct to your own house, supposing this will be sent after you, and having no surer way. For the same reason, I have directed a haunch of venison to be sent Mrs. Dryden, in case you are out of town. It will arrive next Monday early at Lord Cobham's, in Hanover Square: but if you are in town, and would have it otherwise disposed of, you may prevent it by sending thither over night a new direction to the porter. I will send you another from Hagley, if you appoint beforehand where it shall be left.

Your next direction is to Sir Thomas Lyttleton, at Hagley, near Stowerbridge, Worcestershire, where I hope to be on the tenth, or sooner, if Mr. Lyttleton come. Mr. Grenville was here, and told me he expected him in two or three days; so I think we may travel on the eighth or ninth. Though I never saw this place in half the beauty and perfection it now has, I want to leave it, to hasten my return towards you; or, otherwise, I could pass three months in agreeable rambles and slow journeys. I dread that to Worcester and back; for every one tells me it is perpetual rock, and the worst of rugged roads, which really not only hurt me at present, but leave consequences very uneasy to me. The Duke of Argyle was here yesterday, and assures me what Mr. Lyttelton talks of as one day's journey must be two, or an intolerable fatigue. He is the happiest man he ever was in his life. This garden is beyond all description, in the new part of it. I am every hour in it, but dinner and night, and every hour envying myself the delight of it, because not partaken by you, who would *see* it better and, consequently, enjoy it more.

Lady Cobham and Mrs. Speed, who (except two days) have been the sole inhabitants, wish you were here as much, at least, as they wished for their gowns, which are not yet all recovered; and, therefore, I fear yours is not. You might be more at your own disposal than usually; for every one takes a different way, and wanders about till we meet at noon. All the mornings we breakfast and dispute. After dinner, and at night, music and harmony—in the garden, fishing; no politics and no cards, nor much reading. This agrees exactly with me; for the want of cards sends us early to bed. I have no complaints, but that I wish for you, and cannot have you. I will say no more—but that I think *of* and *for* you, as I ever did and ever shall, present or absent. I can really forget everything besides. . . .

I desire you will write a post-letter to my man, John,[1] at what time you would have the pine-apples to send Lady Gerard, and whither he is to send them in town. I have had none yet: but I bade him send you the *very first* that ripened— I mean for *yourself*. But, if you are out of town, pray tell him to whom he shall send it. I have also ordered him, as soon as *several of them* ripen, to inquire of you where and when you would have any, which, I need not say, are wholly at your service. The post comes in crossly here, and after I have written, for the most part: but I keep this to the last, in case I have any letter to-night, that I may add to it, as I sincerely shall, my thanks, whenever you oblige me by writing, but still more by thinking me, and all I say, sincere, as you *safely* may, and *always* may.

Wednesday, 12 *o'clock*.—Adieu. I am going to the Elysian

---

[1] John Searle, whom he mentions in his Will.—C.

Fields, where I shall meet your *idea*. The post is come in without any letters which I need answer; which is a pleasure to me, except with regard to yours. . . . Adieu, once more. I am going to dream of you. Nine at night.

To Miss Martha Blount.

Bristol [Nov., 1739?].

I am glad I sent you my last letter on Saturday, without expecting yours, which did not come till the day after the post, by passing first through Mr. Allen's hands at Bath. I thank you for it, and must now give you some account of this place. I rise at seven, drink at the Well at eight, breakfast at nine, dine at two, go to bed at ten, or sooner. I find the water very cold on my stomach, and have no comfort but in the asses' milk I drink constantly with it, according to Dr. Mead's order. The three days I was at Mr. Allen's I went for two or three hours to Bath; but saw no public place, nor any persons, but the four or five I writ you word of. It grieved me to miss twice of Lady Cox in that time. I had a line from Mr. Slingsby Bethel, to acquaint me his brother was well; and I will write to him from hence, as soon as I can give him a physical account of myself.

I hardly knew what I undertook when I said I would give you some account of this place. Nothing can do it but a picture: it is so unlike any scene you ever saw. But I will begin, at least, and reserve the rest to my next letter. From Bath you go along the river, or its side, the road lying generally in sight of it. On each bank are steep rising hills, clothed with wood at top, and sloping toward the stream in green meadows, intermixed with white houses, mills, and bridges. This for seven or eight miles: then you come in sight of Bristol (the river winding, at the bottom of steeper banks, to the town), where you see twenty odd pyramids smoking over the town, which are glass-houses, and a vast extent of houses red and white. You come first to Old Wells, and over a bridge built, on both sides, like Lon' Bridge, and as much crowded with a strange mixture of seam women, children, loaded horses, asses, and sledges with goods, dragging along all together, without posts to separate them. From thence you come to a key [quay] along the old wall, with houses on both sides, and, in the middle of the street, as far as you can see, hundreds of ships, their masts as thick as they can stand by one another, which is the oddest and most surprising sight imaginable. This street is fuller of them than the Thames, from London Bridge to Deptford; and, at certain times only, the water rises to carry them out: so that, at other times, a long street, full of ships in the middle, and houses on both sides, looks like a dream.

Passing still along by the river, you come to a rocky way on one side, overlooking green hills on the other. On that rocky way rise several white houses, and, over them, red rocks, and, as you go further, more rocks above rocks, mixed with green bushes, and of different coloured stone. This, at a mile's end, terminates in the house of the Hot Well, whereabouts lie several pretty lodging-houses open to the river, with walks of trees. When you have seen the hills seem to shut upon you, and to stop any further way, you go into the house, and, looking out at the back door, a vast rock of an hundred feet high, of red, white, green, blue, and yellowish marbles, all blotched and variegated, strikes you quite in the face; and, turning on the left, there opens the river at a vast depth below, winding in and out, and accompanied, on both sides, with a continued range of rocks up to the clouds, of an hundred colours, one behind another, and so to the end of the prospect, quite to the sea. But the sea nor the Severn you do not see: the rocks and river fill the eye, and terminate the view, much like the broken scenes behind one another in a Play-house. From the room, where I write, I see the tide rising, and filling all the bottom between these scenes of rock: on the sides of which, on one hand, are buildings, some white, some red, everywhere up and down like the steepest side of Richmond to the Thames, mixed with trees and shrubs, but much wilder; and huge shaggy marbles, some in points, some in caverns, hanging all over and under them in a thousand shapes.

I have no more room but to give Lady Gerard my hearty services, and to wish you would see, next summer or spring, what I am sure would charm you, and fright most other ladies. I expect Mr. Allen here in four or five days. I am always desiring to hear of you. Adieu. Remember me to Lord Lyttelton, Lord Cornbury, and Mr. Cleland.

To Miss Martha Blount.

Bristol, Saturday [Nov. 24, 1739 ?].

I have just received yours, for which I most kindly love and thank you. You will have this a post the sooner, by Mr. Allen's messenger coming hither. I have had a kind letter from the Judge,[1] with very friendly mention of you, and concern that he could not see you. As he expects a particular account of myself, I enclose it, to save the trouble of writing it over again to you, who, I know, desire as much or more to know it: and I proceed in my description.

Upon the top of those high rocks by the Hot Well, which I have described to you, there runs, on one side, a large down of

[1] Mr. Baron Fortescue.

fine turf for about three miles. It looks too frightful to approach the brink, and look down upon the river: but in many parts of this down the valleys descend gently, and you see all along the windings of the stream, and the opening of the rocks, which turn and close in upon you, from space to space, for several miles on toward the sea. There is first, near Bristol, a little village upon this down, called Clifton, where are very pretty lodging houses, overlooking all the woody hills; and steep cliffs and very green valleys, within half a mile of the Wells; where, in the summer, it must be delicious walking and riding, for the plain extends one way many miles. Particularly, there is a tower that stands close at the edge of the highest rock, and sees the stream turn quite round it; and all the banks one way are wooded in a gentle slope for near a mile high, quite green: the other banks all inaccessible rock, of an hundred colours and odd shapes, some hundred feet perpendicular. I am told that one may ride ten miles further on an even turf, on a ridge that, on one side, views the river Severn, and the banks steeper and steeper quite to the open sea; and, on the other side, a vast woody vale, as far as the eye can stretch: and, all before you, the opposite coast of Wales beyond the Severn again. But this I have not been able to see; nor would one but in better weather, when one may dine, or lie there, or cross a narrow part of the stream to the nearest point in Wales, where Mr. Allen and Mr. Hook, last summer, lay some nights in the cleanest and best cottage in the world, with excellent provisions, under a hill on the margin of the Severn. Let him describe it to you, and pray tell him we are in much fear for his health, not having had a line since he left us.

The city of Bristol itself is very unpleasant, and no civilised company in it; only the Collector of the Customs would have brought me acquainted with merchants, of whom I hear no great character. The streets are as crowded as London: but the best image I can give you of it is, it is as if Wapping and Southwark were ten times as big, or all their people ran into London. Nothing is fine in it but the Square, which is larger than Grosvenor Square, and well-builded, with a very fine brass statue, in the middle, of King William on horseback; and the Key, which is full of ships, and goes round half the Square. The College Green is pretty, and (like the Square) set with trees, with a very fine old cross of Gothic curious work in the middle, but spoiled with the new folly of new gilding it, that takes away all the venerable antiquity. There is a cathedral, very neat, and nineteen parish churches.

Once more my services to Lady Gerard. I write scarce to anybody, therefore pray tell anybody you judge deserves it, that I inquire of, and remember myself to, them. I shall be at Bath soon; and, if Dr. Mead approves of what I asked him of the Bath water mixed, I will not return to Bristol.[1] Otherwise, I fear, I must: for, indeed, my complaint seems only intermitted, while I take larger quantities than I used of water, and no wine; and it must require time to know whether I might not just as well do so at home. Not but that I am satisfied the water at the Well is very different from what it is anywhere else. For it is full as warm as new milk from the cow. But there is no living at the Wells, without more conveniences in the winter. Adieu. I write so much, that I have no room to tell you what my heart holds of esteem and affection. Pray write to me every Thursday's post, and I shall answer on Saturday: for it comes and goes out the same day, and I can answer no sooner what you write on Tuesday.

[1] In a former letter to Miss M. Blount, Pope tells her that he is "just come from hearing Dr. Cheyne, the eminent Bath physician. I have the headache, which heats my brain, and he assures me I might be inspired, if it had but one turn more."

To Mr. Warburton.[1]

Twit'nam, Aug. 12, [1740?].

The general indisposition I have to writing, unless upon a belief of the necessity or use of it, would plead my excuse in not doing it to you. I know it is not (I feel it is not) needful to repeat assurances of that love and constant friendship and esteem I bear you. Honest and ingenuous minds are sure of each other: the tie is mutual and solid. The use of writing letters resolves wholly into the gratification, given and received, in the knowledge of each other's welfare—unless I ever should be so fortunate (and a rare fortune it would be) to be able to procure, and acquaint you of, some real benefit done you by my means. But Fortune seldom suffers a disinterested man to serve another. 'Tis too much an insult upon her to let two of those, who most despise her favours, be happy in them at the same time, and in the same instance. I wish for nothing so much, at her hands, as that she would permit some great person or other to remove you nearer the banks of the Thames: though very lately a nobleman, whom you esteem more than you know, had destined you a *Living* you never dreamt of, in the neighbourhood where you now are. But the incumbent was graciously preserved by Fortune.

I thank you heartily for your hints; and am afraid, if I had more of them, not on this only but on other subjects, I should break my resolution, and become an author anew: nay, a new author, and a better than I yet have been; or, God forbid I should go on jingling only the same bells!

I have received some chagrin at your delay (for Dr. King tells me it will be no more) of your degree at Oxon. As for mine, I

---

[1] Warburton did not reach the top of the ecclesiastical ladder till nineteen years later.

will die before I receive one, in an Art. I am ignorant of, at a place where there remains any scruple of bestowing one on you, in a Science of which you are so great a master. In short I will be *doctored* with you, or not at all. I am sure, wherever honour is not conferred on the deserving, there can be none given to the undeserving—no more from the hands of priests than of princes. Adieu. God give you all true blessings! I am faithfully yours.

To Mr. Warburton.

Sept. 20, 1741.

It is not my friendship, but the discernment of that nobleman [1] I mentioned, which you are to thank for his intention to serve you. And his judgment is so uncontroverted, that it would really be a pleasure to you to owe him anything, instead of a shame, which often is the case in the favours of men of that rank. I am sorry I can only wish you well, and not do myself honour in doing you any good. But I comfort myself, when I reflect few men could make you happier, none more deserving than you have made yourself.

I do not know how I have been betrayed into a paragraph of this kind. I ask your pardon, though it be truth, for saying so much.

If I can prevail on myself to complete the *Dunciad*, it will be published at the same time, with a general edition of all my verses (for poems I will not call them); and I hope your friendship to me will be then as well known as my being an author, and go together down to Posterity—I mean to as much

---

[1] Lord Chesterfield.

of Posterity as poor Moderns can reach to; where the Commentator (as usual) will lend a crutch to the weak Poet, to help him to limp a little further than he could on his own feet. We shall take our degree together in Fame, whatever we do at the University: I tell you once more,[1] I will not have it there without you.

To Mr. Warburton.

Bath, Nov. 12, 1741.

I am always naturally sparing of my letters to my friends, for a reason I think a great one—that it is needless, after experience, to repeat assurances of friendship; and no less irksome to be searching for words to express it over and over. But I have more calls than one for this letter: first, to express a satisfaction at your resolution not to keep up the ball of dispute with Dr. Middleton, though I am satisfied you could have done it; and to tell you that Mr. Lyttelton is pleased at it too, who writes me word, upon this occasion, that he must infinitely esteem a divine and an author, who loves peace better than victory. Secondly, I am to recommend to you, as an author, a bookseller in the room of the honest one you have lost—Mr. Giles; and I know none who is so worthy, and has so good a title, in that

---

[1] This was occasioned by the Editor's requesting him not to slight the honour ready to be done him by the University; and, especially, not to decline it on the Editor's account, who had no reason to think the affront done him—of complimenting him with an offer [of an honorary degree], and then contriving to evade it—the act of that illustrious body, but the exploit of two or three particulars, the creatures of a man in power, and the slaves of their own passions and prejudices. However, Mr. P. could not be prevailed on to accept of any honours from them, and his resentment of this low trick gave birth to the celebrated lines of Apollo's Mayor and Alderman, in the fourth *Dunciad*.—Warburton.

character to succeed him as Mr. Knupton. But my third motive of now troubling you is my own proper interest and pleasure. I am here in more leisure than I can possibly enjoy, even in my own house—*vacare literis*. It is at this place that your exhortations may be most effectual, to make me resume the studies I have almost laid aside by perpetual avocations and dissipations. If it were practicable for you to pass a month or six weeks from home, it is here I would wish to be with you; and if you would attend to the continuation of your own noble work,[1] or unbend to the idle amusement of commenting upon a poet, who has no other merit than that of aiming, by his moral strokes, to merit some regard from such men as advance truth and virtue in a more effectual way. In either case, this place and this house would be an uninviolable asylum to you from all you would desire to avoid, in so public a scene as Bath.

The worthy man,[2] who is the master of it, invites you in the strongest terms, and is one who would treat you with love and veneration rather than what the world calls civility and regard. He is sincerer and plainer than almost any man now in this world, *antiquis moribus*. If the waters of the Bath may be serviceable to your complaints (as I believe, from what you have told me of them), no opportunity can ever be better. It is just the best season. We are told the Bishop of Salisbury is expected here daily, who, I know, is your friend; at least, though a bishop, is too much a man of learning to be your enemy. You see I omit nothing to add to the weight in the balance, in which, however, I will not think myself light, since I have known your partiality. You'll want no servant here. Your room will be next to mine, and one man will serve us. Here is a Library, and a Gallery ninety feet long, to walk

---

[1] *The Divine Legation of Moses Demonstrated* (1737-41.)

[2] Ralph Allen, the friend and host of Pope, the original of Allworthy, in *Tom Jones*. As Pope represents him, he was used to "do good by stealth and blush to find it fame."

in; and a coach, whenever you would take the air with me. Mr. Allen tells me you might, on horseback, be here in three days: it is less than one hundred miles from Newark; the road through Leicester, Stow-in-the-Wolde (in Glostershire), and Cirencester, by Lord Bathurst's. I could engage to carry you to London from hence, and I would accommodate my time and journey to your conveniency.

Is all this a dream, or can you make it a reality? Can you give ear to me?

> *Audisti? an me ludit amabilis Insania?*

Dear Sir, adieu, and give me a line to Mr. Allen's at Bath. God preserve you ever. I am, yours faithfully, &c.

Mr. Allen's house (where I am, and hope you may be) is less than two miles from Bath: but his brother, the Postmaster, lives at Bath, and takes care of letters to me.

To Mr. Warburton.

Jan. 12, 1744.

An unwillingness to write nothing to you, whom I respect; and, worse than nothing, what would afflict you, to one who wishes me so well, has hitherto kept me silent. Of the public I can tell you nothing worthy the reflection of a reasonable man; and of myself only an account that would give you pain: for my asthma has increased every week since you last heard from me, to the degree of confining me totally to a fireside, so that I have hardly seen any of my friends but two, who happen to be divided from the world as much as myself, and are constantly retired at Battersea. There I have past most of my time, and often wished you of the company, as the best I knew to make me not regret the loss of all others, and to prepare me for a nobler hope than any mortal greatness can open to us. I fear, by the account you gave me of the time you design to come this way, one of them (whom I much wish you had a glimpse of, as a being *paullo minus ab angelis*) will be gone again, unless you pass some weeks in London, before Mr. Allen arrives there in March.

My present indisposition takes up almost all my hours to render a very few of them supportable. Yet I go on softly to prepare the great edition of my things, with your notes, and, as fast as I receive any from you, I add others in order, determining to finish the *Epistles* to Dr. Arb[uthnot] v. 2; two or three of the best of Horace, particularly that to Augustus first, which will fall into the same volume with the *Essay on Man*. I determined to have published a small number of that *Essay*, and of the other *On Criticism*, ere now as a sample of the rest; but Bowyer advised to delay,—though I now see I was not in the wrong.

I am told the Laureate [1] is going to publish a very abusive pamphlet. That is all I can desire: it is enough if it be *abusive*, and if it be *his*. He threatens you: but I think you will not fear, or love, him so much as to answer him, though you have answered one or two as dull. He will be more to me than a dose of hartshorn; and, as a stink revives one who has been oppressed with perfumes, his railing will cure me of a course of flatteries. I am much more concerned to hear that

---

[1] Colley Cibber. The piece which procured for him the Laureateship was his *Nonjuror*, an adaptation of Molière's *Tartuffe*. It had a great run, and was known, at a later period, under the title of the *Hypocrite*. Cibber produced, altogether, some twenty-five Plays—tragedies and comedies. He continued to act on the Stage up to a very advanced age. Pope, between whom and himself there was war à *outrance*, made him the principal personage in the Second Part of the *Dunciad* (1743). Two "Expostulatory Letters" were addressed by him to his satirist.

some of your clergy are offended at a verse or two of mine, because I have a respect for your clergy (though the verses are harder upon ours). But, if they do not blame *you* for defending those verses, I will wrap myself up in the layman's cloak, and sleep under your shield.

Have you forgot, as I did in my last two letters, the debt I owed you ever since November was twelvemonth, and some little matter you undertook to pay for a saddle and apothecary's bill, when I left you at Bath? Pray send me word, if I shall pay the whole, or the interest, to any person before you come to town. I am sorry to find, by a letter two posts since from Mr. Allen, that he is not quite recovered yet of all that remains of his indisposition, nor Mrs. Allen quite well. Don't be discouraged from telling me how you are, for no man is more yours than, &c.

To Mr. Ralph Allen.

March 6 [1744].

I thank you very kindly for yours. I am sure we shall meet with the same hearts we ever met,[1] and I could wish it were at Twickenham, though only to see you and Mrs. Allen twice there instead of once. But, as matters have turned out, a decent obedience to the Government has since obliged me to reside here, ten miles out of the Capital; and, therefore, I must see you here or nowhere. Let that be an additional reason for your coming and staying what time you can.

The utmost I can do, I will venture to tell you in your ear.

---

[1] Alluding to the unhappy disagreement which had occurred between them, and to the reconciliation which had taken place.—R.

I may slide along the Surrey side (where no Middlesex Justice can pretend any cognisance) to Battersea, and thence cross the water for an hour or two, in a close-chair, to dine with you, or so. But to be in town I fear will be imprudent, and thought insolent. At least, hitherto, all comply with the Proclamation.[1]

I write thus early, that you may let me know if your [fixed] day continues, and I will have every room in my house as warm for you as the owner always would be. It may possibly be, that I shall be taking the secret flight I spoke of to Battersea before you come, with Mr. Warburton, whom I have promised to make known to the only great man in Europe, who knows as much as he;[2] and from thence we may return the 16th, or any day, hither and meet you, without fail, if you fix your day.

[1] On the invasion, at that time threatened from France and the Pretender.—Warburton. Warburton's note is vague and insufficient. Pope was no more concerned with the threatened invasion than any other Englishman, than Allen himself, who was travelling, and might go to Twickenham, or anywhere he pleased. But, consequent on the threatened invasion, the *Habeas Corpus* was suspended; and a Proclamation issued in February (just issued, therefore, when this letter was written) for putting the laws in execution against papists and non-jurors, commanding their departure out of the cities of London and Westminster on or before the 2nd March, and not to remove from their respective places of abode above five miles, &c.—C. W. D. (MS. note.) But, as a (nominal) papist, Pope was, as matter of course, especially obnoxious to the operation of these laws.

[2] He brought these two eminent men together, but they soon parted in mutual disgust with each other.—Warton. Pope lived scarcely three months beyond the date of this letter. The Jacobite Invasion, as is well known, took place in the next year.

The Thirteenth Book of the Iliad.

When Jove's high will, ev'n to ye Sea-beat Coast,
Had borne ~~advanc'd wth conquests~~ of great Hector's Host
He left them ~~there~~ to the Fates, in bloody Fray
to toil and struggle thro' that well-fought day.
Then his eternal Eyes
he cast
along y^e ~~Thracian~~ shores, a desert vast
on Thracia there, a region wild & waste;
where ~~bold~~ Mysians prove their martial force,
& hardy Thracians tame ye savage Horse:
& where ye far-fam'd Hippomolgian strays,
Renown'd for Justice, & for length of days,
~~Thrice~~ happy Race! that innocent of Blood,
from Milk, innoxious, seek their simple food.
Jove sees delighted; & avoids ye Scene
of guilty Troy, of arms, & dying men.
No aid, he deems, is giv'n,
while his high ~~will~~ Law suspends the Pow'rs of Heaven.

Observ'd the Thunderer ye Monarch of ye watry Reign
~~Beheld~~
In Samothracia, from a mountain's brow,
whose waving woods o'erhang ye deeps below,
He sate; & round him cast his azure eyes
where Ida's misty tops confus'dly rise,
Below, fair Ilion's glittering spires were seen,
& the floating Fleets, & sable seas between.

There

From the original MS. of Pope's "Iliad," in the British Museum.

INDEX.

A

Abbreviations, in the English Language, condemned by Swift, in the *Tatler*, 95; in letter to Beach, 245.

Academy of Lagado, referred to by Mrs. Howard, in a letter to Swift, 193, *note.*

Academy for reforming the English language, proposed by Swift, 128.

Account of the Poisoning of Edmund Curll, a burlesque by Pope, 307.

Acheson, Sir A., and Lady, Irish friends of Swift, introduced in his *Grand Question Debated*, 61; mentioned by him in letter to Pope, 212; Swift gives an account to Pope of his "libels" upon Lady Acheson, 214, and *note.*

Achilles, an opera by Gay, 233, *note.*

Addison, Joseph, sends his *Remarks* to Swift, his intimacy with Swift, revises Swift's *Baucis and Philemon*, 16; Secretary of State for Ireland, 23, and *note*; figures in Swift's letters to Esther Johnson, 29; not a Letter-Writer, 66; at the tavern with Swift, 86, 87; letter from Swift to, 89-91; entertains Swift and Jervas in his country-place, 96; coolness with Swift on political grounds, 101; Swift behaves coldly to him at the coffee-house, at a dinner with Swift and Steele at his sister's house, 102; his reconciliation with Swift, who dines with him and Steele at Tonson's, 116; dines, with Swift, at Lord Bolingbroke's, on Good Friday, preparing his tragedy of *Cato*, at a symposium at Lord Bolingbroke's with Swift and others, and discusses politics with them, 135-136; rehearsal of his *Cato* described by Swift, 137; letters of Swift to, on Steele's reflections in the *Guardian*, 141-142; involved in the quarrel between Swift and Steele, 143, and *note*; letter from Swift to, congratulating him on his appointment as Secretary of State, 167-168; his maxim, to excuse nobody, 181; eulogises Pope's *Essay on Criticism*, in *Spectator*, 282; his acquaintance with Pope originates with the *Essay*, 287; letter addressed by Pope to him (but, in fact, written to Steele), Prologue to his *Cato* written by Pope, defended by Pope from the attacks of Dennis upon his *Cato*, 288; fictitious Correspondence with Pope, causes of estrangement from Pope, his patronage of Tickell's *Iliad*, satirised by Pope under the name of Atticus, 289; alleged reason for his resigning Secretaryship, 290; his *Cato* noticed by Pope in a letter to Caryll, 291; disapproves of the revised edition of the *Rape of the Lock*, 297; offends Pope by his preference for Tickell's *Iliad*, 300; his *Dialogue on Medals* inspires one of Pope's *Essays*, 322; fictitious letters to him from Pope, 344, 346; letter from Pope wrongly printed with superscription to him, 360; his criticism on the *Temple of Fame* requested by Pope, 364; his *Cato* eulogised, and its acting described, by Pope in a letter to Caryll, 365-366; his eulogy of Pope causes the poet to be suspected of Whiggism, his name omitted, in favour of Congreve, in Pope's edition of his own Letters of 1735, 379, and *note*; his verses on *Liberty* noticed by Pope in letter to Jervas, 389; regard and respect for him expressed by Pope to Jervas, 390; sends to Pope a poem of Parnell's, 407; curious fatalities in regard to the dedication of his writings noticed by Atterbury, in a letter to Pope, 447, *note.*

Adrian, Roman Emperor, his epigram, *Ad Animam*, imitated by Pope, 368.

Adventurer, The, a periodical edited by Dr. Hawkesworth, his protest against Hunting in, 287, *note.*

Æneis, quoted by Swift, 149; by Pope, 435.

Æsculapius, Pope's sacrifice to, as reported by Lord Chesterfield, 335; work by Walsh, under that title, 353, *note.*

Æsop, the champion of the Ancients, in the *Battle of the Books*, 15, *note.*

Agriculture, Cicero on, quoted by Pope, 477.

Alcina, Astolfo in the palace of, 416, *note.*

2 K

Alexandriana, lampoons, collected by Dean Smedley, on Pope, 319.

Alexandrine verses, according to Swift, brought in by Dryden, and rejected by Pope, Gay, and Young, 244.245.

Allen, Ralph, the frequent host of Pope, 326; Pope's quarrel with, 333; a legatee under Pope's Will, 335; engages to publish Pope's *Correspondence* at his sole expense, 343; letter to, from Pope, on pictures, and on the ill-placed zeal of the ecclesiastical Reformers in regard to them, 489, 490; eulogised by Pope, in a letter inviting Warburton to Bath, 507; his illness lamented by Pope, 510; letter from Pope to, 510, 511.

Allworthy, in *Tom Jones*, suggested by the character of Ralph Allen, 507.

Ambassadors, denounced by Swift as a new word brought in by the War, 95, *note*.

Amicis Prodesse, Nemini Nocere, a sentence in Cicero's *De Officiis*, admired by Pulteney as a *motto*, and approved by Swift, 261, *note*.

Aminta, of Tasso, noticed by Pope, one of the great store-houses of the English poets in xvi. and xvii. centuries, 352, and *note*.

Amphion, Pope's comparison of himself to, 429.

Amusement, denounced by Swift as a new word, 95.

Andromache, Swift's witty derivation of, 58.

Anne, Queen, described by Swift as a female Jehu and Nimrod, 29; her frequent attacks of gout, her select preachers, 31; a Whig, her new favourite Mrs. Masham, 82, and *note*; resolves to dismiss the premier, Godolphin, 81; prorogues Convocation, 87; dismisses the Court-physician, Radcliffe, at her Accession, for his rash candour, 97, *note*; grants the *first-fruits*, and *twentieths* to the Irish Church, 100; delays to give the Treasurer's Staff to Harley, 107; has a "dunce" to preach before her at Windsor, 118; holds a Drawing-room in her bed-chamber, pays £1000 a month for the dinners at the "Green Cloth," meets Swift in company with Miss Forester and Arbuthnot, 120; present at the private marriage of Abigail Hill, 123, *note*; orders £20,000 to be furnished for the continuation of the building of Blenheim, 124; takes too little exercise, in Swift's opinion, her illness alarms Swift and the Tory Cabinet, 128, 130; sends preserved ginger to Swift, 132; her portrait presented by her to the Duchess of Marlborough and despoiled and given away by the Duchess, 138; is, at length, reluctantly persuaded by Harley and Mrs. Masham to give the Deanery of St. Patrick's to Swift, 140, 141; defended by Swift from the charge of making a bad Peace, 265, 267; under the disguise of Belinda, in *Key to the Lock*, 298; her death excites great concern at Oxford, 389.

Annual Register, The, letter of Pope to the Duchess of Hamilton first appears in, 432.

Apollo's Lord Mayor and Aldermen, the Oxford Dons satirised by Pope under these names, 506.

Apology for his Own Life, by Colley Cibber, noticed by Mr. Carruthers, 320, *note*.

Arabian Author, an, on Humaneness, quoted by Pope, 286.

Arabian Tales, criticised by Atterbury, 441.

Arbuthnot, Dr. John, figures in Swift's letters to Esther Johnson, 29; chief author of *Martinus Scriblerus*, 33; his letter to Swift on that satire, in ridicule of Medicine, 35; author of Gulliverian pamphlets, *Gulliver Decyphered*, &c., 45, *note*; could have added many things to *Gulliver*, if he had been in the secret of its publication, 4¹; acts as Swift's *chaperon* at Windsor, 120; dines with Swift and Berkeley, 140; letter from Swift to, 149-151; the only physician who understood Swift's "case," 261; becomes acquainted with Pope, 287; *Epistle* addressed by Pope to, 289; welcomes Pope's *Iliad*, 300; contributes to the Swift and Pope *Miscellanies*, 314; his character of Curll, 307, *note*; supplies Notes to the *Dunciad*, 319; his *bon-mot* on Jervas, 370, *note*; letters from Pope to, 386-389, 397-398; a letter to Pope from, 398, *note*; his letter to Swift on Gay, 400, *note*; his *bon-mot* on the "South-Sea Bubble," 443, 444; alleged by Pope to have contributed to the satire, *Treatise of the Bathos*, 492; his daughter mentioned by Pope, as having the character of her father, 494; *Epistle* by Pope to, noticed in a letter to Warburton, 509.

Arcadia, of Sydney, Swift probably derived his "Stella" from, 25, *note*.

Ardella, Swift's poetic name for Lady Winchelsea, 87, *note*.

Ariosto, his *Orlando Furioso* imitated by Gay, 300.

Arnold, Matthew, quoted, 15, *note*.

Ars Punica, the *Art of Punning*, by Swift and Sheridan, 58.

Art of Criticism in Painting, by Jon. Richardson, noticed by Roscoe, 480, *note*.

Art Poétique, of Boileau, a model of Pope's *Essay on Criticism*, 281.

Articles of Religion, supposed by Pope to be

INDEX. 515

discarded, one by one, by Lady M. W Montagu, as she nears the country of the Turks and Infidels, 418.

Ashburnham, Lady, daughter of the Duke of Ormond, marriage of, noticed by Swift, 98; invites Swift to a dinner, and forgets the engagement, 109; with her sister, Lady Betty Butler, meets Swift at the Vanhomrighs', 111; Swift's remarks on the death of, 33.

Ashe, Dr., Bishop of Clogher, said to have officiated at the (supposed) marriage of Swift and Esther Johnson, 37, 90, 95, 97, 98, 158, and note.

Astolfo, a hero of the *Orlando Furioso*, his wife alluded to by Pope, 416.

Asturias Prince of, receipt for a, 74, note.

Athenæum, The, some of Pope's letters published in, by C. W. Dilke, 289; quoted by Carruthers, 293, note; 302, note.

Atossa, Duchess of Marlborough satirised by Pope under that name, 323.

Atterbury, Bishop, reports the great success of the *Tale of a Tub*, and guesses its authorship, 14; his lodgings at Chelsea near those of Swift, 28; figures in the journal-letters of Swift, 29; involved in the Jacobite conspiracy, 35; his anger at the abrogation of Convocation, 87; Swift's visits to, 107, 108; his letter to Pope on the satire on Addison, 290, note; his *Correspondence* with Pope, 344; letter from Pope (on his proposal to Pope to secede to the Established Church) to, 434-437; criticises the *Arabian Nights*, 441, note; letter from Pope to, 441-443; writes to Pope on the latter's *Pastorals* and *Shakspeare*, and remarks on the fatality attending on the dedications of the Works of Addison, 447, note; a letter from Pope to, 447-449; pretended complaint against by Pope, 451.

Atticus, Addison satirised under that name by Pope, 289-290.

Aulus Gellius, used by Pope in his version of the *Iliad*, 385, and note.

Auri Sacra Fames, " a crime common to the greatest and the meanest," 435.

Ayre, William, author of a Life of Pope, 336, note.

B

Ballad, A, on a Westminster Election, by Swift, 99; *A Pastoral*, a parody by Pope, quoted, 280, note.

Balvardo, Dr., with Scaramouch and Harlequin, an allusion to by Lord Bolingbroke, in letter to Swift, 217, note.

Bamboozle, denounced by Swift as a new word, 95, note.

Banter, denounced by Swift as a new word, 95, note.

Barber, Mrs., a Dublin friend of Swift, 59; "chief poetess" in Dublin, 224; unfortunate, 243.

Barber, Alderman, letter from Swift to, 270-271.

Barcelonians, the besieged, patriotism of, commended by Pope, 339, 392, 396.

Barnovelt, Esdras, pretended author of the *Key to the Lock*, 298.

Barrack, The, poem of Swift, 231.

Barrett, Dr., Vice-Provost of Trinity College, Dublin, misrepresents facts in Swift's life, 3; 4, note.

"Barrier Treaty," pretended by Pope to be the object of the satire of his *Rape of the Lock*, 298.

Basset-Table, verses contributed by Pope to the *Town Eclogues*, 307.

Bath, Mrs. Pendarves's opinion of, 241, note; Pope's visits to, notice of under the rule of Nash, 305, and note; Pope the guest of Allen at, 333; according to Pope, could not supply the amount of scandal afforded by circuit-experience, 395; Pope wishes to see Martha Blount at, Bowles's remark upon the change of manners at, 396, and note; Pope invites Gay to join him and Parnell at, 400; describes the society and his manner of living at, 407; prefers Twickenham to, 437; invites Warburton to join him at Allen's house near, 507.

Bathurst, Lord, his remark upon Pope's curiosity, 293, note; a satire, in imitation of Horace, by Pope, dedicated to, 331; frequently entertains Pope at his place near Cirencester, 333; letter from Pope to, 471-474.

Batrachomyomachia, an Homeric mock-epic, translated by Dr. Parnell, alluded to by Pope, 406, and note, 420; Parnell's translation of, commended by Pope, 428.

Battersea, the residence of Lord Bolingbroke, 323; Pope's last visits at, 334.

Battle of the Books, a satire by Swift, noticed 15; 16, and note.

Baucis and Philemon, a witty parody, by Swift, of Ovid's *Metamorphosis*, noticed and quoted, 16-18, and notes.

Bayle, Pierre, his *Dictionnaire Philosophique*, calls forth the apologies of the Optimists, King, Leibnitz, and others, 327.

Beach, Thomas, letter from Swift to, 244-246.

Beach, Mary, Pope's nurse, 385, note.

Beasts' Confession, The, a satirical poem of Swift, mentioned by him, 61.

Beatitude, the ninth, according to Pope, 466.

Bede, "the Venerable," his lamentation that

the Irish keep Easter at the wrong time of the year, quoted by Swift, 186.

Beggar's Opera, The, divides the favour of the town with *Gulliver's Travels,* 49.

Belinda, poetic name of Arabella Fermor, in the *Rape of the Lock,* 297, 298, and *note.*

Bellenden, Mary and Margaret, friends of Pope, commemorated by Gay, in verses to Pope; the former, Maid of Honour to the Princess of Wales, unsuccessfully courted by the Prince of Wales, 191, *note*; her beauty and manners eulogised by Horace Walpole and Lord Hervey, becomes Duchess of Argyll, 300, *note*; 304; commemorated in a Court-ballad by Pope, 305, *note.*

Bentham, Jeremy, enters at the Oxford University at the age of fifteen, 2, *note.*

Bentinck, Isabella, Duchess of Kingston, supposed sender of invitation-note to Pope, 304-5, *note.*

Bentley, Dr. Richard, a champion of the Moderns, satirised in the *Battle of the Books,* 15.

Bergerac Cyrano, *Histoire Comique des Etats et des Empires de la Lune,* &c., one of the models of *Gulliver's Travels,* 47, *note.*

Berkeley, Lord, Lord-Lieut. of Ireland, takes Swift as his private Secretary, 11; brings him to England, 12; his warning to him, 70.

Berkeley, Lady, Swift dedicates to her a parody of Boyle's *Meditations,* the *Meditation on a Broomstick,* 21; 94.

Berkeley, Lady Betty, daughter of Lord Berkeley, a friend and correspondent of Swift, 11; letters to Swift from, 57, 58, 247, 248, and *notes*; a letter from Swift to, 246-250.

Berkeley, Bishop, at the Kilkenny School, 2; introduced by Swift to Lord Berkeley, of Stratton, obtains chaplaincy to Lord Peterborough through Swift, 138, and *note*; dines with Swift and Arbuthnot, 140; with Swift and Parnell at an Alehouse, 141.

Berkeley, G. Monck, a letter of Swift first published by, 9; a witness for Swift's (alleged) marriage, 37, *note.*

Bethel, Hugh, letters from Pope to, 450-452, 484-485; Pope sends a copy of his *Odyssey* to, 452.

Betterton, Thomas, the Actor, Kneller's portrait of, copied by Pope, 301; 370, *note.*

Bevis, Mount, near Southampton, residence of Lord Peterborough, Pope's visits to, 333.

Bickerstaff, Isaac, Predictions of, a Satire by Swift, burned by the Holy Office at Lisbon, as a production of the "Black Art,"

20; Swift apostrophised by Pope under that name, 319.

Big-Endians, and Little-Endians, the two great religious sects in Lilliput, an allusion by Mrs. Howard to, in letter to Swift, 193, *note.*

Bindon, H., three portraits of Swift by, 32.

Binfield, Pope's father buys a house and land at, 276; Pope leaves (1716), 377, offers to Gay a retreat at, 399; the Misses Blount how regarded by Pope at, 403.

Birch, Thomas, editor of *Heads of Illustrious Persons,* 348.

Birthday Poem, A, addressed by Swift to Stella, quoted, 51, *note.*

Bishops, compared to black Rabbits by Swift, 195.

Black Art, The, *Predictions of Isaac Bickerstaff* condemned by the Holy Office as a production of, 20.

Blackmore, Sir Richard, M.D., *Key to the Dunciad,* assigned by Pope to, 318, *note*; immortalised in the *Dunciad,* author of certain popular poems, 320.

Blaney, Lord, Swift complains to the Irish House of Peers of insult from, 236.

Blenheim, Queen Anne orders that £20,000 be expended on continuation of, 124.

Blifil, Capt., the epitaph on (in *Tom Jones*), alluded to, 331.

Blount, Martha, letter from Swift to, 199-201; extract from letter to Swift from, 200, *note*; invited with Pope to Dublin by Swift, 201; mentioned in a letter of Swift to Pope, 215; her family among Pope's earlier (papist) friends, 290; residing at Mapledurham, notice of her and of her eldest sister, picture at Mapledurham of, scandal relating to Pope's intimacy with, 291, 292; extract from letter of Mrs. Caryll to, 293, *note*; letter from Pope to, 295; commemorated, with her sister, by Gay in verses addressed to Pope, 300; *Eloisa to Abelard* dedicated, in first instance, by Pope to, 302; verses *To a Lady on her Birthday* addressed by Pope to, 312; *Of the Characters of Women,* a satire of Pope, supposed to have been dedicated to, 322; with Pope at the Allens at Bath, extracts from letters between Pope and, 333; receives one of Pope's last letters, 334; principal legatee under Pope's Will, character of Pope's letters to, 346; supposed representation, in a portrait of Pope by Jervas, of, 348: letters of Pope to, 401-403, 409-411, (conjointly to herself and her sister) 429-431; "diets on fools," in town, 479; on a visit in Surrey, 489; her unselfishness eulogised by Pope, in letter to Swift, 494; letters from Pope to, 497. 499, 499-501, 501-503.

Blount, Teresa, receives the homage of Pope conjointly with her sister, portrait of (as supposed) by Jervas, 292, and *note*; at first more courted by Pope than her sister, an *Epistle* addressed by Pope to, 293; another poetic *Epistle* dedicated by Pope to, under the name of Zephalinda, 294-295; extract from letter of Pope, on Court-diversions, to, 304; Pope describes fashionable mode of bathing at Bath, in a letter to, 305; letter of Pope, on same subject, to, 395-397.

Blount, Edward, extract from letter from Pope complaining of difficulties in engraving maps for his *Iliad*, to, 299; extract from letter from Pope, describing Twickenham Villa, to, 310; letter from Pope on his *Iliad*, and on sectarian partisanship, to, 392-394; Pope desires to see his daughters at Twickenham, their marriages, 467, and *note*.

Blouzelinda, name of a shepherdess in Gay's *Pastorals*, the *Blouzelindas* of the Hague, allusions of Pope to, 400.

Boileau, Nicolas, his *L'Art Poétique*, a model of Pope's *Essay on Criticism*, 281; his *Lutrin* imitated by Pope in his *Rape of the Lock*, 297; 342.

Bolingbroke, St. John, Lord, described by Swift in letter to Esther Johnson, 27; a member of the *October* and *Scriblerus* clubs, 33; flees to France, 35; extract from letters to Swift regarding Stella, 50, *note*; Swift's affection (mixed with some distrust) for, extracts from letters to Swift from, 56; Queen's confidences to, 83; his damaging speech in the House of Commons lamented by Swift, who fears that he will not be able to keep his place in the Cabinet, 113-114, *note*; Swift lodges in the same house at Windsor with, 117; at Bucklersbury with Swift, fraternising with the Berkshire squires, 119; diplomatic despatches received from, 134; Swift prevails on him to invite Addison to a dinner on Good Friday, 135; entertains Swift and Addison at a dinner, answers the latter's objections courteously, 136; letter from Swift to, 154-156; Swift invites him to the Deanery, 155; letter from Swift to, 216. 219; Lord Chatham's visit to, at Battersea, 219, *note*; extracts from letters to Swift from, 217, 218; marries, as his second wife, the Marquise de Villette, 232, *note*; Swift complains of his beginning to fail him in correspondence, 239; his differences with Lord Oxford, 264; Swift in the greatest confidence of, 265; Swift leaves his *History of the Four Last Years* in the hands of, 267; busy writing his *History of His Own Times* in France, his hatred of the very memory of his former colleague, Lord Oxford, 268; writes to Swift, and announces his sale of Dawley, and departure for France, 270; his first acquaintance and intimacy with Pope, 323; sketch of his life after his conspiracy with the Jacobites and disgrace, inherits his father's estate at Battersea, associates with Pope at Twickenham and at Dawley, 323-324; character of his Correspondence with Pope, inspires Pope's *Moral Essays* and, in particular, the *Essay on Man*, agreement of his *Fragments* and *Minutes of Essays* with the principles of those poems, evidence of his direct influence on Pope given by Spence and Lord Bathurst, first to record the inception of the *Essay* in letter to Swift, 324; his presentation of the optimist system of Leibnitz, 327; Pope dedicates last edition of the *Essay* to, 330; Pope's last letters written to, attends Pope's death-bed, Pope bequeaths his manuscripts to, his anger at the introduction of a priest to his dying friend, 335, and *note*; his indignation at Pope's breach of confidence in regard to his manuscript writings, writes to Lord Marchmont and to Mallet upon the subject, publishes a furious attack upon Pope, publishes a revised edition of his Treatises, chief causes of his anger at Pope's premature publication of them. his fierce controversy with Warburton, and his *Familiar Epistle to the Most Impudent Man Living*, 336-337; *Bolingbroke, a Political Study*, referred to, 446; letter from Pope to, 459-464; alluded to by Pope as better engaged in Agriculture than in Politics, 477, and *note*; report of his way of life at Fontainebleau and his writing his *History* (in letter of Pope to Swift),fears that Swift in his *History* has mistaken some facts in the last years of Queen Anne, Scott's remark upon the reason of his fears, 493-494, and *note*.

Bolingbroke, Lady, Bolingbroke's first wife, daughter of Sir H. Winchcomb, a great favourite of Swift, 119; Bolingbroke's second wife the Marquise de Villette, her ill-health alluded to by Swift, her devotion to her husband, 232; 323; lives partly with her husband, and partly with her daughter, 433, and *note*.

Bonarelli, an Italian *Pastoral* poet of the xvi. century, mentioned by Pope, 352.

Booth, Barton, the Actor, plays the part of

Addison's Cato, presented by Bolingbroke with fifty guineas on that occasion, 365.
Borde, Dr. Andrew, said to be the original of the proverbial "Merry Andrew," 404, note.
Boucle de Cheveux Enlevée La, a French version of the Rape of the Lock, by Marmontel, 297.
Bouchain, Marlborough's action at, one of his greatest military achievements, 124, note.
Boutade, a French term, explained to Mrs. Pendarves by Swift, 239.
Bowles, Rev. Wm., editor and critic of Pope, his enthusiastic eulogy of the Rape of the Lock, 297; his edition of Pope characterised by Mr. Elwin, assails chiefly the moral character of Pope, his judgments sometimes self-contradictory and his method confused, his Edition published in 1806, excites vehement controversy, criticised by Byron and by Campbell, his replies, attacked by a Quarterly reviewer, his retort, 339; his remark upon the story of Mrs. Weston, 362, note; criticised by Roscoe in regard to his charging Pope with altering his letters for publication, 416-417, note; his remark on the junction of the Thames and Severn, 450, note; ridicules Warton for his admiration of Pope's Grotto, 468, note; alludes to Bolingbroke's introduction to George II., 493, note.
Brent, Mrs., Swift's Presbyterian housekeeper, mentioned by Lady Betty Germaine, in letter to Swift, 57; cautioned by Swift not to entertain Father Johnson and Mrs. Dingley at the Deanery in his absence, 206.
Bridges, Rev. Ralph, letter from Pope, on his translation of the Iliad, to. 353-355.
Bridgwater, The Ladies, unsuccessful portraits by Pope of, the charms of one of them (according to Walpole) often used by Jervas in other portraits, 370, note.
Briseis, the captive slave of Achilles, an allusion by Pope to, 423.
Bristol, the road from Bath to, the scenery and appearance of, described by Pope in letters to Martha Blount, 499-502; the city of, described by Pope in the same letters, 502-503.
British Apollo, The, alluded to by Pope as the receptacle of the productions of the versifiers of the time, 356.
Broome, Dr. Wm., collaborateur with Pope in his translation of the Odyssey, 299, 313.
Broomstick, Meditation on a, a parody by Swift of Boyle's Meditations, 21.

Brown, Sir G., the original of "Sir Plume," in the Rape of the Lock, 298.
Bucklersbury, Bolingbroke's country place, Swift entertained at, 119.
Bull-Baiting, denounced by Steele in the Tatler, but sanctioned by the Legislature up to the end of the first quarter of the present century, 286, note.
Bully, a new term, reprobated by Swift in the Tatler, 95, note.
Bunyan, John, his Sermons, an allusion to by Pope, 357; his Pilgrim's Progress alluded to by Pope, 430.
Burlington, Lord, Swift expresses vehement anger against, in a letter to Gay, for neglecting his ancestor's monument in St. Patrick's Cathedral, 221-222; 225, note; a friend of Pope, at Chiswick, 302; letter from Pope to, describing his journey to Oxford with Lintot, 305-306.
Burnet, Dr., Bishop of Salisbury, suspected to be the author of the Discourse of Dissensions Between the Nobles and Commons, 12; his death, damned already (according to Dr. Sacheverell and the Church of Rome, as reported by Pope), 405.
Burnet, Thomas, son of the Bishop of Salisbury, publishes Homerides: a Letter to Mr. Pope on his intended translation of Homer, under the pseudonym of "Sir Iliad Doggrel," attacks, also, Gay's What d'ye-Call It, ridiculed by Pope in letter to Caryll, 404.
Butchers' Corporation, The, St. Patrick's bells ringing in the installation of the Master of, 253.
Butchering, Atrocities of, noticed by Pope in the Guardian, Plutarch's denunciation of, 285, 286.
Button's Coffee-house, the Whig Club, 300.
Byblis and Ianthe, the romance of, in Ovid's Metamorphoses, probably in Pope's mind in his Eloisa to Abelard, 304.
Byron, Lord, discriminates between the Pastorals of Pope and of Philips in his Hints from Horace, 28; the most distinguished eulogist and apologist of Pope, his estimate of Pope's poetry and genius, his Letters to John Murray on the Strictures of the Rev. W. L. Bowles on the Life and Writings of Pope noticed, his admiration of Pope, in great measure, sincere, his opinion as to the highest kind of Poetry quoted, 337, 338, note; the principal combatant in the Bowles and Pope controversy, 340.

INDEX.

C

Cadenus, anagram for Decanus; Cadenus and Vanessa, poem of Swift, quoted 38-39; quoted by Swift, 163.164.

Callières De, Wotton (wrongly) asserts the Battle of the Books of Swift to have been derived wholly from the French satire of. 15.

Campbell, Thomas, defends Pope from the charges and criticisms of Bowles, 339.

Campaign, The, poem of Addison, quoted by Pope, 365.

Cardinalate, Pope declares to Swift that he has no hope of attaining the, 411.

Careless Husband, The, a comedy of Cibber, 308.

Carlingford, Viscount, an ancestor of Swift, 1.

Carlyle, Thomas, the Tale of a Tub suggested the hint for his Sartor Resartus, on the "Philosophy of Clothes," to, 14.

Caroline, The Princess, and Queen, reference to, in (the unprinted version of) Swift's verses on his own death, 64; reported to have offered the Bishopric of Cloyne to Swift, Swift reports an interview with, 189, note; Mrs. Howard Maid of Honour to, 191, note; Swift offers, through Mrs. Howard, a present of Irish Plaid to, he engages to have her health drunk by five hundred Irish weavers, 192; graciously receives (as Mrs. Howard writes to Swift) his present, thinks that he cannot decently appear in high heels in England, 193, note; Swift writes from Twickenham to Sheridan that he purposes to go to London only to see her (who had lately been crowned), 204; pays court to Swift, 222, and note; complained of by Swift to Mrs. Howard for her neglect of him, Swift declares he will be satisfied by nothing less than her portrait by Jervas, desires Mrs. Howard will tell her so, is angry with her for sacrificing Gay to Walpole's piques, wishes she would remember her promises to him about Ireland, he himself has never asked more than a trifle from her, 226, 227; is alleged, as Queen, to have taken pleasure in revenging herself upon her rival (Mrs. Howard), 228, note; Swift expresses his high esteem for, 229; Pope attends the Court of, at Richmond, 302.

Carruthers, Robert, a biographer and editor of Pope, conjectures the portraits of Teresa and Martha Blount, at Mapledurham, to be by Jervas, 292, note; prints a letter from Mrs. Caryll to Martha Blount, 293, note; holds the platonic nature of the friendship between Martha Blount and Pope, 295; paintings by Pope noticed by, 301; the story of Mrs. Weston referred to by, 302, note; a letter to Pope from the Duchess of Kingston quoted by, 305, note; references to Pope's Twickenham grounds and grotto, in H. Walpole and Gentleman's Magazine, quoted by, 309, note; his estimate of Cibber's Apology, 320, note; quotes Lord Chesterfield's testimony as to Pope's deism, 335, note; his (personal) biography of Pope the best, 338; his first edition of the Life and Works of Pope published in 1853, a revised edition, in 1859; fac-simile of sketch of full length portrait of Pope given by, 348, note; alteration of a passage in a letter of Pope to Martha Blount noticed by, 411, note; remarks of C. W. Dilke, on extracts from letter of Pope to the Misses Blount, given by, 429, note.

Carte, Thomas, a Jacobite historian, noticed by Swift as publishing with (Buckley, the Gazetteer) "a most monstrous unreasonable" edition of De Thou's Histoire, flees to France, and sells his materials for the edition to Dr. Mead, author of a History of England, 221, and note.

Carteret, Lord, Lord-Lieut. of Ireland, letter of Swift on behalf of Dr. Sheridan to, 179. 180; Swift considers him to be the happiest man he has known but fears that riches may corrupt him, 239; Swift enquires of Pulteney if he will engage for the probity, but hears reports to the disadvantage, of, 263.

Carteret, Lady, plays a trick upon Swift, 113.

Caryll, John, letters of Pope (printed as addressed to Addison) in fact written to, 289, note; of a Papist family, nephew of the Secretary to James the Second's second wife, an early and principal correspondent of Pope, 290; extract from letter from Pope on political partisanship, and on the popularity of Cato, to, 291; letter from Pope (on the reports as to Martha Blount) to, 293; the Rape of the Lock suggested to Pope by, 296; Pope writes indignantly about Addison to, 300; to soften the impression of his Essay on Man upon his Papist friends Pope writes to, 328; dies before Pope, 331; accidental discovery of the manuscript copies of letters from Pope to, 342, 343; the original of many of Pope's manipulated letters to be found in Pope's correspondence with, only six of Pope's letters (in the published editions) assigned to, 3.4; letters from Pope to, 364.366, 366.

369, 375-377. 403-405, 407-409, 443-444, 481-483.

Caryll, Mrs., extract from letter of, to Martha Blount, 293.

Catholic, true conception of the meaning of a, 437, and *note*.

Cato, a tragedy of Addison, expected, 135; Swift at a rehearsal of, 137; Pope writes the *Prologue* for, and publishes in the *Guardian*, 284; verses quoted from, Dennis's criticisms upon, Johnson's defence of the alleged violation of "poetic justice" in, 288 and *note*; allusions by Pope to (*Epistle to Arbuthnot*), 288; 291; 365; 366.

Catullus, *Ode to Lesbia*, quoted, 315, *note*.

Causeries de Lundi, of Sainte-Beuve, an eulogy of Pope's *Essay on Criticism* quoted from, 283.

Causes of the Wretched Condition of Ireland, a *Sermon* of Swift on, 65.

Cellbridge, a village on the Liffey, the retreat of Hester Vanhomrigh, 36.

Censor, The, Theobald's, quoted by C. W. Dilke, 432, *note*.

Challenge, The, a Court-ballad by Pope, quoted, 306.

Chandos, Duke of, Lord-Lieut. of Ireland, Swift's complaint to Mrs. Pendarves against, 240; Swift's epigram upon quoted by Scott, 249, *note*.

Chapman, George, the dramatist, his translation of the *Iliad* used by Pope, 290; followed in his deviations from the Greek by Pope, claims to have restored the genuine sense of the Homeric epics, author of seventeen dramas, 354, and *note*.

Character of Mrs. Johnson, Swift's sketch of Esther Johnson, her beauty and manners, eulogised in, 9 10; Swift narrates the circumstances of the removal of Esther Johnson and Mrs. Dingley to Ireland in, 13; records his reception of the news of the death of Esther Johnson in, 52.

Charactères de Bruyère, noticed by Pope in a letter to Judith Cowper as the work of a master-hand. an imitation of the work of Theophrastus, 456, and *note*.

Characters of Men, a *Moral Essay* of Pope, noticed, 322.

Characters of Women, quoted, Johnson's eulogy of both *Essays*, especially of the latter, 322.

Charles XII., King of Sweden, the Swedish envoy informs Swift of his fears for the safety of, the great forbearance of the Turks towards, 135, and *note*.

Chatham, Lord, his report of a visit to Lord Bolingbroke, referred to by Scott, 219, *note*.

Chesterfield, Lord, quoted by Pulteney, 261, *note*; visits with Pope the Duchess of Marlborough and Stowe, 333; his remark on Pope's theology, 335, *note*; his character of Pope, 345, *note*; in company with Swift, Arbuthnot, and Pulteney, 467, *note*; Pope's praise of the discernment and judgment of, 505.

Cheyne, Dr. George, his *Essay of Health and a Long Life*, according to Pope, in great favour, at its first appearance, with women, his *Essay* goes through many editions, high praise given by Haller to, his *Essay on Regimen, Natural Method of Curing the Diseases of the Body and the Disorders of the Mind Depending on the Body*, the leading Medical Reformer of the earlier half of the last century, noticed by Horace Walpole, 452, and *note*; Pope reports to Martha Blount an interview with, 503, *note*.

China, Swift reports his mania for as cured, 103.

Chiswick, Pope removes from Binfield to, writes his *Eloisa* and *Elegy* at, 301, 302.

Chloe, Pope's character of Mrs. Howard (Lady Suffolk) in his *Characters of Women*, under that name, quoted, 322.

Christ, attempted picture of crucifixion of, by Pope, 370.

Christiani Morientis Ad Animam, an imitation by Pope of an epigram of the Emperor Hadrian, 369.

Christianity, An Argument Against Abolition of, an ironical piece by Swift, taken seriously by most of its readers, 19.

Christina, Queen of Sweden, Martha Blount compared by Pope with, 396.

Christian Religion, likely to be abolished by the Legislature, according to Pope, 433.

Church, the best reason with some people for going to, 433.

Churches, The, compared by Pope to Banks, 412.

Cibber, Colley, Poet-Laureate, Lady B. Germaine's opinion of, 57; origin of Pope's quarrel with, his place in the *Dunciad*, 308; substituted for Louis Theobald, as the occupant of the throne of Dulness, Carruthers on his *Apology for his Life*, 320, and *note*; Pope learns that he intends to publish an "abusive pamphlet," his *Nonjuror* obtains for him the Laureateship, author of twenty-five Plays, publishes two *Expostulatory Letters* in his defence, 509, and *note*.

Cicero, on Agriculture, quoted by Pope, 477.

INDEX. 521

Cirencester, Pope's visits to, 333, 439, 449.
City Shower, The, a satirical poem by Swift, published in the *Tatler*, Swift inquires from Esther Johnson the opinion in Ireland of, reports to her its popularity in London, noticed by Steele in the *Tatler*, 98, 99, and *note*; Swift remarks his ridicule of the *Alexandrine* verse in, quotation by Scott from, 244, 245, *note*.
Clarissa, poetic name of Lady Masham in the *Rape of the Lock*, 298.
Clarke, Dr. George, Judge-Advocate under George I., entertains Pope at Oxford, Pope's remark on ecclesiastical controversy to, 391; often met by Pope at Oxford, purchases copies of the *Cartoons* of Raffaelle from Jervas, sends Jervas to Paris and Italy, 420, and *note*.
Clifton, village of, near Bristol, Pope visits the Hot Wells of, 332; described by Pope 500-502.
Clogher, Bishop of, Dr. Ashe, a friend of Swift, officiates at the (alleged) marriage of Swift, 37, and *note*; mentioned in letters of Swift, 90, 93, 137.
Cobham, Lord, Pope's visits to, at Stowe, 478, 496, 497.
College Green Club, the Irish Parliament so termed by Swift, 256.
Collins, Anthony, his *Discourse of Free-Thinking* assailed by Swift in a pamphlet, 19.
Comte de Gabalis, a witty romance by the Abbé de Villars, one of the models of the *Rape of the Lock*, notice by Warton of, 297, and *note*; alluded to by Pope, in a letter to Arabella Fermor, 382.
Comus, of Milton, quoted, 448, *note*.
Conduct of the Allies, a pamphlet of Swift, referred to, 129, *note*.
Congreve, William, at Kilkenny School with Swift, 2; visit of Swift to, almost blind and never free from gout; bad *dietetics* of, his comedies, monument in Westminster Abbey put up by the Duchess of Marlborough, to allusion by Gay to, 178, *note*; 103 and *note*; his letters to Lady M. W. Montagu in Turkey sent with Pope's, 424.
Convocation (of Clergy) in Ireland, Swift complains of the ingratitude of, 123.
Cooper, J. G., letters of Pope to the Misses Blount republished by, (in 1737), 429, *note*.
Cooper's Hill, a poem by Denham, the model of Pope's *Windsor Forest*, 284.
Cope, Robert, letter of Swift to, 173-175.
Corisca, a heroine of the *Pastor Fido*, 352.
Coronations, compared by Pope to Puppet Shows and Harlequinades, 475.

Coryate, John, travels of, alluded to by Pope (in letter to Lord Bathurst), publishes an account of his eccentric travels, under the title of *Coryate's Crudities*, Fuller's remark about his appearance, 472, and *note*.
Court News, The, and Newspapers, full of feastings given to the Royal Family, &c., 477.
Court of Death, The, a Fable of Gay, Gout assigned a prominent place at, 404, *note*.
Cowper, Judith, Pope's freedom of style in correspondence with, 292; celebrated by Pope as Erinna, her identity unknown until the investigations of C. W. Dilke, niece of Lord Chancellor Cowper and aunt of the poet, beginning of correspondence of Pope with, eulogises Pope in some verses, verses *To a Lady on her Birthday* sent by Pope to, extract from a letter from Pope to, marries Mr. Madan, 312; letters from Pope to, 453-454, 454-456 457-459.
Coxe's *Memoirs*, referred to by Bowles, introduction of Bolingbroke to George II. stated in, 493, *note*.
Craftsman, The, Bolingbroke's letters to, under the title of *Remarks on the History of England*, 323.
Craggs, The Hon. James, Secretary of State, letter from Pope to (in reference to Mrs. Weston), one of Pope's principal friends, fills several confidential public employments, epitaph of Pope in Westminster Abbey upon, extract from letter to Pope from, 362-363, and *note*; Addison's Works dedicated to, 447, *note*.
Craik, Henry a, biographer of Swift, remarks on Swift's university examination, 4; on the *Tale of a Tub*, 13; on Swift and Hester Vanhomrigh, 29; his remarks on a portrait of Swift by Jervas, 32, *note*; a summary of the conflicting evidence for and against Swift's marriage drawn up by, holds the reality of the marriage, 37; Swift's *Journal* at Holyhead first printed by, 49; his remarks on and paraphrase of Swift's *Modest Proposal*, 54, 55; an interesting letter of Swift's to Arbuthnot first published by, 67.
Crinoline, remarks of Swift on, 31, and *note*.
Criticism, An Essay on, Pope's, compared with the earliest productions of other poets, admiration (sometimes extravagant) of its critics, its models, its principles, quotations from, 281-282; attacked by John Dennis, praised by Addison, hyperbolical praises of later eulogists, Johnson's eulogy of, quoted, Sainte-Beuve's remarks on,

quoted, 282-283; Pope's intention to republish a small number of copies of, 509.

Croker, The Rt. Hon. Wilson, quotes the *Suffolk Correspondence* on the duties of Mrs. Masham, Bed-chamber woman to Queen Anne, *Memoirs of the Reign of George II.* (by Lord Hervey) edited by, 228, *note*; an adverse critic of Pope, 337; *critique* by Macaulay (in the *Edinburgh Review*) on, proposes a new edition of Pope but does not live to complete it, 340.

Cromwell, Henry, a correspondent of Pope, notice of, his correspondence with Pope chiefly noticeable as having been the first published of the Pope Letters, 295, 296; letter from Pope to, 359-360.

Crousaz, Jean Pierre de, a Swiss theologian, his assault upon the *Essay of Man*, Pope's remark on, in a letter to Warburton, 325, 326; denounces not the Optimist fallacies but the *deism* of that *Essay*, 327.

Curll, Edmund, the bookseller and publisher, alluded to by Swift in a letter to Pope, Swift has long had a design upon the ears of, Swift's incredulity as to the poisoning of, publishes a volume of *Town-Eclogues*, Scott's remark upon the story of his poisoning, 161, and *note*; Swift (in a letter to Lady Betty Germaine), expresses his indignation at the indulgence of the House of Lords to (but is at a loss to understand how he could get access to Pope's letters), Lady Betty Germaine's reference to, his boast of the superior number of his friends, his lines upon Pope, Scott's remark on Pope's trick upon, 247, and *note*; origin of Pope's quarrel with, his interview with Pope, vehemently vituperated by Pope in various pamphlets, especially in *A Full and True Account, &c.*, and *A Strange but True Relation, &c.*, his character and appearance, his conspicuous place in the *Dunciad*, 307, and *note*.

D

Dacier, Mde., her translation of the *Iliad* used by Pope, 299, 385.

Daily Post, The, the first edition of the *Dunciad* advertised in, 318, *note*.

Daniel, Richard, Dean of Armagh, Swift's estimate of, as a poet, 213; appears as a witness in a law-suit, referred to by Scott 213, and *note*.

Davila, Enrico Catterino, his *Storia di Francia*, read by Swift and Hester Vanhomrigh, referred to by the latter in letter to Swift 145, and *note*.

Day of Judgment, The, a satirical set of verses by Swift, preserved by Lord Chesterfield, quoted, 61-62, *note*.

Dean and Chapter of St. Patrick's, The, their revenues stated by Swift, in letter to Gay, 222.

Dawley, a residence of Lord Bolingbroke, near Uxbridge, Swift's visit to, in 1726, 43; sold by Bolingbroke, 270; 323, 493.

Debate on Black and White Horses, A, a parody by Pope, in *Miscellanies*, 314.

Defence of Lord Carteret, a pamphlet by Swift, 231.

De Foe, Daniel, on the *Tale of a Tub*, 14; *A Short and Easy Method with Dissenters*, an ironical pamphlet by, referred to, 19.

Delany, Dr., a friend of Swift, 58; his dinners, 235; his house at Delville, 243, Swift remarks upon the expense of visiting him from Dublin, 251.

Delia, a Shepherdess in Pope's *Pastorals*, 279.

Dennis, John, on the Italian Opera, 23; provoked by Pope's satire in the *Essay on Criticism*, author of a tragedy on the story of Virginia and Appius Claudius, retaliates on Pope in a vituperative pamphlet, 282; criticises Addison's *Cato*, assailed by Pope with a vituperative satire, 288; criticises Belinda's action in the *Rape of the Lock*, 298; satirised by Pope as "Sir Tremendous," in *Three Hours after Marriage*, 308; Pope expresses pity for, in letter to Hill, 485.

Desfontaines, Abbé, translates and adapts the *Travels of Gulliver*, reports to Swift the popularity of the book in France, and invites him to Paris, Swift's ironical reply to, misstates certain facts in the *Drapier Letters*, Scott's remark on the translation of, writes a continuation of the *Voyages*, in his Preface apologises for the indecorum of expression in the original, and assures his readers that he has accommodated the incidents to French taste, afterwards editor of the *Journal des Sçavans* and the assailant of Voltaire, 44, 45, and *note*.

Devil, The, his *circuit* compared by Pope with that of the lawyers, 394.

Dialogues des Morts, Les, of Fontenelle, referred to by Hester Vanhomrigh in letter to Swift, her delight in reading, 147, *note*.

Digby, The Hon. Robert, letter from Pope to, quoted, 311; notice of, 422; letter to Pope from, quoted, 440, *note*; letters from Pope to, 422-424, 437-438, 439-440, 449-451.

Dilke, C. W., first to identify the "Unfortunate Lady" of Pope's *Elegy* with Mrs. Weston, 302; minutely investigates the chronology, and examines the genuineness, of Pope's Correspondence, leaves copious and minute manuscript notes, 341; his accidental discovery of the original source of Pope's manufactured letters, 342, 343; MS. note on Richard Nash in Roscoe's edition of Pope, 1847 (in British Museum), 402, *note*; MS. note on a letter of Pope to Martha Blount, 409, *note*; MS. note on a letter of Pope to Lady M. W. Montagu, 413, *note*; remark of, on letter of the same to same, 416, *note*; quotes from letter of Mr. Wortley, 425, *note*; remarks on Lady Masham, 426, *note*; on a letter of Pope to the Misses Blount, 429, *note* ; on a passage in the same letter, 431, *note* ; on letter from Pope to the Duchess of Hamilton, quotes Theobald's *Censor*, 432, *notes*; MS. note on Pope's alleged danger under the Government Proclamation against the Pretender, 511, *note*.

Dilworth, publishes a Life of Pope in 1759, 336, *note*.

Dingley, Mrs. Rebecca, a relative of the Temples, resident at Moor Park, figures frequently in Swift's Correspondence, 5; Swift prevails on her and Esther Johnson to join him in Ireland, 12; in Dublin society, 18; resides with "Stella" at Trim, 34; a witness against the (alleged) marriage of Swift, 37, *note*; Swift gives Dr. Tisdall message to, 76; Swift on the blunders of, 79; references of Swift, in his letters to Esther Johnson, to, 88, 99, 103, 111, 116; letter to Swift from, referred to, 205; Swift writes to John Temple on behalf of, "sunk with age and unwieldness," 257. 258.

Directions to Servants, an ironical piece by Swift, referred to by him in a letter to Gay, 60.

Discourse of the Dissensions between the Nobles and Commons in Athens and Rome, a political brochure by Swift, 12.

Discourse of Free Thinking, A, by Anthony Collins, a pamphlet of Swift upon, 19.

Discourse to Prove the Antiquity of the English Tongue, a satire by Swift, 58, and *note*.

Discovery of Joseph to his Brethren, a picture by one of the Italian Masters, an engraving from, promised to Pope, 489.

Disraeli, Isaac, takes part in the Pope controversy raised by Bowles, 340.

Distich Dick, a satire upon himself by Pope in the *Guardian*, 347.

Diversion, the predecessor of *Amusement*, 170, *note*.

Divine Legation of Moses, The, by Wm. Warburton, the first volumes of, published before his vindication of the *Essay on Man*, 325.

Don Juan, Pope (in his letters to the Misses Blount) characterised by Carruthers as a, 292; Byron's referred to by Professor A. W. Ward, 304, *note*.

Donellan, Mrs., a friend of Swift and Mrs. Pendarves, alluded to, 242.

Donne, Dr. John, Dean of St. Paul's, his *Satires* imitated by Pope, 330.

Dorinda, and Dress, epigram of Swift on, addressed to Hester Vanhomrigh, 164.

Dorset, Duke of, Lord Lieut. of Ireland, Swift's complaint against, in letter to Lady B. Germaine, 249; and to Pulteney, 262.

Double-Dealer, The, a comedy of Congreve, 103, *note*.

Dragon, The, the familiar name of Harley (Lord Oxford) in the *Scriblerus* Club, an allusion to by Swift in letter to Dr. Arbuthnot, 149, 150.

Drapier, The, a pseudonym of Swift, addressed by Lady B. Germaine, as the, 58; apostrophised under that name by Pope, in the *Dunciad*, 319.

Drapier Letters, The, of Swift, addressed to the people of Ireland, 41, 42.

Drawing-room, at Windsor, account of a, by Swift, 120.

Dryden, John, a relative of Swift, 2; abounds in *triplets*, imitated by all the bad versifiers of Charles II. reign, though his near relative blamed as well as pitied by Swift, finishes his *Plays* in great haste under pressure of poverty, brought in the *Alexandrine* verse, 244; the chief favourite and study of Pope, his estimate of Walsh, 277; his authority quoted by Pope, 354; condemns the use of *hiatus* in poetry, but seldom observes his own rule, 358 ; as a poet cannot be "saved under some hundreds of masses," 273; lines upon his turning to translation quoted by Pope, 408; his *Gorboduc* compared by Pope with his own, 423.

Dublin, the birth-place of Swift, Esther Johnson and Mrs. Dingley dislike, 12; Swift resides alternately at Laracor and at, 18; returns to, on taking possession of his Deanery, his annoyances at, 34; Hester Vanhomrigh follows him to, 36; Swift's friends in, 58, 59; buried in St. Patrick's Cathedral in, 65; his dislike for, 147, how it looks to Hester Vanhomrigh, 157; in what superior to London, 235; printers and publishers of, 245, 246, and *note*.

Dublin, University of, Swift an undergraduate at, 2-4, and *note*; never quite forgets

his humiliations at, 7; the Prince of Wales proposed by Swift to be Chancellor of, 205.
Duchess, invitation to Pope by a, 304, *note.*
Du Guernier, the *Rape of the Lock* illustrated by engravings after, 299.
Dulness, The Progress of, original title of the *Dunciad,* 318.
Dust-Plague, The, Arbuthnot's verses on, sent by him to Swift, 386, *note.*

E

Eclogues, of Virgil, one of the models of Pope's *Pastorals,* 278, 279.
Edinburgh Review, The, article on Wilson Croker's ed. of Boswell's *Life of Johnson* in, referred to, 340.
Elegy to the Memory of an Unfortunate Lady, by Pope, quoted, 302, *note.*
Eloisa to Abelard, a poem of Pope, quoted, 302-303; enthusiastic eulogy by the critics of, the materials and models used by Pope for, their alleged Latin letters assumed to be authentic by many French critics, Mde. Guizot's remarks upon them, Elwin's criticism of them, Professor Ward's observations upon Hallam's charge against Pope in reference to representation of Eloisa, 303-4, and *note.*
Elwin, Rev. Whitwell, editor of Pope, Wakefield's suggestion for the reading of a verse in the *Rape of the Lock,* Pope's reply to a criticism of Dennis on the conduct of Belinda quoted by, 298, 299, *notes*; criticises the Latin letters of Heloisa and Abelard, 303, *note*; his Introduction to *Works of Pope* referred to, 318, *note*; Warburton on Optimism, Louis Racine's verses on the *Tout Est Bien* philosophy quoted by, 328, *notes*; letter of Pope to Caryll on *Essay on Man,* quoted by, 329, *note*; an adverse critic of Pope, accounts for Voltaire's admiration of the *Essay,* and quotes his opinion of it, 337, and *note*; his character of Warburton, 338; characterises Warton's edition of Pope, and that of Bowles, 339; materials for an edition of Pope (collected by Wilson Croker) used by, his edition the most comprehensive of all the editions of Pope, his estimate of the *Rape of the Lock* and the *Eloisa,* 340; indicates some literary and philosophical faults too lightly passed over by former critics, but makes too little allowance for the age and education of Pope, 341; Gay's verses upon Hills, the bookseller and printer, quoted by, 357, *note*; relates the money-investments of the elder Pope, 377, *note*; remarks on the omission of names of Pope's papist friends in favour of Congreve and Craggs, 379, *note*; on a letter of Pope and Parnell to Gay, 380, *note*; notice of Parnell by, letter of Swift to Miss Vanhomrigh quoted by, 386, 387; notices of Thomas Hanmer, John Barber, the Bill of Schism, and Proclamation against the Pretender, 388, 389, *notes*; refers to Philips's charge against Pope, as recorded by the latter, 390, *note*; quotation of Pope's reported reply to Clarke on sectarian controversy by, 391, *note*; remarks on the laws against the papists, the Siege of Barcelona, and Pope's curiosity, 292, 293, *notes*; letter of Arbuthnot to Swift, and Gay's *Epistle to a Lady,* quoted by, 401, 402, *notes*; Burnet's *Homerides,* Lord Landsdowne's imprisonment in the Tower, and Rich's theatre in Lincoln's Inn Fields noticed by, 404, 405, *notes*; Johnson's remarks on the character of Dr. Parnell, frogs unknown in Ireland till the XVIII. century, the *Grumbler* newspaper, Bishop of Salisbury's death, noticed by, 406, 407, *notes*; remarks on Jervas's copies of Raffaelle's *Cartoons,* 420, *note*; letter from Pope to Lord Oxford, Pope's strange assertion as to dedication of his works, noticed by, 444, 445, *notes*; remarks upon Pope's flattery of Lord Oxford, quotes Spence and Lewis on the character of Lord Oxford, 445, 449, *note*; Young's remark on the *Henriade* of Voltaire quoted by, 462, *note*; (supposed) correspondence of Pope with Voltaire noticed by, 464, *note*; the marriages of the daughters of Edward Blount related by, 467, *note*; remark on the Pope-Swift volume of *Miscellanies* by, 469, *note*; on the *Marco-Aurelio* of Guevara, a Spanish bishop, 474, *note*; on Pope's propensity to disparagement of alterations not suggested by himself, 472, *note*; George Fox on steeplehouses, Walpole's toleration of Noncomformists, noticed by, 473, *note*; Lord Bathurst's reason for abstention from the House of Lords, quoted by, 474, *note*; on Pope's disclaimer of the *Essay on Man,* and his studied ambiguity in regard to belief in future existence (in the *Essay),* 482, *notes*; on the non-Christian inspiration of certain verses of the *Essay,* 483, *note.*
Employments, in Ireland, exclusively in English hands, 235.
Encyclopædia Britannica, article on Swift in, referred to, 39.

England, Church of, alluded to, 372, 418.
Englefield, the papist family of, Pope's earlier acquaintance with, Mr. Englefield's incivility to Pope's family, noticed by Pope, 367.
English Bards and Scotch Reviewers, superior to the *Essay on Criticism* in brilliancy and wit, 281.
English Language, The, Swift on the corruptions of, 95, note; proposes the reform of, 128; Pope, in a letter to Bolingbroke, on, 461-462.
Enthusiasm, Letter on, by the Earl of Shaftesbury, attributed to Swift by his correspondent Col. Hunter, Swift deprecates the reputation of its authorship (in letter to Hunter whom he suspects to be the author), complains of the imputation in his *Apology* for the *Tale of a Tub*, 88, and note; Pope to Bolingbroke on, 461, 462.
Epistle of Mary Gulliver, a parody, by Pope, quoted, 316.
Epistle to Arbuthnot, by Pope, referred to, 275; satire of Addison in, quoted, 289: satire of Lord Hervey in, 332; Pope determines to finish, 509.
Epistle to a Doctor of Divinity, by Lord Hervey, a satire on Pope, 331.
Epistle to a Lady, by Gay, addressed to the Princess of Wales, quoted, 401.
Epistle to the Pisos, of Horace, compared with the *Essay on Criticism* by Sainte-Beuve, 283.
Epistles, moral or satirical poems, addressed to various eminent personages, noticed and quoted, 321, 322, 330.
Epistles of the Heroines, of Ovid, Pope's *Sappho to Phaon*, imitated from, 284; a model of the *Eloisa to Abelard*, 304.
Epitaph, on Gay, by Pope, in Westminster Abbey, criticised by Swift in letter to Lord Orrery, 233.
Epitaphs, on his friends, by Pope, one on himself, placed by Warburton in the Twickenham church, quoted, 331; on Mrs. Whitworth, on the public way, at Twickenham, referred to by Pope and by Theobald, 432, and note.
Erasmus, Desiderio, commemorated in *Essay on Criticism*, 282; Im. of Hor. Sat. II., 1., 482, note.
Erick or Herrick, Abigail, the wife of Godwin and the mother of Jonathan Swift, 2.
Erinna, Judith Cowper celebrated by Pope under that name, 312, 454.
Essay Concerning Aliments, by Dr. Arbuthnot, referred to, 177, note.
Essay on Criticism, noticed and quoted, 281.
Essay on Flesh Eating, by Plutarch, quoted by Pope in the *Guardian*, the most remarkable moral treatise of Antiquity, 286, note.
Essay on Gardening, by Pope, in the *Guardian*, 310, 311; by Horace Walpole, referred to, 309, note.
Essay on Man, The, by Pope, inspired by Lord Bolingbroke, identity of thought in the writings of the latter with that of, external as well as internal evidence of Bolingbroke's influence on, first appeared anonymously, the authorship for some time concealed even from the author's friends, the Fourth Book published two years later, gradual increase of popularity, alterations of opening verses made by Pope quoted, translated into French, assailed by De Crousaz, defended by Warburton, 324-326; Optimism the leading principle of, the various sources of, the fundamental principle of logically leads to Fatalism, the deism, not the Optimism of, objected to by De Crousaz, and unsuccessfully denied by Warburton, Warburton's original opinion of, Pope sends to Louis Racine an apology for, also to Caryll, the merits of particular parts of, (excepting Shakspeare and Milton) no poem so often quoted, its *ethics* deserving of high praise, in particular its rebuke of human arrogance, its cosmopolitan precepts quoted, the last edition in Pope's life-time, in 1743, with Warburton's Commentary and Notes, and Dedication to Bolingbroke, instance of alteration and doubtful improvement in, quoted, 327. 330.
Essay on Propriety in the Thought and Expression of Poetry, by Aaron Hill, noticed by Roscoe, 491, note.
Eugenia, a Defence of Women, by Wm. Walsh, noticed by Johnson, in his *Lives of the Poets*, 353, note.
Eugenio, a poem, by Thomas Beach, referred to, 244, note.
Eustathius, Archbishop of Thessalonica, the most considerable Commentator on the Homeric Epics, used and referred to by Pope, 385.
Evans, Dr. Abel, an Epigrammatist and friend of Pope, mentioned by Pope, and noticed by Bowles, 422, and note.
Examiner, The, a political periodical, Swift's first overt act of apostasy from Whiggism appears in, under his management asserts its superiority (in ability) over its political rivals, the Duke of Marlborough held up to ridicule and detestation by Swift

in, 26, 27; the Tory rival of Steele's *Guardian*, 116, *note*; reported by Swift to be "deadly sick," 129; Swift denies to Addison that he is the editor of, 142, declares to Steele that he seldom reads, Steele writes to Swift that he believes him to be an "accomplice" of, the latter asseverates that he had had no hand in writing any of the papers of, 143.

F

Fable of the Bees, The, of Bernard de Mandeville, the *Essay on Man* indebted to, 327.
Fables, The, of Gay, Swift's encomium on, written for the young Duke of Cumberland, 227; a Second Series of (left by Gay), Swift prophesies no good of, 234.
Faith, Modes of, 291, 436.
Familiar Epistle to the Most impudent Man Living, addressed by Lord Bolingbroke to Dr. Warburton, 336.
Fan, The, a satirical piece, by Gay, alluded to by Swift in letter to Mrs. Pendarves, 239; Pope's allusion to, in letter to Gay, its use in China, 370.
Farewell to London, verses by Pope, quoted, 301, *note*.
Faulkener, Alderman, a Dublin publisher, a friend of Swift, 59; Swift complains of his *Works* hav ng been printed without his consent by, 246, *note*.
Favourites, ladies at Court, as, usual fate of, 229.
Fenton, Mrs., only sister of Swift, her unsuitable marriage opposed by him, left dependent upon him, lives with Lady Giffard at Moor Park, 11; mentioned by Swift in letter to Esther Johnson, dies at Farnham in the house of Esther Johnson's mother (1739), her brother's reported harshness to, 132, and *note*.
Fermor, Arabella, her quarrel with her lover Lord Petre, the heroine of the *Rape of the Lock* under the name of Belinda, resents her first presentment in the original edition of the poem, Pope appeases her anger by an improved edition, 296, 297; marries Mr. Perkins, her portrait at Tusmore, Mrs. Piozzi's report of an interview with the niece of, 298; letters from Pope to, 381-383, 383-384.
Fit of the Spleen, an imitation of Shakspeare, by Judith Cowper, published afterwards in the *London Magazine* (1737), praised by Pope, 455.
Flams, term applied by Swift to the verses written by Ambrose Philips on Miss Carteret, 187, and *note*.

Flamnap (Sir R. Walpole), a character in the *Travels* of Gulliver, introduced by Pope in the *Epistle of Mary Gulliver*, 316.
Flying Island, The, in the voyage to Laputa, alluded to by Swift in letter to Pope, 197; its illustration suggested to Motte, the publisher, by Swift, 208.
Flying Post, The, a newspaper, referred to by Arbuthnot in letter to Pope, 393.
Floyd, Mrs., mentioned in a letter of Swift, the subject of some lively verses of his, 87, and *note*.
Fontainebleau, Bolingbroke's life at, described by Pope to Swift, 493.
Fontenelle, Bernard de, Hester Vanhomrigh delighted with the *Dialogues des Morts* of, 147.
Ford, Charles, a friend and publishing agent of Swift in Dublin, editor of a Government newspaper, 59; conveys the MS. of *Gulliver's Travels*, with mysterious secrecy, to Motte, the publisher, 67.
Forester, Miss, a Maid of Honour to Queen Anne, accompanies Swift and Arbuthnot in a riding-party, character by Swift of, married at the age of thirteen to Sir John Downing, divorced at the age of fifteen, 120, 121.
Forster, John, the most elaborate biographer of Swift, prints a *fac-simile* of the registry of the results of Swift's examination at the Dublin University, letter to Worral from Swift (on Swift's love-affair with Betty Jones) quoted by, 4, and *note*; letter from Sir W. Temple to Southwell quoted by, Macaulay's representation of Swift's and Esther Johnson's position at Moor Park criticised by, letter from Swift to John Temple quoted by, 6, 7, and *notes*; early letter from Swift to Mrs. Johnson quoted by, refutes charge against Swift of harshness to his sister, 11, and *note*; notice of the *Tale of a Tub* by, 14; MS. copy of the *Baucis and Philemon* found at Narford, and account of the poem, by, 16, 17; remarks on differences between the original and printed poem, 18, *note*; an unprinted letter of Swift to Philip's quoted by, 23; *fac-simile* of Swift's *Note-books*, letter of Lord Halifax to Swift, given by, 24, and *notes*; conjectures the origin of Swift's name of "Stella" for Esther Johnson, the original spelling of the *Journal to Stella* first restored by, 25, *notes*; MS. of Swift's *Diary at Holyhead*, formerly in possession of, 50, *note*; opportunity of inspecting a large number of unpublished letters of Swift afforded to, the large interleaved paper

INDEX. 527

copy of *Gulliver*, in manuscript, noticed by, 67, 68.

Fortescue, Wm., a friend of Pope, 371, and *note*; a judge, and Master of the Rolls, life-long friendship between Pope and, Pope addresses First *Satire* of Second Book of Horace to, a remark of Bowles on the Pope-letters to (first part of them first published in Polwhele's *History of Devon*, second part by Miss Warner), 394, *note*; letters from Pope to, 394-395, 465, 466-467; Pope, in letter to Martha Blount, refers to, 501.

Fountaine, Sir Andrew, Forster discovers MS. of Swift's *Baucis and Philemon* at the house of (at Narford), 16; mentioned by Swift, 111.

Fox, George, the founder of the Society of Friends, gives the name of "Steeple-Houses" to churches, the steeple-houses and pulpits why offensive to, his *Journal* quoted by Elwin, 473.

Fragments and Essays, by Lord Bolingbroke, their ideas correspond with Pope's *Essay on Man*, 327.

France, flight of the heads of the Tory and Jacobite factions to, 35; reception of *Gulliver's Travels* in, 43; Col. Hunter, a correspondent of Swift, a prisoner in, 85; intended visits of Swift to, 207, 226; Bolingbroke's exile in, 323; Pope's report of Bolingbroke's life in, 493.

French, *Gulliver's Travels* translated into, 43; letters in, from Swift to the Abbé Desfontaines, 44, from Swift to Hester Vanhomrigh, 168-170; Swift's difficulty in conversing in, 213; *Essay on Criticism*, *Essay on Man*, and *Rape of the Lock* translated into, 283, 297, 325.

Frederick, Prince of Wales, gives to Pope some marble heads of poets for his Library, and urns for his Grotto, 495.

Frogs and Mice, Battle of the, translated by Dr. Parnell from the Greek, 406, *note*; eulogised by Pope, 428.

Frogs, when first imported into Ireland, 406, *note*.

Froude, Philip, a friend of Swift and Addison, a Government official, author of two tragedies, referred to by Swift, 86, and *note*.

Fuller, Dr. Thomas, on John Coryate, the Odcombe traveller, 472, *note*.

G

Gabrielle, d'Estrées ("la belle Gabrielle"), the heroine of the *Henriade*, alluded to by Pope, 463.

Gage, Miss, daughter of Mr. Gage, owner of Sherbourne Castle, marries Mr. Weston of Sutton, separates from and afterwards (by Pope's mediation) reconciled to her husband, dies in 1725, the heroine of the *Elegy* of Pope, 302, and *note*.

Gage, Mr., Pope meets at Bath, 402.

Galland, Antoine, translator of the *Arabian Tales*, noticed, 441, *note*.

Gardening, *Essay on*, by Horace Walpole, referred to, 309, *note*.

Gardening, absurdly artificial styles of, ridiculed by Pope, in the *Guardian*, 310, 311.

Garth, Sir Samuel, M.D. (author of the *Dispensary*, a satire), figures in the journal-letters of Swift, 29; his *bon-mot* on *Cato*, 366; on Dr. Radcliffe, 431, and *note*.

Gay, John, a member of the *October* Club, letter to Swift on *Gulliver's Travels* from 45, 46; Swift's correspondence with the Duchess of Queensberry and, extracts from letters of Swift to, 55, 56; letter from Swift to, quoted, 60; *Eclogues* of dedicated to Bolingbroke, 177; extracts from letter to Swift from (on Congreve, Pope, the South Sea Bubble, Opera, &c.), 178, 179, *note*; letters from Swift to, 176-173, 219-223; his *Opera* bought by Swift for sixpence, 201; his second Opera (*Polly*) prohibited by the Lord Chancellor, complains of persecution in the cause of virtue, 212, and *note*; his congratulatory verses to Pope on the completion of the *Iliad* quoted, 300; a poem on *Wine* attributed to, verses upon Hills, the publisher, by, 357, *note*; writes *Pastorals* during time of "divine service," and spends his money on dress, Pope's consequent anxiety as to his redemption from Purgatory, 374; letters from Pope to, 369-370, 371; Pope's remembrances to, as the "true genuine shepherd," 386; loses his Secretaryship to the Hanoverian Embassy, and continues his contributions to *Martin Scriblerus*, 397, 398, and *note*; letter of Pope to, 399-401; going to France with Pulteney, 429; Pope sends to Bishop Atterbury two volumes of the Works of, 441; at Bath, with Dr. Arbuthnot, 465; extract from letter to Fortescue from, 466, *note*.

George I., King of England, satirised in *Voyage to Lilliput*, 45; Swift's hopes of preferment raised by the death of, 49; giving audience to his Vice-Chamberlain, 304.

George II., ironical eulogy of, by Pope in his *Imitations* of the *Satires* of Horace, 331.

Gerard, Lady, widow of Sir W. Gerard, of

New Hall, Lancashire, a friend of Martha Blount, 334, *note*, mentioned in letters of Pope, 498, 501, 503.

Germaine, Lady Betty, daughter of Lord Berkeley, meets Swift first at the Castle, Dublin, in later years corresponds with him, 11; extracts from letters to him from, 57; invites him to Drayton, 94; Swift's account of a dinner with, 112; letter from him to, 246-250.

Gery, Mrs., wife of the incumbent of Letcombe, Swift a guest in the house of, Swift's reference to (letter to Miss Vanhomrigh), Molly Gery an old acquaintance of Swift's at Farnham, 387, *note*.

Ghosts, the Island of, in *Gulliver's Travels*, Swift does not know how to illustrate, in a wood-cut, 209.

Gibbon, Edward, his remarks on Pope's *Iliad*, 301, *note*; on the romance-view of the Pastoral Life, 352, *note*; his temporary conversion, at the age of sixteen, to the Papal Church, 435, *note*.

Giffard, Lady, a sister of Sir W. Temple, at the head of the household at Moor Park, Swift's occasional quarrels with, 5; Swift will not see her until she asks his pardon, she quarrels with him about the publication of Temple's *Works*, much at Court, 94, and *note*; in debt to Esther Johnson, 104.

Gifts of Preaching, Dr. Wilkins's, recommended to Swift by Archbishop King, 33,

Gil Blas, and the Archbishop of Granada, allusion to, 364, *note*.

Gilchrist, J., editor of the *Quarterly Review*, one of the combatants in the Pope Controversy, 340.

Glubbdubdrib, the Island of Magicians, visited by Gulliver, alluded to by Pope, 470, and *note*.

Glumdalclitch, the Brobdingnagian Maid of Honour, Lamentation of, a parody by Pope, quoted, 315-316.

uttony, the selfish cruelty of, remarked upon by Pope, 285.

omes and Sylphs, who, explained by Pope in a letter to Miss Fermor, 382.

dolphin, Lord, the Whig Premier, Swift's introduction to, 12; characterised by Swift as the worst dissembler of his Cabinet, 92; Swift regards it as a good jest to hear the Tory Ministers talk of his death with pity, 131.

Golden Age, The, ironically applied to the South Sea Bubble period by Digby, 440, *note*.

Golden Age Restored, The, by William Walch, noticed, 353, *note*.

Goldsmith, Oliver, his description of a "Visitation Dinner" in the *Citizen of the World*, 212, *note*; his *Life of Richard Nash*, quoted, 305, *note*; letter from Pope to Parnell published in *Life of Parnell* by, 334, *note*; his *Life of Nash* quoted by Dilke, 402, *note*.

Gorboduc, by Thos. Sackville, the first regular English tragedy, Pope claims to have derived great credit from his edition of, compares it with that of Dryden and Oldham, and accuses them of ignorance of the sex as well as sense of, 423, and *note*.

Gout, frequent mention in the correspondence of the last century of, prominent place assigned in Gay's *Court of Death* to, 403, 404, *note*.

Grace and *Right Honourable*, Pope's criticism on the prefixes of, 477.

Grand Question Debated, The, a poem by Swift, quoted, 61, *note*.

Granville, Mary, her parentage and correspondence noticed, 237, *note*.

Great Britain, Swift anathematises the term, 271.

Gregg, a Government official, sentenced to death on the charge of traitorous correspondence with the French Government, referred to by Swift, 84, and *note*.

Green Cloth, The, at Windsor, Swift dines at, "the best table in England," costs the Queen £1,000 a month, designed to entertain Foreign Ministers and people of quality, 120; noisy company of people from the Races at, 121.

Grierson, Mrs., a Dublin friend of Swift, dies at the age of twenty-seven, famed for her extraordinary learning, 59, 223, 224.

Griffiths, Miss, a correspondent of Lady M. W. Montagu, 426.

Grildig, the Brobdingnagian name of Gulliver, lamentation of Glumdalclitch over, 315, 316.

Grotto, The, at Twickenham Villa, described, 309, and *note*; in a letter from Pope to Edward Blount, 310, 467-469; opinions of his critics upon, intended verses for an inscription on, 468, 469, and *note*.

Grub Street Journal, The, Pope's assaults upon his enemies in, its reputed editors, 321.

Grub Street, literature of, extinguished by taxation, 128-129, *note*.

Grumbler, The, a weekly periodical, on Gay, referred to, 407.

Guarini, Battista, his *Il Fido Pastor*, its surprising discoveries the effect of design, a great store-house of the English poets of the xvi. and xvii. centuries, 352, and *note*.

Guardian, The, a daily paper, founded by Steele, noticed by Swift, 136; Swift complains to Addison and Steele of being attacked by the latter in, 141-144, and *note*; Pope's rival (Philips) highly eulogised in, Pope inserts ironically eulogistic notice of Philip's *Pastorals* in, quoted, 278-280, and *note*; Pope contributes a number of papers (on various subjects) to, the most meritorious of them his Essay on "Sport," and on the cruelties of Butchering, 284-286; publishes his *Prologue to Addison's Cato* in, 288; inserts a caricature of himself, under the name of "Dick Distich," in, 347; Steele writes to Pope of his design to bring out, and asks him to contribute to, 363, *note*; Pope assures Caryll that he writes very seldom for, 367.

Guclti, G., an Italian sculptor, artist of a statue to Craggs in Westminster Abbey, alluded to by Pope in letters to Mr. and Mrs. Knight, 475, and *note*.

Guevara, Antonio de, a Spanish Bishop, his *Marco Aurelio* alluded to by Pope, 470, and *note*.

Guizot, Mde., her remarks on the Heloisa of the Latin Letters of Heloisa and Abelard, 303, *note*.

Gulliver, The Travels of Lemuel, Dr. Barrett infers Swift's authorship of a College exercise from its resemblance to a passage in, 3; published anonymously in 1726, under the title (in full) of The *Travels into Several Remote Nations of the World by Lemuel Gulliver*, excites extraordinary sensation, printed editions abound in England and Ireland, the first classical work of fiction to appear periodically in a newspaper, goes through many revisions, references in letters (before publication) to, 43; translated in France by the Abbé Desfontaines at the suggestion of Voltaire, its popularity in France, correspondence of the Abbé and Swift respecting, letter from Gay to Swift reporting universal popularity of, 44-46; Swift's ironical complaint to the publisher on account of certain excisions or alterations in, 46, 47; critical remarks upon, Swift publishes maps in, a copy (in the South Kensington Museum) of the first edition of, manuscript revisions of the author, a revised passage quoted, 47; theories as to the purpose of, the author's own declaration of the object of, letter to Motte (the publisher) from the author supplying hints for the illustration of, 48; letter from Swift to Pope upon, 184-185; extracts from letter of Mrs. Howard to Swift respecting, 193, *note*; letter from Swift to Mrs. Howard allusive to, 194-195; extracts from letter of Lord Peterborough to Swift reporting an universal mania regarding, 196, *note*; Swift wishes his friends to give out that his book has been unwarrantably altered by his publisher, 198; allusions (in a letter to Mrs. Howard) to, 198-199; Pope's parodies on, 315-317; refers to them, in a letter to Swift, 470.

Gulliver *Le Nouveau*, a continuation of the *Travels*, by Desfontaines, Scott's notice of, 45, *note*.

H

Habeas Corpus, Writ of, suspended by the Government, during the panic from the expected rising of the Jacobites, 511, *note*.

Halifax, Lord, makes the acquaintance of Swift, 12; his letter to Swift in reply to a request for preferment quoted, Swift's remark upon, 24, and *note*; out of office, 26; figures in the *Journal Letters*, 29; Swift burns all the letters (but one) received from, 248; Pope refers to subscription to the *Iliad* by, 372.

Hallam, Henry, his remark upon the Eloisa of Pope criticised by Prof. A. W. Ward, 303, *note*.

Haller, Albrecht von, the Swiss physiologist, his praise of Dr. Cheyne's *Essay of Health and a Long Life*, 452.

Hamilton, The Duchess of, grief of, at the death of her husband in a duel with Lord Mohun, Swift's description of, 131, *note*; letter from Pope to, 432-434, her portrait alluded to by Pope, compared by him to an elephant, 432, 433.

Hamilton, Anthony, translates (but does not publish) the *Essay on Criticism* into French, 283, *note*.

Handel, Georg Friedrich, alluded to by Gay, 179, *note*.

Hanmer, Thos., Speaker of the House of Commons, his name how treated by Swift, 388.

Harcourt, The Hon. Simon, son of the Lord Chancellor (the first Lord Harcourt), a friend of Pope, referred to in Pope's letters, 380, 391, 404, 410.

Harley, Robert, Earl of Oxford and Mortimer, succeeds Lord Somers in the premiership, 26; complains that he can keep no secret from Swift, 23; a con-

2 L

spicuous figure in the *Journal Letters*, 29 ; one of the first members of the *October*, 33 ; and of the *Scriblerus* Club, 34 ; compromised in the Jacobite intrigues, 35 ; the seals taken from, his skilful intrigues to alter the Ministry, the Duke of Somerset's insult to, related in a letter of Swift's to Archbishop King, 83 ; Swift addresses his *Proposal for Correcting the English Tongue* to, 95, *note* ; references to Swift's interviews with. 97, 93, 99 ; Swift's high credit with, 100; Steele writes a *Tatler* against, 101, and *note* ; raised to the peerage, expects the Treasurer's Staff, 107 ; will not allow Swift to address him as " My Lord," 103 ; Swift's candid remark to, 114, *note* ; goes every Saturday to Windsor, can be seen only at his *levées*, his joke with Swift about the Queen, 119, 120 ; entertains Swift and Mrs. Masham at a dinner, his procrastination in business matters, 123 ; Swift remonstrates (against the law on the Press) with, 126 ; his critical position in the Cabinet, his enemies fully resolved to have his head, 127 ; A Letter (proposing an Academy for reforming the English language) dedicated by Swift to, 128; takes into his counsels Lady Orkney, 131 ; goes to Wimbledon to his daughter, Lady Carmarthen, 137; buys a portrait of the Queen (Anne), 133; long interview with Swift, dines with Swift at the Duke of Ormond's, 139; offers to him a *prebend* at Windsor, and thus " perplexes things," Swift informs him that he will see him no more, unless the expected Deanery be given to him, 140, 141 ; reproaches Swift for Steele's ill-returns for the office conferred upon him, 142 : alluded to by Swift under the name of " the Dragon," in retreat in Herefordshire, Swift writes to, in a style " very odd and serious," 149, 150 ; Swift expresses his affection for, imprisoned in the Tower two years, 153, and *note* ; never Swift's " hero," Scott's comment upon this remark of Swift, 217, and *note* ; Swift's narrative of his attempt to reconcile Bolingbroke with, Swift's expression of extraordinary regard for and high character of, (in letter to the second Lord Oxford), 264.265 ; Swift (in letter to Lewis) asserts that, in his *History*, he has drawn, with partiality, his character of, declares Bolingbroke's hatred of, 267, 268 ; his health drunk by Swift and Pope at Letcombe, 387 ; favours the South Sea Company. 440 ; letter from Pope to, 444.446 ; Pope's character of (as given by Spence), Queen Anne's character of (as given by Erasmus Lewis), 445, 446, *note;* letter to Pope from, 446, *note*.

Hawkesworth, Dr. John, Editor of Swift's *Works*, publishes the twenty-five letters of Swift to Esther Johnson, and deposits them in the British Museum, 67 ; notes to letters of Swift by, 188, 207 ; Editor of the *Adventurer*, denounces the cruelties of " Sport," 237.

Haymarket Theatre, Masquerade in, introduced by Heydegger, or Heidegger, alluded to by Pope, in letter to Lady M. W. Montagu, 426.

Heads of Illustrious Persons, Edited by Thos. Birch, an engraving by Houbraken of a portrait of Pope by Pond, referred to, 343.

Hedge Tavern, A, Swift, Addison, and Garth dine at, explanation of the term, 105, and *note* ; Hedge Chapter, 221.

Helsham, Dr., a Dublin physician, a friend of Swift, lives in the same house with Dr. Delany, 59 ; character by Swift of, " the true happy man," 211 ; referred to, 239, 251.

Henley, Anthony, of the Grange, Hampshire, contributor to the *Tatler*, discarded, among other Whig acquaintances, by Swift, 109, 110, and *note*.

Henriade, The, an epic poem, by Voltaire, Pope's criticism on, in letter to Bolingbroke, 462-434 ; noticed by Aaron Hill, in letter to Pope, 436, *note*.

Hero and Leander, the story of, alluded to by Pope, in letter to Lady M. W. Montagu, the poem of, by Ovid and Musæus, 425, and *note*.

Hervey, Lord, Pope's attacks on, and his *Epistle*, 275, *note* ; 331, 332.

Heroic Epistle to Mrs. Gulliver, sent by Pope to Swift, 470.

Hesiod, his poem, *Works and Days*, quoted. 442.

Heydegger, Johann, a Swiss settled in England, introduces the Masquerade, 426, and *note*.

High Heels, and Low Heels, the two chief religious parties in Lilliput, 75 ; alluded to by Mrs. Howard, in letter to Pope, 193, *note*.

Hill, Aaron, a dramatic writer, and manager of Drury Lane Theatre, &c., figures in the *Dunciad*, 320 ; letter from Pope to, 435-486 ; contributes to Pope's *Grotto*, and sends him his translation of Voltaire's *Zaïre* ; letters to Pope from, expressing his delight with *Zaïre*, and anxious for its success upon the London stage, quoted, 436, *note*.

INDEX. 531

Hills, Henry, a pirate publisher, referred to by Pope, Gay's lines upon, 356, 357, and *note*.

Hippokekoana, Countess of, the Duchess of Monmouth satirised by Pope under the name of, 308.

History of English Poetry, full account of *Gorboduc* in, by Thos. Warton, 423, *note*.

History of the Four Last Years of Queen Anne, by Swift, written at Windsor, the Tory Ministers not agreed upon the propriety of printing, Swift now determines to publish (1737), he has all the requisite materials for, is ready to print, in an Appendix, any matter supplied by the second Lord Oxford, one great design of it, 264-266, 267-268; criticism of the Tory authorities upon, 269, *note*; Pope hints to Swift Bolingbroke's fear that some facts are not exactly stated in, 493, 494.

History of his Own Times, projected by Bolingbroke, Swift's high expectations from, and wish to see, 270; the Introduction to, noticed and eulogised by Pope, 493.

Hoare, William, portrait-painter in *crayons*, notice of a portrait of Pope, in the National Portrait Gallery, by, 348.

Hobbes, Thomas, of Malmesbury, his translation of the *Iliad* used by Pope. 299; his probable influence on the *Essay on Man*, 327; the Cambridge Editors of *Homer* confess their large obligations to, 354.

Hogarth, William, a satirical print upon the "South Sea Bubble" by, 440.

Holyhead, Swift's *Journal* during his detention at, 49, and *note*.

Homer, quoted, 10; imitated by Pope, at the age of twelve, Ogilby's translation used by him, 277; publishes in Tonson's *Miscellany* a translation of an episode in the *Iliad*, 281; canvasses for subscriptions to the *Iliad*, alluded to in a letter to Swift, 287; the preference of Addison for Tickell's version of, 289; Pope publishes (1715) the first four books of the *Iliad*, commentators and assistance used by him upon, his correspondence relating to, pecuniary profits derived from, the *Odyssey* begun in 1723 finished in 1725; his entire profits from the two poems, 299, 300; enthusiastic welcome from his friends of, Addison's attitude in regard to, specimens of Pope's *Iliad* printed by Johnson (with the manuscript variations), Johnson's estimate of, Gibbon's remark upon, Professor Newman's *Iliad* referred to, 300, 301, and *note*; Pope's remarks upon in letter to Bridges, 353-255; thinks it will be better worth his while to raise a subscription for a change of religion than for a translation of, 372; desires Caryll to send him a list of subscribers to, expects to be warmly supported, on all sides, in his translation of, 376; flatters himself that he is secretly favoured by, remarks on the commentators on, 373, 385; " curses them all religiously," and "even blasphemes Homer himself," 335; goes to Oxford to consult books on, his trouble with the maps for, 391, 392; near completion of the *Iliad* of, 397; writes each day fifty verses of, as well as notes, claims Gay's congratulations upon the achievement of, 400; references to, 404, 408, 422, *note*; Pope heartily wishes the death of all the heroes of, 423, 424; thinks that Lady M. W. Montagu, in Turkey, could enlighten many passages in, sends her the third vol. of the *Iliad* of, 426; praises Parnell's translation of the *Batrachomyomachia* of, asks Parnell's assistance on the *Iliad* of, 428; on the immortality of the language of, 461; reports to Fortescue his progress on the *Odyssey* of, 465; comparison of men to grasshoppers by, 487.

Homerides, a Letter to Mr. Pope, occasioned by his intended Translation of Homer, by Sir Iliad Doggrel (Thos. Burnet), Pope's remarks upon, 404, and *note*.

Horace, quotations by Swift from (*Ep.* II., 2), 158; (*Ep.* I., 1), 176; 213, and *note*; Swift considers Pope's *Imitation* of one of his best things, 233; thanks him for his English version of some verses of, 260; surpassed by his imitator Pope, 342, his *Odes* III. 4 quoted by Pope in letters to Bolingbroke, 464; Pope refers to his *Imitation* of one of the *Satires* of, 481; quotations from, 481, 482; Pope quotes *Odes* III., 4, in letter to Warburton, 503.

Hot Wells, The, of Clifton, noticed by Pope, 500, 502.

Houbraken, W., engraver of a portrait of Pope, referred to, 348.

Houghers, and *Houghing*, the barbarous cruelty of, in Ireland, compared by Swift with the English *Mohawks*, 126, and *note*.

Houyhnhnms, The, remark upon the *Voyage* to, all but one of the revisions of Swift of the *Travels* occur in that part of the book, 47; passage quoted from, how pronounced, 47, and *note*; Swift's suggestion to

532   INDEX.

the publisher for illustrations of scenes among, 48 and 209.
Houyhnhnms, Grateful address of the unhappy, now in Slavery and Bondage in England, to Mr. Lemuel Gulliver, by Pope, quoted, 317.
Howard, The Hon. Mrs. (afterwards Lady Suffolk), on friendly terms with Swift, 43; disappoints the hopes of Swift, 49; letter from Swift to, 191-193; notice by Scott of, 193, 194, *note;* Lady of the bedchamber to the Princess of Wales, a *favourite* of the Prince of Wales (George II.); anecdotes in Horace Walpole's *Reminiscences* respecting, 192, *note;* extracts from letter to Swift from, 193, *note;* letters from Swift to, 194-196; 198-199; Swift complains of want of memory of, 215; 225-229; letters to Gay from, quoted, 225, *note;* position at the Court of George II. and Queen Caroline of, Thackeray's character of, 228, *note;* commemorated in Gay's verses to Pope, 300, *note;* a friend of Teresa and Martha Blount, 292; with other Maids of Honour patronizes Pope, 304; Pope's representation (in his *Characters of Women*), of, 322; Pope, in letter to the Misses Blount, alludes to a conversation with, 430; refers, in letters to Miss Cowper, to, 453, 454, 457; requests his correspondent to send on a copy of verses to, 459.
Howard, Edward, author of a poem entitled *The British Princes,* figures in the *Dunciad*, 320.
Howell, James, noticed as the best letter-writer of the first half of the XVII. Century, 66.
Howth Castle, near Dublin, portrait of Swift by Bindon at, 59.
Howth, Lady, a friend of Swift, commemorated by him as "the blue-eyed nymph," 59.
Hudibras, of Samuel Butler, alluded to by Pope, 289.
Hudson, W., the portrait-painter, successor to Jon. Richardson, and the master of Reynolds, referred to, 480, *note.*
Hughes, John, Swift's contemptuous notice of a volume of Poems by, 251; translator of the French version of the *Letters* of Eloisa and Abelard, 303.
Humanity, the remarks of Plutarch (in his *Life of Cato*) on, 286.
Hunter, Col., a correspondent of Swift, extract from letter from Swift to, 23; letter from Swift to, when prisoner in France, 85-88.
Hunting, Pope, in the *Guardian*, on the Cruelties of, 285.

Hyde Park, a Military Camp in, described by Pope, 450.
Hypocrite, The, the alternative title of Cibber's *Non-juror,* referred to, 509.

I

Ianthe, a heroine in the *Metamorphoses* of Ovid, referred to, 304.
Idylls of Theocritus, The, the models of the later *Pastoral Eclogues,* imitated by Pope, 278; allusions by Pope, in essay in the *Guardian,* to, 279.
Iliad, see under *Homer.*
India, the estimate of feminine charms in, according to Pope, 415.
Ingoldsby Legends, The, the receipt for a Prince of the Asturias in, 74.
Intelligencer, The, a periodical started by Sheridan, in Ireland, and contributed to by Swift, 214.
Inquiry into the Expediency and Propriety of Public Worship, An, by Gilbert Wakefield, referred to, 339, *note.*
Ireland, Jonathan Swift the Elder, migrates, with others of the family, to, 2; Swift, in his twenty-first year, leaves, but returns to, after a year's absence, 4, 5; in anger quits Moor Park again for, 8; sets out for England, after two years' residence in, 8; accepts secretaryship to the Lord Lieutenant of, 11; prevails on Esther Johnson to take up her residence in, 12; resides in during 1707; his changes of residence between England and, 18; goes back to, in 1709, leaves in Sept., 1710 for London, 26; sets out to take possession of his Deanery in (1713), after a few months' interval leaves again for London, 34; after the death of the Queen retreats to, 35; at the death of Hester Vanhomrigh goes into the South of, 40; the grossly bad government and consequent miseries of, Swift engages (anonymously) in a war of pamphlets on behalf of, 40-42; returns to (not again to leave), 49; impresses upon Hester Vanhomrigh that it is "not a place for freedom," or secrecy, 153; reminds Pope that it is not Paradise, 161; no conversable creature in, want of cleanliness in, 171; Swift's definition of, woollen exports prohibited from, 220; represents to the Queen the miserable condition of, 227.
Island of Ghosts, The, in *Gulliver's Travels,* allusion by Swift to, 209.
Issachar, the example of, quoted by Pope, 418.
Italy, described by Pope as the ladies' climate, 416.

J

Jacobites, the leading, seek refuge in France, 35, 323; expected rising of, 511.

James II., King of England, characterised by Swift, 245.

Jaques, his denunciation of Deer Hunting in *As You Like It*, 456.

Jervas, Charles, the portrait painter, Swift sits for his portrait to, 31, 32; Swift requests the Queen (Caroline) to sit for her picture to, 326; Pope makes the acquaintance and places himself under the tuition of, 301; Pope's letters to, noticed, 346; paints the earliest portrait of Pope, portrait by, described, 347, 348; Pope expresses his obligations, in the way of lessons in painting, to, 365; Pope at the house of, in Cleveland Court, St. James's, 367; Pope refers to his instruction in painting by, 369, 370, to variety of portraits by, 374; letters from Pope to, 389-391; 420-422, goes to Rome and Naples in search of health, 494.

Job (in the Jewish Sacred Scriptures), quoted by Pope, in reference to the South Sea Speculation, 442.

John Bull, a Satire by Arbuthnot, allusion to by Swift, 129, *note*.

Johnson, Esther, her parentage, lives with her mother and sister, sometimes in the house of Sir W. Temple, sometimes in a cottage, at Moor Park, 5; Macaulay's representation of the position of at Moor Park, at the age of fifteen, remarkable for charms of manner, one of the *belles* of the London drawing-rooms, Swift's description of, 9, 10; Swift acts as her preceptor, her passion for him (apparently), of later date, 10, 11; removes to Ireland, 12; Swift's series of letters to, commonly known as the *Journal to Stella*, begun in the autumn of 1710; Swift describes his friends, the Tory Ministers, to, 27; describes St. John to, 28; alleged coolness in Swift's letters to, 29; a *résumé* of the contents of the letters of Swift to, 29-31; in Swift's society at Laracor, 34; her reproaches and entreaties to Swift long unheeded; her alleged marriage to him, conflicting evidence for and against it, 36, 37, and *note*; her death, her will, 50, 51; remarkably rare references in the correspondence of Swift to, Bolingbroke's allusion to, Johnson's notice of her position at Swift's table, 50, *note*; Swift's poems addressed to, 51, *note*; his notice of her death (*Character of Mrs. Johnson*), her burial in St. Patrick's Cathedral, Swift's inscription on a lock of her hair, 52; Swift buried in the same grave with, 65; letters from Swift to, 93-98, 98-107, 107-114, 114-121, 121-124, 124-128, 128-133, 135-138, 138-141; conjectures as to the meaning of his familiar expressions to, 133, *note*; Swift's alarm about illnesses of, 188, 189, 190, 202, 206.

Johnson, Mrs., the mother of Esther Johnson, notice of, 5; her position at Moor Park, according to Scott, 7, *note*; Swift refers to, 94; marries a Mr. Mose, land agent of Sir W. Temple, 11; Swift's sister (Mrs. Fenton) lives at Farnham with, 11, *note*; reference to, in a letter of Swift to Esther Johnson. 94.

Johnson, Samuel, a biographer of Swift, on Swift's fancy as to the surfeit of fruit, 5; revives the controversy as to the authorship of the *Tale of a Tub*, 13; his opinion of that Satire, 14; affirms the marriage of Swift, on the reasons for the (alleged) marriage, 37, and *note*; on the fancied origin of Swift's maladies, 120, *note*; his eulogy of the *Essay of Criticism*, 283; on Vivisection and other experimental torture in the *Idler*, 287, *note*; on "poetic justice, 288; his estimate of Pope's *Iliad*, 301, *note*; on his *Shakspeare*, 313, and *note*; his high praise of the *Characters of Men* and *of Women*, 322; his remarks on the *Letter to a Noble Lord*, 331; notice of *Life of Pope* by, 338; relates the effect of the publication of Pope's Letters, 343, *note*; remark on the character of Parnell by, 406, *note*; speaks with contempt of Pope's Grotto, 468.

Jones, Betty, a cousin of Swift, her love-affair with Swift at Leicester, marries an innkeeper at Loughborough, 4; a letter from Swift to the Rev. J. Kendall, in regard to, 69-71.

Jones, Inigo, his designs for Whitehall, shewn to Pope by Clarke at Oxford, 420.

Jonson, Ben, his comedy of the *Tale of a Tub*, referred to, 13, *note*.

Journal of a Modern Lady, The, a poem by Swift, referred to, 61.

Journal of a Dublin Lady, The, a set of verses by Swift, published in the *Intelligencer*, 214.

Judges, The, interpreted by Swift to be allegorised under the appearance of Rabbits, 195.

Jupiter, derivation of the word by Swift, 58, *note*.

K

Kelly, Capt. Dennis, an agent in *Sayer's Plot*, 175, note.

Kelly, the Rev. George, an Irish clergyman, a Jacobite agent of Bishop Atterbury, 175, note.

Kendall, The Rev. John, writes a letter of advice to Swift, on his love affair with Betty Jones, letter of reply from Swift to, 69-72.

Kerkopes, a comic-heroic epic, in parody of the *Iliad*, referred to, 406, note.

Key to the Lock, A, by Esdras Bavnevelt (a *nom de plume* of Pope), noticed, 293; reprinted in the *Miscellanies*, 314; alluded to by Arbuthnot, 398, note.

Key (Complete) to the Dunciad, with a character of Mr. Pope and his Profane Writings, by Sir W. Blackmore, Knight, M.D., an ironical publication by Pope, 318, note.

Kildrohod, the Irish name for Cellbridge, the residence of Hester Vanhomrigh, 156.

Kilkenny, the School at, famous for educating three great literary celebrities, 2.

Kilmansegg, Madame, Pope invited to an *Assembly* by, 431.

Kilroot, near Belfast, prebend of, held by Swift, 8.

King, Dr. Wm., Archbishop of Dublin, author of a defence of Optimism (*De Origine Mali*), a correspondent of Swift, 16; extract from letter to Swift from, 33; character of Swift's correspondence with, 60; letter from Swift to, 80-83; Swift reports to Esther Johnson receipt of letters upon the "First-Fruits" business from, 93, 122; Swift defends his ecclesiastical dominions from the encroachments of, 160; letter from Swift (on his suspected Jacobitism) to, 155-167; Swift purposes to "elude" his ecclesiastical mandates, 204, and defies him, 205; his *Origin of Evil* used by Pope in the *Essay on Man*, 327; reference of Pope to, 406, and note.

King Dr. Wm., Principal of St. Mary Hall, Oxford, a friend of Swift, revises for him his *Verses on his Own Death*, extract from letter to Swift from, 64; mentioned by Pope, 504.

King, Dr., a friend or client of Lintot the publisher, reported by the latter to Pope to be able to "write verses in a tavern three hours after he could not speak," 306.

Kingston, the Duke of, (Lord Dorset), father of Lady M. W. Montagu, "nobody's favourite," 87; marries Isabella Bentinck, 305, note.

Kit-Cat Club, The, Mrs. Long the chief toast at, 106, note.

Kneller, Sir Godfrey, a saying of, quoted by Pope, a note from, quoted, 480, and note.

Knight, John, letters from Pope to, 474-476, 478-479, a notice of, 478.

Knight, Mrs., a correspondent of Pope (wife of the preceding), letter from Pope to, 488-489.

L

Ladies, of Swift's acquaintance, unable to write and spell, 243.

Lady at Quadrille, a poem attributed to Swift and denied by him, 214.

Lady's Dressing Room, The, a poem by Swift, a stolen copy, mentioned by him in letter to Pope, 231.

Lady's Journal, The, poem of Swift, referred to by him, 231.

Lagado, Academy of, allusion to, 193, note.

Lamentation of Glumdalclitch for the Loss of Grildrig: a Pastoral, a parody by Pope, 315.

Langallerie, Philippe de Gentils, Marquis de, Swift dissuades Pope from taking a post under, in the Turkish service, 162; Pope announces to Swift the prospect he has of securing some place under, 412.

Lansdowne, Lord, Pope invited to see the lions at the Tower by, expects to be lodged in the Tower, 405.

Laputa, Voyage to, referred to, 193, note.

Laracor, near Trim, the living of, given to Swift by Lord Berkeley, 12; Swift's life and his parishioners at described, 18; in the society of Esther Johnson at, writes to "Vanessa" from, 34; describes to Dean Sterne the employments of his parishioners of, 89; describes to Lord Bolingbroke the ruinous condition of his "country-seat" at, 155, 156; writes to Esther Vanhomrigh from, declares his intention of passing most of his time in Ireland at, reports the latest news of their common friends at, 147, 148.

La Rochefoucald, Duc de, his *Maximes* and *Mémoires*, consulted by Hester Vanhomrigh, 145, note.

La Source, the place of residence of Bolingbroke, near Orléans, 323, 464.

La Valterie, a commentator on the *Iliad*, used by Pope, 299.

Leach, Wm., a cousin of Swift, the printer of the Tory *Postman*, Swift's dinner in the City with, 103, 104.

Lectures on the English Humourists, by W. M. Thackeray, his estimate of the theological

INDEX.   535

sincerity of Swift in, 20; his eulogy of Pope's *Ethics* in, 345.

Lectures on the Four Georges, by the same, his character of Lady Suffolk, quoted, 228, *note.*

Legion Club, The, a satirical poem by Swift, remark on, 62, *note;* referred to by Mrs. Whiteway and Swift (in a humorous joint-letter to Sheridan), 254-255.

Leibnitz Gottfried Wilhelm, his *Theodikée,* used by Bolingbroke, and by Pope in the *Essay on Man*, 327.

Leicester, Swift's visits to, 4; his uncomplimentary character of, 70.

Leicester House, the Opposition Court of the Prince and Princess of Wales held at, Swift a welcome guest at, 43.

Lely, Sir Peter, a portrait of Lady Giffard by, referred to by Swift, 253.

Lepell, Mary, (Lady Hervey), commemorated by Gay, in his *Verses to Pope*, 300; one of the Maids of Honour who took Pope under their protection, Pope's walk with, 304; Pope's commemoration of (in his Court-Ballad), 305; alluded to by Pope, 430.

L'Estrange, Sir Roger, why his political friends should buy him out of Purgatory, 373.

Letcombe, near Berkshire, retreat of Swift in 1714, Swift visited by Pope and Parnell at, 387.

Letter on the Sacramental Test, A, by Swift, against Noncomformity, referred to, 18.

Letter to a Noble Lord on Occasion of Some Libels Written and Propagated at Court, Pope's reply to Lord Hervey's *Epistle,* noticed, 275, 331.

Letter to the Editor of the Letters on the Spirit of Patriotism, addressed to Bolingbroke by Warburton, 336.

Letters of Abelard and Heloisa, noticed, 303, 304, and *note,*

Letters of the Heroines, by Ovid, referred to, 304.

Letters on the Spirit of Patriotism, by St. John, Lord Bolingbroke, entrusted to Pope, and published by him without authorisation, 335, 336.

Letters to John Murray, &c., by Lord Byron, referred to, 337, *note.*

Letters of Pope, the Collected, an account and criticism of, 242-246.

Letters of Swift, the Collected, an account of, 66, 67.

Letter-writing, Pope's opinion on the use of, 504.

Lewis, Erasmus, Secretary to Lord Dartmouth, an intimate friend of Swift, Swift talking politics with, 101; references to, 103, 110, 139, 140, 145; letter from Swift to, 267-269, extracts from letter to Swift from, 269, 270, *note.*

Liberty, Verses on, of Addison, quoted by Pope, 389.

Ligue La, the first title of the *Henriade* of Voltaire, noticed by Pope, 462.

Lilliput, High-heels and Low-heels, Bigendians and Little-endians in, alluded to by Mrs. Howard, 193; the *Voyage* to, Swift thinks, will bear woodcuts better than the Brobdingnagians, suggestions by him for illustrating, 208.

Lintot, Bernard, one of Pope's publishers, various translations from the Latin poets, and first edition of the *Rape of the Lock,* inserted by Pope in the *Miscellanies* of, *Windsor Forest,* &c., published by, 284; *Rape of the Lock,* 299; sums received by Pope for his *Iliad* and *Odyssey,* from, 299, 300; Pope's relation of his journey and dialogue with, 305, 303.

Lions, at the Tower, The, Pope invited by Lord Lansdowne to see, 405.

Little Language, used between Swift and Esther Johnson, referred to, 35, 133.

Lives of the Poets, The, by Samuel Johnson, Cunningham's edition of, referred to, 6; the biography of Pope the best in the series of, 333. (For various references to, see under Johnson.)

Logg, Dr. (or Legg), confessor, or chaplain, to the Blounts, humourously characterised by Pope, 433.

Long, Mrs. Anne, Swift's reference to, "the most beautiful person of the age she lived in," a notice of her, 103, and *note.*

Longitude, proposed method for finding, alluded to by Swift, 128.

Longleat, Mrs Pendarves refers to a visit to Lady Weymouth at, 237, *note;* Pope going to take a trip to, 403.

Lowell, James Russell, a critic of Pope, referred to, 337.

Love for Love, a comedy of Congreve, referred to, 103, *note.*

Lucian, the Greek Satirist, a volume of, appears in the portrait of Swift by Jervas, 32; Swift indebted to, in *Gulliver's Travels,* 47, *note.*

Lucretius, *De Rerum Naturâ,* used by Swift in the *Tale of a Tub,* 15.

Lutrin, the satirical poem by Boileau, a model of the *Rape of the Lock,* 297.

Luke, St., referred to as a painter by Pope, 370.

M

Macaulay, Lord, his representations of the positions of Swift and Esther Johnson at Moor Park (in *Ed. Rev.* and his *Hist. of England*) disputed by Forster, 6, *note;* an adverse critic of Pope, 337; criticises Croker's *Boswell* in *Ed. Rev.*, 340.

Macfarland, Mrs., immolating her lover, Pope (in letter to Lady M. W. Montagu) refers to, 417.

Mac Flecknoe, The, a Satire by Dryden, a model of the *Dunciad*, 318.

Macchiavelli, Nicolo, *Il Principe*, quoted by Swift, 196.

Machinery, in Poetry, explained by Pope to Miss Fermor, 382.

Macrobius, *Saturnalia*, used by Pope in translating the *Iliad*, 385.

Madonna, Pope attempts a picture of the, 370.

Mahomet, his Paradise, referred to by Pope in letter to Lady M. W. Montagu, 419.

Maids of Honour, Swift threatens a History of, 30; how regarded by Swift, 60, *note*.

Maintenon, Mde. de (Frances d'Aubigné), Lord Bolingbroke's second wife a niece of, 323.

Malherbe, François de, the French poet, his authority as not using *hiatus*, quoted by Pope, Balzac's witty allusion to his tyranny in Grammar, Boileau's high praise of, 358, and *note*.

Mallet, David, letter on Warburton from Lord Bolingbroke to, quoted, publishes for Bolingbroke a revised edition of Bolingbroke's *Letters on Patriotism*, 336; one of the best correspondents of Pope (in describing landscape scenery), two letters from referred to, 347.

Mandeville, Bernard de, the influence of his *Fable of the Bees* on the *Essay on Man*, noticed, 327.

Manley, Mrs., a novelist and play-writer, succeeds Swift in the editorship of the Tory periodical, *The Examiner*, 26; Addison's character in the *Memoirs of Europe* by, Swift's remarks to Addison on the book, 91.

Mapledurham, on the Thames, the residence of the Blounts, 291; a portrait of Teresa and Martha Blount by Jervas at, 292; the original of letter of Pope to Martha Blount, on his journey to Oxford, at, 409, *note.*

Mapp, Mrs., the famous "bone-setter," a story of, by Pulteney, in a letter to Swift, 262, *note*, 263.

Marble-Hill, near Richmond, the residence of Mrs. Howard, afterwards Lady Suffolk, referred to by Pope, 465.

Marchmont, Lord, an executor of Pope, Lord Bolingbroke writes to, requesting the immediate destruction of the printed copies of his Treatises, 336; his remark to Pope in regard to Warburton as editor, 338.

Marlborough, John Churchill, Duke of, satirised by Swift in the *Examiner*, 27; figures in the journal-letters, 29; references to, 83, 86, 90, 127; Swift has defended him from many "hard things said against him," 144; Swift's reflections in his forthcoming *History*, on the personal courage of, objected to by the historian's friends, 269, *note*.

Marlborough, Duchess of (Sarah), her opinion of *Gulliver's Travels*, 46; puts up monument to Congreve in Westminster Abbey, 103, *note*; supplanted in the Queen's favour by her relative and dependant, Mrs. Masham, 123, *note;* an anecdote of the meanness of, 138; figures in the *Rape of the Lock* as *Thalestris*, 299; as *Atossa* in the *Characters of Women*, 322; entertains Pope and Lord Chesterfield, pays court to the former, 333.

Marrowfat, Dr., at the "Visitation Dinner," described by Goldsmith in his *Citizen of the World* (LVIII.), 212, *note.*

Marshall, Judge, an executor of Hester Vanhomrigh, takes copies of her MS. letters before they were destroyed, 38.

Martyn, Dr. John, a Cambridge Professor, a reputed editor of the *Grub-Street Journal*, mentioned, 321.

Masham, Mrs. (afterwards Lady), Swift's notices of her in the journal-letters, 29; her "lying-in" troubles at Kensington Palace, 31; comes to town to "lie in," Swift expresses a fervent wish for "a good time" for, dines with, 122, 123; a notice of, 123, *note;* one of a riding-party with Swift, Arbuthnot, &c., 125; makes the Queen send to Kensington for preserved ginger for Swift, 132; accident at Windsor, and Swift's anxieties as to the consequences to, 133; her great friendship for Swift, sheds tears at his approaching departure from England, entertains him at a dinner, speaks to the Queen for him, 140; informs Mrs. Howard as to the duties of bed-chamber woman, 228; Swift endeavours to effect a reconciliation between Lords Bolingbroke and Oxford at the residence of, at St. James's, 264.

Masquerades, introduced by Heydegger, 426, *note*.

INDEX. 537

M.D., initials used by Swift in letters to Esther Johnson, conjectured meaning of, 93, *note.*

Mead, Dr. Richard, Pope under the medical treatment of, 499, 503.

Medals, The, Swift's ironical allusion (in his *Verses on his own death*) to the Queen Caroline's forgetting omitted in the revision of Dr. King, omitted passage quoted, 64, *note;* Swift's complaints to Lady Suffolk that the Queen has not sent him them, 226.

Medley, The, a periodical of the day, noticed by Swift as amalgamated with the *Flying Post,* in consequence of the newspaper-tax, 129, *note.*

Meditation on a Broomstick, a parody by Swift, 21, *note.*

Memoirs of Europe, by Mrs. Manley, ridiculed by Swift, 91.

Merry Andrew, alleged origin of the term, 404, *note.*

Messiah, The, an *Eclogue* or *Pastoral* poem by Pope, originally published in the *Spectator,* Steele's high praise to the author of, its models, the justness of the general eulogy of, by the critics, first questioned by Wordsworth, 283, 284.

Middleton, Dr. Conyers, a witness to the *deism* of Pope, 328; Pope expresses his satisfaction that Warburton has abandoned the field of controversy to, 506.

Milton, John, his *Paradise Lost* quoted by Swift; Warton's assertion as to Swift's indifference to, controverted by Nichols, 161; his *Hymn to the Nativity* referred to, 281; his *Par. Lost* quoted by Pope, 439, and *note; Par. Regained* quoted by Pope, 448; his *Comus, Par. Lost,* quoted, 448, *note.*

Mirror of Magistrates, The, by Thos. Sackville, assisted by Thomas, referred to, 423, *note.*

Misanthropy of Swift, defined by himself, as general, not particular, 185.

Miscellanies, The, jointly contributed to by Swift, Pope and Arbuthnot, 43; Swift desires Sheridan to send him to Twickenham his *Verses to Stella* for insertion in, 205, 206; the greater part contributed by Swift who refuses remuneration for, 209; Pope's *Pastorals* and his imitations of Chaucer, &c., appear in Tonson's, 278, 281; his translations of Statius and Ovid and the *Rape of the Lock* appear in Lintot's, 284; Pope contributes further translations and adaptations from Chaucer and Homer to Steele's, 299; refers to Tonson's, 356; and to his specimens of his Homeric translations in Steele's, 379; announces to Swift the completion of their joint-labours in, refers to the character to 470; Ford's remark upon, 470, *note.*

Miss, in the first half of the last century, of uncomplimentary meaning, 79.

Mist's Journal, Theobald (according to Pope) "crucifies Shakspeare once a week" in, 313.

Mob, a newly-introduced word, Swift protests against, 95, *note.*

Modest Proposal for Preventing the Poor People in Ireland from being a Burden to their Parents or Country, and Making them Beneficial to the Country, an ironical Essay by Swift, quoted, 53-55.

Mohawks, or Mohocks, unpunished licentious savagery and insolence of (in the London streets), noticed by Swift in letters to Esther Johnson, 31, 126, 127.

Mohun, Lady (widow of Lord Mohun, the hero of a duel with the Duke of Hamilton), her marriage with Col. Mordaunt, her third husband, alluded to by Pope in a letter to Lady M. W. Montagu, 426.

"Moll," the familiar name of Mary Vanhomrigh, used by Swift, 135, 145, 146, 147, *note,* 152.

Montagu, Lady Mary Wortley, resents Pope's innuendoes, 275, *note;* his free expressions of admiration for, 292; commemorated by Gay (in verses to Pope), rivalled by Mary Bellenden in beauty, 300, *note;* the *Epistle of Eloisa to Abelard* dedicated by Pope to, 302; authoress of the *Town-Eclogues,* 307; her correspondence with Pope referred to, 343, 344, 348; letters from Pope to, 413-416, 416-419, 424-427; Pope regrets the absence of, 443.

Montagu, Edward Wortley, husband of Lady M. W. Montagu, Swift in the company of, 99; references of Pope to, 414, 426, 415; official letter of, quoted, 425, *note.*

Montaigne, Michel de, his device to induce ladies to keep his *Essays* in their closets alluded to by Swift, 77; referred to by Bolingbroke, 217, *note;* his denunciations of the cruelties of hunting quoted by Pope, 285; Pope quotes a remark of, 375.

Moor Park, the residence of Sir Wm. Temple, Swift finds an asylum at the household of, Esther Johnson's position at, 5; Swift returns to, his life at, 7-11; his reminiscences of, in letter to John Temple, 258.

Moore, Thos., *Life and Letters of Byron,* quoted, 337, *note.*

Moral Essays, of Pope, noticed, 322, 324, 324-330.

Moralist, The : A Philosophical Rhapsody, by Lord Shaftesbury, republished in his *Characteristics*, one of the sources of *The Essay on Man*, referred to, 327.

More, Sir Thomas, uses the proverbial phrase "Tale of a Tub," 131, *note*; his *Utopia* (on the evils resulting from the conversion of arable into pasture land), quoted, 53, *note*.

Mose, Mrs., the mother of Esther Johnson, her second marriage, 11; Swift's only sister lives at Farnham with, 132, *note*.

Motte, Benjamin, the publisher of *Gulliver's Travels*, letter from Swift to, 43, 68, 207-209; his final settlement with Swift, purchases the copyright of *Gulliver* and *Miscellanies*, 224 and *note*; recommended by Swift, 246 ; letter from Swift to, noticed,314, *note*.

Mourning Bride, The, a tragedy by Congreve, referred to, 103, *note*.

Muses' Mercury, The, a periodical, an allusion to by Pope, 356.

N

Nash, Richard, (commonly known as Beau Nash), autocrat of Bath in the last century, his reign of nearly fifty years, his request to Pope for a set of verses, described by Goldsmith, 305, *note*; Pope makes his acquaintance at Bath, remarks on his impudent air, notice of by Dilke, his behaviour to the Duchess of Queensberry related by Goldsmith, 402, and *note*.

Narcissa, the poetic name given by Pope to the Duchess of Hamilton, in his *Characters of Women*, 322.

Narrative of Dr. Robert Norris on the Frenzy of J. D. [John Dennis], a satire by Pope, 288.

National Gallery of Portraits, The, a portrait of Swift by Jervas in, 32, and *note*; of Ann Oldfield in, 37, *note*; of Pope by Jervas in, 292; earliest portrait of Pope by Jervas and another by Hoare in, 347, 348.

Newgate Pastorals, the composition of, suggested by Swift to Pope, 162.

Newman, F. W., his *Essays on Diet* referred to, 53; his *Iliad of Homer*, referred to, 301, *note*.

Newmarket, the "annual cheat" at, stigmatised by Pope (in his *Grateful Address of the Houyhnhnms*), 317.

Newsham, Mrs., a correspondent of Pope, marries (as second husband) Mr. John Knight, (as third husband) Mr. Nugent, 478, *note*.

Newspapers, a stamp-tax on, by the Tory Cabinet, noticed by Swift, 128, 129, *note*.

Nichols, John, *Literary Anecdotes*, controverts Warton's remark as to Swift's quotations from Milton, 161, *note*; an account of Hills, the pirate-publisher, by, 356, 357, *note*.

"Noll," condemned by Swift, as too much of a *cant* word for poetry, 245.

Nonjuror, The, a comedy by Cibber (in imitation of *Tartuffe*), gives offence to Pope, 308; alluded to by Pope, 438, and *note*; obtains for its author the laureateship, 509.

Notes and Queries (Feb. 5, 1881), King's omission of Swift's ironical reference to the Queen (Caroline) in his *Verses on his Own Death* remarked in, the omitted verses quoted in, 64.

Nugent, Mrs., a correspondent of Pope, (see under Knight and Newsham), 478, *note*.

O

Observations on the Second Iliad, by Pope, referred to by him, 292, *note*.

Observator, The, a periodical, its collapse alluded to by Swift, 123, *note*.

Occasional Conformity, the Bill against, extraordinary excitement regarding, a favourite measure of the Tories, 75, and *note*; Swift writes, but does not print, a pamphlet in opposition to, 80.

October Club,The, a sort of caucus of the ultra-Tories, the original members of; places of meeting of, reconstituted as a Literary Club, 33.

Ode to Temple, by Swift, quoted, 7.

Ode to Congreve, by Swift, quoted, 8.

Ode on Solitude, An, said to be Pope's earliest attempt in Poetry, 277.

Ode for Music on St. Cecilia's Day, an early poem of Pope, 284.

Odyssey (see under *Homer*).

Of False Taste, a poetical Essay by Pope, 321.

Of the Use of Riches, a poetical Essay by Pope, 321.

Ogilby, John, Pope's first acquaintance with *Homer* made in the English version of, 277.

Ogygia, the Island of Kalypso, an allusion by Pope to, 418, and *note*.

Old Bachelor, The, a comedy of Congreve, referred to, 103, *note*.

Oldfield, Mrs., an eminent actress, takes the part of Cato's daughter in *Cato*, contemptuous reference of Swift to, buried in Westminster Abbey, a portrait in the National Gallery, at South Kensington, of, 137, and *note*; noticed by Pope in the part of Cato's daughter, 366.

Oldfox, in Wycherley's *Plain-Dealer*, an allusion by Pope to, 357.

Oldham, John, a writer of dramas, contemptuous reference of Pope to the presentation of *Gorboduc* by, 423.

Old Wells, Bristol, described by Pope, 500.

Ombre, a fashionable Spanish game at cards, Swift complains of his losses at, 134.

On the Science of a Connoisseur, an Essay on Pictures, by Jon. Richardson, eulogised by Roscoe, 480, *note*.

Opera, Italian, The, Dennis's denunciation of, a good story told by Swift of a Mrs. Malaprop and the, 23; Swift reports the rage for us at its height, notices a *castrato* (Nicolini) as the reigning favourite of, 87.

Optimism, the characteristic doctrine of the *Essay on Man*, the sources from which Pope and Bolingbroke drew their beliefs in, the essential fallacy and weakness of the ordinary, a true and a false, 227; Warburton's perception of the essential weakness of the creed of, 328, *note*.

Origin of Evil, The, a treatise on, by Dr. King, referred to, 327.

Orkney, Lady, Swift's intimacy with, "the wisest woman he ever saw," the oracle of Lord Oxford, formerly mistress of King William III., £20,000 rental settled by the King upon, "squints like a dragon," her bad understanding with her sister-in-law the Duchess of Hamilton, 131, and *note*; an unflattering reference by Pope to (in letter to the Duchess of Hamilton), 423.

Orlando Furioso, of Ariosto, imitated by Gay, 300, *note*; the adventures of Astolfo in, alluded to by Pope, 416, and *note*.

Ormond, The Duke of, a friend of Swift, Lord-Lieutenant of Ireland in the Tory Government, 26; compromised in the Jacobite intrigues, 35; competitor with the Duke of Shrewsbury for Vice-Royalty, 92; Swift high in the regard of, 97; entertains Swift and Lord Oxford at a dinner, assures Swift of St. Patrick's Deanery, arranges with the Queen as to the preferments of Dromore and St. Patrick's, 139, 141; Swift expresses to Pope his affection and fears for, 158.

Orrery, Lord, a biographer of Swift, originates the story of Swift's ignominious career at the Dublin University, publishes his *Remarks on the Life and Writings of Swift* in 1751, Mrs. Delany's observations upon it, 3, and *note*; his description of Hester Vanhomrigh, Mrs. Delany's comment upon it, 36, *note*; the first to assert the marriage of Swift, 37, *note*; his representation of the character of Swift's connexion with Hester Vanhomrigh, 39; letters from Swift to, 233-234, 250-252; Swift invites him to consider the misery and poverty of the people on his estates, 251; Pope at the house of, 496.

Ovid, the story of Baucis and Philemon (*Metamorphoses viii.*), parodied by Swift, 16; Pope makes the acquaintance of, in the version of Sandys, 277; parts of his *Metamorphoses* and *Letters of the Heroines* translated by Pope, 284; the latter poem a model of the *Eloisa*, which, also, probably is indebted to the romance of Byblis and Ianthe of, 304.

Owl and the Nightingale, The, an early English poem, referred to, 280.

Oxford, Lord, see under Harley.

Oxford, the University of, Swift takes the *degree* of Master of Arts at, does not forget his good reception at, 7; Pope's visit to, 305, 311; his character of the members of, concern at the Queen's death at, 389; his visit (to consult books for his version of the *Iliad*) to, 391; his life at, meets Dr. Clarke and sees Jervas's copies of Raffaelle's *Cartoons* at, 420; Pope (letter to Warburton) declares he will not accept an honorary degree unless Warburton also receives one from, 504, 505, 506; Warburton's comments on the refusal of a *degree* to him by, 506, *note*.

P

Paine, Thomas, Replies to his *Age of Reason* by Gilbert Wakefield, 339, *note*.

Palladio Andrea, an eminent Italian architect, his *Trattato del L'Architectura* referred to by Pope, 440.

Palmerston, Lord, correspondence of Swift with, referred to by Scott, 258.

Pamphlets, a War of, recorded by Swift, 92.

Papist, Swift's first reference to Pope as a, 27; Pope, in his youth, alternately Protestant and, 435; professes himself to be not a, 436.

Papists, laws against, put in force, 292, *note*; laws against harbouring, allusion to, 304; a proclamation issued for putting the laws into execution against, 511.

Paradise, the Persian name for garden, Swift enquires how often it is brought back by wives, 242.

Paradise Lost, quoted by Swift, 161; twice alluded to (with praise) by him, a copy of, annotated by Swift in manuscript, 161, note; quoted by Pope, 439; quoted, 448, note.

Paradise Regained, quoted by Pope, 448.

Parker's Penny Post, publication of Gulliver's Travels in, 43.

Parliament men, all employments go to the friends of, 178.

Parnell, Dr. Thos., dines with Swift and Berkeley at an ale-house, 141; has some ideas for Scriblerus 150; assists Pope in his Iliad, 299; at Pope's request contributes to Tonson's Miscellany, 371; in friendly alliance with Pope, mixes up the prayer to Apollo (Il. I.) with the Pater Noster, 380; letter from Pope to, 384-386; accompanies Pope on a visit to Swift at Letcombe, 387-389; joint-letter from Pope and him to Arbuthnot, 397; with Pope at Bath, 100; letter from Pope to, 405-406; receives a prebend and the vicarage of Finglass from King (Archbishop of Dublin), remark on his character by Johnson, translates the Batrachomyomachia, 405, note; letter from Pope (on the Iliad and the Battle of the Frogs and Mice) to, 427-429; Pope edits the Remains of, 445.

Parsons, held by Swift to be not bad company, 156.

Party-Spirit, Pope's reflections on, 303.

Party-Writers, the English language corrupted by, 462.

Partridge, John, the almanack manufacturer and prophet, editor of the Merlinus Liberatus, ridiculed by Swift in his Predictions for the year 1708, 20, 21.

Pascal, Blaise, his Pensées, influence on the Essay of Man of, 327.

Pastoral Ballad, a pretended Somersetshire, by Pope, quoted, 280.

Pastoral Poetry, a Discourse on, by Pope, referred to, 278.

Pastoral Life, fitted for fostering fierce habits, 354, note.

Pastorals, The, of Pope, first composed at the age of sixteen, patrons and eulogists of, 277; appear in the Poetic Miscellanies of Tonson, the sources of, 278; Byron's estimate of, 280; alluded to by Pope in letter to Walsh, 351-353; Bishop Atterbury promises to return to the author the volume of, 477, note.

Pastorals, The, of Philips, appear in the same volume of Miscellanies with Pope's, Pope's ironical critique upon, quoted, 278-280.

Pastor Fido, Il, of Guarini, alluded to by Pope, 352.

Patrick, Swift's Irish servant, allusions of Swift to his drinking habits and incorrigible negligence, 30; reports to Swift the indifference of his acquaintance as to the change of place-holders, 92; drunk about three times a week, has got the better of his employer, who determines to turn him off, 96; neglects to appear with Swift's gown and periwig, 108; does not present himself until the next day, his suit of clothes at the tailor's counter-ordered, 109; an inefficient guard at Swift's bathing-place at Chelsea, 113; absents himself all night and leaves Swift without linen, &c., 115; neglects his duties again at a critical moment, 117; drunk three days out of five, has lately had his suit of clothes, and now has the "whip-hand" of his employer, Swift is resolved to part with him without pity, 118; keeps Swift waiting, his punishment 124.125.

Patrick, Saint, the miracle of, recommended by Pope to Jervas, 421.

Peel, Sir Robert, a bust of Pope by Roubiliac in the Art Gallery of, referred to, 348, note.

Pelters and Roasters, the World divided into (in respect to eggs), 195.

Pembroke, Lord, a friend of Swift in Ireland, speaks against Harley, 83; makes puns with Swift, 105, 113.

Pendarves, Mrs., (Mary Granville), her interesting references (in her Letters) to Swift, 59; extracts from a letter to Swift from, 237, note; letter from Swift to, 237-241; extract from letter to Swift from, 241; letter from Swift to, 241-243.

Penelope, described in Odyssey, Stella compared by Lord Orrery to, 10.

Percy, Lady Elizabeth, her three marriages alluded to, 243, note.

Perrault, Charles, a champion of the Moderns as against the Ancients referred to, 15.

Persian Tales, The, recommended to Judith Cowper by Pope, 312; Atterbury's criticism on, 441, note.

Persius, the Stoic Satirist, an English translation by Dr. Sheridan of, alluded to by Swift, Swift's advice to the author upon it, 204; quoted (on the use of the letter Y by Pythagoras) by Warburton, 320, note.

Peter the Great, Russian Tsar, his visit to

INDEX.

England noticed by Swift (in a letter to Mrs. Mose), 11.

Peterborough, Lord, a friend of Swift, brought over by him to the Tories, Swift's witty verses descriptive of, quoted, 27, *note;* his impeachment threatened, 84, and *note;* dines with Swift, Bolingbroke, &c., 118; letter to Swift from, quoted 196, *note;* a visitor at Twickenham Villa, 309; visited by Pope at Bevis Mount, 323; Horace Walpole's description of, his enmity to the Duke of Marlborough, marries Mrs. Robinson, his *Memoirs* destroyed by her, 476, *note;* letter from Pope to, 476-478; extract from letter to Pope from, 478, *note;* at sea with Pope, 496.

Petis de la Croix, François, the Persian Tales of, appear (in 1720) in five volumes, noticed by Atterbury, 441.

Pheidias, the Greek Statuary and Sculptor, an allusion by Pope to, 376.

Philips, Ambrose, extract from a letter from Swift on the Italian Opera to, 23; writes "little *flams*" to Miss Carteret, a contributor to the *Freethinker,* 187, and *note;* his *Pastorals* published at the same time with Pope's, 278; accused by Pope of misrepresenting him to Addison, 390, and *note;* ironical reference by Pope to, 400; his *Pastorals* more true to Nature than those of his rival, 400, *note.*

Philips, the Rev. J., an episcopal chaplain, fears the inopportune death of his bishop, 251, 252.

Physicians, Swift's opinion of, 261; compared by Pope to asses, 422.

Pilkington, Mrs., an Irish friend of Swift, her *Memoirs* of Swift referred to, 59; commended by Swift, her account of Mrs. Grierson's extraordinary learning, 224, and *note.*

Pindaric Odes, by Swift, quoted, 7.

Piozzi, Mrs. (*Observations and Reflections*, &c.), reports a remark of the niece of Miss Fermor on the latter's self-consciousness, 298, *note.*

Plain Dealer, The, a comedy of Wycherley, allusion by Pope to, 357, 369.

Plea of the Damned, The, a poem by Swift, referred to, 55, 61; mentioned by Swift as a stolen copy, printed in London, 231.

Plutarch, his Moral Essay *On Flesh-Eating,* and his *Life of Cato* (in the *Parallel Lives*), quoted by Pope, 286; his Essay *On Flesh-Eating* quoted by Rousseau and by Shelley, the English version of Philemon Holland, and that "by several hands," noticed, 286, *note;* referred to as a humanitarian moralist, 329.

Poetry : *a Rhapsody,* a poem by Swift, referred to, 61.

Poets, how they fail as flatterers, 177; how they resemble deity, 220.

Polite Conversation, a satirical piece by Swift, mentioned by him in a letter to Gay, one of his wittiest productions, in its full title, *A Complete Collection of Genteel and Ingenious Conversation, according to the most Polite Mode and Method, now used at Court, and in the best Companies of England,* 60, and *note;* an allusion by Swift, in a letter to Lord Orrery, to, 252.

Polly, a comic opera, by Gay, not allowed to be acted, Croker's remarks on it, 212, *note;* the Duchess of Queensberry becomes its champion, and quarrels with the Court respecting it, 223, *note.*

Polwhele, R., the first portion of the letters of Pope to Fortescue published in the *Hist. of Devon* of, 394, *note.*

Pond, Arthur, a portrait painter, an engraving from a portrait of Pope by, noticed, 348.

Pope, Alexander, the father of the poet, a linen-draper in Lombard Street, a papist, upon the Revolution of 1688 gives up his business and lives at Binfield, 275, 276; his death in 1716 alluded to, 301.

Pope, Mrs., of a Yorkshire family, her social position, her son's strong affection for her, belongs to the Papal Church, 275, 276; her gradual decay, her death, noticed by Swift in letters to Pope, 232, 234; Pope announces her death to Richardson and requests him to make a sketch of her face, a *facsimile* of the etching in Mr. Elwin's *Works of Pope,* 483, 485, and *note.*

Pope, Alexander (see *Contents*).

Popery, satirical allusions by Pope to, 372, 373.

Porphyry, his humane teaching, referred to, 329.

Portraits of Swift, noticed, 31, 32, and *notes;* of Mary, Queen of Scotland, peculiarities in, 32, *note;* of Teresa and Martha Blount, 292, *note;* various portraits copied by Pope, 301; of Pope, 347, 348.

Post-Boy, The, a newspaper, Swift inserts a paragraph on Mrs. Long in, 106, *note.*

Postman, The, a rabid Tory paper, printed by Leach, a cousin of Swift, Lady Giffard accuses Swift of mis-editing Sir W. Temple's Writings in, 104, and *note.*

Predictions of Isaac Bickerstaff, satires by Swift, noticed, 20, 21.
Presto, a name given to Swift by the Duchess of Shrewsbury, first appears in the twenty-seventh letter of Swift to Esther Johnson, 95, *note;* Swift relates the occasion and reason of the bestowal of the name, 118.
Pretender, the (Elder), allusions of Swift to, 150, 165, 166, 175; of Pope to, 388, invasion threatened by, 511, *note.*
Prior, Matthew, dedicates his poems to Lord Dorset, 87; dines with Swift and Rowe, eulogises Swift's *City Shower*, 105; his imitation of Hadrian's *Ad Animam*, quoted by Pope, 368; author of a poem entitled *Merry Andrew*, 404, *note.*
Prior Park, Bath, the residence of Ralph Allen, visits of Pope to, 332, 333, 507, 508.
Prodigal Son, The, a satirical picture by Pope of, 301 and *noto.*
Progress of Poetry, The, verses by Judith Cowper, a eulogy of Pope in, 312; quoted, 457, *note.*
Project for the Advancement of Religion and the Reformation of Manners, an ironical piece by Swift, quoted, 21-23.
Project for Eating Children, A, an ironical pamphlet by Swift, alluded to by him, 231.
Projectors, The, in *Gulliver's Travels* ("Voyage to Laputa"), the part of the book least liked by Arbuthnot, 197, *note.*
Proposal for the Universal Use of Irish Manufactures, a pamphlet by Swift, noticed, 40.
Proposal for Correcting, Improving, and Ascertaining the English Tongue (1712), addressed to Lord Oxford, quoted, 95, *note;* Steele reminded of the celebration of his name by Swift in, the first piece of writing published by Swift with his name, two Replies to it, 144 and *note.*
Psalms of David, The, a parody by Pope of one of, affectation of denial by him (in a letter to Swift), Warburton believes Pope be the author of, printed in *Additions to Pope's Works*, 412, and *note.*
Pulteney, William, letter from Swift to, 260.263; extract from letter to Swift from, 261; allusion by Pope to, 496.
Punch and the Puppet-Show, popularity of, the most important news from the metropolis, 475.
Purchas, Samuel, his *Pilgrimage, or Relations of the World,* &c., alluded to by Pope, 430, and *note.*
Purves, D. L., a biographer of Swift, quoted, 118, 121, 124, 125, 138, *notes.*

Pyrenees, Treaty of the, Lord Bolingbroke begins his *History of His Own Times* from, 493.

Q

Quaker Pastorals, suggested by Swift to Gay, who takes the hint and writes one, 162, and *note.*
Quarles, Francis, an allusion of Pope (in a letter to Bishop Atterbury) to the *Devil at Bowls* in the *Emblems, Divine and Moral*, of, 448, and *note.*
Quarterly Review, The, July, 1883, article on Swift (in regard to his alleged marriage) referred to, 37, *note;* the publication of *Gulliver's Travels* in Parker's *Penny Post* noticed in, 43; the close resemblance of a passage in the *Voyage to Brobdingnag* to one in the *Mariners' Magazine*, 1679, pointed out in, 47, *note;* its editor takes part with Campbell and the partisans of Pope against Bowles, 339, 340.
Queen Mab, Shelley's, referred to, 281.
Queensberry, Duchess of, the patroness and hostess of Gay, Swift addresses letters in part to Gay, and in part to her at Aimsbury, 55, 56; alluded to, 212, *note;* Swift regrets that he does not know her, apologises to her (through Gay) for a breach of good manners in his manner of eating, begs that she will be the guardian of Gay's purse, and felicitates her upon the cause of her disgrace at the Court, 222, 223, and *note;* canvasses for subscriptions for Gay's Opera, *Polly*, in the drawing-room at St. James's, and is forbidden to appear at Court, her reply to the Vice-Chamberlain's message, 223, *note;* Goldsmith's anecdote of the insolence of Beau Nash to, 402, *note.*
Quickly Mistress, A, suspected by Swift, "by her eyebrows" (letter to Esther Johnson), 122, *note.*
Quilca, the residence of Dr. Sheridan, in County Cavan, Swift's visit to, 180, and *note.*
Quincey, Thomas De, his opinion of the *Rape of the Lock*, quoted, 297; an adverse critic of Pope, 337; errs on the side of depreciation, contradictory judgments (in regard to Pope) of, 340.

R

Rabelais, François, Swift indebted to his *Gargantua et Pantagruel* in the *Tale of a Tub*, 14; a model of *Gulliver's Travels*, 47, *note;*

Swift's allusion to the Giant Longaron in, 154; represents the interpreters of the Laws as "Furred Cats," 196, *note*.

Racine, Louis, author of a poem entitled *La Religion*, its ironical allusion to the Optimism of the *Essay on Man* quoted, sent by Pope a letter defending himself from the charge of heterodoxy to, attributes the popularity of the *Essay* in France to its "infidelity," 323, and *note*.

Radcliffe, John, M.D., referred to by Swift, Court physician to William III., loses his place at Anne's succession by his candour, founder of the library of that name at Oxford, 97, and *note*; orders Martha Blount to Bath, 336.

Raffaelle, Sanzio, his *Cartoons* copied by Jervas, 420, *note*.

Ram, Squire, Swift complains in his *Intelligencer* of having been almost ridden over by the carriage of, 238, *note*.

Rape of the Lock, The, a poem by Pope, first appears in Lintot's *Miscellany*, 284; revised and enlarged in 1714, origin of, dedicated to Miss Fermor, the additions and improvements of, its models, surpasses them all, its parody of the epic style, universal praise given to it by the critics. Marmontel's French version of, 296, 297; quoted, a *Key* to, pecuniary profits brought to Pope by, illustrated by engravings, 298, 299; its eulogies by Pope's critics quoted, 340; Pope reports to Swift the completion of, 375; skilful dedication of, 376; letters from Pope to Miss Fermor upon, 331-334.

Rapparees, The, wild Irish outlaws, an allusion by Pope to, 461.

Rawlinson, R., his translation of the Latin Letters of Heloisa and Abelard, probably used by Pope, 303, 304.

Raymond, Vicar of Trim, a friend of Swift, Esther Johnson and Mrs. Dingley occasional boarders at the house of, 18; Swift's reason for recommending him to the Duke of Ormond for the living of Laracor, 132.

Redriff, Gulliver's birthplace, an allusion in the *Epistle of Mary Gulliver* to, 316.

Reformed Church, The, will not permit legacies for redemption of souls from Purgatory, 374.

Rehearsal, The, a drama by Cibber, the author's *vivâ voce* interpolation of a speech in, the alleged ground of the quarrel between him and Pope, 308.

Religion of Nature Delineated, The, by Wm. Wollaston, noticed by Pope as having lately appeared, and as popular with women, the Queen (Caroline's) patronage makes it fashionable, 452, and *note*.

Rentes Viagères (French Government Annuities), Pope expresses his anxiety about his father's investments in, 377, and *note*.

Resignation of the Captive by Scipio, of Ricci, reference to the picture, belonging to Lord Burlington, 489.

Rhymes, jocular, by Swift, sent by him to Sheridan, 253.

Rich, Lady, a correspondent of Lady M. W. Montagu, allusion by Pope to, 424, 426.

Rich, Thos., turned out of Drury Lane, builds a theatre in Lincoln's-Inn-Fields, intends to act Gay's *What-D'ye-Call-It* without Steele's consent, 405, and *note*.

Richardson, Jonathan, the painter, a friend of Pope, Roscoe's character of, 480, *note*; letters from Pope to, 480-481, 487.

Richardson, Samuel, the novelist, his letter respecting Swift's life at the Dublin University quoted, 3.

Rickett, Magdalen, the only (half) sister of Pope, referred to, 276, *note*.

Riding-Party, A, at Windsor, described by Swift, 125.

Robinson, Mrs. Anastasia, a celebrated singer, marries Lord Peterborough, an allusion by Pope (letter to Peterborough) to, burns her husband's *Memoirs*, 476, and *note*.

Rolt, Patty, a cousin of Swift, mentioned by him in a letter to Esther Johnson, 103, and *note*.

Rome, the Church of, Pope judges, from modern symptons and ancient prophecies, to be in a declining condition, 412.

Roscoe, William, a biographer and editor of Pope, his *Life and Writings of Pope*, letter from Pope to Martha Blount published by, 334, and *note*; quoted, 362, 394, 417, 422, 437, 476, 478, 490, 491, 496 510.

Rosalind, a Shepherdess in Philips's *Pastorals*, quoted by Pope, 279.

Rosicrucians, The, described by Pope in a letter to Miss Fermor, etymology of the word, 382, and *note*.

Roubiliac, Louis François, a distinguished French Sculptor, resident in this country, his bust of Pope referred to, 348.

Rowe, Nicholas, a dramatist and poet-laureate, Under-Secretary of State, entertains Swift and Prior at a dinner at his office and afterwards, with the guests, to a "blind" tavern, 104, 105.

Ruffhead, Owen, his *Life of Pope* (1759) referred to, obtains his material from Bishop Warburton, the first biography of Pope of any value, 336, *note*.

544　INDEX.

Ruffs, German, an allusion by Pope to, as being introduced into England, 396.

S

Sacheverell, Dr. Henry, the ecclesiastical and political agitation caused by, 25; figures in the journal-letters of Swift, 29; extract from letter to Swift from, 31, *note;* Swift reads his "long, dull sermon," printed and sent to him by the preacher (the first since his suspension), entitled *The Christian Triumph, on the Duty of Praying for our Enemies*, Swift reports to Esther Johnson an account of its publication, 136, 137; his opinion upon Dr. Burnet the Bishop of Salisbury's future destination, 405.

Sainte Beuve, Ch. A. (*Causeries de Lundi*), controverts Taine's estimate of Pope, his opinion of the *Essay on Criticism* quoted, 283; a favourable critic of Pope, 337.

Salamanders, in the Rosicrucian system, explained by Pope, 382.

Sancho Panza, an allusion by Pope to his ravenous eating, 454.

Sappho, Lady M. W. Montagu satirised under that name in the *Dunciad*, 319, in the *Characters of Women*, 322; Pope (apparently) interpolates passages in the letters of Lady M. W. Montagu to justify the appellation of, 346; the name first applied by him to Mrs. Thomas (the mistress of Henry Cromwell), 357; Lady M. W. Montagu commemorated, under the name, in verses addressed by him to Judith Cowper, 454.

Sappho to Phaon, a poem by Pope, in imitation of the *Epistle* of Ovid, published in Lintot's *Miscellany*, 284.

Sarpedon, the episode of (*Iliad* xii., xvi.); Pope notices his version of, in Tonson's *Miscellany*, 379, *note.*

Sartor Resartus, by Thomas Carlyle, indebted to the *Tale of a Tub* for hints for the Philosophy of Clothes, 14.

Satires of Pope, in imitation of Horace and Donne, noticed, 330-331.

Savage, Richard (the poet), a friend and agent of Pope, lends his name as the pretended author of a narrative of the publication of the *Dunciad*, 319; dies in Bristol Jail entirely destitute; owes his burial to his jailor, his extraordinary career narrated in detail by his friend Dr. Johnson, 332, and *note.*

Scheme of Paying Public Debts by a Tax on Vices, by Pilkington, inspired by a passage in *Gulliver*, 231, and *note.*

Scriblerus, Cornelius, the father of Martin, alluded to, 34.

Scriblerus Martinus, the Memoirs of, an unfinished Satire by Swift, Arbuthnot, Pope, and Gay, so called from the Club of that name, 33; the first hint for it attributed by Swift to Pope, Swift concedes the honour of its completion to Arbuthnot, why Pope, Gay, and Parnell are disqualified for continuing, 149, 150; Swift himself not easy enough in mind for, 159.

Schism Bill, The, to disqualify all Nonconformists for being teachers of the young, Swift's conduct in regard to, 388, and *note*.

Scotland, how regarded by Swift as many times worse than Ireland, 219.

Scott, Sir Walter, a principal biographer and editor of Swift, remarks on the position of Esther Johnson's mother at Moor Park, 7, *note;* on the letter from Swift to Miss Waring, 9, *note;* describes Swift's figure and features, 32; maintains the reality of Swift's marriage, 37; the letters of Hester Vanhomrigh printed (from copies taken by his friend Mr. Berwick) by, 38, and *note;* criticism upon Desfontaines' *Le Nouveau Gulliver* of, 45; gives high praise to Swift's *The Grand Question Debated*, 61, *note;* alleges the only excuses for the publication of the grossest of Swift's poems, 62; Swift's manner of letter-writing remarked by, very few additions to the Swift Letters published since the edition of, 67; his *Life and Works of Swift* quoted, or referred to, 69, 71, 72, 75, 76, 77, 79, 80, 82, 84, 85, 87, 88, 89, 91, 102, 116, 127, 134, 145, 146, 148, 151, 152, 153, 156, 157, 158, 159, 161, 162, 163, 167, 172, 174, 175, 180, 182, 183, 185, 188, 189, 190, 191-192, 194, 197, 198, 202, 213, 214, 217, 219, 229, 236, 244, 245, 247, 248, 249, 258, 260, 264, 269.

Seasons, The, of Thomson, the greatest humanitarian poem of the last century, referred to, 287, *note;* said to have been contributed to by Pope, 486, *note.*

Secchia Rapita, La, of Tassoni, noticed, 297.

Select Preachers, Swift's remark upon, 31, *note.*

Seneca, *Morals*, on the retribution of gluttony, quoted by Pope in the *Guardian*, 285; an allusion by Pope to, 371.

Sermons of Swift, given by him to Sheridan, quoted, 65.

Sermons, general contempt for, alluded to by Pope, 438.

Settle, Elkanah, the City Laureate, ridiculed by Pope in the *Dunciad*, 320.

INDEX.   545

Seven Times Shorn Goat, The, a comic-heroic Greek poem, referred to, 406.

Shaftesbury, Lord, his *Letter on Enthusiasm* attributed to Swift, who complains of this ascription in his *Apology* for the *Tale of a Tub*, 88, and note.

Shakspeare, William, his *King Lear*, referred to, 211, note; Tonson engages Pope to undertake an edition of, its little popularity, Pope's pecuniary profits from, Theobald contributes articles to *Mist's Journal* on, criticises Pope's edition in his *Shakspeare Restored*, Pope's remarks upon the criticism, Johnson's opinion of the Pope edition, 313, and note; quotation by Pope from, 430; Atterbury promises to return Pope's annotated copy of, and intends to read him once more, 447, note; an imitation of, by Miss Cowper, commended by Pope, 455; reflections of Jaques on Deer-Hunting (in *As You Like It*) referred to, Pope's emendation of a word in *Twelfth Night*, noticed 456, notes.

Sham, newly-introduced word, objected to by Swift, 95, note.

Sheen, near Richmond, a residence of Sir William Temple, allusion to, 5.

Shelley, Percy Bysshe, his *Address to the Irish People* quoted, 42, note; his *Queen Mab* referred to, 281; *Revolt of Islam* quoted, 448, note.

Shepherd's Week, The, a *Pastoral*, by Gay, 280, note.

Sheridan, Dr. Thomas, a friend and correspondent of Swift, letter from Swift (on the illness of Esther Johnson) to, quoted, 50; one of Swift's most intimate friends in Dublin, a notice of, joins with Swift in a volume of *Miscellanies*, ruins his chances of preferment, 58, and note; Swift gives his *Sermons* (in manuscript) to, 65; some of the best Swift letters written to, 67; Swift's petition to Lord Carteret on behalf of, 91; has a school at Quilca in Cavan, Swift's visits to, 180, note; letters from Swift to, 180-181, 182-184, his unlucky *Discourse*, 183, note; letters from Swift to, 190-191, 200-203, 203-206; entertains Esther Johnson and Mrs. Dingley at the Dublin Deanery, Swift's notice of his *Persius*, 203, 204; conjointly with Swift writes a weekly paper, the *Intelligencer*, 230; his departure from Dublin lamented by Swift, 251; jocular letters from Swift to, 252-253, 254-255, 255-257.

Sheridan, Thomas, son of Dr. Sheridan, a biographer of Swift, publishes his *Life of Swift* in 1787, repeats the story of Swift's idleness at the Dublin University, 3; his remarks on the beginning of Swift's attachment to Hester Vanhomrigh, quoted, 30, note; a principal witness for the (alleged) marriage of Swift, his evidence quoted, professes to have had his account from his father, 37, and note; his report of a visit to Hester Vanhomrigh, quoted, 38, and note; alleges the refusal of Swift to acknowledge the marriage, 51.

Shower, A City, verses by Swift, quoted, 245, note.

Shrewsbury, the Duchess of, daughter of the Marchese Paleotti, gives the Italian name of *Presto* to Swift, 118, and note; on a riding-party, with Swift and others, in Windsor Park, 125; expected popularity in Ireland of, 131.

Shute, Mr., a Presbyterian, Secretary to the Irish Viceroy, noticed by Swift as the "shrewdest head in Europe," 87, note.

Sid Hamet, a verse-Satire by Swift on Lord Godolphin, alluded to by Swift, 96; attributed either to himself or to Prior, 99.

Sieve Yahoo, signature of Mrs. Howard, derived by her from the *Voyage to Laputa*, 193, note.

Silvia, the Story of, and her murdered Fawn, the most charming episode in the *Æneis*, referred to, 285, note.

Sir Ralph, the Patriot, a set of verses by Swift, allusion by Swift to, first appears in the *Country Journal* (Aug. 1728), in full, *The Progress of Patriotism: A Tale*, a Satire on Walpole, 214, and note.

Sirrah, substituted by the editors of Swift for *Sollah*, the word which really appears in the MS. letters of Swift to Esther Johnson, 96, note.

Smedley, Dr., Dean of Clogher, editor of a collection of lampoons on Pope entitled *Alexandriana*, figures in the *Dunciad*, 319.

Smythe, James Moore, a friend of the Blounts, noticed, 292; immortalised in the *Dunciad*, 320.

Sollah, the familiar name given to Esther Johnson in Swift's Letters, by the editors printed Sirrah, 56, note.

Solomon, the Song of, an allusion by Pope (letter to Lady M. W. Montagu) to, 416; *Solomon* quoted by Pope, 470.

Somers, Lord, Lord Chancellor, an early patron of Swift, 12; suspected of the authorship of *A Discourse of the Dissentions Between the Nobles and Commons of Athens and Rome*; the *Tale of a Tub* dedicated to, suspected to be the author of that Satire, 13; appears in the early journal-letters of Swift, vacates office, 26; his confidence

2 M

to Swift on the Bill against Occasional Conformity, 76 ; Harley's intrigues against, 83 ; references of Swift to, 87, 136.

Somerset, the Duchess of, her hatred of Swift, exerts her influence with the Queen to prevent his preferment, 25, *note.*

Somerset, the Duke of, his attack upon Harley in the Privy Council, 83.

South Sea Company's Bubble, The, an allusion of Swift to, 154 ; Pope reported by Gay to have lost money in, 178, *note ;* Swift's narrative of its establishment (in his *History*) objected to by his Tory friends, 269, *note ;* an allusion of Pope to, extract from letter from Digby respecting, Hogarth's engraving in satire of, 440, and *note ;* allusions of Pope to, 142, 144 ; Arbuthnot's *bon mot* upon, 443.

South Sea Project, The, a satire by Swift, referred to, 60.

Sparrow, the, a conventional representative of the Latin *Passer,* impropriety of the translators and poets respecting, 315, note.

Spectator, The, started and edited by Steele, references of Swift in his journal-letters to, reports (Nov., 1711) the probable cessation of, as readers begin to weary of them, ridicules the frequent recurrence of the *fair sex* in, supplies a hint to Steele for No. L, 31, and *note ;* Swift reports that it keeps up and doubles its price, 129, *note ;* Addison's eulogy of Pope's *Essay on Criticism,* in, 282 ; Pope publishes his *Messiah* in, 283, "certain honest country-gentlemen" of Pope's acquaintance never see it, 238, 360.

Spence, Joseph, a friend and anecdotist-biographer of Pope, author of *Observations, Anecdotes, and Characters,* &c., Pope's statement of his first literary efforts to, quoted, 277, and *note ;* relates Pope's or Tonson's remark on Addison's *Defence of the Christian Religion,* 290 ; origin of Pope's acquaintance with, 313 ; records Pope's declarations of his obligation to Bolingbroke in the *Essay on Man,* quoted, 324 ; attends Pope on his death-bed, 335 ; prints an edition of *Gorboduc,* Professor of Poetry at Oxford, 423, *note.*

Sports, of Hunting, stigmatised by Pope, 284.

Sporus, Lord Hervey satirised by Pope under that name, in the *Dunciad,* 319, in the *Epistle to Arbuthnot,* 332.

Squire, The, the familiar *Scriblerus* name of Lord Bolingbroke, an allusion by Swift to, 149.

Stage, The, Dr. Johnson on, 288 ; Pope's account of the use made of, 438.

Stanhope, Sir William, the purchaser of Twickenham Villa, 220.

Stanhope, Lady Lucy, mentioned by Swift, 109, 110, *note.*

Statius, a Latin poet, his *Thebais* imitated and translated by Pope, 277, 284 ; quoted by him, 347.

Steele, Sir Richard, his first acquaintance with Swift, 16 ; joins with Swift in the satire of Partridge the astrologer, 21 ; starts the *Tatler,* suggested by the production of *Bickerstaff,* and secures the assistance of Swift, 25 ; appears in the journal-letters, 29, 30 ; Swift sends a letter for the *Tatler* to, 95, references of Swift to, 88, 98, 101 ; his quarrel with Swift, his paper in the *Tatler* attacking Harley, 101, and *note ;* references of Swift to, 102, 116 ; accused to Addison by Swift of assailing him in the *Guardian,* 141, 142 ; letter from Swift, on the same subject to, 142-144 ; extracts from a letter to Swift from, 143 ; publishes a paper by Pope on *Pastoral* poetry for the *Guardian,* 278 ; writes to Pope in high praise of his *Messiah,* 283 ; protests against the savagery of Bull-baiting (in the *Tatler* Feb. 1709), 286, *note ;* expresses his admiration of Pope's poetic genius, 287 ; receives a letter from Pope thanking him for his favourable *critique,* 288 ; conveys to Pope Addison's disapproval of the attack on Dennis, 289 ; brevity of his correspondence with Pope, 290 ; Pope's connexion in the *Guardian* with, 291 ; a volume of *Miscellanies* edited by, 299 ; only two letters from Pope to, 344, 360-361 (his reply, quoted, 361, *note*), 363-364 ; writes to Pope complimenting him on his *Temple of Fame,* and asking his assistance in the *Guardian,* 363, *note ;* Pope reports the displeasure of his Tory friends at his writing for, 367 ; Gay's Farce, *What-D'ye-Call-It,* discountenanced by, 404, 405, and *note.*

Stella, the poetic name given by Swift to Esther Johnson, his series of letters to her (1710-1713) wrongly entitled the *Journal* to, does not once occur in the manuscript journal-letters, inserted by the editors, 25, and *note ;* 28 ; 37, and *note ;* 50 ; Bolingbroke's use of the name, 50, *note ;* Swift's verses addressed to, 51, *note ;* occurs in printed letters, 65, and *note,* 96, 97, 99, 100, 103, 107, 110 ; occurs in MS., 180, 181, 204, 205, 206 (letters to Sheridan).

Stephen, Mr. Leslie, a biographer of Swift and of Pope, his remark on the three distinguished *alumni* of the Kilkenny School,

INDEX. 547

2; on Swift's *Modest Proposal*, 53; a favourable critic of Pope, 337; his high estimate of the interest of the Swift and Pope correspondence, 346, *note*.

Sterne, Dean of St. Patrick's, a friend and correspondent of Swift, letters of Swift to, 18, 88-89, 92-93; references to, 96, 98; promoted to the Bishopric of Dromore to make way for Swift, 139, 140, 141.

Sternhold, Thos., Groom of the Robes to Henry VIII., versifier of the *Psalms*, an allusion by Pope to, 418, and *note*.

Stewart, Dugald, an admiring critic of Pope, 337.

St. John, Sir Henry, Lord Bolingbroke's father, Swift's description of, tried for murder in a duel, 23, and *note*; allusion of Swift to, created Baron St. John, of Battersea, and Viscount St. John, 262, and *note*; reference to, 323.

Stowe, in Buckinghamshire, Lord Cobham's place at, visits of Pope to, 333; his praises of the beauty of, 478; Lord Peterborough's notice of, 478, *note*.

Stoyte, Alderman (and Lord Mayor of Dublin), a friend of Swift, frequent references in the journal-letters to, 18.

Suits of Clothes, term improperly applied, what in reality, 15.

"Sweetness and Light," an expression employed by Swift in his *Tale of a Tub*, 15, *note*.

Swift, Godwin, the father of the Satirist, noticed, 1, 2.

Swift, Deane, a second cousin of the Satirist, biographer and critic of Swift (*Essay on the Life, Writings, and Character of Swift*), repeats the story of Lord Orrery, 3; criticised by Mrs. Delany, 3, *note*; publishes earlier part of journal-letters, 67; quoted, 72, *note*; 74, *note*; 114, *note*; 155, *note*; 268.

Swift, Jonathan, Dean (see Contents).

Swift, Thomas, Incumbent of Goodrich, grandfather of the Satirist, noticed, 1.

Swift, Thomas, a cousin of the Satirist, at the Dublin University with him, 3; chaplain at Moor Park, and resident there with his cousin, 5; pretends to part authorship of the *Tale of a Tub*, 14; an allusion by his cousin to, the latter's dislike for, 108, and *note*.

Sylphs, who, explained by Pope in a letter to Miss Fermor, 382.

Sylvia, a Shepherdess in the *Pastorals* of Pope, 279; Pope addresses Teresa Blount by the name of the Lady, 395.

Sympson, Cousin, Swift addresses a remonstrance to his publisher (in a preface to the second edition of *Gulliver's Travels* under the name of, 46.

T

Taine, Henri, his criticisms on Pope disputed by Sainte-Beuve, 283; among the unfavourable critics of Pope, 337.

Tale of a Tub, The, a Satire by Swift, 3, 11; origin of the title, 13, *note*; an account of, 13, 14, quoted 14-15; referred to, 108.

Tale of Sir Ralph, a set of verses by Swift, noticed by him to Pope, 231.

Tasso, Torquato, the *Aminta* of, a model of the *Pastorals of Pope*, 278; Pope's remarks upon, 352, and *note*.

Tassoni, Alessandro, his *Secchia Rapita*, a model of the *Rape of the Lock*, 297.

Tatler, The, a periodical started and edited by Steele, suggested by the Satires of Bickerstaff, obtains the aid of Swift, the contributions of Swift to, 25, 30; the Bishop of Clogher shews Swift the first volume of the small edition of, in which the latter is highly complimented, Swift disapproves of the reprinting the news of, thinks it a trick of the publishers to increase the bulk and price (letter to Addison), 90; his paper in ridicule of newly-introduced words into the English language, 95, *note*; reports to Esther Johnson the having written a paper in, 96; publishes his *City Shower* in, 98, 99, *note*; Steele loses his place of Gazetteer for writing against Harley in, Steele's paper quoted, 101, and *note*; praise of Philips in, 278; paper by Steele, on bull-baiting and cock-fighting, in, 286, *note*; Swift's *City Shower* first appears in, 245, *note*.

Temple, Sir William, a connexion of Swift's mother, receives Swift into his house, resides alternately at Sheen and at Moor Park, other guests of, scandal in regard to the relationship of Mrs. Johnson with, 4, 5; writes to Sir R. Southwell, on behalf of Swift, Swift re-enters the service of, Macaulay's article on (in *Ed. Rev.*), quoted, 6, and *note*; uses his influence to obtain a degree for Swift at Oxford, an *Ode* addressed by Swift to, 7; deputes Swift to attend on King William III., on his visit to Moor Park, and sends him to 'the Court on business of State, Swift leaves the service of, but received again by, 8; the death of, bequeaths to Swift the labour of editing his works, 11; leaves a small legacy to Esther Johnson, 12; defended by Swift in the *Battle of the Books*, 15; his *Remains* edited by Swift, 23, 24; promises preferment in the Church to Swift, 72; Swift informs his cousin of his quarrel with, 74; referred to, 94, 257, *note*.

Temple, Lady, a relative of Swift's mother,

only the nominal head of the household at Moor Park, 4.

Temple, John, a nephew of Sir W. Temple, extract from letter from Swift to, 7, and *note*; referred to, 257, *note*; letter from Swift to, 257-259.

Temple of Fame, The, an adaptation from Chaucer by Pope, noticed, 299; Steele's enthusiastic eulogium on (in letter to Pope), 363, *note*; alluded to by Pope, 407.

Terence, his *Andria* quoted by Swift (in letter to Bolingbroke), 216; an edition of, by Mrs. Grierson, referred to, 224, *note*.

Thackeray, W. M., *Lectures on the English Humourists*, holds Swift's theological orthodoxy to have been insincere, 20, *note*; his opinion of Lady Suffolk, 228, *note*; an enthusiastic admirer of Pope, 337; high eulogy of Pope's services in the everlasting war against Falsehood and Superstition, 345, *note*.

Thalestris, the Duchess of Marlborough appears (in the *Rape of the Lock*) under the name of, 298.

Thames, The, three weeks' frost on, alluded to by Swift, 87; Pope's villa on the, 310, 311; a high flood of, 443, and *note*; the junction of the Severn and, alluded to by Pope, 450, and *note*; 464; 468; preferred by Pope to Bath, 487, 511.

Thebais, The, of Statius, Pope's version of, 284; quoted by Pope, 347.

Theobald, Lewis, criticises Shakspeare in *Mist's Journal*, his *Critique* on Pope entitled *Shakspeare Restored*, &c., Pope's remarks on, 313, and *note*; made to occupy the throne of the realms of Dulness in the *Dunciad*, 320, and *note*, 321; a rival of Pope as editor of Shakspeare, 343; defended by Aaron Hill from Pope's criticism, Pope professes to have had no enmity, on account of his *Shakspeare*, to, 491, and *note*, 492.

Theocritus, the *Idylls* of, imitated by Pope, 278, 279.

Thomson, James, the first poet to insist, emphatically, upon the rights of the non-human races, 287, *note*; brings his poem of *Liberty* to Pope, 486; his *Seasons* (morally) the most meritorious poem of the century, appears complete in 1730, 486, *note*.

Three Hours After Marriage, a Farce by Gay, Pope and Arbuthnot, a satire upon certain contemporary personages, noticed, 308.

Tichborne, Sir J., of Tichborne, the brother of Teresa and Martha Blount marries the daughter of, 292.

Tickell, Thomas, a friend of Addison and Steele, and contributor to the *Spectator*, praises Philips in the *Guardian*, 278, translates the First Book of the *Iliad*, announces the reason for his relinquishment of the *Iliad*, the rival of Pope as translator, his version preferred by Addison to Pope's, 300; an allusion by Atterbury to, 447, *note*.

Tisdall, the Rev. Dr., an Irish Church dignitary, a correspondent of Swift, his rival for the affections of Esther Johnson, letters from Swift to, 75-77; 77-80; notice of his courtship of Esther Johnson, 100, *note*.

To a Lady on her Birthday, verses by Pope, sent by him to Judith Cowper, quoted, 459.

Tobacco, excise-tax on, voted by an extraordinary majority, 233; how used by Swift, 114, and *note*.

Tofts, Mary, imposes upon the credulity of the public and the medical profession, an allusion to, 193, *note*.

Toilet, the Royal, at the French and English Courts, 228, *note*.

Tonson, Jacob, the publisher, dines with and pays court to Swift, 116; his *Poetic Miscellanies* referred to, 278, 281, 306, 356, 371; *Woman*, a Tale in verse, published in his *Miscellanies* by, 416.

Tories, The, Swift pities for fools, 175.

Tout Est Bien philosophy, the hollowness of, 327; ridiculed by Voltaire, 337, *note*.

Treatise on the Bathos, A, a satire by Pope, appears in the *Miscellanies* of Swift and Pope, the most important contribution, notice of, 314, 318; an allusion by Pope to, 492.

Tribnia, the Island of, in the *Voyage to Laputa*, a revision by Swift respecting, 47.

Triennial Bill, The, Swift despatched by Temple on a mission to William III. respecting, 8.

Trip, a newly-invented word, objected to by Swift, 95, *note*.

Troy, the Siege of, Pope's principal difficulties in, 378.

Trumbull, Sir Wm., an ex-Secretary of State, Pope's first literary sponsor, 277.

Tunbridge Wells, a lesser rival of Bath, receives its ceremonial laws from Beau Nash, 305, *note*.

Turner, the maiden name of Pope's mother, a Yorkshire family, 276.

Turks and Tartars, The, Pope's estimate of, 414.

Twickenham, Gay alludes to Pope at, 178, *note*; Pope removes to, 308; account of his villa at, 309, and *note*; 310; 314; 326; 335; allusions of Pope to, 447, 450, 457; a description of his gardens and grotto (in a letter to Edward Blount), 467-469.

U

Undine, a fairy-romance of La Motte-Fouqué, the hint for, derived from the *Comte de Gabalis*, 297, *note*.

Universal Prayer, The, epilogue to the *Essay on Man*, added by Pope (in 1738), one of the most widely known of his productions, not the least meritorious part of the poem, 330.

Use of Riches, Of the, a Moral Essay of Pope dedicated to Lord Burlington, originally under the titles *Of Taste*, and *Of False Taste*, 321.

Utrecht, the Treaty of, Swift's remarks on the signing of, 136.

V

Valterie, La, his French version of the *Iliad* used by Pope, 299, 385.

Vanbrugh, Sir John, the Architect and Comedy-writer, satirical poem by Swift on, 16.

Vanessa, the poetic name given by Swift to Hester Vanhomrigh, 28, 34, 36, *note*, 38, 39, 164, *note*, 151, *note*, 153, *note*, 156, *note*, 163, 164, 172, *note*.

Vanhomrigh, Mrs., Swift's visits to (in 1709), 23; his first acquaintance with the family of, a notice of, 28, 30; her death, 35; notices, in Swift's journal-letters, of, 98, 106, 110, 111, 122; letter from Swift to, 145-146.

Vanhomrigh, Hester, daughter of the preceding, her accomplishments, in his letters to Esther Johnson Swift mentions her only twice, the nature and extent of the intimacy between them a matter of doubt, letters of the most passionate kind to Swift from, 28, 29; Swift's embarrassment from his connexion with, letters from him to, quoted, 34; left dependent for protection on Swift, claims his protection, her appeals and protestations of affection become more passionate and despairing, extracts from letters to Swift from, 35, 36; in Ireland usually resides at Marley Abbey near Cellbridge, Lord Orrery's character of her, Mrs. Delany's criticism upon it, 36, and *note*; the news of the marriage of Swift said to have caused the death of (1723), Sheridan's report of a visit from Swift and a friend to, she rejects the proposals (of marriage) of the latter with disdain, and retires to Cellbridge, her original manuscript letters destroyed, but copies taken, 38; Swift's poem *Cadenus and Vanessa* (on her), noticed and quoted, 38-39; Orrery's theory of the relations of Swift to, and Sheridan's remarks upon it, 39; said to have left instructions for the publication of all her letters to Swift, leaves her property to strangers, 39, 40; letter from Swift to, 134-135; extracts from letters to Swift from, 135, *note*; 145, *note*; letter from Swift to, 147-148; extracts from letter to Swift from, 147, *note*; letters from Swift to, 151-152, 153, 156-157; extracts from letter to Swift from, 157, *note*; letters from Swift to, 163-165, 168-170 (French), 170-172, and *note*; extracts from letters to Swift from, 172-173, *note*; extract from letter from Swift to, 387, *note*.

Van Loo, Jean-Baptiste, a French painter, mentioned by Pope, 489.

Varina, poetical name given by Swift to Miss Waring, 8, 9, 11.

Vere, Lady, niece of Lady Betty Germaine, in the habit of calling Swift "parson Swift," alluded to by Swift, 249, and *note*.

Verses on the Death of Dr. Swift, by Swift, noticed, and quoted, 62-64, and *note*.

Vertumnus and Pomona, a story in the *Metamorphoses* of Ovid, a version of, by Pope in Lintot's *Miscellany*, 284.

Vienna, the Court of, an allusion by Pope to, in letter to Lady M. W. Montagu, 414.

View of the State of Ireland, A, a pamphlet of Swift, mentioned by him, 231.

Villars, the Abbé de, his *La Secchia Rapita* imitated by Pope, a notice by Warton of, 297, *note*.

Villiers, Lady Elizabeth, afterwards Lady Orkney, the mistress of King William III., 131, *note*.

Villette, La Marquise de, a niece of Mde. de Maintenon, the second wife of Lord Bolingbroke, an allusion of Swift to, 213; Bolingbroke's reference to, 217; Swift's concern at news of ill heath of, 232; brings a large fortune to her husband, 323; writes Swift a long letter, 471.

Virgil, quoted by Swift *Æneis* XI., &c., 86, 89; imitated by Pope, 277; the *Pastorals* of Pope an imitation of the *Eclogues* of, 278; his *Æneis* VII. (episode of Silvia), II., IX., II., quoted by Pope, 285, 421, 435.

Virgil Travesty, quoted by Swift, 257.

Virtues of Sid Hamet, the Magician's Rod, The, a verse-satire on Lord Godolphin by Swift, 96.

Visitation Dinner, A., described by Goldsmith, 212, *note*.

Vital Spark of Heavenly Flame, Pope's imitation of the Epigram of Hadrian, 368; undergoes two or three revisions, 369, *note*.

Vivisection, the barbarity of, and other

experimental torture, denounced by Johnson in the *Idler*, 287, *note*.
Voiture, Vincent, a French poet and letter writer of the XVII. century, a copy of his works sent by Pope to Teresa Blount, 293.
Voltaire, François Marie Arouet de, suggests the translation of *Gulliver's Travels* into French, 43; extract from a letter to Swift from, 44, *note*; Lord Chesterfield sends verses of Swift to, 61; his *Œdipe* quoted, 282, *note*; on a visit to Dawley, writes a letter of condolence to Pope, compliments him upon his *Essay on Criticism* and *Rape of the Lock*, alleged dislike of Pope for, the guest of Bolingbroke, admired by the Princess of Wales, 318; an enthusiastic eulogist of Pope, his opinion of Pope quoted, his hatred and ridicule of the Optimistic creed, Mr. Elwin's remarks upon the reason of his admiration for the *Essay on Man* noticed, 337, and *note*; notice of the *Henriade* of, Bolingbroke writes to Pope to be prepared for a visit from, and that he is reading the *Mariamne* of, Bolingbroke's high praise of it, 462, *note*; eulogistic notice by Pope of the *Ligue (Henriadé)* of, its "spirit of true religion" commended by Pope, 462-464; probable correspondence of Pope with, 464, *note*; Pope returns thanks to Hill for his translation of the *Zaïre* of, letter from Hill to Pope expressing his delight in reading that tragedy, and intention of placing it on the London stage, 486, and *note*.

W

Wagstaff, Humphrey, a *nom de plume* of Swift, used by him as a signature to the *City Shower*, quoted by Steele, in the *Tatler*, 98, 99, *note*.
Wakefield, Gilbert, an Editor of Pope, remarks on a verse in the *Rape of the Lock*, 298; a favourable critic of Pope, 337; publishes an unfinished edition of Pope, in 1794, abandons his work to Warton, maintains the "inculpable perfection" of all Pope's compositions, did much to lighten the labours of succeeding editors, 339, a Fellow of Jesus, Coll., Cambridge, a Greek critic, author of *An Inquiry into the Expediency and Propriety of Public and Social Worship*, incarcerated in the Dorchester Jail, joins a Nonconformist body, 339, and *note*.
Walls, Archdeacon, Swift's agent in Ireland, one of his Dublin friends, 18; 97; meets Swift in the city, lodging in Aldersgate Street, buys his wife a new gown, &c., 115.
Walls, Mrs., familiarly called by Swift "goody," for what remarkable, 18.
Waller, Edmund, his *Saccharissa and Amoret* alluded to by Lord Peterborough, in a letter to Pope, 478, *note*.
Walpole, Horace, on the beauty of Mary Bellenden, 300, *note*; his remarks on Pope's Twickenham Villa, quoted, author of an *Essay on Gardening*, 309, *note*; on Jervas and Lady Bridgwater, 370, *note*; his description of Lord Peterborough, 476.
Walpole, Sir Robert, an interview of Swift with, 43; satirised in *Gulliver's Travels* under name of Flamnap, 45; visited by Swift twice, 189, *note*; accused of corruption by Swift, 202; his pique against Gay noticed by Swift, 227; presents a copy of the *Dunciad* to George II. and Queen Caroline, 319; swears Mrs. Howard shall have the Grounds she wishes for, his visit to Pope not returned, 466; favours the toleration of Nonconformists, 473, *note*.
Walsh, William, literary patron and correspondent of Pope, Dryden's estimate of him as a critic, his place in Johnson's Lives, resides in Worcestershire, invites Pope to Abberley, his eulogy of the *Pastorals* to Wycherley, 277; letters from Pope to, 278; Pope's Correspondence opens with his letters to, 343; 351-353; the expense of his redemption from Purgatory as a Socinian and a Whig, 373.
Warburton, Rev. J., Swift's curate at *Laracor*, 18; 148.
Warburton, Dr. William (afterwards Bishop of Gloucester), remarks upon Sir G. Brown in *Rape of the Lock*, 298; a rival of Spence in Pope-worship, 313; suggests to Pope the addition of a Fourth Book to the *Dunciad*, his enemies assailed in that poem, his remark on the authorship of the *Essay on Man*, suggests the alteration of the opening verses of the *Essay*, publishes his first volumes of the *Divine Legation of Moses*, steps forward as the champion of Pope's orthodoxy, inserts a series of vindications of it in a periodical of the day, 325; receives a letter of grateful recognition from Pope, his first meeting with Pope, formerly an adverse critic of Pope, firm alliance between Pope and, the great advantages from Pope's friendship resulting to, the rival of Bolingbroke, correspondence of Pope and, characterised, 326; is at pains to deny the *deism* of Pope, formerly charges the *Essay on Man* with atheism;

his Apology for Pope translated into French, 327, 328; discerns the essential weakness of Optimism, 328, *note;* the edition of the *Essay,* of 1743, published with the Commentary and Notes of, 330; puts up in Twickenham Church the cynical epitaph of Pope on himself, 331; with Pope at the Allens', at Prior Park, Martha Blount complains to Pope of the incivility of, termed a "sneaking parson" by Pope, 333, 334; last letters of Pope written to, Pope bequeaths his library, and the property of all his poems commented upon by his friend, to, 335; origin of the furious controversy between Lord Bolingbroke and, meditates a Life of Pope, but does not carry out his intention, his *Letter* addressed to Bolingbroke, in defence of Pope, 336; among the eulogistic critics of Pope, quotes Voltaire as a eulogist of Pope, 337; his edition of Pope appears in 1751; his character as given by Mr. Elwin, Lord Marchmont's allusion to, places his portrait in the frontispiece to his edition, supplies Ruffhead with materials for a Life of Pope, 338; his edition criticised by Warton, 339; character of the correspondence of Pope with, 346; suggests an edition to the *Dunciad,* 408, *note;* remarks on Wollaston's *Religion of Nature,* 452, *note;* his praise of Pope's *Grotto,* 468, *note;* letters from Pope to, 504-505, 505-506; his remark on the slight shewn to him at the University of Oxford, 506, *note;* letters from Pope to, 506-508, 508-510.

Ward, Prof. A. W., a biographer and editor of Pope, criticises Hallam's remark on the *Eloisa,* 304, *note;* a fallacy of the Optimist creed pointed out by, 327; a favourable critic of Pope, 337.

Ward, E. W., his picture of the *South Sea Bubble,* referred to, 440, *note.*

Waring, Miss, a young lady of Belfast, Swift pays his addresses to, 8; his letters to, quoted, 8, 9; he breaks with, and sends her an insulting letter, 11.

Warner, Miss, her publication of the second part of Pope's letters to Fortescue (in 1817) referred to, 394, note.

Warton, Dr. Joseph, an editor of Pope, his opinion of the *Rape of the Lock,* account of the Abbé de Villars, 297, *note;* a favourable critic of Pope, 337; publishes his edition of Pope in 1797, 339; remarks by, or references to, 391, 423, 431, 438, 452, 468, 511.

Warton, Thomas, brother of the preceding, Professor of Poetry at Oxford, 339, *note;* his *History of English Poetry* referred to, 423.

Water-Drinkers, among the Poets, 160, *note.*

Weather, The, the superiority of, in former times, imaginary, 107. *note.*

Weekly Papers, The, what full of, 477.

Wesleys, The, Dublin friends of Swift, 18; their occupations alluded to by Swift, 89.

Weston, Mrs., the heroine of the *Elegy* of Pope, her identity long a subject of dispute, at length discovered by Mr. Dilke, an account of, the *Elegy* to, quoted, 302, and *note;* allusions by Pope to (in a letter to Craggs), 362; he refuses to satisfy Caryll's curiosity as to the name of, related to the Duke of Buckingham, 362, *note;* letter from Craggs to Pope respecting, quoted, 363, *note.*

What-D'ye-Call-It, a Farce by Gay, an allusion by Bolingbroke and by Swift (in letter to Bolingbroke), to, 217, and *note;* attacked by Burnet, 404; an allusion by Pope to, 406.

Whifflers, The, Swift out of patience with, and their new-fangled politeness," 251.

Whigs and Tories, Pope upon, 393.

Whiteway, Mrs., a niece of Swift, and his housekeeper, his last words in writing addressed to, 64; a joint-letter to Dr. Sheridan from Swift and, 254-255; her regard for Sheridan, 256.

Whitworth, Mrs., her epitaph on the high road at Twickenham, alluded to by Pope (in a letter to the Duchess of Hamilton), reference in Theobald's *Courier* to, quoted, 432, and *note.*

Wife of Bath, The, a comedy by Gay, imitated from Chaucer, noticed by Swift, represented unsuccessfully at Drury Lane, revised by the author, Gay's allusion (in letter to Swift), to, 220, and *note.*

Wilde, Dr., a biographer of Swift, in his *Closing Years of Swift's Life* controverts the common theories as to the causes and character of Swift's mental disease, 64, *note;* the origin of his *Closing Years,* 65, *note.*

Will, Hester Vanhomrigh's, 40; Esther Johnson's, 57; Swift announces to Lord Orrery his having drawn up his, settles his whole fortune in founding a Hospital for Lunatics, 250; legacies and provisions of Pope's, 335.

William III., King, received by Swift at Moor Park, Swift sent to conduct political business with, 8; Swift sends his "love" to, 11; a *prebend* promised to Swift by, 72; settles an estate in Ireland of £20,000 rental on Lady Orkney, 131.

Will's Coffee-house, the Tory Club, Pope frequents, 296; the rival of Button's, the Whig Coffee-house, 300.

Winchcombe, John, the ancestor of Miss Winchcombe, first wife of Lord Bolingbroke, noticed, 119, note.

Windsor, Swift's life at, 30, 31, 33; 114. 124; 128-135; Lord Oxford offers him a Prebend at, 140; 157, and note, 172.

Windsor Forest, Pope's father settles on the borders of, 276; allusions to, 304, 305.

Windsor Forest, a poem by Pope, noticed, and quoted, 284.

Windsor Prophecy, satirical verses of Swift upon the Duchess of Somerset, alluded to by Sheridan, 25, note.

Witchcraft and Diabolism, the annals of, not attentively studied by Swift, 74, note.

Wollaston, William, author of the *Religion of Nature Delineated*, alluded to by Pope, 452, and note.

Woman, a tale in verse, published in Tonson's *Miscellany* (1709), an allusion by Pope to, 416, and note.

Women, the prayers of, Swift's idea of, 78.

Women, theory of the inferior intelligence of, why not combated by Swift, 233.

Wood, William, patentee of halfpence coinage in Ireland, obtains his privilege by a bribe at Court, assailed by Swift in his *Drapier Letters*, 41; represented, in a picture by Bindon, at the feet of Swift, 59.

Woodward, John, M.D., author of a *Natural Theory of the Earth*, his antiquarian researches ridiculed in *Three Hours After Marriage*, 308.

Wordsworth, William, the poet, criticises the *Messiah*, 284; praises the *Eloisa*, 303; generally adverse critic of Pope, 337; classes the *Eloisa* as a monodrama, 340.

Works of the Learned, The, a literary periodical, contributed to by Warburton, 325.

Works of the Unlearned, The, a proposed ironical periodical, designed by Pope and approved by Swift, but never started, alluded to by Pope, 371.

Worrall, an agent and correspondent of Swift, letter from Swift (respecting Betty Jones) to, quoted, 4; respecting Esther Johnson's Will, 51; letters from Swift on the illnesses of Esther Johnson, 187-190, 206-207.

Wotton, William, a champion of the Moderns as against the Ancients, publishes a commentary to expose the mischievousness of the *Tale of a Tub*, Swift ironically retaliates upon, 14; charges Swift with plagiarism in his *Battle of the Books*, 15.

Wotton, John, a painter, referred to by Swift, criticises the illustrations to *Gulliver's Travels*, 208.

Wrongs of Africa, The, a pamphlet by William Roscoe, referred to, 340, note.

Wycherley, William, a literary patron of Pope, Pope submits his *Pastorals* (in manuscript) to the judgment of, 277; an early correspondent of Pope, reciprocal compliments, coolness, and final reconciliation between Pope and, 295, 296; notice of the published correspondence of Pope with, 343, 344; allusions of Pope to, 357, 408.

Y

Y, the letter, how used by Pythagoras, the reference of Persius (*Sat.*) to that Pythagorean symbol, 320, note.

Yahoos, the, a species of animals who do not improve, 46; Swift (in the person of Sympson) considers he has reason to complain when he sees them carried by Houyhnhnms, 46, 47; illustrations of, 48; allusions by Mrs. Howard to, 193, note; Swift's suggestions for illustrations of, 209; allusions in the *Grateful Address of the unhappy Houyhnhnms* to, 317.

Young, Dr. Edward, referred to by Swift as rejecting the *triplet*, 245; an allusion to Dr. Radcliffe in a Satire of, 431; relates his acquaintance with Voltaire (with praise of him), recognises the merits of the *Henriade*, 462, note.

Z

Zaïre, a tragedy of Voltaire, Pope returns his thanks to Aaron Hill for a copy of his English version of, highly praised by Hill in a letter to Pope, Hill announces his intention to prepare the London audience for the favourable reception of, 486, and note.

Zephalinda, Teresa Blount celebrated under that name by Pope, in a poetic Epistle addressed to her, 294.

Zoilus, an allusion to Dennis, the hostile critic of Pope, as a modern, 282.